E Y A L   R E G E V is professor of Jewish studies in the department of Land of Israel Studies and Archaeology and the director of the Helena and Paul Schulmann School for Basic Jewish Studies at Bar-Ilan University. His books include *The Sadducees and Their Halakhah*, *Sectarianism in Qumran*, and *The Hasmoneans: Ideology, Archaeology, Identity*.

The Temple in Early Christianity

THE ANCHOR YALE BIBLE REFERENCE LIBRARY is a project of international and interfaith scope in which Protestant, Catholic, and Jewish scholars from many countries contribute individual volumes. The project is not sponsored by any ecclesiastical organization and is not intended to reflect any particular theological doctrine.

The series is committed to producing volumes in the tradition established half a century ago by the founders of the Anchor Bible, William Foxwell Albright and David Noel Freedman. It aims to present the best contemporary scholarship in a way that is accessible not only to scholars but also to the educated nonspecialist. It is committed to work of sound philological and historical scholarship, supplemented by insight from modern methods, such as sociological and literary criticism.

John J. Collins
General Editor

THE ANCHOR YALE BIBLE REFERENCE LIBRARY

The Temple in Early Christianity

Experiencing the Sacred

EYAL REGEV

Yale
UNIVERSITY
PRESS

NEW HAVEN
AND
LONDON

Published with assistance from the foundation established in memory of Amasa Stone Mather of the Class of 1907, Yale College.

Yale University Press books may be purchased in quantity for educational, business, or promotional use. For information, please e-mail sales.press@yale .edu (U.S. office) or sales@yaleup.co.uk (U.K. office).

Set in Adobe Caslon and Bauer Bodoni types by Newgen North America. Printed in the United States of America.

Library of Congress Control Number: 2018952551

ISBN 978-0-300-19788-4 (hardcover : alk. paper)
A catalogue record for this book is available from the British Library.

This paper meets the requirements of ANSI/NISO Z39.48-1992 (Permanence of Paper).

10 9 8 7 6 5 4 3 2 1

To the memory of my mother, Hannah Regev (Buchman)

Contents

Preface

This book discusses the Temple, its meaning and function and how it was viewed by early Christians. It shows how early Christian self-identity developed through the relationship with and attitude toward the Temple and the sacrificial cult.

I was not always consciously aware of my interest in the Temple. It took several years for me to realize that most of my research relates to it despite my not having any particular intention or agenda. It would seem that the Temple is present almost everywhere in Second Temple Judaism, whether or not one is aware of it. Could studying the Temple still be counted as offering a sacrifice, as some ancient rabbis argued long ago?

I began studying the New Testament (NT) when I wrote my doctoral dissertation on the Sadducees. At first I treated it as a direct source for the Sadducees and Pharisees. Reading the NT in a Jewish Israeli so-called orthodox contemporary milieu elicited some critical comments from friends. Nonetheless, the text piqued my curiosity about the creation of a new belief system in first-century Judaea. I realized that the study of early Christianity has the potential to contribute to a deeper understanding of Judean society and religion. Only at a later stage did I become interested in understanding early Christianity for its own sake, as a fascinating, extremely complex socioreligious phenomenon, similar to my interest in the Dead Sea Scrolls and the Qumran sectarians.

The intersection of early Christianity and the Jerusalem Temple presents diverse potential directions for understanding the past and looking at the present and future of Judaism and Christianity. However, my intentions are restricted to the study of ancient history in as accurate and as learned a manner as possible, primarily through a textual-critical attitude but also employing a social-scientific approach. Any implications of this study for our contemporary religious thinking and dialogue are beyond my scholarly scope.

This book originated with several articles published in the *Harvard Theological Review*, *New Testament Studies*, and *Cathedra* (in Hebrew) and in the edited volumes *Text, Thought, and Practice in Qumran and Early Christianity*, *Studies in Rabbinic Judaism and Early Christianity*, and *Soundings in the Religion of Jesus*. In the course of writing this book, which took four years, I revised my earlier treatments of the subject. The various NT texts and the vast number of books and articles on the subject in different languages demanded a substantial amount of time and effort to produce a readable, sensible monograph which presents the texts and my study of them in detail while also providing a fresh perspective on approaches toward the Temple in early Christianity. I can only hope that I have done justice to the complexity and richness of the early Christian discourse about the Temple and subsequent scholarship on the topic.

Many teachers, colleagues, and friends deserve my gratitude. First and foremost, my *doctorvater*, Professor Joshua Schwartz, of the Department of Land of Israel Studies and Archaeology at Bar-Ilan University, who not only introduced the academic world to me and guided me all the way from junior student to full professor, but also taught my first course on the NT. Other prominent teachers at Bar-Ilan University who encouraged and inspired me as a historian and interpreter of ancient texts are Professors Al Baumgarten, James Kugel, Zeev Safrai, and the late Hanan Eshel. Professor Helmut Koester taught me some of the basics of NT scholarship when I was a Fulbright postdoctoral fellow at Harvard University. I have also benefited from the friendship of Professors John Kloppenborg and Loren Stuckenbruck.

Special thanks are due to Professor John Collins, the editor of this series, for his wisdom and kindness. This book was actually John's idea, and his guidance and encouragement are what have made it possible. Heather Gold of Yale University Press also helped me throughout the project, and the rest of the team at Yale University Press made every effort to publish the manuscript professionally.

I would also like to thank my friend Dr. Stephen Arnoff, who helped improve my writing. Dudi Benyem and his team at the Wurzweiler Central Library at Bar-Ilan University, as well as the interlibrary loan service, made every effort to purchase or borrow the many books I needed for my research. Tamar Magen-Elbaz, the vice chair of my department, made it easier for me to devote my time to writing. The publication of this book was supported by research grants from the Koschitzky Chair of the Department of Land of Israel and Archaeology at Bar-Ilan University and from the Dr. Irving and Cherna Moskowitz Chair in Land of Israel Studies.

Last but not least is my family. My dear wife, Tanya, and our children, Nadav, Tomer, Ori, Yotam, and Amit, were supportive during my work on this book and waited patiently for its completion. My father, Zvi, also encouraged me and expressed interest.

This book is dedicated to the memory of my late mother, Hannah. Long ago she gave me my first copy of the NT (in Hebrew), which she kept next to her bed. To her, the NT was part of the history of the Jewish people and the Land of Israel. My mother was born in Tiberias in 1929 and educated in Kibbutz Mishmar ha-Emek. She established Kibbutz Revadim in Gush Ezion in 1947 and was injured by an Arab bullet in the first attack on Gush Ezion on February 14, 1948. Ever since, despite her injury, she continued to walk through and learn about the Holy Land. This book is a tribute to her intellectual interest in Jesus and his followers.

Editions and Translations

The Greek text of the New Testament follows Aland-Metzger, 4th edition (1993).

Unless otherwise noted, translations of the New Testament follow the New Revised Standard Version, with slight stylistic modifications.

Unless otherwise noted, translations of the Dead Sea Scrolls follow García Martínez and Tigchelaar, *The Dead Sea Scrolls Study Edition* (2000).

The Temple in Early Christianity

Introduction

Jesus is on the cross. People pass by, mocking him: "Aha! You who would destroy the Temple and build it in three days, save yourself, come down from the cross!" (Mark 15:29–30). Several years later Paul, standing on the steps of the Roman castle in Jerusalem after being arrested, addresses the crowd who attacked him a short while earlier in the Temple courtyard. He speaks of Jesus's revelation to him on the road to Damascus, stressing that when he had returned to Jerusalem "and while I was praying in the Temple, I fell into a trance" (Acts 22:17). In the Letter to the Hebrews, "Christ came as a high priest . . . through the greater and perfect Tabernacle not made with hands . . . he entered once for all into the Holy Place . . . obtaining eternal redemption (Heb 9:11–12).

In these three passages Jesus is crucified as the enemy of the Temple, Paul declares his devotion to the Temple, and Hebrews introduces a Temple in heaven where Christ serves as a high priest. The passages illustrate the importance of the Temple for the early Christians and also indicate diversity in the attitude toward the Temple found in the New Testament (NT). This book examines the Temple in early Christianity from two perspectives: the attitude toward the Temple as an institution where pilgrims visit, meet one another, and offer sacrifices; and the Temple as a symbol of commitment and proximity to God. Sometimes these two aspects appear to be in conflict, when the Temple as an institution does not fulfill its destiny as a symbol. One of the aims of this book is to demonstrate the significance of these two aspects and their complex relationship.

My analysis is based on four criteria for classifying attitudes toward the Temple: attendance (visiting the Temple), analogy (modeling religious ideas and rituals after the Temple or sacrifices), criticism, and rejection. In the following chapters I explore the aspects of the Temple cult that appeal to the NT authors, what characteristics of the cult are challenged, and why.

The Temple is the heart of ancient Judaism, in both an institutional and a symbolic sense. But what about the Christians? I regard the NT authors and readers—I refer to them as Christians, which is indeed an anachronism for the believers in Jesus—as inherently related to Jewish civilization.[1] They believe in the one and only God of Israel, frequently cite the Hebrew Bible, and relate to Jewish beliefs and practices (such as the Sabbath and Passover). Early Christian discourse about the Temple engages with Judaism or, according to another scholarly perspective, with early Christianity's own Jewishness. This discourse is laden with deep religious sentiments, both positive and negative. Most NT texts allude to the Temple at a time when the physical structure is no longer in existence, and yet the Temple remains significant and even central to the authors of Luke, Hebrews, and Revelation. What aspects of the Temple and the sacrificial cult are relevant to NT authors? Why do they still engage with these issues when they are no longer practical? In what sense is the Temple cult rejected or replaced by early Christian religious innovations, and in what manner does the Temple theme serve as a continuation of Jewish tradition in the formation of early Christianity?

This book attempts to study virtually all the explicit treatments of the Temple and the Temple cult in the NT. My method is conventional textual criticism, and my general approach is historical, aiming to understand not merely texts but the people who wrote and read them during the first century CE. I am less interested in the theological concerns of Christians or Jews after the first century CE.[2] I seek to understand early Christianity as a religious movement in the first century CE. The book has two objectives: to offer the reader an accessible presentation of the texts and their meaning according to current scholarship; and to provide a systematic analysis which presents my own interpretation of the various attitudes toward the Temple in the NT.

While working on this book I have found a vast amount of scholarship on the subject, in several languages. To corroborate the information in even half of these books and articles would have made this book not only difficult to write but also difficult to read. Therefore, in the interest of clarity and accessibility, I present only that information which I find to be the most relevant, omitting many interesting studies and restricting others to references in the notes.

Although many monographs on the gospels, Hebrews, Revelation, and the Pauline letters are dedicated to the Temple, very few attempt to impart a panoramic view of the Temple and the cult throughout the NT.[3] None actually discuss all the relevant NT texts, hence the synthesis they present is far from conclusive. They do not present the entire spectrum of NT approaches to the cult, and at times they are heavily influenced by a theological rather than a historical critical approach. Therefore, these discussions cannot accurately account for the diversity and historical development of early Christian approaches to the Temple. In other studies, too, scholars pay insufficient attention to the historical setting of the Temple in ancient Judaism or to early Christians' adherence to basic Jewish ideas and practices.

In many studies the main thrust is aimed at whether or not the early Christians of the first century CE are committed to the Jerusalem Temple, either practically or symbolically. Most NT scholars stress the early-Christian negative approach to the Temple: Jesus, the evangelists, and the author of Hebrews reject it, while Paul and 1 Peter "spiritualize" it, creating alternatives to the cult.[4] It is commonly argued that there are at least four ways in which the Temple is superseded in the NT texts: the church is the new Temple, the individual believer is the Temple, the Temple is in heaven, and the Temple is Jesus's body.[5] Some commentators even assume that the break with the Temple should be traced to the very origin of the Christian movement: the Historical Jesus already regarded himself or the church as the new Temple or believed he was the new high priest (see chapter 1). However, recent scholarship evinces more sensitivity toward the complex treatment of the Temple theme in the NT. Certain studies indicate that even Paul and John expressed appreciation of the Temple, tracing the manner in which Temple themes influenced early Christianity.[6]

The Assumed Tension Between Christ's Atonement and Sacrifices

Why do so many NT scholars regard the early Christians as rejecting, challenging, or replacing the Temple? What assumption underlies the so-called supersessionist approach? Many of those who write about the Temple assume that there is tension between the sacrificial system and early Christian belief. The core of this tension is theological, pertaining to the role atonement plays in both. The basic purpose of sacrifice is to atone for sin, and Jesus died to atone for the sins of his believers. Following are three views of this conflict:

1. According to Philip Esler, "It is, indeed, very difficult to imagine how a theory of the atoning death of Jesus, already present in Paul and Mark, and indeed, in Pre-Pauline and Pre-Marcan traditions, could have arisen among Jews who preserved close links with the sacrificial cult."

2. Since Jesus provides direct access to the Father (e.g., John 14:6–11; 16:26–27), Andreas Köstenberger maintains that "no longer must worshipers come to God by sacrificing in the temple; they can simply approach God through prayer in Jesus' name."

3. Similarly, Martin Hengel contends that since Jesus's death brought universal atonement once and for all (e.g., Rom 6:10; 1 Pet 3:18) there is "a fundamental break with the atoning and saving significance of sacrifice in the worship of the Temple in Jerusalem. . . . Atonement through the Temple cult finds its *end* and at the same time also its *fulfillment* in the eschatological saving event on the Golgotha."[7]

However, there is only one NT text which explains the transition of the role of atonement from the sacrificial cult to Christ: the Letter to the Hebrews. The author argues that effective atonement is achieved only through Christ and not by the high priest and animal sacrifices, which needed to be repeated time and again (Heb 7:26–27). Furthermore, while the blood of sacrifices purifies the soul, Christ's blood purifies the conscience (Heb 9:12–14).

One can also refer to Paul's outright assertion against the Law: "For if justification comes through the Law, then Christ died for nothing" (Gal 2:21). This may be interpreted as if Christ's "justification," which is related to (but not identical with) atonement, also replaces the sacrificial cult (Paul states this in the course of his marginalization of the Jewish Law). Paul may be hinting that adherence to the Temple cult along with the belief in Jesus as "ransom for the many" is a sort of "double booking" and attests to imperfect Christian faith. Yet Paul's intention in these passages may not be as straightforward as it appears when read out of context.[8] Paul never speaks directly about the question of observing the Temple practice. His approach is reflected in his cultic metaphors and deserves a detailed analysis. The tension between Christ and the Temple is therefore poorly demonstrated in the NT and is mainly a matter of later theological interpretation.

There is another good reason to dispense with the equation (and the resulting replacement) of Christ's atonement with the sacrificial cult: The Temple serves functions other than atonement. While many sacrifices are offered to atone for the individual or the entire Jewish people (such as in the Day of Atonement),[9] it would be wrong to reduce the entire purpose of the cult to atonement. Sacrifices carry other meanings as well; above all, the maintenance of the dwelling of God's presence.[10] In Psalms, for example, the cult has several meanings: acknowledging God's supremacy and righteousness, thanking God, adherence to God's commandments, and, above all, visiting the Temple as an experience of the sacred.[11] My point is that even if Christ atones for one's sins, the Temple is not necessarily superfluous. A Jew who believes in Jesus may nevertheless feel the need to visit the Temple and offer sacrifices to fulfill other aspects of cultic worship. It is also not inconceivable that some people would prefer to pursue multiple means of atonement at one and the same time. Furthermore, if certain followers of Jesus sense tension or even a contradiction between Christ and the Temple as agents of atonement, this would hardly apply to all or perhaps even most of them. We shall see that just as there are various approaches toward the Temple in ancient Judaism, there are also diverse voices within early Christianity.

It would be methodologically wrong to assume, before actually examining the evidence, that for first-century believers in Jesus the Temple was redundant. One should not presuppose the outcome of such an investigation. And one should try to examine the sources free of theological or any other predispositions. Scholarly assumptions and tendencies are unavoidable, especially when the evidence is scarce and one can complete the picture only through theory and intuition. However, this is not the case here because the NT text contains many passages which engage with the Temple explicitly and in detail.

I therefore find the replacement-of-atonement theory very disturbing, and not only because it is supersessionist, arguing that Christianity is the heir to Judaism. If this is indeed the view of the first-century Christians, the historian cannot argue against his own research subject. The problem is that first-rate scholars assume that atonement moved from the Temple to Christ before reading the text carefully, and they interpret the NT passages in this light. I think one should have as few presuppositions as possible before approaching the evidence and let the ancient authors speak for themselves.

I am not suggesting that we put aside the question of how belief in Christ conflicts with worship in the Temple, but rather that we approach it from a historical perspective, with much sensitivity for the text itself and its literary context, and that we remain aware of the complexity of religious ideas. One example of this complexity is the fact that Luke's Paul was devoted to the Temple and purified himself before entering it (Acts 21:26; 22:17), although Luke probably knew that, for Paul, Christ atones for sin, and Luke himself regards the coming of Christ as a means of forgiveness of sin (Acts 5:31).

Excursus: John the Baptist and the Temple

The theory of a contrast between the sacrificial cult and the independent-individual forgiveness-atonement system also characterizes scholarship on John the Baptist. Since the Baptist grants his followers remission of sins (Mark 1:4; Luke 3:3), recent scholars assume that this must have been at the expense of the Temple.

John Dominic Crossan maintains that while sacrifices in the Temple were expensive, John proposes a rite both inexpensive and available, one which is effective for absolution from all sins. John's innovation was that the average person can do something to prepare himself for the catastrophic coming of the Kingdom.[12] According to Robert Webb, John's baptism functions in a manner similar to sacrifices (Webb also recalls that John is a priest)—serving as absolution of sin. John "offered an alternative to a primary function of the Temple, and so was a threat to the temple establishment." John's baptism was "probably a replacement for the temple rite, at least temporarily," since "receiving John's baptism probably functioned as a form of protest against the temple establishment."[13] Others also reconstruct a cold relationship between the Baptist and the Temple authorities, surmising that John's eschatological beliefs are probably also directed against the Temple hierarchy.[14]

However, others do not concur in this view. Friedrich Avemarie compares the Baptist with the Qumran sectarians and contends that the ablutions are the only aspect that offers an alternative to the Temple, but they are not sufficient to incur active tension.[15] Joan Taylor believes there is no evidence for immersion as a substitution for sacrifice in Second Temple Judaism. She points to the call to repent in prophetic tradition, which is also not related to sacrifice.[16]

John draws on the immersion in water as a symbol of "cleansing" from sin (cf. Ezek 36:25). This, however, has nothing to do with sacrifices. Interestingly, the metaphoric equation of ritual immersion with sacrifices is attested to in a purification liturgy (4Q512) found in Qumran. Here the purpose of the immersion is both physical and moral purification, aimed at atonement. Sacrificial imagery appears in one of the blessings recited by the immersed person, addressing God: "[forgave me al]l sins and purified me from impure immodesty and atoned so that can enter[...] purification. And the blood of the *burnt offering agreeable to you [and the pl]ea[sa]nt (aroma) agreeable* to You."[17] Here purification does not explicitly substitute for sacrifice, yet the text does relate it to the aroma of burnt offering. Since the purpose of immersion and prayer in this liturgy is repentance from sin and attaining atonement, it is possible that in a certain sense ritual purification from sin takes the place of sacrificial rites.

In contrast, such a substitution is hardly implied in the gospels' tradition on John the Baptist or in Christian baptism in the NT. The first evidence for baptism replacing sacrifices is found in the anti-Temple Pseudo-Clementine's *Recognitions* 1.39. It would be wrong to attribute to John the Baptist ideas that were developed in second- or third-century Christianity. There is no reason to presuppose that there is direct tension between earliest Christianity and the Temple, and there is no evidence that Jesus inherited this approach from his teacher, the Baptist.

Jewish Attitudes Toward the Temple

Almost every book on the Temple in NT scholarship begins with a long introduction on the Temple cult in ancient Judaism. There is no need to repeat it here. It is well known that in the Hebrew Bible and sources from the Second Temple period the Temple is regarded as the link between heaven and earth, the navel of the world, a representation of the entire cosmos, and the dwelling place of God's presence.[18]

Instead of pointing to the common Jewish attitude toward the Temple I prefer to introduce the diversity of Second Temple attitudes toward the Temple and the sacrificial cult. Focusing on the attitudes of four religious or social groups or schools—the traditional priests and the Sadducees, the Qumran sectarians, Diaspora Jews, and the rabbis after the destruction of the Temple—illustrates the diverse ways in which the Temple was viewed. Even within these four general groupings one finds differences.

PRIESTLY JUDAISM AND THE SADDUCEES

It is natural to begin a survey of Jewish attitudes toward the Temple with priestly authors—Ben Sira (admittedly, his priestly descent remains uncertain) and Flavius Josephus. Jesus son of Eleazar Ben Sira, writing in ca. 180 BCE, regards Aaron as the ideal religious leader (45:6–22). For Ben Sira, sacrifice evinces religious piety and commitment to the Law (35: 1–2, 8). He stresses the need to honor the priest as a holy person because this is an integral element in worshiping God, and he calls upon the people to give the priests their dues (7:29–31). The "holy tent" is the dwelling place of the divine wisdom (24:10), and the Second Temple is designated for ever-lasting glory (49:12).

Josephus is proud that the Jews are scrupulous in preserving the purity and holiness of the Temple. He writes specifically of the priestly divisions into four courts, the regulations concerning the priestly duties, and the various taboos restricting persons and objects from the sacred area (*Against Apion* 2.102–109). He regards priestly devotion to the sacrificial cult as a supreme ideal (*War* 1.148, 150). For Josephus, the Temple should always be pure (for instance, Pompey orders the priests to purify it after he enters the sancta, *War* 1.153). When accusing those who rebel against Rome and fight each other for control of the Temple Mount, Josephus displays sensitivity toward the Temple's pollution. He blames the rebels for killing innocent people in the holiest place of all and using the sacred precincts for military purposes. This impurity is one of ritual (e.g., corpse impurity), but also it is mainly a moral issue: evil conduct defiles the cult.[19]

The Sadducees, one of the two leading religious movements along with their rivals, the Pharisees, maintained strict halakhic positions regarding purity, with special attention paid to the Temple. They also aimed to restrict laypeople from being within the sacred domain. For example, they rebuke the Pharisees for permitting the laity to touch and defile the Temple Menorah during the festival (t. *Hagigah* 3:35). They also emphasize the central-ity of priesthood and the high priest in relation to the laity and sages. New Pharisaic cultic practices, such as the libation of water on the altar during the Feast of Tabernacles, were rejected (t. *Sukkah* 3:16).

The high priests, most of whom are probably Sadducees, defend the sacredness of the Temple against Agrippa II and the Roman governors. Ishmael son of Phiabi and others of the high priestly class build a wall to prevent Agrippa II from observing the sacrificial cult from his palace and even travel to Rome to obtain Nero's approval for this screening wall (*Ant.* 20.189–195).[20]

These priestly views regard the Temple cult as the heart of religious piety, and they are also proud of the extensive boundaries with which they have surrounded the sacred realm. Nothing should mar this ideal situation, and no one should question the priestly authority, as long as they perform the rites appropriately. One cannot, therefore, expect the Temple institutions to display religious tolerance. According to the priestly and Sadducean Temple ideology, the Temple cult is viewed from the practical perspective of the priests and is associated with sacrifice and, especially, purity. The present cult is regarded as an ideal, and the serving priests are the only agents standing between God and His people. We may designate this priestly approach as *realistic and performative.*

QUMRAN I: STRINGENT TEMPLE LAW

Among the Dead Sea Scrolls found at Qumran are documents that reflect the views of secluded sects who reject the Temple, but there are also earlier scrolls detailing the laws that formed the foundations of the Qumran movement. These scrolls—the Temple Scroll and 4QMMT (the halakhic letter called *Miqsat Ma'ase ha-Torah*)—discuss laws of purity and sacrifices. They demand a higher degree of scrupulousness in the practice of Temple rituals than those prescribed by the Priestly Code in the Pentateuch and later rabbinic halakhah, since they adhere to a stricter interpretation of the laws of the Torah. These laws pertain to protecting the purity of the Temple from defiled persons, restrictions as to where priestly dues should be eaten, and how sacrifices should be offered (for example, slaughtering an animal outside the Temple is prohibited, since any such slaughter is sacral and requires bringing portions of the animal to the altar). The Temple Scroll also contains an extensive plan of the Temple courts which reflects the boundaries of sacred space as well as new rites of atonement and the festival calendar.

The authors of the Temple Scroll and MMT follow the theology of the so-called Priestly Code, but they augment the scope and intensity of its purity restrictions, ritual taboos, and ceremonies of atonement. This rigorous pursuit of purity, sanctity, and atonement derives from the idea that the sancta is extremely sensitive to threats of pollution and desecration, and any violation of cultic holiness imposes blame upon Israel, leading to divine wrath and punishment. Thus one should keep away from impurity because one must "be full of reverence toward the sanctuary" (MMT B 48–49). The authors are concerned with the risk that "the priests shall not cause the people to bear sin" (MMT B 12–13, 26–27). If Josephus and the Sadducees are restrictive in their approach to the cult, these scrolls show that there are others who wish to be even stricter. Their authors presuppose a vulnerable, dynamic Temple holiness that is very susceptible to desecration. The cultic system, it appears, may be extremely sensitive. In comparison to the former priestly attitude, the basic Qumranic approach may be designated as *demanding* and in a sense even *utopian*. It is based not on the present Temple practice but on the ideal of a higher standard of holiness and purity and also greater sensitivity to sin.

QUMRAN II: SEPARATION, SUBSTITUTIONS FOR SACRIFICES, AND THE ESCHATOLOGICAL TEMPLE

According to the so-called sectarian scrolls, the Qumran movement withdraws from Jewish society and does not participate in the Temple cult in Jerusalem. The Temple and its sacrifices are condemned because the Jewish leaders, who are morally corrupt and defiled, pollute the Temple cult. In *Pesher Habbakuk*, the authors accuse the Hasmonean high priest and leader, "the Wicked Priest," saying he was "arrogant, [had] abandoned God, and [had] betrayed the laws for the sake of wealth. He stole and amassed the wealth of men of violence who had rebelled against God, and he took the wealth of people to add himself guilty of sin. And abominated ways he practiced with every sort of unclean impurity." The Wicked Priest was also accused of having "committed abominable deeds and [having] defiled God's Sanctuary. He stole the wealth of the poor ones."[21] In the Damascus Document (CD 6:11–17) the sect's members are called upon to refrain from impure dedications and engagement with the wealth of the Temple because of the wicked social conduct of "the sons of the pit" toward the poor, widows, and orphans.

Apparently, the Qumran sectarians refrain from worshiping in the Temple in Jerusalem. This is probably why they develop substitutes for the sacrificial cult. In the Community Rule, the authors proclaim that moral behavior and prayer can replace atoning sacrifice. "The perfection of the way" performed by the *yahad* serves as an offering which pleases God (1QS 9:3–5).[22] In the penal code of the Damascus Document the authors link communal punishment with the sacrifices of atonement and purgation of sin at the altar. The punished transgressor should accept his punishment and feel remorse, as if he is bringing atoning sacrifices to the altar.[23]

In several scrolls the Temple is mentioned in relation to eschatological events. The War Rule (elaborating the war of the Sons of Light against the Sons of Darkness) envisions that after the first phase of the eschatological war with the *kittyim* (Seleucids or Romans) and other neighboring enemies, the priests and the elders of Israel will return to the Temple and offer sacrifices "in order to prepare the pleasant incense for God's approval, to atone for all His congregation and to satisfy themselves in perpetuity before Him at the table of glory."[24] For the Qumran sectarians, this means that the Temple plays an important role in their plans and dreams for the future. 4Q Florilegium, an exegesis on the End of Days, mentions the eschatological hope for "the house which [He will establish] for [Him] in the last days." It seems that this Temple, which will be established by God's own hands (following Ex 15:17), will not be entered by foreigners, and they will not desolate it as happened before.[25] The Temple Scroll 29:9–10 mentions the sanctuary which God himself will establish on "the day of creation." Both passages attest to a miraculous foundation of the eschatological Temple.

Evidence from Qumran indicates that purity and sacredness are not merely a matter of legal conduct and bodily immersion. Morality and social values also play a critical role in the Temple. The Qumran sectarians are harshly critical of the Temple leadership. They refrain from the cult and establish substitutions for sacrifices not because they do not care for the Temple but because they care too much. Their dualistic worldview, sectarian separation, and quest for immediate atonement lead them to seek new cultic avenues. Nevertheless, they are waiting to return to the Temple on their own terms and believe that an eschatological Temple structure would descend from the skies at the End of Days. Paradoxically, their intense interest in the Temple draws them away from it and raises their expectations for the future. It is sometimes assumed that the Qumran sectarians had some degree of influence on the early Christians. Current scholarship, however, usually rejects the possibility that the NT authors were directly affected or even aware of these scrolls.[26]

The Qumranic sectarian approach can be termed *polemical, moralized, and eschatological*. It denies the validity of the current Temple cult and creates substitutions which compensate for the overwhelming gap between the present and the utopian-eschatological cult.

DIASPORA JUDAISM

It is sometimes assumed that the Jews of the Diaspora had less of an interest in the Temple. Owing to their distance from Jerusalem, the influence of Hellenism, and the need for more accessible religious modes, they found alternatives such as prayer.[27] The evidence, however, shows otherwise. Jews from the Greco-Roman world donate money to the Temple, especially the annual half-shekel tribute. This is an act of identification with the Temple cult.[28] Furthermore, several Jewish writers from Egypt show interest in and even admiration for the Temple.

Aristeas's letter to Philocrates (*Pseudo-Aristeas*), which purports to tell the story of the translation of the Torah into Greek in Alexandria, was written during the second century BCE, probably in Alexandria. Aristeas describes his journey to Jerusalem to bring back qualified translators, including a detailed description of the Temple and its holy vessels (83–106). Much attention is paid to the altar, the manner in which the veil is moved by the wind, the priestly vestments, and the priestly service. The sacrificial cult arouses astonishment, wonder, and marvel in the eyes of the beholder (*Ps. Arist.* 84–99). Aristeas praises the high priest Eleazar for his integrity, reputation, and honor, as the supreme authority in matters pertaining to the Torah.[29]

2 Maccabees, written by Jason of Cyrenaica in the mid-second century BCE, places the Temple at the heart of the narrative. The official subject of the book is "the purification of the greatest Temple and the rededication of the altar" (2 Macc 2:19). The Temple is mentioned forty times in the book, and the festival of Hanukkah, celebrating the purification of the Temple, plays an important role (2 Macc 10:1–8). The narrative depicts the threats and attacks on the Temple and stresses that Judah Maccabee strives to defend the Temple and its sanctity. The Maccabees demonstrate piety toward the Temple. For instance, they utter a prayer at the Temple altar before going into battle (2 Macc 10:26).[30]

In the Third Sibylline Oracle, which dates to the second century BCE, reverence to God is manifested by offering sacrifices at the Jerusalem Temple. Worship at the true Temple is a necessary requirement for salvation. The Greeks are also told to bring gifts to the Jewish Temple.[31] The Fifth Sibylline Oracle, written between 70 CE and the reign of Hadrian, complains bitterly about the destruction of the Temple despite Israel's piety and also envisions the rebuilding of the Temple.[32]

Philo's treatment of the Temple cult is extensive and complex. There are more than one hundred references to the Temple in his writings.[33] His comments on the Law and the Torah include the necessity of sacrifice.[34] He praises sacrifice as a proper means of worship, representing righteousness and praise of God.[35] For Philo, sacrifice has moral symbolism, such as humility before God. He believes that God is interested not in the sacrificed animals but in the pure spirit of the sacrifice.[36]

Philo is well known for his spiritualization of the Temple and sacrifice.[37] He argues that the soul is the true house or Temple of God.[38] He also introduces a cosmological understanding of the cult. Heaven, or the entire cosmos, is a Temple.[39] Still, humans need the earthly Temple in order to worship and access God.[40] Cultic objects in the Temple, such as the high priest's vestments, represent the cosmos.[41] Thus Philo uses the allegorical method to seek the ultimate meaning of the Temple. Using symbolic allegorical interpretation, he makes a transference of visible phenomena, applying a Platonic dialectical method (in which there is an ontological dualism between the empirical and ideal worlds), inferring from the specific to the universal or cosmic categories.[42]

The fundamental question, then, is, Where does Philo's heart lie? Does he adhere to the practical aspects of the cult or merely admire its symbolism? Erwin Goodenough concludes that while Philo is loyal to the literal commands, he is mainly attached to the sacramental or ritualistic symbolism, the philosophy it invokes. What Goodenough finds appealing in the cult is not its underlying idea, but its emotional and aesthetic association.[43] Nonetheless, Philo's allegoric interpretation of sacrifice does not come at the expense of adherence to the Jerusalem Temple.[44] Philo seeks the true meaning of sacrifice without discrediting its importance to religious life.[45]

Philo's twofold approach is important for assessing the use of the Temple and sacrifices as an analogy, as is found in Paul's cultic metaphors. Using the cult to represent something else does not necessarily deprive the basic practical aspects of their value. It makes more sense that appreciation of the Temple and sacrifices leads the author to develop their symbolism in new religious messages.

Although it is impossible to claim that the Jews of the Diaspora have a uniform approach, many texts from Hellenistic-Egyptian Judaism show the immense impact of the Temple on Jews living outside of Judaea. They feel committed to the sacrificial system, and they also regard the Temple as the symbolic center of Jewish belief, practice, and collective identity. The Temple defines their identity, especially when they annually contribute money for its upkeep. The attitude of the Hellenistic Jews in the Diaspora is not as specific as that of those of the priests and the Qumranites. Rather, it is a more general admiration of the cult, to which Philo adds Temple symbolism. It seems that both the realistic and the symbolic attitudes toward the Temple are regarded from an ethnic perspective, in which the Temple *designates and symbolizes the essence of Jewish identity* in relation to the pagan Gentiles. Can this also be applied to the early Christians in Syria, Asia Minor, Greece, and Rome?

RABBINIC APPROACHES TO THE TEMPLE AFTER 70 CE

The early rabbis share this Jewish appreciation and devotion to the Temple. A large portion of their halakhah pertains to the sacrificial system. For instance, the earliest layers of rabbinic literature regard pilgrimage as the essence of the festivals, with the emphasis on visits to the Temple, sacrifices, and special rites.[46] After the destruction of the Temple, it is difficult for certain rabbis to come to terms with its loss. R. Yeshua mentions that some rabbis intend to continue to offer sacrifices without the Temple (m. *Eduyot* 8:6.), while others pray for its restoration (m. *Pesahim* 10:6).[47]

The rabbis also employ Temple symbolism in everyday life. For instance, in their discourse relating to the practices of the festival of Tabernacles (*Sukkot*), some laws pertaining to building the domestic *sukkah* relate to it as a Temple.[48] The commandment regarding the four species in this festival is perceived as building an altar (b. *Sukkah* 45a), and they should be without blemish, like animal sacrifices (b. *Sukkah* 35a). Waving the four species is even listed along with explicit cultic practices.[49]

Rabbinic sources testify to several substitutes for the Temple cult after 70 CE. Giving charity, as an act of commitment to the Law, replaced some festival sacrifices, and, according to R. Yohanan b. Zakkai, the leader of the rabbis after 70 CE, it even atones for sins.[50] He also maintains that good deeds (*gmilut hasadim*) atone for sins in place of sacrifices.[51] Prayers are instituted to replace sacrifices, and they are sometimes regarded as superior to offerings. Prayer and the study of the Torah are termed 'avoda, like the sacrificial cult.[52] Another substitution is the heavenly Temple. This concept is developed in later rabbinic literature, and the sage Rav (ca. 250 CE) already mentions that the angel Michael offers sacrifices on the altar in heaven (b. *Menahot* 110a).

For the early rabbis, Torah and the rabbinic ethos replace the Temple cult. The rabbis fill the vacuum left by the Temple, seeking substitutes for the precepts associated with the Temple. The sages and their teachings are regarded as analogous to the Temple, in order to justify and enhance their claim of religious authority.[53] They believe that "two who are sitting [together] and words of the Torah pass between them—the Divine presence [*shekhinah*] resides between them" (m. *Avot* 3:2). The (study of the) Torah is regarded as more sacred than the Temple vessels.[54] R.

Simeon b. Yoḥai (ca. 140 CE) says that, for God, the words of the Torah (as studied by the sages) are more precious than burnt offerings and sacrifices.[55] It is even claimed that the study of the Torah atones for sin (b. *Rosh ha-Shana* 18a).

For the rabbis of post-70 CE, the sage is comparable to the Temple: "The Sons of Torah are atonement for the world."[56] They also act accordingly in regulating their religious institutions. For instance, the rabbinic court at Yavneh assumes the status of the Temple in regard to festival ceremonies.[57] The laws pertaining to sacrifice which describe the cult in legal terms actually permit the Jews to experience the cult through its laws. While the Temple cannot be regained, it can at least be remembered in the vivid detail supplied by the sages.[58]

The rabbinic approach is therefore *substitutional.* The religious void left by the absence of the Temple is seen by the rabbis as a challenge and an opportunity to enhance their authority. Unlike the Qumran scrolls, these substitutions are not a matter of choice. They are an attempt to contend with the historical reality, although the rabbis also take into account their ideological agenda and social interests in introducing the substitutions. And as with any alteration to the cult, the rabbis build on certain symbolic understandings of the essence of the Temple. Rabbinic literature illustrates the intriguing dynamics of cherishing the Temple cult while also developing substitutes for it. The role and status of the early rabbis are based on their claim that the study of the Torah comes in place of the Temple. They are able to commemorate and replace the Temple at one and the same time. This substitution does not necessarily attest to a lack of appreciation, although it does reflect the cultural transformation of values and social norms.

This survey of attitudes toward the Temple during a period roughly contemporary with the composition of the NT texts may be helpful in assessing early Christian treatments of the Temple theme. These include observance and restriction, admiration and commemoration, criticism, and replacement. One attitude I have not been able to trace in Second Temple Judaism before 70 CE is a total rejection of the Temple cult as unnecessary. It will be interesting to seek such a view in the early Christian sources.

Method of Research

Examining the various treatments of the Temple theme in the NT demands religious and historical sensitivity. One needs to pay attention to the meaning of rituals, symbols, and the diverse perspectives and approaches to those cultic acts and symbols in first-century Judaism. NT authors perceive certain aspects of the Temple in very different ways. As I have mentioned, the most basic step is to distinguish between the Temple as an institution and the Temple as a symbol. The latter is more flexible and invites a variety of approaches.

In order to classify and interpret the vast corpus of NT material related to the Temple, I divide it into four categories: participation, analogy, criticism, and rejection. *Participation* texts present the Temple as the center of Judaism. We see this, for example, in those passages in gospels and Acts that describe Jesus and the apostles attending the Temple on a regular basis. Do these narratives imply that the Temple was a legitimate and highly relevant institution, one that merited the attention and respect of pre-70 CE Christians? *Analogy* texts draw parallels between believers and the Temple/priests/sacrifices. This kind of Temple imagery—on display in, among other works, Paul—builds on the Temple's symbolism (i.e., holiness, religious devotion) in order to inject a *new* sense of sacredness into the early-Christian community. *Criticism* texts, such as Jesus's "cleansing" of the Temple (Mark 11:15–17 and par.), are an attempt to restore the original status of the cult, not to altogether refute the idea of an earthly Temple. Finally, *rejection* texts assert that Jesus in effect replaces the Temple cult (or the high priest), for example, one may assume, in Hebrews. It will be interesting to see to what extent rejection of the Temple cult can be discerned elsewhere in the NT.

The study of the Temple in early Christianity is closely linked to the attitude toward the Jewish Law, the observance of halakhah. We need not link them too closely, since the Temple theme not only is a matter of legal observance but also represents religious devotion and identity (and even

Gentiles may attend it). Still, when discussing each NT text, it is necessary to examine its more general approach to Judaism, or at least to the question of Jewish versus Gentile identity, and the best marker for this is the author's approach to the Law.

My discussion will go beyond the question of whether early-Christian attitudes toward the Temple were in favor of or hostile to the sacrificial cult. I intend to show that in discussing the Temple, the NT authors were negotiating their relationship with the institutional and symbolic center of Judaism as well as with their own Jewishness.

1 Jesus: "Cleansing," Trial, and Last Supper

Introduction: On Methods and General Assumptions

THE HISTORICAL JESUS: A METHODOLOGICAL TRAP

Jesus's attitude toward the Temple plays an important role throughout the gospels' narratives. The gospels seemingly describe a relationship of conflict between Jesus and Temple authorities but lack any straightforward statement by the evangelists about Jesus's attitude toward the Temple. It is commonly held that Jesus commits a hostile act in the Temple itself and proclaims something about its destruction.[1] But what is this act and why does it take place?

Getting to the bottom of what actually occurs in this context is virtually impossible. We do not have any direct historical evidence concerning Jesus, only subsequent theological traditions. The field in NT scholarship, commonly known as "the quest for the Historical Jesus," attempts to overcome this obstacle, trying to determine what portions of the gospels' narratives, sayings, and parables attributed to Jesus by its authors can be reasonably traced back to Jesus himself. While there is agreement on several criteria—such as multiple attestations, embarrassment, discontinuity, etc.[2]—each scholar offers his or her own reconstruction of the Historical Jesus. Furthermore, there is disagreement on the historical value of the Passion Narrative, the main source employed as evidence of Jesus's arrest and crucifixion, incorporated into the gospel of Mark.[3]

My discussion focuses on three episodes upon whose authenticity most scholars agree: the act of "cleansing" the Temple; the accusation that Jesus says he will destroy (and rebuild) the Temple; and the Last Supper. These episodes offer sufficient opportunities to reconstruct Jesus's understanding of the problems related to the Temple of his day, his expansion of cultic symbolism, and the reactions he engenders as a potential enemy of the Temple. While the literature on these three episodes is vast, I think there are very general directions to which some scholars would agree. My own conclusions will focus on how the Jewish establishment—the chief priests of the Temple, in particular—responds to Jesus's approach to the Temple.

GENERAL APPROACHES TO JESUS, JUDAISM, AND THE TEMPLE

As I stressed in the introduction, many Christian scholars claim there is an inherent tension between Jesus and the sacrificial cult. This tension is expressed in some of the studies that ascribe to Jesus a generally negative approach to the Temple. Some scholars reason that when Jesus forgives sins (Mark 2:5, 9; Luke 7:48–49), he takes upon himself the role of the Temple as an institution providing atonement. Thus, in a way, Jesus identifies himself with the cult. But when he grants forgiveness without sacrifice, he actively distances people from the Temple cult.[4] Scholarly animosity toward the Temple increases when Jesus's death is deemed a conscious act meant to replace or supersede the sacrificial cult due to his ability to facilitate atonement.[5] Perhaps this theological framework lies behind the scholarly view that the cleansing marks the end of the Temple, while the Last Supper launches the beginning of a new Temple in which bread replaces animal sacrifice.[6] Some also conclude that the concept of the Christian community as a Temple—as attributed to Paul, Mark, John, and other texts—begins with Jesus himself.[7]

N. T. Wright, for example, understands Jesus as inviting his followers to join him in the establishment of the true Temple (Matt 7:24–27, where "house" refers to the Temple and "rock" to its foundation stone). For Wright, because the Jerusalem Temple is under judgment and soon to be desolate (Matt 23:38//Luke 13:35), there is no longer a need for sacrifices (Matt 9:13; 12:7), which will be replaced by mercy (cf. Hos 6:6). Jesus inaugurates a way of life in which there is no further need for the Temple because the love commandment supersedes it (Mark 12:28–34). He takes upon himself the Temple's role, thereby implicitly making it redundant and forming a counter-Temple movement around himself.[8]

Recently, it has even been argued that Jesus thinks of himself as the eschatological high priest. Based on Mark's story, it is claimed that Jesus acts as a high priest, forgives sins, regards himself as a holy person, possesses priestly contagious holiness (1:40–45; 5:25–34; 5:35–43), and attends the Temple as the Messiah. Jesus therefore suggests that he is destined to be the nation's king and priest in alignment with the order of Melchizedek.[9]

This approach assuming that Jesus consciously serves as a replacement for the sacrificial cult may be criticized on several levels. First, according to Acts, the early Christians—Paul included—continue to attend the Temple on a regular basis; hence they do *not* view Christ as taking the place of the Temple cult.[10] Second, those maintaining that Jesus intends to substitute for sacrifice rely solely on Mark without engaging any arguments that trace these traditions back to the Historical Jesus. Finally, it seems unwarranted to ascribe to Jesus a radical departure from traditional religious and historical Jewish contexts when he does not explicitly spell out such a shift in any of his teachings. If Jesus is not cited as presenting his acts and intentions as a full-blown replacement of the sacrificial cult, then the gospels' authors do not have such a tradition. In other words, the "replacement theorists" lack definitive proof.

Indeed, in the view of some scholars, Jesus's approach to the Temple cult is basically positive, since the gospels contain several such statements. In Matt 5:23–24, Jesus calls for reconciling with one's brother and sister before offering a sacrifice. In Mark, Jesus visits the Temple several times and teaches there when he makes his only visit to Jerusalem. But Jesus may change his mind when he visits there in his last week, assuming he believes that the Temple's destruction is imminent and that the chief priests are unworthy of their respective posts.[11] (These views are discussed further below.)

JESUS AND THE LAW

Naturally, one's approach to the question of Jesus and Jewish Law affects conclusions about Jesus and the Temple. Current scholarship tends to see Jesus as more supportive of Jewish legal practices than previous generations. Namely, the cases in which he departs from the Law are seen as exceptions rather than the rule. It is customary to understand Jesus as a Jewish scribe or rabbi teaching at a synagogue, discussing the meaning and application of the commandments.[12] Much has been written about the Historical Jesus's relationship to the Law, and it is impossible to address this subject adequately here. I wish only to illustrate this question with some halakhic examples closely associated with the Temple—purity laws.

E. P. Sanders concludes that Jesus generally does not transgress the Law even though he regards Mosaic Law as neither final nor absolute since a new age is at hand. Jesus does not break the laws of impurity when he eats with sinners because sin does not produce impurity within the teachings of rabbinic Judaism.[13] There is a common premise that Jesus is a relatively normative Jew of his time—otherwise he would not attract contemporary Jewish followers. That he does not address purity rules or specific purity instructions should not lead us to assume that he ignores or opposes Jewish purity codes but rather that he takes them for granted.[14]

Other scholars are more skeptical. Thomas Kazen argues that Jesus is indifferent to some purity concerns, including skin disease, menstrual blood, and corpse impurity. In the case of Mark 7:15, Kazen discerns a relativizing perspective on the part of Jesus with regard to his use of the language of inner and outer purity. This potentially denotes a somewhat indifferent attitude to the specific issue of bodily transmittable impurity. Sanders, in contrast, interprets this approach as a "not only [purity laws are abiding] . . . but even more [moral demands should be observed]" rigid approach to the Law.[15] There are also more negative approaches according to which Jesus rejects the laws of purity entirely. According to Gerd Theissen and Annette Merz, Jesus relaxes legal norms, and in Mark 7:15 in particular he denies external uncleanness.[16] However, as we shall see in the following chapters, many maintain that the authors of Q, Matthew, and perhaps even Mark and Luke do not deny the validity of Jewish Law so bluntly. There is no reason to assume that Jesus is more lax than his later followers.

The "Cleansing" of the Temple

"Then they came to Jerusalem. And he entered the Temple and began to drive out those who were selling and those who were buying in the Temple, and he overturned the tables of the money changers and the seats of those who sold doves; and he would not allow anyone to carry anything through the Temple. He was teaching and saying, 'Is it not written, "My house shall be called a house of prayer for all the nations (Isa 56:7)"? But you have made it a den of robbers' (Jer 7:11)." (Mark 11:15–17)

This famous episode is commonly called the cleansing because scholars have previously held that Jesus regards the Temple as defiled and wants to purify it.[17] What is the reason for the tension between Jesus and the Temple? Does this cleansing reflect a broader conflict with contemporaneous Judaism, or is it rather an attempt to act within the traditional framework of the Temple cult? Is Jesus for or against the Temple?

Almost all Historical Jesus scholars think that this act actually took place.[18] Even the highly critical Jesus Seminar agrees on the likelihood that "Jesus precipitated some kind of temple incident by his aggressive criticism of the commercialization of the temple cult."[19] There are, however, some who regard it as a nonhistorical event invented by Mark or a pre-Markan source.[20] A different version of this cleansing appears in John 2 at the beginning of Jesus's career (see chapter 6). While several researchers regard this instance as being independent of Mark 11,[21] it is much more common to see it as secondary and dependent upon Mark.[22]

Most scholars accept the authenticity of this description, but there is a debate as to whether Jesus really cites Jer 7:11 and Isa 56:7. Against the long list of those who reject the authenticity of these verses,[23] some insist that these scriptural citations are authentic because they find it reasonable that Jesus would make claims that can be linked to the interpretation of these verses.[24] As we will see below, conclusions about this episode impact any interpretation of Jesus's intentions, since its omission usually leads to a softening of Jesus's criticism of the Temple.

A SYMBOLIC ACTION AND ITS DIRE CONSEQUENCES

It is common to speak of Jesus's act as "a symbolic action" or "a prophetic demonstration," meaning it has no real practical goals but rather aims to send a message by means of a public performance. Sanders champions this interpretation, arguing that it is impossible for Jesus to occupy the Temple or to really stop the cultic practices: "It was a gesture intended to make a point rather than to have a concrete result."[25] It is a demonstration of the need to reform rather than an attempt at taking action—a threat and a hope but not implementation.[26]

Nevertheless, the cleansing has severe consequences for Jesus, leading in one way or another to his arrest, trial, and crucifixion. Assuming that the high priest and other Jewish authorities see Jesus's act as offensive or even threatening to the stability of the existing religious and political order, it requires a severe reaction.[27] Yet, according to the Passion Narrative, authorities in the Temple display a delayed reaction.[28] Below I will suggest why both the high priests and Pilate react as they do.

In what follows I will survey nine possible intentions or meanings for Jesus's act prevailing in current scholarship.[29] As we shall see, some researchers claim more than one explanation, and some views are inherently linked to others. Finally, I will propose my own interpretation, relating the cleansing to the message of the Historical Jesus.

AGAINST TRADE IN THE TEMPLE

The simplest interpretation of Jesus's Temple cleansing is that he objects to trading on the Temple Mount because it is a holy place. The first to introduce this explanation is the author of the gospel of John: "He told those who were selling the doves, 'Take these things out of here! Stop making my Father's house a market-place!'" (John 2:16). Jesus overturns the tables of the money changers who are converting local coins to Tyrian shekels, which are mandatory for paying the half-shekel tribute required every year from every Jew (apart from the priests).[30] He also turns over the chairs of those who sell doves, which are the cheapest and most popular sacrifice. Therefore, Jesus's basic objection to trade in the Temple is the obvious rationale for this episode.

Jesus's strange prohibition of carrying a vessel (*skeuos*) into the Temple during the cleansing can be interpreted in several ways. Many maintain that it upholds the halakhic prohibition against shortcutting through the Temple, which implies using the Temple as a place of everyday activity.[31] It is more plausible, however, that he is referring to a vessel containing money, flour, oil, or wine—perhaps donated to the Temple.[32]

Several scholars consider it reasonable that Jesus resists trade in the Temple. Market activity threatens the holiness of the sanctuary and disturbs worship.[33] He may be influenced by the eschatological banishment of "traders" in the Temple in Zech 14:21, believing that in the eschatological era the distinction between both holy and profane and pure and impure will be transcended.[34] Or he may follow Ezekiel and the Temple Scroll, which hold that the outer court should be a sacred space devoted to prayer and teaching, not profane activities.[35]

These suggestions presuppose that Jesus is not anti-Temple. On the contrary, he cares about the Temple and the cult, defending its holiness from the profanation of trading, and ultimately wants to make it better or more sacred. As we shall see, this basic view is shared by most of the scholars who discuss the "cleansing."[36]

However, it is not reasonable that Jesus would oppose trade in the Temple Mount because it would not be practical. It is impossible to carry on a sacrificial cult of this magnitude without supplying suitable animals, and it is difficult for the pilgrims to bring the sheep or doves from afar.

Mass pilgrimage to a sacred place requires trade.[37] Furthermore, it is unlikely that Jesus sees the Temple as defiled or impure, since, according to
Acts, his followers continue to worship there. The only possible clue that
the cleansing targets the priests and is intended as a cultic reform is the
passage "You have made it a den of robbers" (following Jer 7:11), which is
probably a Markan addition.[38] As we shall see below, opposition to trade
in the Temple is embedded in other, more specific and complex interpretations of the "cleansing."

SYMBOLIC DEMONSTRATION OF DESTRUCTION (AND RESTORATION)

According to Sanders, the cleansing symbolizes destruction. An attack
on the Temple service is "a gesture towards disrupting the trade [and] represented an attack on the divine ordained sacrifices." However, "destruction
symbolized restoration," since Jesus probably expected a new Temple building to be given by God from heaven. The demonstration in the Temple
probably "prophetically symbolized the coming event." Jesus's message is
that the end is at hand and that the Temple will be destroyed so that a new
and perfect Temple can arise. Sanders needs to explain why the gospels do
not make this point clear, *and for this reason he* argues that Mark and Matthew are embarrassed about Jesus's threat to the Temple *and explain* the act
otherwise as an act of cleansing or purification. The reference to a "den of
robbers" is intended to make the action "relatively innocuous." Sanders also
adds that perhaps the people do not understand the symbolic message of
Jesus's Temple act. He insists, however, that the theme of destruction and
rebuilding is supposed to be familiar, even if it is also offensive.[39]

Sanders supports his thesis by reviewing the Jewish restoration theology of the Temple. He asserts that in Hebrew Bible prophecies, the expected
restoration of Zion is related to the Temple; Zion is sometimes equated
with the Temple (Jer 50:28; 51:10–11) and the New Zion (New Jerusalem)
denotes a new Temple. Hope for the rebuilding of the Temple also appears
in several early Second Temple sources.[40] Sanders therefore contends that
when Jesus speaks of this destruction people understand that "the end was
at hand and thus redemption was near. . . . the connection between disaster,
God's chastisement, and the subsequent redemption of a remnant was so
firmly fixed in Judaism that we should assume that even a bare statement of
destruction would not be altogether misunderstood."[41]

Sanders has had an enormous impact on contemporary scholarship.[42]
Wright embraces his view that Jesus prophesies that Israel's sins will lead

to the coming destruction and replacement by the Kingdom—not just reformation of the cult. He argues that nowhere does Jesus predict the physical rebuilding of the Temple.[43] Paula Fredriksen also sees the cleansing as a symbolic enactment of an apocalyptic prophecy that God will destroy the current Temple and build an eschatological Temple. But she adds that Jesus's act is hardly noticed by the crowd due to the commotion at the Temple Mount on the eve of the festival. The priests are not particularly troubled by it.[44]

There is, however, a crucial weakness in Sanders's thesis. While he assumes that predicting the fall of the Temple naturally implies its rebuilding, the sources to which he refers mention only rebuilding. At times even this is merely implied. There are no predictions of destruction of the Temple between Jeremiah and the 60s CE. Also, no Second Temple text refers to the rebuilding of the Temple by the Messiah—and certainly not its destruction by him.[45] There are no real grounds to expect that anyone would understand that overturning the tables stands for the rebuilding of the Temple in the coming Kingdom.[46] A further problem is that Sanders does not explain why the symbolic demonstration of the Temple's destruction should take place among the money changers and dove sellers.[47]

It seems to me that Sanders actually bases his theory on false testimony attributing to Jesus a declaration that he will destroy and rebuild the Temple in three days (Mark 14:48). However, his methodology of reconstructing the Historical Jesus, based on actions rather than on a disputed saying, does not allow him to acknowledge the essential role of Mark 14:58 as support for this interpretation.

AGAINST CORRUPTION OF THE CHIEF PRIESTS

For Craig Evans, the cleansing is directed against corrupt chief priests. Whereas Sanders claims there are no authentic traditions concerning Jesus's critique of the priesthood, Evans refers to several such traditions in Mark: the cursed fig tree (Mark 11:12–14, 20), which he thinks symbolizes a "fruitless and doomed Temple"; the Parable of the Wicked Tenants (Mark 12: 1–11); the question of authority (Mark 11:27–33, which takes place at the Temple); and even the Widow's Mite (Mark 12:31–44). Evans adds that when Jesus opposes the oppression of the poor or elderly for the sake of religiosity he is actually lamenting a religious establishment that contributes to the hardship of the poor. In addition, in Jesus's predictions the chief priests are among his main antagonists. All of this implies criticism of the Temple and the priesthood, demonstrating that Jesus probably says and does things

that provoke the priesthood. Ultimately, according to Evans, there is controversy and animosity between Jesus and the priests. The cleansing is a
direct attack by Jesus on the integrity of the priesthood.[48]

Evans then turns to another proof that Jesus's act is anti-priestly. He
points to criticism of the cult and the priesthood in the Hebrew Bible as
well as in Second Temple period documents and rabbinic sources. He argues that scriptural expectations and contemporaneous approaches would
make the cleansing an act comprehensible to Jews of the time. Evans's
long list includes accusations against the immorality of the priests and
high priests as well as condemnations of the present Temple as polluted.[49]
These admittedly biased sources portray various high priests or priestly
families as being wealthy, corrupt, greedy, and sometimes violent. Hence
"the high priesthood of Jesus' time was in all likelihood corrupt (or at
least was assumed to be so) . . . [and] Jesus' action in the temple is direct
evidence of this." In turning over the tables of the vendors and accusing
them of robbery, he is actually condemning the high priests. Furthermore,
some of these texts suggest—even if they do not make it explicit—that
the Temple would be purified in the eschaton and that this would be the
Messiah's task.[50]

Evans also proposes a historical context for the cleansing in alignment
with Victor Epstein. According to Epstein, Jesus reacts to the political and
economic reform of Joseph Caiaphas, the High Priest at the time, which
includes moving sacrifice vendors to the Temple Mount.[51] Yet Epstein's
theory is based on an idiosyncratic exegesis of a very late and perhaps legendary rabbinic source, and he conjectures that Jesus's act is directed against
Caiaphas's supposed economic reform at the Temple Mount.

While this view is quite common among scholars,[52] it falls into the trap
of following hostility against the high priests as expressed by contemporary
rivals. Despite the long list of accusations against the high priest's immorality, criticism of the high priest's economic abuse and corruption in Josephus
and rabbinic literature pertains to the period around the fifties CE, later
than Jesus's lifetime.[53] There is also no evidence of exploitative conditions
at the Temple market, and it is hard to see Jesus's act as representing such a
message.[54] In fact, in some of the sources, such as the Psalms of Solomon,
the Temple and the priesthood are not mentioned explicitly. In others, the
accusations are pointed at specific high priests. Furthermore, as Sanders
explicates, "If Jesus were a religious reformer . . . we should hear charges
of immorality, dishonesty and corruption directed against the priests. But

such charges are absent from the gospels (except for Mark 11:17) and that is not the thrust of the action in the temple."[55] If Jesus's act is directed against the priesthood, why doesn't he attack the priests in the Temple?[56]

There is hardly any evidence in the gospels of Jesus rebuking the priests or high priest by mentioning them *explicitly*. Although Q and Mark detail Jesus's attack on the Pharisees and the Scribes (Luke 11:38–52; Mark 12:38–40), there is no parallel attack, direct and specific, on the chief priests, despite their role in Jesus's arrest and his being turned in to Pilate. The accusation of denying and executing Jesus is directed at Jewish leaders and the Jewish people in general.[57] Furthermore, the Markan sources that Evans (like many others) interprets as anti-priestly can also be read as a more general protest against Jewish leadership (see chapter 3).

SOCIOPOLITICAL RESISTANCE TO THE ROMANS, THE HERODIAN ORDER, OR THE ELITES

Several scholars interpret the cleansing as an act of resistance or protest against the political domination of those who rule Judaea, namely, the Romans, the Herodian political order, or the governing elites.

Given the social and economic tension between rural dwellers and the Jerusalem aristocracy, Jesus's protest at the Temple may represent the outlook of a Galilean Jew visiting Jerusalem. He voices conflict between rural and urban societies. Indeed, prophetic protests and other opposition to the Temple usually come from the countryside in this era.[58] Crossan, who stresses Jesus's egalitarianism, argues that his active protest explodes when he reaches the hierarchical, oppressive Temple. His symbolic destruction actualizes a message of open commensality. Jesus is the opponent, the alternative, and the substitute for the Temple all wrapped in one.[59]

Jesus may also protest against "Herod's subjection of the Temple to the political purpose of glorifying his kingship and by the intrusion of commercialism." Commercialism in the Temple area is a form of Romanization and paganization of the Jewish cult.[60] The cleansing is therefore a socioeconomic act of resistance to the aristocracy that the Temple represents, since it is "an instrument of Imperial legitimation and control of a subjected people."[61]

Certainly, the Historical Jesus opposes the social and economic situation in his environs. However, these scholarly views lack support from Jesus's sayings linking the Temple to the rejection of the elites or the Herodian or Roman political order, since they assume that this is obvious.

Nowhere in the gospels does he correlate the teachings about sinners or the poor to the Temple or the high priests.

AGAINST HUMAN FIGURES ON TEMPLE COINS

Peter Richardson and Adela Yarbro Collins point to a very specific explanation of Jesus's overturning of the tables: he opposes pagan figures on Tyrian coins used for the half-shekel tribute.

The Tyrian tetradrachmas are not mentioned in the NT, but according to rabbinic sources the Temple tax was paid in Tyrian coins because they had the highest percentage of silver and are therefore the most reliable financial value.[62] Strangely, the Jews did not mind the figures of the god Melkartt and an eagle. Still, we find Jewish rejection of iconic representations,—for example, in the act against the placement of Herod's eagle at the Temple Mount (*Ant.* 17.149–167). In Mark 12:13–17, Jesus is asked about paying tribute to the Roman emperor and responds, "Give back to Caesar what is Caesar's and to God what is God's" (v. 17). This shows that, for Jesus, imagery entails ownership—hence the coin belongs to its owner, and he should pay God what belongs to God. Thus, one may conclude, paying the Temple dues in Tyrian shekels is not acceptable to God, since they belong to another god.[63]

Jesus may reject the use of the Tyrian shekels because he is concerned about the holiness and purity of the Temple. He insists on stricter regulations regarding holiness than the priests administering the Temple, placing "the honor and dignity of God above human convenience." Jesus aims not to abolish the commercial activity related to the Temple but to extend the holiness of the inner court to the whole Temple Mount, including the outer court.[64]

I think that although the focus on the coins is a good start, this explanation is too specific for such an extraordinary and risky act as overturning the tables. Jesus is not cited as an opponent of idols elsewhere. His response about the tribute to the emperor concerns politics and taxation, using the human figure only as a symbol of Roman domination. It does not necessarily follow that Jesus specifically opposes human figures on coins.

A PROTEST AGAINST THE TEMPLE TAX

William Horbury and Richard Bauckham argue that the tradition in Matt 17:24–27 questions the validity of the so-called Temple tax of half a shekel, thus reflecting the Historical Jesus. Here Jesus is reluctant to pay it, as the tax should be paid from lost property rather than from the common fund.[65] Bauckham adds that Jesus objects to the selling of doves, which is probably a monopoly of the Temple treasury, because it makes the sacrificial system a burden on the poor, creates oppressive financial demands, and gleans profits from the commercialization of sacrifices. Jesus objects to the Temple treasury turning the sacrificial system into a profit-making business, even if this is done for the sake of the Temple and not for personal profit. Nevertheless, these elements do not necessarily make the Temple morally corrupt.[66]

Even though Jesus disturbs the collection of the Temple tax, one could make the argument that since Jesus's reservations appear only in Matthew, Matt 17:24–27 reflects a later perception stemming from a pre-Matthean tradition.[67] Furthermore, the view that Jesus rejects the half-shekel tribute is not particularly strong since Peter pays it eventually (see chapter 4). In any event, this seems too marginal of an issue to lead Jesus to engage in a violent and risky act.

SACRIFICIAL REFORM CONCERNING THE OWNERSHIP OF SACRIFICE

Bruce Chilton devotes an entire book to a thesis which links the cleansing to Jesus's special approach to sacrifices. He posits similarity between the context of the cleansing and the halakhic view of Hillel the Elder, a contemporary of Jesus, who holds that the owner of an *olah* (whole burnt) sacrifice should lay his or her hands on a sacrifice before giving it to the priest as an offering on the altar. This act expresses the intention of the offerer's participation by virtue of his ownership of what is offered. Jesus's presence at the Temple should therefore be understood as embodying the same point of view as Hillel's notion—an attempt to claim that the offerer's actual ownership of the offering is a vital aspect of the nature of the sacrifice itself. In this sense, Chilton links the personal nature of the sacrifice to its purity.[68] Furthermore, beyond his concerns about the element of ownership in sacrifices, Jesus does not attack the sacrificial system itself. He wants to prevent the sacrifice of animals acquired at the Temple Mount through trade and commerce.[69]

Chilton's thesis has not garnered support. He has not been able to show coherence between this framing of Jesus's acts and sayings and the messages actually conveyed. One may also ask why the House of Hillel, whom

Jesus supposedly follows, never acts at the Temple in a manner that embodies their halakhic view.

REFORMING THE CULT: A NEW HOLINESS SYSTEM FOR THE ESCHATOLOGICAL AGE

Marcus Borg advances a thesis that in the cleansing Jesus is in fact calling for a new religious system of holiness that rejects Jewish separatism. Building on the authenticity of the saying about the "den of robbers," Borg posits that Jesus acts against improper commerce in the Temple, referring to violent people and perhaps even anti-Roman rebels. In doing so, Jesus objects to the use of the Temple as well as to any hopes resting upon it with regard to resistance against Rome. Relying on the citation of the "house of prayer for all the nations" (Mark 11:17; Isa 56:7), Borg's Jesus insists that the Temple should be open to all nations. He resents the separation from the Gentiles within it.[70]

Borg writes, "The money changers and sellers of sacrificial birds were there in service of the ethos of holiness. . . . The activity of these 'ecclesiastical merchants' manifested the clear-cut distinction between sacred and profane, pure and impure, holy nation and impure nation that marked the ethos and politics of holiness." The money changers protect the Temple's holiness by exchanging profane money for holy animals supplied for sacrifices. They thus stand for the separation between holy and profane that is the basis of the resistance against Rome. Jesus, however, supports universalism and opposes resistance. He believes that the exclusivity of the Temple's system of holiness is destined to bring punishment—the banishment of God's dwelling in it—even though this may be remedied by repentance.[71]

Still, reliance on Jesus's disputed scriptural allusions to Jer 7:11 and Isa 56:11 as a starting point for his hypothesis leads Borg astray from accurate interpretation of the act itself. Moreover, the Historical Jesus probably does not pay any special attention to the Gentiles, including their inclusion in the Kingdom.[72] It is anachronistic to trace the early Christian mission to the Gentiles back to Jesus's lifetime as an attempt to make up for the lack of his sayings about them in the evidence we have.

A CALL FOR A NEW TEMPLE?

A minority of scholars believe that Jesus expresses his call for or anticipation of a new kind of Temple—one that is different from the physical building—through the "cleansing." Some argue that it symbolizes the end of sacrifices with the arrival of the messianic era.[73] Crossan maintains that in the cleansing Jesus symbolically destroys the Temple by stopping its fiscal, sacrificial, and liturgical operations. Jostein Ådna concludes that Jesus expects that the new Temple will be the center of God's eschatological reign, based on biblical and Second Temple traditions. Jesus claims that he will establish the eschatological Temple based on Exod 15:17–18, hence the current Temple is a den of robbers. He admonishes the people to repent in order to get into the Kingdom, but they continue to hold on to the Temple. Through the cleansing Jesus wants to demonstrate that the old atonement cult must be brought to an end. It is inappropriate in the dawning eschatological era and must be replaced by eternal worship by the redeemed representing all nations. However, the renewed Temple (following Isa 56:7) will not follow the traditional sacrificial cult. Jesus offers himself as a replacement for the Temple cult as the means of atonement. The post-Easter Christian community continues this understanding.[74] Simon Joseph suggests that Jesus's act relates to his objection to animal sacrifices in the Temple because God does not demand them.[75]

Such suggestions can hardly be taken seriously by anyone holding that Jesus follows the Jewish Law (notwithstanding some reservations) and accepts the sacrificial cult.[76] In terms of method, it seems that the idea of Jesus's new unearthly Temple is a misguided projection of later Christian ideas (such as in the Letter to the Hebrews) onto Jesus himself.

CRITIQUE AND ALTERNATIVE: MONEY AND RIGHTEOUSNESS—A GENERAL CALL

The previous discussion demonstrates how most of the interpretations of the cleansing contain some kernel of truth—an element of historical evidence, a generally accepted view of Jesus's message, or an ideological motivation. Yet each contains weaknesses as well.

Many of these views suffer from the underlying problem that the intended meaning of Jesus's act cannot be clear to the audience that witnesses it. It's hard to believe that a random crowd in the Temple would understand monolithically that overturning the tables definitively symbolizes either the Temple's destruction and subsequent rebuilding, rejection of the Herodian/high priestly dominance and its corruption, or the separation between Jews and Gentiles. At best, this audience can be assumed to grasp only that Jesus's protest is related in a general sense to the presence of money in the Temple.

The most fundamental flaw in most of the reconstructions surveyed above is a pattern of attributions to Jesus of concepts about the Temple not recorded elsewhere in the synoptic tradition. There are no attestations in the NT of opposition to commerce on the Temple Mount, no direct condemnations of the chief priests despite their active role in Jesus's execution, no sources of evidence for the inclusion of Gentiles in the Temple, and no hopes for the erection of a Temple building. Some of the general cultic or political ideologies that are read into Mark's short description might be characteristic of certain radical Jewish groups—such as the Zealots—or of later Christians, including Mark himself. In fact, Jesus hardly mentions the Temple at all either before and after the "cleansing." Even the saying about destroying and building the Temple in three days is attributed to him by false witnesses (Mark 14:58; 15:29, see below). Is it possible that the initial subject of his act was not the Temple?

My own interpretation of the cleansing is grounded in recognizing that common to all of the details of Jesus's act is *money*. Namely, all of these descriptions and sources refer to the buying, selling, changing, and (according to many interpretations) prohibiting of a vessel from entering the Temple—a vessel which probably contains money or goods.[77] Jesus is addressing a specific problem of money in the Temple. In another tradition, Jesus does not object to money in the Temple. He praises the small donation of a poor widow to the Temple's treasury (Mark 12:41–44; see chapter 3). Money in the Temple, therefore, is not inherently good or bad. If a donation to the Temple can be an act of religious piety, the problem does not lie in the basic institution of money and the Temple. And we should also note that Jesus attacks both sellers *and* buyers, all of whom are Israelite laypeople.

If Jesus's act targets money in a very particular context, we should look at his other teachings about money (of which there are many in both Q and Mark) as well as what their general thrust may tell us about the Historical Jesus. In these as well as in the Sermon on the Mount and in the parables Jesus teaches against the accumulation of wealth and the destructive force of money. He also stresses that the destitute are potentially more righteous than the rich.[78] Wealth and materialism lead one astray from both true worship of God and moral behavior: "No one can serve two masters. . . . You cannot serve God and *Mammon*."[79]

Another key issue rooted in both Mark and Q is Jesus's preaching on the need for moral behavior, emphasizing that immorality produces (metaphoric) impurity, "the things that come out are what defile."[80] This idea is probably also related to the view that wealth leads to unrighteousness and corruption. Both show Jesus's ethical sensitivity. It is likely that money leads to unrighteousness and produces moral impurity in Jesus's worldview.[81] If wickedness is defiling, then money used to accomplish wickedness—or money earned by wickedness—may be both contaminated and contaminating.

I propose that Jesus's message in the cleansing is that the money of unrighteous people corrupts or defiles the Temple cult. His protest is not directed against the Temple. He calls for protecting the Temple from the unrighteousness transmitted to it through money contributed to the Temple that had previously been used for changing coins for the half-shekel tribute or buying an animal for sacrifice.

In the cleansing of the Temple, the concept of wealth as a vehicle for corruption is interwoven with the idea of the defiling force of sin. Although there is no direct combination of the two ideas in the gospels or any clear statement that the money of the wicked is metaphorically defiled by their moral impurity, I maintain that these two ideas are logically related.

The object of Jesus's wrath is the money itself, its essence contaminated by its use in the financing of sacrifices and offerings before being delivered to priestly officials. His act is directed not just against the trading adjacent to the Temple's sacred courts, but specifically against money that is tainted by injustice and corruption. Corrupted wealth is morally impure in a metaphorical sense, blemishing the sacrificial rite. The sanctity of sacrifices and rituals is compromised by the money that finances them.

If I am correct, Jesus protests against neither the Temple itself nor the priests but against the unrighteous activity that employs or generates corrupted money. This seems to be the same abstract immorality against which Jesus preaches over and over again without singling out any specific group or class. The reason for his protest on the Temple Mount is that when this money is being used for buying sacrifices, it threatens the moral—not the ritual—purity of the Temple cult. Perhaps the reason he attacks the sellers is that it is easier to overturn their tables and chairs than to disperse the coins of the individual buyers. Hence he may be more concerned with the overall moral pollution of the Temple than with the unrighteousness of those buyers.

Like all of the scholarly views on the cleansing cited thus far, mine is an interpretation, a conjecture without proof. Nonetheless, it offers two advantages. First, it attributes to the Historical Jesus two ideas that are well attested to elsewhere tying them together in the Temple act. Thus I regard the cleansing as the continuation and practical application of views Jesus has expressed before the event. Second, there is a close parallel to the view in Qumran that unrighteous money defiles the Temple. In the *Damascus Document* VI, 13–17, the authors call on the members of the sect to "separate [themselves] from the sons of the pit and to refrain from the wicked wealth [which is] impure due to oath[s] and dedication[s] and to [its being] the wealth of the sanctuary, [for] they (i.e., the sons of the pit) steal from the poor of his people, preying upon wid[ow]s and murdering orphans." Here the "wicked" stolen money is contaminated by impurity. When it is donated to the Temple's treasury, it causes the pollution of the cult. Thus the explicit cause of the Temple's impurity is the fact that the money donated to the Temple is "money of wickedness."[82] It seems that if one deems certain acts or people to be corrupt, one is likely to declare the money associated with them to be taboo as well.

Jesus's Trial and the Saying on the Temple's Destruction

"They took Jesus to the high priest; and all the chief priests, the elders, and the scribes were assembled. . . . Now the chief priests and the whole council were looking for testimony against Jesus to put him to death; but they found none. For many gave false testimony against him, and their testimony did not agree. Some stood up and gave false testimony against him, saying, 'We heard him say, "I will destroy this Temple that is made with hands, and in three days I will build another, not made with hands."' But even on this point their testimony did not agree. Then the high priest stood up before them and asked Jesus, 'Have you no answer? What is it that they testify against you?' But he was silent and did not answer. Again the high priest asked him, 'Are you the Messiah, the Son of the Blessed One?' Jesus said, 'I am'; and 'you will see the Son of Man seated at the right hand of the Power,' and 'coming with the clouds of heaven.' Then the high priest tore his clothes and said, 'Why do we still need witnesses? You have heard his blasphemy! What is your decision?' All of them condemned him as deserving death." (Mark 14:53, 55–64)

"As soon as it was morning, the chief priests held a consultation with the elders and scribes and the whole council. They bound Jesus, led him away, and handed him over to Pilate. Pilate asked him, 'Are you the King of the Jews?' He answered him, 'You say so.' Then the chief priests accused him of many things. Pilate asked him again, 'Have you no answer? See how many charges they bring against you.' But Jesus made no further reply, so that Pilate was amazed" (Mark 15:1–5).

THE REASONS FOR JESUS'S ARREST: THE CONFLICT WITH THE HIGH PRIESTS AND PILATE

Much has been written about the trial of Jesus.[83] In his trial Jesus (and, for later readers, the early Christian movement) urges full conflict with the Jewish establishment. Our concern is the question as to why Jesus is arrested and executed, and how this is related to his attitude toward the Temple.

The major historical source for the trial, the Markan Passion Narrative, is usually regarded as partly authentic in its general narrative, although it surely includes a theological reworking by Mark.[84] Most scholars accept the general historicity of both the high priestly and Roman involvement in the arrest.[85]

Sanders puts the focus of the trial on Jesus's attitude about the Temple. According to Sanders, the most crucial aspect in Jesus's life is that he acted and spoke in relation to the Temple in a manner that is interpreted as a threat to this most sacred place. Many follow Sanders, either fully or partly. Crossan, James Dunn, and others assert that the charge of a threat against the Temple is the main reason for his arrest and execution.[86] Paul Winter notes a central component of the trial tradition throughout its various versions is the role of the high priest (later to be identified with Joseph Caiaphas) as being the one who interrogates Jesus in court.[87] It is commonly agreed upon that the arrest by the Jewish Temple police and the subsequent hearing before a council convened by the high priest have a historical basis.[88] Since the high priest is the leader of the Temple, his role also links Jesus's arrest to the Temple.

Almost anyone who accepts the cleansing as historical assumes that its inevitable consequence is Jesus's conflict with the chief priests and the Temple establishment.[89] Indeed, even if Jesus's acts and words in the Temple are hardly noticed, he is still regarded as a threat to peace and order.[90] Many see the Roman intervention in the plot as natural, since the cleansing—or any threat to the Temple—concerns Pilate.[91] The best proof that Jesus is judged and executed by the Romans, not the Jews, is that crucifixion is a Roman punishment. This is probably because Jesus poses (or is accused of posing) a threat to Roman rule.[92] John points to the Roman interest in getting rid of Jesus and its relation to the Temple when he adds that Roman soldiers are involved in Jesus's arrest in tandem with servants of the chief priests (John 18:3); and he mentions Caiaphas's concern that belief in Jesus will cause Roman destruction of the Temple (John 11:48).[93]

IS THE MESSIANIC ACCUSATION AUTHENTIC?

The traditional view that Jesus is crucified because his disciples and followers believe he is the Messiah while his accusers regard him as a Messianic pretender is still held by many modern scholars.[94] For those who regard the coming of the Kingdom as Jesus's main message (Mark 1:15)—even if it is not necessarily political—it is quite natural to think that Jesus is accused of being a royal aspirant who threatens Roman rule because of his call for the "kingly rule" of God. He poses a threat because he might spark messianic expectations among his disciples and other Jews, and some may even think he is the Messiah himself.[95]

In the contemporary quest for the Historical Jesus, scholars typically question whether the Markan narrative of the trial represents Jesus's original message. Dunn, for example, concludes that Jesus never claims to be the Messiah, son of David—especially not during the trial. Nevertheless, since his disciples think he is the Messiah immediately after his death, it seems reasonable to suppose they already suspect this before it.[96]

Some see the charge of blasphemy leveled against Jesus in Mark 14:64 as authentic, detaching it from the accusation of false messianism in Mark 14:61. They attribute the blasphemy charge to Jesus's cleansing or his statements regarding the Temple's destruction. Sanders maintains that the charge of blasphemy originates with his speaking and acting against the Temple, leading to Jesus's death.[97] Others claim that the saying attributed to Jesus regarding destroying and building the Temple is his actual blasphemy. They suggest that it has strong messianic overtones—assuming that the Messiah is expected to build a new Temple.[98] But as we will see, it is unlikely that the saying that Jesus will destroy and rebuild the Temple is authentic. It is also doubtful that Jews expect the Messiah to build a new Temple as long as the Herodian Temple is still standing.

In fact, I think we should reject the historical value of the legal hearing at the high priest's court, especially the messianic accusation. From a literary perspective, the scenes of Jesus's dialogues with the high priest and Pilate are too detailed to be remembered or recorded by Jesus's disciples, who are not present in the court.[99] The structure of the two questions by both the high priest and Pilate, of which Jesus answers only one, seems to be the result of a literary reworking.[100]

The trial scene contains Christological titles that are historically suspect. The high priest's question, "Are you the Messiah, the Son of the
Blessed One?" and Jesus's announcement, "I am; and you will see the Son
of Man seated at the right hand of the Power and coming with the clouds
of heaven" (Mark 14:61–62) conform precisely with Markan Christology.
They contain the markers of Jesus being Christ, Son of Man, and Son of
God, following Ps 2:2, 7. The passage therefore probably results from a later
reworking.[101]

From a historical perspective, even if one assumes (along with most
scholars) that Jesus is an eschatological prophet,[102] he clearly continues
a long tradition of messianic expectations. Proclamations of the coming
messianic age are quite common in Second Temple writings (e.g., Daniel, Jubilees and Psalms, and Solomon). Jesus's teaching that the eschatological Kingdom is coming can hardly explain his execution. Furthermore,
despite Mark's hints, Jesus is never proclaimed to be the Messiah. When
Jesus is asked at the Temple, "By what authority do you so act?" he refuses
to answer (Mark 11:28–33). According to Mark, only Peter recognizes that
Jesus is the Messiah but must keep this secret (Mark 8:29–30). Therefore,
I think it unlikely that the Jewish and Roman authorities prosecute Jesus
solely as a false Messiah.[103] True, Jesus is crucified as "the king of the Jews"
(Mark 15:26; John 19:19–21). Nevertheless, there is much irony in this inscription on the cross, which leaves room for speculation as to the motivation for the Roman charge against Jesus as a would-be Messiah. From the
Roman point of view, it may be related to the Temple charge. Below, I suggest that a threat to destroy (and rebuild?) the Temple may be understood
as bold resistance to Rome.

THE AUTHENTICITY OF THE TEMPLE SAYING

The saying "I will destroy this Temple that is made with hands, and in
three days I will build another, not made with hands" (Mark 14:58) has a
seminal role in the historical reconstructions of the Jesus trial. Many maintain that Jesus predicts the destruction or even threatens to destroy the
Temple. This also implies its rebuilding. Such a prediction or threat relates
to Mark 13:2, where Jesus says, when leaving the Temple, that no stone
will be left on another. As I have already noted, Mark 14:58 has a major
role in Sanders's thesis that the demonstration in the Temple "prophetically
symbolized the coming event," since it provides him with a link between
destruction and rebuilding/ or restoration. Still, this saying does not necessarily imply a condemnation of the Temple cult because it still intimates a

desire to build a better Temple.[104] For others, the saying indicates an early transformation of the Temple into something else, whether a community of believers in Jesus or Jesus as a temple (following "the temple of his body" in John 2:21).[105]

But can we trust this saying to be authentic? Mark 14:48 is attested to elsewhere although in partial forms: "Aha! You who would destroy the Temple and build it in three days, save yourself, and come down from the cross!" (Mark 16:29b-30); "For we have heard him say that this Jesus of Nazareth will destroy this place and will change the customs that Moses handed on to us" (Acts 6:14); "Jesus said, 'I will destroy [this] house, and no one will be able to build it [. . .].'" (Gos. Thomas 71);[106] and many would add another saying: "Do you see these great buildings? Not one stone will be left here upon another; all will be thrown down" (Mark 13:2).

Surely these many attestations—and especially the mocking of Jesus on the cross (Mark 15:29)—increase the possibility of the authenticity of the saying in question.[107] But do the multiple attestations of the saying apply to the Historical Jesus's own words? Does the most detailed version, Mark 14:58, reflect his apocalyptic hope for rebuilding the Temple by himself, rather than by God?[108] If so, Jesus may say it after the cleansing and before his arrest, when the leaders do not accept his previous message.[109] For Sanders, the charge encapsulated in Mark 14:58 "is based on an accurate memory of the principal point on which Jesus offended many of his contemporaries," even if the entire trial scene is fictional. Still, he doubts Mark's narrative of the trial because the charge leads nowhere and, according to Mark, it is apparently dropped since the testimonies of the witnesses do not agree.[110]

Yet the exact wording of Mark 14:58 is confusing and does not seem to be authentic. The saying may contain Markan reworking in an attempt to water down its implications.[111] The destruction portion seems much more authentic than that of the rebuilding.[112] The words "made with hands . . . not made with hands" and "in three days" are likely Markan additions, since this distinction does not appear in all of the versions—therefore raising suspicion. As for the three-day deadline, one may suspect that Mark attempts to bring the saying into line with resurrection predictions (Mark 8:31).[113] But is this a prediction or a threat of the destruction or both?

Those who maintain that Jesus proclaims the rebuilding of the Temple rely on what they regard as a common expectation in ancient Judaism for a new Temple as well as the hope that the Messiah will be the one to build it (in 1 En 90:28–29; Temple Scroll 29:7–10; 4 Ezra 10:25–54; 2 Bar 6:7–9; Sib Or 5:397–423).[114] They assume that Jesus continues these expectations.

This argument is false. While there is certainly hope for a new Temple at the End of Days (e.g., Tob 14:5), it is not a common belief. Most of the texts that are usually referred to in this regard do not actually mention the eschatological Temple. 1 Enoch refers to the city of Jerusalem ("the house") but not to the Temple (the "tower"). 4 Ezra does not mention the Temple at all. The Temple Scroll predicts a Temple made by God in the Day of New Creation (cf. Jub 1:27), not its rebuilding by the Messiah. The only text that links the Temple directly to the figure of the Messiah and predicts that it will be built by him is the Fifth Sibylline Oracle 397–423. However, it is written in the wake of the destruction of the Temple by the Romans—or even later, which is close to the date of the gospel of Mark.[115] This idea is therefore unattested to in the days of Jesus. The idea that the Messiah will first destroy the Temple before he rebuilds it is, to say the least, unfounded and strange. Indeed, it is difficult to understand why Mark would even invent it. Nowhere else in the NT do we find a hope for a new and better *physical* earthly Temple.[116]

Certain scholars reject the authenticity of the saying attributed to Jesus by the false witnesses. It does not cohere with Jesus's other positive sayings about the Temple, is contradicted by the fact that Peter and the apostles still attend the old Temple, and reflects later accusations against the church (I discuss these accusations in chapter 5).[117] Along this same line of thinking, some also dispute the authenticity of Jesus's prediction of the supposed destruction of the Temple in Mark 13:2 (discussed below).[118] These queries as well as the previous ones are resolved if we see Mark 14:58 not as the authentic words of Jesus but as an accusation by the false witnesses, whether or not Mark alters it.

ACCUSING JESUS OF PLANNING TO DESTROY AND REBUILD THE TEMPLE

Despite Mark's introducing of Jesus's saying on destroying and building of the Temple as false testimony, some argue that Mark actually wants the reader to think that Jesus says it.[119] This position may be supported by the predictions of "no stone upon another" (Mark 13:2) and Jesus straightforwardly saying, "I will destroy this house" (Gos Thomas 71).

However, this evidence is weaker than typically admitted. In Mark 13:2 Jesus predicts the destruction but does not say he will destroy the Temple himself; nor does he say when it would it happen. Strikingly, the Temple is not mentioned here at all, and it seems that the prediction concerns Jerusalem in general (see chapter 3). As already noted, these sayings may be Markan. As for Thomas, there is debate as to whether this gospel predates or postdates the synoptic tradition. It would therefore be unwarranted to base an argument solely on this passage. Even if one holds that Thomas precedes Mark, Jesus's disciples may erroneously attribute words to him only because the accusation becomes common. In any case, there is no other sign of hostility toward the Temple in this noncanonical gospel.

Jesus's declaration that he will destroy and rebuild the Temple appears as an *accusation* against him in three traditions: false witnesses (Mark 14:48); mockery when Jesus is on the cross (Mark 15:29–30); and accusations against Stephen, again, made by false witnesses (Acts 6:14). The charge's format is neither the literary craft of a single author nor a single channel of tradition. There are a multitude of attestations pointing to an early and solid tradition of such an accusation, which resonate later as well.[120]

Later evangelists also are very cautious not to attribute to Jesus a direct threat on the Temple. Matthew 26:61 tones down this charge, saying that the false witnesses only claim that Jesus says, "I am *able* to destroy the Temple of God and to build it in three days." Luke omits it from the trial altogether, later denying it when it reappears in the charges against Stephen. John 2:19–21 omits this accusation from the trial and places it in the context of the cleansing of the Temple, transforming its meaning to a positive one while interpreting it as an analogy: "Jesus answered them: destroy this Temple, and in three days I will raise it up. . . . But he was speaking of the temple of his body." Here Jesus would not destroy the Temple but only rebuild it if others would destroy it, and the pronouncement also loses the concrete sense of the Temple when Jesus's body is introduced.

In all of these cases the authors convey a message that Jesus never says he will destroy the Temple. Nevertheless, their attempts to deny this show that non-Christians indeed accuse Jesus of threatening to do so! Notably, none of the four canonical evangelists believes that Jesus proposes a straightforward assault on the Temple, even when they are writing after 70 CE! Two conclusions thus emerge: Jesus is *accused* of threatening to destroy the Temple, and the later Christians deny that he threatens it. I think their denial stems from a common belief among non-Christians that Jesus is anti-Temple, and/or because the Christians themselves are not. The four evangelists resist the opportunity to set Jesus boldly in opposition to the Temple, either as the founder of a new Temple of the Church or as a replacement for the destroyed Temple. We must bear this in mind throughout the next chapters.

From a historical perspective we can confidently conclude that regardless of what Jesus actually says or does not say, the chief priests and the Romans accuse him of threatening to destroy the Temple. The exceptional, unprecedented, and violent act of cleansing the Temple may reasonably lead to this accusation.[121] It is difficult to determine whether Jesus also says something interpreted as anti-Temple or as a verbal threat to it, since the literary evidence about this is obscure.

Admittedly, accepting this Temple saying as an accusation and not as the authentic word of Jesus does not solve a number of problems: Why would anyone accuse Jesus of claiming to both destroy *and* rebuild the Temple? Why limit this claim to three days? Why distinguish between a manmade Temple and one that is divinely made? These questions require broader consideration. I suggest that the development of the tradition girding Mark 15:29–30 and 14:58 is complex. First, Jesus is *accused* of threatening to destroy the Temple (which may serve as the background of Mark 13:2); then, Christian tradition, as reworked by Mark, adds the first three days motif to intersect with Jesus's resurrection and the later concept of a Temple not made by human hands.[122] The post-Easter concept of the Temple not made by human hands resembles the ideas of the divinely made but still physical Temple of the Temple Scroll 29:9–10 and Jubilees 1:29 and those of Jesus as a Temple and the Christian community as a Temple. I do not think the two latter ideas are attested to in Mark (see chapter 3). I prefer to draw a link to the less radical anticipation of some Christians that Jesus would bring about the eternal Temple at the End of Days.

THE TEMPLE CHARGE: THE CHIEF PRIESTS' PERSPECTIVE

Jesus's audience at the Temple Mount's "cleansing," his adversaries, and the Jewish leaders who hear about it all probably have a completely different impression of the turning over of the tables. Given the ambiguity of the Temple act, its violent character, and the sacred place in which it takes place, Jesus's contemporaries probably viewed it as extremely offensive. Those who witnessed it were unaware of Jesus's intentions and former teachings. All they see is a Jew violently interfering in daily worship. Jesus may also say something critical of the Temple or the people who participate in the cult. But does this warrant a death sentence?

Why does the high priest react so harshly? The high priest before whom Jesus is brought at the hearing (who is probably also the one who orders his arrest) is identified in Matt 26:57 as Joseph Caiaphas.[123] He is a Sadducee.[124] In fact, most of the members of the high priestly elite are Sadducees. The Pharisees, on the other hand, are not mentioned in the synoptic versions of Jesus's "trial" at all.[125]

The Sadducees, and the Sadducean high priests in particular, are more sensitive to any violation of the Temple's sacredness. In comparison to the Pharisees, the Sadducees hold a stricter approach to the Temple's ritual purity and give greater significance to the priestly cult.[126] They regard the Temple and the sacrificial cult as more sensitive and vulnerable—and in a certain sense more sacred—than the Pharisees. Any possible violation of the cultic order or any potential desecration of the Temple is regarded as dangerous.[127] The Sadducees believe that the masses should be restricted from approaching the sacred. Thus, for example, they complain about the Pharisees permitting the laity to approach the Temple candelabrum (the Menorah) within the Temple's sacred precinct, thereby defiling it and requiring its purification.[128]

Sadducean high priests are involved in intense political attempts to prevent what a non-Sadducee would regard as a minor violation of the Temple cult. Thus, Ishmael son of Phiabi leads a delegation to Nero applying to keep a screening wall which the priests have built to prevent Agrippa II from observing the sacrificial cult from his palace. Agrippa's staring at the priestly ritual is regarded as sacrilegious since it invades the sancta.[129]

It therefore appears that a high priest who is in charge of the Temple—especially a Sadducean high priest—would be extremely offended and threatened by Jesus's cleansing of the Temple as well as his supposed saying about demolishing it.

THE ROMAN PERSPECTIVE: CULTIC UPRISINGS IN THE ROMAN EMPIRE

The fact that Jesus is sentenced to crucifixion by Pilate is attested to in all four gospels as well as by Tacitus.[130] But what does Pontius Pilate care about the Temple charge, and why does he interfere?[131] If Jesus's offense is indeed related to the Temple, why is he crucified, a penalty which seems to indicate that Jesus is convicted of sedition against Roman rule?[132] Before suggesting an explanation, one should recall an additional case indicating that the Romans are bothered by such prophecies about the Temple's destruction. In 62 CE Jesus son of Ananias cries out in the Temple (*naos*), foreseeing the destruction of Jerusalem and the Temple. He is arrested by the Jewish *archontes* and brought before Albinus, the Roman procurator. Jesus son of Ananias is imprisoned and tortured by the Romans until Albinus pronounces him insane and releases him. Jesus continues his predictions until being struck dead by a stone launched from the Roman ballista (*War* 6.300–309).

The Temple is not restricted to internal Jewish affairs. Viewed from a Roman imperial perspective, Jewish matters concern Roman authorities as much as those of any major provincial cult. Threats on the cult or the violation of its proper performance are considered anti-Roman acts that require a firm reaction by Roman authorities.

From a political perspective, the Jerusalem Temple is a Roman temple. The high priest was nominated by the Roman authorities (in 6–41 CE); the high priestly vestments of the Day of Atonement ritual were held by the Roman governor; a daily sacrifice was dedicated for the sake of the emperor (instead of the pagan imperial cult);[133] and the Roman army was stationed in the Antonia watching the Temple (Acts 21:30–37). Indeed, quite like their approach to imperial cults in other provinces, the Romans regarded the Temple as the symbolic center of their dominion in Judaea, though even more so than in other provinces owing to the central role of the Temple in ancient Judaism.[134] Proclamations about its coming destruction or an act against its status quo would have been taken as attempting to disturb Roman patronage.

Pilate may have been especially sensitive to a threat to this grand symbol of the Jewish acceptance of the emperor's rule. More than his predecessors, Pilate promoted the Roman imperial cult in Judaea. His coinage featured items related to Roman religious rituals, perhaps celebrating the religious role of Tiberius. The Tiberium he dedicated to the emperor in Caesarea Maritima and the shields he set up honoring Tiberius in Jerusalem may both be interpreted as relating to the imperial cult.[135]

Roman rulers and governors had good reasons to be watchful concerning violations of the public order in imperial temples. Several uprisings against Rome were first directed against the Roman imperial cults or a local cult which was enjoying Roman patronage. These cults symbolized the imperialism against which the rebels resist. Comparing Jesus's subversive cleansing of the Temple and the saying that is attributed to him about destroying it (and building a better one) to these other incidents demonstrates how Pilate may understand Jesus's symbolic attack on the Temple. In a revolt in Germania a priest called Segimundus serving at the altar of the Ara Ubiorum cult destroyed wreaths symbolizing his office and joined the rebels.[136] In Britain revolutionaries burned the Temple of Claudius.[137] The Druid revolt in Gaul was accompanied by a prophecy that the (accidental) burning of the Capitoline Temple in Rome would signify the end of Roman rule over the Gauls.[138] Last but not least, the so-called Zealots began the Jewish revolt by cessation of the daily sacrifice for the sake of the emperor.[139]

Indeed, many revolts in the Roman Empire emerged from the native cults.[140] The rebellion of the Bessi in Macedonia in 11 BCE was led by a priest of Dionysus who practiced divinations.[141] The revolt in Britain in 60 CE emanated from the sacred groves of the Druid priests as a reaction to the dedication of a Temple for Claudius, the conqueror of Britain.[142] In 69 CE Julius Civilis gathered his Batavan followers to feast in a sacred grove, where he took a religious vow to grow his hair until he defeated the Legions.[143] And Isidorus the priest led the revolt of the Bucoli near Alexandria in 172–173 CE, which included a ritual killing and an oath.[144]

It follows that Jesus's act and alleged words may also have been regarded by the Romans as resistance to the present state of affairs at the Temple, meaning an uprising not against the Temple per se but for the sake of the Temple and against Roman imperial influence. If Jesus was suspected of calling for the destroying and rebuilding of the Temple, the Romans may have interpreted this as an attempt to begin a revolt around the Temple or perhaps as a cultic reform that might lead to an anti-Roman uprising.

Prophecies and oracles of holy men—particularly those related to future destruction, such as those attributed to Jesus of Nazareth and Jesus son of Ananias—were taken very seriously by Roman rulers, especially the emperors. When directed against Rome, they were considered a potential threat to Roman rule.[145] The Romans paid attention to the words and deeds of those who spoke in the name of the gods, especially when their message was far from flattering.[146] This is another reason the charge leveled against Jesus of threatening to destroy the Temple could not go unnoticed by Pilate.

To conclude, considering the many cases of cultic resistance to cults sponsored or supervised by Rome as well as the cultic motivation of rebellions against the empire, it is likely that—from Roman imperial perspective—Jesus's supposed threat to destroy the Temple was understood as a political attack on Roman rule. Pilate may reasonably have assumed that anyone who begins such a rebellion designates himself as a new ruler. This may explain why the official (yet ironic) execution of Jesus as "King of the Jews" is rooted in the Temple charge, whether or not this was Jesus's intention.

The Last Supper and the Temple Cult

"On the first day of Unleavened Bread, when the Passover lamb is sacrificed, his disciples said to him, 'Where do you want us to go and make the preparations for you to eat the Passover?' So he sent two of his disciples . . . say to the owner of the house, 'The Teacher asks, Where is my guest room where I may eat the Passover with my disciples?' So the disciples set out and went to the city, and found everything as he had told them; and they prepared the Passover meal. . . .

While they were eating, he took a loaf of bread, and after blessing it he broke it, gave it to them, and said, 'Take; this is my body.' Then he took a cup, and after giving thanks he gave it to them, and all of them drank from it. He said to them, 'This is my blood of the covenant, which is poured out for many. Truly I tell you, I will never again drink of the fruit of the vine until that day when I drink it new in the Kingdom of God.'" (Mark 14:12–16, 22–25)

AUTHENTICITY

Many NT scholars maintain that the Markan narrative is a primitive report of the Last Supper. When Jesus speaks of his blood of the covenant shed for the many, he believes that his death will bring universal atonement.[147] The earliest attestation in the NT for the Last Supper is Paul's description of the Eucharist in 1 Cor 11:23–26, where he refers to an earlier tradition.[148] The similarities between 1 Cor 11:23–26 and Mark 14:22–25 are used as proof for a pre-Pauline and pre-Markan version of the Last Supper, one upon which the Markan account, also containing Hebraisms, is based.[149]

Some employ the criteria of embarrassment as proof of the authenticity of Jesus's words. Drinking blood (Mark 14:15) is repulsive for Jews. Therefore, Christians would preserve this tradition only if they believed it can be traced directly to Jesus. Furthermore, this tradition has multiple attestations in 1 Cor 11:23–26 and a slightly different version in Luke 22:13–20.[150] Not all scholars accept the authenticity of the words Mark cites as Jesus's words.[151] Crossan, for example, considers Mark 14:22–25 to be later then 1 Cor 11:23–26 (which is from the earliest historical stratum) but believes that neither of these are attributable to Jesus.[152] As we will see below, Jonathan Klawans's interpretation of the Last Supper as a ritual metaphor—in which Jesus does not call his disciples to actually eat his flesh and drink his blood (transgressing a Jewish taboo) but rather uses these as symbols—increases the plausibility of its authenticity.

There are several theories on the origins and development of the Eucharist as an early Christian rite: It is celebrated in remembrance of Jesus's daily meals with his disciples and others (Lietzmann, Chilton); it begins as a thanksgiving meal for the deliverance of the crucified Jesus as a thanksgiving sacrifice (Léon-Dufour); it is practiced in light of certain Psalms (Gese); Paul transforms it into a celebration of the death of Jesus, influenced by Greco-Roman cults (Lietzmann); it develops owing to the influence of the more mundane shared meals of Greco-Roman associations (Klinghardt).[153]

CULTIC SETTING: A PASSOVER SEDER?

In Mark and subsequently in Matthew and Luke the context of the Last Supper is the Passover festival.[154] According to Mark 14:12–16, Jesus and his disciples discuss the preparations for eating the Passover sacrifice and finding a place for the Passover ritual meal. Luke 22:15–16 adds Jesus's saying about his wish to eat the Paschal lamb; this may be an interpretation of the Markan passage.

It is quite natural to understand Jesus's words as an integral part of the interpretation over the bread and wine during the Passover meal. The Last Supper's description has a great deal in common with the Passover meal. It is eaten in Jerusalem at night (John 13:30; 1 Cor 11:23; and probably also Mark 14:17) jointly with the twelve apostles in a narrow circle. Also according to John 13:20, it is eaten in a state of Levitical purity required for eating the Passover lamb. Wine is used, common only on festivals and special occasions. The meal ends with the singing of a hymn (Mark 14:26) identified with the *hallel* (Ps 113–118) sung during the Passover meal. Jesus's words over the bread and wine are typical of the Passover seder rite in which homilies, blessing, and songs are recited. None of these characteristics derived from later Christian liturgical practice.[155] Joachim Jeremias regards it not as a historical description but as a cultic formula. He explains that Mark 14:22–25 does not mention the seder explicitly because Mark is interested only in the rites that are continued by the early church.[156]

Some disagree with identifying the Last Supper with the seder. Nowhere does Jesus refer to the Passover during the meal. There is no description of the bringing of the Passover lamb to be sacrificed on the altar by Jesus or his disciples, and Jesus eats bread, not lamb. Perhaps Jesus looks forward to eating the Passover lamb but cannot (Luke 22:15), substituting bread for it.[157] One solution to these queries is that in the Passion Narrative the Passover meal simply precedes the sacramental Lord's Supper—and that the two should be distinguished from one another.[158] Another solution is to suggest that the Supper is modeled after the seder but is in fact an independent ritual meal.[159]

Furthermore, the similarities between Jesus's Last Supper and the ceremonial contents of the Passover seder assume that the rabbinic description of the latter reflects pre-70 practices, a premise that some recent scholars doubt. If the rabbinic seder is established only at Yavneh, it is unlikely that Jesus follows it.[160] In addition, if it is a Passover meal, then the Supper should become an annual meal, not one that is celebrated weekly. Another concern is that if Jesus is crucified on the Passover day, how can Joseph of Arimathea buy linen cloth on the festival (Mark 15:46), as the Law demands that people refrain from commerce? It is more likely that he would buy it on the eve of the festival.[161]

The view that the Last Supper is a traditional Passover seder is also challenged by a different Johannine chronology of the Passion Narrative. In John, Jesus is put on trial by Pilate and crucified *before* Passover, at the "day of Preparation," namely, at the Passover eve (John 18:28; also in rabbinic tradition in b. *Sanhedrin* 43a). The Last Supper occurs a day earlier. Is John wrong?[162] There is one major reason for preferring the Johannine chronology: Mark's sequence of events placing the arrest on Passover eve and the trial on the festival is improbable, since the legal proceedings occur on the night of the Passover festival. This supports the Johannine chronology of crucifixion on the eve of Passover, and the trial's taking place before the festival.[163]

But even if one concludes that the Historical Jesus's Last Supper is not a seder, it is quite obvious that Mark (14:12–16, and then Matthew and Luke) consciously introduce it as such.[164] In order to gain a perspective on the meaning of the Passover context for Mark we need to compare it with John. John (18:28; 19:14) contextualizes Jesus's execution at the time of the Passover sacrifice, thus equating Jesus with the Paschal lambs and thereby making a theological point. Mark, however, does not mention the Passover characteristics—either in the bread and wine passage or afterward. Outside of the synoptic narrative, no early Christian source attempts to link the Supper to Passover. By 70 CE the Eucharist is already an established rite with no relation to Passover. So why does Mark introduce this setting to begin with? The simplest explanation is that Mark is following an earlier tradition, one which Paul probably finds irrelevant and does not mention in his epistles.

It is true that there is no other evidence for the Passover seder before the late first century CE rabbinic tradition at Yavneh. Nevertheless, Second Temple sources mention not only the sacrifice but also the drinking of wine, praising of God, and reciting of prayers and hymns.[165] This may be a reasonable setting for the Historical Jesus with regard to Jesus's blessings and words at the Last Supper.[166]

All of these elements are relevant to Jesus's approach to the Temple because of the possibility that he eats a Passover sacrifice right before or exactly when he speaks of eating and drinking his flesh and blood and discussing the covenant for the many. The context of this sacrificial ritual is crucial to understanding the Last Supper. We cannot ignore the possibility that Jesus says these words during or immediately after the traditional Passover sacrificial meal. Is it possible that Jesus initiates a substitution for sacrifice while he is actually eating one?

In any event, if Mark's story about the disciples' preparations for bringing the Passover sacrifice is authentic,[167] it demonstrates Jesus's general adherence to the sacrificial cult, notwithstanding the Last Supper.

ALTERNATIVE SACRIFICIAL CULT OR ITS REPLACEMENT

In his own words, Jesus makes the broken bread a metaphor for the flesh of his body, the wine a metaphor for his outpoured blood.[168] It is customary to understand his language as alluding to himself as a sacrifice.[169] For many, this means that Jesus introduces a substitute for sacrificial worship and the Temple cult.

Many believe that the sacrificial character of the Supper entails Jesus offering his own death as the ultimate sacrifice.[170] Jeremias comments that "it is a likely assumption that in the preceding Passover devotions he had also interpreted the Passover lamb in terms of himself," and this is why Paul identifies him as a Passover lamb (1 Cor 5:7). Jesus describes his death as an eschatological Passover sacrifice, a saving event. This parallels the Passover meal, which commemorates the original Passover of the Exodus and God mercifully "passing over" the house of the Israelites—since in Egypt the blood of the slaughtered lamb has redemptive power causing God to revoke their death sentence. In the same way, the people of God at the End Time will be redeemed by the merits of the Passover blood.[171] For Scott McKnight, the cup is connected to sacrificial death just as sharing the bread denotes participation in the death. Jesus offers himself to his followers in a sacrificial death. Jesus's body and blood become more effective substitutes or extensions of the Temple cult. Thus the Supper is the foundation of the abandonment of the Temple—a "fundamental reorientation of the Temple order" as the Temple is about to be destroyed. Those who eat Jesus's body and drink his blood are "passed over" from suffering.[172]

In fact, one may doubt whether the Historical Jesus actually refers to his coming death at the Last Supper. It is sometimes argued that "the blood poured for the many" is added after Jesus's death, thus reducing the Supper's sacrificial meaning. And even if these words are authentic they may nonetheless lack any expiatory or cultic meaning.[173]

Chilton maintains that Jesus's reference to his body and blood does not mean that he is a sacrifice, a victim. Such a doctrine can emerge only after the destruction of the Jerusalem Temple. Nevertheless, blood and body can be read sacrificially as referring to offerings one brings to God without being identified with Jesus's death. Jesus uses formulas for sacrifices that he himself forsakes (recall Chilton's thesis on Jesus's reform of one's ownership of sacrifice). He sets up an alternative cult of the Supper, a surrogate for sacrifice. This innovation of pure wine and bread shared in a community created by mutual forgiveness as a substitute for sacrifices leads to his arrest by the high priests and consequently to his death.[174] His "creation of alternative cultus"—the claim that God prefers a pure meal to impure sacrifice in the Temple and that eschatological purity becomes more important than a holy place—is regarded as a blasphemy of the Law.[175]

Theissen and Merz conclude that the Last Supper is the symbolic action of founding a cult that Jesus offers in place of the Temple, though he does not intend to found a cult that will last through time. He simply wants to temporarily replace the Temple cult, which has become obsolete. Jesus offers his disciples a replacement for the official cult in which they can no longer take part or which will not bring them salvation until a new Temple comes. They also suggest that the bread, not Jesus's own body, replaces the sacrifice; the cup symbolizes a new covenant. This covenant is built (following Jer 31:31–33) on the will of God being put in human hearts as well as God forgiving them of their sins.[176]

All in all, it is necessary to bear in mind one simple fact: Jesus does not refer to sacrifice directly during the Last Supper, nor is the Eucharist called a sacrifice anywhere in the NT, only later in the second century CE.[177] Paul equates it to sacrifices on the altar only to stress the feature of collective sharing (1 Cor 10:17–18). It is the Didache 14:2–3 which alludes to the Eucharist as sacrifice ("that your sacrifice be not defiled") without explanation. This certainly cannot be projected back to Jesus.

CULT AND SACRIFICE AS INSPIRING JESUS

Do these readings of the Last Supper as a substitute for sacrifices hold water? Does the description in Mark attest to a substitute for sacrifices? Klawans introduces an alternative view in which Jesus employs a sacrificial metaphor—nothing more, nothing less. Klawans states, "It is difficult to conceive of any understanding of Jesus' words at the Last Supper which does not grant on some level (stated or not) that Jesus' equation of wine with blood and bread with flesh is a metaphor of some sort."[178] Indeed, sacrifices in general and in Judaism in particular have a symbolic dimension.[179] As Klawans explains, "Sacrificial metaphors operate on the assumption of the efficacy and meaning of sacrificial rituals, and hope to appropriate some of that meaning and apply it to something else."[180]

The sacrificial aspects of Jesus's words include flesh and blood; the symbolic act of giving (as in offering the sacrifice to God through the altar); sharing it with others, as in the *shelamin* (well-being) sacrifice, which results in a ritual meal; the expressions "for you/many," which may echo expiatory implications; the juxtaposition of blood and covenant (cf. Exod 24:5–11); and the Paschal context. All but the Paschal event appear in 1 Cor 11:23–26, hence we can determine that Paul also models the Eucharist after sacrifice.[181]

Klawans maintains that Jesus's purpose in viewing the Last Supper along the lines of sacrifice is to show that the Supper, too, is a divine service. This may be equated with the manner in which Temple purity is applied to both meals and prayer as an effort to expand the realm of holiness. Meals and prayer do not set an alternative or critique to the cult when they imitate it. Rather, that may even be seen as "sacrificialization" (*imitatio Templi*) of nonsacrificial worship.[182] Therefore, the Eucharistic sacrificial overtones do not reject the Temple but, on the contrary, appropriate it when they borrow from the cult as a model for divine service.[183]

A good example of this approach is 1 Cor 10:14–18, where Paul draws an analogy between the Eucharist and sacrifice, arguing that the believers share the cup and bread just like Israel shares the sacrifices offered on the altar. Klawans notes that this analogy is not drawn to make the Eucharist a better alternative or even a replacement for Israel's service in the sanctuary. Rather, it aims "to underscore the seriousness, legitimacy, and efficacy of Israel's sacrificial service, and to present the Eucharist as similarly serious, legitimate and efficacious" and to "claim that Christian worship—like its analogue in Jerusalem—is not disembodied or abstract, but physical, tangible, and even threatened by defilement and profanation."[184]

Although Klawans's view is a minority one, I fully agree with it. Jesus's sayings may be compared to the Psalmist's: "Let my prayer be counted as incense before you, and the lifting up of my hands as an evening sacrifice" (Ps 141:2). This does not mean he would like to stop offering incense at the Temple and replace it exclusively with prayer. He introduces prayer as a cultic act, wishing to give it a holy status similar to incense.[185] Furthermore, the fact that the synoptic evangelist and Paul do not explicitly refer to Jesus's meat/flesh and wine/blood as a sacrifice also shows that they do not equate them with animal sacrifice.

Sometimes it seems that NT scholars read into the Last Supper ideas they find elsewhere in the NT. This replacement framework is not attested to in the Last Supper passage and is imported by commentators because of their understanding of other passages or general ideas about Jesus. Such claims, however, need to be substantiated by literary analysis.

The context of the Passover sacrifice, when Mark describes Jesus's preparation for eating the Passover lamb, overrules a full-blown anti-sacrificial reading of the Last Supper. When Mark portrays Jesus as sending his disciples to prepare the Passover ritual meal in which the Paschal lamb is eaten after being slaughtered at the Temple, he does not appear to think that Jesus claims that sacrifices are passé. Consequently, it is likely that Jesus, who stands closer to traditional Judaism than his post-Easter followers and interpreters, approaches the cult even more favorably. Therefore, it is possible that Mark 14:12–25 is authentic and that Jesus actually ate the Passover lamb during the Last Supper.

Conclusions

Jesus's cleansing of the Temple is usually seen as a protest in defense of it, not a rejection of the necessity of the sacrificial cult. Yet there are several suggestions as to what motivates Jesus to confront the cult: trade on the Temple Mount; the chief priests' immorality and politicization; the coming destruction (and rebuilding) relating to the Kingdom; the use of human and animal figures on the half-shekel Tyrian coins; the Temple tax itself;

or the division between holy/Jew and profane/Gentile. My own interpretation is that Jesus protests (or tries to halt, albeit symbolically) the pollution of the Temple via wicked money that is being transmitted to the Temple through the buying of animals for sacrifices or contributing of the half shekel.

Many scholars agree that Jesus says he will destroy the Temple, but some doubt that he also says he will rebuild one not made by human hands in three days. In my view, there is no sufficient evidence for either hypothesis. All four evangelists resist attributing this position to Jesus. There is very solid evidence that Jesus is accused of threatening the Temple, and this may be the Temple establishment's conclusion from his overturning of the tables. Jesus may not intend to threaten to destroy the Temple, but the thought that he does (whether sincerely or as an excuse) is, in my mind, a main reason for his arrest and crucifixion. Both the Sadducean chief priests and Pilate are very sensitive to such Temple issues. The Temple is also the last place the Romans would tolerate a rebel's yell. But Jesus may only want to oppose the unrighteousness of the laypeople reaching the most sacred place.

It is very common to interpret the Last Supper as a rite in which Jesus introduces his bread/flesh and blood/wine as a substitute for sacrifice. This innovation, however, does not appear explicitly in Jesus's own words, but rather, as Klawans suggests, as a sacrificial metaphor. Jesus uses the model of flesh and blood to imply sacrifice in order to give his ritual meal a sense of sacredness. He does not wish to replace sacrifice but to expand it to a new realm. Mark describes the Last Supper as occurring on Passover night, perhaps even during the seder, and mentions the preparations to bring the Paschal lamb to the Temple. Mark does not portray Jesus as being anti-sacrificial. It is even possible that the description is historical and that Jesus uses a sacrificial metaphor while eating the Paschal lamb.

Jesus is using the Temple and the cult to transmit some of his messages. He is committed to the cult, but not in the usual manner. He does not mean to threaten to destroy the Temple, although others think he does. He leaves his followers a heritage of unique, complex, and obscure approaches to the Temple that is continued in a rich variety of traditions.

2 Paul's Letters: Temple Imagery as Religious Identity

Introduction

PREVIOUS SCHOLARSHIP

Paul mentions the Temple and sacrifices several times in his un-contested letters, in different senses and contexts. This chapter examines themes that have already been extensively explored by previous scholars: Paul's analogy of the Christian community as a Temple, and his referring to Christ as a sacrifice. My aim is to examine Paul's preconception of the Temple cult when he coins these cultic ideas that are central to his theology and rhetoric. Several recent monographs on this topic have advanced the discussion considerably, but none gives equal attention to the entire spectrum of Paul's ideas of the Temple and sacrifices.

The modern study of the subject begins with Hans Wenschkewitz's concept of spiritualization, arguing that Paul's use of the temple language is not literal, that is, it does not refer to the actual Temple.[1] Rather, the temple theme represents the idea of numinous awe, for the sake of ethical admonition, influenced by Stoic philosophy and Jewish Hellenism.[2] Wenschkewitz concludes that Paul loses interest in the Jerusalem Temple and the sacrificial cult, since he believes that Jesus was the last sacrifice.[3]

Many modern scholars were influenced by Wenschkewitz.[4] According to Georg Klinzing, Paul's idea of atonement replaces the sacrificial cult, and instead of spiritualization he suggests the concept of *Umdeutung* (re-interpretation).[5] One may criticize the concept of spiritualization of sacrifice, since it builds on an assumption that favors the liberation of the worshiper from the "external, national cult and its institutions" so as to achieve a higher and better form of worship. Instead, an alternative term was suggested: "transference" of the Temple and cultic terminology, in which such concepts are shifted to designate noncultic reality.[6] Another possibility is that Paul redefines not the Temple cult itself but the situation of the Gentiles in relation to salvation, which he expressed in cultic terms. Yet it is still argued that in the end (Rom 15:16) Christ is substituted for the Temple cult.[7]

Most scholars simply take it for granted that for Paul the Church is the new Temple and that belief in Christ takes the place of the sacrificial cult in the Jerusalem Temple. Recently, however, there has been growing recognition of a more positive approach to the Temple cult in Paul's letters.[8] According to this trend of thought, Paul does not aim to set apart his addressees from the Temple cult, and his use of the cultic metaphors is constructive.[9] Some also argue that Paul uses cultic language because it offers a common idiom for Jews and Gentiles, since Paul's cultic language is not distinctively Jewish. He uses Temple imagery to illustrate God's acceptance of Jews and Gentiles alike—a sense of belonging to God.[10]

AIMS AND METHODS: THE ROLE OF METAPHORS

In this chapter I discuss all the references to the Temple, priests, sacrifices, and related cultic terms in Paul's letters, in the Deutero-Pauline letters, and in 1 Peter. The discussion follows a thematic order. Philological concerns will be reduced to a minimum (building on previous research) because of the vast amount of evidence and scholarship that exists on the subject. My aim is to suggest a synthesis of how Paul works with Temple/sacrifice imagery to advance his theological claims. I seek to reconstruct the basic concept of the Temple cult he has in mind and how this concept affects his theology and rhetoric. My hypothesis is that there is an inner logic behind Paul's rhetorical use of cultic imagery that reveals his attitude toward the Temple, whether theoretical or practical.

Like previous studies, mine will gather the pieces of his imagery scattered in many passages in his authentic epistles and identify the exact cultic image and its usage, while remaining sensitive to Paul's rhetoric and theology. In each passage I will examine why this imagery is necessary or useful in its current context. At the end of each section and in the final discussion concluding this chapter I will attempt to deduce Paul's approach to the religious or practical root of this image or analogy—the Jerusalem Temple and the actual sacrificial system.

Paul's biography is exceptional: a zealous persecutor of the followers of Jesus, he becomes one of the leading apostles. His attitude toward traditional Judaism is unclear and debated among scholars (see below). Three theoretical possibilities for schematizing his attitude toward the Temple may be found in his letters. Paul's use of Temple-related themes may

A. transform the concept of holiness and the worship of God from the Jewish sacrificial system to the belief in Christ and the life of the Christian community, thus denying the relevance of the Temple. This is indeed the most common view.
B. convey the sense of holiness and ritual to the Gentile Christians who lack such terms, being devoid of both pagan rites and Jewish Law. For Paul's Gentile readers, the Temple imagery is a substitute for the actual cultic system in which they cannot participate. The question remains whether Paul himself is more committed to the substitution he creates than to the original Temple cult on which it is based.
C. import terms of holiness and ritual to the spiritual life of the Christians, without substantial implications for the Jerusalem Temple, to which Paul remains fully committed.

Judging which of these three possibilities is correct is not an easy task. Paul's discourse is replete with metaphors, and his Temple-related imagery is only one of several groups of metaphors relating to the city, agriculture, marriage and family life, body, clothing, slavery, market, debt, travels, warfare, theater, and more.[11] My inquiry will therefore focus on the meaning and use of the relevant metaphors.

Every metaphor contains two parts, a source domain (Temple, sacrifice) corresponding to constituent elements of the target domain (the community, Jesus).[12] In his series of Temple and cultic images Paul uses "conceptual structural metaphors," in which the structure of the source domain is projected onto the structure of the target domain.[13] Such metaphors are based on both knowledge and image.

How do such metaphors operate in theory? Constituent elements of the source domain (Temple, sacrifice) correspond to constituent elements of the target domain (the community, Jesus). Elements of the source domain are mapped onto elements of the target domain. The elements of the target domain are not always present, and the metaphor does *not* follow preexisting similarities between elements in the two domains. These elements are created by the metaphor, when the target domain is structured by the source domain. The application provides a new concept with a particular structure or elements (e.g., romantic relationship described as a journey: "We're not going anywhere"). It is difficult to think of the target domain in the same manner without using the elements of the source domain, that is, it is not structured independently, as the elements of the target domain are based on language taken from the source domain. Such mapping is usually only partial, since the conceptual domains cannot be exactly the same.[14]

In the following sections I will attempt to evaluate what is the force of the cultic metaphor Paul is using. I will try to measure the extent of the hermeneutical gap between the source domain of the Temple-related metaphor and its target (community, believer, Christ, etc.), or the extent of the spiritualization process.[15] I will examine the connection between the substance of the Temple/sacrifice and the sense of Pauline imagery: Does Paul mention cultic *details* or only a general concept? Does he relate the Temple or cult to specific details in the Christian realm (such as behavior or practices)? In other words, how thick is the spiritualization or metaphor, and how far, for example, do the ties between the Temple and the community extend? The thicker and more detailed the analogy or metaphor, the more remote from the actual cult the imagery becomes, until it is a substitution. According to this methodology, the transference of the cultic imagery is achieved through channels of appropriation: the question is, To what extent is a specific component of the cult transferred to the Church, and where exactly is it situated in its new realm; is it marginal or given a central role?

There are two further criteria for measuring the cultic transference effected by these metaphors: Does the *context* of Paul's use of imagery have any connection to the Temple theme, or is it a more general or even mere rhetorical use of the Temple imagery? Furthermore, viewing the entire spectrum of Paul's use of cultic imagery, do these metaphors relate to each other in a way that reflects a *system*, comparable to the sacrificial system in the Temple, or are they isolated or even coincidental assertions? Only in the event that the context attests to an interest in the cult, and Paul's cultic metaphors culminate in an alternative cultic system, is it possible to claim that Paul replaces the Temple cult with new religious concepts modeled after the Temple.

Paul's Temple-related discourse cannot be isolated from his general approach to the Law and Judaism as a religion. The problem is that if Paul rejects the Jewish Law and commandments, if he regards himself and his

Gentile addressees as being outside Judaism in the practical sense of the term, why does he use the imagery of Temple and sacrifice? Does his cultic discourse prove that he nevertheless thinks highly of the Temple, or the opposite, that he wants to replace it? My study must relate to the scholarly debate on Paul's attitude toward the Law and Jewish identity—but without depending on it! These matters must await the results of an examination of Paul's discourse on the Temple, priests, and sacrifices and will be discussed in the concluding section of this chapter.

Temple

I COR 3:16–17: THE BELIEVERS ARE GOD'S TEMPLE

"Do you not know that you are God's temple [*naos*] and that God's Spirit dwells in you? If anyone destroys God's Temple, God will destroy that person. For God's Temple is holy, and you are that Temple."

Paul's message is that the community should regard itself as a dwelling place of God's Spirit.[16] The dwelling (*oikein*) holiness in the Temple is a Jewish concept found in Josephus, Qumran, and so forth.[17] Here Paul creates a threefold analogy: holiness, spiritual empowerment (God's spirit), and (in v. 17) the judgment cast on one who destroys the Temple.[18]

The common view is that here the Church is a substitute for the Temple or serves as a new Temple.[19] However, the metaphor does not necessarily imply any antagonism toward the Jerusalem Temple. Paul may merely mean that God's presence resides in the Christian congregation.[20] Albert Hogeterp maintains that Paul makes positive use of the concept: "The idea of the Temple provided a strong theological model for the appeal to holiness and unity."[21] Paul uses the concept only in order to show that the Corinthians are called upon to be holy and not behave like ordinary people obsessed with strife, factionalism, and pride. There is no sign that they are superior to the Temple or that they are a substitute for it.[22]

Paul specifies the common domain shared by the community and the Temple: God's Spirit resides in both. If Paul attempts to create a sense of the community to serve as a real Temple instead of the one in Jerusalem, he should provide more details, such as arguing that in the community the sacrifice of Christ takes the place of animal sacrifice. Furthermore, the analogy may be limited to its specific context, namely, the danger of strife and factionalism within the community. The implication of the analogy is too narrow for a complete equation of the community with the Temple.

Nevertheless, the very idea that the Holy Spirit dwells in the Corinthian community as it does in the Temple is certainly radical.

In this passage the Temple is perceived as a locus of God's spirit, where conflicts and divisions between the worshipers disappear. These features are not attributed to the Temple in the Hebrew Bible,[23] at least not explicitly. Rather, the spirit dwells in the *people of Israel*.[24] In a sense, the basic concept that God's *spirit* (and not merely His dwelling or presence) resides in the Temple is Paul's innovation. But here and elsewhere in the Corinthian correspondence, the Temple is where God dwells and not necessarily where sacrifices are offered. For all these reasons, it seems that Paul's metaphor is mainly a rhetorical tool for arguing for general sanctity within the community.

I COR 6:19: THE BELIEVERS' BODY AS A SANCTUARY

"Or do you not know that your body is a sanctuary [*naos*] of the Holy Spirit within you, which you have from God, and that you are not your own?"

It is not clear whether "your [plural] body" means the individual bodies of the Corinthians or a corporate communal body. If Paul relates to the sanctity of the physical bodies of the individual members, he is denying the contrast between body and spirit in relation to holiness and using the human body to express the reality of the presence of God's Spirit within that community.[25] Support for this reading may be found in the context of sinning against one's own body in the previous passage (6:13).[26] One might suggest that since the individual body is part of the community, his or her defilement is contagious for the whole community, the communal body.[27]

Robert McKelvey concludes from the conjunction of the Temple in 1 Cor 6:19–20 that the new Temple is also a new cult, a new sort of sacrifice.[28] But is there such total transference or identification of the Corinthians' bodies with the Temple? To what extent does Paul use the image of the Temple as containing God's Holy Spirit to create the analogy with the bodies of the believers? The context of the passage indicates that he calls upon the Corinthians to shun fornication and prostitution.[29] He contrasts sexual sins with the sanctity of one's body in God's Spirit, which is mandatory according to Jewish tradition.[30] The sense of sacredness is limited to refraining from prostitution. Paul's accusation to the owners of body-sanctuary of *porneia* is indicative of the low level of sanctity embedded in this Temple imagery. There is no other aspect of holiness in this passage, as we might expect if Paul actually applied the religious aspect of holiness to the Corinthians. Once again the concept of the Temple as a Holy Spirit is unique to Paul and even more limited than in 1 Cor 3:16–17.

2 COR 6:14–16, 7:1: THE COMMUNITY AS A TEMPLE— A NON-PAULINE PASSAGE?

"Do not be mismatched with unbelievers. . . . For what agreement has the Temple of God with idols? For we are the temple [*naos*] of the living God." . . . "Since we have these promises, beloved, let us cleanse ourselves from every defilement of body and of spirit, making holiness perfect in the fear of God."

Continuing the sweeping identification of the Corinthians with God's Temple in 2 Cor 6:16, in 7:1 the community becomes the bearer of purity, holiness, and the promise of an everlasting future.[31] The passage highlights the concept of purity in relation to the Temple in other ways as well. 6:17 refers to Temple purity, which is delineated as the communal boundary of a state of holiness, while in 7:1 it is assumed that without purity the glory of God will leave the Temple.[32]

Here the characterization of the Christians as a Temple is not limited to the Holy Spirit. In both the community and the Temple purity of body and soul is necessary to create the holiness in which God dwells. Several features of the Temple are detailed—the most important is the contrast between the Temple of "the living God" and idols—and a number of scriptural citations support these features. There is a real sense of equating the community with the Temple, and there is a practical implication for the Corinthians: They must separate themselves from idolatrous Gentiles.

The differences between this analogy and the metaphors of 1 Cor 3 and 6 are obvious. The Temple imagery is not merely a rhetorical phrase but the essence of the entire passage. The transference from the Temple to the believers' social behavior is more detailed, involving patterns of behavior in relation to purity, several explanations (God's dwelling, holiness), and several scriptural justifications.

Some scholars conclude that the presence of God had moved from the official Jerusalem Temple to the new people of God.[33] That is, the association of the community with the Temple is not an analogy. Paul's use of Scripture (Lev 26:11–12 and Ezek 37:26–27) shows that the Christians *are* the Temple, "the church being the actual beginning fulfilment of the end-time Temple prophesied in the Old Testament."[34]

Nevertheless, it is also possible to interpret Paul's statement as transference from the Temple to the community, but not as a total replacement of the Jerusalem Temple. Notably, the biblical passages cited do not refer specifically to the Temple. The analogy is deep in its expression but still restricted in its content: God's presence within the Corinthians, which *seems* similar to God's dwelling in the Temple, demands purity in relation to "outsiders."

Is this passage written by Paul? There is a resemblance to the dualistic theology of the Community Rule and the War Rule from Qumran (especially the contrast between light and darkness and God and Belial).[35] One may therefore speculate that Paul uses earlier ("Essene") material in his composition of 2 Cor.[36] The passage carries a separatist ideology which may not suit Paul. It seems to indicate that the Corinthians do not accept the need to draw the boundaries between pure and impure etc. that are related to the Temple concept. They become too universal and foster their relationship with unbelievers too much. The author's bold denouncement of outsiders is uncharacteristic of Paul and recalls the Qumranic attitude.[37]

Whether Paul or a later editor positions or reworks this passage, its non-Pauline origin/character is also attested to by the unusual use of Temple imagery in comparison to 1 Cor 3 and 6 (and, as we will see below, the entire imagery of Temple priests and sacrifice in Paul's letters). 2 Cor 6:16–7:1 provides us with a valuable tool. It shows that typical Pauline Temple imagery is restricted and thin in relation to the thicker and more extensive metaphor(s) in the present passage. Nevertheless, even here the community-as-Temple imagery does not stand alone but has a specific rhetorical function. It serves the author's call for the Corinthians to separate themselves from idolatry because they are holy.

I now turn briefly to two non-Pauline epistles which also portray the community as a Temple.[38] It will be helpful to compare their use of Temple imagery to Paul's.

EPH 2:20–22: JESUS AND THE COMMUNITY AS A TEMPLE

". . . with Christ Jesus himself as the cornerstone; In him the whole structure is joined together and grows into a holy Temple [*naon hagion*] in the Lord; in whom you also are built together spiritually into a dwelling-place [*katoikētērion*] for God."

Ephesians is commonly viewed as Deutero-Pauline (post-70 CE?). In verses 19–20 the Ephesians are called holy citizens and members of the household of God. These passages are intended to elevate them spiritually as intimates of God and to establish that their spiritual edifice is based on belief in Jesus. The entire section describes closeness to God through imagery such as cornerstone, building, sanctuary, dwelling place, and city. Ephesians thus employs more substantive architectural and Temple imagery than 1 and 2 Corinthians.

In contrast to Paul's relationship to the community as a Temple, here the Temple of believers does not stand by itself; rather, the believers are identified with a sanctuary whose foundation rests on Jesus. Unlike 1 and 2 Corinthians, here the Temple imagery is closely related to Christology. The imagery of the holy building is what connects the believers and Jesus. But here as well, the result is that God dwells with the believers.[39] The Temple is a model, one of many, for holiness. These images are introduced after the author emphasizes the transition of the Ephesians from sinful Gentiles and those who hunger for bodily desires to a people close to the savior. Here we see that the imagery of the Temple is intended to infuse them with a sense of belonging to the Christian movement.[40]

1 PET 2:4–6: THE BELIEVERS AS A SPIRITUAL HOUSE

"Come to him, a living stone, though rejected by mortals yet chosen and precious in God's sight, and; like [*hōs*] living stones, let yourselves be built into a spiritual house [*oikos pneumatikos*], to be a holy priesthood [*hierateuma*], to offer spiritual sacrifices [*pneumatikas thusias*] acceptable to God through Jesus Christ; For it stands in scripture: 'See, I am laying in Zion a stone, a cornerstone chosen and precious; and whoever believes in him will not be put to shame.'"

1 Peter, another post-70 writing, contains a complicated structure of Temple ideas of dwelling/Temple, priests, and sacrifices. Most scholars identify the "spiritual house" as a Temple. This is consistent with the references to the priesthood and sacrifices later in the verse.[41] In a sense, the community of believers is the new Temple in which the believers are serving as priests.[42]

This is the only section in the NT that ties together references to Temple, priests, and sacrifices, rendering them "spiritual" and connecting them to believers in Jesus. The "spirituality" of the believers is translated into three images—building/Temple, priests, and sacrifices. None of these refer to actual Temple rituals; rather, they transport the Temple-ritual symbolism to another realm, namely, to the members of the community to which the epistle is addressed. In contrast to 1 and 2 Corinthians and to Ephesians, where only the Temple is mentioned in relation to the community, here the author is not satisfied with transferring only one cultic element to the spiritual sphere. Instead, he lists them all, emphasizing that he offers a parallel system equivalent to the priestly sacrifices in the Temple. From this it can be assumed that he was aware of Paul's imagery but expanded upon it.

Why does the author introduce this complex Temple imagery? The association is an attempt to preach morality (2:1, 11–12) and to call for the elimination of evil, deceit, jealousy, and lust. Prior to this (1:14–15) the author creates a conflict of values between lust and being counted among the holy believers. This link between the Temple imagery and the moral behavior already appears in 1 and perhaps in 2 Corinthians as well. However, the broader context is a call to be holy, quoting the commandment for holiness made to Israel in Ex 19:6 and Lev 19:2 (1 Pet 1:16; 2:9). The determination that the audience is holy like the Temple is not superficial, as it is in 1 Corinthians; it is more developed, listing the elements of the cultic system and pointing out the commandment in the Torah to be holy. This indicates that the intention of the Temple-priests-sacrifice imagery is to reinforce and enhance the value of holiness and closeness to God in the eyes of the readers so they will be scrupulous in their interpersonal relationships and imbued with a consciousness of holy community, similar to the sanctity of the People of Israel to God.

1 Peter is therefore unique in its elaborate cultic imagery and the development of its theological implications. 1 and 2 Corinthians and Ephesians do not explain how the community becomes similar to the Temple, and no cultic function is mentioned beyond the metaphor itself to create a link between the community and the Temple. Unlike 1 Peter, Paul and the author of Ephesians do not specify how the community is characterized as a Temple and what Temple functions it replaces or imitates. Like Ephesians and, again, unlike Paul's letters, in 1 Peter the cultic imagery is closely linked to Christological worship.[43]

EXCURSUS: QUMRANIC INFLUENCE ON PAUL'S COMMUNITY-AS-A-TEMPLE MODEL?

There is a common thesis that Paul's community-as-a-Temple image follows an idea previously found in Qumran, in the Community Rule (1QS) and 4Q174 Florilegium.[44] I have discussed the Qumranic community-as-Temple metaphor elsewhere in detail.[45] Here I would like to discuss briefly

Table 1.

Text	Temple Terminology	Cultic Function
1QS 8: 6–7	**holy house** (*bayit*) for Israel and the foundation of **the holy of holies** for Aaron	To **atone** for the land
1QS 8: 8–10	most **holy dwelling** (*ma'on*) for Aaron, a **house** of perfection and truth in Israel	in order to **offer a pleasant aroma** and these will be accepted in order to **atone** for the land
1QS 9: 3–5		in order to **atone** for the guilt of iniquity and for the unfaithfulness of sin . . . without the flesh of **burnt offerings** and without the fats of **sacrifice**—the **offering** of the lips in compliance with the decree will be like the **pleasant aroma** of justice and the perfectness of behavior will be acceptable like a **freewill offering**.
1QS 9: 5–6	a **holy house** for Aaron, in order to form a **most holy** (literally: "holy of holies") community (*yahad*), and a **house** of the Community for Israel	
4Q174 1: 6–7	a **Temple** of man	to **offer** him in it, before him, **the works of thanksgiving/Torah**

the differences between Pauline and Qumranic Temple imagery. As more and greater differences are found between the passages in the scrolls and the NT, the fewer are the chances that early Christians were influenced by the Qumranic worldview. My analysis relates to three central differences: 1. Temple terminology; 2. Temple functions; 3. Overarching context of the early Christians' conception of the community as a Temple.

Terminology. As opposed to the NT, in the Community Rule there is no use of the explicit term "Temple" or, more precisely, sanctuary, *naos*. Rather, the Community Rule uses other language which only hints at the Temple and even combines the cultic and social/communal meanings, such as house or dwelling. The authors of the Community Rule do not call themselves a Temple or bestow upon their community explicit Temple titles. They do, nonetheless, present their sect as a kind of (temporary) substitute for the Temple while refraining from presenting themselves as equivalent to it in terms of status. Furthermore, in the revolutionary concept "Temple of Man" in Florilegium, *adam* may denote the difference between this temple and the earthly Temple in Jerusalem, implying that the "Temple of Man" is not a real Temple.[46]

It is customary to interpret the Qumranic term "house" in 1QS as being synonymous with "Temple."[47] However, in Qumran "house" embodies both the House of the Lord and the social group. The usage of "house" in the context of atonement for the members of the sect creates a double meaning. Therefore, one should not keep to the narrow meaning of "house" as a synonym for only the Temple's physical structure.[48] Moreover, if "house" were synonymous with "Temple" and nothing more, then "a holy house for Aaron . . . a community [*Yahad*] house for Israel" (1QS 9:6) would necessarily mean two different Temples, one for Aaron and one for Israel! Furthermore, holy and holy of holies are levels of holiness, whereas the Inner Sanctum is called "*the* holy of holies" in the Temple Scroll.[49]

Function. 1 and 2 Corinthians and Ephesians do not explain how the community comes to resemble the Temple. There is no cultic function mentioned beyond the metaphor itself to create a link between the community and the Temple. In general, the aim of the authors of the NT epistles was to instill in their followers a sense of holiness and the Holy Spirit and to imbue them with the identity of a sacred religious community. But beyond that, Paul and the author of Ephesians do not specify how the community is characterized as a Temple and what Temple functions it replaces or copies.

In contrast, the Community Rule mentions "to atone" once and "to atone for the land" twice. 1QS 9:3–6 offers a systematic, alternative system of prayer and justice to replace the sacrifices (see the text in table 1). In Florilegium, I suggest, the purpose of the "Temple of Man" is to observe the laws of the Torah. These functions explain how the community can act as a Temple, and they infuse meaning and tangibility into the Temple terms in the scrolls. The authors of the Qumran scrolls do not use the term "Temple" simply as a description or metaphor for the religious community. Rather, they are declaring that now atonement is achieved through relationships and deeds in the same way it is achieved through sacrificial service.

In the passages in 1 and 2 Corinthians and Ephesians there is no information about what readers need to do in order to become a temple (this is implied elsewhere throughout these epistles: believing in Jesus, distancing oneself from idol worship, and establishing loving relationships among themselves, etc., but without linking these teachings and instructions to cultic imagery). This may indicate that the metaphor of the community as a Temple does not pretend to claim that the community undertakes the role and place of the Temple but is only compared to it for the purpose of glorifying and illustrating its holiness. In this respect, as already noted, 1 Peter is different.

Context. The Temple imagery in the Community Rule and Florilegium is not presented in a limited, concrete context but programmatically, by introducing the basic aims of the sect. 1QS 8:5–6, 9–10, and 9:4–6 are statements regarding the general objectives of the Yahad. They herald the new conditions or guidelines "in Israel" in relation to the rules relevant to the sect's situation at the present time. In the case of the Florilegium the entire passage deals with Temples, including the past and the future and most probably also the present, within the context of threats to the Temple from strangers.

In contrast, we have seen that in the three relevant sections of 1 and 2 Corinthians the metaphors are used in a context that limits their meaning to motivate specific social behavior: preventing internal conflicts, avoiding prostitution, or severing relationships with idol worshipers. In this way the Corinthians do not atone through Temple sacrifices; rather, their existence is like a Temple requiring them not to be defiled. The context shows that Paul does not intend the Christian community to resemble the Temple in every respect. Its members must avoid quarrels, prostitution, and idolatry, as these are forbidden in the Temple. This is probably why cultic functions are absent. Thus the rhetorical and practical goals of these passages limit the religious extent of the metaphor of community as a Temple. It is neither a central religious characteristic of these communities nor a major theological argument for Paul. In contrast, in the Community Rule this is perhaps *the* central tenet of the sect; indeed, the idea of atonement while living in the sect is central and recurs constantly in the Damascus Document, the Hodayot (thanksgiving hymns scroll), and other scrolls.

There are indeed intriguing similarities between 1QS 5:5; 8:6; 9:3, Ephesians 2:20–22, and 1 Pet 2:5. All share allusions to the foundation (*sod* or *yesod*) and/or stone in Isa 28:16 ("I am laying in Zion a foundation stone, a tested stone, a precious cornerstone, a sure foundation *musad musad*") as a symbol of the community.[50] All relate this to Temple imagery, in various forms, although this is not attested to in Isa 28. One may therefore speculate as to whether the authors of Ephesians and 1 Peter are influenced by the Qumranic tradition.

1 Pet 2:5 relates to the cultic function of the community, namely, how it actually operates as a Temple, offering spiritual sacrifices acceptable to God. This is quite similar to "for the approval of the land" and "acceptable like a freewill offering" in 1QS 9:3–5. And yet, in contrast to the Community Rule, which presents new modes of prayer and righteous conduct as a means of atonement, 1 Peter does not specify which sacrifices are offered or exactly how the readers function as priests (although 1 Pet 2:3–4, 6 implies that the concepts of sacrifices and priesthood concern the belief in Christ). 1 Peter also uses the term "house" (*oikos*) as in 1QS for the community, with the possible allusion to Temple imagery. Also, both mention the priests, who are alluded to three times in the Community Rule by the mention of "Aaron." Most important, both 1 Peter and 1QS 9:3–5 refer to the tripartite system of Temple, priests, and sacrifices as being replaced by the community. Allowing for these parallels, it is possible that the author of 1 Peter is familiar with and inspired by the Community Rule 9:3–5, although it seems that he is initially influenced by Paul's community-as-a-Temple metaphor.[51]

In conclusion, there are substantial differences between the community-as-Temple metaphors in Qumran and in the Pauline letters. In the Community Rule the link between the sect and the Temple is the most elaborate. It is intertwined with implications and meaning, and yet it never explicitly uses the term "Temple"/"sanctuary." If there had indeed been a strong Qumranic influence on Paul, it would make sense that his use of the metaphor of community as a Temple would not be so superficial. As I will show, Paul's metaphors of community as a Temple are part of a more complex Pauline system of cultic metaphors with no connection to the scrolls. It appears that Paul developed the metaphors on his own, which attests that the Temple-priests-sacrifices are close to his heart, at least from a conceptual perspective.

PAUL'S TEMPLE IMAGERY: GREEK-PAGAN OR JEWISH?

Since Paul writes in Greek for a Hellenistic and Roman audience, mainly non-Jews, is it possible that he draws on Greek, that is, pagan conceptions of Temples, so that his audience will understand his words better? It is reasonable to assume that Paul speaks to the Gentile Corinthians in their own idiom and using their own imagery and uses Temple metaphors because both Jews and Gentiles could understand them.[52] Thus the Gentile Corinthians would probably not think of the Jerusalem Temple when presented with the verbal image of a temple.[53] For example, Greco-Roman temples in a city like Corinth (including those of the imperial cult) demonstrated civil identity. This sense, with its powerfully evocative visual imagery, may fit Paul's needs.[54]

However, more than mere rhetoric is involved here. Such an approach neglects the fundamental difference between Jewish and pagan conceptions of temples. Gentiles regard the Jerusalem Temple as one among many, dedicated to many gods, while for Jews, Greek temples are the complete antithesis of the Temple of the true and only God. In fact, Paul takes it for granted that his audiences should follow a monotheistic belief and reject other gods, and he calls on them time and again to refrain from sacrificing to idols.[55] The last thing he wants is to stimulate their spiritual imagination and self-understanding with images of local pagan cults and sanctuaries.[56] Furthermore, an analysis of the language and literary context of the passages of Temple imagery reveals that they relate to Jewish scriptural citations, symbols, and ideas. For example, in 1 Cor 3:9 Paul used *oikodomē* for God's building, as in 1 Chron 29:1.[57] The eating from the altar in 1 Cor 9:13 should be read in light of eating sacrifices at the altar in 10:18, which explicitly relates to the people of Israel.[58] Here the primary claim of the passage in 1 Cor 10:14, 20–21 is that the Corinthians must refrain from sacrifice to idols. In Rom 15:16 (discussed below) the offering (*prosphora*) of the Gentiles matches not only Greek parallels but also the usage in the LXX and Josephus. It refers to God (15:16) and Jerusalem (15:19), hence it is entirely Jewish.[59] The libation (*spendomai*) in Phil 2:17 (discussed below) does not pertain to pagan sacrifice because Paul applies it to the children of God (2:15),[60] and 2:14–15 alludes to the Hebrew Bible.[61]

Just as Paul expects his readers to understand the numerous biblical citations and scriptural allusions in his epistles, despite their Greco-Roman background, he also assumes that they know that his Temple imagery pertains to the Jewish sacrificial system and the Jerusalem Temple. The fact that they are already familiar with other Greek (pagan) cults is hardly helpful, since neither Paul nor his audience believe that the Holy Spirit dwells in the Temples of Corinth, Rome, or Philippi. To the contrary, the Christian Gentiles' *desertion* of these pagan cults provides the background and reasoning behind Paul's cultic metaphors.

CONCLUSIONS

It is commonly argued that Paul's Temple language derives from the belief that the Holy Spirit now resides in the midst of the community, in the same way that the presence of God dwelt in the Jerusalem Temple.[62] McKelvey, like many others, concluded that the new Temple replaces the old one and that the church as Temple is the fulfillment of the hope of eschatological indwelling in Jerusalem.[63] Yet he adds that Paul does not regard the new Temple as totally superseding the old one, since the Jerusalem Temple does not cease to have religious significance for Paul.[64]

However, a careful reading of Paul in the context of his own rhetoric and in comparison to the Qumranic explicit transference of atonement from the Temple to the community leads to different conclusions. First of all, in the passages discussed in this section, Paul's purpose is not to define the community as a *new* Temple but to combat dissension and teach ethics. The Temple imagery does not demand that the Corinthians observe ritual purity as in the Jerusalem Temple (with the possible exception of the non-Pauline 2 Cor 6:16–7:1). The Temple imagery remains merely an image of holiness, an analogy without practical cultic implications.[65] Second, the analogy is brief, without explanation or justification, either by Scripture or by Paul's own theology (again, 2 Cor 6:16–7:1 stands out). All this seems to attest to acknowledgment rather than replacement of the Temple.

Paul refrains from linking the community-Temple analogy to other cultic terms he employed in the same manner. For example, he never identifies Jesus with the Temple, as in John 2:21, or equates Jesus with the Temple, as in Matt 12:6. The Corinthians' bodies are imaged as a Temple, and they are also Christ's body (1 Cor 6:15; 12:17, yet the purpose of these analogies is to encourage the unity of the community). One could argue that the implication is that Christ is the Temple. But, curiously, Paul never closes the circle with the image of Christ's body as a Temple.[66]

Paul as Priest

1 COR 9:13: THE APOSTLE AND THE TEMPLE SERVICE

"Do you not know that those who are employed in the Temple service get their food from the Temple, and those who serve at the altar share in what is sacrificed on the altar?"

The entire chapter justifies Paul's material rights as an apostle.[67] Paul refers to the Temple service at the altar as an example of a service which entails certain material rights, an analogy to the material rights of those who proclaim the gospel. At the heart of this analogy lies the equation of

Paul (or any apostle) to a priest serving at the altar, offering the people's sacrifices. The implication is that the Christian mission is like the Temple. While the target metaphor is limited to an economic sense, the metaphor is nevertheless rooted in the holiness of the Christian faith or movement. The rhetorical question introduced by Paul implies that the cultic background of the rules of priestly service is not an innovation, and perhaps Paul's use of such an analogy should not surprise the Corinthians.

According to this metaphor, Paul is like a priest and the gospel is like a Temple service, but not really. This is stated only to justify common, yet disputed economic and social behavior. Reducing the Temple service to its administrative or economic aspect does not really utilize the religious ("spiritual") potential of the analogy to the sacred realm.

ROM 15:16: PAUL AS PRIEST, THE GENTILES AS AN OFFERING

". . . because of the grace given me by God: to be a minister [*leitourgos*] of Christ Jesus to the Gentiles in the priestly service [*hierourgounta*] of the gospel of God, so that the offering [*prosphora*] of the Gentiles may be acceptable, sanctified by the Holy Spirit."

Paul seems to argue, literally, that the gospel is a "sacrifice" and he is its "minister."[68] He may mean that he consecrates the gospel, which is "sanctified by the Holy Spirit." That is, Paul is like a temple servant of Jesus Christ with respect to the Gentiles, who perform the cultic duty of consecrating the gospel of God; hence the offering (*prosphora*) of the Gentiles might be acceptable, as it is sanctified by the Holy Spirit.[69] The cultic metaphor is therefore twofold: for the Gentiles the gospel is a priestly liturgy, and the Gentiles' faith in Jesus is an offering consecrated by the Holy Spirit.[70] Paul is portraying himself as one who serves as a priest in the Jerusalem Temple, with no hint of later Christian leaders designated as priests (as in 1 Peter and Revelation).[71]

Here the analogy is double and therefore thicker than the previously discussed Temple imagery. Paul is a priest because the Gentiles are an offering, and it is his duty to ensure that they are sanctified in the Holy Spirit. The entire Christian mission and perhaps Christian faith in general are described as a sacrificial system. The basic message is that for the Christians holiness is involved here just as it is in the Temple. Nonetheless, the focal point relates personally to Paul: as an apostle he has a major spiritual role, since his work must be executed with care and accuracy, without errors, just like the work of the priest.[72] The metaphor demonstrates that for Paul his mission to the Gentiles is the most important task in the world, and in this sense it is, for him (and probably in his own view, for God), no less important and holy than sacrifices in the Temple. Perhaps Paul uses this grand metaphor because he wants the Christians in Rome to acknowledge his special role and authority as their apostle,[73] since he immediately boasts of his signs and wonders (vs. 17–20). This passage differs from the previous functional analogy of the right of the priest/apostle to earn a living from his service at the altar/mission. When Paul wants to demonstrate the true meaning of his life, he thinks in terms of a priest in the most sacred service of God.

Sacrificial Imagery

I COR IO:I6–I8: EUCHARIST AS SHARED SACRIFICE

"The cup of blessing that we bless, is it not a sharing in the blood of Christ? The bread that we break, is it not a sharing in the body of Christ? Because there is one bread, we who are many are one body, for we all partake of the one bread; Consider the people of Israel [according to the flesh][74]; are not those who eat the sacrifices partners in the altar?"

Here Paul discusses the Eucharist, which sustains a sacrificial meta-phor of flesh, blood, and meal (as in 1 Cor 11:23–26, see chapter 1). He then refers to the sacrifices of the laity and to the actual meal that follows the offering of the sacrifice on the altar, shared by the participants.[75]

Does the reference to Israel's altar carry a negative connotation with pagan cults? This should be considered in the context of Paul's preach-ing against sacrifices to idols and Israel's sin and idolatry in the wilder-ness.[76] Furthermore, the phrase "Israel according to the flesh" is pejorative. There are, however, several arguments to the contrary. Not all Israelites have sinned, and in v. 20 Paul does not condemn Jews but, specifically, pagans (*ethnē*).[77] As for the phrase "according to the flesh," Paul uses it favorably in relation to Christ (1 Cor 9:5) and "my kinsmen" (Rom 1:3; 4:1; 9:3).[78]

But what does Paul actually mean by "partners in the altar"? When the Israelites/Jews offer their sacrifices and partake of them, they are in effect identifying with what is offered on the altar and with the Lord, since the sacrifice is shared between God, the priest, and the offerer.[79] This rite binds them together in common worship of God. The message he wants to stress concerns his opposition to other idolatrous meals and worship (in vs. 7–8, 19–20). The believers cannot attend both rites (v. 21).[80]

The analogy from the eating of the Eucharist—the most important Christian rite which symbolizes the union with Christ according to Jesus's own command—to the sharing of the sacrifice on the altar in Jerusalem is impressive. Nonetheless, it would be wrong to deduce from this passage that Paul regards the Eucharist as equivalent to a sacrifice.[81] Paul's discourse is instructive rather than declarative. He does not deal directly with the Eucharist but merely reminds the Corinthians that idolatrous rituals are prohibited. He uses the analogy that the ritual meal is a communal sharing in order to exclude sharing with outsiders, pagan worshipers. Comparing the Eucharist to the sacrificial meals after they are offered on the altar gives the impression that the Christians are one community under one God, just like the Jews at the Temple. Paul limits the analogy to its practical sense. Yet it rests on the basic assumption, supposedly obvious to the Corinthians, that both the Eucharist and the sacrifices on the altar are sacred rites. Can we learn from this that Paul regards the Eucharist as a sacrifice? Surprisingly, he never makes such a statement.

2 COR 2:14–16: THE GOSPEL / CHRIST AS THE FRAGRANT AROMA OF SACRIFICES

"But thanks be to God, who in Christ always leads us in triumphal procession, and through us spreads in every place the fragrance [*osmē*] that comes from knowing him; For we are the aroma [*euōdia*] of Christ to God among those who are being saved and among those who are perishing; to the one a fragrance from death to death, to the other a fragrance from life to life."

Here the fragrance is both the gospel and the believers who spread it. Paul expresses the power of his gospel of Christ through cultic terms which evoke the idea of a pleasing fragrance to God that rises from the burning sacrifice.[82] This is a cultic metaphor: The smoke that rises from the burning sacrifice (or incense) pleases God. His use of cultic terminology appears to underline his sincere commitment to his mission in relation to God.[83] The technical language of odor and fragrance in the sense of acceptable sacrifice also occurs in Phil 4:18 and Eph 5:2. It is used in the same manner as in Ezek 20:41, where Israel is desired by God as a pleasing odor (the context is sacrificial: "sacred things" are mentioned in the previous verse).[84]

When Paul wants to illustrate that his gospel is confirmed by and pleasing to God, he uses cultic terms. This is not just a common biblical figure of speech—as in Phil 4:18, where "a fragrant offering [*osmēn euōdias*], a sacrifice acceptable [*thusian dektēn*] and pleasing to God," is merely the food sent to Paul by the Philippians.[85] The smoke of the burning sacrifice is a metaphor for the divine character of the gospel. It implies that it is like a sacrifice—an assertion that Paul never actually states explicitly. The metaphor of aroma is repeated in the Deutero-Pauline Eph 5:2, where it is related to Christ as both a sacrifice and an aroma. The author of Ephesians expands the sacrificial connection and creates a twofold sacrificial imagery.

ROM 12:1: THE BELIEVERS' BODIES AS A SACRIFICE

"I appeal to you therefore, brothers, by the mercies of God, to present your bodies as a living sacrifice, holy and acceptable to God, which is your spiritual worship."

Here the believers' bodies are a living sacrifice (*thusia*). This coheres with Paul's statement in Rom 6:12–13 about the consecration of the believers' bodies and perhaps also with their participation as one body in Christ in Rom 12:5.[86]

Does the cultic vocabulary serve the anticultic thrust?[87] Although Dunn notes that there is no reference to Jesus's sacrifice in this passage, he nonetheless argues that the use of sacrificial language here and elsewhere in Paul "implies a *replacement* of ritual sacrifice and indicates an assumption that the death of Jesus had been a *final* sacrifice to end all sacrifices."[88] I discuss this view later, but in the context of the present passage it is clear that Paul is speaking not of Christ but of the Christian faith, the "spiritual [*logikēn*] worship." The *belief* in Christ is one which involves real sacrifice and hardship.[89]

PHIL 2:17: THE PHILIPPIANS' FAITH AND PAUL'S LIBATION

"But even if I am being poured out as a libation [*spendomai*] over the sacrifice and the offering [*thusia kai leitourgia*] of your faith, I am glad and rejoice with all of you."

Paul portrays the Philippians' faith as a sacrifice and offering, and his own endeavor in guiding them as a libation on the altar.[90] Since the context is suffering and being without blemish, Paul may be referring to his own suffering as well as that of the Philippians in cultic terms.[91] The double analogy to the sacrificial rite reinforces the metaphor, which at first glance seems thick and instructive. However, it seems that Paul overloads his metaphor. The libation is relatively marginal to the sacrificial rite, and its metaphorical use is uncommon (and somewhat odd). Therefore, when Paul adds his own work as a libation to the initial, more substantial and common metaphor of the Philippians' faith-sacrifice, it transpires that the entire imagery is mainly illustrative.

CONCLUSIONS

The Pauline allusions to the Christians and to Paul himself as sacrifices or related cultic terms are usually limited in scope and sense. The analogy from Israel's sharing of the sacrifices offered on the altar to the communal sharing of the Eucharist (1 Cor 10:16–18) is functionally limited to the identification of the entire community with the religious rite, which excludes other commitments (namely, idol sacrifices). Paul does not argue that the Eucharist is a sacrifice. Later readers sense the affinity between the two mainly because the sacrificial imagery of the Last Supper in Mark 14:22–24 is in the background.

When Paul says that the gospel and the Christians are the fragrant aroma of sacrifices (2 Cor 2:14–16) he wishes to convey that they are pleasing to God. Similarly, the portrayal of the Philippians' faith as a sacrifice and offering and Paul's ministry to them as a libation on the altar (Phil 2:17) are reflections of their joint devotion and efforts. The context of both passages does not suggest that he really identifies the believers with true sacrifices. There is no reason to see here substitution for the Temple cult.

Paul's treatment of the believers' bodies as a sacrifice in Rom 12:1 may be somewhat different. Paul makes a seminal theological claim. The verse opens a new section in Romans and is therefore somewhat out of context. As an isolated passage it can be read as a claim that the believers' worship is a sacrifice. Nothing in the rhetoric and context limits its scope and meaning. Still, Paul does not develop this metaphor, and the rest of the passage calls upon the Romans to make extensive spiritual efforts in their service of Christ and their intergroup relations. The sacrificial imagery may symbolize these elevated demands from the believers. In order to appreciate the metaphor better, we should examine other senses of sacrifice in Paul's letters.

Jesus as a Sacrifice

1 COR 5:7: CHRIST AS THE PASCHAL LAMB

"Do you not know that a little yeast leavens the whole batch of dough? Clean out the old yeast so that you may be a new batch, as you really are unleavened. *For our Paschal lamb, Christ, has been sacrificed;* Therefore, let us celebrate the festival, not with the old yeast, the yeast of malice and evil, but with the unleavened bread of sincerity and truth." (1 Cor 5:6b–8)

Here we find an identification of Jesus with the Paschal lamb, an image which is implied in John 19:14. Further references to Jesus as a "lamb" (*amion*) are found in Acts 8:32–35, John 1:29; 1 Pet 1:19, and throughout Revelation, sometimes in relation to atonement. Is the Paschal lamb the key metaphor for understanding Jesus in cultic terms?

At first glance Paul appears to regard Christ, instead of the Temple, as the source of communal holiness and mediating atonement. It is also natural to link the Paschal lamb to the Last Supper (the Eucharist is mentioned in 1 Cor 11:17–34), in which Jesus's blood is poured out for many (Mark 14:24) and the language is sacrificial and signifies atonement.[92] Christ is the Paschal lamb because it is a sacrifice that symbolizes redemption, and through Christ redemption is achieved.[93]

The rationale of such readings is, as Paul stresses elsewhere that Jesus died for the believers' sins and that belief in Christ brings atonement, and hence one may think that the Paschal lamb alludes to Jesus's sacrifice as a ransom for human sins.[94] However, this is not supported by the logic of the biblical sacrificial system. There are several differences between the sacrifice of the Paschal lamb and sin offerings: the Passover sacrifice is not a sin offering and does not expiate sins.[95] Unlike sin offerings it is eaten in a feast by its owners. The Paschal lamb is not a communal sacrifice brought in the name of the entire nation, nor is it an individual sacrifice, since it is offered in the name of the family or an association (*havurah*, see Mark 14:12–18). It is not eaten in the Temple but, according to the Pharisees or rabbis, throughout Jerusalem.[96]

Jeremias and Dunn point to the link between the Paschal lamb and atonement in Jesus's own words at the Last Supper. Jesus refers to "the blood poured out for many" (Mark 14:24). This language is unavoidably sacrificial and signifies atonement.[97] Indeed, as we saw in chapter 1, Mark understands the scene as happening while Jesus and his disciples are eating the Paschal lamb. Nonetheless, Jesus never relates these words directly to the Paschal sacrifice. Notably, the blood to which he referred in the Last Supper is not the blood of the Paschal lamb (which could have represented the blood used to save the exempt Israelites from death in Exod 12:7–26), but the wine in the cup! It can be argued that Jesus's disciples made a connection between the Last Supper and the Paschal lamb, but this is merely speculation. A clear connection between the Paschal lamb and atonement is still lacking.

An alternative reading of the passage should concede that Paul's use of the imagery of Jesus as a Paschal lamb is focused and limited by its immediate context. This image is intended to match the metaphor of the Corinthians as "unleavened" that should be (morally) purified.[98] In v. 8 being unleavened is a symbol of justice and truthfulness. The context is not Christological but a moral exhortation regarding the Corinthians' iniquities of sexual immorality. In other words, Paul mentions that Christ is the Paschal lamb only in relation to his point that the Corinthians are special and need to improve their behavior. The key image in his rhetoric is the Passover unleavened bread, not the Paschal lamb.[99] It is even possible that Paul draws on the common association of Jesus as a lamb in general, which was a multiform image, as we shall see in chapters 6 and 7.

The Paschal lamb metaphor as a Christological image related to the Last Supper could have fitted the description of the Eucharist as a ritual commemoration of Christ's death in 1 Cor 11:23–26. However, Paul does not use it there or elsewhere in his letters, despite his frequent mention of Jesus's death as an expiation. Owing to the lack of further evidence in Paul, the thin use of the metaphor in 1 Cor 5:7 attests to a relatively marginal meaning of the imagery. For Paul, the Paschal lamb is merely a designation for Jesus which lacks explanatory force.

2 COR 5:21: JESUS AS A SIN OFFERING

"For our sake, he made him to be sin [*hamartian*] who knew no sin, so that in him we might become the righteousness of God."

Although in most translations *hamartian* is simply a sin,[100] many interpret it as a sin offering.[101] Undoubtedly, Paul actually means that Christ died for our sins. The sin-offering metaphor aims to explain a paradox in his Christology: while Jesus has no sin upon him, he died for the sins of the believers and atones for them,[102] just like the animal that is sacrificed as a sin offering.[103]

This is a powerful and effective metaphor, and it serves Paul well. As is clear from the second part of v. 21, it illustrates how the believers benefit from Jesus's self-sacrifice. They become righteous because the one who brings the sin offering is cleared of blame. This verse closes Paul's argument that "one died for all" (v. 14), that God "reconciled us to himself through Christ," and that "in Christ God was reconciling the world to himself, not counting their trespasses against them, and entrusting the message of reconciliation to us" (vs. 18–19). Thus the Christological context shows that the metaphor is extremely thick, and its explanatory force is maximized.

However, the efficacy of the sin-offering metaphor is limited by its context. The passage is not a Christological or soteriological teaching. Paul's discourse concentrates on his ministry,[104] and it is possible that in calling Jesus a sin offering he demonstrates the link between weakness and power, shame and righteousness, which also applies to his own personal experience as an apostle.[105] Furthermore, in the verse preceding the sin-offering metaphor, Paul has already fractured the reasoning of equating Christ with an expiatory sacrifice and urges the Corinthians: "be reconciled to God!" (2 Cor 5:20). Here it seems that Christ's so-called sin offering does not expiate by itself. Jesus both sacrifices the offering and is the offering itself, but those for whom he is offering himself also need to take an active part and "open wide your hearts" (2 Cor 6:13). That is, the believers' role, which is Paul's main point here is not included in the metaphor. While the imagery of Christ as a sin offering may imply that the believers' sins were expiated, it does not relate to their belief or their actual sharing of the sacrifice. It only demonstrates the idea that death atones for the sins of somebody else.

ROM 8:3: JESUS AS A SIN OFFERING

"For God has done what the law, weakened by the flesh, could not do: by sending his own Son in the likeness of sinful flesh, and to deal with as a sin-offering [kai peri hamartias], he condemned sin in the flesh."

Some scholars take the term "sin offering" in a less specifically sacrificial sense, maintaining that peri hamartias means "for sin" in general. Yet the sacrificial language here is obvious and probably denotes "for sin offering" as in the LXX (e.g., Lev 5:6–7, 11), especially since Paul uses cultic allusions.[106] Indeed, not every sacrifice can purge sins, only the sin offering.[107]

Paul claims that God sent his Son, in the guise of flesh, to erase the sin of the flesh, and he did so because he was a sin offering. This specific sacrifice is envisioned as an efficient and ultimate ritual mechanism for wiping out the sins of the flesh, and Jesus is equated with this sacrificial rite, or rather replaces it. Whether or not Paul uses the concept of sin offering in the accurate sense of the Priestly Code, we shall see below.

It is interesting to observe the theological significance of the sin offering concept for Paul in light of its context. Paul preaches of the end of the Law as the death of sin, and of the flesh as the source of sin (Rom 7:8–25). In 8:3 Christ is the redemption from these sins, and he overcomes the weakness of the Law. Paradoxically, however, when he is envisioned as a sin offering, Christ is modeled after the Law. Paul admits this in the next verse: "The just requirement of the Law might be fulfilled in us" (Rom 8:4). In other words, when Paul treats Christ as a sin offering, he actually acknowledges the validity of the *model* of a sacrifice, and the Law in general, as the only way to overcome sin: instead of a bull, goat, or lamb, the sin offering is Jesus; instead of the Law of the flesh he preaches the Law of the spirit.[108] The core concept for Jesus as a vehicle of atonement for sins remains a sacrifice. Curiously, in this passage Christ's death is not even mentioned explicitly. Paul does not explain how Jesus is able to be a sin offering or how the metaphor actually operates.[109] The sin-offering metaphor is supposed to be clear enough in itself. Yet, as we shall see below, it is generalized and does not accurately apply the Levitical concept to the realm of Christian faith.

EPH 5:2: CHRIST AS AN OFFERING AND SACRIFICE

"Live in love, as Christ loved us and gave himself up for us, a fragrant offering and sacrifice [*prosphoran kai thusian*] to God."

In this Deutero-Pauline letter we find the same metaphor of Christ's self-sacrifice for the sake of the believers, but in a more general form. The author does not refer to the problem of sin or its expiation. However, the general terms of offering and sacrifice are corroborated by adding the cultic expression "fragrant" (*osmēn euōdias*).

Unlike 2 Cor 5:21, here the sacrificial metaphor is made in passing. It is mentioned only to remind the Ephesians of Christ's death, from which they have benefited so that they will live lovingly.[110] There is no attempt to draw on the metaphor, and its use is merely as *a label* for Christ's death without explaining its sacrificial meaning and its soteriological implications. It seems that the author is already aware of a previous use of the metaphor of Jesus as a sin offering.

ROM 3:23–25: CHRIST AS A KAPORET

"Since all have sinned and fall short of the glory of God; they are now justified by his grace as a gift, through the redemption [*apolutrōsis*] that is in

Christ Jesus; whom God put forward as *a sacrifice of atonement* [*hilastērion*] by his blood, effective through faith. He did this to show his righteousness because in his divine forbearance he had passed over the sins previously committed."

The NSRV translates *hilastērion* as "a sacrifice." Most scholars agree that it is not a sacrifice but a cultic object. Following its sense in the LXX, it is identified as the *kaporet* ("the mercy seat"), the covering, the golden plate upon the Ark of the Covenant in the holy of holies at the Tabernacle, which was considered "the place of atonement."[111] Josephus uses it as a general term of cultic appropriation or means of propitiation.[112]

Thus hilastērion represents the presence of God and the place of the atonement, the sacrificial system, the spatial pinnacle of the cult, and Paul refers to it in relation to blood.[113] The only rite in which the high priest approaches it is on the Day of Atonement, when he sprinkles blood on it to cleanse it of Israel's impurities and sins (Lev 16:14–16). Paul's metaphor therefore envisions Christ's death as purifying the Temple.[114] NT scholars tend to regard Paul's kaporet as standing for the Temple and its rituals in general, reflecting means of expiation, as a "medium of atonement," parallel to Jesus's death as a sacrifice offered by God, in which Jesus atones by his own blood.[115]

How literally does Paul intend the metaphor to be understood? For some, Christ's death "parallels and replaces" the cultic action carried out at the kaporet because it cleanses the impurity that sin has brought upon the sanctuary. According to this full-blown analogy, Jesus replaces the entire cultic system. Christ serves as both high priest and sacrifice.[116] Dunn is more cautious. He leaves open the question as to whether Paul regards Jesus's hilastērion as validating the sacrificial system or as indicating its merely provisional character, that is, if Jesus's death and resurrection are more effective than the cult. Textually, he says, Paul is too brief to tell.[117]

While Paul certainly argues that the believers now have a hilastērion of faith, where the properties of the kaporet are applied to Christ, there are reasons to see this not as a total replacement of the Temple cult but as a more limited metaphor. First, Paul never equates Jesus with a Temple, and his readers have no preliminary inclination for such an association. In Romans he also does not use the community-as-Temple metaphor.[118] The metaphor of Christ as a hilastērion is restricted to expiation from sin in relation to the death of Christ as a saving event.[119] Still, if Paul means that

"Jesus is the new place of atonement for the whole human race,"[120] it would seem that Jesus takes the place of the Temple's paramount function!

Paul's use of the hilastērion is not restricted to its actual role in the Temple, since there are considerable differences between Paul's idea of atonement and the original rite in which the kaporet functions. Paul stresses the effective expiation of Jesus's sacrifice without limiting it to one place or object, referring to "passing over [*paresin*] the sins" in the sense of letting them go unpunished, remission of penalty. Unlike the expiation by blood in the inner sanctum, the atonement through Christ is accessible to all.[121] Moreover, Jesus's atonement is not limited to one specific day, while the kaporet is ritually used only on the Day of Atonement. Furthermore, Paul dwells on the association of the hilastērion with blood ("put forward as a *hilastērion* by his blood") when he later relates to Jesus's blood as expiatory in Rom 5:9 (cf. Eph. 1:7; 2:13; Col 1:20; 1 John 1:8–9). Yet the biblical hilastērion is also used as the object upon which the incense was burnt at the very same rite, although this is probably not related to the elimination of sin,[122] which goes unmentioned by Paul.

In a sense, the nature of the hilastērion does not correspond with Paul's theology of the death of Jesus as atoning. Unlike Jesus, it is not killed or does not die; it is only a vessel. This fact leads Paul to skip over Jesus's death in this passage, using the blood imagery merely to demonstrate Jesus being the ultimate means of atonement. Since he does not explain what exactly "hilastērion" means or represents, understanding this metaphor demands the Romans' familiarity with the Day of Atonement ritual and its meaning.

Paul barely utilizes the full potential of the hilastērion as a metaphor. He does not draw on other major features of the hilastērion that may be related to Jesus: its being (with the Ark and the Cherubim) the most sacred object in the Tabernacle and a vehicle of God's revelation to Moses (Lev 25:22; Num 7:89). He restricts the metaphor to Jesus's blood as representing atonement and renders the imagery functional and inconclusive. Therefore, I suspect he does not really see Jesus as the new and real kaporet but only draws on its ritual sense to introduce a compelling metaphor of atonement.

The context of the passage, the Law as leading to sin (Rom 2:27–3:20) and the revelation of righteousness without the Law (3:21–23, 28), may lead to the conclusion that Jesus has become the new kaporet while the original one (and hence the Day of Atonement) is no longer necessary. From now on, sins are expiated through belief in Jesus. But Paul does not say this. He even takes a step back: "Do we then overthrow the Law by this faith? By no means! On the contrary, we uphold the Law" (Rom 3:31). But even if one were to understand that Jesus takes the place of the Temple cult, still the template for Jesus's atoning role remains within the sacrificial realm. For Paul and probably for early Christian tradition before him,[123] in order to understand Jesus as the agent of remission of sins, one must first think of the Day of Atonement ritual at the Temple, as the primary model.

When Paul writes Romans, the kaporet has long since disappeared in the Babylonian destruction of the Temple in 586 BCE.[124] This fact makes Paul's metaphor extraordinary. On the one hand, Jesus is like a kaporet, providing what is missing in the Second Temple. He stands for a more authentic and true atonement which is not available in the present priestly cult. Jesus may even represent the Levitical ideal of atonement, when the Ark of the Covenant exists and God's presence at the Temple is more substantial. On the other hand, when Paul draws on an object that no longer functions in the Jerusalem Temple and is now merely a symbol, he may be aware that he is dealing with a mere concept and symbol and thus does not argue that Jesus represents an actual rite.

CONCLUSIONS: JESUS, SIN, AND SACRIFICE— EXPLORING THE METAPHORS

Paul relates to Jesus as the Paschal lamb, a sin offering (twice), and kaporet. The latter two are linked to his atoning force, either his death for the sake of others or his blood. I now turn to general observations on Paul's use of these sacrificial metaphors: Why does he choose images of sacrifices in relation to Jesus, and to what extent do they transform the meaning of sacrifice as it relates to the figure of Jesus?

For Paul, Jesus's death bears several similarities to a sacrifice offered on the altar. His blood is stressed because he was a sacrifice—although Christ's death was not remembered as being particularly bloody, since he was crucified, not slaughtered.[125] He died for a purpose—"for sins"[126] or "for us."[127] The concept of a sacrifice links both aspects, since the blood of the sacrifice atones.[128] Dunn therefore concludes that Paul appeals to sacrifice because both sacrifice and the death of Christ atone for sin, and for both death is necessary.[129]

Nevertheless, Christ's blood does not necessarily allude to atoning sacrifice in Paul, although it does relate to atonement (but not sacrifice) in latter NT texts (1 Pet 1:2; 1 John 1:7; Rev 7:14; Heb 9:12–14, 22, 25–26; 12:24). Importantly, he never alludes to Jesus's death as a sacrifice.[130] For

Paul, blood may be merely a synonym for Jesus's life and death (cf. 1 Cor 11:25) because elsewhere it denotes life and death in a general sense simply because blood symbolizes life (Lev 17:14).[131] An intermediate approach is to restrict the sacrificial sense of Jesus's death to a ritual mechanism of ransom. In the Pauline concept of salvation, Jesus's death functions as a payment or ritual action. Paul thus chooses the substitution mechanism of sacrifice as a ransom payment, while the other senses of sacrifice are overlooked.[132]

The question is whether Paul sees Christ as a cultic sacrifice to begin with, or whether he uses it only as a literary or theological means to demonstrate the core idea that belief in Christ leads to atonement for sins. If the latter is the case, then the sacrificial meaning is secondary. In other words, Is Jesus a new and ultimate type of sacrifice, or can he be understood only as *modeled after* sacrifice? Is the sacrificial metaphor fundamental to his theology, or is it of restricted meaning, merely illustrative?

If sacrifice is the key model for understanding Jesus's death and its atoning force, one would expect that the most common or central cultic imagery would be related to the Eucharist. One would expect this because the Eucharist is the earliest major Christian ritual to use sacrificial imagery, going back to the earliest Jesus traditions. Surprisingly, Paul never refers to the Eucharist as a sacrifice! Moreover, when discussing the Eucharist or Jesus in general, Paul does not refer to ordinary sacrifices in which the worshipers share the meat,[133] which the Eucharist could have been modeled after. Instead, the most prevalent and substantial sacrificial metaphor for Jesus is the sin offering (*hamartias*), which is not eaten by the lay Israelites.

When Paul relates sacrifice to Jesus, he uses it in different forms and contexts. There is no one model of Jesus as a sacrifice: he is envisioned as a Paschal lamb (which does not relate to expiation), and in the very same letter to the Romans he is both a sin offering and the kaporet. While in Rom 3:25 and 8:3 the metaphor has a valuable explanatory role, in 2 Cor 5:21 the context attests to a more marginal sense which is related to Paul's ministry rather than to Christological teaching. In these three passages Paul relates the sacrificial sense to Jesus releasing from sins, whereas in 1 Cor 5:7 he simply states it without further observations. The eclecticism of Paul's temple imagery will be discussed further.

Paul's sense of the sin offering and the kaporet is intriguing. To what extent does he really exploit their original Levitical symbolism? Unlike the author of Hebrews, nowhere does Paul explain to his readers how exactly the sin offering or the kaporet expiates sins and exactly how they are related to Christ. He mentions only the common function of expiation and details his concerns regarding the Christian faith. This minimal attention to the sacrificial system is telling. The linkage to Jesus is based not on common ritual forms but on the general idea: atonement.

The cultic theology of the sin offering is debatable. Jacob Milgrom maintains that the correct translation of the ḥattat sacrifice is "purification offering." He understands the sacrificial blood to be a ritual detergent which does not atone for personal sin but rather cleanses the sanctuary which has been polluted by sin. The personal sin of the inadvertent offender is atoned for by remorse.[134] This would leave Paul's metaphor devoid of its target of atonement.[135]

In contrast, Bernd Janowski argues that the ḥattat is an offering for sin, a kind of ransom. The Israelite identifies himself with the sacrificial animal, and his laying of hands on the sacrificial animal is an act of identification (but not a transfer of sins). Through the application of the ḥattat's blood on the altar and sanctuary, a representative giving-up-of-life is carried out through which the sin-calamity-connection is abolished.[136]

Although I accept Milgrom's interpretation of the ḥattat in the Priestly Code, for our discussion the question is, How does Paul understand the ḥattat? Milgrom sees the origin of the confusion of the ḥattat as a sin offering (*peri hamartias*) in the LXX.[137] Josephus (*Ant.* 3.230) and Philo (Spec. 1.226) also use the term for the ḥattat in Leviticus 4 and Numbers 15. Therefore, it is possible that Paul's use of the ḥattat is closer to that of Janowski than to that of Milgrom. Yet that the shedding of blood marks the onset of atonement was acknowledged by the author of Hebrews (9:12–13, 22; cf. Tit 2:14; 1 John 1:7, 9).

It is therefore reasonable to apply Janowski's understanding of the sin offering to Paul, illuminating Jesus's dying for the sins of others. One could argue that the entire argument in 2 Cor 5:14–21 may be rooted in Paul's understanding of Christ's death as a sin offering which brings new life to the one who offers it. In 2 Cor 5:15 Paul expresses the goal of Christ's sacrificial death—to give life. Just as in the Priestly Code the Israelite is identified with the sin offering (by the laying on of hands), for Paul the believer is identified with Christ in his death, through faith in Christ.[138]

Strikingly, however, in 2 Cor 5:21 and Rom 8:3 Paul does not bother to describe the relevant regulations or scriptural citations, nor does he explain the features common to the sin offering and Christ. He does not refer to rituals of the sin offering such as the laying on of hands or confession of sins. In fact, he does not add any detail apart from the overall result of atonement for sins.

When Paul refers to *hamartian* in 2 Cor 5:21 and Rom 8:3, it is not clear what kind of sin offering he has in mind: communal (Lev 4:3–21) or individual, inadvertent or intentional (ḥattat of the Day of Atonement). Each relates to different sins and expresses different theological perceptions. While Paul is surely aware of the diverse types of ḥattat, he does not mention any of them because he does not mean to imply that Jesus is like a certain type of ḥattat. Jesus is like the very general *concept* of sacrifice offered to expiate a very general notion of sin. Any further details are missing because they do not serve Paul's overwhelmingly general analogy.

Paul's use of "hilastērion" in Rom 3:25 also lacks the description of the high priest's shedding of blood, its relation to the Day of Atonement as judgment day, the sacredness of the kaporet, or even its being part of the Ark of the Covenant. Unlike Philo's cultic symbolism, no biblical allusion or explanation of the function or symbolism of the kaporet is given. These probably do not matter to Paul, not because he is indifferent to them (otherwise he would not mention hilastērion to begin with). Some of these details are not helpful in spelling out the meaning of expiation. But the main reason for his disregard, I suggest, is that this metaphor is not important enough for Paul to pay more attention to it. The thin description diminishes the thick sense of the metaphor. Paul could have exploited it better. In the end, it is more a slogan than a theological argument.

As Dunn maintains, Paul's use of sacrificial and cultic metaphors is far from systematic. He uses metaphors obscurely. He uses different metaphors and descriptions of Jesus's death in a manner which is less clear than elsewhere in the NT (1 Pet. 1:18–19; John 1:29; Hebrews).[139] The rationale of the core idea that Jesus died as a sacrifice for the sins of humankind "cannot be traced back firmly to a Hebrew theology of sacrifice."[140]

Paul's use of cultic metaphors for Jesus is also very eclectic and general. He uses different analogies from the Temple cult to Jesus in order to associate Christ with atonement.[141] I want to turn now to the question of the extent to which he regards these metaphors as introducing Jesus and the Christian community as a full blown substitution to the cult. This will lead to Paul's more general approach to the Jerusalem Temple and the sacrificial system.

Temple and Sacrifice: Symbols or Substitutions?

PAUL'S CULTIC METAPHORS: SYSTEM AND STRUCTURE

Despite the numerous studies that discuss Paul's treatment of Temple, sacrifices, and priesthood, none tries to examine all of them together as a system. I want to evaluate here the entire spectrum of this imagery: How do the images relate to each other? Do the different analogies coalesce into a whole, with connections and a structured relationship, or do they end up as a list of sporadic and isolated pieces of discourse? Does Paul have a comprehensive metaphoric cultic system in mind, or does he use these analogies ad hoc, without being aware of his other analogies to the Temple cult?

Table 2 presents a summary of Paul's metaphors or analogies of Temple, sacrifices, priests, and related cultic themes pertaining to Jesus, the Christian community, and Paul himself.

We can see that Paul uses the entire cultic system as a metaphoric field: Temple, sacrifices, priest, libation, kaporet, and even fragrant aroma. He applies them to three components of his gospel: Jesus, the believers, and himself as the messenger. At first glance it seems that for Paul the so-called

Table 2. Cultic and Sacrificial Metaphors in Paul's Letters
(and Deutero-Pauline Epistles)

Jesus	Temple	Sacrifice	Priest	Varia
		Sin offering: 2 Cor 5:21 Rom 8:3 Paschal Lamb: 1 Cor 5:7 [Eph 5:2 1 Pet 2:5]		*kaporet:* Rom 3:25
The Community	1 Cor 3:16-17 1 Cor 6:19 2 Cor 6:16-7:1 [Eph 2:21-22] [1 Pet 2:5]	Rom 15:16 (offering) Rom 12:1	[1 Pet 2:5]	Fragrance Aroma: 2 Cor 2:14-16 Sharing the altar in the Eucharist: 1 Cor 10:16-18
Paul			1 Cor 9:13 Rom 15:16	Libation: Phil 2:17

Christian faith has the characteristics of a Temple and the sacrificial cult. Christ and the Christian community parallel, and perhaps are even able to take the place of, the Temple cult. Such a detailed and extensive subordination of the cultic system to another, nonsacrificial field is found only in Philo and Hebrews.

At second glance, however, the structure of Paul's system of cultic metaphors is confusing. It is perhaps not unreasonable to simultaneously think of Jesus as a Paschal lamb, a sin offering, and kaporet (the latter two appear in Romans), since Jesus bears an ultimate soteriological function. Yet how can the Christian believers in Rome be a sacrifice while the Corinthians are a Temple? How could the Romans serve as a sacrifice while they are told that Jesus is the sacrifice? Can the addressees of the second letter to the Corinthians function as both the entire Temple and merely the sacrifice's fragrant aroma?

Paul never links one metaphor to another and never hints to his readers that he has an image of an alternative and complete cultic system in mind. A verse like 1 Pet 2:5, which postulates a cultic triangle of community-Temple, believers-priests, and Jesus-sacrifice, or Heb 8:1–2 or 9:11–2, in which Christ is a high priest offering his own blood in the heavenly Temple, would let his readers perceive his Temple imagery as a system. Paul, in contrast, does not seem to have in mind a new cultic *system* analogical to the Temple cult.

The Pauline cultic images are too multiple, diverse, and duplicated and do not cohere in a holistic, integral whole. Paul does not introduce a systematic web of Temple-priest-sacrifice. Rather, he uses a sporadic and somewhat incidental list of metaphorical imagery. When he draws on one Temple image, he seems to be unaware or uninterested in other cultic metaphors that he uses elsewhere even in the very same letter.

So why did Paul use them so frequently in various forms and contexts?

PAUL'S METAPHORS AND THEIR APPLICATION

The striking feature of Paul's Temple and sacrificial imagery is that he hardly ever specifies the common traits that are transferred from the Temple realm to the community or Jesus. He mentions only such objects as *naos, hamartia*, or *hilastērion* and relates each to his gospel. He usually does not elaborate on the exact sense of the linkage and does not draw a comparison between the cultic and the Christological spheres. As already noted, in his metaphors the structure of the source domain is projected onto the structure of the target domain and creates a mapping of the latter (Christ, the community, etc.) based on prior knowledge of the readers about the source domain (the Temple cult).

These are the cultic elements that are mapped from the Temple source domain to the Christian target domain:

Temple—*God's spirit, holiness*[142]—Community
Sacrifice—*submission to God, holiness*—Community
Sacrifice—*bearing of sin, righteousness*[143]—Jesus
hilastērion—*shedding blood, atonement, righteousness*—Jesus.

In the cases of the Paschal lamb (1 Cor 5:7) and the fragrant aroma (2 Cor 2:14–16) the mapping is implicit and based on the readers' understanding of the source domain.

Paul limits the scope of the metaphor to a specific functional, rhetorical role. In referring to the community as a Temple he draws the attention of his readers to the characteristics of the Temple in their communal identity. The aim of this metaphor is to support his call against internal strife (1 Cor 3:16–17), *porneia* (1 Cor 6:19) and associating with idolatrous neighbors (2 Cor 6:16–7:1, where the sense of the metaphor and its practical implications are detailed as a contrast to relations with pagans). Metaphorical mapping does not detail common attributes or provide practical guidance. Readers are supposed to comprehend the missing details based on their familiarity with the concept of the Temple. This also applies to the other metaphors of sacrifice, priesthood, libation etc.

When Paul portrays the community or Jesus in these passages he does so in a very abstract manner. He characterize them as holy and sinless without going into details which the images could provide in the cases of the Temple (pillars, walls, priests, worshipers) and sacrifice (slaughter, flesh, blood, smell, meal). He does not utilize their explanatory potential. This is characteristic of a metaphor, since metaphors are used in the abstract domain. Furthermore, metaphorical projection is *from the concrete to the abstract*.[144] The Temple realm always remains more vivid than the Christian realm. The full implication of the imagery should be drawn not in Paul's words, but in his readers' mind.

Paul uses Temple-sacrificial imagery through metaphors, *mapping a relationship between the Temple and Christianity*. He does not usually go into the details of both fields and does not refer to their attributes. Thus he builds on his addressees' previous knowledge.[145] These are not necessarily means of transference of the cult to another realm, since it would be wrong to assume, on the basis of these metaphors only, that the source domain of the Temple no longer stands as before the analogy is made. The correct word is "mapping": viewing Jesus and the community in *general* terms of Temple-sacrifice. If these are indeed metaphors, just as we refer to love as a journey without practically treating it as a journey, then Paul, when mapping the belief in Jesus as a sacrifice, does not necessarily regard it as fully equivalent to an animal sacrifice on the altar.[146]

This should be compared to the explicit transference of the sacrificial cult to the realm of Christology in Hebrews, where the author does not leave room for metaphors or imagination but identifies specific components in the Temple realm with Jesus (see chapter 8). The same can be demonstrated in the Qumranic substitution of the sacrifices with communal punishments (based on the idea that morality and judgment serve to atone). In the penal code of the Damascus Document, transgressing members are said to regard their punishment as atoning, imagining that they were actually offered as sin or guilt offerings (*ḥattat* and *asham*). Thus one should accept one's punishment and feel remorse, similar to one who brings an atonement sacrifice to the altar.[147] Here there is no metaphor and no mapping of concepts from source to target, merely practical application. Both the Qumranic penal rite and the sin offerings relate to a sinner. The judicial process is equated with sacrifices in terms of remorse and expiation. This is an analogy which applies to religious practice.

We do not find similarly direct application of the Temple realm in Paul. The cultic language is never related to actual worship and Christian cultic institutions. There are no Christian priests or alternative sacrificial rituals. Like the community-Temple association, the use of cultic terms is general.[148]

Paul's use of cultic metaphors can be compared with that of Philo, in the course of his allegorical symbolism. When Philo says that the human body or the human soul is a temple, his point is that one should grasp the meaning of the body or soul in light of the familiar concept of the Temple.[149] Yet despite his transference of temple symbolism, such as referring to the temples of the universe and of the soul, Philo accepts the validity of sacrifices in the earthly Jerusalem Temple and pilgrimage practices.[150]

The implication is that relating Temple symbolism to noncultic subjects—the so-called spiritualization of sacrifices—does not necessarily involve abandoning the original sense of Temple-sacrifice. If Philo can regard the soul as a Temple and yet still worship God through animal sacrifices, perhaps Paul can view Jesus as a sin-sacrifice and kaporet but nevertheless continue to offer sacrifices at the Temple and consider the Temple cult as atoning.

PAUL'S APPROACH TO THE JERUSALEM TEMPLE AND ANIMAL SACRIFICES

As I mentioned at the beginning of this chapter, several scholars argue that in Paul's letters the Temple was spiritualized to the point of replacement. In a similar vein, some maintain that since Jesus's death is a sacrifice for sin, the implication is that "no other sacrifices for sin were thereafter necessary for those who believed in Jesus."[151]

Some recent studies, however, resist the view that Paul is anticultic or suppresses the sacrificial cult. First of all, unlike the gospels (such as in the cleansing), nowhere in his letters does Paul criticize the Herodian Temple.[152] If the Temple cult has no theological relevance, this would make Paul's labeling of Christ as sin offering or atonement inexplicable, since the cultic metaphors imply that God still responds to some kind of cultic mechanism. Paul thus develops a cultic metaphor which perpetuates cultic thinking, though in an altered form, and he develops new cultic forms, borrowed from the conceptual matrix of the old cult.[153] As Fredriksen puts it, "Paul praises the new community by likening it to something that he values supremely. If he valued the temple less, he would not use it as his touchstone. This is not an either/or situation: for Paul, God's spirit dwells both in Jerusalem's Temple and in the 'new temple' of the believer and of the community."[154] "Paul uses the Temple and its cult to make these analogies because he *values* them; . . . their *continuing* sanctity and probity is precisely what commends them as analogous. . . . Paul has no reason to think that the Temple and its altar could ever be irrelevant to the message of Christ."[155]

Pauline systematic use of metaphors of the Temple and sacrifices does not leave any doubt that Paul regards them as the model for Christian religious life and thought. His repetition and the variety of metaphorical projections from the Temple to the community or Christ reveals a high appreciation of the Temple and its sacrifices. But can we infer from this Paul's actual attitude toward the Temple in Jerusalem?

There is no sign that Paul wants to leave or replace the Temple cult. He only applies its religious principles of holiness, commitment to and devotion to God, and divine atonement to the belief in Christ. However, from the perspective of his readers, when the believers are holy and God's spirit resides within them and especially when their faith is like a sacrifice, and even more so when Christ's death atones like a sin offering or the kaporet (on the Day of Atonement), the religious role of the Jerusalem Temple diminishes. Although the community and Jesus are only *like* a Temple or sacrifice (because they are only metaphors), the number of metaphors and the continuous thinking of Christian worship in terms of the Temple cult divert attention from the Temple to Christian life. True, the Jerusalem Temple is not replaced, and only some aspects of its sanctity and atonement are fulfilled by the Christians and Jesus.[156] Paul's Jewish readers of Romans, for example, may still attend the Temple—as Paul himself does, according to Acts—and offer sin offerings. Yet when the Temple is not the sole place of God's dwelling place and the animal sacrifices are not the only way to achieve cultic atonement, they are no longer the same.

Ultimately, the Pauline use of the Temple realm as a model for sanctity and atonement does indeed create a certain competition with the Temple cult, but it does so somewhat unwittingly and in a relatively delicate manner.

CULTIC SUBSTITUTES FOR NON-JEWISH-CHRISTIANS IN THE DIASPORA

The paradox in Paul's metaphors of the Temple and sacrifices is this: on the one hand, he highly appreciates the Temple cult when he conceptualizes holiness and atonement in nascent Christianity using these cultic models, without doubting the validity of the physical Temple. On the other hand, once he and his readers perceive their religious life in these cultic terms, the necessity for the Jerusalem Temple and animal sacrifices decreases. In the end, for Paul's readers, the community and Christ may indeed fulfill the role of the Jerusalem Temple and all it represents.

This paradox derives from the fact that in Judaism there is only one Temple and one way of practicing sacrificial rites. As long as the physical Temple continues to stand, pluralism and variations weaken the power or credibility of the Jewish cultic system, which resists competition. And yet for those whom Paul addresses, the paradox I have just noted of reducing the cult to a metaphor *because* it matters is mainly theoretical. The Corinthians, Philippians, and many of the Romans are Gentiles. They cannot enter the holy courts and cannot really offer sacrifices. And in any event, like the Jewish Romans, they live far from the Temple.

Paul's cultic metaphors do not replace the practical role of the cult[157] but fill a religious vacuum. Paul's non-Jewish readers are joining a religious movement without a temple of their own, without a cult, and with minimal rituals related to the sacred or ceremonial connection to any God. They have deserted their pagan cults (and Paul urges them to completely turn their backs on idols), but they do not participate in other cults instead. They are far from the Temple of the one and only God they now believe in, and even if they live in Jerusalem they cannot approach the sacred Temple as Jews do. They are caught between paganism and Judaism with no sense of the holy, a state highly common in Greco-Roman life when temples flourished in every city.

In regarding their community as holy, like the Temple, their belief as a sacrifice, and Jesus's death as a sacrifice of atonement, these Gentile Christians experience the sacred in a new way. Beliefs can hardly replace public rituals at the Jerusalem Temple. The Pauline cultic metaphors are merely partial, albeit accessible, substitutions. Paul does not indicate that he intends for the cultic metaphors to become full replacements for the Temple cult. If he had thought otherwise, he would have claimed that the Eucharist is a sacrifice in the full sense of the word, continuing the metaphor that probably goes back to the Historical Jesus.

In calling for his Gentile readers to think of their religious life as Christians along the lines of Temple and sacrifice, Paul actually transforms the basic and unique trait of the Jewish cult—its being exclusively Jewish and unavailable to non-Jews. Through his use of metaphors Paul has made the virtual Temple and sacrifice accessible to non-Jewish-Christians.[158]

Paul's cultic metaphors serve several functions. They make sense of religious Christian concepts (first and foremost Jesus's death), provide models for ethical behavior and social identity,[159] and, most important, create a sense of holiness.[160] There is hardly any other realm of meaning that can fulfill so many functions. Virtual as it may seem, the metaphoric sense of Temple and sacrifice was essential to the religious life of his addressees.

PAUL, JUDAISM, SCRIPTURE, AND THE LAW

Interpreting Paul's approach to the Temple cannot be separated from the general question of Paul, the Law, and Judaism. In what sense, if any, is the Temple cult practically relevant to him?

Although Paul plays down Jewishness as an ethnic identity in relation to the belief in Christ,[161] in Rom 9–11 he associates himself with the people of Israel and regards his gospel as continuing the Israelite tradition. Several times Paul identifies himself with the Jews, the Hebrews, the Torah, and the Temple cult.[162] Paul legitimizes the observance of food strictures among the "weak" Roman Jewish-Christians (Rom 14), and in general he regards Jewish identity as an abiding reality which the "strong" must accept and protect.[163] He also maintains that the gifts and calling of the Jews are irrevocable (Rom 11:28–29). In Rom 11:1 Paul regards himself as an Israelite and claims to express an authentically Jewish viewpoint, speaking as a Jew.[164]

Paul's use of Scripture provides a basic indication of his approach to Judaism. In his undisputed epistles Paul cites more than eighty passages from the Hebrew Bible.[165] He also uses many implicit allusions to Scripture (echoes), taking possession of the biblical verses by parenthetical interpretative comments and transforming their sense to bear witness to the gospel.[166] Paul's speech is scripturally oriented, and the vocabulary of Scripture is deeply imprinted on his mind.[167]

Paul bases his Christological arguments on biblical prophecies (e.g., Rom 15:8–12). He reads the Exodus and wilderness trials as prefigurations of the Church's life (1 Cor 10:1–10). He employs a "vigorous and theologically generative reappropriation of Israel's Scriptures."[168] Scripture also shapes Paul's ethical instructions. When Scripture is quoted in Paul's ethic, it is often at the heart of his argument.[169]

In his epistles to the non-Jewish-Christians, Paul discusses the Jewish Law extensively, introducing complex, perhaps even contradictory, approaches. He speaks boldly against the Law when he says it is impossible to observe the Law completely.[170] Being "in Christ" releases one from the Law (Rom 8:2). Believers are no longer under the Law but under grace (Rom 6:14–15). Not the Law but belief in Christ is an adequate means of righteousness (Rom 3:20).[171]

On the other hand, Paul appreciates the Law when he says that it is holy (Rom 7:12) and that "the law was our *paidagōgos*," namely, the Law instructs the Jewish people.[172] Some passages suggest Paul believes that the Law must be fulfilled in a certain sense: the biblical command to love your neighbor sums up all the commandments and fulfills the Law (Rom 13:9–10), and, after all, Christians do fulfill the Law (Rom 8:1–4; cf. 13:8). Paul also regards the moral norms of the Law as obligatory for the church.[173] Brian Rosner elaborates on Paul's reappropriation of the law as prophecy and wisdom. The Law has ongoing value and validity "for us" (1 Cor 9:8–10; 10:11; Rom 4:23–25), it provides teaching and instruction (1 Cor 10:11; Rom 15:4), it is relevant as a prophecy (Rom 10:6–10), it discloses God's righteousness (Rom 3:21), and, finally, it is fulfilled by the Christian Gentiles (Rom 2:13–14).[174] Rosner concludes that the Law is a formative source for his moral teachings on theft, sexual ethics, idolatry, and other social vices. Paul reads the Law as wisdom for living and makes a reflective application of it to his churches.[175]

True, Paul rejects several times the "works of law." But according to Sanders and Dunn, he does so because the "works of law" constitute a barrier between Jews and Gentiles. The Law restricts the people of God to the Jews, whereas the death of Christ on the cross makes salvation available to all people, both Jews and Gentiles, by faith.[176] The implication is that Paul rejects not the validity of God's commandments in the Torah for Jews but their being the sole means of a covenant with God and salvation. Still, his views about the need for Jewish-Christians to practice the Law remain obscure, as his epistles (with the exception of Romans) are addressed to non-Jews.

Paul seems to be proud of his being blameless in relation to the Law, a Pharisee (Phil 3:5–6; cf. Gal 1:14). But does Paul practice the Law in his personal life? While Paul insists that the Galatians should not practice circumcision, elsewhere he argues that those who are already circumcised should remain in circumcision and should not put on a foreskin (1 Cor 7:17–20).[177] And he also testifies that anyone who is circumcised must observe the entire Law (Gal 5:3). Hence a Jew converted to Christianity should remain obedient to the Law.[178] This may be why, according to Acts 16:3, Paul circumcises Timothy, the son of a Jewish mother and a Greek father.[179]

Some infer from Gal 2:14 that Peter (and Paul) lived like Gentiles with regard to kosher food, etc.[180] Yet Peter merely eats with Gentiles, and Paul's language here seems like an exaggeration.[181] In fact, Paul immediately declares the opposite: "We ourselves are Jews by birth and not Gentile sinners" (Gal 2:15). One should also bear in mind that the controversy in Antioch is merely about table fellowship with Gentiles,[182] and hence it attests to Paul's laxity in observing certain laws of purity, not his total nonobservance of them.

The Acts of the Apostles provide a straightforward albeit secondhand portrait of Paul as committed to the Law and the Temple. According to Luke, Paul attends the synagogue regularly and even cuts his hair after completing a Nazirite vow he made.[183] The claim by some Christians that Paul calls upon Jews, not only Gentiles, not to observe the Torah and circumcision is a matter of some concern to James and the elders. They suggest that Paul disprove it by sponsoring the Nazirite sacrifices of four people at the Temple. Paul agrees. He purifies himself before entering the Temple and announces to the Temple authorities the fulfillment of these Nazirite vows.[184] As we shall see in chapter 5, the narrative in Acts introduces several visits by Paul to the Temple, and his speeches manifest Temple piety. Paul also declares that he still believes in the Torah and the prophets (Acts 24:14) and has not in any way gone against the customs of the ancestors (Acts 25:8).

But is Luke's portrait of Paul historical? How can it be reconciled with Paul speaking against the Law in his letters to his Gentile readers? One could argue that Luke tries to conceal the fact that Paul does not follow the Law, owing to his own rhetorical bias against the Jews' acts against the Christians. Perhaps Paul lives among the Gentiles and eats with them, renouncing the Levitical food laws?[185]

Yet even those who are cautious about the historicity of Acts do not regard Paul's purification and entry to the Temple as fictitious but assume that Paul agrees to display legal observance.[186] Others try to harmonize the letters and Acts on the basis of some parallels in his biography and regard Acts as a reliable portrait of him, with different perspectives and aims than the letters. As for Paul's observance of the Torah, Frederick Bruce thinks that among Jews (and particularly in Jerusalem) Paul conforms to the Jewish food laws, living according to the Jewish calendar, in terms of festivals.[187] Comparing Paul's portrait in Acts with his letters, Porter finds even that in terms of theology there are no significant differences between the Paul of Acts and the Paul of the letters. There is a large degree of continuity and similarity and some close line of connection between the authors of the letters and Acts, whereas the differences are natural owing to the different authors and literary genres. True, the contents of Paul's speeches in Acts do not rehearse Paul's Christology in his letters, but this may be the result of different genres. While much of the contents of the letters is unattested in Acts, there are hardly any contradictions between the two. Hence, according to this approach, there is no reason to doubt the portrayal of Paul as a law-observant Jew who worshiped at the Temple.[188]

Acts contains considerable evidence concerning Paul and the Temple. Many think that the passage in which Paul sponsored the Nazirite sacrifices and purified himself before entering the Temple in Acts 21:17–26 is historically authentic.[189] In addition, the description of Paul's prior purification and paying for the Nazirites' sacrifice in Acts make sense in view of Jewish halakhah and the archaeological evidence.[190]

Scholars find several possible reasons why this evidence of Acts should nonetheless raise doubts in relation to Paul's Temple piety. One may suspect that the Nazirites' sacrifices, which Paul sponsored, were actually a trap set by James and the Jerusalem Church.[191] The episode, even if authentic, perhaps merely shows that Paul conforms to the Jewish way of life only when he is in Jerusalem, behaving like a Jew to win over the Jews, as he declares in 1 Cor 9:19–23. Following 1 Cor 9:19–23, Paul may behave as an observant Jew only among Jews and like a Gentile among Gentiles.[192] This later passage is indeed cryptic, since the meaning of *become as* outside the Law can be interpreted in several ways. Some think it seems compatible with viewing Paul as a Torah-observant Jew who uses different rhetorical tools when addressing Jewish and Gentile audiences.[193] True, Paul's private adherence to the Temple and the Law in Acts does *seem* to be the opposite of his call to his Gentile addressees not to observe it. But we have seen sufficient evidence in both his letters and Acts to suggest that his belief that the Law does not lead to justification—but only to Christ—does not mean that Paul thinks Jews should no longer observe it.

THE ROLE OF CULTIC ELEMENTS IN PAUL'S GOSPEL

What implications does Paul's approach to the Law have with regard to his metaphoric use of Temple and sacrifice? As we have seen, Paul uses Scripture as a didactic tool. He reappropriates the Law as theoretical and practical wisdom for church ethics and vices. Now we can also conclude that he does the same for the Temple cult. Leaven (1 Cor 5:7) and first fruit (1 Cor 15:20; Rom 8:23; 16:5) are Torah-based elements that are applied to the gospel, and so too are the cultic elements. "Temple" and "sacrifice" do not carry their original legal meaning but instead portray a new symbolism.

The non-Jews of the Pauline communities are not supposed to attend the sacrificial rite, but Paul takes it for granted that they view it as holy and Godly. He thus relates to the cult in the same manner that he uses the moral ethics of the Torah—by interpretation and appropriation. Paul uses the general and symbolic characteristics of the Jewish sacrificial system and relates them to the Christian community, Jesus, and himself in order to attach to them similar values, although only in a metaphorical sense. Paul never discredits the sacrificial cult. Had he done so, it would not have served him well as a key concept. Paul's view of the Temple is so different from that of Hebrews' renunciation of the earthly cult that it is possible even that the author of Hebrews reacts to it.

As for Paul's personal devotion to the Temple cult, despite his preaching to the Gentiles against the Law, his approach to Jewish legal observance is more complex and does not negate the possibility that he regards the Temple positively. Paul's Temple-related metaphors are based on the centrality of the sacrificial system in his worldview, showing that he regards it as sacred and inspiring. Nothing in his Temple imagery points to a rejection or conscious replacement of the Jerusalem Temple. Even if the stories in Acts about his adherence to the Temple cannot be trusted as independent sources, they support Paul's positive approach to the Temple.

This leads me to conclude that there is no essential contradiction between Paul's belief in Christ and worship in the Temple. Despite Paul's own words about the tension between the Law and Christ as means of justification (Gal 2:16; 3:21), the evidence shows that he does not see Christ and the Temple cult as competing ways of atonement. Rather, I suggest that he regards the two as somewhat complementary. In a sense, thanks to the Temple and sacrifices, Paul knows the notions of sacredness and atonement. For Paul, the Temple becomes the source domain of his cultic metaphors. However, for his Gentile readers the Temple cult becomes merely a theoretical model for the new faith.

3 Mark: Criticism or Rejection?

Introduction: Double Reading vs. Plain Reading

THE CONSENSUS: THE END OF THE TEMPLE
AND JESUS REPLACING IT

The Temple plays an important role in Mark 11–15. It is central in Jesus's cleansing of the Temple, the reference to the "abomination of desolation", the purported prediction of the destruction of the Temple in Mark 13, and several additional passages—all of which leads interpreters of Mark to conclude that Mark holds a completely negative view of the Temple. Important commentators think that Mark introduces Jesus as a new Temple ("not made with hands") that substitutes for the old one. Others argue that Jesus's mission in Mark is "anti-Temple"—that the Temple "stands condemned of corruption by trade and politics," leading to Jesus's "disqualification" of it since "the Kingdom has been dissociated from the Jerusalem Temple."[1]

It is interesting to elaborate on some of these scholarly views on Mark's hostility toward the Temple. Mark's Jesus "brings to an end the commercial and cultic activities of the Temple . . . he replaces Israel's cult with a new approach to God."[2] For Mark, "Jesus challenges the authority of the order of sacred violence represented by the Temple, and Mark narrates the challenge in terms of the conflict between Jesus and the religious, legal, and political representatives of sacred authority . . . the sacrificial system is to be replaced by faith and prayer."[3] Evans lists several anti-Temple motifs in Mark's Passion, concluding that Mark wants to show Jesus's opposition to the Temple and his role in replacing it. The destruction encourages Mark to stress the prediction of the destruction.[4] As in the case of the Historical Jesus, few even see Mark's Jesus as a new type of priest who declares the leper clean, forgives sins, offers forgiveness, and interprets the Law (such as in relation to the Sabbath). By taking on these priestly functions, Jesus replaces the Temple.[5]

METHODOLOGY

In this chapter I will survey this consensus in detail and examine the sources and interpretive approaches guiding it. However, at the same time, I will also consider an alternative approach which views Mark as less critical of the Temple. While it is possible to understand why so many scholars read this gospel as a call for the rejection and replacement of the Temple, one should also ask whether too much is read into the text. Given Mark's explicit statements about the Temple as well as the religious circumstances in Jerusalem during the First Revolt against Rome, I suggest distinguishing between criticism and rejection as well as between condemnation of Jewish leaders and replacement of the Temple cult.

Recall that I am using several conceptual tools in this study. These include considering the Temple as both an actual, functional institution and as an abstract symbol of religious worship in ancient Judaism. In the analysis of the texts, I employ four categories of approaches toward the Temple: involvement, defined by attending the Temple; analogy, designated by employing Temple or sacrificial imagery to portray concepts not related to Temple service; criticism of the Temple; and rejection of the Temple. Only the fourth category corresponds to the commonly held belief that Mark subscribes to the position that the Temple cult has become irrelevant.

In approaching the gospel of Mark, I consider the entirety of the final text an expression of the evangelist's ideas and intentions—notwithstanding the author's use of a variety of sources and redactions—without concern for those elements of the narrative and sayings that go back to the Historical Jesus or earlier literary or historical phases. This chapter addresses Mark's message to his readers. What impression could these readers obtain about the Temple by reading Mark immediately after its composition in approximately 70 CE?

READING A SECOND LEVEL OF MEANING IN MARK

The most systematic and careful analysis of Mark's hostile approach to the Temple is Donald Juel's published dissertation on the trial of Jesus, entitled *Messiah and Temple*. Juel's discussion represents the typical reasoning and methodology of current NT scholarship concerning Mark.

Juel begins with the Temple charge in Jesus's trial: "For many gave false testimony against him, and their testimony did not agree; Some stood up and gave false testimony against him, saying; 'We heard him say, "I will destroy this temple that is made with hands, and in three days I will build another, not made with hands;"' But even on this point their testimony did not agree." (Mark 14:56–59). Juel admits that in a plain reading of these verses, Mark denies that Jesus says this. He also notes that "in Mark's account of Jesus' ministry, Jesus has never said such a thing as the witnesses report." He also rejects the possibility that the charge recalls the prediction of the destruction in 13:2 ("no stone upon another"), which he regards as related to a different context.[6] Juel than compares the charge to the mockery, "Aha! You who would destroy the Temple and build it in three days, save yourself, and come down from the cross!" (Mark 16:29b–30). He argues that the latter would better fit the trial scene since the distinction made/not made with hands is irrelevant to the trial. This leads him to suspect that Mark uses 14:58 as a clue to the reader beyond the plain reading of the story, namely, that it reveals a special message about Jesus and the Temple.[7]

Juel then makes a methodological shift, building upon Mark's use of two levels of meaning concerning Jesus's identity and fate. The reader knows more than the characters in the story when Mark uses the literary motif of the so-called messianic secret alongside the theme of the resurrection-vindication of the Son of Man (8:31; 9:31; 10:33): "The reader is expected to interpret the events in light of what has come afterwards, and he is able to understand the events in a different level." Mark also uses irony in describing the rejection of Jesus (such as the mockery when Jesus is hailed as "King of the Jews," 15:16–20), since the reader already knows that Jesus is raised from the dead.[8] Therefore, Juel thinks that a similar double meaning or irony can be found in the Temple charges described in 14:58 and 15:29, just as Mark, perhaps, "views it as true in some sense at another level of the story."[9]

Following this two-tiered reading, Juel turns to the theme of the Temple throughout Mark in order to affirm signs justifying reading the Temple charge with irony and double meanings.[10] First, he sees a relationship between the cleansing and the Temple charge "at a deeper level." The use of "house of prayer" (Mark 11:17 citing Isa 56:7) in the cleansing shows opposition to the Temple. "Den of robbers" (following Jer 7:11) means that the leaders of the Temple misuse their privileges. Hence their Temple is to be destroyed. The tearing of the veil is another symbol of this destruction. Furthermore, Mark's framing of the cleansing within the episodes of the cursing of the fig tree implies the rejection of the leaders of the Temple establishment. Jesus's teaching regarding prayer (11:25–26) and the saying that love is greater than burnt offerings and sacrifices (12:33) suggests an alternative for the Christian community that practices them. The wicked tenants (12:1–11) should be identified with the Temple establishment, and the parable hints at the destruction of the Temple.[11]

Returning to the obscure charge in 14:58, Juel concludes that the phrase "Temple not made with hands" indicates a successor to the Temple establishment. The Temple is to be destroyed (13:2) and "replaced by a new reality."[12] The (old physical) Temple is symbolically destroyed through Jesus's death. Then the resurrection in three days embodies the new Temple not made with hands, which should be identified with the Christian community replacing the Temple establishment.[13]

Note that Juel, like many others, does not clearly define the new Temple as the resurrected Jesus or the Christian community.[14] Can the two be identical? The reason for this obscurity is that Mark never defines either Jesus or the community as the new Temple either.

John Paul Heil's oft-cited article is another example of reading an anti-Temple stance when it actually does not appear in the text. Heil concludes that "the Markan narrative invites its audience to become the community that supplants and surpasses the temple by implementing in their lives Jesus' teachings" through prayer and forgiveness. Jesus is the Lord of the Temple.[15] Heil's methodology focuses on the "house of prayer" saying (11:17) as a cornerstone through which Jesus establishes a prayer community as a substitute for a Temple doomed to become a den of robbers. Then he interprets many passages in this light, including the prayer in the cursed fig tree episode 11:24 (see below). He also argues that the expectation for Jesus's return in 13:34–35 is a substitute for the Temple and interprets other passages accordingly—as if Jesus takes the place of the Temple even though the Temple is not mentioned in these passages.[16]

In the course of this chapter I will refer to commentators who follow this line of anti-Temple interpretation based upon such implicit language and double readings. But before we turn to detailed analysis of Mark, I would like to frame my methodological critique and suggest an alternative approach.

A PLAIN READING OF MARK

Juel's discussion is informed and intelligent but prefers double readings over simple facts in Mark's narrative. He makes several interpretive steps I find unwarranted. My critique of Juel serves as an introduction to my own plain reading of Mark, upon which I elaborate in the following sections.

Juel suggests that the falseness of the witnesses in the Temple charge requires interpretation. It is not clear whether their testimony is untrue or if their intention is only to convict Jesus.[17] I disagree. The falseness is a matter of fact. Mark repeats the false nature of the charge in several ways. First, he notes that there are false testimonies that do not cohere and that falsehood is evident by the simple fact of these contradictions. Then Mark specifies one such testimony about the Temple, remarking that this is also a false testimony wherein the testimonies of the witnesses contradict each other once again. They do not agree on what exactly Jesus is alleged to have said. The fact that the trial then proceeds to another charge—this one being false Messianism—shows that even the high priest does not find this legal case convincing.

Thus Mark stresses that the witnesses are lying, explaining why—in legal terms—no one can accept their claim. Mark therefore makes a considerable effort to convince the reader that the charge has no legal basis. If he had wanted the reader to think otherwise, he would not have narrated the scene with such a strong denial of the charge.

When the reader encounters the concept of a Temple not made with hands, he cannot understand it and finds it absurd. Mark does not offer any hint of this. Such a claim holds logic for scholars only because they are familiar with similar concepts found in Qumran (see the introduction), and especially the theology of the Temple in Hebrews and Revelation. In addition, for Mark's readers during or immediately after the First Revolt (see below) who face the danger of the destruction of Jerusalem by the Romans, blaming Jesus for the coming destruction would appear to be unreasonable. After all, when Jesus dies, the Temple still stands.

While Mark uses irony and double readings about Jesus's messianic identity and the plot to kill him, Juel's assumption that his approach toward the Temple has the same features remains mere conjecture. There is no proof that the Temple charge plays such a role. Such a reading is possible only with the community-as-Temple concept in mind. In contrast to the concept of Jesus as the Son of Man, the reader of Mark does not find this claim spelled out anywhere else in the gospel.

Furthermore, asserting an anti-Temple reading of the cursed fig tree, the parable of the wicked tenants, or other such episodes is questionable since the Temple is not mentioned at all in these passages. In effect, in this interpretation the double reading is embraced owing to an agenda to find clues for Jesus's rejection of the Temple in Mark. Such a reading is legitimate as a modern hermeneutical theological approach but is problematic as a historical method for understanding Mark in ca. 70 CE. For this reason we must consider a fundamental hermeneutical question: Does Mark expect his readers to make such a double reading of an anti-Temple approach throughout the gospel?

There is counterevidence for Jesus's positive attitude toward the Temple, which surfaces when one reads Mark plainly, without searching for double meaning. First, the Temple plays an important role in the narrative, as Jesus visits and teaches at the Temple several times. As soon as Jesus reaches Jerusalem he enters the Temple and looks around (Mark 11:11). Jesus visits the Temple again in the famous "cleansing" (Mark 11:15), after which he leaves the city, returning to the Temple later (Mark 11:27) and defending his authority as a sage against scribes and elders (11:27–28). Jesus teaches at the Temple once again about the relationship between the Davidic descent of the Messiah and his being the Son of God, criticizing the scribes' social behavior and praising the poor widow's donation to the Temple treasury (12:35–44). Finally, when he has been arrested by the chief priests, scribes, and elders, he says, "Have you come out with swords and clubs to arrest me as though I were a bandit? Day after day I was with you in the Temple teaching, and you did not arrest me" (Mark 14:48–49). In this last passage Mark probably tries to stress that Jesus does not pose any threat to Temple authorities. Such visits do not seem to introduce a concept of a new Temple but rather concern for the current one.

These instances of attending the Temple attest to the category of *participation* in the Temple. But what does this involvement actually mean? Jesus never participates in the sacrificial cult itself. Nowhere in the gospels is it mentioned that he enters into the sacred domain of the inner court, where only pure Jewish people can enter (as Paul in Acts 21:26–28). Might this indicate that he is indifferent or even hostile to the Temple rites? Surprisingly, Josephus, who is a priest, never mentions his taking part in offering sacrifices. In rabbinic texts there are hardly any references to the early rabbis' respective roles in the sacrificial cult. They merely teach or study on the stairs of the Temple Mount or order laws in relation to the cult. One cannot assume that they refrain from offering sacrifices because of hostility toward the Temple. Therefore, the omission of an active role by Jesus—or the early Christians in general—in the Temple rites is not telling.[18]

Since he visits it time and time again, Jesus, according to Mark, is very much interested in the Temple. Most of Jesus's acts and teachings in Jerusalem take place at the Temple, and all but the cleansing are uncritical of it. Although he has several opportunities to do so, Mark's Jesus does not confront or rebuke the high priest or the Temple authorities openly—apart from the cryptic act of "cleansing," in which Temple authorities are not directly mentioned. Jesus continues to walk and teach in the Temple (12:27, 35, 41), making the preparation to eat the Passover lamb (14:12, 14, 16), probably after it is slaughtered in the Temple. The impression the reader gets from the narrative is that the Temple serves as the setting of his teachings in Jerusalem.

A second type of counterevidence is that Mark's Jesus shows direct concern about the Temple at two critical points. In the act of "cleansing," Jesus protests against making it "a den of robbers." As shown in chapter 1, most scholars regard the overturning of the tables not as a total rejection of the Temple but as an act protecting the integrity of the sacrificial cult. The Markan critique of the Temple being a "den of robbers" means that violence and unrighteousness take over and that Jesus tries to remove it. Mark, I suggest, sees this as an act protecting the Temple against such external forces. The other crucial point is the prediction in 13:14 about the "abomination of desolation," which regards the desecration of the Temple as one among several horrors in the eschaton. It is listed along with wars, earthquakes, trials, false prophets, and as a sign for the readers to flee to the mountains. Violation of the cult is perceived as a religious disaster.

One cannot expect Mark's readers to take for granted a concept of a new Temple not made with hands—meaning the resurrected Jesus or the Christian community—without preparation and elaboration, as if the reader is already familiar with other NT texts. A double reading as suggested by Juel and others is possible, for example, only by a reader who is familiar with these concepts after reading Paul.

Mark, Judaism, and the Law

It is commonly argued that Mark is a Gentile or writes mainly for a non-Jewish audience. One reason for these assumptions is found in the evangelist's presumably erroneous remarks on the date of the Passover ("On the first day of Unleavened Bread, when the Passover lamb is sacrificed," 14:12, when the sacrifice actually takes place on the previous night) and the explanation about the practice of hand washing in 7:3, imputing it to "all the Jews."[19] However, the author may date the Passover not from sunset to sunset but from sunrise to sunrise in order to make the account tangible to a wider audience.[20] The fact that Mark distinguishes his potential readers from the Jews does not mean he estranges them from Judaism and the Law.[21] He is simply aware of them being non-Jews and needs to introduce them to some basic Jewish practices essential to the story.

In fact, Mark stresses Jesus's Jewishness. For example, he introduces the question of the greatest commandment (12:28–34) and values the commandments (10:18–19). William Loader summarizes Mark's attitude toward the Law as affirmation *and* suppression: Jesus's authority depends upon the Torah, but at times the Torah itself is subordinated to his authority as the Son of God.[22]

Scholars debate whether or not Mark's Jesus actually transgresses Sabbath and purity laws.[23] Here I will discuss briefly two issues of purity regulations that may provide legal background for Mark's attitude toward the sacrificial cult.

"SHOW YOURSELF TO THE PRIEST!"

When Jesus begins healing people, a leper (lepros, suffering from a skin disease) on his knees implores him, begging him to "make me clean." Jesus touches the leper and says, "be made clean!" Then Jesus warns him: "'See that you say nothing to anyone; but go, show yourself to the priest, and offer for your cleansing what Moses commanded, as a testimony to them" (Mark 1:40–44).

Does Jesus take the place of the priest in a manner that subverts purity regulations, as he is willing to defile himself by touching this afflicted person?[24] By making the leper "clean," Mark suggests that Jesus heals him, therefore paving the way for his purification.[25] Jesus does not take the place of the priest. Priests declare the afflicted person to be defiled, and once the person is cured the priests announce that he or she can be purified ritually, ordering the healed person to bring a special purification offering in the Temple. Jesus's healing act is as unnatural and subversive as any of his other miracles. However, by ordering the person to appear before a priest and bring a sacrifice, Jesus leaves the final word on announcing the healed person's purity to the priest. What is interesting here is that Mark, by virtue of mentioning Jesus's reference to the Mosaic commands, shows that Jesus acknowledges the priestly purity system, priestly authority, and the sacrificial system.[26] He is concerned not only with the leper's affliction but also with his ritual status.

HAND WASHING AND PURITY OF FOOD IN MARK 7

In Mark 7, Jesus's disciples do not wash their hands before the meal. The Pharisees complain about this to Jesus. His reply is that "there is nothing outside a person that by going in can defile, but the things that come out are what defile" (7:15). Some regard Jesus's reply as an example of Markan opposition to purity regulations.[27] However, it seems more reasonable to suggest that Jesus's point is that moral purity is more important than ritual purity—and that it demands greater attention. The "not ... but ..." antithesis need not be understood as an "either ... or" but as having the force of "more important than."[28] Indeed, the saying would not be understood as so radical if not read in light of "making all food clean," (19c) which comes from the evangelist, not Jesus.[29]

In Mark 19c, following Jesus's condemnation of moral sins, the evangelist adds that Jesus declares all food clean.[30] Scholars usually interpret this as Jesus's abrogation of laws concerning the purity of food, which are mostly Mosaic Laws. Joel Marcus argues that this is Mark's interpretation of the saying in v. 15. Here Jesus declares that all food is now become pure, changing the status of food in accordance with Rom 14:20.[31] Loader concurs, noting that the statement in v. 19c coheres with Mark's stress on the inclusion of Gentiles in the Kingdom by removing the barrier of the purity of food.[32] But he also adds that this is the only place in Mark where Jesus challenges the basics of Jewish (written) Law.[33]

Nonetheless, there is another possible explanation, confining its significance by distinguishing between Mark's Jewish and non-Jewish audiences. "Declaring all food clean" may pertain only to Mark's non-Jewish readers. Dunn concludes that "this unit is directed toward a Gentile audience: verses 3–4 explain Jewish customs ('all the Jews!'); and most commentators agree that verse 19c ('cleansing all foods") is designed to point out or serve as reassurance to Gentile believers that Jewish food laws are not obligatory for them."[34] This would align with the exemption of Gentiles from Jewish Law in the Apostolic Decree (Acts 15:19–29) and in Paul (cf. Rom 14:20).[35] Support for this view emerges from Matt 15:10–20, where the remark of Mark 7:19c is omitted, probably because he writes for an audience that abides by Jewish Law.[36]

There are other reasons to qualify the meaning of v. 19c and not to read it as an overall rejection of the biblical purity system. First, elsewhere in Mark (10:3, 5) as well as in Mark 7 specifically (Mark 7:9–10), the authority of the Torah is affirmed. Denying the validity of many dozens of scriptural rules of purity seems unreasonable and also does not cohere with the acknowledgment of the priestly role in declaring the leper pure (see 1:44, referring to Mosaic commandments). Jesus's disciples violate only nonscriptural laws (plucking heads of grain in 2:23). Second, the controversy with the Pharisees about whether hand washing (or immersion) before a meal is necessary concerns not purity in general (which in the Priestly Code is related mainly to Temple, sacrifice, and priests) but daily, profane, and nonpriestly purity.[37] Therefore, the context of vv. 15 and 19c does not appear to justify an abrogation of purity laws in general but merely of such ordinary, nonsacred activities, which not all Jews observe.[38]

In light of these two examples of Mark's approach toward the Law in general and purity in particular, there is no reason to assume that Mark rejects the Temple or challenges its cultic role as a result of a negative stance toward the Jewish Law.

Jesus's "Cleansing" of the Temple, the Rebels, and the Jewish Leaders

OVERTURNING OF THE TABLES: A SIGN OF THE COMING DESTRUCTION?

The cleansing scene in Mark 11:15–17 has already been cited in chapter 1 and need not be reviewed again here. Understanding Mark's intentions in this passage, however, varies considerably from reconstructing the aims of the Historical Jesus. Many interpreters of Mark understand the act of overturning the tables as a rejection of the Temple, since the traders degrade the Temple into a den of robbers, and any business there robs people of their authentic prayer. Thus Jesus teaches the replacement of the Temple.[39] It is actually a prophecy of destruction since "the corruption of the self-serving leadership is poignantly judged by bringing the temple institution to an end."[40] For Werner Kelber, in the cleansing Jesus "disqualified the Temple as the locus of Eschatological fulfillment."[41] David Seely admits that at first glance this act seems like a reform, hence it is less shocking to the reader than an overt call for destruction. However, in light of the next chapters, it also carries undeniable implications for the Temple's end, a symbol of the cessation of Temple service.[42]

What is intriguing in this line of interpretation is that when scholars read the very same passage in search of the Historical Jesus, most understand it as an attempt to reform the cult in order to defend its sacredness and integrity. How does adding the accusation of making the Temple into a den of robbers change the meaning of the cleansing to a prediction of the Temple's total destruction and end?

Jesus does not relate here to the future of the Temple. A prediction concerning its destruction presumably appears only in 13:2. The demolition comes to mind only because of an intertextual reading of the accusation about making it a den of robbers alongside the warning in Jer 7:3–15 claiming wickedness will lead to the destruction of Temple. However, I doubt whether Mark really expects his readers to read his gospel intertextually with the books of the prophets in lieu of making his message explicit through the narrative itself. In any event, Jer 7 contains a warning as well as a call for repentance, not a simple prediction of doom.[43]

It is not clear how the biblical citations are related to the money changers and buying and selling on the Temple Mount. In Jer 7:11, the crimes that precede the claim about the Temple being a den of robbers include stealing, killing, adultery, and idolatry. If Mark treats the selling and buying of sacrifices and changing of money as robbery, he exaggerates the social injustice of cultic commerce at the Temple. Below, I will turn to an alternative interpretation which links Jesus's cleansing to the social and political events of the First Revolt and the Zealots' rise to power.

HOUSE OF PRAYER

Although Juel admits that the house of prayer in and of itself need not imply opposition to the sacrificial cult (since it does not do so in Isa 56:7), he still concludes that Mark opposes the cult—on the basis of the saying in 12:33 that love is greater than burnt offerings and sacrifices.[44] There is an inherent double contradiction in this claim. First, the term "my house" designates the Temple as the house of the Lord, referring to it in emphatic fashion. Second, Isa 56:7 relates to the Temple as a house of prayer in addition to the site of the bringing of animal sacrifices. Furthermore, these offerings of the Gentiles precede prayer even though they appear in the very same verse. Prayer is one of the major rites of the Temple, accompanied by sacrifices.[45] True, Mark points to the failure of the current Temple to fulfill its ideal goal of being a universal sacred center. But he does not reject or alter this ideal. Actually, he confirms its validity.

Mark cites Isa 56:7, including the words "for all the nations," which Matthew and Luke omit. This may rightly be connected to the mission to the Gentiles in 13:10 (and the confession of the centurion, the first to acknowledge Jesus in 15:39).[46]

DEN OF ROBBERS

Robbers (*lēstai*) are used here to denote not only people engaged in economic dishonesty in the Temple but also brigands using violence.[47] Josephus uses the term to refer to the rebels against Rome.[48] Mark does not state who the robbers are, only complaining that "you made it a house of robbers." Since in the next verse (11:18) the chief priests and scribes seek to get rid of Jesus, the reader may identify them with the rebuked "robbers."[49]

Since Mark was written during or immediately after the First Revolt, when *lēstai* are the rebels against Rome, it is customary for scholars to link the accusation of turning the Temple into "a den of robbers" to the events of the First Revolt in Jerusalem and the Temple. Particularly relevant are the revolutionary anti-Roman rebels (the so-called Zealots) who take over the Temple in 68 CE, removing the official aristocratic high priest from office.[50] Marcus provides a detailed discussion viewing Mark as a counter-Zealot, protesting against the Zealots' violent occupation of the Temple and the radical ideology of purifying the Temple.[51] (Additional strong indications for a 68–70 CE setting in Mark 13 will be discussed below.)

Yarbro Collins also alludes to the Zealots' takeover of the Temple, where they find refuge from their opponents in the Temple fortress. In Josephus's words, "They made the holy place the headquarters of their tyranny" (*War* 4.151). It is possible to see Mark's Jesus as contrasting the nationalism of the Zealots with the universalism of Isaiah. Collins also mentions the corruption and violence among the chief priests and their associates in the 50s and 60s (*Ant.* 20.179–181, 206–207), suggesting that Mark may implicitly accuse them of responsibility for the crisis of the revolt which emerges owing to their failure to maintain political order based upon social justice.[52]

OPPOSING THE LĒSTAI AND THE CHIEF PRIEST

Lēstēs is a key word in Mark 11–15, bearing a special political meaning. In 14:48 Jesus says, "Have you come out with swords and clubs to arrest me as though I were a bandit [*lēstēs*]?" Later on, Jesus is jailed with Barabbas the rebel (15:7) and crucified with other bandits (15:27). Mark understands the term as indicating both violent bandits and nationalistic Jewish rebels. Mark therefore contrasts Jesus with the bandits he condemns in 11:17.[53] Jesus is the opposite of these rebels, but ironically both the chief priests and the Romans treat him as if he is one of them.

Jesus's conflict with the Jewish religious leaders and chief priests in particular is central to Mark. The chief priests' prosecution of Jesus is foretold in the prediction of the passion in 8:31 and 10:33–34. I have already mentioned the leaders' reaction to the cleansing in planning to destroy Jesus, followed by his arrest, hearing before the high priest, and turning in to Pilate.[54] We should examine the conversation between Jesus and the chief priests, scribes, and elders, all of which take place in the Temple (11:27–33) in this conflictual context. The leaders ask him upon what authority he is doing "these things."[55] Since they refuse to acknowledge that John's baptism is "from heaven," Jesus also refuses to defend his authority.

This scene suggesting the questioning of Jesus's authority at the Temple bears special importance given the preceding overturning of the tables. Temple authorities question the legitimacy of Jesus's actions. It appears that Mark wants to show Jesus's takeover of the authority of the Jewish religious leaders in their own center of power.[56] Jesus's acts and words at the Temple (see below concerning Jesus's other teachings at the Temple) grant him religious *authority* over the current leadership of the Temple, but it is unwarranted to see this as a condemnation of the Temple cult in general.

For Mark, therefore, Jesus confronts two competing and opposing groups—traditional Jewish leaders headed by the chief priest and the rebels that turn against them during the war with Rome. Jesus thus challenges two opposing powers striving for control of the Temple. Each holds a different agenda concerning Roman rule, with the rebels also casting aspersions on the Temple cult. Mark poses Jesus as a third alternative. Indeed, granting that Mark writes after the rebels take control of the Temple, the condemnation of the rebels seems more acute and relevant than rebuking the old regime of the chief priests and their associates, who have already lost control over the Temple in 68 CE, many being killed by the Zealots during the revolts. Perhaps Mark accuses them of being responsible for the crisis which sparks the Zealots' rise to power. Or perhaps Mark connects the masses' lack of support for these old leaders to their social behavior.[57]

In any event, the cleansing (which Mark designates as being against the rebels), the dispute with the Jewish leaders taking place in the Temple, and the general clash between Jesus and the chief priests who head the Temple do not concern the essence of the sacrificial cult, but rather relate to moral and political realms of religious leadership and authority. The Temple serves as the background in this complex power struggle, where the chief priests and rebels strive for rule. Mark's Jesus denounces both parties, probably implying that they are all unworthy of governing the Temple. Faith in Jesus is the alternative. Staging Jesus's confrontation with Jewish traditional leaders at the Temple shows that Mark is concerned about the Temple. The question of who governs the Temple is on Mark's mind midst concerns about it becoming a den of *lēstōn* or, as we will see below, the "abomination of desolation." Obviously, the Temple cannot fulfill its sacred potential when violent, dishonest, or ignorant leaders control it.

The Cursing of the Fig Tree

The cursing reads as follows: "On the following day, when they came from Bethany, he was hungry; Seeing in the distance a fig tree in leaf, he went to see whether perhaps he would find anything on it. When he came to it, he found nothing but leaves, for it was not the season for figs; He said to it, 'May no one ever eat fruit from you again.' And his disciples heard it" (Mark 11:12–14).

Then there is the lesson: "In the morning as they passed by, they saw the fig tree withered away to its roots; Then Peter remembered and said to him, 'Rabbi, look! The fig tree that you cursed has withered'; Jesus answered them, 'Have faith in God; Truly I tell you, if you say to this mountain, "Be taken up and thrown into the sea," and if you do not doubt in your heart, but believe that what you say will come to pass, it will be done for you; So I tell you, whatever you ask for in prayer, believe that you have received it, and it will be yours; Whenever you stand praying, forgive, if you have anything against anyone; so that your Father in heaven may also forgive you your trespasses'" (Mark 11:20–26).

For many commentators, the cleansing condemns the Temple to destruction because it is framed within the double-cursed fig tree episode.[58] The leafy fig tree with no fruits represents the Temple. Its cursing represents its destruction. The split episode of cursing the fig tree therefore serves as an interpretation of the "cleansing," representing eschatological judgment on the Temple.[59] If this is correct, the story of the fig tree provides Mark with a symbolic and indirect way of intimating the Temple's end.[60]

The cursing of the fig tree culminates in a lesson on prayer as well as a call to belief (11:22–25). Jesus's teaching in relation to prayer and belief is regarded by many as posing an alternative to the supposedly cursed Temple that fails because of the commercial business of sacrifice. While Jesus protests that the Temple is not fulfilling its destiny to become a house of prayer, he teaches his disciples to pray by themselves. This prayer is actually a restoration of authentic Temple worship.[61] Jesus's call to forgive one's fellows so that God will forgive one's sins (11:25) is also interpreted as taking the place of the role of forgiveness in the sacrificial cult.[62]

Here it is argued, Jesus shows his disciples the way forward to a future without the Temple, when the Christian community will be a new place for prayer and forgiveness.[63] Some go even further in arguing that the teaching about prayer and faith represents the Christian community as the new Temple ("not made with hands") becoming "the communal household of authentic and effective prayer."[64] If this is correct, "the temple has been censured without even being mentioned."[65]

Only a few reject this line of thought, concluding that the fig tree represents not the Temple but Temple authorities. These leaders fail to measure up to messianic inspection.[66] Yarbro Collins insists that condemnation of the leaders by cursing the fig tree does not imply that Mark rejects sacrifice or denies the validity of the priestly service in the Temple. I find support for this view of the imagery of a fruitless tree in the parable of the trees, the so-called Jotham's fable (Judg 9:7–15). Here olive and fig trees as well as the vine refuse kingship because they are busy making fruits. Only the fruitless bramble is willing to rule.

I doubt that Mark's readers can understand that the fig tree represents the Temple if the latter is not mentioned in the episode. Moreover, since in the cleansing and its aftermath Mark's polemic is directed against the leaders—the robbers/rebels or the chief priest and scribes—it is more reasonable to suppose that the cursed tree alludes to them. This would also cohere with the parable of the wicked tenants that appears a few verses later. In addition, readers would not see Jesus's teaching about prayer as an alternative to the Temple cult since they are already familiar with prayer practices introduced earlier in 1:35; 6:46; 9:29, and reappearing in 13:33; 14:38 (cf. 12:40). Communal prayer is a common characteristic of the early Christians, but it never serves as a replacement for the Temple cult.[67]

The Parable of the Wicked Tenants

"A man planted a vineyard, put a fence around it, dug a pit for the wine press, and built a watch-tower; then he leased it to tenants and went to another country; When the season came, he sent a slave to the tenants to collect from them his share of the produce of the vineyard; But they seized him, and beat him, and sent him away empty-handed; And again he sent another slave to them; this one they beat over the head and insulted; Then he sent another, and that one they killed. And so it was with many others; some they beat, and others they killed; He had still one other, a beloved son. Finally he sent him to them, saying, 'They will respect my son'; But those tenants said to one another, 'This is the heir; come, let us kill him, and the inheritance will be ours'; So they seized him, killed him, and threw him out of the vineyard; What then will the owner of the vineyard do? He will come and destroy the tenants and give the vineyard to others; Have you not read this scripture: 'The stone that the builders rejected has become the cornerstone; this was the Lord's doing, and it is amazing in our eyes'?; When they realized that he had told this parable against them, they wanted to arrest him, but they feared the crowd. So they left him and went away" (Mark 12:1–12).

Although the Temple is not mentioned in the parable, many find an implicit allusion to it. It is widely agreed that the tenants who kill the son of the lord of the vineyard should be identified with Jewish leaders, particularly those from within the Temple establishment. It is also natural to link the parable to the plot to kill Jesus after the cleansing (11:18), which is repeated at the conclusion of the parable (12:12). The wicked tenants who refuse to deliver the fruits to the owner's servant are equated with those who presumably abuse the people using their privileged role in the Temple (turning it into "a den of robbers"), and in particular the chief priests.[68] The parable professes that they will be punished and put to death (note that during the civil war with the rebels, many of the chief priests and aristocrats are indeed killed).

Many have found a hint for the Temple itself in the word "tower," which is built by the owner in 12:1 (the tower is mentioned in Isa 5:2). This is because in the Aramaic Targum to the parable of the vineyard in Isa 5—the parable upon which Mark 12 is modeled—the tower is both identified with the Temple and related to predicting its destruction.[69] Furthermore, in an earlier Qumranic text designated 4Q500 the tower seems to be "the gate of the holy height," suggesting that it also probably relates to the Temple.[70] Therefore, the conclusion emerges that Mark situates the parable of the Wicked Tenants in the context of the Temple and that Jesus is addressing the chief priests and elders. Thus the parable relates to the cleansing and the prediction of the Temple's destruction, becoming another indication of Jesus's anti-Temple stance.[71]

This use of the Aramaic Targum to interpret Mark leads some commentators to draw insights from the last part of the parable on Jesus's new Temple despite the fact that a Temple is not mentioned here at all. The Lord's giving of the vineyard to others as well as the reference to the cornerstone (12:9–11; cf. Ps 118:21) are interpreted as transference of the vineyard and the tower to the Christian believers. Jesus is the cornerstone of a new (eschatological) Temple.[72]

However, too much weight is given to external texts in interpreting what is not spelled out by Mark explicitly. I doubt that Targum Isiah and 4Q500 prove that Mark is actually referring to the Temple. The Targum postdates 70 CE, and Mark is probably not aware of it. 4Q500 relates to an ideal Temple and praises it. Namely, its contents are probably very different from those of Isa 5 and the Targum.[73] Furthermore, without being fully aware of these texts, Mark's readers cannot relate the parable of the Wicked Tenants to the destruction of the Temple or to the theme of the Temple in general. They can understand only that those who run Jewish society, including the Temple as an institution, would lose their position—with Jesus taking their place. The implications for the destiny of the Temple remain open.

Commentators' treatment of the parable demonstrate the problematic approach of assuming that Mark (like any early Christian author) holds a certain worldview and then finding evidence for it in a text where it is in fact absent. Echoes of this approach are then found in unrelated documents in order to substantiate this conclusion. Yet Mark's readers cannot think of a new Temple when the parable concerns only the Jewish leaders, and a cornerstone cannot stand for a new type of Temple if the concept is not introduced earlier.

Love Is More Important than Sacrifices

In a conversation with Jesus regarding the question of "which commandment is the first of all," a certain scribe agrees with Jesus and replies, "To love him with all the heart, and with all the understanding, and with all the strength, and to love one's neighbor as oneself—this is much more important than all whole burnt-offerings and sacrifices." Jesus approves (Mark 12:32–34).

Should this passage serve as an indication that Mark opposes the sacrificial cult?[74] The preference of obedience to God or morality over sacrifices is an old prophetic tradition in the Hebrew Bible. It does not mean that sacrifices should be abolished.[75] The rabbis also subscribe to it.[76] In fact, in Ps 51:21, the call for an adequately broken spirit and heart is followed by recommending "sacrifices of righteousness." Prioritization of the love commandment is common to Paul, Hillel the Elder, and Rabbi Aqiva. All regard it as the most fundamental commandment, the one within which all others are included.[77]

Returning to Mark, the scribe does not invalidate sacrifice altogether but merely says that the love of God and fellow humans is even more important than sacrifices. The fact that the evangelist places the juxtaposition of the love commandment and sacrifices in the mouth of the scribe (the archetype of Jesus's religious opponents) rather than attributing this to Jesus shows that Mark regards this teaching as common knowledge—not unique to Jesus but consistent with his attitude.

The Poor Widow's Offering to the Temple

"When Jesus sat near the Temple treasury and saw the crowd, including many wealthy people, putting large sums of money into the treasury, he noted: a poor widow came and put in two small copper coins, which are worth a penny; Then he called his disciples and said to them, 'Truly I tell you, this poor widow has put in more than all those who are contributing to the treasury; For all of them have contributed out of their abundance; but she out of her poverty has put in everything she had, all she had to live on'" (Mark 12:41–44).

This is a key passage with regard to revealing Mark's approach to the Temple cult.[78] It takes place in the Temple precinct opposite the Temple treasury.[79] Taken at face value, Jesus praises the widow's generosity toward the Temple, and it seems that he sees a donation to the Temple as a pious act, recommended even to the poor. The widow demonstrates her love of God with all her strength, as Jesus teaches in 12:30–33.[80]

Addison Wright makes a radical shift in interpreting the passage, reading it not as praise for the widow but as a lament. Jesus does not say that the widow's act should be imitated. His actual opinion is revealed when the passage is read in its immediate context—the denunciation of the corrupt, vain scribes who extort poor widows (12:38–40). In Wright's view, the widow actually accomplishes the scribes' ill intentions. Jesus's teaching is downright disapproval of official devotion. The widow is being taught and encouraged by the religious leaders to donate. Jesus condemns this.[81]

This reading fits Jesus's opposition to the exploitations of the poor as well as his view that human need take precedence over religiosity (e.g., healing on Sabbath, 3:1–5), and the same is true concerning the precedence of love over burnt offerings (12:33).[82] In the same vein, Heil regards that poor widow's donation as an "ultimate waste," since the Temple will be destroyed! He argues that this is a negative example for the disciples, reminding them to detach themselves from the wealth which the Temple establishment seeks.[83]

Wright's clever reading of the passage as a lament expresses Mark's mixed attitude toward the Temple, since the widow's contribution is both a pious act and at the same time the result of the scribes taking advantage of her. However, it has several flaws. His contextual focus is too narrow and perhaps even biased. An adequate contextual approach should consider additional Markan overlapping narratives in addition to the condemnation of the scribes' relationship to wealth.[84] Furthermore, the widow serves as a model for the disciples and does not seem to be abused by the scribes.

Mark 12:41–44 has a seminal significance for understanding Mark's attitude toward the Temple for two basic reasons. First, the episode takes place in the Temple precinct (note that Jesus's long stay at the Temple is stressed in the narrative in 11:27; 12:35; 13:1). Second, it concerns the value of making a contribution to the Temple. Its ideological background is Jesus's favoring of the poor as well as his criticism of wealth in general. Jesus's main point is simply that the true measure of gifts is not how much is given but how much is not given. He also implies the duty of giving alms. But in the narrative context of teaching his disciples in and around the Temple, he also implies that donating to the Temple is a noble cause—and that a poor widow who saves even a minimal amount for the Temple treasury is pious and sincere.

The reader thus gets the impression that a donation to the Temple is a donation to God. Hence the Temple itself is a sacred place. How does this conform with Jesus's cleansing in Mark 11? Turning the Temple into "a den of robbers" may apply either to others whose donations are less sincere than the poor widow's (as I suggest in chapter 1) or to the manner in which the donated money is used, whether by the chief priests or the rebels. The widow's donation therefore qualifies or limits the bad impression about the Temple in the cleansing episode. The Temple is a locus of piety toward God, but something is basically wrong there. In any event, the reader does not have a chance to wonder too long to figure out the complex message about the good and bad sides of the Temple, since the next chapter deals with the coming destruction.

"No Stone Upon Another"

"As he came out of the Temple, one of his disciples said to him, 'Look, Teacher, what large stones and what large buildings!' Then Jesus asked him, 'Do you see these great buildings? Not one stone will be left here upon another; all will be thrown down.'" (Mark 13:1–2)

THE COMING DESTRUCTION—THE TEMPLE OR JERUSALEM?

There is consensus that the "buildings" that will be destroyed in which "not one stone will be left here upon another" refer to the Temple. This passage, in which Jesus foresees the destruction of 70 CE, is generally regarded as proof of Jesus's (or Mark's) rejection of the Temple as well as an indication that he looks forward to its destruction.[85] The fact that Jesus sits on the Mount of Olives "opposite the Temple" (13:3) is a sign that he is distancing himself and his disciples from the Temple.[86]

We can only speculate as to why Mark's Jesus predicts the Temple's destruction. Is it because of commercial activity that defiles it or is it due to the militantly nationalistic (on the part of the Zealots) attitude that transforms the Temple from a house of prayer to a den of brigands? Is it a means of passing judgment on the Temple hierarchy for its rejection of Jesus? Does the Temple fail to bring the Gentiles to worship God as a "house of prayer" as part of the mission to the Gentiles in 13:10? Or perhaps this is a prediction about the Temple's replacement by the new Temple—namely, Jesus and his community. Perhaps it is a call not to cling to the Temple for security in the turbulent war years, but a vision for joining Jesus in abandoning the Temple.[87]

Nonetheless, I follow Lloyd Gaston in refusing to see the passage as predicting the destruction of the Temple in particular, in addition to maintaining that it refers more generally to destruction of the city of Jerusalem. This would certainly also include the Temple itself, but the point is that

Mark has no specific antagonism toward the Temple apart from predicting the general destruction.[88] The reason is that the Temple is not mentioned by name in this passage. Also, there is no further allusion to its destruction. The following verses (13:5–13) indicate that Jesus refers to the destiny of the entire city of Jerusalem and the dire fate of Jesus's followers: wars, earthquakes, and persecutions but no particular stress on the Temple apart from the religious climax of the "desolating sacrilege." This, however, is a cultic matter which does not mean physical destruction. It seems that for Mark the destruction of Jerusalem is an appropriate punishment for sin. Still, this does not necessarily reflect a hostile attitude toward the Temple and sacrifices.

DATING MARK: BEFORE OR AFTER 70 CE?

There is considerable debate about whether Mark 13:2, and indeed Mark 13 in its entirety, were written before the destruction of Jerusalem and the Temple by Titus in 70 CE or immediately afterward. This is usually the main indication for dating the entire gospel. The question is, Does Mark use or compose prophecies about the coming destruction or does he already know the outcome of the First Revolt and reformulate Jesus's words as based upon an already known reality. For our present concern, it is important to determine whether Mark is dealing with the totally new situation of Judaism without a Temple, without a religious, social, and political center; or, if he is reacting to the ongoing crisis of the First Revolt and the civil war between the old elite—the chief priests and aristocrats—and the anti-Roman rebels, the so-called Zealots. Is his perspective on Jewish society and the Temple from within, perhaps as a member of this society? Or is it from without, a point of view from outside the cultic center, reflecting upon its disappearance?

A relative minority of scholars date Mark to the years immediately following the destruction.[89] Most scholars date it to the First Revolt against Rome (66–70 CE), usually arguing that the "no stone upon another" prophecy is a prediction. Their thesis is supported by the inaccuracy of this saying, since Titus does leave some of the buildings standing (indeed, parts of the walls of the Herodian Temple Mount are still standing today).[90] The events of the civil war are hinted at in allusions provided by "many will teach in my name" (13:6) and by the specter of false Messiahs, false prophets, and false omens (13:21–22). These correspond to Josephus's report on many who claim to lead the revolt to victory over Rome, including Menahem the Sicarii (who appears in royal robes in *War* 2.444) and Simon son of Gioras (who after the destruction appears with royal garments where the Temple once stood in *War* 7.29–31) as well as the use of the signs of oracles predicting victory.[91]

Admittedly, the wording "not one stone will be left here upon another" is hyperbolic. It is impossible to determine by comparison with Josephus whether it was coined before or after the destruction.[92] John Kloppenborg shows that the *total* destruction of the Temple might be expected as a result of standard Roman policy documented by Roman historians. In many cases temples would be destroyed systematically, not as part of the collateral or accidental consequences of conflict but deliberately in accordance with the Roman siege practice of *evocatio deorum*. This is the "calling out" of the tutelary deity or deities of a city prior to its destruction, the "devoting" of its inhabitants to death or slavery, and the razing of its buildings and temples. Kloppenborg concludes that the practice of *evocatio* is sufficiently well known and widespread to make it reasonable to surmise that any hostilities with Rome might well eventuate in the abandoning of the sanctuary by the deity and its consequent destruction. Hence it is possible to imagine a pre-70 date for the writing of Mark 13:2.[93]

According to Kloppenborg, the author of Mark 13 is able to use his knowledge of the Roman practice of *evocatio*. He can draw out what it implies regarding the fate of the Temple both as a prediction by a pre-70 source or a historical narrative following the events.[94] There is no clear-cut dating.

In any event, Kloppenborg maintains that Mark 13:1–2 claims that the divine presence is no longer there. It is "a historiographic effort to provide a retrospective account of the dual fates of Jesus and the Temple."[95] This, I think, should be qualified, since Mark does not mention the Temple at all in 13:2. The only implicit reference to the Temple in this prophecy is the "desolating sacrilege" in v. 14. It is inconceivable that the entire chapter discusses the dire fate of the Temple without alluding to it directly even once. The destruction is related to Jerusalem, and, as we shall see below, the desecration (not the physical destruction) of the Temple is the climax of a general narrative of doom.

The "Desolating Sacrilege"

Jesus warns the disciples, "But when you see the desolating sacrilege set up where it ought not to be (let the reader understand), then those in Judea must flee to the mountains" (Mark 13:14). Then Jesus relates in full detail the horror of those future days, referring to false messiahs and false prophets who will try to deceive his followers (13:15–23). Only after that horrible period will the Son of Man come and gather the chosen ones (13:24–27).

The term *to bdelugma tēs erēmōseōs* alludes in the LXX to the profanation of the Temple by the Seleucids in the apocalyptic visions of Daniel (Dan 9:27; 11:32; 12:11). But Mark's use of it is obscure. What event is portrayed here? What kind of approach is expressed toward the Temple? Is it correct to view this passage as an anti-Temple prophecy?[96]

One possibility is that Mark alludes to Titus's occupation of the Temple, when the Roman legionaries take out their standards at the Temple, sacrifice to them, and acclaim Titus as *imperator*. The "desolating sacrilege" thus refers to the pagan Roman cult erected on the Temple Mount after 70 CE.[97] However, the mention of the sacrilege is followed by a call to flee from Judea to the mountains (vv. 14–18). There is no sense in calling for flight to the mountains after the siege is ended and the city is taken. Already in 69 CE there is nowhere to flee outside of Jerusalem when Vespasian occupies Judea. The sacrilege therefore precedes the occupation of Jerusalem and the destruction of the Temple.[98]

Many date the historical setting to 68–69 CE, when the rebels rule the Temple. This is a period of persecution and war. Jerusalem is not yet destroyed but threatened, and the evangelist has only vague ideas of what is happening there.[99] Mark's warnings about false messiahs and prophets correspond to the various leaders and oracles among the rebels.[100]

Marcus interprets this apocalyptic passage as referring to the Zealots' takeover of the Temple in 68 CE, suggesting that the "desolating sacrilege" refers to the Zealots' acts in the Temple and particularly its takeover by Eleazar son of Simon.[101] Marcus notes that according to Josephus the Zealots act violently and viciously against their opponents, defile the Temple, and use some of the sacred articles of the Temple for their own (nonsacred) benefit, thereby desecrating the Temple.[102] The high priest Annaus son of Annaus leads opposition to the Zealots after their takeover of the Temple in the winter of 68 CE. Josephus portrays Annaus as the defender of the Temple, citing a long speech in which his main theme is his call to save the Temple from the hands of the Zealots (*War* 4.162–192). Annaus refers to the defilement of the sanctuary by the Zealots, contrasting their behavior with the Romans' respect and votive donations to the Jewish cult. He laments the abominations at the Temple, since its unapproachable and hallowed places are crowded with murderers.[103]

The Zealots probably also hold certain beliefs about the imminent advent of the Messiah, which may nourish Mark's warnings against false messiahs. The early Christians at the time of Mark (including both Jewish and Gentile believers in Jesus) probably object to the national claims of the Zealots.

Yarbro Collins does not accept this identification of the abomination with the Zealots and Eleazar son of Simon, who take over the Temple and pollute it. She argues that the abomination is "standing," hence located in a specific place, not alluding to the violent Zealots in the Temple courts. It is more likely that it is a "standing" statue of a deity.[104]

The alternative, suggested by Hengel, Evans, Yarbro Collins, and others, is that the "abomination of desolation" does not refer to a historical event but is a prophecy directed at the near future in reaction to the crisis of the First Revolt even as the results are as yet unknown to the author. Mark's pre-70 prophecy alludes to the Antichrist taking over the sanctuary in Jerusalem in order to desecrate it. Mark probably expects the Romans to set up a statue of the emperor as Zeus. Then the risen Jesus as Son of Man will emerge at the climax of the war. Titus does not set a statue at the Temple. Nor does he offer pagan sacrifices. Hence it follows that this is a genuine, unfulfilled prophecy.[105]

Whether Mark sees the rebels as performing an abomination in the Temple or predicting the desecration by the Romans, what can we surmise about his view of the Temple? Does the abomination reflect criticism or rejection of the Temple cult?[106] Does it symbolize the end of the Temple's role in the eschaton, the beginning of a new Temple-less age, in which the community replaces the destroyed Temple? If this is the case, the reader should put his faith in Jesus's final coming instead of in the doomed temple from which people flee.[107] Yet how can readers of Mark in Jerusalem before the summer of 70 CE see here a discourse of farewell for the Temple and a new substitute for it? Something crucial to providing such meaning is missing from Mark 13: the Temple is not mentioned by name in the entire chapter.[108] To the contrary, the allusion to the cult in referring to the "abomination of desolation" expresses disturbance of the integrity of the cult, since it is noted as a bad sign for the coming troubles.

The passage may merely describe a catastrophe for which the "desolating sacrilege" is (quite obscurely) a symbol or a catalyst.[109] Indeed, when Daniel uses the expression, he still hopes for the future end of the desecration.[110] Referring to this symbol does not mean that the Temple is doomed

forever. To the contrary, in using this Danielic term, Mark protests the desecration of the Temple and shows concern for the sacredness of the cult.
Mark uses it only as one detail in describing/predicting the distress of the
revolt as the background to the return of the Son of Man.

I think that Mark 13:14 does not allude to the Temple's final destruction
and does not assume that the days of the sacrificial cult are over. The strife
before the destruction serves as a precedent for the eschatological age. The
Temple merely stands in the background awaiting the appearance of the
Son of Man. A more explicit approach is depicted in the following episode
leading to the Last Supper.

The Last Supper

"While they were eating, he took a loaf of bread, and after blessing it
he broke it, gave it to them, and said, 'Take; this is my body'; Then he took a
cup, and after giving thanks he gave it to them, and all of them drank from
it; He said to them, 'This is my blood of the covenant, which is poured out
for many'" (Mark 14:22–24). This is preceded by a detailed description of
the preparations of Jesus and the apostles for the Passover sacrificial meal,
focusing on finding a place to eat the Passover sacrifice (14:12–16, cited in
chapter 1).

In chapter 1 I discussed at length several issues that are also essential in
understanding Mark's treatment of the Last Supper in relation to his views
on sacrifices. We saw that many scholars of the Historical Jesus comment
on the sacrificial language of eating/drinking flesh and blood, most of them
interpreting it as a replacement of sacrifices with the Eucharist.[111] Commentators on Mark share this view: The bread and wine replace sacrifices
of the "damned temple," and Jesus's blood pours out for the many is like a
covenantal sacrifice of atonement for sins.[112]

The Eucharist, however, is not termed as a sacrifice in the NT writings.
This terminology is particularly conspicuous in its absence in 1 Cor 10:16–18
and 11:23–26. It is first introduced only in Didache 14:2–3. An alternative
interpretation is suggested by Klawans. Jesus's words are metaphors that
should not be taken literally, as if the bread and wine actually replace the
flesh and blood. It creates an analogy without expressing any reservations
whatsoever concerning the real sacrifices. The metaphor appropriates some
of the cultic meaning and applies it to something else, thus demonstrating
that sacrifice is meaningful and symbolic.[113]

The narrative context in which Mark introduces the Last Supper is indicative of his views on its connection to the sacrificial system at the Temple. In chapter 1 we have seen that scholars debate whether the Last Supper of the Historical Jesus is part of the Jewish traditional rite of the Passover seder. Yet as far as Mark is concerned it is likely that he understands it as such because in the preceding verses he describes the preparations for the eating of the Passover sacrifice as a ritual meal in Jerusalem (14:12–16).[114] The Last Supper saying appears immediately after the description of this meal (v. 18) and seems to be a direct continuation of it.

Mark's presentation of the preparations of Jesus and the disciples for eating the Passover sacrifice shows a positive approach to this cultic event.[115] The evangelist presents the eating of the Passover as the highlight of Jesus's own Passover meal. Namely, he mentions *to pascha* four times in the passage preceding the Last Supper (vs. 12 [twice], 14, 16), stressing that Jesus himself should eat it (the disciples use the second person singular in approaching Jesus in v. 12).[116]

If Mark is confined merely to following his tradition or perhaps sources for the Passover sacrifice or seder as the background of the Last Supper, he would not put such stress on practicing the Passover offering. The four-fold repetition of practicing *to pascha* is an editorial decision, betraying an emphatic approach to the sacrifice of the Passover lamb. In Mark, Jesus and the disciples are busy preparing the special rite. There seems to be an atmosphere of a certain excitement or thrill about it. In the course of the narrative Mark thus stresses Jesus's observance of the sacrificial practice shared by many contemporary Jews. If Mark's message is anti-Temple—if he wishes to promote the idea of the Christian community as the new Temple—why does he give attention to Jesus's observing this sacrificial rite? Should not the Last Supper come instead of the Passover offering and not *in addition* to it?

I think that as far as Mark is concerned this narrative framework for Jesus's observance of the Passover rite carries greater weight than any scholarly or theological interpretation of his Eucharistic words as anti-sacrificial. If Mark had understood Jesus's rite as a replacement of the sacrificial cult, he would not have stressed Jesus's involvement in the bringing of the Passover lamb. The context of Jesus's partaking of the Passover sacrifice reveals that Mark does not perceive any tension between consuming Jesus's flesh and blood and the nature of the sacrificial cult. The Last Supper is complementary to the traditional sacrifices and actually builds upon it. Mark comes to intensify the meaning of sacrificial language and symbolism by connecting these two practices.

"I Will Destroy This Temple . . . and in Three Days I Will Build Another"

I have already discussed Juel's methodology of finding double meaning in the saying attributed to Jesus by the false witnesses (Mark 14:58). Juel, followed by many others, argues that despite presenting the saying as a false charge against Jesus, Mark uses it to express a special message to the reader, notwithstanding whether Jesus actually says it.[117] The reasoning is that the charge is false only in the sense that Jesus does not claim himself to be the agent of destruction.[118]

According to the charge, this new Temple "not made with hands" will be built by Jesus, though the precedent or model for such a Temple is built by God in heaven.[119] It is commonly understood that by his death and resurrection ("in three days") Jesus will build a new Temple constructed by God himself, manifest by the power granted to Jesus as part of the resurrection.[120] The power to build a new Temple derives from Jesus being the Messiah,[121] assuming that this is a traditional Jewish expectation[122]—though in chapter 1 we saw that it is recorded only in a single source, the post-70 CE Fifth Sibylline Oracle. This new Temple is identified not with a building in which animal sacrifices are to be offered but with a virtual or "spiritual" one, the Christian community.[123] Thus the saying suggests rejection of the current, corrupted Temple, already called "a den of robbers" by Jesus.[124]

From a strictly literary perspective I cannot find any ambivalence in the narrative of the trial. As I mentioned earlier in this chapter, Mark has two claims: that the charge comes from false witnesses, and that they cannot agree on their testimony (14:57, 59). He precedes this claim with a general introduction about the trial in which there are many false testimonies and charges that do not cohere with each other. In fact, they contradict each other. The narrator cannot emphasize more than that the upcoming accusation is false. Jesus does not say what they attribute to him. Therefore, I disagree with the common assertion that "this accusation is probably meant to be taken both as technically false and, in a deeper sense, as ironically true."[125] Read in isolation with the three days' prediction of the passion and *without assuming* that Mark has in mind a new type of Temple (namely, Jesus or the Christian community), the only possible understanding is that

"Mark wants his readers to think the statement in 14:58 was a total fabrication by the witnesses."[126] Mark 14:58 cannot be read as a Christian proclamation, only as a false charge.

In fact, it is possible that "a Temple not made with hands" is a concept which is rejected as farfetched by the author. Those who express it are denounced as unrighteous and unreliable people. The reader has no way of knowing what "Temple not made with hands" means.[127] There is no hint elsewhere in Mark of the community being Temple-like, and there is hardly a sense of *ecclesia* in Mark or even a close relationship between the disciples independently of Jesus apart from calling the disciples to follow Jesus back to the Galilee (16:7). One should not take the concept of community as a Temple from Paul and attribute it to Mark without sufficient literary justification.

The Tearing of the Temple Veil

When the crucified Jesus gives a loud cry and takes his last breath, "The curtain of the Temple [*katapetasma tou naou*, the *parochet*] was torn in two, from top to bottom" (Mark 15:37–38). Mark undoubtedly regards this as a symbolic occasion reflecting the meaning of Jesus's death. Many interpret the tearing of the curtain as implying the end of the Temple; that the death of Jesus foretells the destruction of the Temple.[128] This is because the (probably inner) veil of the Temple guards the Temple's sanctity.[129] Its tearing implies "a negative, judgmental image" in direct reaction to Jesus's death.[130] Jesus's death actually symbolizes the end of the world and hence the end of the Temple. His resurrection, being the cornerstone, is the beginning of the new Temple.[131] This can be compared to signs marking the Temple's destruction when the massive eastern gate made of brass in the Temple's inner court opens by itself at midnight.[132] Notably, this anti-Temple interpretation is first attested to in the second-century CE Pseudo-Clementine *Recognitions*, which includes a harsh polemic against sacrifices in the Temple.[133]

Parallels between the tearing of the Temple curtain and the sundering of heaven when Jesus is baptized by John (Mark 1:10) may point to a different meaning for this scene.[134] The veil not only symbolizes the Temple but also is a cosmic symbol relating to the firmament of Gen 1:6. According to Josephus, it is colored in blue scarlet and purple, representing the universe and portraying a panorama of the entire heavens. Thus the rending of the veil implies the rending of the heavens, an apocalyptic scene in which the skies are opened.[135] Furthermore, "to tear" (*schizō*) in 15:38 may carry a positive sense of revelation as in Isa 63:18–64:1. Thus Jesus's death opens heaven, as in Mark 1:10, making God's presence felt.[136] The similarity between Mark 15:37–38 and 1:10 shows that it is not a sign of the destruction of the Temple but a nontraditional theophany.[137]

If the tearing of the curtain corresponds to the tearing of heaven, it can hardly be viewed as symbolizing the destruction of the Temple. It more likely reflects a cosmic reaction to Jesus's death, actually attesting to an appreciation of the Temple as a divine institution. Indeed, there is a rabbinic saying in a similar spirit: "If a man divorces his first wife, even the altar sheds tears."[138] Perhaps the tearing of the curtain is a sign of grief, since tearing one's clothes is a customary Jewish ritual of mourning.[139] In fact, since in Judaism the Temple, the *heikhal* (*naos*), and the altar reflect the relationship between God and His people,[140] portraying the Temple's response to Jesus's death makes sense.

Conclusion: The Temple as a Setting for Jesus

The prevailing scholarly view that Mark opposes the Temple and introduces Jesus or the Christian community as its substitute is based upon explicit critique of the Temple in the cleansing and "den of robbers" sayings in addition to reading the prophecy "no stone would be left on another" as a prediction of the Temple's destruction. These, however, may be interpreted not as a rejection of the Temple but as a criticism of how it is currently being operated. Several passages in which the Temple is not mentioned at all—such as the cursing of the fig tree and the parable of the wicked tenants—are read as implying such an anti-Temple stance.

There are two general considerations that counter the replacement theory. Mark's approach toward the Jewish Law, although somewhat critical, is far from being overly negative. It is therefore difficult for the evangelist to deny the necessity of the Temple. In addition, Mark is written before the fall of the Temple. Mark and his readers are not ready for Jewish life without the Temple. Judaism without a Temple, as both an institution and a symbol, is a new situation that demands the rethinking of concepts such as holiness and atonement.

I suspect that those who think Mark substitutes Jesus for the Temple are guided by an implicit presupposition that since Mark wants his readers to believe that Jesus is the eschatological Son of Man, this also necessitates estrangement toward the Temple. Thus Mark's anti-Temple stance should be revealed simply by exegesis. I doubt that such estrangement actually exists, and it is unfortunate that many commentators do not consider alternative approaches to the Temple. According to this consensus, Mark is writing, or being read, as if the Temple no longer exists; or if it still exists, its coming destruction is obvious. Mark is a gospel for Christians without a Temple. The author claims that the belief in Christ makes the Temple cult irrelevant.

I agree that Mark is being read in such a way some time *after* it is written.[141] However, this is not what the author means *at the time* of writing. We have seen indications that Mark 13 reacts to the events of 68 CE, and the gospel is probably written before the destruction. Thus we cannot assume that Mark deals with a situation in which the Temple no longer stands. To the contrary, during the First Revolt the control and fate of the Temple are at the heart of the conflict between the rebels against Rome and the Jewish moderate party which opposes them. Its future is in danger, but this only makes it all the more important, both religiously and politically. Being the first gospel, and actually inventing this literary form, if Mark wants his readers to understand that the cult is no longer relevant since Jesus takes its place, he needs to stress and explain it (as in Hebrews!) and not hint at it. Mark's readers in 69–70 CE cannot grasp the double reading that scholars find in Mark. They do not hold the key notion that the Temple is irrelevant before or after the destruction, since no Christian source tells them so. At least not yet.

In this chapter I have tried to make a case for a very different reading of Mark and to show that Mark hardly draws such a stark contrast between the Temple and Jesus.[142] True, Jesus rebukes the situation in the Temple when he overturns the tables of the money changers and calls it "a den of robbers." But Mark puts the blame on the robbers—the rebels who use it or take control of it—not on the sacrificial cult. Jesus is in conflict with the chief priests and their associates in Jerusalem, who also run the Temple (before the rebels conquer it). Mark's polemic against Jewish traditional leadership is also attested to in the cursing of the fig tree and the parable of the wicked tenants. Indeed, Mark is occupied deeply by Jesus's conflict with competing religious leaders.[143] But this is a struggle over religious authority related to the Temple only indirectly. Jesus hardly deals strictly with the cultic issues that challenge the chief priest. Jesus himself is the challenge, a new religious master who teaches on the Temple Mount.

Mark associates Jesus with the Temple when he repeats several times that Jesus acts and teaches at the Temple. For the reader in 69–70 CE,

Jesus's attendance implies *interest* in the Temple. His acceptance of priestly authority in relation to skin disease purity (1:44) and the disciples' preparations for eating the Passover sacrifice (14:12–16) reflect adherence to cultic practices. Jesus also relates to the Temple when he warns or mourns about the "desolating sacrilege" (13:14) and when his death causes the tearing of the Temple veil (15:37–38). I thus conclude that Mark seems to use the Temple as a background for Jesus's teachings. This location increases his authority and poses him as a threat to the chief priests and scribes.

The reason Mark ties Jesus to the Temple in these various ways is not a polemic against the Temple and the sacrificial cult, but, on the contrary, an attempt to associate Jesus with the Temple. For the reader who views the Temple as the religious and political center of Judaism, this link means authenticity, credibility, and authority. In a period when Jews are fighting for control of the Temple and debating who is to blame for its pending destruction, no legitimate Jewish leader can afford to be detached from the Temple.

Mark wants the reader to think of Jesus in relation to the Temple, to understand that he is a sacred figure who is part of the heart of Jewish religiosity and has authority in the sacred center. By placing Jesus in the Temple and relating him to the cult in the preparation for the Passover sacrifice and the tearing of the veil, some of the attributes of the cult are symbolically transmitted to Jesus without disqualifying the Temple. But this does not mean that Jesus takes the place of the Temple. Mark probably is not sure that the Temple will soon be destroyed. He hesitates to predict it straightforwardly (as Matthew and Luke do).[144] Later, when the Temple falls, Mark's readers are left with Jesus as the closest symbol to the Temple, a holy man who has had special religious authority in the Temple and warns against its chief priests and the rebels, who, according to Josephus, fight against each other to lead to its destruction.

Mark does not reject the Temple cult, does not foresee Jesus as its replacement, and makes positive use of the Temple as a setting for Jesus's authority.

4 Q and Matthew: The Sacred Temple

This chapter unites discussions of Q and Matthew, not only because Q is part of Matthew (as well as Luke) but also because both of these discussions are relatively short.

Section I. Q: Temple Practice and Polemic

The so-called Q source (or Saying Source) preserved in Luke and Matthew—and usually cited from Luke—has little to say about the Temple. Owing to its importance as an early document (ca. 50s of the first century CE) and its influence on both Matthew and Luke, clarity concerning Q's attitude toward the Temple, implicit as it may be, is crucial for understanding pre-70 early Christian approaches to the Temple as a whole.

The Law and the Temple

Unlike Mark, Q lacks disputes on legal matters such as the Sabbath and purity laws. There is no trace of overt criticism of the Torah. When the subject arises, Q underscores the complete authority and validity of the Torah.[1] Scholars usually claim that in Q Jesus obeys the Law and does not dispute it. The author does not often address legal matters. It also seems that the author is close to the Pharisees.[2]

Q 16:16–17 declares the status of the Law under the Kingdom of God unequivocally: "The law and the prophets were until John. From then on the Kingdom of God is violated and the violent plunder it; But it is easier for heaven and earth to pass away than for one iota or, one serif of the law to fall."[3] It is natural to infer from this statement that the Law must still be obeyed in the new era.[4]

However, there is a different scholarly opinion concerning Q's approach to the Torah. Kloppenborg notes that the Torah is scarcely mentioned in Q and that Q's authors generally have limited interest in the Law. Q does not say that one needs to observe the Law in order to be saved or that its wisdom is built upon the foundation of the Torah. At best it is indifferent to the Torah.[5] According to his reconstruction of the Q document, nomistic concerns are foreign to the formative components of Q tradition and appear only at a later stage."[6]

Naturally, these two conflicting approaches relate to different views concerning Q's attitude toward the Temple as well. For David Catchpole, general regard for the Law in 11:37–52 and 16:17 implies an appreciative attitude to the Temple and its cult. The conflict with the Pharisees is an internal Jewish debate, and the definitive place of the Temple is not challenged. Hence the Q community is "Temple-centered" and expects its restoration, even though it also criticizes the Temple. For Kloppenborg, however, it is significant that the Q document does not appeal to the priesthood, the Temple, or purity distinctions. He comes to the far-reaching conclusion that "the redemptive significance of the Temple has been already abandoned." Kloppenborg relates Q's point of view to the Galileans' ambivalent attitude toward the Temple and the Torah, most particularly purity and tithing (which I think should not be exaggerated). Yet he admits that in a certain portion of Q's latest layer—which includes the passages I am about to discuss—there is a shift in the attitude toward the Temple: the Temple is a place where angels are naturally present to assist holy persons, a holy place.[7]

The reconstructed text of Q is relatively short and contains a variety of detached units. It lacks a narrative and contains no systematic treatment of the Temple. Even if we agree about which verses in Matthew and Luke are to be included in the reconstructed Q source and their exact wording, we do not have sufficient evidence to evaluate its attitude toward the Temple, because it is too short and its language is somewhat cryptic. Here one's basic assumptions regarding Q's approach to contemporary Judaism as well as one's understanding of the author's distinctive style of sapiential and apocalyptic rhetoric is crucial. We need to pay special attention to what the text doesn't say in equal measure to what it does say.

Q 4:9–12: Satan's Temptation of Jesus in the Temple

"The devil took him along to Jerusalem and put him on the pinnacle of the Temple and told him: If you are God's Son, throw yourself down; For it is written: He will command his angels about you; and on their hands they will bear you, so that you do not strike your foot against a stone; And Jesus in reply, told him: It is written: You shall not test the Lord Your God."

Jesus's temptation by Satan includes three scenes: the wilderness, a high place or mountain, and the Temple in Jerusalem. But why does the author place the temptation at the Temple?[8] On the one hand, it is possible that this serves as a negative setting for Jesus's teachings. Namely, Jesus refuses to perform miracles in the Temple despite the devil's promise of protection, thus implying a rejection of the Temple's symbolism as a place of divine protection.[9] On the other hand, it is also reasonable to hold that Q's Satan takes Jesus to the Temple's pinnacle because it is a symbolic place of divine protection attended by angels, more likely to tempt Jesus to rely on divine aid.[10]

Reading the temptation story as a whole, one sees clearly that Jesus refuses to perform any such miracles because he is committed to obeying the commandment not to test God.[11] His insistence is not related to the Temple, since he remains steadfast in the other locations as well, including the desert and the mountain. So how is the pinnacle of the Temple special?[12] This high (perhaps the highest) place in the Temple is especially impressive and safe and may represent God's protection.[13] Instead of seeing Jesus as doubting the sanctity of the Temple and the divine protection it harbors, I think we should understand the plot as the devil's attempt to use the idea of the Temple's pinnacle as a safe place. Jesus does not jump from it *despite* the assumption about the special protection of God found there. Therefore, Q may be employing this common knowledge intentionally, placing the temptation at the pinnacle as a means of demonstrating that *even there* Jesus is not tempted to disobey God.

Q 11:42: Rebuking the Pharisees' Practice of Tithing Everything

"Woe for you, Pharisees, for you tithe mint and dill and cumin, and give up justice and mercy and faithfulness. But these one had to do, without giving up those."

In ancient Judaism tithes are given to the priests and Levites directly or brought to the Temple and distributed there.[14] Tithes should therefore be associated with the Temple system and priesthood. Giving tithes to a priest or bringing them to the Temple means accepting and supporting the cultic system.

The nature of Jesus's critique of the Pharisees is not entirely clear. The words "these one had to do" seem to show that he approves of tithing even mint, dill, and cumin. Yet merely raising the subject sounds like a critique of the Pharisees for meticulousness resulting in tithing virtually every herb. According to Kloppenborg, the passage does not correct pharisaic lifestyle but rejects it. Q's description ridicules the Pharisees, using hyperbole and rhetorical lampoon to criticize the Pharisees' meticulous *lifestyle,* not a specific practice.[15] Although the final portion of the verse does indeed confirm strict observance of tithing, Kloppenborg marginalizes it by labeling it a secondary addition since it does not cohere with previous portions of the narrative in which the Pharisees' tithing is critiqued. Kloppenborg maintains that this latter portion stressing commitment to the Law may be an attempt to reduce tension between the Pharisees and the Q community.[16]

As the part of the verse reading "these one had to do" demonstrates, despite its criticism, Q approves the *general* Jewish practice of giving tithes to the priests and Levites.[17] While it is natural to make assumptions about Q's Temple practice or Temple alliance based on this point of view, such an approach is questionable. Kloppenborg argues that acknowledging tithes does not necessarily imply loyalty to the Temple; neither does it definitively suggest that the Q community accepts Temple-centered socio-symbolism.[18] Nevertheless, I would require clear evidence in order to argue for a position holding that tithing is *not* directly related to the Temple. Q lacks any such evidence.

The author of Q presents strict pharisaic tithing in order to distance Jesus from the Pharisees, while still associating him with the Law. Unlike the Pharisees, Jesus emphasizes the Law's ethical dimensions. There is a passive or implicit acceptance of the system of the Temple and priests but nothing more than that.

Q 11:49–51: The Murder of Zechariah in the Temple

"Wisdom said: I will send them prophets and sages, and some of them they will kill and persecute; so that a settling of accounts for the blood of all the prophets poured out from the founding of the world may be required of this generation; from the blood of Abel to the blood of Zechariah, murdered between the sacrificial altar and the House. Yes, I tell you, an accounting will be required of this generation!"

One might wonder whether mention of the killing of Zechariah at the Temple (*oikos* in Q; *naos* in Matt 23:35) implies a negative perception of it. This Zechariah should probably be identified as the son of Jehoiada, the priest who is stoned during the reign of King Joash in the outer court of the Temple. He is a distinguished priest warning against leaving God in favor of idols and is stoned by the king's command (2 Chr 24:17–21).[19]

Zechariah's killing is mentioned in Q in the context of the woes against the Pharisees (Q 11:38–52) in relation to the killing of the prophets by "your ancestors." The Pharisees are accused of approving a killing perpetrated by their ancestors ("for they killed them, and you build their tombs," 11:48), even though this event happened more than five hundred years earlier. Thus there is a certain indirect rhetorical link between the bloodshed in the Temple and the Pharisees. What bearing does this have on Q's view of the Temple? Referring to murder in the Temple and the profanation of the sancta by innocent blood is meant to shock his audience. The author probably cares about the integrity of the cult and seems to associate it with the Pharisees' hypocrisy, even if for merely rhetorical reasons.[20]

Q 13:34–35: "Your House Is Forsaken"

"O Jerusalem, Jerusalem, who kills the prophets and stones those sent to her! How often I wanted to gather your children together, as a hen gathers her nestlings under her wings, and you were not willing! Look, your house is forsaken! . . . I tell you, you will not see me until the time comes when, you say: Blessed is the one who comes in the name of the Lord!"

This lament over Jerusalem is a prophecy by which Jesus reacts to his rejection by the Jews. Although the prophecy expresses deep feelings toward the city, Jerusalem is guilty and will be punished. It is customary to see the prediction "your house [*ho oikos humōn*] is forsaken" as referring to the coming destruction of the Temple. The word *oikos* (Hebrew *bayit*) sometimes means "the Temple," and the Temple is located in Jerusalem. And so the question arises: Is it merely a prediction of the divine punishment of the entire city, or does Q reject the Temple?[21] Certainly, if one is looking forward to the city's destruction for whatever reason, this entails a critical approach to the Temple, even if it does not mean that the author believes that sacrifices are no longer necessary.

The point of the passage is the destruction of the city of those who reject Jesus—and Jerusalem is not alone. It joins two cities of the Galilee, Chorazin and Bethsaida, for which Q predicts destruction for the same reason (Q 10:13–15). In fact, the motif of judgment of "this generation" is fundamental to Q.[22] The reference to "your house" does not stand alone since it is a direct continuation of the sad prophecy about the coming destruction of Jerusalem. If the Temple is destined to be destroyed, it is because it is physically inside of the city, not because the cult is flawed.

But does "your house" actually refer to the Temple at all? Weinert argues that—at least for Luke—it does not. It implies a simple residence, a domestic house. Moreover, it may be that Q is inspired by and perhaps even alludes to Jer 22:7 ("this house shall become a desolation"), which refers not to the Temple but to the king's house, namely, the palace (Jer 22:1, 4).[23] This interpretation makes the link between Jerusalem and "your house" more coherent: the house refers to a house in the city. For this reason I cannot justify Hann's conclusion that the author distances itself from the Temple or that for Q "allegiance to the Temple has been lost."[24]

Conclusions

In the temptation story (4:9–12) the Temple is a place of divine protection. In the criticism of the Pharisees' meticulous tithing at the expense of ethical behavior based upon justice, mercy, and faithfulness (11:42) there is nonetheless acknowledgment of the need to give tithes ("these one had to do"); hence at the very least there is an implicit acceptance of the system of the Temple and the priests.

Mention of Zechariah's murder "between the sacrificial altar and the House" (11:50) is linked to the rhetorical polemic with the Pharisees. It assumes care for the Temple's sanctity, but it would be too extreme to deduce from this supposed allegation that the Temple is morally polluted because of the Pharisees (or their forefathers). After all, this refers to an event from the monarchic period. The lament over Jerusalem and the prophecy that "your house is forsaken" (13:34–35) may not refer to the Temple at all—at least not in the sense that Luke interprets it. And even if the lament and prophecy do assume a link to the Temple, its physical destruction is the result of its location in the city of Jerusalem, not of the nature of the sacrificial cult itself.

Is it possible to present a coherent view of the Temple in Q, our earliest source for the sayings attributed to Jesus? Q pays limited attention to the Temple. The author's attitude is quite positive but includes a certain ambivalence. The sanctity of the Temple or the acceptance of the priestly system is assumed in the temptation story, the murder of Zechariah, and perhaps also the criticism of the Pharisees' stress on strict tithing in the context of ethical concerns.[25] The Temple's holiness is taken for granted, and the Q traditions build upon it to convey other, mostly critical, messages. Yet owing to the tension with the Pharisees inherent in these sayings—in the course of Q's polemics against "this generation" and especially the Pharisees—there may be critical reflections on the Temple because it is under the domain of those who reject Jesus. For Q, the problematic nature of the Temple is not related to an attitude toward the cult itself; but surely, if "this generation" and Jerusalem are doomed, this brings ill consequences upon the Temple as well.

Section II. Matthew: Temple Piety

Relationship with Other Jews, the Torah, and the Law

The gospel of Matthew reached its final form in the 80s or 90s, perhaps in the Galilee. It combines elements embracing main aspects of contemporary Judaism with extremely harsh polemics against the Jews, particularly the Pharisees.[26] Because of this exceptional combination of traditional practice and social conflict there is scholarly debate about Matthew's position in relation to Jewish religion and society. Situating Matthew in relation to first-century Judaism is a complex challenge.

Some current scholars, such as Graham Stanton, continue an older view by which Matthew distances himself from other Jews (the so-called *extra-muros* approach). Matthew stresses a parting of the ways with Judaism as a separate "church," manifested by a deep rivalry with the Pharisees, scribes, and "their synagogue." He sets against them the alternative of the *ecclesia* (a term that does not appear in the other gospels). For Matthew, the Kingdom is given to a new people, including Gentiles. This hostility toward the Pharisees and scribes stems from Matthew's communities' separation from Judaism after a period of hostility, opposition, and persecution on the part of some Jews. Israel's continued rejection of Jesus leads to the departure of the Matthean Christians from Jewish society.[27] Matthew's community has only recently broken with the parent body of Judaism (or "the synagogue") and now lays claim to a common prehistory.[28]

A growing number of scholars now view Matthew as being shaped by inner-Jewish conflict and competition with other Jews (the so-called *intra-muros* approach). While Matthew's main concern is attacking the Pharisees as Jewish leaders, there is no definitive opposition between Matthew and Judaism in general and no rejection of the Jewish People as a whole.[29] In fact, there is an intriguing reason why the author aims to distance his readers from the Pharisees: "The tension of the Matthean community with . . . the Pharisees and 'their synagogues' was born of proximity rather than distance, of similarity rather than difference."[30]

This relationship between Matthew and the Pharisees and the synagogue is examined by Anders Runesson. He demonstrates that general references to synagogues (6:2, 5; 23:6) indicate that the Mattheans regard the public synagogue as the normal, accepted venue for worship in local public contexts. The conflict with the Pharisees therefore takes place in the synagogue. He concludes that the Mattheans are initially part of the pharisaic association. The author's community is in the process of leaving the larger Jewish community after the war of 66–70 CE.[31]

Matthew is extremely preoccupied with questions relating to the Law. Few see this as a reflection of the rejection of Jewish legal practice.[32] The consensus is that Matthew confirms the validity of the commandments. Matthew insists strongly on the continuing importance of the Law: "Do not think that I have come to abolish the law or the prophets; I have come not to abolish but to fulfill; For truly I tell you, until heaven and earth pass away, not one iota, not one stroke of a letter, will pass from the law until all is accomplished; Therefore, whoever breaks one of the least of these commandments, and teaches others to do the same, will be called least in the Kingdom of heaven; but whoever does them and teaches them will be called great in the Kingdom of heaven" (5:17–19). The time limit of "until heaven and earth pass away" may relate to the eschatological age, the Parousia. Yet Jesus has his own authoritative interpretation of the Law (7:26–29; 28:20), which is related to the conflict with the Pharisees.[33]

Commitment to the Law is further demonstrated in Matthew's revision of Mark's treatment of the laws of purity and Sabbath. Matt 15:11, 17 omits the remark in Mark 7:19b about declaring all foods clean, and it seems that he accepts the purity laws. Matt 12:3–8 also omits the saying that the Sabbath is made for man and not man for the Sabbath (Mark 2:27) because it might promote general laxity in keeping the laws of the Sabbath. In 24:20 Matthew adds that the flight from Jerusalem would not happen during the Sabbath (cf. Mark 13:18). Although there are other interpretations, the simplest one is that he does not want to breach the Sabbath laws.[34]

Interestingly, Matthew combines legal observance with criticism of the Pharisees and scribes: "The scribes and the Pharisees sit on Moses' seat; do whatever they teach you and follow it; but do not do as they do, for they do not practice what they teach" (23:2–3). Surely Matthew admits their powerful social and religious position. Yet he calls upon his readers not to follow their behavior. Scholars disagree about the extent to which Matthew accepts the pharisaic legal doctrine.[35]

Matthew and the Temple: General Approaches

Matthew's attitude toward the Temple is a bone of contention among scholars. Some believe that the Temple is rejected and replaced by Jesus because, as in Mark, it is a place of conflict with the Jewish authorities. Furthermore, Jesus heals in the Temple in Matt 21:14, which may make it seem as if he is fulfilling the function of the cult. Then Jesus leaves the Temple, professing its destruction, and sits directly opposite it on the Mount of Olives (24:1–3).[36] In addition, Matthew presents Jesus's role of saving Israel from its sins (an angel tells Joseph that "he will save his people from their sins" 1:21), Jesus offers his blood as a means of forgiveness of sins for the many in the Eucharist (26:28), and, finally, he gives his soul as a ransom for the many (20:28). All of these acts may be seen as substitutes for sacrifices.[37]

Others contend that Matthew's portrayal is consistently positive and that he accepts the legitimacy of the Temple. Despite his criticism of the Jewish leaders who run it, for Matthew, the Temple remains an appropriate setting for Jesus's teachings (21:23; 26:55). Offering sacrifices is still recommended (5:23–24; 8:4), although Jesus remains superior to it (12:6).[38] Jerusalem is the holy city before as well as after the death of Jesus (Matt 4:5; 5:35; 27:53).[39] The destruction of Jerusalem and the Temple, of which the final author/redactor is certainly aware, does not affect the holiness of the Temple or the respect for it. Rather, the destruction is used to blame the leaders who had been appointed by God but had used their position in ways contrary to God's purposes.[40]

In what follows I want to discuss not only Matthew's approach to the Temple but also whether or not he attempts to suggest a certain balance between belief in Jesus and adherence to the Temple.

Sacrifice Needs Reconciliation First

"So when you are offering your gift at the altar, if you remember that your brother has something against you; leave your gift there before the altar and go; first be reconciled to your brother, and then come and offer your gift." (5:23–24)

This passage at the beginning of the Sermon on the Mount continues instruction on not getting angry or insulting one's brother and sister (5:21–22). In our passage, the need to reconcile with an offended brother takes priority over the sacrifice for unwitting sins. While there is a priority for personal piety or proper ethical behavior, this does not diminish Temple worship. Matthew assumes the validity of sacrifice and participation in the cult. Still, the plain, practical meaning of leaving the sacrifice with the priest and returning later is not reasonable.[41] The rationale of the saying, in which morality takes precedence over sacrifice, is rooted in ancient Judaism, probably reflecting, along with the entire Sermon on the Mount, a pre-70 tradition from an era when the Temple still stands.[42]

There is another case in which Jesus orders the bringing of a sacrifice: When Jesus heals the leper, he sends him to the priest to bring sacrifice, as in Mark 1:44. Matt 8:4 adds "and offer the sacrifice . . . as a testimony to them." Unlike in Mark, sacrifice (*dōron*, literally, "gift") is explicitly mentioned in order to stress cultic fidelity.[43]

Mercy Is More Important than Sacrifice

"When the Pharisees saw this, they said to his disciples, 'Why does your teacher eat with tax-collectors and sinners?'; But when he heard this, he said, 'Those who are well have no need of a physician, but those who are sick; Go and learn what this means, 'I desire mercy, not sacrifice [*thusian*].' For I have come to call not the righteous but sinners." (9:11–13)

In the course of his conflict with the Pharisees, who rebuke Jesus for associating with the religiously inferior sinners and tax collectors, Jesus justifies his acts by citing Hos 6:6, saying, "I desire mercy, not sacrifice" (*eleon thelō kai ou thusian*). Matthew uses a literary translation of the Hebrew instead of the LXX, introducing a tension between sacrifices and mercy or compassion (Heb. *hesed*).

The complete verse in Hosea is, "For I desire mercy and not sacrifice, the knowledge of God rather than burnt-offerings." The prophet condemns not sacrificial worship as such but faulty reliance upon it amidst moral corruption and religious ignorance. Such rituals are meaningless without the faithful love of the worshipers. *Hesed* in Hosea is related to truth and knowledge (Hos 4:1), righteousness (Hos 10:12), and justice (Hos 12:7). Any of these may suit Jesus's saying, in which sacrifice represents general strict obedience to the commandments.[44]

Since the context does not refer to the cult apart from citing the verse, it is difficult to maintain that Jesus speaks against sacrifices. Rather, as in Hosea, the negation is far from being absolute. Matthew thinks that cultic observance without inner faith and heartfelt covenant loyalty is vain.[45] The Hebraic locution *kai ou* is not a starkly contrastive assertion, but an idiom of "dialectical negation" meaning "I desire mercy *more* than sacrifice." Cult cannot be separated from morality.[46] Matthew's Jesus thus affirms that God requires faithful adherence to and love for God in addition to merciful actions, not heartless sacrifice or mere formal religious piety. Jesus does not downplay the Law and sacrifices but argues that adherence to the Law starts with a compassionate heart.[47]

A further argument against an anti-Temple reading of the citation of Hos 6:6 is its occurrence in Matt 12:6. Here it is cited in the course of an analogy between Jesus performing healing on the Sabbath and the priestly service at the Temple during the Sabbath (12:5), aiming to legitimize his healing on the day of rest (see below). This context implies that Matthew affirms the legitimacy of the cult.[48]

Greater than the Temple

"At that time Jesus went through the cornfields on the Sabbath; his disciples were hungry, and they began to pluck heads of grain and to eat. When the Pharisees saw it, they said to him, 'Look, your disciples are doing what is not lawful to do on the Sabbath.' He said to them, 'Have you not read what David did when he and his companions were hungry? He entered the house of God and ate the bread of the Presence, which it was not lawful for him or his companions to eat, but only for the priests. Or have you not read in the law that on the Sabbath the priests in the Temple break the Sabbath and yet are guiltless? I tell you, something greater than the Temple is here. But if you had known what this means, "I desire mercy and not sacrifice," you would not have condemned the guiltless. For the Son of Man is lord of the Sabbath.'"(12:1–8)

It is intriguing that a controversy about plucking grain on the Sabbath turns into a discussion of four issues relating to the Temple cult: David

eating of the bread of the Presence; the priestly service at the Temple during the sacred day; the phrase "something greater than the Temple is here";
and, again, the phrase stating that mercy is more important than sacrifice.
Matthew brings these elements into a discussion that is entirely different
from the issue of the Sabbath law, while the Markan source mentions only
David's eating of the bread of the Presence (Mark 2:23–28). The author is
therefore concerned about the Temple and sacrifices, and this seems to be a
key passage for understanding Matthew's approach. I want to discuss each
element separately and then turn to Matthew's general argument.

The Pharisees see Jesus's disciples plucking grain and rebuke their lack
of observance of the prohibition on harvesting during the Sabbath, the
day of rest. Jesus responds (as already recorded in Mark) by mentioning
another, much bolder case of breaking the law: David and his men, who are
also hungry during their escape from Saul, eat from the bread of the Presence at the Sanctuary of Nob, the priestly town, since there is no ordinary
bread available (1 Sam 21:4–7). It is unlawful for a nonpriest to eat of the
bread of the Presence (see Lev 24:9, where it is called the "holy of holies").
David's lack of observance therefore serves as a precedent for hunger le-
gitimizing breaking the Law.[49] This Markan passage probably encourages
Matthew to continue on to other arguments relating to the realm of the
Temple.

Jesus draws another analogy to justify his disciples' plucking grain, this
one directly related to the Sabbath laws. Just as the priests "violate" Sabbath
rest in order to fulfill the more important task of making sacrifices man-
dated for the Temple—technically the priests desecrate the Sabbath commandments while remaining "guiltless"—so Jesus's disciples pluck grain to
assuage human hunger. Matthew apparently argues that Jesus and his disciples represent a similar special instance of the work of God and thus are
not bound to the Law.[50]

Then Matthew introduces the catchy slogan "something greater than
the Temple [hieron] is here." Although he does not say so explicitly, it is
clear that "something" implies an act related to Jesus or his ministry,[51] especially since at the end of the passage he repeats the Markan saying "the Son
of Man is lord of the Sabbath." Namely, Jesus's personhood is present in the
entire passage, though not directly. Why is this relevant here? While the
Temple is greater than the Sabbath (since the priests work in the Temple
even on the Sabbath), Jesus is greater than the Temple, which means he too
is greater than the Sabbath. One can infer that Jesus (as the Son of Man

and the interpreter of the Torah) has the authority to determine what loyalty to the Sabbath means.[52] The disciples can pick grain on the Sabbath if they are hungry as long as Jesus permits it.

Does the concept of "greater than the Temple" defy the Temple cult? Stanton and Gurtner believe it does not. Matthew uses this comparison to make a striking Christological claim that *God is present in Jesus to a greater extent than in the Temple*. The Temple remains even if it is considered secondary to Jesus.[53] Read in the context of justifying the disciples' plucking of grain on the Sabbath by pointing out Temple practice, it appears that the existence and legitimacy of the cult are taken for granted (unless Matthew is using a rhetorical trick).

When Matthew repeats Hos 6:6, "I desire mercy and not sacrifice," the contrast comes across as more loaded than his use of Hosea in Matt 9:13, since the Temple service has just been mentioned. But how does this verse confirm that "something greater than the Temple is here?" This biblical verse suggests that mercy is implicitly associated with Jesus. The reasoning for the argument goes as follows: Mercy takes precedence over sacrifice, and sacrifice—as Jesus argues, on the basis of priestly service—takes precedence over the Sabbath. It appears that in Matthew's view the disciples are indeed obeying the commandment of mercy and therefore can pluck grain on the Sabbath if they are hungry. However, this does not mean that the sacrificial laws are irrelevant. It merely demonstrates that there are circumstances in which there is something even more important than the cult.[54] This message is Jesus's innovation: under certain circumstances ethics are more important than the Law and the cult.

Matthew ends the passage by revisiting the statement from Mark 2:28 that "the Son of Man is lord of the Sabbath." Like Mark, he employs the conflict about Sabbath observance to promote a Christological assertion, but this time he also engages with the Temple. But why does Matthew, who is committed to the Law, find it necessary to make such a provocative statement, establishing a hierarchical relationship between Jesus and the Temple? I will return to this question at the conclusion of this chapter.

Peter as the Rock of the Ecclesia—Temple Imagery?

"Blessed are you, Simon son of Jonah! For flesh and blood has not revealed this to you, but my Father in heaven. And I tell you, you are Peter, and on this rock I will build my church, and the gates of Hades will not prevail against it. I will give you the keys of the Kingdom of heaven, and whatever you bind on earth will be bound in heaven, and whatever you loose on earth will be loosed in heaven." (16:17–19)

This passage is important for Matthew's understanding of his community, but it does not mention the Temple. Still, scholars see here implicit Temple imagery which reflects Matthew's transforming the Temple as it aligns to the needs of the Christian community. According to this line of interpretation, the building is associated with Nathan's prophecy of the construction of the Temple in 2 Sam 7:4–16, conceptualizing the people of God as a Temple with the cornerstone (perhaps as the center of the world where heaven and earth meet, expanding upon Ps 118:22 and Zech 4:7). If this is the case, then Matthew accepts the notion of the church as the new Temple.[55] It has even been argued that Matthew's eschatological Christology envisions Jesus the son of David as a Temple builder (26:61; 27:40 where outsiders argue that Jesus said he can demolish and rebuild the Temple), and that in Matt 16:17–19 Peter is assigned a priestly role, implied by the keys of the house (cf. Isa 22:22, whereby the keys of the house are associated with a priest). Peter's authority of binding and loosing, which may be related to the Law or to judgment, is also interpreted as a priestly element.[56]

It is indeed striking that scholars search for substitutes for the Temple in Matthew. Such exegesis is interesting and may carry weight for later readers of Matthew, but the allusions are too intertextual and indirect to substantiate Matthew's original intentions and how they are understood by his original audiences. If Matthew had wanted to introduce the *ekklesia* as a new form of a Temple, the author of the saying "something greater than the Temple is here" would have probably attempted to do so more clearly.[57]

The Temple Tax

"When they reached Capernaum, the collectors of the Temple tax [*didrachma*] came to Peter and said, 'Does your teacher not pay the Temple tax?' He said, 'Yes, he does.' And when he came home, Jesus spoke of it first, asking, 'What do you think, Simon? From whom do kings of the earth take toll or tribute? From their children or from others?' When Peter said, 'From others,' Jesus said to him, 'Then the children are free. However, so that we do not give offence to them, go to the lake and cast a hook; take the first fish that comes up; and when you open its mouth, you will find a coin [*startēra*, which is worth two didrachmas]; take that and give it to them for you and me.'" (17:24–27)

A great deal is written about this passage, probably because it reflects the delicate dilemma of the early Christians: To what extent do they belong to the Jewish people? Are they loyal to Jewish identity? But this may also be a significant passage for reconstructing Matthew's special attitude toward the Temple, even though the Temple itself goes unmentioned. But first we must examine whether it really deals with the Jewish annual tribute of half a shekel to the Temple, the so-called half-shekel tax.

Several scholars interpret this passage as responding to a Roman tax, either a customary civil tax or the *fiscus Iudaicus,* a compulsory tax that replaces the Temple tax, levied by the emperor Vespasian upon all the Jews in the empire in order to fill the coffers of the temple of Jupiter on the Capitol. This is because taxing terms appear in the passage: *telos* refers to various taxes, customs, and duties, while *kenson* is a poll tax paid on the basis of a census. Furthermore, since Matthew writes when the Temple (and the Temple tax) are no longer extant, the Temple tax is not relevant for Matthew's readers.[58] The problem with these suggestions, I think, is that the local subjects, especially the rebellious Jews, have no choice but to pay what the Romans demand. So in such cases the collector's question to Peter is hypothetical.

Most scholars, however, agree that Matthew actually refers to the Temple tax, the annual half-shekel tribute paid voluntarily by every Jewish adult male, as is established by the Hasmoneans and which conforms with the Pharisees' view.[59] It matches the amount of the payment (two drachmas, a half shekel) and coheres with the parable creating an analogy from a secular situation to a religious one: "the kings of the earth" do not take tax from their children, only from others. According to the common interpretation, the kings are analogous to God, and their children—who are free from having to pay—are analogous to Jesus, Peter, Matthew's church, or perhaps all of Israel. Indeed, if the one who sets the tax is God, the tax cannot be identified with the Roman fiscus Iudaicus—and the only tax of didrachmas attributed to God is the Temple tax.[60]

Nonetheless, it is somewhat strange that Matthew would discuss the validity of the tribute of the half shekel, which is already ended owing to the destruction of the Temple and the resulting Roman reformulation of tax to the fiscus Iudaicus. What is its relevance after 70? This question remains important even if one assumes that Matthew incorporates a pre-70 tradition.[61] First, this is not the only uniquely Matthean tradition that concerns

Temple practice. Sacrifices and oaths related to the Temple are mentioned in 5:23–24 and 23:16–21. Matthew is concerned with religious memory as a means of conveying his message, perhaps even to shape a sense of identity. The Temple tax tradition functions as a parable about the relationship of Matthew's followers to other Jews. It is meant to show that, either in the past or present, the followers of Jesus are within Israel, expressing conciliation toward the Jews. Readers are urged to avoid unnecessary provocation of hostile Jewish neighbors from whom they have parted company.[62]

Curiously, Matthew provides us with a genuine dilemma concerning the question of whether or not the Christians should pay the Temple tribute. Why is this question raised to begin with, and why does Matthew affirm a positive answer? What are the reasons not to pay, and what reasons ultimately lead Matthew to recommend paying it?

The answer lies in the identity of the children of the kings of the earth who are not obliged to pay their father. Are they all of the Jews or only the Christians? Let us first assume that the parent-child relationship applies to all of Israel, but for some reason most of the Jews do not accept the notion that a tax dedicated to God can be invalidated. They pay it, while Matthew's Jesus thinks they should not. Matthew may follow the common notion that the priests are exempt from payment.[63] He may reject the Temple tax as an unfounded innovation of the Pharisees, as implied in the Qumran scrolls.[64] Yet Matthew does not wish to offend these Jews (including the Pharisees?) or to estrange potential followers who favor the Temple tax—so he approves the payment.[65]

We can also identify the children of the kings with Jesus's followers, since Jesus is designated as the Son of God. His father would never make him pay a tax, and so too, perhaps, his followers.[66] While the result is similar, in this case Matthew actually might relinquish his own views and religious identity, recommending paying it even though the Christians alone are God's sons, exempted from the payment. Such a yielding or concession is less likely.

The miraculous ending of the passage is awkward. Why should Peter pay with a coin (a double didrachma) found in a fish's mouth? This is not a practical possibility for Matthew's readers! Perhaps the practical question is no longer relevant for them anyway, so Matthew can have it both ways, paying without spending anything and at the same time reflecting Jesus's special relationship with his father in heaven.[67] Of course the bottom line is, whatever reservations there may be, the Temple tax must be paid. In fact, in the very beginning of the passage Peter answers the collectors that Jesus does pay the tax. All in all, one might wonder what exactly is the offense to which Jesus refers when he explains that the tax should be paid "so that we do not give offence to them" (17:27).[68] The answer, it seems, is related to the Temple.

Once we accept that the tax discussed here is the Temple tax, the reservations about it highlight Matthew's approach to the Temple. Does the illegitimacy of the payment to the Temple cult reflect criticism or estrangement toward the cult?[69] Hardly. The consensual understanding of the parable in which the children are not required to pay their father represents how the concept of Jews and Christians paying for the Temple manifests the idea that the tax reflects a relationship with God and is associated with God. This suggests a positive view of the Temple cult, one that negates reducing it to a mere fiscal relationship between God and his people.[70] Matthew criticizes not the Temple and its worship but the relationship with God, implying an idealistic model of God's relationship with Israel.

Remarkably, the decision to pay the half shekel despite these reservations (even if this remains a theoretical step on Matthew's part) attests to alignment with the Temple. At least on the declarative level, Matthew is ready to put aside the religious reasons for not paying the tax in order to demonstrate conformism with the sacrificial cult. The fact that this is still important for Matthew after the destruction of the Temple proves that the Temple remains a symbol of Jewish religion and identity. Matthew reminds his readers that if the Temple had existed in his day, they would need to compromise their distinctive views in order to share the cult with other Jews. The parable thus stands as a compromise in favor of taking part in the Temple cult.

Cleansing, Curing, and Conflict in the Temple

"Then Jesus entered the Temple and drove out all who were selling and buying in the Temple, and he overturned the tables of the money-changers and the seats of those who sold doves; He said to them, 'It is written, "My house shall be called a house of prayer"; but you are making it a den of robbers'; The blind and the lame came to him in the Temple, and he cured them. But when the chief priests and the scribes saw the amazing things that he did, and heard the children crying out in the Temple, 'Hosanna to the Son of David,' they became angry." (21:12–15)

Matthew revises the scene of the cleansing of the Temple, adding a number of significant elements. Matthew does not diverge much from

Mark in the description of Jesus's driving out those who are buying and selling in the Temple; nor the overturning of the tables of the money changers and the seats of those who sell doves; nor the citation of the prophetic saying concerning the house of prayer and a den of robbers. Nonetheless, some read these verses quite differently from those commentators who interpret Mark 11:15–18 as offering an anti-Temple stance. After all, Matthew's stress on Temple observance in 5:23–24 and 8:4 and the use of Temple practice as a model in 12:5 suggests that Matthew accepts the role of the Temple. Very similar to the cases of most interpretations of the cleansing of the Historical Jesus, it is reasonable to read Matthew's cleansing as an attempt to correct cultic flaws without changing the system too radically.[71]

Most important, Jesus heals blind and crippled people in the Temple (21:14). In Mark Jesus acts as a healer several times, but only outside of the Temple (Mark 3:1–6; 8:22–23; 10:46–52; the first case leads to a conflict about the Law). Matthew deliberately places this healing immediately after the overturning of the tables. Jesus's healing at the Temple attests to his special authority and holiness. He restores not only the Temple but also the pilgrims. This act does not really challenge the credibility of the Temple since there is no special Temple rite for healing. His act is complementary to the cult.[72]

In Matt 21:15 the children at the Temple call Jesus "the son of David." This means that even children, who are untainted (in 18:1–5 those who become humble like children should enter into the Kingdom of heaven first) notice his messianic identity. Placing this "crowning" at the Temple makes it more effective. Once again Matthew uses the setting of the Temple incident to increase Jesus's authority. This authority is questioned or rejected by the chief priests and the elders in 21:23.

Matthew lowers tensions in relation to the sacrificial cult in another passage in Matt 22:37–40, the discussion of the great commandment, that seems to take place in the Temple (Jesus returns to the Temple in 21:23 and leaves it in 24:1). Matt 22:37–40 omits Mark 12:33, in which loving God "is more important than all burnt offerings and sacrifices." This may indicate that he views the statement as potentially nullifying the sacrifices that he affirms elsewhere.[73]

Swearing by the Altar and Sanctuary

"Woe to you, blind guides, who say, 'Whoever swears by the sanctuary [*naos*] is bound by nothing, but whoever swears by the gold of the sanctuary is bound by the oath.' You blind fools! For which is greater, the gold or the sanctuary that has made the gold sacred? And you say, 'Whoever swears by the altar is bound by nothing, but whoever swears by the gift [*qorban*] that is on the altar is bound by the oath.' How blind you are! For which is greater, the gift or the altar that makes the gift sacred? So whoever swears by the altar, swears by it and by everything on it; and whoever swears by the sanctuary, swears by it and by the one who dwells in it; and whoever swears by heaven, swears by the throne of God and by the one who is seated upon it." (23:16–22)

Jesus debates the pharisaic laws concerning oaths that pertain to the Temple, specifically the inner building, the *naos*, and the altar. The Pharisees do not consider an oath upon architectural elements to be binding, their sacredness notwithstanding; only an oath upon materials for which financial value can be easily estimated is held to be binding. Their approach is practical. Jesus, in contrast, argues that even though the value of the sanctuary and altar cannot be estimated, because of their holiness such oaths are binding—and because of this it is better not to take a vow (Matt 5:33–37). Jesus regards the Pharisees' rejection of such oaths as disrespectful to the sacredness of the Temple, or even an insult to people's religious sentiments in relation to the Temple.[74]

For our purposes, this controversy reveals Matthew's special concern for the Temple, despite the fact that in his era the Temple as a building no longer stands. He stresses the sanctity of the altar and the sanctuary's shrine, that is, God's presence there ("whoever swears by the sanctuary, swears by it and by the one who dwells in it").[75] Furthermore, Matthew blames the Pharisees for misappropriation of the Temple with respect to their rules of oaths, for which they see only the material or financial aspects of the holy place. Matthew's Jesus is more sensitive to the image of the Temple than the Pharisees are.[76]

The Destruction of "Your House" and "No Stone Upon Another"

Here I discuss two passages allegedly predicting the Temple's destruction that reflect how Matthew deals with the loss of the Temple.

In 23:38, at the end of the long list of woes against the Pharisees and in continuation of a reference to Jerusalem killing its prophets, Matthew recalls Q 13:35: "See, your house [*oikos*] is left to you, desolate." As in the case of Q or Luke, it is customary to interpret "house" as the Temple. Yet some commentators on Matthew consider the possibility that Matthew is referring to Jerusalem. As far as philology is concerned, Matthew does not call the Temple *oikos* elsewhere, only *naos* or *hieron*.[77] Interpreting "house" as the Temple relies heavily on the next passage in 24:1–2, where Jesus departs from the Temple and refers to the destruction of the buildings of the Temple.[78]

Matthew 24:1–2 repeats Mark 13:1–2 but adds one important detail. When Jesus says, "You see all these, do you not? Truly I tell you, not one stone will be left here upon another; all will be thrown down," he does not address merely "those buildings," as in Mark. Matthew specifically adds that the prophecy applies to "the buildings *of the Temple* [*hieron*]." It is the Temple that will be destroyed. Is it possible that Matthew is more explicit about the destruction of the Temple because he is more critical of it? Hardly. Unlike Mark, who probably writes during the First Revolt, for Matthew the fall of the Temple is a given, a fulfilled prophecy. He cannot ignore it.

The prophecy concerning the end of the Temple does not in and of itself question the legitimacy of the cult. This is because, as we have seen, the Matthean Jesus teaches that cultic laws should be observed. He should be read with biblical prophets in mind, since they foretell the doom of the Temple without attacking the Pentateuch. This passage is actually a lament which "expresses uttermost devastation" (as in Jer 26:18). Matthew presents "not repudiation of a divinely founded institution but a tragic forecast . . . of a disaster fostered by human sin."[79]

Positioning these two passages after the woes against the Pharisees, as well as implicitly situating chapter 23 in the Temple (between Jesus entering and leaving it in 21:23 and 24:1), gives the reader the impression that the sins of Jerusalem and the punishment of the destruction are directly related to the behavior of the Pharisees, and not the rejection of Jesus by the chief priest and the leaders (as in Mark). Matthew uses the Markan narrative of coming doom as a weapon against the Pharisees. But beyond the controversy concerning oaths in the altar or sanctuary, the complaints against the Pharisees are not related to the Temple at all. Their immediate setting is the local synagogue.

The Temple Charge: "I Am Able to Destroy the Temple"

"Now the chief priests and the whole council were looking for false testimony against Jesus so that they might put him to death, but they found none, though many false witnesses came forward. At last two came forward and said, 'This fellow said, "I am able to destroy the Temple of God and to build it in three days."' (26:59–61)

Matthew inserts several changes in the description of the charges against Jesus in Mark 14:56–59, and by doing so he alters the attitude toward the Temple attributed to him in Mark. The main question is whether his blame is true or false for Matthew.

Matthew uses the phrase "I am able [*dunamai*] to destroy the Temple" instead of Mark's rendering of "I will destroy" (14:58). "I am able" mutes hostility against the Temple, corresponding with Matthew's positive approach to the Law in general and cultic laws in particular. But there is another, more trivial reason for this change. While Mark probably writes, "I will destroy" prior to the destruction, it is inappropriate for Matthew to write it in the years after 70, since by then everyone would know that culpability does not lie with Jesus.[80] Furthermore, because the fall of the Temple is so devastating to the Jews and also a symbol of their defeat by the Romans, it is too abusive even to mention such an outright threat. Yet by mentioning Jesus's capacity to destroy the Temple, Matthew may be hinting to the reader that even Jesus's foes must consider the possibility that he has special abilities.

Mark not only introduces the search for false witnesses against Jesus (repeated by Matthew) by the chief priests and the council but also specifically notes the fallacy of the testimony of Jesus's statement about destroying and rebuilding the Temple in which he mentions that the testimonies do not agree. Matthew, however, omits the latter, leaving us with the question of whether he believes that Jesus actually says that he could have destroyed the Temple. Does the evangelist accept their testimony? One may suggest that this change is merely stylistic, a means to avoid redundancy. Matthew's readers probably do not compare Matthew's version with Mark's, so they cannot sense that there is a hint that the testimony is true. But there is another, more serious consideration that I will need to examine below: Does the charge, as rephrased by Matthew's witnesses, make sense to Matthew's readers?[81]

As in Mark, the charge contains not only destroying but rebuilding: "I am able to . . . build it in three days." Scholars disagree whether or not this is a hint for Matthew's readers that Jesus is described as a new kind of a Temple—be it his body or the Church.[82] If we regard this testimony as false, Matthew denies such a possibility, and no alternative to the Temple is in fact introduced.

Matthew 26:61 omits Mark's distinction between destroying a Temple "made with hands" and building a Temple "not made with hands." Some think that he simply follows an earlier version. Others speculate about Mark's hidden apocalyptic message, which Matthew rejects.[83] But it is possible that Matthew simply does not understand the phrase "not made with hands" and finds it confusing. In any event, if—as many commentators of Mark hold—the second evangelist hopes for an eschatologically divine-made Temple, Matthew does not follow his lead.

Instead, he designates the Temple that is supposed to be destroyed as "the Temple of God." He switches a critical portrayal of the current Temple as manmade ("made with hands") with another one which reminds the reader of its holiness. In Matthew's version of the charge, God takes the place of man. In doing so, Matthew mutes Mark's polemic against the Temple, since, after all, it belongs to God, and God dwells in it. This alternation strengthens the impious character of the saying, emphasizing the illegitimacy of speaking against the Temple.[84] It appears that Matthew actually defies the charge from within: the reader should understand that Jesus does not really want to destroy God's house, to which he shows commitment throughout the gospel. This leads me to conclude that Matthew regards the witnesses as false and their charges fictitious, even though he does not stress this as much as Mark does.

Judas Returns the Blood Money to the Temple

"When Judas, his betrayer, saw that Jesus was condemned, he repented and brought back the thirty pieces of silver to the chief priests and the elders. He said, 'I have sinned by betraying innocent blood.' But they said, 'What is that to us? See to it yourself.' Throwing down the pieces of silver in the Temple, he departed; and he went and hanged himself. But the chief priests, taking the pieces of silver, said, 'It is not lawful to put them into the treasury, since they are blood money.' After conferring together, they used them to buy the potter's field as a place to bury foreigners." (27:3–7)

Judas Iscariot has regrets and returns to the chief priests the thirty shekels they give him (Matt 26:14–16, 47–50). Then he hangs himself. Our concern relates to the following questions: Why does he throw the coins into the Temple? Why are the chief priests unable to keep them there? And how is the Temple portrayed in this strange episode?

Since the chief priests refuse to receive the returned money, Judas throws down the pieces of silver in the Temple, the inner building (*naos*).[85]

He regards the money as coming from the Temple because he associates the chief priest with this place. Throwing the money not into courts of the Temple (*hieron*) but into its most sacred location (where money is probably not deposited) increases the anomaly of corrupted wealth in the holy place and creates circumstances leading to desecration of the sacred.[86] Another attractive interpretation, although perhaps less convincing, is that Judas may be trying to repent, throwing the money as some kind of sin offering or donation to the Temple.[87]

The chief priest, however, cannot countenance keeping money responsible for spilling innocent blood, not even in the Temple's treasury (*eis ton korbanan*).[88] It is regarded as morally defiled and as a result must be spent on a good, though nonsacred, cause.[89]

In any event, Matthew's criticism is directed not at the Temple as an institution but at the chief priests.[90] Their efforts to get rid of Judas's money show that this is blood money, even according to their own cultic criteria. They understand that the money derived from Judas's betrayal of handing over Jesus is contaminated and cannot be used in the Temple. This passage demonstrates their hypocrisy since they are aware that their arrest of the innocent Jesus is indeed, at the very least, unrighteous. At the same time, however, it is assumed that Temple sacredness must be maintained.

The Tearing of the Temple Veil

"Then Jesus cried again with a loud voice and breathed his last. At that moment the curtain of the Temple was torn in two, from top to bottom. The earth shook, and the rocks were split. The tombs also were opened, and many bodies of the saints who had fallen asleep were raised. After his resurrection they came out of the tombs and entered the holy city and appeared to many." (27:50–53)

The tearing of the veil of the sanctuary (*to katapetasma tou naou*) "from top to bottom" is similar to Mark 14:38. The results, however, are much more far-reaching. Here Matthew adds an exceptional apocalyptic scene. An earthquake occurs, which probably symbolizes an apocalyptic event of divine wrath in addition to being a symbol of the cosmic power of Jesus as the Son of God (as acknowledged by the Roman centurion and the guards in 27:54). But then Matthew also describes an even more significant apocalyptic event: the resurrection of the dead. This seems to indicate that Matthew understands the tearing of the veil as leading to a positive event equated with new life. This sheds a different light on the meaning of the tearing of the veil.

Recall that the veil is a curtain restricting access to the presence of God. Its function is probably to reflect separation between the most holy and the less holy. It prohibits physical and visual accessibility to God enthroned in the holy of holies.[91] Most scholars interpret the tearing as symbolizing the end of the Temple, an act of judgment against the priests. It shows that by his sacrificial death, Jesus obviates both sacrifices and priesthood, making available to all people new, bold, unrestricted access to God's presence.[92] For the Matthean reader who already knows about the destruction of the Temple and reads Jesus's alleged predictions of it as well as the saying that he has the ability to destroy the Temple, the destruction is predicted by the tearing of the veil. Yet it could also express a divine lament over the destruction (as I suggest in relation to Mark 14:38).[93]

However, Gurtner suggests a different interpretation. He argues that there is no need to see the veil as representing the Temple in toto. The veil is torn (*schizō*) following Jesus's death as an eschatological event of opening (as in the opening of heaven in Mark 1:10), a revelation of Jesus's identity as the Son of God. There is no further need for veiling the presence of God or making a distinction between the holy and the less holy. With his atonement through his death, Jesus also achieves accessibility to God, demonstrated by the visual tearing of the veil.[94]

As I have already noted, the relation to the people's resurrection seems to show that Matthew understands this tearing as a positive event. The use of the Temple in this apocalyptic context demonstrates the importance of the cultic system. The veil is a religious symbol that the first evangelist finds helpful in creating a religious message that is not directly related to the Temple itself. Later readers can easily find here an urge for a new reality without a Temple, but the passage itself does not necessarily express a message of Jesus's death as taking the place of the Temple.

Conclusions: Something Greater than the Temple

Matthew mentions several Temple practices and stresses Jesus's teachings of ethics in relation to the cult. The acceptance of sacrifice is conditioned upon reconciliation with one's brother (5:23–24), stressing cultic allegiance though prioritizing ethics. Jesus's debate with the Pharisees, arguing that oaths which pertain to the Temple inner building and altar are binding (23:16–22), stresses Temple piety and sacredness. These passages show that Matthew is sensitive to the image of the Temple. Matthew's

Jesus points to the tension between cult and ethics even when the context does not invite mentioning of the Temple. Twice he cites Hosea 6:6, "I desire mercy *more* than sacrifice" in relation to two controversies with the Pharisees (9:13; 12:7). The message is that adherence to the cult (which seems to represents the Law in general) first requires a compassionate heart or moral behavior.

Temple sensibilities appear further in the narrative. For Matthew and his readers, it is obvious that the Temple shrine or its treasury cannot be contaminated by Judas's blood money (27:6). The tearing of the Temple veil (27:51–53) is not necessarily connected to the end of the Temple; rather, it is a cultic object with religious symbolism of revelation and transformation which conveys the message of a new religious era (including the resurrection) which begins with Jesus's death

Matthew's readers know that the Temple is destroyed. Matthew refers to the destruction of the Temple explicitly (in 24:1 and possibly in 23:38). So why are these Temple practices which no longer exist relevant for Matthew? I suggest that the evangelist aims to transmit a message of embracing Jewish religious and legal traditions, albeit with the twist of Jesus's special understanding of them. In so doing, Matthew reinforces the Jewishness of his message and also highlights a special Christian doctrine which revises Jewish practices and ideas. This trend of continuity with Judaism is also the point of paying the half-shekel tax to the Temple in 17:21–24 (which, again, can no longer be paid): Sometimes Jesus's followers need to compromise their distinctive views in order to show that they share respect for the Temple with others; that is, to identify themselves with "official" or "common" Judaism.

At the same time, the Temple is used to demonstrate Jesus's supreme identity. In the rewriting of the cleansing of the Temple, Jesus's authority vis-à-vis the Temple is stressed. He heals the blind and crippled there (21:14), an act which does not suppress the cult but supplements it. In the next verse the children at the Temple call Jesus "the son of David." Thus the setting of the Temple is used to convey its continuing formal status as the primary religious place.

In an apologetic against viewing Jesus as an enemy of the Temple, Matthew reworks the trial scene to diminish the tension between Jesus and the Temple. When the false witnesses blame Jesus for saying, "I am *able* to destroy the Temple of God and to build it in three days," Matthew lowers the severity of the charge. Jesus can but probably will not destroy the

Temple. Since the Temple is designated as God's Temple, it is inconceivable that Jesus would act against it.

Prioritizing both the Temple and Jesus leads Matthew to explain the relationship between them to his readers. In 12:3–7, the service of the priests at the Temple during the Sabbath is mentioned as proof that Jesus's disciples are allowed to pluck grain on the seventh day. This argument implies acknowledging the sacrificial cult as self-evident. However, the saying, "greater than the Temple is here" although certainly not defying the Temple cult, means that God is present in Jesus to a greater extent than in the Temple.

It is remarkable that Matthew addresses the question of what is greater so directly. Yet we should notice that he is not fully explicit about it. "Something" blurs the meaning of Jesus. Is it Jesus the person, his teachings and doctrine, or the community of his followers? Perhaps, as the context permits, what is greater than the Temple is merely mercy (the disciples' hunger) and human need, which Jesus stresses.

In any event, it is striking that Matthew, who holds a very favorable opinion of the Temple cult, is ready to admit to this tension and declare that Jesus or something related to Jesus has the upper hand over the Temple. This fact is crucial to our understanding of early Christian attitudes toward the Temple. It shows that accepting Jesus does not necessitate a rejection of the Temple. One can have it both ways. Nonetheless, although one can be devoted to both, according to Matthew, a Christian must decide which is "greater!"

5 Luke–Acts: Living and Dying with the Temple

Section I. The Attitude to the Temple in Luke–Acts

Introduction

In this chapter I discuss both the gospel of Luke and the Acts of the Apostles, since both were written by Luke. Despite their similarities in theology and ideology, I do not assume that Luke's gospel and the book of Acts reflect the same approach to the Temple. And even if they do exhibit certain similarities, they differ in both genre and sources: Luke is based on Mark and Q, continuing the gospel biographical genre, while Acts is based on various unknown sources, employing a historiographical genre which requires differences in how it deals with the Temple and the cult.[1]

Luke writes the third gospel and Acts after "investigating everything carefully" (Luke 1:3; cf. Acts 1:1), arguing for historical accuracy. Until recently it has been common to accept Acts' historical credibility and to view Luke as a reliable historian who uses authentic sources.[2] Indeed, Luke seems to be familiar with the reality in the Temple.[3] However, a growing number of scholars are skeptical of this assumption. While he is a skillful author, Luke is also a theologian and thus naturally shapes his narrative to convey certain theological messages. These messages, critics argue, may affect the historical accuracy of his narrative.[4] Therefore, it leaves one to wonder whether Luke's competence as a historian is an indication of his reliability or of his literary skill.

In contrast to the format of previous chapters in which I have commented on each passage separately, the large number of relevant passages in this chapter requires combining some of them into discussions of issues that repeat throughout Luke–Acts. Unlike my discussions in the chapters on Mark, Q-Matthew, and John, in this chapter I will not limit myself to the author's approach. Owing to the historical purposes and potential of Acts, I will also discuss it from the historical perspective, relating it to the Christian community in Jerusalem. This approach, however, will be limited mainly to section II, which deals with the Temple persecutions.

BETWEEN JEWS AND GENTILES

In his gospel and especially in Acts, Luke promotes one basic idea: the mission to the Gentiles. Both Jews and Gentiles should believe in Jesus, he claims, and the flourishing of this "way" (*hodos*) is only a matter of time.[5] Gentiles should be accepted to Christianity with minimal requirements or conditions concerning Jewish law.

Past generations have seen Luke as being quite critical of contemporary Jews and Judaism because of Jewish rejection of Jesus and persecution of his followers. The most extreme scholarly view is that Israel in Acts is dismissed from salvation history because of its unbelief.[6] Israel is replaced by the Gentiles.[7] The church becomes an independent entity separate from Judaism.[8] The positive aspects of Judaism largely belong to the past.[9] This is attested to by Paul's turning to the Gentiles when the Jews reject his mission (Acts 13:46; 18:6; 28:28), signaling his final failure among the Jews.[10] This so-called anti-Jewish orientation is related to Luke's universalistic ideology of the salvation of the Gentiles (e.g., Luke 2:31–32; 24:47). For Luke, the belief in Christ is much more important than any carnal affiliation to Israel.[11] As the conversion of Cornelius (Acts 9–10) demonstrates, repentance is given to the Gentiles (not to the Jews alone), and the Law is not a condition for salvation (Acts 11:17). These characteristics lead scholars to conclude that Luke's intended audience is mainly Gentile Christians.[12]

Since the studies of Jacob Jervell, an alternative approach has developed and become quite popular. Jervell stresses that the Jerusalem church consists first and foremost of Jews. In his view, Israel in Acts does not reject the gospel but rather is divided over the issue. The Gentiles who accept the gospel are mostly God-fearers. He then concludes that Luke "knows only one Israel, one people of God, one covenant." He maintains that in Luke–Acts "God is the God of Israel alone. There is no salvation outside of Israel." The church is the one and only traditional Israel, the inheritor of God's promises of salvation.[13] Others follow Jervell, although only to a certain extent.[14] Some acknowledge that Paul's rupture with the synagogue, initiated by Jews, does not replace the promises made to Israel. Peter's baptism of Cornelius (10:34) shows not that the status of Israel is abolished but that its holiness is no longer exclusive. It includes all believers in Jesus.[15]

It may be safe to conclude that Luke universalizes salvation without turning his back on Judaism. He tries to have it both ways: continuity *and* rupture. As François Bovon summarizes: Luke–Acts is "the most open to universalism and the most favorable to Israel."[16] Thus Luke–Acts does not polemicize about Judaism as such and is intended not only for Gentiles but also for Jews.

THE LAW

For some, Luke represents an essential break with and freedom from the Law for both Jewish and Gentile Christians. At the very least the Law is "an issue of no immediate concern" for him since he writes for Gentiles.[17] Jervell, however, is probably the first to argue that Luke fully conforms to Judaism and embraces the Law in its entirety.[18] Esler maintains that in his gospel Luke holds an extremely conservative approach to the Law and that Stephen and Paul also remain faithful to the Law in Acts.[19] Loader agrees that Luke does not position Jesus as an alternative to the Torah in terms of the proper way to approach God. Rather, Jews approach God by being Torah observant *and* recognizing Jesus as the Messiah.[20]

Several examples may demonstrate Luke's message that Jews should practice the Law. Jesus as well as other figures are described as Law-observant Jews. Jesus attends the synagogue in Nazareth and reads Scripture "according to the custom" (Luke 4:16.). He also dines with the Law-observant Pharisees several times (Luke 7:38; 11:37; 14:1). In the so-called Infancy Narrative, John's parents and Simon (who blesses Jesus and professes that he will save the people) are portrayed as devoted to the Laws or customs (Luke 1:6; 2:25; cf. Acts 2:25). The women taking care of Jesus's body refrain from work on Sabbath "according to the commandment" (Luke 23:56). Luke mentions that the distance from the Mount of Olives to Jerusalem is a "Sabbath day's journey" (Acts 1:11). He is probably implying that it does not exceed the walking distance permitted during the Sabbath.[21] Some of the priests and Pharisees join the Jerusalem community (Acts 6:7; 15:5). After Jesus is revealed to Paul on the road to Damascus, Paul is guided by Ananias, "a devout man according to the Law and well spoken of by all the Jews living there" (Acts 22:12). This means that following Jesus neither conflicts nor contradicts with traditional Jewish practice. In Acts,

Paul observes the Law. The elders, who are James's associates, say to him that Jewish believers in Jesus "are all zealous for the Law" (21:20).[22]

Paul's purification before entering the Temple offers an interesting illustration of Luke's understanding of legal practice. The elders tell him to pay for the offerings of four Nazirites and to "go through the rite of purification with them" so that "all will know that . . . you yourself observe and guard the law." Then "the next day, having purified himself, he entered the Temple, making public the completion of the days of purification when the sacrifice would be made for each of them" (Acts, 21:24, 26). Finally, "when the seven days were almost completed," Paul enters the Temple and is seized and almost killed by Jews from Asia (21:27).

Commentators find it difficult to understand what type of ritual purification is being referred to here. Do the Nazirites and Paul need similar cleansing? Is it possible that Luke does not understand the halakhic procedure to which he alludes? It is also common to claim that Paul needs cleansing because he comes from abroad and is defiled by Gentile land—although it is not clear how many days such a procedure should take. In any event, his purification period, it seems, lasts seven days.[23]

However, even though Paul is directed to be purified with the Nazirites, his cleansing procedure is different. Although he purifies himself with the Nazirites (Acts 21:26), he enters the Temple "the next day" (probably a day after being cleansed), while the Nazirites are impure for seven days. They are likely defiled by corpse impurity lasting seven days. Furthermore, in the case of Nazirites this requires special sacrifices (two pigeons for a burnt offering and purification offering, *hattat*, and a lamb for guilt offering, *asham*) owing to the Nazirite failing to fulfill his vow of holiness and avoidance of corpse impurity (Num 6:8–12). Paul, I suggest, purifies himself for a different reason and is able to enter the Temple immediately. He probably does not get rid of any specific defilement. I suggest that Paul practices the custom of extra-purification before entering the Temple Mount despite the fact that he is already ritually clean. This kind of ritual bathing permits one to enter the Temple immediately after bathing. Ritual baths found next to the Temple Mount serve as evidence for this practice.[24] Luke, then, may be reporting purity practices quite accurately—and in any case he is interested in them.

Thus the release of the Gentiles from the Law notwithstanding, Luke stresses that Jewish-Christians observe the commandments quite scrupulously, especially in relation to purity in the Temple.

A NEW TEMPLE IN LUKE–ACTS?

Most of the plot in Luke–Acts occurs in Jerusalem, which is both the geographical and religious center of his narrative.[25] The Temple is mentioned in Luke–Acts approximately 120 times. The third gospel's narrative begins with Zechariah serving in the Temple and being told by an angel about the coming birth of his son (John the Baptist). It ends with the apostles attending the Temple regularly (Luke 1:8; 24:53). Luke includes several scenes taking place in the Temple that are unique to his gospel, especially in the Infancy Narrative. Furthermore, significant portions of the narrative of Acts take place in the Temple, which is also often mentioned in speeches in this gospel. The Temple functions as the geographical center of Luke–Acts, and both Jesus and his followers are anchored there.[26] It seems that for Luke the Temple (and Jerusalem in general) represents the universal holy place for the Jews, the center of Jewish worship and the earthly locus of Jewish life and hope.[27]

Some claim that Luke actually contests the holiness of the Temple in Jewish tradition while situating Jesus within it. For Luke, Jesus becomes more important than the Temple. He provides forgiveness (2:38; 3:19), brings peace between God and humankind (10:38), and eventually takes over the function of the Temple, extending it to the Gentiles. The divine presence in the Temple stems from Jesus—and he actually transforms the Temple's sacredness.[28] It is not uncommon to find scholars who argue that from Luke's perspective the Christian community in Jerusalem represents the new Temple.[29] Support for this idea is presented from Acts, but it is not sufficient.[30] Whether or not Luke's understanding of the Temple continues traditional Jewish views or merely uses the Temple as a platform for Christian doctrine will be discussed in this chapter, but it can already be assumed that there is no direct evidence of cultic language transferred from the Temple to a community context.[31]

Many claim that authentic evidence of the self-perception of the community in Jerusalem as the new/eschatological Temple is found not in Acts but in Gal 2:9. Here Paul refers to James, Cephas, and John as being "the reputed pillars" (*stuloi*). Since pillars are identified as part of the Temple building, many point to this designation as an indication of the self-understanding of the church as the eschatological Temple destined to supersede the Temple in Jerusalem. This means that at a very early stage Christians regard their community as a kind of Messianic Temple, the place of God's eschatological presence. It is worth noting that Paul does not specifically refer to the pillars of the Temple. Rather, this scholarly identification is based on the promise in Rev 3:12: "He who is victorious—I will make him a pillar in the Temple of my God."[32]

However, it still needs to be made clear that Paul does not explicitly relate these pillars to Temple symbolism. Among his many cultic metaphors he does not refer to architectural elements—and he does not call the Temple *oikos,* "house"—even though he does use other architectural metaphors (e.g., 1 Cor 3:10). In ancient Jewish sources, pillars are at times employed as a building metaphor with no connection to the Temple. While a pillar is associated with the Temple in Revelation, that book is rich in cultic metaphors and does not explicitly introduce the idea of the Christians as the new Temple (see chapter 7). Moreover, the meaning of Rev 3:12 does not prove that pillars carry a similar meaning in another, earlier text. Indeed, the imagery in Revelation consists of many pillars in the Temple (equaling many triumphant members), while Paul refers to three major or monumental pillars which support the entire structure.[33] The fact that new Temple symbolism is absent from Acts weakens considerably the possibility that this idea is central for the early Christians under the leadership of those "pillars."

John Elliott also attempts to demonstrate the diminished role of the Temple in Acts. He suggests that for the early Christians in Jerusalem, gatherings in private houses and domestic activities take the place of the cult. Household scenes frame much of Acts, demarcating differentiated communities with unique social institutions and contrasting loyalties. If the Temple aligns with the center of political and religious control as well as conflict, the household connotes assembly, prayer, receiving the spirit, breaking bread, and sharing all things. While at the beginning the community gathers both in the Temple and in individual households (Acts 2:46; 5:42), after Stephen's death the Christians do not engage together at the Temple *as a group.* This is natural since only the household is capable of socially and ideologically embodying the structures, values, and goals of an inclusive gospel of universal salvation.[34]

These conclusions notwithstanding, it remains to be seen if there is a transformation in the perception of the Temple throughout Acts. To this end, one query can already be raised: If, as Elliott argues, the house takes the place of the Temple, why is the Temple so prominent—it is mentioned much more often than the house—in both Luke and Acts?

The Infancy Narrative: The Temple as the Origin of John the Baptist and Jesus

The Temple provides the main setting for the scenes which open Luke's gospel—the birth of John the Baptist and Jesus. This portion of the gospel (Luke 1–2) is called the Infancy Narrative and contains material unique to Luke. Some regard it as a Lukan composition with Lukan character.[35] It is here that news of the pending birth of John is revealed to his father during his Temple service, and baby Jesus and his parents come to the Temple bringing a sacrifice immediately after his birth. They visit there once again on Passover when Jesus is twelve years old, at which point he stays to study at the Temple. Since Luke begins and ends the Infancy Narrative with the Temple, the Temple becomes both a literary thread binding together the birth narratives of John and Jesus and a focal point for their respective ministries.[36]

JOHN'S BIRTH

Zechariah the priest, while offering incense on the altar, is told by an angel that he is about to have a child after years of barrenness. This happens in the Temple, which is portrayed as a place of prayer, revelation, and God's presence. In the opening verse it is mentioned that both John's father and mother are of a priestly stock, and Zechariah's priestly stock is specified—the order of Abijah (Luke 1:5).[37] They are also portrayed as being law observant, "living blamelessly according to all the commandments and regulations of the Lord" (1:6).

The rite which serves as a background for the angelic revelation is described in great detail (1:8–11, 21, 23).[38] Zechariah's priestly service is described positively "before God" (1:8), echoing Ex 30:8. Luke notes that Zechariah's particular priestly section is on duty—probably referring to his priestly family—which is meant to serve on that specific day. He is chosen to enter the sanctuary (*naos*, i.e., the *heikhal*) by lot "according to the custom of the priesthood" to offer incense (as in m. *Tamid* 3:1; 5:4). At the same time, an assembly of people prays outside of the building of the sanctuary (1:9–10). This offering of incense is part of the regular, twice-daily rite of the offering of the Tamid daily sacrifice, and communal prayer is an integral part of the daily sacrificial rite.[39] Luke specifically mentions that Gabriel the angel is revealed to Zechariah while he is "standing at the right side of the altar of incense" (Luke 1:11) so that the reader can actually visualize the scene.

While Gabriel's message aims to show that John the Baptist is a holy man, the priestly setting gives it a unique and authentic character. Not only is his birth announced by God's angel—characterizing him quite like Elijah the prophet and Samuel the Nazirite child (1:15–17)—but his birth is foretold in the midst of a central Jewish religious practice. John's parents represent priestly origins and blameless observance of the Law. The Temple is used not only to stress John being sent by God but also to situate him in the context of the heart of Jewish tradition. Given the plot throughout Luke–Acts, it is also possible to understand this stress on the priesthood in light of the forthcoming opposition between Jesus and the Temple leaders. Luke wants to affirm that this clash with the chief priests is not owing to an inherent contradiction between Christianity and the cult of Israel.[40]

BABY JESUS IN THE TEMPLE: LAW AND PRAISE

After Jesus's birth his parents come with him to the Temple and offer the *hattat* sacrifice for his mother (Luke cites Lev 12:8). This is known as the childbirth sacrifice. The author certainly wants to demonstrate that Jesus's parents observe the Torah (Luke 2:22–24). Strangely, he deems this rite "for their purification" even though, it seems, Scripture designates it as a sacrifice of atonement. Specifically, the days after birth are called days of purification in Lev 12:4 and are necessary only for the mother.

Luke 2:22–23 weaves into the childbirth sacrifice another rite, that of presenting the firstborn in the Temple. He says that the purpose of the visit in the Temple is "to present him to the Lord," citing the command that "every firstborn male shall be designated as holy to the Lord" (Ex 13:1; cf. Num 8:17). Scholars usually regard this as a Lukan fiction. No such custom of presentation of the firstborn is known, and there is no need to bring baby Jesus to the Temple as a firstborn. Luke conflates two different sacrifices that are originally distinct, perhaps during his reworking of sources.[41] Indeed, although Luke mixes two different rites, the bringing of the baby Jesus to the Temple is not farfetched. First, when the mother is nursing, her visit at the Temple to offer a childbirth *hattat* sacrifice necessitates carrying the newborn with her. Second, firstborn sons may in fact be expected to be brought to the Temple in Neh 10:35–36. Even if the Law does not require it, we can understand why parents might very appropriately present their firstborn son at the Temple as a gesture of gratitude to God.

For Luke, the presentation of baby Jesus at the Temple is not necessarily derived from Jewish Law or practice. This ceremonial act is an opportunity for the author to praise Jesus and proclaim his destiny. He uses it for the Christological characterization of Jesus, showing that Jesus is holy and belongs to God. Bovon argues even that Luke prefers this narrative quality over being legally precise.[42]

In the Temple Jesus the newborn is praised by Simon as the coming savior of Israel and the Gentiles (Luke 2:25–35). This Simon is described as "righteous and devout, looking forward to the consolation of Israel, and the Holy Spirit rested on him" (2:25). Then Jesus is also praised by Anna the widow as the one who will bring redemption to Jerusalem (2:36–38). Anna "never left the Temple but worshipped there with fasting and prayer night and day" (2:37). Both Simon and Anna are designated as pious Jews expecting a savior while located in the Temple. Anna's devotion to the Temple is stressed even further: she never leaves it, practicing fasts and prayers. The two seem to represent the atmosphere at the Temple, and Luke uses them to show the acknowledgment of Jesus as a holy person designated to bring consolation and redemption to the center of Judaism and its most sacred place.[43] It is interesting that Luke chooses pious lay figures rather than formal Temple figures such as priests or high priests. Perhaps this narrative choice reflects Jesus's future conflicts with the chief priests. In the future he would not be praised by the Temple establishment.

PILGRIMAGE AND STUDY IN "MY FATHER'S HOUSE"

Luke 2:41–50 depicts how Jesus at the age of twelve years old goes up to the Temple in Jerusalem for the Passover pilgrimage "as usual." By the end of the festival his parents forget their child and find him in the Temple after three days. He is "sitting among the teachers, listening to them and asking them questions." When his mother disciplines him, Jesus the boy replies, "Why were you searching for me? Did you not know that I must be in my Father's house?' But they did not understand what he said to them" (2:49–50).

This scene may not be a natural continuation of the birth of Jesus,[44] but it does follow the theme of Temple setting and piety. Luke wants to situate the young Jesus in the Temple for the second time in his lifetime. For this reason Jesus and his mother join his father for the pilgrimage despite the fact that Scripture commands only male adults to come to the Temple. But many women and children participate in such a pilgrimage even if they are not obligated to do so.[45] When Jesus listens to the teachers in the Temple and asks them questions, the Temple is portrayed as a place of teaching and learning. Jesus's study there anticipates his later teachings in the Temple described in chapters 19–21. His listening to the teachers of the Law and asking them questions also foreshadow future debates about the Law, while at the same time reflecting Temple piety.[46]

Jesus's statement about being in his father's house (*en tois tou patros mou*, 2:49) mentions the Temple only indirectly, but it does clearly relate to the Temple, since this is where he has been.[47] Indeed, the Temple is also designated as God's house in Luke 19:46. What Jesus means is that his vocation in service of God demands his presence as close as possible to God. Hence it is only natural that he finds himself in the Temple.[48] It is significant that Jesus's first words in the gospel are said in the Temple and affirm Jesus's relationship not only to God, his father, but also to the Temple.

We may conclude that throughout the Infancy Narrative the Temple is portrayed in an extremely positive manner. It is a place where Zechariah sees an angel envisioning the birth of John the Baptist, pious people profess Jesus's future and destiny, and the young Jesus himself learns and demonstrates his wisdom.[49] Jesus will teach time and time again in the Temple later in the gospel. The Temple not only represents the Law by its very nature as the site of the sacrificial cult, but Luke makes clear that the people in the Temple, such as Zechariah, Jesus's parents, Simon, and Anna, all observe the Law. Luke's Temple is the traditional Jewish Temple, and Jesus's parents conform to legal practice with unadulterated enthusiasm.

Jesus and the Apostles in the Temple

In both Luke and Acts there are numerous mentions of Jesus or the apostles teaching in the Temple. While there are certainly differences between the activities of Jesus and the apostles while in the Temple, the author stresses in both cases that the Temple is a natural setting for their respective activities.

JESUS'S TEACHING IN THE TEMPLE

Jesus's first visit to the Temple as an adult immediately follows his arrival in Jerusalem when he overturns the tables. Jesus then continues to teach there even after the cleansing of the Temple: "Every day he was teaching in the Temple . . . and all the people were spellbound by what they heard" (Luke 19:47–48). The next conflict, with the chief priests and scribes, happens immediately afterward: "One day, as he was teaching the people in the Temple and telling the good news …" (Luke 20:1). In fact, it is likely that the entirety of the conflict and teaching scenes in chapters 20–21 also occur in the Temple. As described in Luke's summary statement, this seems to be Jesus's routine: "Every day he was teaching in the Temple, and at night he would go out and spend the night on the Mount of Olives, as it was called; And all the people would get up early in the morning to listen to him in the Temple" (21:37–38).[50] Jesus mentions this fact when the chief priests and the Temple police arrest him, using swords and clubs as if he is a bandit: "When I was with you day after day in the Temple, you did not lay hands on me" (Luke 22:53, following Mark 14:49).

How should we understand Luke's approach to Jesus vis-à-vis the Temple? Why is he teaching there? Does the Temple serve as a public stage that has no religious meaning for him?[51] Does he mean to challenge the Temple by his authority? Or perhaps his activity there means that his words are meant to conform to the cult? These same questions will soon be applied to the apostles in Acts.

Despite his ongoing presence in the Temple, Jesus does not participate in the sacrificial cult or even public prayer. Besides teaching, he only debates with the chief priests and other leaders in addition to overturning the tables. It is not unreasonable, therefore, to argue that Jesus challenges the Temple from within. But the very nature of Luke's decision to stress the location of Jesus in the Temple more than Mark affirms that he associates Jesus with the Temple. If Luke's Jesus wants to oppose the Temple he should be active outside of it. In a literal reading, Jesus's activities there are understood as the result of his valuing it as a holy place[52]—and he never claims otherwise. (On the prophecy of destruction, see below.) Another argument concerns the nature of the meaning of "teaching" (in the Temple) for Luke. One may argue that the very act of teaching is closely related to the Law (compare Gamaliel, a teacher of the Law in Acts 5:34).[53]

THE APOSTLES' TEMPLE ATTENDANCE

By the end of the third gospel Jesus tells his disciples to stay in Jerusalem since it is there that repentance and forgiveness to the Gentiles will be proclaimed (Luke 24:47–48). In the final verses of his gospel Luke says that they "returned to Jerusalem with great joy; and they were continually in the Temple blessing God" (24:52–53). The disciples' continuing presence at the Temple is important for Luke's narrative since it forms an *inclusio*, connecting the end of the gospel's story to the beginning. The apostles'

Temple attendance is connected to Jesus's message about future expectations, associated with general piety toward God.[54]

Acts 3 and 5 describe two instances in which the apostles attend the Temple. Peter and John go to the Temple for afternoon prayer, subsequently healing a lame man there after which Peter makes a speech there (3:1–26). Later, the apostles assemble in the Temple and heal many others (Acts 5: 12–16). Another activity in the Temple takes place in Acts 21 when Paul facilitates Nazirite sacrifices (see above).[55] Interestingly, at least once (Acts 5:19–20) the apostles' preaching at the Temple is guided by an angel. Thus the Temple continues to be related to angelophany in a manner similar to the angel's apparition to Zechariah.[56]

Two Lukan summaries show the apostles attending the Temple as common practice: "Day by day, as they spent much time together in the Temple, they broke bread at home and ate their food with glad and generous hearts" (Acts 2:46); "And every day in the Temple and at home they did not cease to teach and proclaim Jesus as the Messiah" (Acts 5:42). The summary accounts of this way of life prove that the events in the Temple depicted by the author are not the only occasions in which the Christians visit there. Some conclude from this evidence that the primitive community remains loyal to the Temple as a matter of principle. Given the Lucan style of summaries, these verses represent Luke's main message on the centrality of the Temple in the life of the apostles.[57]

Whether we approach the activity of the apostles from a historical or a literary perspective matters a great deal.[58] From a historical and functional point of view, it surely is a convenient place of assembly for engaging with the masses, but it is also—as we shall see below in the discussion of Temple persecutions—a very dangerous place. It is quite reasonable that the apostles continue Jesus's teaching there. From a literary or theological point of view, Luke certainly is trying to make a point about the Christians' relationship to the Temple. It is premature to determine the nature of his message at this point. We need to examine his entire discourse about the Temple in order to offer a thorough analysis.

Interestingly, Luke specifies distinct sites on the Temple Mount attended by the apostles. When Peter and John go up to the Temple for the daily afternoon prayer, they meet the lame man at the Beautiful Gate (Acts 3:1). This gate may the same one referred to as the Corinthian Gate at the eastern entrance to the Women's Court in rabbinic sources.[59] Another site is Solomon's portico, the colonnade where the crowd gathers around Peter and John after this healing (3:11). Later, the apostles visit this place on a regular basis (5:12). The colonnade may be identified with the one along the eastern wall of the Temple Mount.[60] While the readers do not visit the Temple and are not familiar with these locations, Luke gives them the impression that he knows the Temple. By naming these sites Luke makes his descriptions more vivid. Note, however, that while both sites are public venues where people gather, they are outside of the sacred precincts.

PRAYER AT THE TEMPLE

Prayer at the Temple is mentioned three times in Luke–Acts. These three episodes show Luke's concern for the cult and how it affects the piety of his characters.

In one case the time of prayer is indirectly related to the sacrificial cult. Here in Acts 3:1, Peter and John "were going up to the Temple at the hour of prayer, at three o'clock in the afternoon [literally, "the ninth hour"]." This timing is important to the story, since many people are gathered in the Temple at this moment (Acts 3:9, 11), probably for the public prayer. Such prayer is also mentioned in relation to Gabriel's revelation to Zechariah "at the time of the incense-offering" when "the whole assembly of the people was praying outside" (Luke 3:10).

Luke also pays specific attention to the exact time of prayer when presenting Cornelius, the Roman centurion and a God-fearer who "gave alms generously to the people and prayed constantly to God" (Acts 10:2) and is later converted by Peter. The story begins when "one afternoon at about three o'clock he had a vision in which he clearly saw an angel of God" (Acts 10:3)—that is, at the same time as the public prayer at Temple mentioned above.[61] Cornelius mentions his prayer at this specific hour again later when telling Peter about his angelic revelation (Acts 10:30), which makes this detail even more important to the reader. It is not a coincidence that Cornelius prays at the time when the afternoon daily Tamid sacrifice is offered at the Temple. Judith's timing is exactly the same: "At the very time when the evening incense was being offered in the house of God in Jerusalem, Judith cried out to the Lord with a loud voice" (Judith 9:1). So too Daniel is "speaking in prayer . . . at the time of the evening sacrifice" when he sees Gabriel in a vision (Dan 9:21). Thus Cornelius's prayer is positioned in relation to the sacrificial cult.[62]

The public prayer in the Temple during the twice-daily Tamid sacrifice in the morning and afternoon is an important liturgical event. During the

Hellenistic and early Roman period until the destruction of the Temple in 70 CE, a ritual and public prayer—consisting of a fixed text recited at fixed times—takes place only at the Temple, not in the synagogue, at least not in Judaea. This public prayer is related to the sacrificial cult, and all of the people in the Temple take part in it. It is first documented in Ben Sira (ca. 180 CE) and mentioned in other sources from the Second Temple period such as 1 Maccabees and Josephus. Its contents, which include reciting Scripture and specific blessings, are detailed in the Mishnah. Public prayer develops from the sacrificial rite, ultimately becoming an integral part of the cult. It draws its sacredness from the sacrificial cult (and the words recited also address the sacrifices themselves).[63] Thus when Luke mentions that key figures practice this prayer or consider it important, he actually regards the Temple cult not just as background for his story but as a core element of the narrative.[64] Interestingly, in his speech before the crowd as he stands on the stairs of the citadel (the Antonia), Paul wants to demonstrate his Temple piety, pointing out that after being called by Jesus, he prays in the Temple (Acts 22:17). This, however, is most likely a private prayer.

Another case of prayer in the Temple involves private prayer. It appears in the parable of the Pharisees and the tax collector (Luke 18:9–14). Both "went up to the Temple to pray" (v. 10), and their confessions make clear that this is a private prayer.[65] The differences in their religious status or essence are apparent in their location at the Temple: the Pharisee is "standing by himself," while the shamed tax collector is "standing *far off*" (18:11–12). Luke's depiction makes the scene more realistic, the Temple setting ensuring that it is more concrete.[66]

For Luke, the Temple is a place for both a Pharisee and a tax collector (whom the gospel classifies among the sinners because he makes his living by taking people's money) to come to on a regular basis when the need to express piety toward God arises. It is the most appropriate place for individual prayer and repentance—but also a place where a person like the Pharisee shows his pride.

Luke does not mention the sacrificial cult. Is this intentional and/or significant? The tax collector specifically pleads for atonement that would normally be associated with sacrifice. We are also told that he goes down from the Temple "justified." So why doesn't the tax collector offer a sacrifice?[67] For Luke, the Temple is "a house of prayer" (Luke 19:46), but he also mentions the offering of the incense (Luke 1:9) and sacrifices of a Christian Nazirite (Acts 21:26). It is inconceivable that he ignores sacrifice altogether.

Perhaps this omission has something to do with the fact that sacrifices are irrelevant after 70 CE, while prayer is all the more valid.

Furthermore, mentioning the tax collector's sacrifice may not suit the parable's message. It is God who affects justification owing to the tax collector's sincere repentance (and Luke thinks highly of repentance, e.g., Acts 2:38; 3:19). The perfect passive participle *dedikaiōmenos* ("justified") in this passage supports such a reading. Yet God's justification occurs in the Temple, hence the Temple's significance remains.[68]

To conclude, one may argue that the Temple serves here as a third character in the parable, along with the Pharisee and tax collector. The outcome of the parable indicates something about the institution in whose shadow this drama unfolds. In a way, the Temple is the concrete embodiment of Jewish identity and tradition.[69] It is where both repentance and pride play a role.

Cleansing and Trial: The Disappearance of the Temple Charge

Luke's description of the cleansing of the Temple (19:45–48) follows Mark 11:15–17, but both omit some things and add others to this source. Luke mentions only Jesus's driving out of "the sellers." He omits Mark's detailed depiction of Jesus's banishment of the buyers, his overturning of the tables of the money changers and of the seats of those who sell doves as well as his prohibition to carry anything through the Temple.[70] Luke seems to minimize the extent of Jesus's act, reducing its violent character. He does not want the reader to think of Jesus as aiming to damage the Temple or the cult.

Immediately after the act, Luke adds a scene in which Jesus teaches at the Temple: "Every day he was teaching in the Temple. The chief priests, the scribes, and the leaders of the people kept looking for a way to kill him; but they did not find anything they could do, for all the people were spellbound by what they heard" (19:47–48). In this manner Luke swiftly moves the reader's attention from driving out the sellers to the much more generative act of teaching. While this might mitigate negative impressions engendered by the destructive nature of the cleansing scene,[71] it is actually not the overturning of the tables that disturbs Jewish leaders in the Temple (as in Mark 11:18), but the fact that Jesus establishes himself as an authoritative teacher there.

As in Mark, Jesus cites two biblical verses: "My house shall be a house of prayer" (Isa 56:7) and "But you have made it a den of robbers" (Jer 7:11). In the first he omits Isaiah's original words about a house of prayer "for all the nations" (cited by Mark but also omitted in Matthew 21:13). This is surprising because Luke stresses that the gospel is meant for all of the nations (e.g., Luke 2:32; Acts 28:28). Some suggest that Luke thinks the Temple is not relevant to the Gentiles who join the Christian movement because the Temple no longer exists or because—unlike Isiah—Luke does not believe that the Temple will have a role in the eschatological age in which worshipers from all nations will gather there.[72] However, this approach would not cohere with the importance of prayer in the Temple (see above) or with the prayers of the apostles outside of it (Acts 2:42; 16:13, 16).

I suggest that Luke does not want the reader to think that Jesus cleanses the Temple in order to make it possible for Gentiles to enter it. We should bear in mind that despite his interest in Gentile Christians, Luke never mentions Gentiles at the Temple Mount and rejects the accusation that Paul brings a Gentile into the Temple courts (Acts 21:28–29, and see below). As we have already seen, Luke portrays the Temple as the heart of Jewish religion and devotion, describing Temple practices in detail. He does not want to confuse this message by hinting at Gentile interference in the authentic, genuine cult—as if this is the intention of the Christians. This would seem to be a sensitive matter, especially shortly after the Romans have turned the Temple into a ruin.

The exact meaning of the cleansing for Luke is debated. Does Jesus take possession of the Temple as if it belongs to him, preparing it for his stay and activity there? This suggests that Jesus may relate to the Temple on a functional basis, not necessarily valuing it for its own sake. Such a reading may also explain confrontations between Jesus and the chief priests in the Temple (Luke 19:45–20:47). Alternatively, Luke's Jesus may not think that the Temple is profaned. Perhaps for Luke Jesus *restores* the Temple, rendering it fit to fulfill its eschatological role as a decisive center of God's saving work.[73]

Given that Luke minimizes the Temple act and deletes the over turning of the tables, it seems obvious he attempts to avoid a negative stance toward the Temple. He is compelled to follow the general tradition introduced by Mark (which is probably already familiar to at least some of his readers) and cannot erase the cleansing altogether. But for Luke, as we have already seen, Jesus is first and foremost a teacher in the Temple.

The short trial scene has something in common with Luke's "cleansing." Unlike in Mark 14:57–58 and Matthew 26:61, in Luke 22:66–71 Jesus is asked at the beginning of the hearing if he is the Messiah. Nothing is said about the false witnesses' accusations that he says he will destroy the Temple made with hands and build a Temple not made with hands in three days! Luke also omits the claim of rebuilding the Temple in three days from the scene of the mocking of Jesus on the cross (Mark 15:29 and Matthew 27:40), though he does enhance this scene with other verbal abuse of Jesus (Luke 23:35–42).

Surely Luke knows this tradition from Mark, which is his primary source. He even implies as much in Stephen's trial and speech, where he mentions the accusation by false witnesses that Jesus says he will destroy the Temple. Stephen also speaks against the Temple "made by hands" (Acts 6: 13–14; 7:48). But in Acts these accusations concern Stephen and indirectly refer to Jesus only after the reader has already established his or her opinion about Jesus and his approach to the Temple.

The omission is therefore intentional and telling.[74] The Temple charge in both the trial and crucifixion present Jesus as an alleged enemy of the Temple. This might put at risk Luke's special message about the Christians' unique and sustaining attitude toward the Temple. Instead of denying it (as Mark and Matthew do), he simply prefers to omit it altogether, probably because the reader might otherwise wrongly suspect that it is true (as modern commentators of Mark certainly do!).

Predicting the Destruction and Its Aftermath

As in Mark 13:1–2, in Luke 21:6 Jesus predicts that "the days will come when not one stone will be left upon another; all will be thrown down." There is, however, one difference between these two accounts. In Mark, Jesus responds to a general comment on "buildings." In chapter 3 I suggested that since the Temple is not mentioned explicitly in this case, a reference to the Temple should not be inferred. In Luke, however, the introduction to the following saying leaves no doubt as to its focus: "When some were speaking about the Temple, how it was adorned with beautiful stones and gifts dedicated to God" (21:5). Unlike Mark, Luke knows about what takes place in 70 CE. Despite his feelings about the Temple, no one can deny that it has been destroyed, and hence the tradition concerning Jesus's prediction should be more precise.

Another difference from Mark is that in Luke Jesus proclaims this not after leaving the Temple (Mark 13:1) but while standing inside of it (cf. Luke 21:1, 37).[75] The prophecy of destruction may sound less offensive from within, although Luke may have another literary concern when he reshapes Mark's narrative: to place Jesus's teaching and activity within the Temple.[76] In fact, he readily expands the theme of the destruction of Jerusalem. He has already introduced the destruction of "your house" in Luke 13:35 (see the discussion of Q in chapter 4) and includes another version of the "no stone" saying in another prophecy, predicting the Roman siege of Jerusalem in 19:42–44. There he adds that the reason for its destruction is "because you did not recognize the time of your visitation." He also corroborates a lament on the women and children of Jerusalem in 23:28–31.[77]

In Luke 19:42–44 Jesus is not pleased with the coming destruction. He weeps for Jerusalem. Luke interprets the past event of the destruction along the lines of Jesus's oracle. He expresses genuine lament and grief, reflected by an abundance of scriptural allusions.[78]

NT scholars tend to see Luke's understanding of the destruction as a result of or even a punishment for the rejection of Jesus.[79] Some read the scene in which the Temple's gates are being shut on Paul in Acts 21:26 as a representation of the destruction of the Temple. It is understood as the result of the rejection of Jesus and the mob's violence toward Paul. According to Frederick Bruce, "For Luke himself, this may have been the moment when the Jerusalem Temple ceased to fill the honorable role hitherto ascribed to it in the twofold history. The exclusion of God's message and messenger from the house once called by his name sealed its doom: it was now ripe for the destruction which Jesus predicted for it many years before (Luke 21:6)."[80] However, Paul continues to declare his loyalty to the Temple in Acts 22:17; 24:12, 17–18; 25:9. Despite his exclusion from the Temple, an attempted lynching there by the mob, and continued attempts by the high priest to put him on trial (cf. Acts 23:12–15, 29), he argues that his past actions prove his piety toward the Temple (see also below).

In the speeches of Peter, Stephen, and Paul, Luke has several opportunities to add—in the context of their description of the disbelief in or even killing of Jesus (e.g., Acts 4:10–12; 5:30–32; 7:51–53)—a threat of punishment and a hint about the coming destruction. Obviously, Luke resists this temptation. I think he has two reasons for this. First, he too is devastated by the loss of the Temple. In Luke 19:41–44, Jesus weeps because of the coming destruction of Jerusalem. In Luke's eyes, the transition from divine abode to divine abandonment is far from being a positive development. Otherwise there is no reason for him to give the Temple so much attention and credit. Second, Luke wants to show his readers that there is no truth to the common Jewish accusation that Christians oppose the Temple or threaten it.

For these reasons I hold that the text does not substantiate the view that for Luke the destruction is a positive turning point for Christianity—not that its ties to its geographical center in the form of the Temple and the city are now broken or (even more so) that blood sacrifice must end.[81] Throughout the gospel the reader is shown that the Temple is the origin and basis of Jesus, supporting a key mode of piety and devotion. The reader is supposed to feel devastated when he reads about the coming destruction, not to think about the dawn of a new age. Even when Jesus ascends, the apostles remain in the Temple as if nothing has changed.

Luke may hint even that the judgment and destruction of Jerusalem and the Temple are not final, stating "and Jerusalem will be trampled on by the Gentiles, *until the times of the Gentiles are fulfilled*" (21:24). When God punishes the Gentiles, the Temple may be restored.[82] If Jerusalem and the Temple are as central to Luke's worldview as they are for the prophets, this would suggest such hope for restoration. This also depends on whether or not Jesus's resurrection and the coming of the Holy Spirit replace the Temple after it is already gone.[83]

The Torn Veil

"It was now about noon, and darkness came over the whole land until three in the afternoon, while the sun's light failed; and the curtain of the Temple was torn in two. Then Jesus, crying with a loud voice, said, 'Father, into your hands I commend my spirit.' Having said this, he breathed his last. When the centurion saw what had taken place, he praised God and said, 'Certainly this man was innocent.' And when all the crowds who had gathered there for this spectacle saw what had taken place, they returned home, beating their breasts. But all his acquaintances, including the women who had followed him from Galilee, stood at a distance, watching these things." (Luke 23:44–49)

The tearing of the Temple veil while Jesus takes his last breath signals for some just what it does for many commentators on Mark 15:37–38: that the coming destruction of the Temple and the symbolic termination of the cult are directly aligned with the death of Jesus.[84] However, Luke alters the order of things in relation to Mark in a manner that seems meaningful and may hint at a different message about the Temple.

In Mark the veil is torn (*eschisthē*) after Jesus dies, hence it seems to represent the outcome of his death. Luke, in contrast, dates the tearing of the veil earlier than Jesus's last cry and breath, suggesting that it is not torn because he cries or dies. Distancing the veil from Jesus's death attests to a more remote connection. Furthermore, the thought that the Temple falls into ruins with the crucifixion flies in the face of the apostles' continued attendance at the Temple and Paul's participation in the cult. Surely, granted Luke's special interest in the Temple, the scene must have a role in Luke's general portrayal of the Temple.[85]

The episode contains additional significant elements that are not found in Mark 15:37–38: the darkness (Matthew 27:45–54 adds here earthquake and resurrection), the timing "in the ninth hour," and a reworking of the centurions' reaction. All of these may shed light on the meaning of the tearing of the Temple veil. Darkness in the middle of the day is an apocalyptic sign. It may signal destruction because of the rejection and crucifixion of Jesus, so that the torn veil stands for the end of the Temple. However, if this is the case, the fact that Luke changes the order of the scene and describes the tearing of the veil as coming prior to Jesus's death becomes almost meaningless. It may be suggested that both the darkness and the torn veil attest to a cosmic and religious change, the coming of the "last days." Another possibility is that the torn veil is connected not to the fact that the sun's light fails but to Jesus's cry. Both options signal the revelation of God and the opening of the heavens.[86]

Another interesting component of the scene is that it happens between noon and three in the afternoon (that is, the ninth hour during the day). This specific hour is also mentioned in Acts 3:1 and 10:3, 30. As I have already noted, it relates to the time of the afternoon public prayer at the Temple during the offering of the Tamid daily sacrifice. Thus Jesus's death is coordinated with the Temple cult! This does not seem to be an appropriate way to argue that Jesus's death brings the end of sacrifices. It may suggest exactly the opposite. It is a sacred time, not a time of grief.[87] Indeed, Jesus's death is followed by positive events which are expanded on by Luke. The centurion not only acknowledges Jesus but praises God.[88]

The tearing of the veil therefore relates not to a situation which is destructive but to a colossal event that leads to the spread of belief in Jesus. Still, while it is obvious that Luke sees Temple symbolism in this scene, its exact meaning remains vague.

The Authority of the Priesthood

Not only the Temple but also the priests appear in Luke frequently. We must distinguish between Luke's presentation of the priests, priesthood, and the Levites on the one hand and the chief priests—the leaders of the Temple—on the other. When he alludes to the first group, Luke expresses a general attitude toward the Temple and the cult. His approach to the second group may also be related to their political power as leaders, their confrontation with Jesus, and the persecution of the Christian leaders.

Are there any indications of criticism of the ordinary priesthood? In two cases a priest behaves in an improper manner. In the parable of the Good Samaritan, the priest (and also the Levite) ignore the miserable man (Luke 10:31–32). The sons of a Jewish "high priest" named Sceva are involved in exorcism using Jesus's name in vain (Acts 19:13–17). One may also view in a negative light the fact that Zechariah does not believe Gabriel the angel and that Zechariah and Elizabeth are unable to bear children (Luke 1:7, 18).[89] Nevertheless, I am not sure that it is their priesthood that affects these priests in this way. Furthermore, Luke portrays John's parents as "righteous before God, living blamelessly according to all the commandments and regulations of the Lord" (1:6). Disbelief in the angel's message about having children in old age is a familiar phenomenon for Luke and his readers (Gen 18:12–15).

Luke shares some favorable assertions in relation to the priests and their priesthood. Luke 5:12–14 reiterates Mark 1:40–44, in which Jesus cures a leper and tells him to show himself to the priest and offer sacrifices according to the Torah. But Luke adds another scene of his own in which Jesus cures ten lepers and orders them to go and see the priests (17:12–14). This seems not only to stress Jesus's power but also to recognize priestly religious authority.[90]

More significant is the comment that "a great many of the priests became obedient to the faith" (Acts 6:7). For Luke, this indicates Christianity's success among the circles of mainstream Judaism, quite like his comment that there are also Christian Pharisees (15:5). Some might argue that this is meant to show that these priests lose their faith in the Temple. But it is far more likely that Luke wants to prove that even priests, the most traditional, conservative, and Temple-oriented class within Jewish society, may and in fact should be attracted to believe in Jesus without seeing in this a turning back to their heritage.[91] Yet despite Luke's interest in the Temple there is no basis to argue that he himself is a priest.[92]

Besides ordinary priests, Luke frequently mentions the chief priests (*archiereis*). They belong to five major families whose members are nominated to the office of the high priesthood by the Herodian rulers and the Roman governors from the rise of Herod to the First Revolt (ca. 37 BCE— 68 CE). They are the leaders of the Jewish people and especially of the Temple.[93] They appear in Luke's reworking of the Passion Narrative, and even more prominently in the conflicts with Christian leaders in Acts. In section II, I analyze these stories in relation to the Temple persecutions, but here I want to introduce some general observations about Luke's approach to their authority.

We need to distinguish between two aspects in Luke's approach to the chief priests. On the one hand, they oppose Jesus, arresting him and turning him over to Pilate; and later they bring the apostles, Stephen and Paul to trial. They can certainly be viewed in a negative light for these reasons. On the other hand, and quite surprisingly, Luke does show respect for them as the leaders of the Jews and the Temple and does not deny the legitimacy of their authority or office. They are at the center of God's presence.[94]

Consider, for example, the confrontation between Paul and the high priest Ananias (son of Nedebaeus, cf. *Ant* 20.103). At Paul's hearing before the Sanhedrin, the high priest Ananias orders those standing near him to strike Paul on the mouth. Paul then curses the high priest and rebukes his departure from the Law: "Are you sitting there to judge me according to the Law, and yet in violation of the Law you order me to be struck?" (Acts 23:3). When admonished by others for insulting the high priest, Paul expresses regret since he is told that he has abused the high priest in breach of the law of Ex 22:28: "I did not realize, brothers, that he was high priest; for it is written, 'You shall not speak evil of a leader of your people'" (23:5).[95]

Furthermore, Luke highlights the high priests' part in the arrests and trials of Jesus, Peter, Stephen, and Paul.[96] He also mentions several times the Temple officers (*stratēgoi*, Luke 22:4, 52) and the Temple's chief captain (*stratēgos*, Acts 4:1; 5:24, 26), who is in charge of the Temple's guard or "police" and may be considered the deputy of the chief priest.[97] He thus shows special interest in the Temple leadership.

Significantly, Luke never accuses the chief priests and their associates, either specifically or directly, of unrighteousness, nor does he condemn them for hating the Christian leaders.[98] The accusations of rejecting Christ and persecuting his followers are instead directed at the Jerusalemites and *their leaders*.[99] He does not wish to specifically condemn the leaders of the

Temple or the high priests, despite their role in the persecution of Jesus, Peter, the apostles, Stephen, and Paul. In so doing, I suggest, Luke wants to confirm the credibility of the Temple in the eyes of the Christians.

Luke's strategy is not limited to the Temple authorities and applies to all Jewish leaders. Despite Jesus's moral criticism of Jewish leaders, Luke's Jesus prays for their forgiveness because they do not know what they are doing (Luke 23:34; and so does Stephen in Acts 7:60). Despite their acts against him, Jesus preaches to the leaders and even heals the high priest's slave (Luke 22:50–51).[100]

All of this demonstrates that Luke exhibits religious concerns in portraying the chief priests and Temple leadership in a relatively neutral fashion, beyond politics and persecution.

Stephen's Speech: Does God Dwell in the Temple?

Stephen—one of the so-called Hellenist members of the Jerusalem community and a man full of faith and the Holy Spirit (Acts 6:1, 5)—is accused of wrongdoing by other Jews from the Hellenistic Diaspora. They instigate false witnesses to claim the following in a trial before the Sanhedrin and the high priest: "This man never stops saying things against this holy place and the law; for we have heard him say that this Jesus of Nazareth will destroy this place and will change the customs that Moses handed on to us" (6:13–14). Stephen responds with a long speech about Jewish history and Israel's disobedience to God since the period of Israel's wandering in the wilderness. It includes this comment on the Temple:

> "Our ancestors had the tent of testimony in the wilderness, as God directed when he spoke to Moses, ordering him to make it according to the pattern he had seen. Our ancestors in turn brought it in with Joshua when they dispossessed the nations that God drove out before our ancestors. And it was there until the time of David, who found favour with God and asked that he might find a dwelling-place for the house of Jacob. But it was Solomon who built a house for him. Yet the Most High does not dwell in houses made by human hands; as the prophet says, 'Heaven is my throne, and the earth is my footstool. What kind of house will you build for me, says the Lord, or what is the place of my rest? Did not my hand make all these things?'" (Acts 7:44–50)

Stephen concludes by accusing the audience of not keeping the Law, opposing the Holy Spirit, and betraying and murdering the Righteous One (7:51–53).

AGAINST THE TEMPLE "MADE WITH HANDS"

It is common to see in Stephen's speech a straightforward, harsh criticism of the very existence of the Temple. Marcel Simon champions this approach, concluding that Stephen expresses "fierce hostility towards the Temple" and "considers [it] almost as a place of idolatry." The Temple means, from the very beginning, "a falling away from the authentic tradition of Israel."[101] Although Stephen refers to Solomon's Temple, there is no doubt that he intends to address the Herodian Temple of his time. For some, this rejection of the very notion of the Temple as a divine residence prepares the reader for "Luke's account of the dissemination of the divine presence with the spread of the Church which follows Stephen's death," or the idea that Christ is the new Temple, not made by hands.[102]

The thrust of this interpretation relates to the opposition between the Tabernacle (representing Israel's wandering in the Sinai desert) and the building of the Temple. David, who finds favor with God, seeks a dwelling place (*skenoma*) for the divine, while Solomon builds God a house (*oikos*) (Acts 7:46–47). This is seen as a condemnation of the building of the Temple. Solomon is presented as having erred in building God a Temple, whereas David seems to represent the ideal king, "who found favour with God" and wants to build only a tent, not a Temple. God, it seems, is pleased by a mere tent and does not ask for Solomon's house/Temple. The opposition between tent and Temple is found in v. 47 by virtue of the word *de* ("*But* it was Solomon who built a house for him").[103]

Another lexical aid for condemning the Temple is the phrase "made with hands" (*en cheiropoiētois*). Stephen declares, "The Most High does not dwell in houses made by human hands" (7:48). This term is used in the LXX to describe temples for idols, but here Solomon's Temple is considered as such! The Tabernacle, however, is not, because it is made according to the fashion that God shows Moses (Acts 7:44). It is made due to God's will.[104] And if Stephen actually opposes the Temple so radically, it indicates that the accusations leveled against him in the trial are probably true, despite being hostile and malicious.[105]

What flaw does Stephen find to justify such a bold attack on the very notion of an already-built Temple? To be sure, Luke's Stephen quotes Isa 66:1–2, which originally targets cultic and moral transgressions. This is understood as relevant to first-century Judaism: "God's transcendent majesty, His ubiquity . . . forbid us to think of Him as dwelling in a house."[106]

Esler suggests that a particular social background leads to this claim. It originates among God-fearers forbidden to enter the interior precincts of the Temple. These individuals are limited to entering the court of Gentiles, which is located outside of the Court of Women. They are excluded from the sacred experience. We might assume that a God-fearer who stays in Solomon's portico while his Jewish associates enter the Temple courts during the Tamid sacrificial rite might become ambivalent about the Temple. He can sense the beauty of the Temple but is prevented from approaching closely the presence of God and participating in the cult. He remains an outsider, experiencing marginalization. Perhaps God-fearers convince their Greek-speaking Jewish friends that they too should accept discipleship, resulting in some Christians adopting antipathy toward the Temple in solidarity with their Gentile colleagues.[107]

For Luke's readers, such an approach might justify the destruction of the Temple—or at least encourage religious life without it. One may even expect that the author would mention the destruction. In fact, it is this speech that leads some to conclude that Luke's general approach to the Temple is not at all favorable, despite the positive evidence I have already discussed.[108]

Simon also points out the source of the hostility toward the Temple: Hellenistic Judaism. It is the religious tradition of the Greek-speaking Diaspora Jews—immersed in Greek culture and philosophy—that turns some Christians against the Temple and sacrifices. Other scholars follow this approach.[109] Even those who do not accept such a critical interpretation of Stephen's view of the Temple relate the idea of *holiness outside of the Temple* to Hellenistic Judaism.[110]

REVISING THE ANTI-TEMPLE STANCE: READING WITHOUT PREJUDICE

Recently, a growing number of scholars have come to disagree that the plain meaning of Stephen's speech rejects the very notion of the Temple.[111] It seems that the setting of the speech as a reply to accusations during a trial about declaring the destruction of the Temple is misleading. There is no correspondence between Acts 7:44–50 and earlier testimony in which Stephen claims that Jesus will destroy the Temple. Luke stresses that these accusation are made by false witnesses and that Stephen is innocent. It is therefore unreasonable that Luke would support this allegation throughout his speech.[112]

Distinguishing between Tabernacle and Temple is also groundless. The meaning of the Greek *de* which separates them (Acts 7:47) is not "but" as a negation; it means "and" as a consecutive connective. In the next verse—as part of the conclusion about the dwelling of God not manifesting itself in houses made by human hands—the opening word *alla* is not a regular contrast but rather a concessive sense like "though" or "yet." Thus the statement about Solomon is not negative, and there is no distinction between David's Tabernacle and Solomon's Temple. God does not dwell in handmade *things*—neither tent nor house. God cannot be localized, and the use of the term "the Most High" stresses this.[113]

Understanding David's building of the Tabernacle as positive in nature in contrast to Solomon's Temple building being bad is a farfetched notion. In 2 Samuel 7 it is David who initiates the building of the Temple. There is no justification for arguing that David plans to build only a sturdy tent and not a building, and there is also no reason a tent would suit God's dwelling better than a solid building in the very same place.[114]

When Stephen opposes the Temple because it is made by (human) hands (*cheiropoiētos*) he cannot distinguish between the Temple and the Tabernacle, since the latter is also built by humans. Only the heavenly Temple is not made by human hands. In the Septuagint this word refers to "idol-houses" as well as similar cultic buildings, but such a reading cannot be applied here. The correct translation may be "human handiwork," i.e., material sanctuaries.[115]

In making this claim and quoting Isa 66:1–2, Stephen rejects confining God to the Temple, but this does not mean that God cannot be encountered there. The issue is not "tent" versus "house" but rather true and false thinking about God's presence. God should not be *confined* to a Temple. This view is already found in Solomon's prayer at the inauguration of the First Temple (1 Kings 8:27). Thus Stephen does not reject the Temple but rather warns against restricting God to the Temple: God is available to all with or without the Temple.[116] Indeed, this notion is fundamental for the early Christians, especially with regard to Luke's stress on the Holy Spirit within the community.

Still, there is certainly a polemical tone in this portion of the speech which matches the polemical nature of the entirety of the text. One theme unites this speech at every level: Israel's disobedience of God. Past generations are not without their sanctuaries, but in all of these cases a sanctuary does not mitigate the consequences of disobedience. In the same way, the Temple does not guarantee God's savings. Tabernacle and Temple are listed together in reviewing the history of sanctuaries and rebellion (Acts 7: 39–43).[117]

As far as Luke is concerned, Acts 7:46–50 actually responds to the accusations against Stephen, showing that he follows prophetic tradition and is loyal to the Torah. He is not anti-Temple, but he does criticize an overdependence on the Temple as the only mode of communicating with God.[118]

Section II. Temple Persecutions and Alignment in Acts

According to the Book of Acts, the early Christian leaders in Jerusalem are brought to trial before the Temple's high priests: Peter and the apostles are flogged, Paul is arrested and charged, and Stephen is executed. Josephus (*Ant.* 20.200) adds that James is sentenced to death by stoning, a scene that is dramatized in later Christian legends. Different explanations are offered for the persecution of these Christian leaders.[119] I would like to show that the narrative suggests that all are related to the Temple. My analysis will be carried out on two levels: narrative and historical. First, I will try to interpret the messages conveyed in these narratives; then I will attempt to evaluate their historical basis.

Temple-Related Conflicts and Prosecutions in Acts

PETER AND THE APOSTLES

In Acts 4 and 5, Peter and other apostles are arrested and brought before the Sanhedrin (*sunedrion*, NSRV: "council," a judicial committee headed by a high priest or king). According to Acts 4:1–3, "While Peter and John were speaking to the people, the priests, the captain [stargtēgos] of the Temple, and the Sadducees came to them; much annoyed because they were teaching the people and proclaiming that in Jesus there is the resurrection of the dead; so they arrested them and put them in custody." At the judicial hearings the chief priests Annas, Caiaphas, and John as well as other members of the high priestly families are present (Acts 4:7). To be sure, the charges are not baseless: Acts 3 describes how Peter and John go up to the Temple for the afternoon prayer, and Peter heals a crippled beggar "in the name of Jesus, near the Temple's 'Beautiful Gate.'" When news of his action spreads, a crowd gathers around Peter and John in "Solomon's portico" at the Temple Mount (*hieron*), where Peter delivers a speech about the failure to believe in Jesus. As a result, the Sanhedrin decides to warn the apostles "not to speak or teach at all in the name of Jesus" (4:18).

A similar story is recounted in Acts 5:12–42, although the consequences of Peter's actions are quite different.[120] Here the apostles continue to heal, preach, and gather in Solomon's portico (5:12). In response, "the high priest and all who were with him (that is, the sect of the Sadducees), being filled with jealousy, arrested the apostles and put them in the public prison" (5:17). The apostles then flee and "entered the Temple at daybreak and went on with their teaching" (5:21). The high priest, the captain of the Temple, and the other chief priests bring them back before the Sanhedrin, where Peter defends himself with a speech on the salvation of Israel through Jesus. As a result, the apostles are flogged and ordered to halt their teaching in the name of Jesus—although, as Luke makes clear, they continue preaching at the Temple nonetheless (5:42).

In both descriptions the high priest and the Temple officers arrest and charge Peter and the other apostles with healing and preaching in the name of Jesus. Some scholars suggest that the reason for the arrests is the apostles' belief in resurrection or even black magic as well as inappropriate spreading of apocalyptic expectations.[121] Yet instances of healing and preaching appear elsewhere in Acts 2, 8–10, and in all of these cases the high priests take no judicial measures against them. What, then, accounts for this different response?

Examination of Luke's narratives shows that he connects the arrests to the Temple. His frequent mention of the Temple in relation to these episodes suggests that he associates the prosecution of the apostles to the *location* of their activity—namely, the Temple Mount. Luke seems to make the implicit claim that the chief priests are concerned not merely about the apostles' teachings about Jesus and their demonstrations of the power of healing through the use of Jesus's name. Rather, the priests are concerned because these teachings and demonstrations are carried out in the Temple, making the acts a public desecration of a holy place. This claim is supported by the direct involvement of the high priest (who is in charge of the Temple cult) in the legal measures taken against the apostles and by the presence of the captain of the Temple at the trials. In comparison, when King Agrippa I executes James, son of Zebedee, and persecutes Peter (Acts 12:1–5), he is not concerned with such cultic or religious issues.[122]

STEPHEN

Stephen is brought before the Sanhedrin, where false witnesses declare, "This man never stops saying things against this holy place [namely, the Temple] and the law; for we have heard him say that this Jesus of Nazareth will destroy this place [*ton topon touton*] and will change the customs that Moses handed on to us" (Acts 6:8–14). The high priest asks Stephen if this is true. At the end of his long speech (Acts 7:2–53) Stephen declares, "I see the heavens opened and the Son of Man standing at the right hand of God" (7:51). The people regard this statement as blasphemous; they rush at Stephen, drive him out of town, and stone him to death in a kind of public lynching (7:57–58).[123]

Significantly, however, even though Stephen is killed on account of blasphemy, the *original* charge leveled against him is that he had declared that Jesus would destroy the Temple and change the Law. The first part of this accusation echoes the one attributed to Jesus about destroying and rebuilding the *naos* (Mark 14:58; 15:29) by the false witnesses. Nevertheless, Luke makes it clear that Stephen has not said what the witnesses argue he has said. And, as I showed earlier, there is no need to see Stephen's speech as anti-Temple; he criticizes only the belief in a restricted abode for the Divine Presence. Nonetheless, Stephen is arrested and brought to trial owing to his alleged rejection of the Temple; that is, the claim of its imminent destruction, which is based upon Jesus's prophecy.

PAUL

When Paul returns to Jerusalem he is suspected by other Jewish-Christians of warning Jews not to obey the Torah. The elders among James's associates insist that Paul will disprove this accusation and demonstrate that he "observes and guards the law," specifically through his sponsorship of the sacrifices (i.e., Nazirite vows) of other Christians. Paul purifies himself along with the Nazirites and enters the Temple (Acts 21:18–26).

As Paul enters the Temple he is seized by Jews from Asia who declare, "This is the man who is teaching everyone everywhere against our people, our law, and this place [*tou topou toutou*]; more than that, he has actually brought Greeks into the Temple [*hieron*] and has defiled this holy place [*hagion topon touton*]" (Acts 21:28). Luke here adds an explanatory comment meant to undermine the accusation: "For they had previously seen Trophimus the Ephesian with him in the city, and they supposed that Paul had brought him into the Temple" (21:27–29). Paul is dragged out of the Temple and is not killed only because Roman troops are stationed nearby. Hearing the commotion, they intervene and arrest Paul (21:30–36). It is possible that the crowd is following a legal practice, acknowledged by the Romans, according to which a Gentile who enters the courts of the Temple is to be executed immediately, even without the benefit of a trial.[124] Yet in this case, we must remember, it is a *Jew* who is accused of responsibility for such a sacrilegious act.

There ensues a long, winding path of legal procedures under the leadership of the high priest Ananias son of Nedebaus in partnership with the Roman procurators Felix and Festus as well as King Agrippa II. The Jewish crowd, led by the high priest and the Sanhedrin, demand enforcement of the death penalty, but the Roman procurator is not convinced of any actual guilt. Therefore (and since Paul is a Roman citizen), he is taken into Roman custody until his appeal to Nero.[125]

At first glance, the Temple accusation against Paul may seem like a mere excuse to punish him for his teachings against the Torah. Consider, however, that Paul visits Jerusalem in Acts 15 without encountering any such enmity. Furthermore, Luke mentions the violation of the Temple's sacredness time and again, both in his descriptions of the charges brought against Paul and in Paul's own speeches. After Paul is transferred to Caesarea, a delegation headed by the high priest Ananias approaches Felix, accusing Paul of trying "to profane the Temple" (24:7). Paul replies that he "went up to worship in Jerusalem" but is not—in what would seem to be a reference to the acts of Peter and the apostles—"disputing with anyone in the Temple or stirring up a crowd either in the synagogues or throughout the city" (24:11–12). Later, he states to Festus in response to the subsequent accusations against him, "I have in no way committed an offence against the law of the Jews, or against the Temple, or against the emperor" (25:8).

In Paul's speeches, Luke portrays Paul as devoted to the Temple cult. According to Luke, Paul points out that after being called by Jesus, he prays in the Temple (Acts 22:17). Paul stresses that he comes to Jerusalem "to bring alms to my nation and to offer sacrifices; while I was doing this, they found me in the Temple, completing the rite of purification, without any crowd or disturbance" (24:17–18). It seems likely that Luke is here attempting to convince the reader that the Temple charge is false—an implicit acknowledgment that the Temple is a focal point in the conflict between Paul and the Jerusalem Jews.

The Temple Conflicts in Acts: Message and History

A theme emerges from the survey of measures taken against the early Christian leaders above: Peter and the apostles as well as Paul are all arrested and put on trial on account of their having allegedly committed forbidden actions in the Temple. So too Stephen is prosecuted following his supposed statement about Jesus's destruction of the Temple.

The historical credibility of Acts notwithstanding, there is no doubt that Luke employs narrative history in an effort to convey certain messages. What lessons are implied in the Temple conflicts involving Peter, Stephen, and Paul? Ostensibly the Temple conflicts described in Acts would seem to support interpretations of implied criticism of the Temple. After all, according to Acts, while the Temple is undoubtedly a holy place, its establishment—namely, the chief priests and their associates—stands in opposition to belief in Jesus and the mission of the apostles. Hence the Temple is designated as a negative entity deserving condemnation and rejection.[126] Stories of Temple persecution may in fact serve as a form of protest against the Temple establishment.[127]

This reading, however, contradicts Luke's favorable approach to the Temple—the frequent visits, the teaching and prayer of Jesus or the apostles he describes there and his omission of the signs for Jesus's challenging of the Temple and its leaders in the "cleansing," trial, and crucifixion. It also does not cohere with our earlier findings about Luke's respect for the priesthood and the lack of a direct attack on the chief priests concerning their responsibility for Jesus's execution. Significantly, in Paul's speeches Luke stresses his devotion to the sacrificial cult (Acts 22:17; 24:17–18; 25:8, all quoted above), showing that the Christians' commitment to the Temple remains undiminished despite the tribulations they suffer at the hands of the high priests following their visits to the Temple.[128]

These stories in Acts demonstrate that despite Christians' desire to take part in Temple worship, they are nonetheless maltreated on account of baseless suspicions. In other words, Luke uses the Temple episodes to demonstrate that Christianity is *not* a dissident Jewish faction. His apologetic purpose in the Temple conflicts is to show the *unjustified refusal of the Temple authorities to let the Jewish-Christians engage with the Temple. Their teachings and activities (such as healing) are taken as illegitimate.*[129] The chief priests and their followers among the Jews want to exclude the Christians from the Temple and therefore accuse them with trumped-up charges.

Now I will move from narrative to history and address the historical reliability of these Temple incidents and persecutions. We cannot find external evidence to confirm them, and it is impossible to conclude that they are all historically accurate. Nonetheless, the four conflicts with the Temple establishment stand in tension with Luke's main theme of appreciation of the Temple as the most sacred place representing God's presence as well as his muting of Jesus's alleged threat to the Temple in his gospel.

It is therefore unlikely that Luke would conjure episodes with such clear anti-Temple overtones if they are contrary to his own purposes. It is also unreasonable to argue that Luke introduces the Jewish (or high priestly) conception of the early Christians as enemies of the Temple—a conception to which Luke is wholeheartedly opposed—if it is not based on historical fact. We may thus conclude that his presentation of these events is biased but not fictitious.

Luke is likely replying to allegations against the Christians. In order to argue for their innocence he must first introduce the allegations. The basic facts are probably that while the Christians in Jerusalem cherish the Temple and want to attend it and preach there the chief priests joined by a Jewish mob suspect their intentions.[130]

Before I turn to the reasons that lead the chief priests to act against the Christians, I need to engage with another incident not recorded in the NT but relevant to James's attitude toward the Temple.

Excursus: James's Execution and the Temple: Narrative and History

According to Josephus, in 62 CE the Sadducean high priest Ananus son of Ananus "convened a Sanhedrin of judges and brought before them a man named James, the brother of Jesus who was called the Christ, and certain others. He accuses them of having acted illegally [*paranomēsantōn*] and delivered them up to be stoned."[131] And with this pithy description Josephus leaves the question of *why* James is prosecuted—and ultimately executed—open to intense scholarly debate.

It is suggested that James is executed because he is the leader of a messianic/apocalyptic movement that is regarded as politically dangerous, perhaps even revolutionary.[132] The fact that he is convicted of an illegal act leads other scholars to infer that he does not observe Jewish law strictly enough.[133] Some deduce from Josephus that James is executed not because of his Christian beliefs or his possible status within the nascent Christian community but because of prosaic political reasons: James's political alliance with Ananus's opponents (either rival high priests or common priests who are exploited by the high priesthood).[134] This alliance may be the result of James's criticism of the priestly aristocracy or of his support for the poor and the needy;[135] it may also simply be due to a personal rivalry between himself and Ananus.[136]

All of these explanations for James's execution are problematic for several reasons. First, James can hardly be regarded as lax with regard to the Law, since he is described as strict in his observance of purity restrictions in Gal 2:11–14 and also in Acts 21:24. Second, if the mission to the Gentiles or Jews is the reason for the charges against him, the high priests would be expected to act much earlier than 62 CE, probably closer to the Apostolic Council in ca. 49 CE. Third, deducing James's role in the political scene from Josephus's account of tension between high and common priests, or between aristocrats and Zealots, is highly hypothetical since we have no information whatsoever about James's relations with any of these parties. The fact that there are some priests among the Christians (Acts 6:7) and that the Christians in Jerusalem associate themselves with the poor are not sufficient grounds for arguing that the high priests are determined to rid themselves of James. After all, there are many other poor people and anti-aristocrats in Judaean society at the time.

Ananus's convening of a Sanhedrin of judges and the execution of a death sentence are extremely unusual steps. Josephus does not mention any other high priest who acts similarly. True, both Herodian rulers and Roman governors execute opponents, but these are all revolutionary Jews charged with sedition. Never in the years preceding the Great Revolt, when political or personal conflicts turn violent, do the high priests carry out trials and executions.[137] James's alleged offense must therefore be graver than the ones mentioned above. Josephus thus leads us to a dead end regarding the actual charge against James, apart from the sole hint provided by the penalty of stoning.

Some scholarship on the reason for James's execution focuses solely on Josephus's account, ignoring four later Christian sources that are regarded—quite rightly—as legendary.[138] Nevertheless, these sources are critical to understanding the event in question, and even more so with regard to how this event is understood by later Christians. I will now turn to an examination of these texts in the context of several overlapping lines of thought: the narrative construction provided by their authors (which also shows second-century interest in the Temple) and their possible reflection of historical reality. I will focus both on the geographical setting of the conflict between James and his opponents in the Temple and on his execution by means of stoning or being thrown down from a great height.

The initial and probably earliest source depicting James's conflict with his fellow Jews and subsequent martyrdom is Hegesippus, cited in Eusebius's *Historia Ecclesiastica* II, 23.5–18. Hegesippus portrays James as a Nazirite ascetic, explaining that "he alone was allowed to enter into the Sanctuary [*ta hagia*] . . . and he used to enter alone into the Temple [*naos*] and be kneeling and praying for forgiveness for the people" (23.6). The scribes and Pharisees ask James to persuade the crowds not to believe in Jesus as a messiah and "to stand at the battlement/pinnacle of the Temple" (*pterugion tou hierou* [11]) so that everyone is able to hear him. Yet when they ask him, "What is the gate of Jesus?" James replies that the Son of Man in heaven will come on clouds. They then, according to Hegesippus, throw James down and stone him, "since the fall had not killed him" (16). When this too proves ineffective, a certain laundryman finally beats James on the head with a club (17). He is then buried "on a spot by the Temple" (*naos*), and his gravestone remains there (18).[139]

A somewhat similar story is presented in the second century CE in Pseudo-Clementine *Recognitions* I. 66–70. In this telling James ascends to the Temple with his congregation (including Gamaliel) and encounters there a large crowd led by the high priest Caiaphas. He enters into a discussion with Caiaphas concerning belief in Christ and various scriptural matters, a discussion that ends in bloodshed as a massacre of the Christians in the Temple ensues. The person who orders the massacre enters the Temple near the altar and brandishes an altar brand (1.70.1, 6). James is then thrown from the top of the stairs, although it is not stated that he is put to death (1.70.8).[140]

A third and even more obscure description is introduced in the Second Apocalypse of James from Nag Hammadi. There James announces, "Behold, I gave you your house, which you say that God has made. Did he who dwells in it promise to give you an inheritance through it? This [house] I shall doom to destruction and derision of those who are in ignorance." Consequently the priests say, "Come, let us stone the Just One." They "found him standing beside the columns of the Temple beside the mighty corner stone.[141] And they decided to throw him down from the height, and they cast him down. . . . They seized him and [struck] him as they dragged him upon the ground. They stretched him out and placed a stone on his abdomen. They all placed their feet on him, saying 'You have erred!' Again, they raised him up, since he was alive. . . . After having covered him up to his abdomen, they stoned him in this manner."[142]

The fourth relevant source is Eusebius's quotation of Clement of Alexandria, stating that "James the Just . . . was thrown down from the pinnacle [*pterugion*] of the Temple and beaten to death with a fuller's club."[143]

Hegesippus, the Pseudo-Clementine *Recognitions, 2 Apoc. Jas,* and Clement of Alexandria contain both similarities and differences. First of all, they are all based, directly or indirectly, on an early second-century CE source, or at the very least on a common ancient tradition containing remnants of a Jewish one.[144] The result, as we shall see below, is that all four narratives include two basic common features: the preaching in/about the Temple and the stoning of James.

On the literary level all of these sources place the conflict between James and his opponents (whether they are the high priest, the priests, the scribes and Pharisees, or simply the crowd) in the Temple. James commits several forbidden acts there: Hegesippus argues that James enters into the *naos* when praying for the forgiveness of the people, thus implying that he acts like a priest—which would be considered a grave transgression against the Temple cult.[145] *2 Apoc. Jas* specifically mentions that James preaches that the Temple is "doomed to destruction and derision" while standing within it; and finally, in both Hegesippus and *Recognitions,* James preaches about the belief in Christ in the Temple. No doubt Hegesippus and *Recognitions* call to mind the preaching of Peter and the apostles in the Temple that lead to their arrest and flogging in Acts 4–5. Hegesippus, *Recognitions,* and *2 Apoc. Jas* agree, then, that the very presence of James in the Temple, along with his actions therein, lead to the zealous measures taken against him.

The Pseudo-Clementine *Recognitions,* Hegesippus, and *2 Apoc. Jas* portray the Temple as the locus of the conflict between Jews and Christians, which in turn elevates it to a symbol of the rejection of Christ. However, on the basic narrative level, all of these sources assume interest on the part of James in attending the Temple Mount. Hegesippus even describes him as acting like a (high?) priest. These sources thus imply an attraction on the part of James and his followers to the Temple, either as a place of worship or as a venue for preaching as attested to by Acts. Only *2 Apoc. Jas* describes an explicit anti-Temple stance by recounting James's prophecy of its destruction as God's punishment of the Jews for their "ignorance" (of Christ).

On the historical level only a few scholars consider Hegesippus and, to a certain extent, *2 Apoc. Jas.* to be possible keys to understanding the offense for which James is executed by Ananus.[146] According to Bauckham, since James is executed by stoning he must have been charged either with blasphemy or with leading the people to apostasy. He suggests that the charge against James is based on his Christological interpretation of "the gate of God" as "the gate of Jesus" as well as James's preaching that Jesus is the gate of the eschatological Temple through which the righteous enter the presence of God.[147] Evans, by contrast, *does* associate James's execution directly with the Temple even though his aim is purely exegetical. He does not attempt to draw actual historical conclusions from this fact.[148]

As far as we are concerned, it is important that Hegesippus, Clement, *Recognitions,* and even *2 Apoc. Jas* detail James's activities and interest in the Temple despite the fact that these authors no longer value the Jewish cultic system. Thus their descriptions are likely based on an older tradition rather than simply invented to suit their own contemporary agendas.

One aspect of possible historical value is the *means* of James's execution. In *2 Apoc. Jas* the priests literally want to stone James but throw him down from the height of the Temple instead and then "placed a stone on his abdomen." James is likewise thrown from the Temple in Hegesippus and Clement. In *Recognitions* he is thrown from the top of the stairs. According to Hegesippus, he is also stoned afterward. This type of punishment probably represents an early rabbinic version of the biblical stoning penalty: According to Mishnah *Sanhedrin* 6.4, someone condemned to be stoned must be pushed down from a place that is twice the height of a man. If this does not kill him, a witness must drop a large stone on his chest (as mentioned in *2 Apoc. Jas*); and if *that* does not kill him he must literally be stoned to death (as in Hegesippus). Thus all four sources describe the stoning of James, which is already mentioned by Josephus! We can conclude that they do provide at least a kernel of historical truth, albeit with changes and adjustments that reflect later rabbinic law.[149]

Significantly, however, all four sources place the stoning or throwing down in the Temple—which seems historically impossible. Their purpose is to relate as directly as possible the cause of James's execution to his involvement in the Temple even if this information is conveyed via fictitious narratives. Yet both the location of the execution and the transgressions attributed to James hint that the *real* reason for the stoning is in truth an illegal act on James's part that has something to do with the Temple. I therefore suggest that later authors transform an original conflict *related to* the Temple into a dramatic and legendary confrontation *inside* the Temple.

Indeed, the very manner in which James is put to death is connected to transgressions against the Temple: The final beating with a club described in both Hegesippus and Clement, as well as the use of an altar brand wielded by a priest described in *Recognitions,* is reminiscent of the ancient Jewish penalty for Temple transgressions. According to Mishnah *Sanhedrin* 9.6, a priest who serves in a state of impurity is executed by fellow priests outside of the Temple "by splitting his brain open with clubs." Furthermore, in the early, nonrabbinic penal code, trespassing the Temple's sacred domains (ascribed to James by Hegesippus) requires the death penalty, which is probably carried out by stoning (perhaps even without a trial).[150]

It is possible to conclude, then, that three of these texts attest to different sorts of offenses carried out either against the Temple or within it. Moreover, all four of them recall sanctions taken against transgressions of the Temple's sacredness. This common theme may point to an earlier Jewish-Christian tradition that connects James's execution to the Temple—one that, I believe, has historical roots. I find it reasonable to conclude that James preached the Christian doctrine *in the Temple*—much like Peter and the apostles—and perhaps said something that was interpreted as a declaration *against* the Temple (such as its coming destruction) in a manner reminiscent of his more famous brother. This leads to his being sentenced to stoning by Ananus son of Ananus, as recorded by Josephus.

The Historical Background of the High Priestly Prosecutions: Jesus's Anti-Temple Charge and the Sadducees' Sensitivity

Much like the high priestly persecutions and legal prosecutions of Peter, Stephen, and Paul in Acts, the traditions on James's execution regard the Temple as the locus and substance of the early Christians' conflict with Jewish leaders. Scenes of Christian interest and activity in the Temple as well as sanctions against and trials of Christians carried out by the high priests run across too many different texts and events to be regarded merely as a literary fiction. This tradition must contain some truth.

We have seen that, according to Luke, the apostles hold a positive view of the Temple, and in the preceding chapters we have seen that Jesus, Paul, Mark, and Matthew are all far from holding anti-Temple stances or aiming to replace it. There is no reason to think that the historical apostles felt otherwise. So why do the chief priests suspect that the early Christians endanger the Temple?

Turning to the historical aspects of these narratives, I will now examine two issues that may affect the harsh reactions of the Jewish leaders to the acts of the early Christian leaders in the Temple: accusations that Jesus threatens the Temple and the Sadducees' extreme sensitivity to any violation of the Temple's sacredness.

JESUS AS THE ENEMY OF THE TEMPLE

For the high priest, the chief priests, and their associates, Jesus is known as an enemy of the Temple. The very same high priest who tries Peter and the apostles also delivers Jesus to Pilate: Joseph Caiaphas.[151] Recall that Jesus is charged with leveling a threat against the Temple: "I will destroy this Temple that is made with hands, and in three days I will build another, not made with hands" (Mark 14:58), the content of which is repeated in the mockery of Jesus on the cross in Mark 15:29–30. This accusation is probably related to Jesus's cleansing of the Temple when he clashes with buyers and sellers of sacrificial animals and the money changers (Mark 11:15–17). As far as Caiaphas and the chief priests are concerned, he threatens the Temple in both deeds and words, perhaps calling for its destruction or anticipating it. As we saw in chapter 1, this charge is modified by the evangelists. Luke omits it from Jesus's trial and mockery, though it is implied in Stephen's trial. Matthew and John downplay it, and Mark, Matthew, and Luke (in Stephen's speech) argue that it is made by false witnesses. Their treatment of the charge shows that the evangelists are reacting to a real charge leveled against Jesus and/or his followers and subsequently attempt to deny it.

Reflections of Jesus's Temple charge can be found in later traditions, suggesting that the Jewish-Christians are suspected of plotting against the Temple. According to the gospel of Peter, the apostles stand accused of attempting to burn down the Temple, and a similar charge is made against Jewish heretics (*minim*) in early rabbinic literature.[152]

Returning to the Temple incidents described in Acts, these narratives would seem to provide a response to accusations of Jesus's sacrilegious intentions, showing that despite the severe measures taken against Peter, Stephen, and Paul, suspicions that they reject the Temple cult or seek its destruction are false. To the contrary, Peter and the apostles, like Paul (and, according to Hegesippus, James), actually want to participate in Temple rituals at any cost.

Moreover, Jesus's alleged anti-Temple stance increases the historical plausibility of the narratives of the Temple conflicts in Acts as well as the association of James's execution with the Temple. Given the unsavory reputation of the Christians in the eyes of the Temple authorities, it is understandable that the chief priests and their followers would regard Peter, Stephen, Paul, and James with suspicion and hostility when they enter the Temple or preach about it.

THE SADDUCEES IN DEFENSE OF THE TEMPLE

The chief priests' behavior can also be explained in light of the attitude of the Sadducean chief priests toward the Temple cult. In Acts, Hegesippus, *Recognitions,* and *2 Apoc. Jas,* the preaching and actions of the Christian leaders in the Temple are met with extreme sanctions by the chief priests or other Jewish leaders in the Temple. They are portrayed as hard-hearted defenders of the Temple against somewhat insignificant or merely symbolic threats. This, I maintain, results from the sensitivity of the Sadducean high priests to any possible violation of the sacredness of the sacrificial cult, as I discussed in chapter 1.

Here I will demonstrate that these are indeed Sadducees. Ananus son of Ananus, the high priest who executes James, "followed the school of the Sadducees" (*Ant.* 20. 199). The unnamed high priest who leads the prosecution of Peter and the apostles is also associated with the Sadducees ("the high priest and all who were with him, that is, the sect of the Sadducees," Acts 5:17) and should be identified with Joseph Caiaphas (note that Caiaphas also confronts James in *Recognitions*).[153] It is more than possible that the unnamed high priest who prosecutes Stephen as well as Ananias son of Nedebaus, who heads Paul's hearing before the Sanhedrin (Acts 23:2), are also Sadducees.[154]

The Pharisees, who oppose the Sadducees on legal matters and compete with them for religious influence, are not involved in the measures taken against the Christian leaders in Acts (although they do take part in James's execution in Hegesippus). In fact, Luke describes the Pharisees as *defending* the Christians: During the second judicial act against Peter and the apostles, when the members of the Sanhedrin express their willingness to execute them, Luke assigns to Gamaliel, "a Pharisee in the Sanhedrin," a speech in which he calls for releasing them without penalty. Consequently, the final punishment is reduced to flogging.[155] In Paul's hearing before the Sanhedrin, he declares himself a Pharisee who believes in resurrection, thus sparking a dispute between the Pharisees and the Sadducees, resulting in the following pronouncement by an unnamed pharisaic scribe: "We find nothing wrong with this man." In this instance the hearing ends without a decision (Acts 23:6–11). Indeed, the characterization of the Pharisees in Acts is always positive.[156]

According to Josephus, James's trial and execution by Ananus are opposed by "those of the inhabitants of the city who were considered the most fair-minded and who were strict in observance of the law." These people inform King Agrippa II and the Roman governor Albinus of Ananus's unacceptable deed, leading to his dismissal from the high priesthood (*Ant.* 20.201–202). Josephus's wording is similar to his usual characterization of the Pharisees.[157] Since this passage deals with a legal case led by a Saducean high priest, it is likely both that Ananus's opponents are none other than the Pharisees and that they resist the Saducean law invoked by Ananus.[158] Therefore, it seems that the Pharisees object to the severe punishment of James for his alleged act against the Temple.

Why are the Saducees particularly hostile concerning the involvement of Christian leaders in the Temple?[159] As I stated in chapter 1, the Saducees and especially the Saducean high priests have heightened sensitivity to any violation of the Temple's sacredness. In comparison to the Pharisees, for example, the Saducees hold a far stricter approach to the Temple's ritual purity and ascribe greater significance to the priestly cult. They regard both the Temple and the sacrificial cult as more sensitive and vulnerable to desecration and, in a certain sense, more sacred than do the Pharisees. To the Saducees, any possible violation of the cultic order or any potential desecration of the Temple is regarded as extremely dangerous.[160]

This Saducean cultic strictness demystifies many of the Temple episodes in Acts and underscores our reconstruction of James's execution; it also supports their historical reliability. It helps explain why the Saducees react so harshly and maliciously to the acts of Peter, Paul, and James in the Temple and to the supposed sayings of Jesus, Stephen, and James against it. It is not, therefore, the Saducees' rejection of Christian belief per se that underlines these conflicts, but their special sensitivity to threats against the Temple and to any possible violation of its sacredness.

Results: The Consequences of Temple Attendance

On the narrative level, my analysis of relevant texts shows that the Temple incidents described in Acts in which Peter and the apostles as well as Paul are involved—in addition to the one described in Hegesippus concerning James—all attest to concern for the Temple. True, James's condemnation of the Temple is found in the second-century *2 Apoc. Jas*, but even here and in *Recognitions* the authors presume a certain interest on the part of James in the Temple. It therefore appears to be true that the earliest traditions concerning the early Jerusalem church largely regard the Temple in a favorable manner.

The Temple conflicts described in Acts and the connection between James's actions and a certain transgression against the Temple all seem historically plausible for several reasons: (1) Luke's extraordinary appreciation of the Temple runs counter to Temple conflicts described in his narrative in which Stephen and Paul are accused of holding an anti-Temple stance. Since Luke's narrative aims to defy these accusations, it is virtually impossible that they are figments of his imagination. (2) The pattern of Christian attendance in the Temple leading to an arrest, trial, and punishment is repeated too many times—both in Acts and in later traditions about James— to be regarded as merely a literary device. Indeed, even if certain episodes are reproduced or exaggerated, it is nonetheless reasonable to conclude that they are based on older traditions that emerge from historical experience. (3) These conflicts cohere with the Jewish perception of Jesus and his followers as enemies of the Temple. (4) The Sadducean sensitivity to possible threats to the sacrificial cult explains the chief priests' persecutions of the early Christians leaders.

If we take this conclusion one step further, there is reason to believe that the actual attitude toward the Temple displayed by Peter, Paul, and James is not very different from that of their fellow Jews.[161] Indeed, the sources discussed here do not justify the assumption that the Christian leaders' clashes with the high priests derive from the formers' attempts to gain a measure of control over the Temple.[162] Nor do they support the view (refuted above) that the Jerusalem community regards itself as a "human Temple" that can serve as a substitution for the physical one"

It is ironic, then, that, according to Acts and the traditions about James, attempts by early Christians to involve themselves in Temple life or to use its setting or ritual cult for their own interests result in clashes with Jewish leaders, particularly the Sadducean high priests—and with tragic results. It is tempting to conclude that their somewhat naïve attempt to combine Christian belief with common Jewish religious devotion is in fact what gets them into trouble.

Conclusions: The Temple as a Jewish Identity Marker

I am now in a position to summarize the findings of sections I and II. In the gospel of Luke, Jesus visits and teaches at the Temple more than in any other gospel. Tensions in relation to the Temple are reduced, including the shortening of the cleansing and complete omission of the charge about threatening to destroy the Temple. In the Acts of the Apostles, the apostles and Paul teach or heal in the Temple. Paul purifies himself before entering it and takes care of the sacrifice of Christian Nazirites. Even Stephen's speech need not be interpreted as the rejection of the cult. Luke stresses the hour of the Tamid daily sacrifice and prayer in the Temple, both public and private. The importance of the Temple and its cult and the loyalty of Jesus—and even more so that of the apostles—to the Temple is one of Luke's major themes.

Luke is also at pains to show that accusations of mistreatment of the Temple against Peter and the apostles, Stephen, and Paul are completely false. They are interested in being at the Temple or express positive views about it but are nonetheless persecuted and prosecuted by the chief priests and their associates. And still Luke shows respect to the chief priests and never condemns them directly.

This focus on the Temple and its cult may attest to Luke's embracing of one aspect of the priestly worldview within Second Temple Judaism.[163] Luke is more occupied than the other gospels with the notion of repentance and forgiveness of sins.[164] My point is not that he believes that the Temple cult is an exclusive or primary mode for attaining atonement. Indeed, he never relates atonement to the Temple. Coping with sin is common to both Luke and priestly circles, including the Sadducees and the Qumran sects. Luke simply holds that the best place and way to be close to God is the Temple.

Luke's gospel gives the Temple more weight than Mark and Matthew, although he rewrites Mark and Q in a later period, when the Jerusalem Temple has been in ruins for at least a generation. He develops the role of the Temple in his history of the Jerusalem community in the Acts of the Apostles. Despite the persecutions of Jesus and the Christian leaders by the chief priests, he does not condemn them as unworthy of their office. While there is implied criticism of the Temple establishment in his narrative in Luke–Acts, there is no sign of its rejection or posing of new alternatives to take its place.

Why is Luke, of all the NT authors, so favorable of the Temple and the cult when they no longer exist? Why is the Temple so important to him? Hans Conzelmann, who maintains that Luke sees Christianity as the heir of Judaism, concludes that Luke focuses attention on Jerusalem and the Temple in order to grant continuity to Israel's salvation history. Christianity is a Gentile phenomenon free of the Law and the Temple, but the church aims to be the legitimate heir of Israel. Thus Luke uses the Temple as a means of legitimation of a new religious phenomenon, a bridge between Judaism and Christianity.[165]

This explanation is not accepted by a more recent scholarly trend. As already mentioned, recent scholarship (following Jervell) disagrees with Ernst Haenchen, Conzelmann, and many others that Luke aims to dissociate Christianity from Judaism. It seems more accurate to regard Luke's view of Judaism in a more favorable light: as an integral part of the Jewish world, announcing God's salvation of both Jews and Gentiles.[166]

Rather than seeing apologetics here Esler points to the positive symbolism of the Temple for Luke. The theme of the Temple actually substitutes for the now-destroyed Temple. It is a central component of the symbolic universe of the early Christians. Esler, I think, reaches the right answer but for the wrong reason. He argues that the advantage of transforming the Temple from reality to a symbol is that it suits the needs of the non-Jewish (God-fearers) Christians: they cannot be banned from a symbolic Temple. He suggests that a God-fearer who stays at Solomon's portico while his Jewish associates are getting into the Temple courts at the Tamid sacrifice rite becomes ambivalent toward the Temple. He sees the beauty of the Temple but is prevented from approaching closely to the presence of God and participating in the cult. He remains an outsider, experiencing marginalization. This may lead Luke to a certain reluctance or remoteness toward the Temple.[167]

This explanation does not hold for Luke, who, in ca. 90 CE, writes for readers who do not visit the Temple. Luke does not need to address the problem of non-Jews' inaccessibility to the sacred, since nobody can approach it anyway, especially if he writes in the Diaspora, outside Judaea. Furthermore, Luke does not try to relate non-Jewish-Christians to the Temple (in Acts 21:29 he denies that Paul let Trophimus the Ephesian into the Temple). He even omits from Jesus's reciting of Isa 56:7 that the Temple will be a house of prayer "for all the nations" (Luke 19:46)!

We must assume that the Temple is a key symbol for Luke's readers, and there is no reason to think it is relevant only for the Jews among them. It is rooted in Luke's message no less than the notion that non-Jews can and should join Christianity without circumcision. And since the Temple is no longer a living institution but a symbol of the relationship between God and Israel, it can apply to both Jews and non-Jews. Admittedly, it does give Jewish members a preference, albeit theoretical, since they feel "at home" there. Perhaps this is somewhat balanced by Stephen's speech, but when the Temple is transformed into a memory or a concept, the non-Jews can feel attached to it as much as they like.

The Temple is not only a Jewish symbol. For Jewish and Gentile Christians alike it symbolizes Judaism. That Jesus and the apostles attend the Temple and respect the cult are, for Luke and his readers, indications that they are Jews both pious toward God and faithful to the Jewish tradition. As we saw in section II, Acts has a very apologetic flavor, showing that Peter, Stephen, and Paul do not do or say anything offensive in or about the Temple. Luke also omits signs of Jesus's alleged threat to the Temple.

But it is not enough to say that Luke wants to protect Christians from charges made by other Jews. There must be a reason why Luke is so protective and wants to reject accusations of disloyalty to Judaism. The reason is, I suggest, that Luke sees himself attached to Judaism, whether or not he is of Jewish origin or circumcised. His message is that Christianity is not only loyal to its Jewish roots; it *is* Judaism! The Temple belongs to the Christians as much as to other Jews. The idea of the Temple connects his readers to Judaism. Through the stories about the Temple and the sensibilities expressed toward it, readers can and should feel like Jews whether or not they actually are Jews. The Temple theme enables Luke to present Christianity as if it is mainstream Judaism.

6 The Gospel of John: Temple and Christology

Introduction

JESUS REPLACES THE TEMPLE

Jesus visits the Temple several times in the gospel of John and relates to the Temple directly in two sayings. Scholarship on the Temple in John is almost unanimous in seeing Jesus as a replacement for the Temple[1]—though some recently published work joins an opposing minority view.[2]

According to the replacement theory, "the Johannine Jesus replaces and fulfills the Jerusalem Temple and its cultic activity . . . there is therefore no future for the old Temple and its sacrifices. God no more dwells within its walls, and its sacrifices have been replaced by Jesus . . . Jesus is now the house of the Father."[3] The religious (or perhaps theological) justification for assuming such a far-reaching transformation from ancient Judaism to Johannine Christianity is that Jesus is consecrated by God (10:36), possessing both the divine glory and the divine name (17:1–26).[4] This radical shift is sometimes compared to that of the early rabbis in Yavne after the destruction of the Temple in 70 CE. They replace a Temple-centered religion (or belief system) with a Torah-centered religion, whereas John replaces this iteration of the religion with Jesus.[5] John thus reacts to the destruction by searching for another substitute for the lost Temple. Indeed, the entire gospel may be viewed as a response to the religious vacuum or trauma left by the destruction of the Temple.[6] However, it is not totally clear what John introduces in place of the Jerusalem Temple. Is it a heavenly Temple such as the one described in Hebrews and Revelation? (While such a Temple is not described in John, some think that it is presumed.) Or is it an eschatological Temple, such as the one depicted in Ezekiel 47:1–11?[7]

Despite relative consensus about Jesus replacing the Temple in some form, the manner in which Jesus is described as fulfilling the function of the Temple and the sacrificial cult is not explored in depth. In what sense are the parallels or equivalences between Jesus and the Temple established by John? Are there cultic symbols or biblical terms related to the Temple that shift the role of the Temple to Jesus? When does John explicitly present Jesus as a replacement for the Temple, and when is this role merely reconstructed by theological exegesis?

John is a highly complex gospel. It can be understood at various levels of narrative and meaning.[8] It sometimes conceals or intentionally complicates its message. Readers must distinguish between plain and concealed messages, determining for themselves the exact meaning of what is layered within the text. Its language is full of symbols and imagery.[9] Jesus Christ's extremely close relationship with God—as the Father's Son, logos, and divine light—is the central message of the gospel. This, I suggest, may also be the key to understanding the relationship between Jesus and the Temple.

In trying to understand what the author thinks about the Temple, we need to agree on the context guiding our analysis: What previous knowledge does John assume that his readers already have about Jesus when first encountering this gospel? What are readers' backgrounds and approaches toward Jewish tradition, Law, and identity? My working hypothesis holds that John's readers are already familiar with the story of Jesus from texts such as Mark, which supports the belief that Jesus is Christ and the Son of God.[10]

JOHN AND JUDAISM: THE LAW AND THE JEWS

The fourth gospel is well known for its religious innovation, spirituality, and "high Christology."[11] This fact, I suspect, leads many to think that John rejects the Law, or the Torah either partly or entirely.[12] Nevertheless, John alludes to many Jewish institutions and practices which he seems to believe carry validity, as he does not question them.[13] When it comes to direct evidence, John does not posit any explicit criticism of Jewish legal practices or traditions.

According to John, following Jesus means abiding by the Law (7:17, 19). Jesus fulfills the Law, and his opponents misunderstand this (7:23). Yet in order to do the will of God and reach salvation it is not enough to obey the Law; one must also believe in Christ. The Law has a positive function as long as it leads to Christ. The Jews, however, understand the Law as the opposite of Christ.[14] John thus has a different understanding of the Law than "normative Judaism" owing to its relationship with Jesus.[15]

According to Loader, John holds not only that Jewish legal and religious practices have validity but also that Jesus is associated with the Torah. And yet the author uses the Law to legitimize the authority of Christ: "John has Jesus claim the Jewish heritage, but as something both preliminary and inferior to what he brings." Law and Scripture are only "a pointer to Christ."[16] In a sense, John "reflects the strongest Jewish ethos of all of the gospels as well as the sharpest break from Judaism."[17]

The term "the Jews" (*Ioudaioi*) is used in John more than thirty times in a polemical manner, showing enormous hostility toward non-Christian Jews (or at least some portion of them). But at the same time, Jesus himself is identified as a Jew (4:9b, 22; 18:35). Scholars debate if the gospel's negativity concerning "the Jews" relates to Jewish leaders and authorities, the people of Judaea but not all Jews, all Jews everywhere or Jesus's adversaries—the elitist Jews in contrast to the nonelite Judeans, or Israelites.[18]

The theme of Jewishness is complex. Religious innovations of John are often fundamental and far-reaching, suggesting that John is far removed from traditional Judaism. After the "cleansing," Jesus proposes new rites of membership (3:3–5), new feasts, new benefits prayed for and given at feasts, and new food, including both bread and lamb.[19] And Johannine Christology is revolutionary in attributing divine status to Jesus (1:17; 6:38–40; 17:5; 20:28).

At the same time, John's outlook is essentially Jewish, and his main audience probably consists of Jews.[20] In fact, the author hardly mentions Gentiles at all. His main reference group is "Israel" (1:31, 47; 3:10; 12:13). John addresses the question: Who is the "True Jew?" (The answer is the one who believes in Christ.) Moreover, if Judaism is condemned, it is always from within and not from without.[21] Johannine polemics against contemporary Jews does not negate their common ground. For instance, Jesus says to the Samaritan woman that "salvation is of the Jews" (4:22). Unlike Josephus, for example, John never mentions the corruption of the priesthood, the defilement of the Temple, or the ineffectiveness of sacrifices.[22]

Some explain the contradiction between traditional Jewish and "anti-Jewish" or innovative characteristics by assuming two chronological layers in the gospel. John reflects a period after a break with Judaism, and his audience includes non-Jewish-Christians—especially if one reads John in light of the Johannine epistles (though they probably represent a later phase!). But his gospel also contains earlier phases of inter-Jewish conflict and discourse, including the issue of exclusion from the synagogue.[23]

Instead of making a preliminary judgment concerning this complexity, I prefer not to take for granted that the traditional sacrificial system is irrelevant for John or his audience. John and his readers are still not (fully?) detached from commitment to the Law and their Jewish religious identity, practically or symbolically. They surely complicate this commitment, but they do not forsake it.

The "Cleansing" of the Temple and the Temple of Jesus's Body

"The Passover of the Jews was near, and Jesus went up to Jerusalem. In the Temple he found people selling cattle, sheep, and doves, and the money-changers seated at their tables. Making a whip of cords, he drove all of them out of the temple, both the sheep and the cattle. He also poured out the coins of the money-changers and overturned their tables. He told those who were selling the doves, 'Take these things out of here! Stop making my Father's house a market-place!' His disciples remembered that it was written, 'Zeal for your house will consume me.' The Jews then said to him, 'What sign can you show us for doing this?' Jesus answered them, 'Destroy this Temple, and in three days I will raise it up.' The Jews then said, 'This Temple has been under construction for forty-six years, and will you raise it up in three days?' But he was speaking of the temple of his body." (2:13–22)

In contrast to the synoptic gospels, in which the cleansing appears in the final third of the narrative, John places it near the beginning of his gospel. There are some significant differences in the details as well. As we saw in chapter 1, most scholars regard the synoptic version as being closer to historical events, while few think that John's version of the cleansing is more accurate.[24]

THE CLEANSING AS A REJECTION OF THE TEMPLE CULT

It is almost a given in NT scholarship that the cleansing in John is an anti-Temple act.[25] But perhaps John's Jesus protests only against the profanation of the Temple by commerce (2:16), while still acknowledging the cult. Or does he express total rejection of the sacrificial cult that will be replaced by Jesus himself?[26] Since trade is inevitable at the Temple, the rejection of trade signifies, according to some commentators, the end of animal sacrifices![27] In addition, Jesus's phrase "my Father's house" (2:16) allegedly indicates that the Temple is Jesus's own house. Hence he has authority over the Temple and also becomes the alternative to the Temple.[28]

Jesus's provocative saying "destroy [*ean lusate*] this Temple and in three days I will raise [or restore] [*egerō*] it up" (2:19) is a complex one. Is it an ironic remark suggesting that if the Jewish leaders continue their behavior, the Temple will be destroyed? Or does Jesus actually foresee the destruction, expecting its replacement rather than renewal?[29] According to Raymond Brown, it contains two levels of meaning: While the Jews understand Jesus to be referring to the messianic rebuilding of the Jerusalem Temple, he is referring to himself, namely, his resurrection.[30] Indeed, the question is what is destroyed and rebuilt here: Jesus or a physical Temple.[31]

This interpretation builds on the phrase "the temple of his body." When the Jews at the Temple doubt how the physical Temple—"which has been under construction for forty-six years"—can be raised up in three days, John 2:21 interprets Jesus's saying about destroying and raising "this Temple" as a reference to "the temple of his body" (*tou nauo to sōmatos hautou*). There is a parallelism or at least a linkage between the destruction of the Temple (*naos*) and Jesus's body: the moral or figurative destruction of the Temple parallels the destruction of the body of Jesus, and the building of the new Temple takes place via the resurrection of Jesus—perhaps "the Temple of the new age is Christ."[32] This may be a simple replacement, so that believers enter into a living communion with the Father through Jesus[33]—the new heavenly Temple[34] or the eschatological Temple.[35] But in what sense is Jesus's body a Temple? The simplest explanation seems to be that the flesh/body of Jesus reveals the divine glory, just as the Temple reveals the glory of God for Israel (cf. Isa 6:1–5).[36]

We have seen two general typical readings of the Johannine "cleansing." One assumes a negative stance toward the Temple from the start, holding that the episode "inaugurates a theme of 'replacement' by Jesus in regard to Israel's sacred space, feast days, and sacred object petitioned."[37] The other shifts from the present Temple to the eschatological one, which will be without blemish and perhaps where no sacrifices will be offered.[38] However, the question remains as to how far this eschatological Temple is identified with Jesus and on what basis.

A NEW READING: JESUS'S PARADOXICAL INTERACTION
WITH THE SACRED

I would like to suggest a systematic interpretation that challenges this approach, dividing the episode into five parts and examining each one of them independently: the physical act; the disciples' reflections upon Jesus's zeal for the Temple; Jesus's saying against commerce; Jesus's declaration concerning his ability to rebuild the Temple from ruins; and John's explanation that Jesus actually refers to the "temple of his body." My point of departure is that we should not interpret the previous parts in light of the last one against their plain and literal meaning but see them as a part of a narrative arc built gradually.

The Act of "Cleansing"

The banishment of the sellers of doves and animals alongside the turning back of the money changers in John is quite similar to the description in Mark 11:15–16. John stresses Jesus's violence, adding that he drives all of them out of the Temple using a whip of cords. John's interpretation of the cleansing should not be substantially different from that of Mark: a physical act directed at the Jerusalem Temple as a religious institution.

The plain narrative of Jesus coming to the Temple Mount as a pilgrim (as indicated by the use of *anebē* in v. 13) before Passover reflects customary worship by the Jews at the Temple. Jesus's efforts to change the manner in which money and animals designated to be offered on the altar change hands before entering the inner courts attest to his desire for reform. It shows that the cult matters to Jesus. Or perhaps Jesus actually rejects the entire concept of animal sacrifice but is only initially able to interrupt the sellers and money changers.

Zeal for the Temple

If Jesus rejects animal sacrifice in general, the author needs to state such an extremely revolutionary message explicitly, since it is unexpected by the reader. Here reflecting upon zeal for the Temple becomes meaningful. John notes that the disciples recall Ps 69:9 that "zeal for your house will consume me," not zeal against the house/Temple.[39] That is, they think Jesus cares for the integrity and sacredness of the cult and wants to protect it. They also regard his act as the one that finally leads to his crucifixion. The disciples' perspective is important since it is assumed to precede the author's. John's decision to use this tradition in this specific context demonstrates that he shares a similar perspective: Jesus is zealous in his support for the Temple.[40]

Against Commerce in the Temple

The saying "Stop making my Father's house a market-place" (2:16) that John attributes to Jesus is missing from the synoptic gospels. This early interpretation of Jesus's act is also a reasonable one. Namely, Jesus protests against the exchange of animals and money near the sacred place of worship. I suggested in chapter 1 that the Historical Jesus takes issue with the problem of immorality and wealth in the "cleansing." John's criticism of trade at the Temple reflects his own interpretation of Jesus's approach toward the Jerusalem Temple.

That Jesus opposes trade on the Temple Mount does not mean that he also rejects the sacrificial cult.[41] Nor does it necessarily imply wishing for an alternative eschatological Temple. His action may be a specific and relatively limited criticism, though practically unrealistic owing to the enormous numbers of visitors and sacrifices brought to it. Yet John writes decades after the destruction, when this impractical aspect no longer plays a role. His message is that Jesus wants the Jerusalem Temple maintained without the involvement of commercial self-interest or monetary profit, preserving the ethical integrity of the sacred.

This passage does not relate to the eschatological Temple.[42] The event described takes place in the earthly Jerusalem Temple. It is a practical and physical protest against commerce at the Temple's margins. John's Jesus seems to demand that this situation be fixed immediately, not in an abstract future. Later, Jesus returns to the Temple several times during the festivals without further criticism of the cult, attesting to his interest in the Temple cult.

Jesus refers to the Temple as "my Father's house" (2:16). This is a very emphatic way to express his relationship to the Temple. The Temple is of the Father—meaning God—and Jesus is God's son. He feels at home in the Temple and cares for its sacredness. He is not identical with the Temple since the Temple is "the house." Jesus expresses attachment to the earthly Jerusalem Temple owing to his closeness to his Father, but this is also the very same "house" he attempts to "cleanse" of commerce. There is no hint of religious critique of animal sacrifices and priestly rites. Rather, the present Temple is still the House of God. And, as we have seen, the disciples recall Jesus as being zealous for the Temple, that is, enthusiastic about maintaining its sacredness. Thus far we see no sign of spiritualization of the Temple or reference to either an eschatological or heavenly Temple. The problem addressed in this text exists in the here and now, at the Jerusalem Temple.

Destroy and Rebuild the Temple

The turning point occurs when the Jewish leaders ask for "a sign." Jesus is asked to explain the awkward act of the turning back and banishing of the traders. His provocative statement that he can rebuild the Temple is a version of an accusation found in the Jesus trial scene in Mark 14:58, which is also reflected in Stephen's trial in Acts 6:14. Here it is put in the mouth not of (false) witnesses but of Jesus himself, who declares, "Destroy this Temple, and in three days I will raise it up" (2:19). He does not say he intends to destroy it. If, for some reason, the Jewish leaders destroy the Temple,[43] he will be able to rebuild it. Up to here the passage deals with the earthly Jerusalem Temple, and the leaders naturally understand Jesus's saying as referring to the rebuilding of the Herodian Temple. They reply that it is impossible to rebuild the Temple within three days since it took forty-six years to build it.

Echoes of parallel passages in other gospels complicate Jesus's saying for later readers. John is using the saying attributed to Jesus by his opponents and, as we saw in chapter 1, Mark, Matthew, and Luke deny its credibility. Mark and Matthew use the version that Jesus will rebuild the Temple "in three days," and Mark also adds that this will be a Temple "not made with hands." The nonphysical character of the rebuilt Temple may provide an answer to the puzzlement of the Jewish leaders. That is, *if* John and his readers have the earlier Markan version in mind, they may think that Jesus does not plan to rebuild the Temple by his own hands—and perhaps the new Temple that he will build is not made with hands at all. In any case, Jesus's saying implies a certain challenge to the Jerusalem Temple, yet it is phrased in a way that suggests Jesus does not threaten to destroy the Temple (as seen in the accusation posed against Jesus in Mark, Matthew, and Acts). He only has the ability to restore it after its destruction.

The puzzlement of the Jewish leaders underscores their failure to understand that Jesus does not mean to rebuild the earthly Temple. Still, the magnificent Jerusalem Temple built by Herod and his successors no longer existed when the gospel was written. The "destroy" part had already occurred. It is time to see how Jesus rebuilds the Temple. Here—between "destroy" and "rebuild"—the transformation of the meaning of the word "Temple" takes place.

"The Temple of His Body"

The Temple that Jesus claims to rebuild is not a building. Next, John identifies it with Jesus's body. But the destroyed Temple is indeed the Jerusalem Temple. In "destroy this Temple" John uses a double meaning. The gospel refers to the destruction of the Temple in 70 CE, but at the same time it refers to the death and resurrection of Jesus.

The message of this statement is not that the Temple cult is no longer legitimate but that it no longer exists. After 70 CE, when the Herodian construction no longer stands and the sacrificial cult does not function, Jesus is the alternative. Given the circumstances at the time in which John is written, Jesus is the alternative to the worship of God in the Temple.

When reading the act of cleansing again in this context, one may object and argue that Jesus foresees the destruction coming because of trade on the outskirts of the Temple—that something inappropriate happening in the Temple years before justifies Jesus becoming a substitute for the Temple later. But if this is true, John's narrative also shows that Jesus does his best to remedy the situation but fails.

When John creates this complex construct of double meaning, we should bear in mind that he already holds two key traditions: first, Jesus's act in the Temple is historical; and, second, that the accusation of the destruction/rebuilding of the Temple described by Mark is regarded by most Christians as false and attributed to false witnesses. John ties them together in one episode, which is a logical step. If Jesus actually says something like this, it most likely takes place on the Temple Mount when he gets furious and overturns the tables. Nonetheless, many fail to see both the "stitches" or gaps between the different elements of the passage. There is nothing in the act of the cleansing itself that hints at the rebuilding of the Temple or at the identification of Jesus with the Temple. John needs to cite the misunderstanding of the Jewish leaders, their mention of the Herodian Temple, and the odd presentation of the Temple as Jesus's body in order to encourage this connection.

As much as its intent to identify Jesus as the Temple seems logical, the innovative phrase "the temple of his body" should be somewhat qualified. While John implies a catchy analogy paralleling the destruction and rebuilding of the Temple with Jesus's death and resurrection, we should not make too much of it. Nothing in the episode leads the reader to believe that an earthly Temple is invalid. Jesus's body is associated with the Temple after the reader has already been informed that he very much cares for the integrity or moral stance of the Temple cult when he banishes the traders and after John implies that the Herodian Temple is already destroyed.[44]

The reference to the body as representing Jesus seems to hint at his bodily resurrection and perhaps also to the rite by which one interacts with Jesus's body—the Eucharist.[45] Paul already associates the believer's body with Jesus's body as well as with a temple (*naos*) of the Holy Spirit

(1 Cor 6:15, 19). As we saw in chapter 2, the believers are not actually equal to the Jerusalem Temple but possess some of its sacred features, parts of Jesus's body in a figural speech.[46]

If John's understanding of the imagery of Jesus's body resembles that of Paul, the implication is that John means that Jesus's body is *like* a Temple. This corresponds with his zeal for a Temple without trade, referring to the Jerusalem Temple as "my Father's house" and stressing the holiness of the earthly Temple. If Jesus is to be the true Temple—better than the earthly one—this would contradict the previous positive outlook on the Temple. When Jesus is described as the protector of the Temple cult, it is difficult to see him as suddenly better than the Temple.

The reader's response to the destroy/rebuild saying is that Jesus provides a certain solution to the fact that the Temple is destroyed. The transference from the Temple to Jesus operates in an intriguing and paradoxical way. As Jesus's attachment and devotion to the Jerusalem Temple are stressed, the analogy of the Temple to his body becomes more charged and powerful. He is worthy of becoming like the Temple because of his piety toward the Temple.

The manner in which he rebuilds the Temple turns out to be symbolic. Jesus's Temple is ultimately manifest in his body, but only in a figurative sense. The Temple that Jesus will build turns out to be not a real Temple but one that relies upon the real Temple as a symbol or template. The sense of Jesus's body should be grasped in light of other Johannine symbols. These include the bread of life (6:35), the good shepherd (10:11), the light of the world (8:12), the door for salvation (10:9), and the vine (15:5)—all metaphors that cannot be taken literally. Indeed, they are meaningful only if understood figuratively.[47] The Temple of Jesus's body is introduced in the same vein, although the metaphor is structured differently.

"The temple of his body" is therefore a metaphor or an analogy. John is able to introduce this symbol as a message of Jesus's destroying/rebuilding saying by employing conventional narrative tools, inserting it into the cleansing episode using the narrator's voice. It is a striking analogy for the reader but is meant to set the tone for the understanding of Jesus throughout the gospel. Yet its meaning still remains obscure at that early stage. Does it mean that Jesus is holy like the Temple? Or should the Jews worship God through Jesus—at least in some sense—just as they used to do in the Temple? John develops this perspective further in chapter 4.

Gerizim, Jerusalem, or Spirit and Truth (John 4:20–24)

In John 4 Jesus passes through a Samaritan village and meets a Samaritan woman. Their conversation concerns the relationship between Jews and Samaritans and eventually broaches the topic of their holy places. The episode discusses the legitimacy of the Jerusalem Temple and also shows the Samaritans' acceptance of Jesus as "the savior of the world" (4:42). The encounter with the Samaritan woman highlights the Jewishness of Jesus. She notices immediately that he is a Jew (4:9). She also states that "our ancestors worshipped on this mountain, but you [namely, the Jews] say that the place where people must worship is in Jerusalem" (4:20). The relationship between Jews and Samaritans lies in the background of this scene, which ends when the Samaritans accept a Jew as their messiah.

GERIZIM OR JERUSALEM? "SALVATION IS FROM THE JEWS"

Jesus turns to the Samaritan woman, who has just associated Jesus with the Jews and their sacred center at Jerusalem, and says, "You worship what you do not know; we worship what we know, for salvation is from the Jews" (4:22). Here Jesus juxtaposes implicitly the Samaritan belief in or worship on (*proskunein*) Mount Gerizim with Jewish belief in the sacredness of Jerusalem and the Temple on Mount Zion. This is an issue Jews and Samaritans had been debating vigorously since the Hellenistic period.[48] The first part of the sentence juxtaposes both places—each ethnic group worships what they "know" or "do not know,"[49] namely, following their respective traditions. The second part of the sentence gives preference to the Jewish sacred place. There is a kind of criticism of the Samaritan religious ethos, since their place of worship is based on an error: they worship what they "do not know."[50] Then comes the surprisingly bold declaration that "salvation is from the Jews" (*hē sōtēria ek tōn Ioudaiōn estin*). This Judeo-centric slogan criticizes Samaritans for their religious beliefs[51] but may also apply to Gentiles—some of whom are probably among the readers of the gospel. The phrase is also exceptional since on other occasions in John "the Jews" do not really "know" crucial things about faith in God.[52]

The statement "salvation is from the Jews" regards Judaism as being superior to Samaritan belief and religious practice and once again gives preference to the Jerusalem Temple over the one on Mount Gerizim (which is destroyed by the Hasmoneans). But John's Jesus may also hint about himself both as a Jew and as a savior. Salvation is *from* (*ek*) the Jews because Jesus is a Jew. And while salvation comes from the Jews—or at least one specific individual Jew—this statement does not deny the possibility that non-Jews will also be saved.[53] Indeed, the episode shows that the Samaritans accept Jesus as a savior. But at the same time, John seems to imply that in doing so the Samaritans implicitly acknowledge the superiority of Judaism. All of these factors implicitly support the religious validity of the Jerusalem Temple in comparison with that of its major competitor, the Samaritan sacred place, the ruined Temple on Mount Gerizim.

WORSHIP IN SPIRIT AND TRUTH

Jesus says to the Samaritan woman, "But the hour is coming, and is now here when the true worshippers will worship the Father in spirit and truth, for the Father seeks such as these to worship him; God is spirit, and those who worship him must worship in spirit and truth" (4:23–24).

"Worship in spirit and truth" may be read in a general sense as sincere faith in God, as both spirit and truth allude to God. Spirit (*pneuma*) is the means of God's operation in the world, an expression of God's immanence. God communicates with humans through the spirit. It is the highest element in the human being, not requiring the aid of corporal objects and fixed cult (or a certain place).[54] Truth is also one of God's main characteristics.[55] In John, truth (*aletheia*) means eternal reality as revealed to men. The spirit is an experience of this truth.[56] Spirit and truth are thus introduced by John's Jesus as the true Temple of God, and this seems to be preferable to the Temple.[57]

More popular, however, is the view that true worship of the Father "in spirit and truth" refers to belief in Jesus as Christ. In John, truth is achieved through Jesus (1:17; 8:32), and the spirit testifies to Jesus and glorifies him (15:26; 16:13–15). It is even argued that the Holy Spirit, who is the Paraclete, is a kind of manifestation of Jesus. Jesus's message is also said to be truth in 17:17 as well as in 14:6.[58]

The author uses "but" (*alla*) when turning from discussing the places of worship of both Samaritans and Jews to the spirit and truth. This implies that the former lack such spirit and truth. It therefore seems that the latter is a better alternative than both places of worship. The "true worshipers" (*ampelos alēthinē*) are those who worship "in spirit and truth"—because "God is spirit," implying the denial of locative worship. Jesus speaks of the coming of "the hour," a realized eschatology of worship in spirit and truth.

Some see this as a reference to the "hour" of Jesus's death, resurrection, and ascension (12:27; 13:1; 17:1), yet another proof that worship in spirit and truth is akin to worship of Jesus.[59] The narrative thus transforms a locative category (Gerizim vs. Jerusalem) to a spiritual one that maintains eschatological hope: spirit and truth meant for Jews and Samaritans alike, not bounded by geographical limitations.[60] At the same time, spirit and truth concern both Jesus's future and the present of the author and his readers.[61]

Here John's Jesus challenges the very concept of the Jerusalem Temple, even regarding it as any other locus or space of worship.[62] But is Jesus the new Temple, perhaps the eschatological one? Is Jesus, the spirit and truth, "the eschatological replacement of the temporal, earthly sanctuary of the Jerusalem Temple . . . a different type of worship in a new kind of Temple?"[63] If John wants to introduce Jesus as a new kind of Temple which usurps the previous one, why would he stress that Jesus prefers the Jewish mountain of worship over the Samaritan one: "You worship what you do not know; we worship what we know, for salvation is from the Jews"? It is unlikely that John wishes to show that the cult in the Jerusalem Temple is not valid to begin with, as the passage uses the Samaritan place of worship to credit the Jewish Temple as the better one.[64] And since 4:23 relates to when "the hour is coming" in the future, "spirit and truth" should be connected to the future from the perspective of Jesus. This future pertains to the destruction of the Jerusalem Temple in 70 CE, at which point "Jesus is the answer to the fall of the Temple."[65]

Another indication of the post-70 *Sitz im Leben* of the alternative to the Temple is the comparison of this Jewish holy place to that of the Samaritans. The Temple on Mount Gerizim is destroyed completely by John Hyrcanus in 111 CE.[66] Nonetheless, the Samaritans continue uninterruptedly to worship at the place it had stood (and not the Temple itself), developing their self-identity in contrast to the Jews vis-à-vis its sacredness. Jesus refers to the two *mountains* (4:20–21), not to either of the temples. Thus the author seems to take for granted that these sites have the same status—that of a holy place on which a temple used to stand.

When John equates the Jerusalem Temple Mount with Mount Gerizim (which even the Jews acknowledge as a sacred place, as it is the mountain of blessing in Deut 11:29; 27:12), he reduces the Jewish Temple to a mountain. But John does not degrade the sacredness of the Temple Mount, since spirit and truth do not replace a functioning cult. Spirit and truth are an alternative to a Temple that no longer exists.

John therefore uses the meeting with the Samaritan as a setting for posing an alternative—namely, spirit and truth—to Jewish devotion toward the Jerusalem Temple after it is already in ruins. Since the woman as well as many later Samaritans from that city believe that Jesus is the Messiah, John surely means that alternative worship is through/in Jesus. But John is careful not to claim crudely that Jesus is the new Temple. He poses spiritual worship as preferable to *locative* worship, relating to holy places rather than actual sanctuaries. If one would follow the Johannine Christology of Jesus · as spirit and truth (as well as logos, bread, etc.), one would find that Jesus is the substitution for the Temple *Mount.*

John 4 uses the Samaritan faith to show that Jesus is the spiritual alternative. The reason for this, I suggest, is not merely John's appeal to Samaritans or a recollection of the mission to the Samaritans.[67] When John compares the Jerusalem Temple Mount with Mount Gerizim, he reduces the (destroyed) Temple to a mere sacred mountain. To replace a sacred mountain with spirit and truth is a completely different matter than arguing that Jesus takes the place of the Jerusalem Temple while the sacrifice cult and pilgrimage are still practiced. In a sense, the Samaritan faith is John's straw man.

Jesus as Tabernacle?

In his famous prologue John introduces the word/logos as residing within the Johannine community: "And the Word became flesh and *lived* among us, and we have seen his glory, the glory as of a father's only son, full of grace and truth" (1:14). The Greek word for "lived" is *eskēnōsen.* Since the verb *skēnoō* evokes the noun *skēnē,* "Tabernacle," many translate it as "tabernacling."[68] Several scholars thus draw the connection between the logos, which is Jesus, and the Tabernacle, which is the Temple of the wilderness of Sinai.

Given the central place of this verse within the prologue, if Jesus is introduced as the true Tabernacle, it depicts Jesus in a very specific way throughout the entire gospel: The rationale for "Temple Christology" is that just as God reveals himself to Moses in the Tabernacle, so he manifests His presence in Jesus. It shows that Jesus is "the true temple of God's presence," surpassing the Temple.[69] According to Craig Koester, tabernacle imagery portrays Jesus as the locus of God's word and glory among humankind. Hence John replaces the Temple with Jesus.[70]

Nonetheless, I doubt that *eskēnōsen* alludes to the Tabernacle. The verb *skēneō* means that God reveals His glory, referring to the *Shekhina*. Only from this connection can one possibly draw the implication that John implies the Tabernacle. It may carry a noncultic use (meaning "dwells"), referring to the Logos in a tent, as demonstrated in the LXX.[71] Furthermore, it sometimes denotes God dwelling within Israel, though not in reference to the Temple.[72] Thus *eskēnōse* in John 1:14 means that the Word (Jesus) dwells in a sacred manner "among us" with "glory." It manifests the divine essence of the Word but not the wilderness Tabernacle.

Such usage of *skēnē* without explicit reference to the Tabernacle is found in Ben Sira. Here wisdom dwells in heaven, though it also resides in the Tabernacle and later in Zion (Ben Sira 24:4, 10). In Ben Sira 24, the logos wanders in the world and can dwell in more than one place simultaneously. Wisdom is not limited to one and only one place. It resides in Israel—at the Temple, in the Torah, and in the prophets all at the same time (Ben Sira 24:8, 10, 23ff., 33). In the same manner, it can also reside in Jesus.

Similarly, when John introduces the logos as dwelling among the believers, it may relate Jesus to the Tabernacle, but it does not imply that the logos or Jesus is the true Tabernacle. There is a much simpler explanation for John's language, according to which the logos dwells in sanctity, like a heavenly inspiration. Furthermore, if John attempts to convey here the claim that Jesus is the true Tabernacle, this kind of message can hardly be absorbed by the reader. This would be a single clue—based upon the double meaning of the verb—without any further indication in the prologue, which is already heavy with other extremely complex concepts. It would be misguided to argue that John hints here that Jesus is the true Tabernacle only because this possibility may be relevant to other passages in John in which the subject of the relationship between Jesus and the Temple is straightforward.

The House of Many Rooms—The Heavenly Temple?

"In my Father's house there are many dwelling-places. If it were not so, would I have told you that I go to prepare a place for you?; And if I go and prepare a place for you, I will come again and will take you to myself, so that where I am, there you may be also; And you know the way to the place where I am going." (John 14:2–4)

Several scholars interpret "my Father's house" (*oikia*) with "many rooms" (*monai*) as the new Temple, which replaces the ancient one.[73] James

McCaffrey devotes an entire monograph to arguing that the house of many rooms is the heavenly Temple. Examining "my Father's house" (2:16) as the heavenly Temple, he notes the use of a house (*oikos*) of God as a Temple in biblical writings and identifies the "many rooms" with chambers or apartments within the Temple.[74] The place (*topos*) in vv. 3–4 that Jesus prepares for his disciples at his Father's house is probably identical with the "many rooms." Indeed, *topos* is one of the names for the Temple in several NT passages, and the same meaning may apply here.[75]

One general flaw in this suggestion is that the term *oikia* with *monē* is never found in the Jewish tradition with reference to the Temple, either earthly or heavenly.[76] McCaffrey may be aware of some weakness in his thesis, as he limits the relevance of his conclusion to the second ("post-Paschal") level of meaning of the gospel.[77] However, "dwelling" in John 14–15 is a spiritual experience ("the Father . . . dwells in me," 14:10) relating to fellowship after Jesus's departure.[78] This is a "pictorial representation of the transcendent dwelling of God," such as the heavenly Jerusalem (Heb 12:22)—perhaps an eschatological one—as the eternal house in heaven in 2 Cor 5:1.[79]

Commentators who see a Temple here take for granted that such a heavenly Temple is characteristic of John and seek it out whenever possible. Yet a plain reading of John does not associate the "house of many rooms" with a heavenly Temple. The passage does not contain hints of a Temple or its attributes. Rather, John associates Jesus with the Temple in a more delicate, complex manner, and it is not his way to simply assume that Jesus dwells in a heavenly Temple. Rather, the purpose of John 14:2–3 is similar to that of John 14:23, whereby Jesus and the believers dwell with the Father.

The Festivals: Passover, Tabernacles, and Hanukkah

John describes Jesus's visits to the Temple during (or immediately before) three Jewish festivals—Passover, Tabernacles (Sukkot), and Dedication (Hanukkah). It is sometimes argued that, in John, Jesus does not participate in the Temple cult or behave like a pilgrim; the feast no longer concerns him and his disciples, and the Passover merely offers Jesus an occasion for his proclamation.[80] So why does John's Jesus visit the Temple so frequently? Are these merely opportunities to present himself and his teaching in addition to waging conflict with the Jewish leaders?

Many commentators infer that Jesus becomes a substitute for the Jewish festivals in these passages. Because the festivals are related to the Temple this reflects John's approach toward the Temple. During the Passover Jesus offers bread to replace the manna; during the festival of Tabernacles he replaces the water and light ceremonies. On the festival of Dedication, Jesus is consecrated instead of the altar.[81] He appropriates to himself cultic symbols of bread (6:35, 48, 51), water (7:37–39), light (8:12), and sacred place (10:36) in the Jewish festivals of Passover, Tabernacles, and Dedication.[82] I shall now review these passages in more detail and examine their cultic symbolism.

PASSOVER (JOHN 6:51–71)

John 6:4 remarks that the following narrative about Jesus's miracles and teachings takes place "now the Passover, the festival of the Jews, was near." This is taken to be the setting of chapter 6, in which Jesus identifies himself with the true bread from heaven and calls upon the disciples to eat his flesh and drink his blood.

It is sometimes taken for granted that, in John, Jesus is the Passover lamb who atones for the world's sins, since Jesus is referred to as "the lamb" in 1:29. The Passover festival is superseded by Jesus becoming the Passover lamb. The "flesh" of the Passover is of no avail; it is the spiritually ingested Jesus—the Passover lamb—appropriated by faith that begins life.[83] This is substantiated when Jesus orders the disciples to eat his flesh and drink his blood (6:51, 53–57), as if he is a sacrificial victim. Later, Jesus is arrested right before the Passover (11:55; cf. 12:1), portrayed as the Paschal lamb when none of his bones are broken (19:36; cf. Exod 12:46). Thus one could say that John presents Jesus as "the fulfillment of the Passover," which also relates to the "temple of his body" in 2:21, mentioned in the cleansing that also occurs before the Passover (2:13). Since the Passover lamb is slaughtered and eaten in the Temple, it is argued that this could indicate that he is also the true Temple, the designated place of sacrifice.[84]

TABERNACLES (JOHN 7:37–39)

In John, Jesus goes to Jerusalem as a pilgrim for the festival of Tabernacles while the Jewish leaders look for him during the festival (7:2, 10–11). At about the middle of the festival Jesus goes up into the Temple (*hieron*) and begins to teach about the Law (7:14). John mentions once again that he preaches at the Temple (7:28). Later, he teaches there "on the last day of the festival, the great day . . . 'Let anyone who is thirsty come to me; and let the one who believes in me drink; As the scripture has said, "Out of the believer's belly/heart shall flow rivers of living water"'" (7:37–38). Jesus departs to the Mount of Olives, returning to the Temple on the next morning (8:2). While teaching in the treasury of the Temple (8:20), he says, "I am the light of the world. Whoever follows me will never walk in darkness but will have the light of life" (8:12). Jesus continues to talk about the truth of his message—his Father and Abraham—and finally leaves the Temple when his adversaries threaten to stone him (8:59).

Two issues discussed by Jesus in this scene may be linked to the celebrations and rituals in the Temple during the festival of Sukkot: the water ceremony, in which water is drawn from a nearby spring and poured on the altar;[85] and the use of fireworks in the Court of Women. Both of these take place during the celebration of "the house of shoevah."[86]

Interpreted in light of passages from the Hebrew Bible, the living water that flows out from Jesus may allude to the eschatological flow of water in Ezek 47:1–11 and Zech 14:8.[87] Does this mean that Jesus is the eschatological Temple, fulfilling the expectations of water from the rock of the eschatological Temple?[88] Jesus's claim to be the guiding light (8:12) is also read with eschatological trust: light has eschatological meaning (e.g., Isa 60:3), and the Temple is a locus of light for the world. This leads certain scholars to conclude that it is possible that the Temple is also replaced as the place for seeking God's light.[89]

The plain narrative is sometimes interpreted as holding an anti-Temple stance. The scene where Jesus leaves the Temple (8:59b) reflects deliberate rejection of the Temple. Namely, God's presence departs from the Temple and is found whenever Christ is found. Later, Christ himself becomes sanctified (10:36). Note, however, that there is no public act of rejection of the Temple here and Jesus returns there on the Dedication (10:22).[90]

DEDICATION (JOHN 10:22–11:53)

In John 10:22–23, Jesus walks in the Temple in Solomon's portico at the time of the festival of the Dedication (*egkiania*, lit. "renewal"; namely, the dedication of the Temple). He preaches there about his authority, and, accused by the Pharisees of blasphemy, Jesus replies, "Can you say that the one whom the Father has sanctified [*hēgiasen*] and sent into the world is blaspheming?" (10:36). When they try to capture him he runs away and stays in the Transjordan (10:39–40).

It is sometimes speculated that since Jesus claims he is consecrated by God in a scene that occurs on the Dedication (10:36), it follows that this consecration happens on this festival. Hence Jesus is consecrated/dedicated

by God "in the place" of sacrifice and presented as the fulfillment and replacement of the festival of Dedication, echoing the consecration of the
Temple courts celebrated on Hanukkah.[91] The question remains as to how
crucial the timing of Jesus being sanctified is. After all, he is already designated as being "holy to God" in 6:69.

Once again, Jesus's departure from the Temple (permanently this time)
to the desert of Jordan recalls the departure of God's glory through the east
gate (Ezek 10:18–19; 11:23). The glory of God, revealed in Jesus, "permanently leaves the Temple. The cultic institutions of Israel are left emptied of
the reality they once symbolized and celebrated."[92]

THE FESTIVALS LINK JESUS TO THE TEMPLE

I have surveyed several readings of the narrative of Jesus's proclamations in light of John's placing Jesus in the Temple at the time of (or before)
a festival. Jesus relates to the characteristics of the festival, such as the eating
of the Paschal lamb, the rite of prayer for water, and the celebration of fire,
and stresses his being consecrated during the festival of the dedication of
the altar. According to these readings, the meaning of this relationship is
always interpreted in a similar fashion: He is about to replace the Temple
and, it appears, the festival itself.

I have two general reservations about these inferences from the festive
motifs. First, these interpretations neglect the role of the narrative situating Jesus at the Temple time and again. Second, they assume a monolithic
meaning for the motifs assigned to Jesus's words.

Jesus visits the Temple in John at least three times—on Passover (2:13–
14), Tabernacles, and Hannukah—while in the synoptic gospels he attends
the Temple only at some point before Passover, the time of his arrest. John
mentions his presence there nine times.[93] Jesus says something or acts directly in relation to the Temple only once (2:13–17), in the "cleansing," but
he also shows his concern (one might even say zeal) for the appropriate
cult there. In a plain reading, Jesus's repetitive appearances at the Temple
—especially on the major pilgrimage festival of Tabernacles—probably
seems like conventional attendance at the Temple rites. The message seems
to be that Jesus cares about the Temple, at least as much as any ordinary
Jew does, even though he never takes an active part in it, as Paul does
in Acts.

Jesus's presence in the Temple during these festivals is narrated in order
to transmit a certain message about Jesus's attitude toward the Temple.[94] I

would like to suggest an alternative reading of the festival motifs and their relationship to the Temple.

In John 6:22–59, the Temple is not mentioned at all. The exposition of the Eucharist rite (6:53–58) can be related to the Passover only if one bears in mind the close connection between the two in Mark, where the Last Supper occurs in conjunction with the Passover ritual meal of the Paschal lamb (see chapter 1). The relationship between the Passover festival and the Eucharist can probably be seen only in John 19 (see below).

Since Jesus presents himself as the true bread of life (6:35), the main theme of John 6 is food, especially bread. The association of this theme with Passover is not clear at all. (One can barely see here an allusion to the Passover bread, the Matza, since the explicit image is the Manna, which is not related to the Passover.) If one reads John without having Mark in mind, there is no indication of Jesus taking on the functions of the Passover and certainly not of the Temple.

John 7:10 mentions the pilgrimage of his brothers in the background of Jesus' appearance at the Temple on Tabernacles. Jesus goes up (*anebē*) to the Temple as a pilgrim, giving the impression of traditional observance of the commandment of pilgrimage.

Jesus introduces two characteristics of the Temple specifically related to Tabernacles—flowing water and light, both celebrated at the Temple in the celebration of the house of *shoevah*. Ascribing these symbols to Jesus, however, still does not introduce him as the new Temple.[95] Water and fire are marginal attributes of the Temple, and the ritual celebration of the house of shoevah is a popular but not integral part of the sacrificial cult.[96] It is more reasonable that John wants to show that Jesus promises water and light in order to stress his giving spiritual life to believers. Perhaps John implies that, in a concrete and limited manner, Jesus is *like* the Temple during the Tabernacles, when the Jews pray for rain in the upcoming winter. Still, it is difficult to see Jesus as the total replacement of the Temple on the basis of this imagery.

Viewing Jesus as the eschatological Temple from which rivers will flow is also problematic because of the exact contents of John 7:38: "Out of the believer's heart [lit. belly] shall flow rivers of living water." The water flows not from Jesus but from anyone who believes in him.[97]

Hanukkah is a Temple festival in its very essence. It commemorates the rededication of the Temple by Judah Maccabee in 164 BCE, modeled upon the Days of Ordination (*millu'im*) of the Tabernacle and the Temple.

Its original theme is the holiness of the Temple.[98] Nevertheless, we have no information on special rites at the Temple during the festival. When Jesus refers to himself as being sanctified (*hēgiasen*), the dedication of the Temple and Jesus's sanctification have something in common—holiness—but this does not make them the same. Many things are sanctified at the Temple —sacrifices, priests, sacred objects and spaces, and sacred times.[99] Jesus's sanctification still does not designate him as the Temple.[100] And Jesus is not the only one to be sanctified in John. He prays, "Sanctify them [the disciples] in the truth . . . I sanctify myself, so that they also may be sanctified in truth" (17:17, 19).

The characteristics of the festivals to which John alludes, implicitly but consistently, are related to the Temple in different ways, but they do not point to a replacement or transformation of the Temple. Rather, they imply that certain features, in most cases not the fundamental ones, are common to the Temple or its festivals and Jesus. They do not introduce an either/or relationship between Jesus and the festivals and the Temple.

Jesus Is Like a Temple

PLACING JESUS IN THE TEMPLE

Any attempt to understand John's attitude toward the Temple must consider the role of the Temple in John's narrative. While in Mark Jesus visits the Temple only once, John depicts four visits—on Passover, an unidentified festival, Tabernacles, and Hanukkah. Jesus's presence there is mentioned nine times.[101] In two cases John gives the direct location of Jesus within the Temple realm: in the treasure house (8:20) (which is probably inside the Temple courts) and in Solomon's portico (10:23). It is important for John to show that Jesus acts at the Temple.

Furthermore, John stresses four times that Jesus teaches in the Temple.[102] This means that Jesus's religious message should be heard at the religious center of Judaism; that is, John regards Jesus as the leader of the Jews. In his trial before the high priest Jesus declares, "I have always taught in synagogues and in the Temple, where all the Jews come together" (18:20). In the fourth gospel, Jesus's teachings are more substantial and complex than in the synoptic ones. His teachings stand at the focus of the gospel because during the trial the high priest asks him specifically about his teachings. It is therefore significant that John associates Jesus's teachings with the Temple.

This linkage between Jesus and the Temple empowers the Temple in the eyes of readers. It does not imply that Jesus takes the place of the Temple, since when Jesus acts there it seems he shares the view that the Temple is the most sacred place.[103] Whoever comes to the Temple, even a Gentile, is attracted to its sacredness. Substitutions for the cult, such as in Qumran, take place far away from the Temple and in modes which are unrelated to sacrifices and offerings (see the introduction).

One crucial point that is usually overlooked is that, unlike Mark 13:2 (and Matthew and Luke), John's Jesus does not anticipate the destruction of Jerusalem. Nobody claims that he says he will or can destroy the Temple. Unlike in Mark and perhaps even Matthew, in John, Jesus does hardly criticize the cult and priesthood; nor does he discredit them.[104]

I thus suggest that in his treatment of the Temple theme John wants his readers to understand belief in Jesus in light of the Temple, treating him as a generator of holiness and an agent of worshiping God, just as the Temple is before 70 CE. John merely uses characteristics of the Temple that are familiar to his readers in order to shed light on Jesus and let the reader understand his sacred character. He wants to show Jesus's holiness as a source of life and spirit, one that connects the believer with God. John wants the reader to understand that Jesus is somewhat similar to the Temple.

Our evangelist is cautious not to argue that Jesus is the true or new Temple. He uses the Temple as an interpretive tool for grasping Jesus's role as God's sacred agent. He plays with Temple imagery so that those who still cherish the cult are able to understand his message about Jesus. Perhaps John does not intend for readers to forsake their feelings toward the Jerusalem Temple but only to find some comfort with Jesus. Given the positive, central role of the Temple in John, it is even possible that some readers still hope for its restoration even if they do believe in Christ. If Jesus attends the Temple several times and cares for it, is it reasonable to await Jesus's return to the renewed Temple in the future?

In this respect, it is necessary to mention Fuglseth's comparison of John's attitude toward the Temple with both Philo and Qumran. He shows that John does not reject the Temple cult or manifest a social tension in relation to it. Rather, John introduces a "conjunctional" relationship to the Temple, a "transference" of some aspects of the Temple to Jesus. This transference, he rightly claims, does not mean neglecting the Temple cult. Furthermore, similar transference is also evidenced in Philo (a nonsectarian author who upholds Temple practices), whereas in the sectarian scrolls from Qumran the Temple is explicitly (but temporarily) replaced.[105]

This Temple transference is therefore the result of the central role of the cult for John and his readers. It does not point to rejection or replacement. Yet, as in the case of the rabbis after 70 CE, when such transference takes place and the original Temple no longer exists, the new concept which is built upon it becomes more valid and substantial. For the readers of John, especially in the following years, what is left from the Temple is this transferred Temple Christology.

EXCURSUS: THE PASCHAL LAMB AND THE HIGH PRIESTHOOD

John 1:29 introduces another cultic image, wherein John the Baptist refers to Jesus: "Here is the Lamb of God who takes away the sin of the world." The meaning of the lamb in John 1:29 (repeated in 1:35) raises a great variety of interpretations. Such a kosher animal which removes sins may allude to expiatory sacrifice.[106] If Jesus is a sacrifice of atonement, this should be a core element in the Johannine view of the Temple cult. However, such an interpretation falls short of the fact that the sin offering (or the purification offering) consists of goats, not lambs. Furthermore, the image of Jesus's death as an atoning sacrifice is not developed in the fourth gospel.[107] Another interpretation is that the image of the lamb carrying the sins builds upon the Suffering Servant who suffers the sins of his people as a lamb (Isa 53:7).[108]

In the Johannine Passion Narrative also Jesus is portrayed, implicitly but systematically, as the Paschal lamb. In John 19:14 the date of the trial and crucifixion is Passover eve, creating a parallel between Jesus's death and the slaughtering of the Pascal lambs at the Temple.[109] When Jesus dies on the cross the soldiers do not break his legs (in contrast to the request of the Jewish leaders), and John connects this to the biblical commandment: "So that the scripture might be fulfilled, 'None of his bones shall be broken'" (19:36; cf. Exod 12:46). Indeed, the identification of Jesus as the Paschal lamb goes back to Paul (1 Cor 5:7). But does this image relate to John's approach toward the Temple?

It is sometimes argued that the Johannine image of the Paschal lamb symbolizes an expiatory sacrifice in which Jesus atones for sins instead of the offerings on the altar.[110] However, the Paschal lamb is not a sacrifice of atonement. It is offered like a well-being (*shelamin*) sacrifice, brought to the Temple by every family or group and slaughtered there. Furthermore, its flesh is not burnt on the altar. It does not expiate any sins but commemorates Israel's Exodus from Egypt.[111] Each family or group has its own Paschal lamb and eats it throughout Jerusalem.

When John treats Jesus as a Paschal lamb, I suggest, he actually relates it to the Eucharist, the symbolic consumption of Jesus's flesh. Jesus as a virtual Paschal lamb is central to Last Supper imagery, not to the ultimate Temple sacrifice that atones for the world's sins. Thus John 1:29 goes back to Jesus's death and does not relate to the Temple.[112]

I now turn to John's approach toward the high priest(s) in terms of his treatment of the Temple theme. There is a theory that John portrays Jesus as a high priest: He is consecrated by God (17:19). Caiaphas the high priest speculates that Jesus will save the people (11:50–51) and that Jesus is a high priest because he sacrifices himself.[113] However, John's portrayal of Caiaphas is much more positive than in the synoptic gospels. He is gifted with a prophecy that enables him to acknowledge that Jesus is about to die for the sake of the "nation." This means that Caiaphas is almost a believer in Christ.[114] One of the disciples is even "known to the high priest" (18:15), thus creating a certain relationship between Jesus's followers and the high priest. In any event, it is awkward to see Jesus as both the sacrifice and the high priest at the same time.

I think the reason for some of the confusion engendered by associating Jesus with the Temple or the high priesthood lies in the holiness of Jesus in the gospel of John. Jesus is "the Holy One of God" (6:69), not only consecrated by God (10:36) but probably *the* most Holy since "I and the Father are one" (10:30). He is God's exclusive mediator: "No one comes to the Father except through me (14:6). In addition, Jesus is glorified and exalted by God.[115] Therefore, it is unnecessary to relate Jesus's sacredness directly to the Temple.[116] His holiness is inherent in his divine nature ever since his preexistence as logos. John's Temple imagery is not the main means of ascribing holiness to Jesus but merely a complementary one in which this holiness operates and how it relates to the fact that the Jerusalem Temple no longer stands.

CONCLUSIONS: TEMPLE SYMBOLISM IN THE FOURTH GOSPEL

Two arguments lead me to reject Johannine replacement theory in its current form. First, John does not explicitly state that Jesus is the new

Temple. Second, John deals with the Temple extensively in a manner which implies that this symbol is very important. If the Temple as a symbol is not valid anymore, why use it and remind readers about the irrelevant sacrificial cult which no longer exists?

John relates Jesus to the Temple, attributing to Jesus certain features of the Temple. He does so since he uses the Temple as an *explanatory model for understanding Jesus*. Jesus's role and character are explained in terms of several characteristics that are also shared by the Temple. Portraying Jesus as analogical to the Temple does not aim to show that the Temple is no longer relevant. Instead, the Temple is used as a model by which to comprehend Jesus's religious function. Jesus is the means to reach God and in this sense has something in common with the pre-70 CE Temple.

In order to define John's use of the Temple theme more clearly, I suggest treating it as a symbol. A symbol is not a decorative means of language (like an allegory) or an abstract, pedagogical device. It conveys a reality and aims to transfer the self into an experience. It invites subjective participation and the reader's response. This symbol cannot be articulated or substituted for something else.[117] John's Christology is complex and difficult to understand. The Temple, its sacredness and rites, are more familiar to the reader. For this reason John uses the Temple to illuminates Jesus's sacredness and closeness to God by introducing Jesus as relating to it. This also means that the symbol cannot be replaced by what it symbolizes. As long as it is a symbol and not a reality its validity is never questioned.

This "Temple Christology" provides a more flexible model that corresponds with the literary evidence. The result is a less radical relationship between Jesus and the Temple. Jesus is neither the new Temple nor a full replacement of the Temple. He is *like* the Temple—serving similar religious functions but certainly not all of the Temple's functions. He should not be equated with the Temple in a full sense. Nonetheless, when the Temple becomes both a symbol and a memory, the reader is left with Jesus embodying a vivid, effective mode of worshiping and getting close to God.

7 The Book of Revelation: The Alternative Temple

Introduction

The book of Revelation to John is exceptional within the NT not only because of its genre and rich imagery but also because it introduces a unique approach to the Temple. On the one hand, it portrays an alternative heavenly Temple, while on the other it argues that in the eschatological age the New Jerusalem will lack a Temple altogether.

The author's use of the genre of an apocalypse, not a gospel or letter, provides him with the opportunity to introduce radical approaches to the Temple. An apocalypse is revelatory literature with a narrative framework in which a revelation is mediated by an otherworldly being to a human recipient. It discloses a transcendent reality including eschatological salvation and/or a supernatural world.[1] In the book of Revelation the secrets of the heavenly Temple and its impact on the earthly world are revealed, thus reflecting the author's conventions about the meaning of the Temple cult.

The context of Revelation is undoubtedly the great cities of Asia Minor to which the seven letters are sent (chs. 2–3). Most scholars regard it as a reaction to Roman rule and the imperial cult in the region (see below). Nonetheless, David Aune lists several possible indications of the author's Judaean origins: familiarity with the Old Testament and the Temple cult; writing in Semitizing Greek; and the use of the apocalypse genre, which had developed in Judea. Both Aune and Yarbro Collins suggest that the author of Revelation was a refugee who reached Asia Minor after the First Revolt against Rome. The many similarities to the Qumran scrolls—especially the Songs of the Sabbath Sacrifices and the New Jerusalem scroll—as well as to the eschatology of the New Zion in 2 Baruch and 4 Ezra also point to the Judean origins of Revelation.[2]

It is commonplace to base the dating of Revelation upon Irenaeus's view that it is written by the end of Domitian's reign (81–96 CE), even though his evidence is far from reliable.[3] However, post-70 dating may be confirmed by internal evidence from the text. The name Babylon denotes Rome only in post-70 CE writings such as 4 Ezra and 2 Baruch. According to this line of thinking, just as Babylon destroys the first Temple, Rome destroys the second. The motif of the Beast suffering a wound that is healed (13:3, 12, 14) hints at the legend of Nero *redivivus* on which the author/editor seems to depend. This legend is attested to as early as 69 CE, hence Revelation was written somewhat later.[4]

An apocalypse written a generation after the destruction of the Jerusalem Temple that discusses Temple imagery and cultic themes is most likely a reaction to the loss of the earthly Temple, a response to a crisis within Judaism. And yet scholarship on Revelation stresses its Greek and Roman contexts, assuming a Greco-Roman audience.[5] But, as I will demonstrate here the Temple theme in Revelation is not related to the Greco-Roman cult and culture. Rather, Revelation's religious ideas and imagery are based upon Jewish traditions.

JEWISH IDENTITY

As is true of most NT texts, it is usually assumed that the author of the book of Revelation is addressing both Jewish and Gentile Christians. Thus Gentiles from every nation stand before the Lamb and worship God in His Temple (7:9, 14–15). Still, there is no admonition against specific Jewish values or practices. Furthermore, there is an emphasis on continuity between the Jewish people and the messianic movement centered on Jesus.[6] There is more evidence for Jewish readership or at the very least Jewish motifs as well.

Indirect reference to Israelite descent is found in the list of the 144,000 faithful people, God's servants "who were sealed," consisting of 12,000 from each of the twelve tribes of Israel (7:3–8). The number 144,000 is therefore symbolic, a multiple of twelve representing the twelve tribes. Scholars debate whether this number includes only Jews or includes Gentiles as well.[7] It seems that the church is identified here as Israel. After the conclusion of the list of the people of the twelve tribes, John sees "a great multitude that no one could count, from every nation, from all tribes and peoples and languages" standing before the throne and the Lamb. These appear to be Gentiles annexed to the chosen Israelites. Thus the chosen people of God also includes a crowd from every nation, and the entire list represents Israel, uniting both Jews and Gentiles.[8]

The author discusses other non-Christian Jews directly on only two occasions—the letters to Smyrna and Philadelphia: "I know the slander on the part of those who say that they are Jews and are not, but are a synagogue of Satan" (2:9); "I will make those of the synagogue of Satan who say that they are Jews and are not, but are lying, I will make them come and bow down before your feet, and they will learn that I have loved you" (3:9). Who are those adversaries that "say that they are Jews and are not?" They are probably not apostate Jews but rather Jews who oppose Christianity. They are condemned by the author owing to an intra-Jewish debate. It is even possible to find here a claim by the author that only his movement represents the true Judaism.[9]

It appears that the Jews of Smyrna and Philadelphia are vilified as blasphemers or slanderers. This vilification may be reflective of conflict between Christians and Jews in Asia Minor, shedding light on the message of the entire book: a conflict with neighboring non-Christian Jews. On the basis of Coser's conflict model, Yarbro Collins suggests that this vilification defines who the Christians really are. They are the genuine Jews, the heirs of the promises to Israel. But there is a boundary between those who accept Jesus and those who reject him.[10] John's apocalyptic message is therefore related to hatred of other non-Christian Jews and is used to gain legitimacy for believers in Jesus.

The Heavenly Temple

After the conclusion of the seven letters to the communities in the cities of Asia Minor in chapter 4, John sees an open door in heaven. His spirit goes up, and he discovers the heavenly throne where God is worshiped by the heavenly creatures. It is here that the rest of the Revelation to John takes place. Among these creatures he sees the Lamb, Revelation's designation for Jesus. In Rev 5:8 John sees bowls of incense, the first indication that the heavenly throne is also a heavenly Temple. In 6:9, John first sees an altar.

The Temple in heaven is explicitly mentioned for the first time in 7:15. Here the "sealed" ones (the 144,000 of the twelve tribes along with the multitudes from the nations, all wearing white robes) are "before the throne of God, and worship him day and night within his Temple [*naos*]." The next episode in which this Temple is referred to occurs when the seventh angel blows his trumpet to call for the final judgment: "Then God's Temple in heaven [*ho naos tou theou ho en tō ouranō*] was opened, and the ark of his covenant was seen within his Temple; and there were flashes of lightning, rumblings, peals of thunder, an earthquake, and heavy hail" (11:19).[11]

Following the visions of the woman and the dragon and the two beasts, "another angel came out of the Temple [*naos*], calling with a loud voice to the one who sat on the cloud, 'Use your sickle and reap, for the hour to reap has come, because the harvest of the earth is fully ripe' and another angel came out of the Temple in heaven" (14:15, 17).[12] Then, when the seven angels carry the seven plagues to pour God's wrath on earth, "the Temple of the tent of witness [namely, the Tabernacle] in heaven was opened, and out of the Temple came the seven angels . . . And the Temple was filled with smoke from the glory of God and from his power, and no one could enter the Temple until the seven plagues of the seven angels were ended" (15:5–6, 8). John still hears a "loud voice from the Temple calling the angels" to pour the plagues (16:1). After the seven angels pour the bowls of plagues, a loud voice comes out of the Temple from the throne, saying, "It is done" (16:17).[13]

In these passages *naos* refers to the heavenly Temple as a whole without mentioning other architectural elements. I want to examine now the activities and objects related to this Temple.

THE FUNCTIONS OF THE HEAVENLY TEMPLE

The heavenly Temple in Revelation is a place of worship for God and the Lamb (God is present in the Temple in 7:15; 15:8). It is also a place from which God rules the world and executes divine judgment. It embodies both transcendence and transformation of the sacred in mediating the presence of God among humans. Access to the Temple means access to God's presence, power, and revelation. These cultic objects and related activities have the effect of making it function like a real Temple. Temple language offers conceptualization of a new sacred place which is altered in highly effective ways.[14] In this context the heavenly Temple plays a dual role. On the one hand, it is a source of hope for the faithful. Here God is worshiped as the Creator of all things (4:11; cf. 10:6; 14:7), and the faithful are promised that they will join the heavenly company in God's Temple (7:15). On the other hand, the Temple is a source of threat for God's foes. God opposes the forces that now ruin the world. Lightning and thunder come from the Temple as signs of God's judgment against the destroyers of earth (11:18–19). Plagues are sent from the Temple (15:5–8) as well.[15]

There are several ideal characteristics of this heavenly Temple which resemble the New Jerusalem (21:1–22:5). Both are God's throne and God's dwelling with the faithful. In both cases God's name is sealed on the forehead of the chosen ones (7:3–4; 22:4), the names of the twelve tribes appear on the city's gates (7:15; 21:13), and God wipes away the tears (7:17; 21:4).[16] Some commentators seem to confuse the two, which represent two distinct concepts. The eschatological scenario is reserved for the New Jerusalem.[17] Other heavenly Temples in ancient Judaism are also noneschatological: there is no sense of eschatology in 1 Enoch 14, Testament of Levi 3:5–8, or the Songs of the Sabbath Sacrifices. Later Heikhalot literature (such as 3 Enoch) also describes the heavenly Temple not in the future but in the present.[18]

Since the heavenly Temple represents a reality understood as already present, some regard the heavenly Temple as a symbol or metaphor for the Christian community, using the Pauline community-as-Temple metaphor. Thus the cultic details of the heavenly Temple are symbols of God's real presence in the church. Like this Temple, the church is where the Christians encounter God and Christ without separation between God and humans. The church is where God is present. It is God's chosen abode.[19]

This understanding is exegetically problematic. If the church is the heavenly Temple, what is the difference between the present situation and the eschatological age when God and the Lamb will be a Temple in the New Jerusalem (21:22)? Since the church—God's people—will prevail in the millennium (22:3–5), and John says that in the New Jerusalem there will be no Temple but that God and the Lamb will be the Temple, does John mean that in the eschaton the church will no longer be the Temple? These difficulties demonstrate that the church–Temple model does not mesh with the Temple symbolism of Revelation. The notion of the Temple is much more significant for John than the notion of the church (which is only implicit, with no specific designations for the community.) The community-as-Temple model unnecessarily reduces the meaning of the heavenly Temple, which centers on God and the Lamb. It is true that John wants to show that believers in Jesus are closest to God by placing them in the heavenly Temple, but he does not identify them as *the* Temple.

The heavenly Temple is at one point designated as the Tent of Meeting, Israel's Tabernacle in the wilderness: "The Temple of the tent of witness [*ho naos tēs skēnēs tou marturiou*] in heaven" (15:5) uses one of Tabernacle's designations (Num 1:53; 17:22 MT). John 13:6 also calls it a dwelling, a term which is used for both the Tabernacle and the Jerusalem Temple.[20] This gives the Temple in heaven an authentic flavor. It may also remind the reader of the giving of the Torah to Moses, since "witness" (Hebrew *'edut*) alludes to the designation of the tablets of the covenant (Ex 25:21; 30:6; 31:18).

When the seven angels receive the bowls of wrath with the plagues thrown on the people of the world, "the Temple was filled with smoke from the glory of God and from his power, and no one could enter the Temple until the seven plagues of the seven angels were ended" (15:8). This description of divine theophany recalls the inauguration of the Tabernacle (Ex 40:34–35) and Temple (1 Kings 8:10–12). However, unlike these biblical passages, the manifestation of the divine here is related to heavenly punishment. God is temporarily unapproachable because His presence has become one of wrath and judgment or because of the full manifestation of His majesty and power.[21]

THE THRONE

As I mentioned above, the divine throne, the seat of the Lord, has a central role in Revelation and functions as the center of the universe.[22] In chapter 4 John reaches it through a door, hears a voice calling him, sees "the one" seated on the throne with twenty-four elders seated around it dressed in white robes and a golden crown worshiping God. Flashes, lightning, and thunder come from the throne, and seven torches burn in front of it (identified as the seven spirits of God). On each side of the throne there are four living creatures that look like a lion, an ox, a human, and an eagle. Each of them has six wings and is full of eyes all around and inside. Day and night they sing, "Holy, holy, holy, the Lord God the Almighty," giving glory, honor, and thanks to God.

Undoubtedly, the idea of God's throne in heaven goes back to 1 Kings 22:19–23, Isaiah 6, and Ezekiel 1. It is a symbol of God's sovereignty in heaven. This appearance of the divinity demonstrates God's power on earth.[23] In a sense, such a manifestation of God's glory anticipates God's final victory and the revelation of God's epiphany in the New Jerusalem in the End of Days.[24]

The throne and the heavenly Temple are interrelated phenomena. Both are in heaven (4:2; 11:19). Both exhibit lightning, rumblings, thunder (4:5; 11:19) and involve praise and service day and night (4:8; 7:15). In both there are seven angels and four living creatures (4:6; 7:9; 8:2–3; 11:16; 14:3; 15:1, 6, 7), and a voice comes forth from each (16:1, 17; 19:5). Some passages identify the Temple and throne quite explicitly. In Rev 16:17 a voice comes "out of the Temple from the throne." In 7:15 the multitude are both "before the throne of God" and "serve him . . . in his Temple." John therefore conceives the throne as if it is in the Temple. One might say that the Temple is the place of the throne. According to Stevenson, the throne functions like a cult statue. It is a physical object that represents the presence of God. Its appearance is a form of epiphany.[25]

Cultic Objects and Rituals in the Heavenly Temple

Throughout the descriptions of the heavenly Temple many cultic elements are mentioned: the altar, burning incense, prayer, the lampstands of the Temple, and the holy Ark of the Covenant.

THE ALTAR

The altar (*thusiastērion*) of the heavenly Temple has a major role in Revelation. It first appears in the book when the fifth seal is opened. John sees "under the altar the souls of those who had been slaughtered for the word of God and for the testimony they had given" (6:9). The souls' location under the altar symbolizes the martyrs' closeness to God.[26]

Later, when the seventh seal is opened and the seven angels are given seven trumpets, "another angel with a golden censer came and stood at the altar; he was given a great quantity of incense to offer with the prayers of all the saints on the golden altar that is before the throne. . . . Then the angel took the censer and filled it with fire from the altar and threw it on the earth; and there were peals of thunder, rumblings, flashes of lightning, and an earthquake" (8:3, 5). Interestingly, the one who serves at the altar is an angel. The altar is similar to the incense altar in the Jerusalem Temple, an object made of gold and placed inside the sanctuary.

During the harvest of grapes, which is perhaps an act of judgment, "another angel came out from the altar, the angel who has authority over fire, and he called with a loud voice to him who had the sharp sickle, 'Use your sharp sickle and gather the clusters of the vine of the earth, for its grapes are ripe'" (14:18). There may be a relation between the fire for which the angel is responsible and his place by the altar, on which, we may suppose, the fire is burning. Here this altar seems to represent an act of divine punishment.

John also hears voices coming from the altar. When the sixth angel blows his trumpet, "I heard a voice from the four horns of the golden altar before God, saying to the sixth angel who had the trumpet, 'Release the four angels who are bound at the great river Euphrates'" (9:13–14). Also, when the bowls of plagues are poured on the earth on those who shed the blood of the saints and the prophets, John says that he "heard the altar respond, 'Yes, O Lord God, the Almighty, your judgments are true and just!'" (16:7). It is not clear whether the altar itself is being personified or only represents someone by the altar, such as an angel (as in 9:13–14) or perhaps the martyrs buried under it (as in 16:7).[27]

Nonetheless, when cultic imagery is at stake, especially in the case of a heavenly Temple, there is no reason to doubt that the cultic object is endowed with speech. Its words convey the divine will, quite like angels. Similar personalization of cultic elements, in this case architectural ones in the heavenly Temple, are found in the Songs of the Sabbath Sacrifices found in Qumran. Here the foundations of the holy of holies, along with the Temple's pillars and corners, are living creatures that join with the heavenly hosts and sing praises to God.[28]

Although the altar is a major component of the Temple structure, its exact location is unclear. In another scene John is called to "measure the Temple of God and the altar and those who worship there" but not the outer court (11:1, see below). It is noteworthy that the altar is specified as something that should be measured independently of the Temple itself. The obscurity about the function and location of this altar results from the fact that in the Jerusalem Temple there are two altars: the altar on which animal sacrifices, cereal offerings, and libations are offered, which is made of stone and located in the inner court but outside the sanctuary's building (*naos*); and the altar of incense, made of gold, which stands in the *heikhal*, inside the sanctuary. The measuring of the altar separate from the *naos* in 11:1 probably refers to the offering altar, which stands outside the *naos*. The location of the martyrs' souls (6:9) is also more appropriate under this altar, since they are slaughtered like a sacrifice.[29]

Still, the altar of incense is explicitly mentioned in 8:3, 5 (and, as we will see below, incense has a special role in Revelation). Some scholars think that both types of altar are referred to in Revelation, while others see here only one, since only the incense altar is explicitly mentioned.[30] This assumption about the lack of an altar for offering sacrifices also leads some to argue for the spiritualization of sacrifices; for John, incense is offered in the heavenly Temple instead of animal sacrifices.[31]

The altar has multiple symbolic meanings. It represents the sanctity of the heavenly Temple from which voices are heard, and it is the place from which angels are sent on their mission. No animal sacrifices are mentioned, and owing to the notion of the significance of the death of Jesus for the believers' sins (1:5; 5:9; 12:11), it is natural to assume that the martyrs' souls under the altar imply a sense of atoning sacrifice.[32] Yet the reference to the souls of the martyrs is only one instance among several, and it does not represent John's entire understanding of the altar. In fact, only here and in the burning of incense in 8:3, 5 does the altar serve a role in worshiping God directly. Acts carried out under the dominion of God are common to all altar scenes. Unlike the earthly Temple, the altar is not a passive object. Through the symbol of the altar John wants to show that the heavenly Temple and its beings are acting under God to carry out the divine plan.

BURNING INCENSE

The offering of incense appears twice in Revelation. When the Lamb takes the scroll from the one who is seated on the throne, "the four living creatures and the twenty-four elders fell before the Lamb, each holding a harp and golden bowls [*phialē*] full of incense, which are the prayers of the saints" and sang a new song for the Lamb (5:7–9).[33] Here incense represents the cultic worship of God.

As I've mentioned, when the seventh seal is opened, "another angel with a golden censer came and stood at the altar; he was given a great quantity of incense to offer with the prayers of all the saints on the golden altar that is before the throne. And the smoke of the incense, with the prayers of the saints, rose before God from the hand of the angel. Then the angel took the censer and filled it with fire from the altar and threw it on the earth; and there were peals of thunder, rumblings, flashes of lightning, and an earthquake" (8:3–5). Here incense at first represents worship of God. When the angel takes it and throws it on the earth, it suggests divine judgment of the earth. This results in lightning, thunder, and an earthquake—a theophanic manifestation.[34]

Incense has two cultic uses in Judaism. The most common involves praising God, which is practiced twice daily in the Tamid sacrifice. More rare is its use for atonement, either on the Day of Atonement (perhaps concealing the divine abode in the holy of holies) or for stopping the plague in the wilderness after the uprising of Korah and his followers.[35] While Rev 5:7–9 corresponds to the first meaning of worship, Rev 8:3–5 coheres with the uses of incense which relate to judgment and punishment, but in reverse fashion. Instead of stopping God's wrath, throwing it represents a spreading across the earth, like a plague.

Interpreters of Revelation sometimes understand the sense of incense as representing something else.[36] It is certainly related to prayer, as I will explain in the next section. It is even argued that John replaces animal sacrifices, which he rejects, with incense.[37]

PRAYER AS A CULTIC ACT

Revelation alludes twice to prayer in relation to sacrifices and incense. In Rev 5:8, the living creatures and elders fall before the Lamb, holding a harp and "golden bowls full of incense, which are the prayers of the saints." And in Rev 8:3–4, the angel stands at the altar holding "incense to offer with the prayers of all the saints on the golden altar that is before the throne. And the smoke of the incense, with the prayers of the saints, rose before God from the hand of the angel."

In both passages the saints' prayers are described as a kind of offering akin to the incense offering at the Temple. In the first passage incense is intended as a direct metaphor for prayer, while in the second the metaphor is merely contextual: the prayers are "offered" *with*—not *as*—the incense; that is to say, prayer is *associated with* incense but does not substitute for it.[38] This metaphor is already introduced in Ps 141:2, where prayer is depicted as an offering that *adjoins* the incense (which is the most elevated or "spiritual" among the different offerings), as if the words of prayer, too, are a tangible thing that can be placed inside a vessel or offered on the golden incense altar in the sanctuary.

The content and meaning of the prayers of the saints are not specified. They may praise God or ask to punish the wicked on earth from whom the saints suffer. In the next chapter we will see a similar prayer in Heb 13:15. Notably, unlike the prayers of the Qumran sectarians, the prayers of the saints in Revelation do not presume to substitute for the sacrificial cult, but are—albeit in a metaphorical manner—integrated into the ritual offerings at the heavenly Temple. Revelation thus refrains from replacing cultic acts with prayer and instead connects prayer to the Temple rite. This, however, changes in Didache 14:1–3, where prayer is designated simply as sacrifice.[39]

Intriguingly, John needs cultic context and imagery to introduce these prayers, connecting the prayers of the saints to the bowls of incense and making them seem like holy offerings acceptable to God. This makes these prayers appear to be holy, likely encouraging readers to relate them to their own communal ritual prayers. John can give the prayer scenes a place independent of the sacrificial cult (cf. the martyrs' prayer for justice in 6:10). He relates prayer to cultic acts to give them a higher status in addition to suggesting that prayer is one of the activities in the heavenly Temple. Yet— in comparing Revelation to the Songs of the Sabbath Sacrifices found at Qumran—while the angelic prayers and blessing are the main issue in the Songs, in Revelation, prayer is relatively marginal.

In fact, these two scenes of prayer (along with the souls of the martyrs under the altar) seem to be the only ones in which the saints take part in the cultic acts of the heavenly Temple. (In Rev 7 the Temple is not mentioned, but rather the throne). Even in these two passages the saints are not involved directly, and their prayers are like passive objects, as if they are collected by the angels.

THE LAMPSTANDS

Lampstands, in both plural and singular, are mentioned several times in Revelation—most likely referring to the Temple Menorah. At the very beginning, when John hears a voice in his first vision, he sees "seven golden lampstands, and in the midst of the lampstands I saw one like the Son of Man" (1:12–13). The lampstand, which gives everlasting light inside the Jerusalem Temple, is placed inside the sanctuary "before the Lord" (Ex 27: 20–21; Lev 24:2–4). In Zech 4:10, it represents "the eyes of the Lord."[40]

Then John sees the "one like the Son of Man," who explains the mystery of this vision, which also includes seven stars that this heavenly creature holds in his hand: "The seven stars are the angels of the seven churches, and the seven lampstands are the seven churches" (1:13, 20). These are probably the seven communities in Asia Minor to which John is sending letters in chaps. 2–3.

For John, this vision is formative, since it enables him to introduce his letter to Ephesus as the words of the one like the Son of Man, designated as the one "who holds the seven stars in his right hand, who walks among the seven golden lampstands" (2:1). In so doing, he draws an analogy between the lampstand and the Christian community. This identification continues when he threatens the angel of Ephesus that unless he repents, "I will come to you and remove your lampstand from its place" (2:5).

The fact that John sees seven lampstands before writing to the seven urban communities of Asia Minor is probably not a coincidence. The identification of the community as a lampstand is important. Stevenson even argues that the lampstand represents Christ's presence within the church.[41] The implication is that there is a connection, albeit symbolic, between John's vision (and ultimately the heavenly Temple) and the Christian reality or identity on earth. The symbol of the lampstand is a divine affirmation of the Christians' good standing before the Lord in the heavenly Temple.

Later on, the lampstands appear again as the representation of God's two witnesses, who profess, "These are the two olive trees and the two lampstands that stand before the Lord of the earth" (11:4). Once again the lampstand appears as a symbol of closeness to God. John's use of the olives alludes to the olives branches or trees on the two sides of the Menorah (which seems to allude to the two leaders of the Judean community) in Zech 4:3, 11–14.

THE ARK

The Ark of the Covenant—the most holy vessel in the sanctuary, containing the tablets of the covenant and covered by the golden Cherubim (Ex 25:11–22)—is described in Revelation in relation to the theophany in heaven. The seventh angel blows the trumpet while the twenty-four elders sit in their seats worshiping God. "Then God's Temple in heaven was opened, and the ark of his covenant was seen within his Temple; and there were flashes of lightning, rumblings, peals of thunder, an earthquake, and heavy hail" (11:19).

Not only is the holy Ark the most sacred cultic object John can imagine, but this vision has a special meaning since the Ark is lost when the Temple is destroyed by the Babylonians in 586 BCE. There are traditions about its hiding place and expectations for its return.[42]

Viewing the Ark may have two complementary meanings. Because of the resemblance of earthly and heavenly sanctuaries as well as the idea that the one in heaven is the model for Moses's Tabernacle, it is possible that John is implying that he sees the original Ark.[43] Thus the vision is another way to stress the authenticity of the heavenly Temple as resembling the one on earth—but in an idealized form.

Some suggest that this vision is a distinctive Christian idea. Namely, since the Ark is a sign of the covenant at Sinai, the Ark in heaven stands for the new covenant under Christ. While viewing the old Ark is forbidden, the Ark comes to symbolize salvation through Christ.[44] The saints, however, do not see the Ark, and neither the Lamb nor any other Christian marker is found in the scene—all of which suggests the unlikelihood that this proposed message is John's intention.

The New Priesthood

Revelation opens with a declaration that Jesus is the ruler of the kings of the earth who frees the believers from their sins by his blood and "made us to be a Kingdom, priests serving his God and Father" (1:6). Later, the living creatures sing to the Lamb: "You have made them [the saints from every tribe and language and people and nation] to be a Kingdom and priests [*basilian kai hiereis*] serving our God, and they will reign on earth" (5:10). Here John thinks that all Christians are included in the new priesthood.[45] This idea is also found in 1 Pet 2:9, where the author argues, "You are a chosen race, a royal priesthood, a holy nation, God's own people, in order that you may proclaim the mighty acts of him." These passages follow Ex 19:6, according to which all Israel are "a priestly Kingdom, a holy people." The notion that the believers become priests means that, just as the priests are chosen from the Israelites, they too are chosen from other humans and subsequently are separated by God to become holy people.[46]

After the fall of Babylon and the capture of the dragon, John sees the divine judgment and the martyrs' souls reigning with Christ (20:4–5). Then he adds his own message about their status as priests: "Blessed and holy are those who share in the first resurrection. Over these the second death has no power, but they will be priests of God and of Christ, and they will reign with him for a thousand years" (20:6). The idea that the people of God will be redeemed, their enemies will be punished, and they will be called Priests for the Lord and servants of God is found in Isa 61:6.[47] In both passages victory and ruling are connected with the official role of serving God. John's proclamation of their priestly status is certainly related to the fulfillment of messianic promises. The priesthood reflects perfect closeness to the Lord.

It is commonly argued that the believers' priesthood is implied earlier in a number of passages. The angels, living creatures, or martyrs execute cultic, priestlike acts, serving and worshiping God in the heavenly Temple as if they are priests.[48] Nevertheless, although these elements have some common ground with priest and priesthood, they are not designated as priestly markers.

There are exegetical and theological difficulties in understanding the relationship between the concepts of priesthood in these passages. In 1:6

and 5:10 the believers are already priests, since the author uses the past tense. In contrast, in 20:6 they will become priests in the future.[49] There seem to be two different types of priesthood in Revelation. The priesthood in the present is not related to the heavenly Temple. The Kingdom of priests modeled after Ex 19:6 is merely a designation for the people of God. Nothing in Rev 1:6 and 5:10 or their literary context suggests that the believers are acting as priests. Like the people of Israel in the wilderness, they are designated as priests only as a means of demonstrating that they are the chosen ones—priesthood is a metaphor. This priestly designation or metaphor should be contrasted with the believers' priesthood in 1 Pet 2:5, where the author tells his readers, "Let yourselves be built into a spiritual house, to be a holy priesthood [*hierateuma*], to offer spiritual sacrifices." Unlike Rev 1:6 and 5:10, in 1 Pet 2:5 the author does not merely refer to the priestly *status* but instructs the addressees to *act* as spiritual priests—to offer sacrifices—even though this seems to amount to belief and the telling of God's glory (1 Pet 2:9).

In contrast to Rev 1:6 and 5:10, where only the holy status of the priest is at stake, in Rev 20:5–6 believers in Jesus are found in heaven. They are nominated as priests of God and Christ (and not merely a "Kingdom of priests," which originally refers to the entire people of Israel) and reign with Christ for a thousand years. It therefore appears that they actually serve as priests by the throne. Thus the difference between the two priestly types not only is a matter of present–future[50] but also concerns the identity of the new priests and the essence of their priesthood. In addition, those ministering as priests in the heavenly Temple cannot be traditional Aaronite priests, since the latter serve only on earth. Heavenly priesthood is "new"; namely, these priests are different from those in the Jerusalem Temple because they are chosen by merit, not by descent. By comparison, in the Songs of the Sabbath Sacrifices the ministering angels in heaven serve as priests.[51]

In all of these passages the new priesthood of the believers or martyrs is interwoven with a complementary one: their being like rulers. Rev 20:6 refers to priests who reign for a thousand years, and this is mentioned in the context of their refusal to serve the beast and its image (20:4), implying the Roman ruler cult.[52] This may hint that they rule instead of the emperor. The concept of reign is also implied by the designation of "a Kingdom of priests" in 1:6 and 5:10. This slogan is not only confined to the priestly domain but also contains the aspect of Kingdom (*basilea*)—the power to rule and the freedom from subordination to foreign kings and rulers.[53] Thus I suggest that by using the term "a Kingdom of priests" John claims that the believers are already sovereign and free in spirit and that the martyrs will join God and the Lamb in heavenly rule.

The Lamb: Sacrifice or Deity?

While John stresses the basic familiar notion that Jesus's death—and especially his blood—is a ransom for believers' sins (1:5; 5:9; 7:14; 12:11), his treatment of Christ is unique. Among the many designations of Christ, he makes extensive use of the term "the Lamb" (*arnion*), both standing by God and being worshiped.[54]

The Lamb is a sacrificial symbol. It is designated as "the Lamb standing as if it had been slaughtered" (5:6). The four living creatures and the twenty-four elders praise him, singing "for you were slaughtered and by your blood you ransomed saints for God" (5:9). Yet it is not really slaughtered since it is, after all, resurrected and alive.[55] It functions very much like a sin offering: the blood of Christ is mentioned as having a ransoming (1:5), purifying (7:14), and conquering (12:11) effect.[56]

The heavenly company declares that the slaughtered Lamb is purchased for God as well as for the people of every tribe, people, and nation (5:9). The victim is the one worthy of power. Losing his life brings salvation to others (7:9–10), and his blood brings the cleansing that allows access to God (7:14).[57] The implication may be that it replaces blood sacrifice[58]—though this is never stated.

The sacrificial symbol of the Lamb is developed in Revelation more than in any other NT text.[59] However, nowhere in Revelation does the Lamb function as a sacrifice offered in the heavenly Temple. It is glorified and worshiped along with God[60] but is not related to the altar, and it has no special role in the rituals of the heavenly Temple. Its sacrificial character appears as a symbol or archetype, a matter of the past. In a sense, its being slaughtered and serving as a ransom serve only as background and explanation for the author with regard to its divine status in heaven.[61]

The worship of the Lamb is fully expressed in 5:8–12. When the Lamb takes the scroll, "the four living creatures and the twenty-four elders fell before the Lamb, each holding a harp and golden bowls full of incense, which are the prayers of the saints. They sing a new song: 'You are worthy to take the scroll and to open its seals, for you were slaughtered and by your blood you ransomed for God saints from every tribe and language and people and nation; you have made them to be a Kingdom and priests serving our God, and they will reign on earth'; And all the angels stood around the throne and around the elders and the four living creatures, and they fell on their faces before the throne and worshiped God; singing, 'Amen!' Blessing and glory and wisdom and thanksgiving and honor and power and might be to our God for ever and ever! Amen."

The relationship of the Lamb to the throne is quite complex. The Lamb stands next to the throne "between the throne and the four living creatures" (5:6). Then it sits at the center of the throne (7:17), and the shepherd selects it from there. It shares the throne with God when the water of life flows from the throne of God and the Lamb (22:1). In the New Jerusalem the throne belongs to both God and the Lamb (22:3).

Being a Pillar in the Temple

One puzzling passage in Revelation refers to the believer as a pillar in the Temple of God. This is an intriguing piece of Temple imagery. It raises the question of the relationship between the members of the Christian community and Temple and cult in Revelation.

In the letter to the angel of the congregation of Philadelphia, John encourages the addressee who keeps Christ's word, adding, "If you conquer, I will make you a pillar in the Temple of my God; you will never go out of it. I will write on you the name of my God, and the name of the city of my God, the new Jerusalem that comes down from my God out of heaven, and my own new name" (3:12).

What does being a "pillar," especially one in the Temple, mean? Pillar is a common metaphor for good standing in the Hellenistic world. It shows that a person is of central importance to the community.[62] It is usually assumed that the pillar at stake is the one placed inside the *naos*.[63] God's name is written on it. Such an inscription is a metaphor for divine ownership and dedication to God. In the present case, inscribing the name of the New Jerusalem signifies citizenship in the heavenly city.[64]

The one who conquers is a designation for remaining faithful to Christ despite oppression—as if the believer conquers the world by his faithfulness.[65] The meaning of this phrase can be compared to another reward that is promised "to everyone who conquers:" "I will give permission to eat from the tree of life that is in the paradise of God" (2:7). One may assume that being a pillar in God's Temple is similar to eternal life in the heavenly world.[66]

Special scholarly attention is paid to the question of which Temple John is alluding to here. Is it earthly, heavenly, or eschatological—or perhaps merely a metaphorical Temple, such as the Christian community itself?[67] I think John refers to a pillar in the heavenly Temple, the one he describes in detail. Being such a pillar may serve as a metaphor for eschatological salvation.[68]

An interesting perspective on the meaning of pillars in the heavenly Temple is found in the description of the heavenly Temple in the Songs of the Sabbath Sacrifices. As already mentioned, here the Temple's pillars and corners are animate beings joining with the heavenly hosts and singing praises to God. If the pillars of the heavenly sanctuary are alive and capable of lifting up their voices to give glory to God, then the believer made into pillar in Rev 3:12 is promised a place in the heavenly choir, the angelic hosts worshiping God.[69] The believer-pillar probably joins the chosen ones by the throne with God's seal on his head (as mentioned in Rev 7).[70] Thus the promise relates to the heavenly Temple and may refer to the believer's afterlife.

Measuring the Temple

Following the opening of the seventh seal, the angels' blowing of the six trumpets, and the killing of a third of the people by plagues, an angel opens a small book. John then describes the strange scene of the measuring of the Temple: "Then I was given a measuring rod like a staff, and I was told, 'Come and measure the Temple of God and the altar and those who worship there; But do not measure the court [aulē] outside the Temple; leave that out, for it is given over to the nations, and they will trample over the holy city for forty-two months'" (11:1–2). In the next verses John describes the death of the two witnesses as caused by the beast and the angels' war against the dragon.

Here there is a separation between two domains of the Temple. The naos and the altar are secured, whereas the outer court is trampled by the nations for forty-two months. This means that the Temple and the worshipers escape the control of the Gentiles—namely, profanation and destruction.[71] The act of measuring is common in prophetic literature, serving as a symbolic act. Note, for example, the measuring of the New Jerusalem in 21:15–17. Measuring stands as a sign of either destruction or preservation. In our case, what is measured cannot fall to the nations, hence the worshipers will remain safe.[72]

Still, the context of this prophecy raises several issues. First, the command is not carried out but only given. Second, it is not clear how John can have access to the Temple to measure it, especially if this applies to the heavenly one. And if the command relates to the Jerusalem Temple, this would also be strange because the earthly Temple is not mentioned at all in Revelation. Neither is its destruction by Rome.[73]

There have been several opinions concerning which Temple is referred to here: the Jerusalem Temple before it is destroyed by Rome, the Christian community as the true or metaphorical Temple, or the heavenly Temple. Since the passage relates to the coming conquest by the nations, some argue that it concerns the Jerusalem Temple while it is still standing. Some even regard the passage as originating from the Zealots' prophecy before 70 CE. The logic of such suggestions is that only a physical Temple can be measured. In this context, John the seer probably descends to earth to measure the Temple. This interpretation also draws on the fact that another earthly location, Mount Zion, is mentioned in 14:1. Admittedly, the threat of being trampled by the nations seems tangible and relevant during the First Revolt against Rome.[74] However, current scholarship does not accept this suggestion since the Jerusalem Temple is not mentioned elsewhere in Revelation, and there are good reasons to date the text after the Temple's destruction.[75]

Contemporary scholarship usually views John 11:1–2 as applying to the Christian community, as if this community is a symbolic Temple: the inner court represents the Christians, while the outer court stands for those who do not believe in Jesus. This interpretation builds on the Pauline metaphor of the community as a Temple and also regards the symbolic Temple as a locus of salvation despite the destruction.[76] Thus the outer court is the vulnerable realm, the unbelieving world, while the naos is the worshiping community.[77]

Others suggest that the passage describes the heavenly Temple.[78] This is plausible because the heavenly Temple is the author's major concern, and he has already described its altar. No other Temple is mentioned in the book, at least not explicitly. Obviously, its location in heaven along with its divine character means that it is protected (as in 7:14–17). Nonetheless, those who support the identification of the Temple in 11:1–2 with the community raise a number of reservations. The existence of the outer court does not correspond with the notion of a heavenly Temple, which does not seem to have one. Furthermore, it is inconceivable that part of the Temple would be left to the nations.[79] Angels are not mentioned in our passage, and, unlike other cases in which the Temple is in heaven, there is no mention of its location in heaven either.[80]

Surely the image of measuring the Temple and distinguishing the naos and the altar from the outer court is a complex one. Each of the above interpretations poses difficulties. My own suggestion is that the scene alludes to the heavenly Temple. It uses the image of the Temple allegorically. The inner court represents the heavenly Temple, the location of some of the chosen believers—namely, those who have God's name sealed on their forehead. The outer court stands for the rest of the world, including the earthly Jerusalem, in which evil forces still rule and even the witnesses are in danger (11:7–10). I see no contradiction between referring to the outer court as "the holy city" (11:2) and the statement that "the great city that is spiritually called Sodom and Egypt, where also their Lord was crucified" (11:8). Evil prevails in both cases. The holy city relates to the past and future—to the city's religious potential—while Sodom and Egypt are designations that represent its present citizens. Note that in the renewal of the cosmic war against Satan after a thousand years, the saints and "the beloved city" will be besieged again (20:9). Thus the city is the earthly location of the believers, unlike the safe place in heaven.

What John wants to argue is that the naos area, the heavenly Temple, is the only safe place until the End of Days and the coming of the New Jerusalem. This passage marks the difference between the situation in the present, when the divine realm is limited to heaven, and the future, when it will come down to earth.

The New Jerusalem and the Absent Temple

THE NEW JERUSALEM AS GOD'S DWELLING PLACE

The culmination of Revelation's discourse is the coming of the New Jerusalem from the sky in 21:1–3: "Then I saw a new heaven and a new earth; for the first heaven and the first earth had passed away, and the sea was no more. And I saw the holy city, the new Jerusalem, coming down out of heaven from God, prepared as a bride adorned for her husband. And I heard a loud voice from the throne saying, 'See, the dwelling [*skēnē*] of God is among mortals. He will dwell [*skēnōsei*] with them; they will be his people, and God himself will be with them as their God.'"[81]

Consequently, the one who is seated on the throne declares, "I am making all things new." Only "those who conquer," namely, the ones who hold fast in their faith, will inherit the new things. The faithless and wicked will be destroyed (21:5–8). In the verses that follow, the angel shows John the

Lamb's "bride," the holy city of Jerusalem. It has the shining glory of God, a great wall, and twelve gates—each with the name of one of the twelve tribes of Israel.[82] It is built with precious stones or gems, and its street is made of gold (21:10–21). Most of the stones in this list of twelve precious stones resemble one of the stones on the high priest's breastplate (Ex 28:17), in which each gem represents one of the tribes. It is possible to interpret the list of gems as priestly imagery, as if the city bears the identity of the entire people of Israel like the gates' names.[83] Furthermore, the New Jerusalem may be considered the opposite of Babylon in terms of purity vs. uncleanness and the exclusion of abomination and falsehood.[84]

In the description of the New Creation, the New Jerusalem comes down from heaven as a city of heavenly origins whose builder and maker is God.[85] The New Jerusalem is new not only in time but also quality.[86] It is possible to see here a transformation of the divine throne, which is relocated since God now dwells with humans (21:3). In fact, John hears a voice from the throne telling him about this transition.

The New Jerusalem belongs to the Christian believers: John refers to "those who conquer" (21:7) and mentions God's servants who have God's name sealed on their foreheads (22:5–6). It therefore symbolizes Christianity as the heir of ancient promises concerning Israel at Endtime and the identification of the Christians with Israel.[87]

We have seen that the New Jerusalem is based upon the model of the twelve tribes, bearing a clear Israelite identity (and perhaps also implying the gathering of the exiled Jews in the End of Days). Yet special attention is given to the Gentiles: "The nations will walk by its light, and the kings of the earth will bring their glory into it. . . . People will bring into it the glory and the honor of the nations" (21:24, 26). In addition, the leaves of the tree of life "are for the healing of the nations" (22:2). Yet it would be an exaggeration to argue that John is universalizing the Jewish traditional idea of the End of Days.[88] John follows the prophetic idea of the Gentiles joining the worship of God without having status equal to that of the Jews (Isa 2:2–4; 60:3; Jer 3:17; Zech 14:16–19). The Gentiles are positively affected by the light of the New Jerusalem and show respect for it, sharing at least some of its special benefits. But the New Jerusalem is not their own. They will come into it from the outside to share in its holiness.

The New Jerusalem is the culmination of the description of God's throne, the heavenly Temple, and the cosmic combat against the forces of evil. It shows that God rules history. It also symbolizes the union of God's people in heaven (by the throne and in the heavenly Temple) and earth, two domains which had been described as separate previously. It is the manifestation of the ideal Christian community and is even called the Lamb's bride (21:9).[89]

John does not invent the idea of the new and perfect holy city coming down from the sky.[90] The cosmic event of the creation of a new heaven and earth as well as a new Jerusalem is first mentioned in prophetic literature from the postexilic period, during which time the Judean restoration under the Persians takes place (Isa 65:17–25; 66:22). The building of the New Jerusalem with precious stones expounds upon Isa 54:11 ("lay your foundations with sapphires . . . your pinnacles of rubies, your gates of jewels, and all your wall of precious stones").[91] The portrayal of the New Jerusalem as paradise (including the tree of life) is rooted in the prophecy on Zion in Isa 51:3 ("make her wilderness like Eden, her desert like the garden of the Lord"). The idea of the descent of the New Jerusalem surfaces again in the Hellenistic period in Enoch's Animal Apocalypses (1 En 90:29, 33–35) and later as a reaction to the fall of Jerusalem to the Romans in 70 CE, especially in 4 Ezra and 2 Baruch.[92]

Revelation 21:3 explicitly introduces the religious meaning of the New Jerusalem: God will dwell with mortals, and the people of God will be with Him. This intimate relationship is conceived of as the fulfillment of God's promises to Israel. In Lev 26:11, God promises to the Israelites that if they keep the commandments "I will place my dwelling in your midst." Ezek 37:27 concludes the prophecy with the restoration of Judah and Israel under David by promising, "My dwelling-place shall be with them."[93]

Thus the notion of the New Jerusalem and God's dwelling within it is the reworking of an old Jewish tradition that has several versions. Interestingly, John is not the only one who finds it both appealing and necessary after the destruction of the earthly Jerusalem and the Temple in 70 CE. However, John has a distinctive approach to the Temple.

THE ABSENCE OF THE TEMPLE

Rev 21:22–23 notes the absence of the Temple from the New Jerusalem: "I saw no Temple in the city, for its Temple is the Lord God the Almighty and the Lamb. And the city has no need of sun or moon to shine on it, for the glory of God is its light, and its lamp is the Lamb." In this Endtime there is no distinction between heaven and earth, and it seems that the heavenly Temple comes down from the sky, even though this is not explicitly stated. There is, then, no further contrast between earthly and heavenly Temples.

While it was customary for Jewish sources to imagine the new Temple in the End of Days,[94] John boldly diverges from this convention. He seems to acknowledge the expectation that a Temple will stand at the heart of the New Jerusalem. According to his vision, expectations of the new Temple throughout redemptive history will be consummated in the New Jerusalem by the most intimate dwelling of the Lord Almighty God and the Lamb with God's people.[95]

Some commentators have identified the New Jerusalem as the new Temple. There are certainly several similarities between the two. The city has a cubiform, like the holy of holies;[96] heaven and earth meet there; it is the center of God's rule; it is on a high mountain (21:10, as in Isa 2:2; Ezek 40:2); impure and immoral people are excluded from it (21:27);[97] and God's servants have God's name sealed on their foreheads, somewhat like the rosette (*tzitz*) of the high priest (Ex 28:36–37). However, even though the shape of the New Jerusalem is influenced by myths and traditions about the Temple, the author's explicit words deny the possibility of regarding the New Jerusalem as a broadening of the concept of the Temple. Revelation introduces a brand-new concept according to which the eschaton will lack a Temple.

How can John overtly reject the necessity of the Temple in the ideal future? Not only are temples the ultimate means of worshiping the gods, serving as the basic religious establishments of the Hellenistic world, but also the very sanctity of Jerusalem seems to be grounded upon the existence of the Temple within it. What makes Jerusalem holy is David's bringing of the Tabernacle and the Ark into the city.[98]

Some have concluded that Revelation simply rejects the very idea of the Temple. It is easy to relate this to the supposedly anti-Temple stance contained in other early Christian texts—from Jesus's cleansing of the Temple onward—and to argue that Christ or the Lamb is the new Temple.[99] Nevertheless, the detailed presentation of the heavenly Temple negates this viewpoint. The author sees the Temple cult as a symbolic system that operates even in heaven. Access to God and the Lamb comes through a cultic realm.[100] It is therefore impossible to attribute to the author an opinion about the lack of necessity of the Temple, as is found later in the Epistle of Barnabas and Justin Martyr (see chapter 9).

Although Revelation's rejection of the Temple in the End of Days is the boldest, it is not completely unique. There are non-Christian Jewish precedents for it. Jer 3:16 does not expect the return of the holy Ark. Here the Ark (and the Cherubim upon it), which symbolizes God's throne and presence, will cease to be important because Jerusalem itself will become God's throne on earth and the manifestation of His presence.[101] The Animal Apocalypse (1 En 85–90, dated to the mid-second century BCE) presents the most detailed description of the eschatological scenario. It elaborates the rebuilding of the house of the Lord of the sheep (1 En 90:29–34), including the gathering of the other animals (the Gentiles) into it. According to the symbolism of the Animal Apocalypse, "the house" stands for the city of Jerusalem, whereas the Temple is represented by "the tower." Yet no tower is mentioned in the detailed description of the End of Days.[102]

Revelation's approach should be assessed in comparison to Jewish eschatological Apocalypses that also cope with the destruction of 70 CE. 4 Ezra 10:23–34 and 11:23–50 present the eschatological age and the eschatological Jerusalem but do not mention the Temple.[103] 2 Baruch 6:7–8 relates to hiding the holy vessels until the eschatological age, but the existence of the Temple in the End of Days is mentioned only sparsely in 32:3–4 and 65:4. Baruch does not really distinguish between Jerusalem and the Temple. Despite the detailed description of the eschaton (chs. 29–30, 39–40, 44, 51, 70–74), he pays little attention to the Temple.[104] Below I will suggest why the role of the earthly Temple decreases in these writings.

Unlike 2 Baruch and 4 Ezra, Revelation argues that God and the Lamb serve as the Temple rather than as the Temple building. The idea that God is the true Temple can be found in only a single biblical text, although it lacks explicit negation of the Temple as an institution. Isa 8:13–14 reads as follows: "But the Lord of hosts, him you shall regard as holy; let him be your fear, and let him be your dread; *He will become a sanctuary* [*miqdash*; LXX *hagiasma*], a stone one strikes against." It is difficult to interpret this verse, especially since the context is divine wrath against Israel's sins. It is possible the prophet means that if you sanctify Him God will be a sanctuary to you as well and that in God there will be true protection and refuge.[105] Isaiah may have used the Temple as a metaphor for God, implying a direct sanctification of Israel. In the Apocalypse of John, the metaphor is understood literally, suggesting that a Temple will not be needed in the future.

The rationale for the idea that God will take the place of the Temple is that once the barriers of sin and evil are removed there will no longer be a distinction between holy and profane, and all worshipers in the city will be able to see God's face. There will be no need of a meeting place or a human-built structure to mediate between God's presence and humankind because God will be fully present with all of His people, accessible directly to all.[106] Yet there is no need to confuse this concept with the equation of the Christian community and the Temple.[107] In the New Jerusalem the believers will be as close as possible to God and the Lamb, but they are not a Temple since God and the Lamb *are* the Temple. The author is not following the concept of community-as-Temple. His attitude is actually closer to the gospel of John, which regards Jesus as the heir of the destroyed Temple (see chapter 5).

The New Jerusalem is different from the heavenly Temple, and it seems to take its place. God and the throne are no longer remote in heaven but on earth. Additionally, there is no duality or separation between holy and profane or just and evil. However, there are several common traits that show that the New Jerusalem takes the place of the heavenly Temple: worshipers, including Gentiles (7:9; 21:24, 26; 23:2) approach to serve God (7:9–17; 14:2–4; 22:3); God takes care of their being thirsty (7:16; 21:6) and wipes their tears (7:17; 21:4); whatever is impure is excluded (21:8, 27; cf. 14:4), including unrighteousness (14:5; 21:27); and God's name is sealed on the foreheads of the worshipers (7:3–4; 22:4). In both the New Jerusalem and the Temple we find God's presence and glory. Thus the heavenly Temple is transformed. What the heavenly Temple had once symbolized is realized in the New Jerusalem.[108]

For the author of Revelation, the New Jerusalem is both the perfect reality and the perfect Temple. If the Temple provides a means for humans to serve and approach God, the New Jerusalem fulfills this role in the eschaton. The fact is, however, that John envisions this evolution in the very distant future of another thousand years. I think the lack of an earthly Temple in Revelation is *not* the result of a lack of appreciation for the institution or its symbolism. After all, the author describes an alternative but related cultic system in heaven. Still, the notion that a Temple will no longer be necessary in the distant future is revolutionary and provocative. How could John conceive of a religious utopia without a Temple?

One way to interpret Rev 21:22–23 is to view it as a symbolic discourse. In addition to the absence of the Temple, the author maintains that the New Jerusalem "has no need of sun or moon to shine on it, for the glory of God is its light, and its lamp is the Lamb." The natural world will therefore be abolished. Here John probably follows Isa 60:19–20: "The sun shall no longer be your light by day, nor for brightness shall the moon give light to you by night; but the Lord will be your everlasting light, and your God will be your glory; Your sun shall no more go down, or your moon withdraw itself, for the Lord will be your everlasting light, and your days of mourning shall be ended." This is part of an eschatological promise, as in the opening of the prophecy "Arise, shine, for your light has come, and the glory of the Lord has risen upon you" (Isa 60:1; note the mention of the altar and the Temple in 60:7).

The fact that the absence of the Temple is mentioned contemporaneously with the disappearance of the sun and the moon puts this absence in a different context. The New Jerusalem can do without a Temple just as much as it can do without the sun and moon! Only in the utopian circumstances of the very distant future can one find no need for the Temple—and God and the Lamb will embody their respective places only when they also replace the natural luminaries. Read in this manner, John is actually pointing out the necessity of the heavenly Temple for the present age. It will be replaced not in the present but only at the millennium.

Still, there is a certain message that in the End of Days there will be something better than the Temple, and this is, after all, a revolutionary idea. In fact, as we have seen, 4 Ezra and 2 Baruch, written during approximately the same period as Revelation (several years after the destruction), likewise do not give much weight to the eschatological Temple. I therefore suggest viewing the absence of the Temple from the New Jerusalem as a response to its destruction by Rome in 70 CE.[109]

Life without a Temple presents the Jewish people (not only those in in Judaea) with a new reality. On the one hand, the loss of the Temple is both the result and a symbol of their subordination to Rome owing to the failed revolt. Temple ideology is one of the main reasons for the outburst of the revolt.[110] Hence John's transforming of the concept of the Temple to a non-earthly, nonpolitical reality releases his readers both from the motivation to rebuild the Temple and the urge to rebel once again (as the Jews did under Trajan and Hadrian in 115 and 132 CE, respectively). Furthermore, living without a Temple for a generation showed the Jews that, unlike Greco-Roman religions and cults, Judaism could survive without a Temple.[111] John develops this view further when he actually argues that the Temple is not an ultimate necessity—that it has a better alternative, albeit in another dimension of human life in the End of Days.

Conclusions: The New Cultic System

TEMPLE AND CULT IN REVELATION

Many details concerning the Temple in heaven and its cult are spread throughout Revelation. The heavenly Temple is sometimes designated as the Tabernacle, and even the sacred Ark is mentioned, creating a sense of authenticity. The Temple's altar also plays a significant role in the narrative, although sacrifices are not offered on it, only incense. The Temple Menorah, the lampstand, is also an important symbol of the Christian community. The Temple's pillar and the act of measuring the Temple are important symbols as well. Rites of prayer and incense offerings are mentioned, and there may even be allusions to the rites of the Festival of Tabernacles.[112] The religious world of the author is therefore dependent on the Temple cult. Temple rites and objects shape his ideas of worship of God and divine judgment. It is impossible to say that John rejects the Temple cult since he relies on it heavily to express his imagery and message. He creatively transfers cultic imagery and symbolism from the Jerusalem Temple to the one in heaven.

The author's approach to the Temple and its cult becomes clearer once we compare it to other descriptions of the heavenly Temple in Jewish antiquity. First, the concept of employing the Temple as a model for future worship is quite common.[113] Many authors want to teach their readers about the true and perfect worship of God. Although a heavenly Temple's sacredness is superior to that of the terrestrial one, the Temple in heaven provides inspiration for those in the earthly Temple, showing that similar modes of worship exist in both and that the cult does not arise from a merely human need to approach God. Detailed descriptions such as we find in Revelation are rare and actually are found only in the Songs of the Sabbath Sacrifices from Qumran and the much later Heikhalot literature.[114]

It is interesting to compare the descriptions of the heavenly Temple in Revelation and the Songs of the Sabbath Sacrifices, which describe the angels performing the celestial liturgy praising God, including blessings and singing.[115] Unlike the Qumranic Songs, Revelation is not centered on the angelic assembly and the angels' courses (*mishmarot*), activities, and liturgies. It is also much less interested in the architecture of the Temple.[116] On the other hand, John puts more stress on the divine throne.[117] Other, shorter descriptions of the heavenly Temple do not provide as much cultic detail as Revelation. Neither do the much longer Songs, which do not mention the altar, incense, lampstand, or palm branches. This reinforces the impression that the Apocalypse of John takes special interest in the cultic sphere and the Temple rites. More than any other text, it transfers many aspects or symbols of the earthly Temple to the heavenly one.

On the other hand, Revelation does not mention animal sacrifices or contain any other reference to sacrifice and offering (besides incense), whereas one passage in the Songs does mention offerings, sacrifices, and libations.[118] It is difficult to say whether John avoids mentioning these because Jesus's death replaces sacrifice or because such rites seem inappropriate for a heavenly Temple. Such descriptions of actual sacrifices are quite rare in depictions of the heavenly Temple.[119]

All of this leaves us with an important question as to the meaning of the Temple for the author: is it a literary vehicle, a means to an end, or an expression of a major message of its own? On the one hand, Temple imagery contributes to the portrayal of the divine world and the sacred realm in relation to the author's central ideas concerning the faith of believers, the role of the Lamb, and God's control of the human realm. On the other hand, as I will explain below, the idea of the Temple and the heavenly cult bears a religious message of its own, one which fits within the broader message of Revelation.

ANTI-ROMAN CULTIC STANCE

One of the key themes in Revelation is its critique of Roman power and religious institutions.[120] For example, Rev 12 echoes Greek myths that serve as the basis for the Roman imperial cult and the view of a golden age under the emperor's rule. In Rev 13, the beast that all the people of the earth are bowing in front of represents Rome. Similarly, worshiping the beast is akin to participating in the imperial cult. The beast may be identified with both the emperor and Satan.[121] In his discourse about the combat against and defeat of these forces, John is likely reacting to the social pressure experienced by the Christians in Asia Minor.[122]

In Rev 13, the emperor and his allies are vilified. The Christians not only refuse to recognize the emperor as divine but also do not even acknowledge his right to kingship or universal rule. The author discourages practices like speaking of the emperor as Lord or King, swearing by the Genius or Fortune of the emperor, attending banquets or festivals held in honor of Roma or the emperor, and even using coins with the emperor's image. Indeed, the supporters of Rome see the emperor as the primary link between the divine and the human, whereas Christians view Jesus Christ in that role. Some Christians might maintain loyalty to the emperor as God's servant (as implied in Rom 13:1–7; 1 Pet 2:13–17), but for others acknowledgment of Caesar at the same time as Christ is incompatible (as implied by Rev 13).[123]

Thus the key issue is true or false worship—the correct worship of God in contrast to idolatry. Revelation's claim is that Christians must disassociate themselves from the evil of the Roman imperial system, despite their suffering and persecutions by the Romans. In anticipating God's triumph over evil, the author wants to show that God, not the emperor, is the ruler of the world.[124]

This leads us to the essential purpose of the entire book. The anti-Roman stance is shaped in an atmosphere of cosmic war, but Revelation also introduces the reader to a solution. As an apocalypse, Revelation deals with the crisis by creating a new linguistic "world," employing effective symbols and narrative techniques. In doing so, it releases tension aroused by a perceived crisis and provides the reader with a catharsis. It transfers aggressive feelings to another sphere from the present to the future. The apocalyptic discourse includes internalization and reversal of these feelings by means of intensified norms for the Christian way of life. Thus readers are convinced that what ought to be already exists—that the future reality will be fully and manifestly determined by God and Christ.[125]

COMPENSATING FOR THE DESTRUCTION OF
THE JERUSALEM TEMPLE BY ROME

The anti-Roman stance and the aim to overcome political and religious pressures by turning to an alternative, superior reality should be related to the heavenly Temple and new modes of worshiping God. There should be a good reason why the most anti-Roman NT text introduces an alternative Temple in heaven. The answer lies, I suggest, in the fact that Rome destroyed the earthly Temple and halted the sacrificial cult not long before Revelation is written. Note also that the danger that the Temple would be seized by the Gentiles is mentioned in Rev 11:1–2. As we have seen, 4 Ezra and 2 Baruch, which also respond to the tragedy of the destruction by means of apocalyptic eschatology do not pay considerable attention to the Temple, but they also do not stress such an anti-Roman polemic.

In developing the Temple theme, the author seems to react to the Roman destruction of the Jerusalem Temple.[126] John, I suggest, believes that the destruction of the Temple is an attempt to force the Jews to take part in the idolatrous Roman imperial cult. It is a religious threat not only to what is lost now (the sacrificial system and the primary way to worship God) but also to what is coming next. Christians need a new mode of worship to be the focus of their belief. They need a destiny to which they can direct their prayers, feelings, and fears. This is the aim of Revelation's heavenly Temple. Christian Jews need it owing to their loss of the Jerusalem Temple as a symbolic and spiritual center. But non-Jewish Christians, who are also used to having a cultic place, now must create an alternative cultic center. In a sense, Revelation shows that its readers need a Temple, even if a merely symbolic one.

My interpretation builds on the common dating of the book to the 90s CE. This estimate is especially on target if we hold that the author may have experienced the Jewish War personally in Palestine. Hence the "language about a heavenly temple and a new Jerusalem seems to compensate for the loss of the earthly temple and city as a symbolic center."[127]

The heavenly Temple and other cultic elements in Revelation are important to the description of the heavenly world and the divine rule of the cosmos. Following traditional Jewish ideas, the author probably cannot imagine the celestial world without a Temple and the worship of God. He does not make a strong connection between distinctive Christian elements and cultic imagery. In most cases, Christ and the Lamb are only in the background of the Temple system (the closest link is the Son of Man holding the seven lampstands in 1:20). The question remains whether the discourse of the heavenly Temple and its vessels necessarily means that the Christians have a heavenly Temple of their own. In any event, the heavenly cult is an integral part of a more general cosmic worldview of the divine order. It claims that there is an ideal, eternal Temple in heaven and that the Christology fits into this worldview.

This notion of a celestial Temple and its cultic worship plays a major role in Revelation as a response to the loss of the earthly Temple. Implied here is the claim that Rome demolishes the Jerusalem Temple but cannot destroy the heavenly one. Its punishment will come from the heavenly Temple. The righteous, *Jews and Gentiles alike,* will always turn to this Temple, which will be replaced by a better alternative in the form of the New Jerusalem. The author's need to detail such an alternative cultic system while coping with the evil forces in the world shows a core belief about the necessity of the Temple: to worship God, Jews, including the Jewish-

Christians and their Gentile associates, need a Temple, and if not on earth, then in heaven.[128] John builds this heavenly Temple through his own words.

John does limit the idea of the Temple when he eliminates it in the millennium, but this is not because he does not think highly of it, rather because the entire creation will transformed in the New Jerusalem. For him, the end of the heavenly Temple and the disappearance of the cultic symbolism in approaching the sacred is also the end of the world as we know it. Only God is superior to the Temple.

8 Hebrews: The New Heavenly Temple Cult Based on the Old One

Introduction

The Letter to the Hebrews presents the most detailed treatment of the sacrificial system in the NT and also the most radical one. The author declares that Jesus is the high priest in the heavenly Temple. Jesus offers the ultimate sacrifice, his own body, "so that he might be a merciful and faithful high priest in the service of God, to make a sacrifice of atonement for the sins of the people" (2:17). Through Jesus as both a high priest and a sacrifice, forgiveness is promised to the Christian believers.

About half of the contents of this epistle or treaty discusses cultic issues, and I cannot address all of them here. I will focus on the way the author builds on the Levitical system of priests-Temple-sacrifice in order to explain how Christ and his sacrifice lead to forgiveness and atonement. In the conclusion of the chapter I will address the question of why the high priesthood and sacrifice become the author's model for Christology.

It is quite common to read Hebrews as an attack on the validity of the sacrificial cult. William Manson assumes that "a straight line runs from the teaching and apologia of proto-Martyr [Stephen] to the Epistle to the Hebrews."[1] For Manson, Stephen in Acts 6–7 believes that the Temple cult is "transcended and antiquated" and that the church of Jesus should leave behind the Temple and all that it entails. For Stephen, the Temple is not intended to become a permanent institution. He preaches that Jesus has transcended and superseded the cult and the Law.[2] Whether Hebrews actually introduces such a sharp polemic against the Temple cult remains to be seen and will be a subject of discussion throughout this chapter. Alternatively, some believe that the heavenly Temple is a metaphor in which figurative language symbolizes the eschatological dwelling of God with His people.[3]

It is usually assumed that the audience of Hebrews is not Gentiles but Jewish-Christians. Yet this is not because of its title in the NT canon. The title "to the Hebrews" is added to the book at the end of the second century, and there is no guarantee that it is intended by the original. Still, the contents may seem to address readers with Jewish background because of its many Old Testament quotations and allusions as well as detailed and rich Levitical imagery.[4] It is commonly assumed that the entire epistle is written to address a particular crisis in the readers' community.[5]

Since Hebrews views Christ as a complete replacement of the sacrificial system, it is crucial to determine whether it supersedes the Temple while still standing or relates to the cult after its destruction, thus responding to the actual end of the cult by Titus. Unfortunately, dating Hebrews is extremely difficult owing to a paucity of indicative internal evidence. It is clear that the readers are not converts but second-generation Christians (2:3; 5:12; 10:32) whose leaders are already dead (though not necessarily executed, 13:7). Therefore, Hebrews is certainly not one of the earliest NT texts and cannot be dated before 60 CE.[6] It is commonly assumed that the upper limit for dating Hebrews is the date of 1 Clement, since 1 Clem 3:2–6 uses Hebrews 1:3–5. 1 Clement is sometimes dated to 96 CE or, more broadly, to the period spanning 90–120 CE.[7]

There are several considerations regarding the dating of Hebrews either before or after 70 CE. Hebrews' Christology has common characteristics with other post-70 texts, including Luke–Acts, 1 Peter, and the Pastoral Epistles.[8] Quite puzzlingly the author never mentions the Temple, only the Tabernacle of the Priestly Code. He is not interested in the Herodian Temple and the contemporary high priests, only in the Torah and the cultic system of the Tabernacle in the wilderness.[9] This, however, does not require that Hebrews be written when the Temple no longer exists. To the contrary, if Hebrews is written after 70, why doesn't the author mention the destruction to strengthen his argument, showing the inadequacy and outmoded character of the cult and arguing that Christ is the true high priest and sacrifice?

Some claim that the omission of the destruction of the Temple is counteracted by the references to the Mosaic Tabernacle, which constitute a divinely revealed basis for the sanctuary and the priestly practices on which the author builds.[10] Furthermore, as we shall see, Hebrews is not an apologetic or polemical response to Judaism but instead takes interest in the old cult primarily as a foundation for Christological exposition.[11] The author does not tell the audience not to rely on Levitical elements. He does not frame the destruction as a result of Israel's sins or rejection of Christ. Rather, he argues that the Levitical system was never meant to expiate sin in the first place.[12] This fundamental limitation on the sacrificial cult may even console some Jewish-Christians that the loss of the Temple does not mean that Judaism is doomed to fail.

Indeed, some scholars conclude that Hebrews actually copes with the loss of the Temple and aims to move Christians away from hopes for its restoration. The author discusses the Tabernacle *because* the Jerusalem Temple no longer exists. It is the loss of the Temple that leads to the reinterpretation of Judaism's established means of access to God.[13] Hebrews may be a consolation or apology in the absence of the Temple. Facing the destruction, Hebrews steps back and reflects on the nature of earthly sanctuaries and utilizes the wilderness Tabernacle as a prototype.[14]

Hebrews concludes with self-reference to "those from Italy" (13:24). Given the mention of suffering, imprisonment, and the loss of property due to persecutions (10:32–34; cf. 11:35–40), some suggest that it postdates the persecutions of Christians in Rome, especially under Nero in 64 CE. If this is correct, Hebrews may have been written either before or after 70.[15]

To conclude, while there is no definitive evidence to support the dating of Hebrews, the argument for post-70 seems rather strong.[16] Many would agree that it is possible to read Hebrews in light of circumstances after the destruction of the Jerusalem Temple. At the close of this chapter I will explore whether Hebrews' theology is better explained in light of an existent or a nonexistent Temple.

Jesus as a High Priest

Jesus is called a high priest several times in the epistle. Examples include the following: "Jesus, the apostle and high priest of our confession" (3:1); "Christ did not glorify himself in becoming a high priest, but was appointed by the one who said to him, 'You are my Son, today I have begotten you'" (Heb 5:5; cf. Ps 2:7); Christ is a "minister" (*leitourgos*) serving in the heavenly Tabernacle; he is a true one made by God, not by humans (8:2).[17] (I discuss his special characteristics as a high priest below.) First, it is necessary to explain the origins of high priesthood Christology. In other words, how and why does the author portray Jesus as a high priest?

BACKGROUND OF HIGH PRIESTLY CHRISTOLOGY

At first glance there is hardly a connection between Jesus as the Messiah and Son of God and the figure of the high priest. After all, it is the high priest who hands Jesus over to crucifixion. A closer look at the image of the high priest's office in Second Temple sources reveals what attracts Hebrews to portray Jesus as the ultimate high priest.

The high priest holds the most esteemed office in the Second Temple period. Religious functions of ordinary priests during the Second Temple period are twofold: service in the Temple cult and teaching Torah.[18] The high priest enjoys the appreciation of standing at the head of both of these systems.[19] The admiration of his holiness is demonstrated in Ben Sira 50:5–21, where the high priest Simon son of Onias is designated as "glorious" because he heads the daily sacrifices, the burning of the incense, and the priestly blessings in the Temple. In Aristeas's letter 69–99, the high priest's performance is also depicted as "glorious" and "hallowed." In 2 Maccabees, Onias III is not only pious but also "the city's benefactor, the caretaker of the members of his people, and a zealot for the laws" (2 Macc 3:1; 4:2; cf. 15:12). Onias offers an atoning sacrifice for the sake of Heliodorus, who is struck down at the Temple by an angel. The angel tells Heliodorus that the Lord has granted him his life only for the sake of the high priest (2 Macc 3:32–33). Josephus also mentions the legend according to which Alexander the Great bows before the high priest when he sees him in his dreams before going to battle (*Ant.* 11.326–338).

Several documents found at Qumran (some of which are written in Aramaic and are regarded as presectarian) even stress the angelic character of the eschatological high priest, who provides expiation for all of Israel.[20] The Qumran sectarians develop this theme in the blessings of the *Rule of Benedictions*. Here it seems, the priestly Messiah is blessed as being exalted to heaven, functioning like an angel: "And you as the Angel of the Presence in the abode of holiness for the Glory of the God of Ho[st you] will be round about serving in the palace [*hekhal*] of the Kingdom and may you be cast lot with the Angels of the Presence and a common [*Yahad*] council [. . . for] eternal time and for all glorious endtimes."[21] The blessed figure is able to cast lots like the angels and God, and possibly he is transformed into an angel.[22]

For many Jews, the high priest is closer to God than any other human being. He glorifies God's name by virtue of the fact that he embodies it in his diadem, the visible manifestation of the glorification of God's name.

Thus the high priest gives God's most holy name a substantial and tangible presence within the community.[23] The high priestly office also has political power. The Hasmonean rulers and kings are also high priests, becoming high priests before they take the royal title. In the Persian and Hellenistic periods certain high priests also have certain political authority.[24]

Perhaps the supremacy of the high priest as the leader of the Jews sparks the so-called doctrine of the two messiahs, which is attested to by Qumran. In the Damascus Document and the Community Rule from Qumran, the authors anticipate a Messiah of Aaron—probably the future high priest—along with the Messiah of Israel, the offspring of King David. In the description of the official meal in the Rule of Congregation, the priestly Messiah from Aaron enters, blessing the bread and wine before the Messiah of Israel. This attests to his superiority.[25]

Designating the high priest as a Messiah certainly expresses eschatological overtones, but it also has a lexical basis. God commands Moses that the high priest must be anointed with oil; that is, he must be nominated by God in a special ritual (Ex. 29:7; Lev 4:3–5, 16; 8:12). In a sense, Aaron and his successors are the first Messiahs.

Many conclude that Hebrews is heavily influenced by the Qumran sectarians.[26] However, the similarities between these two streams are rather general and do not attest to a direct influence of the scrolls on the author of Hebrews.[27] And yet it is stunning that Qumranic characteristics of the eschatological high priest as being close to God and angel-like are applied to Jesus in Hebrews.[28]

Some scholars argue that Jesus's high priesthood is an early Christian tradition not confined to Hebrews.[29] The main reason for this is that the author declares Jesus to be a high priest before any elaboration of this concept (2:17–18; 3:1–2; 4:14–16). Harold Attridge suggests that the image of Christ as a heavenly high priest is traditional in early Christianity. This is because the title "high priest" is found in early Christian literature outside of the NT, independent of Hebrews, although these sources are dated to the second century. It is difficult to detect the origins of their Christological doctrine.[30] Hebrews remains the earliest text in which Jesus is the high priest, and there is no dispute that the development of this idea in chs. 5–10 is original to the author. As we will see, the author tries to explain and demonstrate that Christ should be considered a priest in various ways, which suggests that this is a new idea for his readers.[31]

HIGH PRIESTHOOD AS A MODEL

The author does not simply transform the high priesthood from Levitical and earthly to Christian and heavenly. He explains to readers the importance and uniqueness of the high priestly office, choosing particular traits that will be further developed in relation to Christ. By doing this, Hebrews uses the high priesthood as a model for Christology. Let's see how the high priest is introduced in the letter.

First, the author introduces the office in general terms: "Every high priest chosen from among mortals is put in charge of things pertaining to God on their behalf, to offer gifts and sacrifices for sins. He is able to deal gently with the ignorant and wayward, since he himself is subject to weakness; and because of this he must offer sacrifice for his own sins as well as for those of the people. And one does not presume to take this honour, but takes it only when called by God, just as Aaron was" (5:1–4). The high priest is God's chosen human being charged with taking away the sins of others. He does so by offering sacrifices for the people's sins, including his own.

Later, in references to the high priest, his sanctuary and sacrifices are employed as a direct model for Christ. The author makes a comparison between the actual Temple and Christ as an alternative: "For every high priest is appointed to offer gifts and sacrifices; hence it is necessary for this priest also to have something to offer. Now if he [Jesus] were on earth, he would not be a priest at all, since there are priests who offer gifts according to the law. They offer worship in a sanctuary that is a sketch and shadow of the heavenly one; for Moses, when he was about to erect the Tabernacle was warned [Ex 25:40], 'See that you make everything according to the pattern that was shown you on the mountain'" (8:3–5).

Once again the divine election of the high priest is stressed, and we are told that sacrifices are his mode of operation. Jesus, however, operates in another realm, which is beyond the Law. While Moses's Tabernacle is indeed planned according to a divine pattern, the author hints that there is a more perfect alternative to it.

Generally, a list of the commonalities between the high priest and Jesus would include the following: being called by God; serving in matters pertaining to God; coping with sin; and, as we shall see below, offering sacrifice for forgiveness.[32] The so-called Priestly Code of the Torah provides comparative categories through which the author validates the *continuity* of the Christ event with Israelite tradition: covenant, priesthood, and sacrifice. This continuity between the old order of Moses and the new order of Christ is established through the use of these three cultic categories. The high priest acts as the mediator between God and the people, gaining access to God's sanctuary and offering sacrifices to bring atonement. At the same time, however, as we will see below, the author points to *discontinuity* between the Israelite high priest and cult in relation to Christ as well as the superiority of the new order.[33]

Throughout this comparison, Hebrews never contradicts the descriptions of sacrificial rites in the Pentateuch. The author accepts the validity of the Levitical system and sacrifices and does not attempt to undermine them. Instead, he uses what might be termed a "sacramental typology."[34] He never criticizes the Levitical priests or high priest by pointing out the failings of particular priests.[35] There is no hint of them treating Jesus and his followers poorly. Nor are charges against the high priest used to justify his replacement by Christ. This method of viewing the high priest as a model and noting appreciation for the Law or the priestly system will be repeated below in my discussion of sacrifice in Hebrews.

Curiously, when the author discusses the role of the high priest, his examples are not only based on Scripture but also reflect contemporary late–Second Temple practice. First, unlike the Pentateuch (Num 18:21), Hebrews says collecting tithes is not limited to the sons of Levi but is shared by the priests (Heb 7:5). Second, whereas in Num 19 it is "a priest" who sprinkles the blood of the red heifer before burning it, in Hebrews (9:13) it seems this is done by the high priest himself. Third, the author regards the high priest as the general representative of all of the Jews.[36]

THE WEAKNESSES OF THE HIGH PRIEST

In the course of introducing the high priesthood as a model for Christ and the comparison between the Jewish high priest and Jesus, the author spells out several weaknesses of the Jewish high priest to show the superiority of Christ as a high priest: "Unlike the other high priests, he has no need to offer sacrifices day after day, first for his own sins, and then for those of the people; this he did once for all when he offered himself. For the law appoints as high priests those who are subject to weakness, but the word of the oath, which came later than the law, appoints a Son who has been made perfect for ever" (7:27–28). In other words, the need to offer sacrifices again and again attests to the relative inefficiency of the high priestly service. In addition, the high priest needs to atone for his own sins before atoning through sacrifices for the sins of the rest of the Jews.[37] But Christ atones for everyone, once and for all, by offering himself. He does not make an offering *for* himself but *of* himself for the sake of others.[38]

Furthermore, in the discussion of Melchizedek, the author mentions a failure of the priesthood which actually relates to the high priesthood itself "if there has been completion through the Levitical priesthood" (7:11). This means that the Levitical priest is not, in fact, perfect and that there is actually a necessity for a new kind of high priest.[39] In addition, there is another quite natural weakness since "the former priests were many in number, because they were prevented by death from continuing in office" (7:23). The ultimate high priest, in contrast, should never be replaced since he never dies.[40]

All of these points of weakness are actually derived from the basics of the Law as well as from nature. There is no personal blame of the high priest. Christ can escape these failures only because he is not a conventional human being. And, as I will show in greater detail in discussing sacrifice in Hebrews, the author does *not* argue that the high priest, the son of Aaron, cannot atone for the people's sin, only that he needs to do so time and again, endlessly. Yet in order to introduce Jesus as the successor of the Levitical high priest Hebrews draws on Melchizedek.

MELCHIZEDEK AS A PRECEDENT FOR JESUS'S HIGH PRIESTHOOD

Jesus's nomination to the high priesthood is the main argument of the epistle, and the author makes a special effort to explain and justify it. One of his key arguments concerns the priesthood of Melchizedek, which serves as a precedent for a non-Aaronite priesthood. Melchizedek's priesthood is introduced in Heb 5:6 using the prooftext "You are a priest forever, according to the order of Melchizedek" (Ps 110:4, repeated in Heb 7:17). The author further asserts that Jesus is "designated by God a high priest according to the order of Melchizedek" (5:10, repeated in 6:20). Melchizedek's priesthood is mentioned four times in Hebrews.

It seems that Ps 110:4 sparks the very characterization of Melchizedek (the king who is also a priest) as a soteriological figure in Jewish tradition (see below) and later draws a similar identification with Christ. Ps 110:1 states, "The Lord says to my lord, 'Sit at my right hand.'" Our author probably interprets the "lord" as referring to Jesus. Connecting Ps 110:1 and 4 leads to the identification of a priestly figure like Melchizedek with the exalted Christ, the Son of God.[41] The "order" (*taxis*) is also a key term which means "shape" or "pattern,"[42] perhaps of a non-Aaronite high priesthood.

More detailed explanation of Jesus's relation to Melchizedek is developed in Heb 7:1–17. The author (following Gen 14:18–20) describes King Melchizedek of Salem, priest of the Most High God, meeting Abraham, and Abraham giving him tithe. His name is interpreted as "king of righteousness." Melchizedek is characterized here as one "without father, without mother, without genealogy, having neither beginning of days nor end of life, but resembling the Son of God, he remains a priest for ever" (7:3). The author then draws a comparison between the "descendants of Levi who receive the priestly office" and "have a commandment in the law to collect tithes from the people" and Melchizedek, to whom a noble figure like Abraham gives tithe even though he "does not belong to their ancestry" (7:4–6). The author sees in Melchizedek a precedent for a non-Levitical priesthood, an anomaly for a high priest who lacks the correct genealogy. Melchizedek is a famous historical figure in the late first century CE. Josephus refers to him as king and priest, the first priest, who inaugurates the Temple in Jerusalem.[43] Hebrews, however, reads the biblical narrative concerning Melchizedek in light of the Psalms' declaration that a priest like Melchizedek will serve forever.[44]

Hebrews draws a comparison between the Levitical priesthood and the need for another priest to arise according to the order of Melchizedek (rather than one according to the order of Aaron). It creates a relation between "our Lord" and Melchizedek—the latter "belonged to another tribe, from which no one has ever served at the altar," while Jesus "descended from Judah," not from the tribe of Levi (7:11, 13–14). For the author, it is obvious that Jesus is the high priest who fulfills the promise of Ps 110:4: "It is even more obvious when another priest arises, resembling Melchizedek; one who has become a priest, not through a legal requirement concerning physical descent, but through the power of an indestructible life; For it is attested of him, 'You are a priest for ever, according to the order of Melchizedek'" (7:15–17).

The use of Melchizedek develops the contrast between Christ and the Levitical priesthood and enhances Christ's heavenly character. Melchizedek exercises a priestly role on the basis of divine appointment. He serves as a precedent for the superior priesthood based on character apart from the descent, ordained by God apart from the Law. His appearance in Gen 14 anticipates the ultimate displacement of the Levitical priesthood, owing to the timeless nature of his office without successor.[45]

Hebrews is not the only text that interprets the Melchizedek in Ps 110:4 as a mythic figure. In 2 Enoch (71:28–29, 33–34 in the longer version), Melchizedek is a mythological high priest who ascends to heaven, will be the head of the priests of the future, and has a key role in the eschatological priesthood. In 11QMelchizedek, he will free the "captives" from the debt of their iniquities. The scroll envisions him conducting the eschatological Day of Atonement sacrifice as well as the final judgment ("the administration of justice"). He is a heavenly figure in the service of God.[46] Surprisingly, when Melchizedek appears as a heavenly character in 11QMelchizedek, the speculations about his divine or heavenly being do not refer to his priesthood (although he does bring atonement); rather, he is a judge and elohim (cf. Ps 82:1), similar to or identical with the angel Michael.[47]

In contrast, in Hebrews the Melchizedek of Ps 110 is not an independent figure, but a model or type. The author uses this unusual text as a kind of a prophecy fulfilled through the coming of Christ as a high priest.[48] The comparison proceeds on a literary level and does not elaborate on his character or explain how his eternal priesthood relates to Christ.[49] In Hebrews, the interest in Melchizedek is confined to his *model* of priesthood "forever."

JESUS THE HEAVENLY HIGH PRIEST

How Did Jesus Become a High Priest?

Hebrews relates to the questions of why and how Jesus becomes a high priest several times from several angles. We have seen that Melchizedek is supposed to explain this as a precedent for a non-Aaronite high priest, an eschatological promise or prophecy. In the same vein, the author also applies the *oath* to the future Melchizedek in Ps 110:4 ("The Lord has sworn and will not change his mind, 'You are a priest for ever according to the order of Melchizedek'") as God's commitment to Jesus: "This was confirmed with an oath; for others who became priests took their office without an oath; but this one became a priest with an oath, because of the one who said to him, 'The Lord has sworn and will not change his mind, You are a priest for ever'; accordingly Jesus has also become the guarantee of a better covenant" (7:20–23). This oath confirms the new eternal priesthood and its special characteristics, since the Aaronite high priests do not have such an oath. The sworn oath apparently is more binding than the Law.[50]

Jesus is "appointed" to the high priesthood, and the prooftext for this is another verse from Ps 2:7: "So also Christ did not glorify himself in becoming a high priest, but was appointed by the one who said to him, 'You are my Son, today I have begotten you'" (Heb 5:5). This stresses that Jesus is called to the office.

The author also uses a more particular explanation pertaining to the life and death of Jesus. His death, resurrection, and exaltation bring him to his new position. The straightforward explanation is that he "has become a priest, not through a legal requirement concerning physical descent, but through the power of an indestructible life" (7:16). This indestructible life probably refers to his resurrection and exaltation.[51]

What prepares Jesus for his new office in his lifetime? According to Heb 5:7–10, "In the days of his flesh, Jesus offered up prayers and supplications, with loud cries and tears," "learned obedience through what he suffered; and having been made perfect, he became the source of eternal salvation for all who obey him." All of this, the author concludes, results in him being "designated by God a high priest according to the order of Melchizedek." This relates to Jesus's suffering as a kind of ransom that provides his followers with forgiveness (cf. 1 Cor 15:3; Gal 3:13). One may also infer that Jesus's merciful behavior as a human being earns him the new title.[52] Furthermore, his prayer for the sake of others recalls the high priest's prayer or confession of Israel's sins in the holy of holies during the Day of Atonement (m. Yoma 6:2). In a sense, Jesus follows the example of the high priest.[53]

The actual rising up to the high priesthood is described in a figurative manner: "We have a great high priest who has passed through the heavens, Jesus, the Son of God, let us hold fast to our confession" (4:14). His passage "through the heavens" probably refers to the resurrection and exaltation and is further related to Christ's service in the heavenly Temple later.[54] Here his priesthood is revealed to be different from the Levitical one, since it is heavenly rather than earthly. Jesus is not a priest on earth but becomes one only when he goes up to heaven.[55] He cannot serve as a priest in his lifetime because "if he were on earth, he would not be a priest at all, since there are priests who offer gifts according to the Law" (8:4). This, however, is complicated by the fact that Jesus's own life's blood serves as the sacrifice he offers before God (9:12, 26, 28). He removes sin by sanctifying his own body, prayers, and supplications (7:5). But all of these pertain to his lifetime and earthly life![56]

This tension between Jesus's earthly death on the cross and his becoming high priest in heaven is crucial. One may wonder whether Hebrews' model of Jesus as a high priest in heaven aligns with the tradition of Jesus's self-sacrifice (suffering, prayer, pouring blood, and final death) on earth (see below). The author does not deal with this issue and does not explain how Jesus's death on earth can function as a sacrifice offered in heaven by the exalted and heavenly high priest. Nevertheless, this tension probably indicates that Hebrews' Christology is not a direct continuation of the earliest understanding of Jesus's death and resurrection. Jesus's high priesthood does not explain his crucifixion and death. It is reasonable to assume that in the course of interpreting Jesus's death and resurrection in cultic terms, the author is sparked by external traditions about a high priest serving in heaven.

Jesus's High Priestly Character
In his new position as a high priest Jesus has special characteristics. Some continue the duties of the earthly, Levitical high priest and others are unique and heavenly.

Christ serves at the most holy place, offering the ultimate sacrifice of his own blood: "But when Christ came as a high priest of the good things that have come, then through the greater and more perfect Tabernacle, not made with hands, that is, not of this creation; he entered once for all into the Holy Place, not with the blood of goats and calves, but with his own blood, thus obtaining eternal redemption; ... For this reason he is the mediator of a new covenant, so that those who are called may receive the promised eternal inheritance, because a death has occurred that redeems them from the transgressions under the first covenant" (9:11–12, 15).

Christ enters the inner shrine, which parallels the earthly holy of holies which the high priest enters on the Day of Atonement (Lev 16:12–13): "We have this hope, a sure and steadfast anchor of the soul, a hope that enters the inner shrine behind the curtain; where Jesus, a forerunner on our behalf, has entered, having become a high priest for ever according to the order of Melchizedek" (6:19–20). According to the Law, approaching holy sancta is considered an extremely severe transgression. According to the Priestly Code (e.g., Num 16:40), no stranger who is not of the seed of Aaron may come near to burn incense before the Lord.

After his exaltation, Christ the high priest makes intercession for the many and remains "holy, blameless, undefiled, separated from sinners, and exalted above the heaven" (7:25–26). It has been mentioned already that he is "without sin" (4:15).[57] Jesus is beyond death since "he continues for ever" (7:24). His high priesthood is therefore unbroken by death, eternal and inviolable, and he thus offers complete salvation.[58]

In Hebrews, Christ achieves a multitude of cultic goals: absolution from guilt (1:3), expiation of sins (2:17), cleansing of one's consciousness (9:14), sanctification (10:10), removal of the barriers between one's soul and God (10:19–23), impartation of the Holy Spirit, and the powers of the World to Come (6:4–5).[59]

To conclude, in Hebrews, Christ's priesthood is not only fundamentally different from the Levitical one; it is superior to it. It is based not on the Law but on the power by which God raises Christ from the dead. It is not "fleshy" but "indestructible" and permanent. It is based not on God's command but on God's gift of indestructible life. In making this gift, God fulfills the promise to raise up a priest like Melchizedek who will serve forever.[60] I now turn to examine Christ's most distinctive act as a high priest—his sacrifice.

Jesus's Sacrifice

More than any other early Christian text, Hebrews develops the theme of Jesus's sacrifice. He makes "a sacrifice of atonement for the sins of the people" (2:17). Unlike Paul, our author does not just state this but explains in detail the origin and consequence of this sacrifice, drawing on concepts of ritual, blood, and atonement.

SACRIFICE AS A MODEL FOR PURIFICATION FROM SIN

Quite similar to the manner in which the author introduces the high priestly office in ancient Judaism as a model for Christ's high priesthood, he puts forward the logic and practice of sacrifice to prepare the ground for discussing Jesus's sacrifice. For this reason, the author begins by describing the Tabernacle and its holy vessels in great detail: "Now even the first covenant had regulations for worship and an earthly sanctuary; For a Tabernacle was constructed, the first one, in which were the lampstand, the table, and the bread of the Presence; this is called the Holy Place; Behind the second curtain was a tabernacle called the Holy of Holies; In it stood the golden altar of incense and the Ark of the Covenant overlaid on all sides with gold, in which there were a golden urn holding the manna, and Aaron's rod that budded, and the tablets of the covenant; above it were the cherubim of glory overshadowing the mercy-seat [the place of atonement, *hilastērion*]. Of these things we cannot speak now in detail" (9:1–5).

As the setting for the sacrificial rite was made—and as the reader visualizes Moses's Tabernacle and its sacred atmosphere—there follows a simplistic description of the priestly service: "Such preparations having been made, the priests go continually into the first Tabernacle to carry out their ritual duties; But only the high priest goes into the second, and he but once a year, and not without taking the blood that he offers for himself and for the sins committed unintentionally by the people" (9:6–7). The terminology of first and second Tabernacle (literally: "tent") is without parallel. This framing helps distinguish between the outer and inner sancta, the *heikhal* and the *devir*. The sacrifice alluded to is derived from the Day of Atonement, and its purpose is to remove sin by blood. This is the beginning of a main mode in Hebrews: sacrifice-blood-atonement offered by Christ. Other types of sacrifices are hardly mentioned at all in Hebrews.[61]

Later, the author describes the use of blood for sacred rituals, arguing that blood is necessary for inaugurating a covenant. He cites verses which describe Moses's sprinkling of the blood of the covenant on Mount Sinai "in accordance with the Law" (Ex 24:5–8). Then he argues that Moses sprinkles blood both in the Tabernacle and on all of the vessels used for worship (Heb 9:18–21) in the same way.[62] The lesson for readers is that "under the Law almost everything is purified with blood, and without the shedding of blood there is no forgiveness of sins" (9:22).

The blood of sacrifice therefore sanctifies and purifies: "For if the blood of goats and bulls, with the sprinkling of the ashes of a heifer, sanctifies those who have been defiled so that their flesh is purified; how much more will the blood of Christ, who through the eternal Spirit offered himself without blemish to God, purify our conscience from dead works to worship the living God!" (9:13–14).

In these two passages (9:13–14, 18–22) the author blends—perhaps even confuses—different ritual uses of blood: inauguration of a covenant, consecration of people to office, ritual purification from corpse impurity (by the ashes of the red heifer, cf. Num 19), ritual purification from sin (on the Day of Atonement), and the purification of conscience through Christ's blood.[63] He may be implying that Christ's blood actually affects all of these ritual uses of blood all at once. Sacrifice-blood-atonement also includes the inauguration of a covenant, sanctification, and purification. (Other aspects of Christ's sacrifice are discussed below.)

Another, more complex use of the model of sacrifice is related to Jesus's death "outside the camp," where Jesus's crucifixion outside Jerusalem is explained by the need for disposal of the remains of the animal sacrifices: "For the bodies of those animals whose blood is brought into the sanctuary by the high priest as a sacrifice for sin are burned outside the camp; Therefore Jesus also suffered outside the city gate in order to sanctify the people by his own blood" (13:11–12). Such a ritual act actually applies to the remains of a sin offering (*hattat*) burned there including on the Day of Atonement (Lev 16:28). On the one hand, Jesus is once again identified with the sin offering; on the other hand, he represents merely the disposable remains of this sacrifice. By the exclusion from the sacred precincts, the metaphor bears a sense of rejection and shame in the act of crucifixion.[64]

Throughout all these passages the author spells out the priestly laws of sacrifice and rites involving blood without criticizing their rationale or practicality and without hinting that they are superfluous. He does not find fault in the earthly sanctuary and its laws and practices. He cites them as a background for the Christian alternative and does not argue that the legal acts and the priests are corrupt. He will later point out their limited effectiveness, though he surely believes they *are* somewhat effective.[65]

But for what purpose? Koester asserts that the earthly Tabernacle signifies a heavenly reality.[66] However, the priestly sacrificial system is more than that. "The language of sacrifice is more than an extended simile: it provides a coherent and nuanced vocabulary for setting out the work's cosmology, encompassing creation, evil, and the nature of humanity within the framework of a doctrine of salvation." Sin and sanctification are ways of perceiving the power which transcends all human life.[67]

In other words, Hebrews' entire doctrine and discourse are guided by drawing on the sacrificial law. It builds upon the priestly understanding of sin and how the Israelites should eliminate it. The model of sacrifice and priestly theology or cosmology is overarching: sin defiles (10:22) and is also contagious (12:15). Christ brings atonement like the sacrificial cult (2:17). Christ's blood is sacred and must not be profaned (10:29), while it sanctifies the believer (10:10; cf. 2:11). Christ's death purifies (1:3; 9:13–14) or sets aside sin (9:26). Indeed, the author is extremely concerned with God's judgment and wrath (3:7–4:13; 10:26–31; 12:29).[68]

The impact of this worldview on readers must be immense. They become more conscious of sin (9:9, 14; 10:2, 12:1) and feel that they need to strive for atonement. They are called to adapt Jewish cultic/priestly ideas in order to come to terms with their sense of sin against God and the need for atonement. Then the author argues for the complete and abiding efficacy of Jesus's death as an atoning sacrifice so that the readers feel that they are forgiven.[69] Let's turn to the description of Christ's sacrifice and its efficacy.

JESUS'S ULTIMATE SACRIFICE

At the beginning of the epistle it is declared that Jesus "had made purification for sins" (3:1). This is achieved through his sacrifice in the heavenly Temple: "He entered once for all into the Holy Place, not with the blood of goats and calves, but with his own blood, thus obtaining eternal redemption; For if the blood of goats and bulls, with the sprinkling of the ashes of a heifer, sanctifies those who have been defiled so that their flesh is purified; How much more will the blood of Christ, who through the eternal Spirit offered himself without blemish to God, purify our conscience from dead works to worship the living God!; For this reason he is the mediator of a new covenant, so that those who are called may receive the promised eternal inheritance, because a death has occurred that redeems them from the transgressions under the first covenant" (9:12–15).

It is stressed that Christ removes sin eternally. He "appeared once for all at the end of the age to remove sin by the sacrifice of himself; And just as it is appointed for mortals to die once, and after that the judgment; So Christ, having been offered once to bear the sins of many, will appear a second time, not to deal with sin, but to save those who are eagerly waiting for him" (9:26–28).

Jesus's offering is characterized as a priestly one, although earlier he offers something different—loud cries and tears as well as supplications for deliverance (5:7).[70] He offers "himself," a blameless sacrifice, which denotes true worship. The term "blameless" is derived from cultic prescriptions about the physical perfection of the victim and is used in NT texts in a more general, moral sense.[71] By the unique offering of sacrificing himself Jesus puts an end to the whole system of Levitical sacrifices.[72] This is not a continual sacrifice but a singular act once and for all (10:12–14), also producing atonement for the present (2:17).[73] Through Christ's priestlike act, the good things that the Law and its cultic system foreshadow become a reality, and the promises of the interior renewal in a new covenant are realized.[74] I turn now to a more detailed examination of the components of Hebrews' doctrine of sacrifice.

Jesus's Blood

Jesus's sacrifice (not his death) atones because of its blood, just as the blood of the sacrifice atones when poured on the altar (Lev 17:11): "He entered once for all into the Holy Place ... not with the blood of goats and calves, but with his own blood thus obtaining eternal redemption ... for if the blood of goats and bulls ... sanctifies those who have been defiled ... how much more will the blood of Christ" (9:12–14). The blood is Christ's ticket of admission into the holy of holies as it is for the high priest, but his blood is said to have greater effect than the blood of goats and bulls.[75] The shading of Jesus's blood stands for purgation from defilement, cleansing the conscience.[76]

But why is Jesus's blood more effective than the blood of animal sacrifices? Perhaps because Jesus's blood consists of his own life or because it is the absolute and final sacrifice.[77] Other possibilities are that Jesus's blood sacrifice is "through the eternal Spirit" (9:14), which relates to Jesus's death and exaltation. It has a spiritual effect to "purify our consciousness from dead works" (9:14), not by physical contact but through proclamation: the conscience is cleansed when faith is evoked through proclamation of Christ's death. In addition, Christ's blood speaks of God's grace and mercy (12:24).[78]

In any event, it is interesting that the author uses blood here and not death, body, soul, or life. He is certainly not the only NT author to do so,[79] but he develops the imagery inspired by priestly sacrificial ideology more thoroughly.

Atonement and the Purification from Sin

Christ's sacrificial blood results in cleansing from sin (e.g., 9:14).[80] Heb 9:23 portrays Christ's sacrifice as purifying the heavenly tabernacle. Christ's sacrifice at once purifies the heavenly tabernacle and inaugurates the new covenant cult. The moral category of sin is the final target of purification and the notion of ransom, life given in death in place of another life.[81] This is, however, only a metaphor, since, unlike the shedding of blood on the altar, Christ's blood is not actually shed on the believers.

Quite like the description of the high priest atoning for the sins of the people, Jesus's death, exaltation, offering of himself, and atonement by his own blood fulfill the Day of Atonement ritual, taking seriously key elements of the Temple cult. In 9:11–14, salvation through self-sacrifice is accomplished as a kind of symbolic reworking of the Day of Atonement ritual ("entered once for all into the Holy Place") in which Christ's blood substitutes for the blood of animals with an effect lasting forever. The entry of the high priest to the inner sanctum fuses with Jesus's entry into heaven:[82] In 6:19–20, Jesus is said to enter behind the curtain to the inner sanctuary, just like a high priest during the climax of the Day of Atonement rite.[83]

Still, Jesus's wiping off sin is different from that of the high priest on the Day of Atonement. Hebrews 9:9–10 argues that earthly high priests could not purify one's conscience, while Christ's sacrifice not only purifies the conscience but also sanctifies and perfects it (9:14; cf. 10:13–14). For the author, there is a crucial difference between Christ and the priestly system: "This is a symbol of the present time, during which gifts and sacrifices are offered that cannot perfect the conscience of the worshipper; but deal only with food and drink and various baptisms, regulations for the body imposed until the time comes to set things right" (9:8–10). There is also a tension between the priestly rite which purifies the body (9:13)—this actually applies to the ashes of the red heifer, *not* to the blood of the animal sacrifices—and Jesus's blood, which purifies conscience.[84] As a matter of fact, however, the conscience of the Jews is essentially cleansed by sin offerings—most specifically the rites of the Day of Atonement: Scripture promises atonement and purification from sin time and time again (Lev 16:30, 32–34).[85]

Complete and perfect forgiveness of sin—through one act that lasts for all time (10:1)—represents Hebrews' most unique contribution. It diverges from the priestly worldview in the Pentateuch, which assumes that humans will always commit sin, making the cult repetitive.[86]

The Failure of the Levitical System

After a detailed and positive presentation of the priestly cult, the author reaches the point where he must establish the advantages of Christ over the Law, showing the shortcomings of the sacrificial system in comparison to the new cult.

One major problem he emphasizes is the fact that sacrifices are offered continuously: "Since the Law has only a shadow of the good things to come and not the true form of these realities, it can never, by the same sacrifices that are continually offered year after year, make perfect those who approach; Otherwise, would they not have ceased being offered, since the worshippers, cleansed once for all, would no longer have any consciousness of sin? But in these sacrifices there is a reminder of sin year after year. For it is impossible for the blood of bulls and goats to take away sins" (10:1–4).

The need to repeat sacrifice for sin points to its ineffectiveness.[87] This problem also relates to the very consciousness of sin in a manner that recalls Paul's equation of the Law with sin (Rom 7:7–25). A similar problem is already raised in Heb 9:9–10: gifts and sacrifices are not able to make one's conscience complete since they concern only the body.[88] The ineffectiveness of sacrifice is enhanced by citing Ps 40:6–8 (Heb 10:5–9).

This imperfectness inherent in the repetitive sacrificial system is explained in a kind of platonic argument: "Since the Law has only a shadow of the good things to come and not the true form of these realities, it can never, by the same sacrifices that are continually offered year after year, make perfect those who approach; otherwise, would they not have ceased being offered, since the worshippers, cleansed once for all, would no longer have any consciousness of sin?" (10:1–2).[89] Hebrews' alternative emerges as the single sacrifice of Christ—a definitive act which leads to perfection, a sacrifice that stands forever (7:28; 10:10–14).

Another problem with the priestly cult is the priestly need to offer sacrifices for themselves, unlike Christ: "Unlike the other high priests, he has no need to offer sacrifices day after day, first for his own sins, and then for those of the people; this he did once for all when he offered himself" (7:27).[90] This "weakness" (as it is called in 7:28) is mentioned earlier, where it also has a positive side. Namely, it affords the high priest a chance to pity the wrongdoers (5:3–4). The author proposes an alternative, contrasting the Law with the "word of the oath" and "the Son who has been made perfect for ever" (Heb 9:28).[91]

Elsewhere the author seems to declare the end of the Levitical system, stating quite harshly that "by this the Holy Spirit indicates that the way into the Sanctuary has not yet been disclosed as long as the first Tabernacle is still standing" (9:8). Christ's sacrifice is not simultaneous with the Levitical system but replaces it.[92] This implies that the heavenly Temple (already introduced in 8:2) is not available as long as the Tabernacle still operates. Assuming that Moses's Tabernacle in the wilderness stands for the Second Temple, this verse hints that the author writes after the destruction of the Temple!

Christ's Alternative to Sacrifice: The New Cult

Jesus is not a sacrifice in the conventional manner. His crucifixion leads to his enthronement and also allows for his followers to enter the heavenly sanctuary (9:11–12, 14). The author points to the singularity and efficacy of his sacrificial act: "It is by God's will that we have been sanctified through the offering of the body of Jesus Christ once for all. . . . But when Christ had offered for all time a single sacrifice for sins, he sat down at the right hand of God. . . . For by a single offering he has perfected for all time those who are sanctified. . . . Where there is forgiveness of these, there is no longer any offering for sin" (10:10, 12–14, 18). There is no longer a need for further sacrifices. When Christ sacrifices himself and purifies the heavenly Temple, he achieves access to God, perfection, and redemption.[93] As the author mentions in 7:25, Jesus "always lives to make intercession for us"—"always" meaning "for all time."[94]

Although the epistle does not mention the crucifixion explicitly, its allusions to Jesus's blood and death ("when he offered himself," 7:27) show that it is ritualized.[95] An interesting yet indirect reference to crucifixion using sacrificial imagery occurs when the sacrificed Jesus is alluded to as a sort of a sin offering disposed "outside the camp" (13:12). Jesus suffers outside the gate like the remains of the sin offering animals being excluded from the city. This profane place contrasts with his ascension to the heavenly Tabernacle in a manner that conflicts with priestly logic. It is suggested that from an earthly perspective Jesus's suffering and death are profane and lack sacrificial characteristics—and as such they occur in a profane place, outside the camp. Yet from the heavenly perspective it is a most sacred self-offering and fittingly occurs in the most sacred place: the heavenly holy of holies.[96]

In a sense, Christ's death is the precondition for the availability of his blood. His priestly work begins only after his death and reaches its terminus in the heavenly sphere. The cross is not the sacrifice but the preparation for the heavenly sacrificial ministry of the high priest. It is not the altar on which the sacrifice of Jesus begins and ends. It is essential but not completely and totally sufficient.[97]

While Jesus's sacrifice is portrayed as both real in and of itself and analogical to priestly rituals, its effect attests to the transformation and "spiritualization" of sacrifice in Hebrews. The believers participate in it or at the very least benefit from it: Through Christ, they themselves draw near to the throne of grace to receive mercy and grace (4:16). Christ's sacrifice also opens the way for the believers to enter into the (heavenly) sanctuary (*tōn hagiōn*), enabling access to the heavenly holy of holies (10:19–25).[98] Interestingly, however, Hebrews does not seem to offer an alternative communal rite to the earthly sacrifice.[99]

CHRIST IN THE HEAVENLY TEMPLE

Even Better than the Earthly Tabernacle

The heavenly Temple is preferred to the earthly Tabernacle: "When Christ came as a high priest of the good things that have come, then through the greater and perfect Tabernacle (not made with hands, that is, not of this creation); he entered once for all into the Holy Place" (9:11–12). The author also compares the two: "For Christ did not enter a sanctuary made by human hands, a mere copy of the true one, but he entered into heaven itself, now to appear in the presence of God on our behalf" (9:24).

We are told that the heavenly Temple is not made with hands. I have already discussed this kind of Temple in Mark 14:58. Here there is no doubt that the Temple not made with (human) hands is the heavenly Temple.[100] Elsewhere in Hebrews the heavenly Temple is designated as "the holy": Christ is "a minister in the sanctuary and the true Tabernacle that the Lord, and not any mortal, has set up" (8:2; cf. 9:8); "he entered once for all into the Holy Place [*ta hagia*], not with the blood of goats and calves, but with his own blood, thus obtaining eternal redemption" (9:12). Nonetheless, the very same designation of "the holy" is also used for the earthly one (9:1–2). The heavenly Temple is therefore a direct heir to the Temple on earth. But the celestial sanctuary becomes effective only from the moment of Jesus's exaltation.[101]

The true Tabernacle is "greater and more complete" (9:11) than the old one because it is permanent and eternal. It cannot be changed because it is made by God as a New Creation and will remain forever. The earthly one is not the true Temple not only because it is a mere shadow of the Temple to come but also because it will someday cease to exist. The new one exists in the midst of God's unfettered glory, ending any need for a new physical Temple because of its "shadowy" stage of Temple existence.[102] This is the place of the new high priesthood and the new covenant, where Christ the heavenly high priest fulfills a superior ministry.[103]

There is disagreement as to whether the Temple is within heaven, a kind of a place like the earthly one, or merely metaphorical, whereby the entire heaven is in fact understood to be a Temple. The idea of the entire heaven as a sanctuary is attested to in Philo. Hebrews does state that Christ "entered into heaven itself" where God is present (9:24), as opposed to entering the built sanctuary on earth. This still does not solve the problem. As we will soon see, there are specific references to parts of the heavenly

Temple, such as rooms and the curtain which divides them. The author therefore does have an image of a building in mind.[104]

The author introduces a sharp conceptual distinction between the Temple in heaven and the one on earth: the earthly high priest serves "in a sanctuary that is a sketch and shadow of the heavenly one; for Moses, when he was about to erect the Tabernacle, was warned, 'See that you make everything according to the pattern that was shown you on the mountain'" (8:5, citing Ex 25:40). The Tabernacle is therefore a sketch and shadow of the heavenly one.

This is not a pejorative comment. The very same concept is attested to in Jewish Hellenistic sources, and it is used by contemporary Jews to highlight the sacredness of the earthly Temple and revere it, implying that there cannot be a better Temple on earth.[105] In Hebrews the tone is much more critical. That Moses's Tabernacle is only a copy of the heavenly reality consigns the earthly sanctuary to the realm of the changing and transitory, which has only limited validity because it must ultimately pass away:[106] "Thus it was necessary for the sketches of the heavenly things to be purified with these rites, but the heavenly things themselves need better sacrifices than these; For Christ did not enter a sanctuary made by human hands, a mere copy of the true one, but he entered into heaven itself, now to appear in the presence of God on our behalf" (9:23–24).[107]

Cultic Symbolism: Sacrifice, Purification, and Architecture

As the last citation shows, in the heavenly Temple sacrifices function like purification rites on earth, but they are "better" than those of the earthly ones (9:23).[108] But why are sacrifices necessary at all? Why, unlike the heavenly Temple in Revelation, does the perfect sanctuary in heaven also need cleansing? Apparently, the Levitical system still applies to it. It is even possible to suggest that the reason for this is that the laws and rites of the priestly system actually derive from a heavenly origin, like the Tabernacle itself. In any event, sacrificial practice or imagery governs Christ's cleansing of the heavenly Tabernacle at the turn of the ages.[109]

This sacrifice is offered when Christ comes as high priest "through the greater and perfect Tabernacle . . . with his own blood" (9:11–12). Here we find a single sacrifice, and the context points to its purpose: the people's sins (9:7) and the purification of conscience (9:14). This sacrifice is compared, although indirectly, with the high priestly rite of the Day of Atonement which atones for the Israelites' sins (9:7) and also with the cleansing of the body (9:13). The author mixes atonement by blood and cleansing the body from corpse impurity, resulting in a vivid image of Christ shedding his own blood for the many.[110]

Is the image of the heavenly Temple merely a metaphor (for example, for Christ), or does the author grasp it as a real Temple in the sky? Some view the sacrificial language as a metaphorical interpretation of the death of Jesus.[111] However, the comparison to the Day of Atonement seems to relate to a concept of an actual Tabernacle, a spiritual archetype of the earthly Tabernacle. Christ really cleanses something in the spiritual realm.[112] But how does Hebrews' image of Christ's sacrifice in the heavenly Temple affect the image of Jesus's death on the cross (cf. 5:7–8)? The relationship between the cross and the heavenly Temple is a bone of contention among scholars. Recent studies suggest that when Christ brings his own blood into the heavenly holy of holies to present and sprinkle it, his death, resurrection, and ascension are all bound together by his singular sacrificial act.[113] After his death at the crucifixion, Jesus's human body rises from the dead. When Jesus then ascends into heaven, he ascends with that body. It is in the heavenly Temple, not on the cross, that he sacrifices himself and purifies the Temple with his blood.[114]

The Tabernacle's image includes rooms and a curtain/veil. Jesus opens for the believers a way to enter the sanctuary "through the curtain [*katapertasmatos*]; that is, through his flesh" (10:20). The author's hopes are focused on the inner shrine "behind the curtain" where Jesus enters (6:19). The curtain undoubtedly recalls the one in the holy of holies, the inner chamber of the earthly Tabernacle (9:3). Since the Day of Atonement rite is hinted at time and time again (5:1–4; 7:27; 9:13; 10:11; and quite explicitly in 9:25), the curtain probably relates to the Day of Atonement rite, in which the high priest goes beyond it to wipe away Israel's sins.[115]

Since the entry into the sanctuary pertains to the place beyond the curtain (9:19–20), some see here a division between outer and inner parts of the heavenly Temple. The description in which Jesus comes through the perfect Tabernacle and "enters once for all into the Holy Place" (9:11–22) also seems to portray a distinction between the outer space/chamber of the Tabernacle and the inner sanctum. This would accord with the division of the earthly Tabernacle into *hagia* and *hagia hagiōn* (9:2–3).[116] Like the curtain, the existence of inner sancta is important for creating the imagery of the Day of Atonement rite. Our author wants the reader to envision the heavenly Temple as a perfect version of the earthly Tabernacle.

The purpose of the concept of the heavenly Temple is to provide Jesus the high priest with a cultic space he needs in order to serve and offer his sacrifice as a means of providing the believers in Jesus with something to hang on to. The new covenant requires a space corresponding to the spaces of the old covenant.[117] Furthermore, the language of cosmic transcendence is the author's way of addressing the purification of believers by conscience and spirit.[118]

The Law: Change and Validity

The author of Hebrews connects its transformation of the sacrificial cult to a change in the Law. But to what extent is there a transformation of the Torah? Is the Torah reduced merely to a guiding theory or to certain practical aspects which remain valid for the readers? Is the change in the Law restricted to the cult, or does it include all aspects of the scriptural commands?[119]

REJECTING THE LAW

The most famous and straightforward assertion about the transformation of the Law relates to Jesus's high priesthood (descending from the tribe of Judah) taking the place of the one traced back to Aaron: "For when there is a change in the priesthood, there is necessarily *a change in the Law as well*" (7:12). But what does this change (*metathesis*) of the Law mean? Koester as well as many others explains that it means removal. He conceives this to be the "the abrogation (*athetēsis*) of an earlier commandment because it is weak and ineffectual (7:18)." Namely, the Law is abrogated, and this is because the author explains that Jesus has become a priest "not through a legal requirement concerning physical descent, but through the power of an indestructible life" (7:16), suggesting a dualism of Law (actually, genealogy or "flesh") vs. life. Moreover, there is a need to replace the priesthood because it is weak and the appointed people are liable to sin and death (7:28).[120]

Thus, according to the author, it is not humans but God himself who decides on changes in the Law because God brings about the completion of his purpose through Christ. This implies that all other means of fulfilling God's mission—including the Law itself—are inadequate:[121] "Since the law has only a shadow of the good things to come and not the true form of these realities, it can never, by the same sacrifices that are continually offered year after year, make perfect those who approach" (10:1).

Many infer a total abrogation of all aspects of the Law as part of this theological approach: "In Hebrews the supersession of the cultus explicitly involves the repeal of the Law."[122] The inadequacy of the cult to take away sin also attests to the inadequacy of the Law more generally, and obedience to the Law is replaced or completed by the new cultic principle of service (*latreuein*) to the will of God.[123] This naturally leads to comparing Hebrews with Paul. One may infer that both reach the same conclusion, but our author's point of departure is the transformation of the Levitical priesthood to reach "perfection" in approaching God.[124]

Nevertheless, whereas Paul argues that the entire Law loses its ability to achieve justification after Christ, Hebrews builds on the cultic Law as a paradigm which applies to Christ's priesthood, referring to the abrogation of the Law only in relation to the priesthood and sacrifices. Examination of Hebrews' other specific critical assertions about the Law reveals that they all concern the cult: The priests are subjected to weakness (7:28); gifts and sacrifices cannot perfect the conscience of the worshiper, since they deal only with food, drink, and ablutions—that is, the regulations of the body (9:10–11).[125] These regulations cannot remove sin. The author's problem with the Jewish halakhah thus pertains only to the sacrificial cult, which, he claims, is transformed.

Admittedly, our author preaches a new covenant that takes the place of the old one, which should already be a thing of the past (8:13). He declares that Zion replaces Sinai. Namely, the new covenant is Mount Zion and the heavenly Jerusalem along with communion with angels (12:18–22). But the term "new covenant" does not necessarily mean the abrogation of all the commandments. The question remains whether the author also wishes to annul noncultic laws as well.[126]

OBSERVING THE LAW?

The change (*metathesis*) of the Law does not necessarily mean annulment but rather alternation or transformation.[127] Furthermore, the context of the critical comments of the Law suggests that they are all related to the sacrificial system of the cult and the Levitical priests.[128] Thus the question remains: What aspects of the Law are still valid?

In fact, Hebrews also expresses a positive stance toward the concept of the Law, citing Jeremiah's prophecy about the new covenant twice (8:10; 10:16): "I will put my *Law* within them, and I will write it on their hearts" (Jer 31:33). Jeremiah's prophecy probably relates to its new covenant as the new Law, God's commandment. Still, it is possible that only some of the precepts of the Law are changed, while others persist. In 2:2, the author says that "the message declared through angels was valid, and every transgression or disobedience received a just penalty." The mention of angels refers to the revelation on Mount Sinai, relating to angelic mediation on that occasion. The author thus stresses the requirement of human obedience and the legal validity of this revelation.

Further references to legal practices seem to be positive. The Sabbath is the day of rest for the people of God (4:9). Although the author develops the theme of rest on the Sabbath as a symbol, he does not hint that it should not be observed anymore.[129] The Levites' collecting of tithes from the people is spelled out without reservation (7:5). Furthermore, when the author warns of sinning against true belief and the awaiting punishment he also alludes to the Law: "Anyone who has violated the law of Moses dies without mercy 'on the testimony of two or three witnesses' [Deut 19:15]; How much worse punishment do you think will be deserved by those who have spurned the Son of God, profaned the blood of the covenant by which they were sanctified, and outraged the Spirit of grace?" (10:28–29).

Here the biblical penal code applies to the Christians' life without reservation, not as a model that may be transformed but as a reminder of divine punishment. This is important, since the author specifically refers to the violation of "the law of Moses" as if it is still obligatory. Understood without recalling earlier impediments to the Law, this passage argues that while transgressing the laws of the Torah requires punishment, acting against Christian doctrine results in even more severe divine reaction.

Admittedly, it is possible to read this positive assertion regarding the law as merely symbolic or rhetorical, not unlike those found in the Pauline letters (Rom 7:14; Gal 3:24). But while Paul approaches the question of the validity and relevance of the Law directly and in great detail, arguing that (Gentile) Christians are released from it, Hebrews discusses only its cultic aspects, leaving us with doubts as to whether or not the nonsacrificial commandments are still binding.

Because of this ambiguity, and in line with Hebrews' extensive application of the sacrificial system as a model for Christ, I suggest reading Heb 7:12 inversely. Rather than viewing the change in the priesthood as one result of the more general change in the Law (a general change which is never spelled out, while there is some evidence to legal continuity), it is possible to see the change in the Law as an explanation after the fact for the change in the priesthood. This is because the belief in Jesus as the heavenly high priest necessitates acknowledging this change in terms of the origin of the high priest from the tribe of Levi to the one of Judah. Nothing else in the epistle attests to a full-scale, definitive cancelation of the noncultic Law. Moreover, "change" (*metathesis*, literally, transposition) may refer to a more limited effect than total abrogation. In fact, this comment on the change in the Law may testify that the author (or his readers) is uneasy with this contradiction with the Torah and needs to justify it explicitly.

My suggestion has implications for Hebrews' attitude toward the Temple. It is possible that Hebrews' alternative cult of Christ as the high priest and sacrifice does *not* derive from a rejection of the Law. It defies the sacrificial law not because of a general or outright rejection of the precepts of the Torah, but transforms the Temple cult owing to a more specific religious concern that results from only partial rejection of Law.

Conclusions: Revitalizing Sacrifices and Temple

Hebrews introduces a new cultic system which symbolizes the new covenant—nothing less than Mount Zion taking the place of Mount Sinai (12:18–22).[130] The aim of this new cult is direct access to God.[131] The imagery of the high priest, sacrifice, and the heavenly Temple is not metaphorical but refers to heavenly realities.[132]

What is the author's attitude to the Jerusalem Temple and its cult? What is the motivation to portray Christological ideas in such a complex and vivid cultic manner?

As I already mentioned, Manson argues that "a straight line runs from the teaching and apologia of proto-Martyr [Stephen] to the Epistle to the Hebrews." Like Stephen, our author thinks that the Temple cult is "transcended and antiquated." Manson maintains that Stephen preaches that Jesus has transcended and superseded the cultus and the Law of Judaism. Similarly, Hebrews puts "an end to the Law and the Cultus of Israel . . . leaving no place in Christianity for Jewish-Christian archaising." The author preaches against remaining Christians under cover of the Jewish religion.[133] As far as Stephen is concerned, we have already seen (see chapter 5) that Luke denies the allegation that Stephen speaks against the Law and the Temple and that his speech does not criticize the Temple as harshly as Manson and others claim.

Hebrews' attitude toward the Temple and the Law can hardly be equated with Luke's Stephen. Koester notes a difference in relation to the relevance of the old covenant, which is more binding in Stephen's speech. Most important, Koester argues, Stephen views the Tabernacle positively as the sanctuary that is prescribed by the Law, recalling the faithfulness of God. In contrast, Hebrews points to its limitations (Acts 7:44–50; Heb 9: 1–14). Hence, "it is not feasible to call Hebrews an outgrowth of Hellenistic theology."[134] This means that Hebrews stands out as presenting the most critical or even negative attitude toward the Temple in the NT. But, para-doxically, it contains the most detailed cultic discourse in early Christianity!

THE PURPOSE OF HEBREWS

Over the years there have been different theories about the hidden background of Hebrews' distinctive cultic theology, assuming that it re-sponds to specific religious tendencies among its readers.[135] I would like to introduce three possible explanations for Hebrews' approach to the Temple and the sacrificial cult which focus on the author's *motives* in creating his alternative cultic system based on the priestly one:

> 1. Superseding the Temple cult in Jerusalem.[136] Hebrews wants the readers to cut their attachments to the Jewish Temple cult and the Law and there-fore shows that their time has passed. The Torah is no longer relevant since Christ offers a better alternative of "eternal redemption" (9:12).

However, if this is the case, the author would hardly need to review the Levitical system in such detail. His use of the high priesthood and sacri-fices offered for sin as well as their rationale and practices all acknowledge the integrity and power of the Temple cult, showing great respect for the priestly system. Whoever wants to suppress the Torah would not give it so much weight. It is also interesting that the author never rejects the *logic* of sacrifice but instead applies it to Jesus. He is not anti-ritualist. He also does not use any allegory of sacrifice like Philo.[137] The author refrains from refer-ring to the Jerusalem Temple and alludes to the Tabernacle (that is, using solely scriptural terms, distancing the impact of his arguments from the present) because he does not want to attack it directly.[138] In fact, reading the epistle might lead the reader to see the similarities between Christologi-cal doctrine and the priestly worldview, thus theoretically strengthening a reader's attachment to Judaism.

> 2. Giving the Christians who are still devoted to the Jewish traditional Tem-ple and sacrificial cult the sense that their cultic needs and feelings are now fulfilled by Christ. The attachment of these readers to the old cultic ways leads the author to model Christianity after the priestly system.[139]

The competition with the Jerusalem Temple—if it is still standing—or with its memory and impact as the primary Jewish symbol may explain why Hebrews focuses on the sacrificial cult and models Christology upon it: Those who desire a Temple can find it in heaven. (This explanation may also apply to Revelation's heavenly Temple as well.)[140]

The problem with this understanding is twofold. First, the author invests too much in reminding the reader of the contents of the sacrificial system and their positive values; and he actually convinces the reader that they were valid and necessary. He raises the problem of attachment to the Temple no less than he solves it! Second, it seems that the author's major concern is to connect the high priesthood and sacrifices to the image of Christ. He could have suggested to his readers an alternative Temple in heaven, using a more traditional and simpler idea of a Temple, such as the one in Revelation. Therefore, I think that more than the author wants to cope with Jewish devotion to the Temple, he is trying to make sense of Christology.

> 3. The author needs to make sense of Christological doctrine and uses the sacrificial system and the role of the high priest—which he highly appreciates—to explain Jesus's expiation for others and his function in relation to God and humans. Jesus's high priesthood and service at the heavenly Temple aims to make sense of his crucifixion and exaltation in the context of Jewish religion, as if they both conform with tradition and continue the priestly system.

The explanatory value of this cultic Christology may be demonstrated in comparison with that of Paul. In Hebrews, Jesus's death atones because of his blood. The blood is the price of Christ's admission into the holy of holies, in the same way that the animal blood was the price for the high priest. The concept of Jesus's blood reflecting his death is used by Paul (e.g., Rom 3:25; 5:9), but in Hebrews it becomes more concrete and understandable.

In Hebrews, Christ's death cleanses the believers from sin and purifies the heavenly Tabernacle (9:14, 23). This is only a metaphor, since, unlike the shedding of blood on the altar (or the *kaporet*), Christ's blood is not shed on the believers. But this metaphor actually develops Paul's idea of Christ's atonement for sins. It explains the relationship between Jesus, sin, and forgiveness or atonement, which Paul did not explain well: What does "die for our sins" mean in 1 Cor 15:3? The concept of sacrifice which eliminates sin (although Hebrews does not refer directly to the sin offering mentioned in 2 Cor 5:21 and Rom 8:3) explains exactly how Christ's death releases the believer from sin in Rom 6:11, 22; 8:1. It also expands the notion of justification (e.g., in Rom 8:10).

When Christ himself becomes a sacrifice that releases from sin, Paul's ransom theology (Rom 3:24: 5:8) also becomes clearer, although a ransom and a sin offering may not be the same thing. Paul explains Jesus's redemption as being outside or beyond the realm of the Law: "For God has done what the Law, weakened by the flesh, could not do: by sending His own Son in the likeness of sinful flesh, and as sin offering, he condemned sin in the flesh" (Rom 8:3). Hebrews, in contrast, regards Christ as a continuation and development of the priestly Law. Although both may have the same meaning, Hebrews elaborates and explains the concept which Paul terms "sin offering" not merely as a cultic metaphor but as a new type of sacrifice for sins.

My argument here is not necessarily that Christ's sacrifice in Hebrews directly develops Pauline Christology. Rather, I think that the use of detailed cultic discourse clarifies doctrines such as Paul's.[141] I also believe that Hebrews' Christology may seem more appealing to a Jewish audience than that of Paul, but the history of Hebrews' reception indicates that mine is a minority view. Hebrews explains Jesus's exaltation to heaven and *why* his sacrifice atones for humanity once and for all. It does so with multiple explanations, building on both the themes of high priesthood and atonement sacrifices which purify sin.

For these reasons, I suggest, Hebrews' cultic discourse is not merely a rhetorical exercise. The author is highly attached to priestly ideas and the sacrificial cult, and his discourse has two complementary aims: First, it makes sense of Jesus becoming a Messiah who atones for people's sins. Second, it revitalizes the sacrificial system, showing that it is still relevant when followed by Christ. In Hebrews, the priestly system continues in a new and better format when it serves as the key for understanding who Christ is and how he saves the world.

HEBREWS IN POST-70 CONTEXT

Hebrews' brilliant and innovative linkage of Christology with the sacrificial cult, however, is not easily reconciled with the theology of the cross. When Hebrews pictures Christ's offering as a sacrifice in heaven (9:25–28), it somewhat marginalizes the meaning of his death on the cross as the symbolic image of the belief in Christ (1 Cor 1:23; 6:12–14). Jesus's death on the cross, including the shedding of his blood there (Col 1:20), is no longer the occasion of his sacrificing himself for the sake of others (Col 2:14) but merely the locus of Jesus's prayers and supplications (5:7), where the process of exaltation and sacrifice only begins. Furthermore, while many NT passages regard Jesus's ascension to heaven as a consequence of his sacrificial death ("for us") on the cross, Hebrews reverses the sequence.[142] His death on earth grants him his exaltation in heaven, and only then does he also offer himself and his blood as a sacrifice in heaven. On top of the traditional, much simpler early Christian understanding of Jesus's single act of dying on the cross, Hebrews creates the picture of a heavenly high priest entering the heavenly sanctuary. Hence from a critical perspective Jesus's self-sacrifice is independent of the idea of Christ serving in the heavenly Temple.[143]

The complex idea of Jesus as both a heavenly high priest and a sacrifice is somewhat contradictory, even though the author, the readers, and many believers probably do not notice it. This complexity enables us to place Hebrews within the history of Christological doctrine. As much as the high priestly Christology is a brilliant explanation of Jesus's status and role as a savior, it is a secondary interpretation that can hardly be formulated in the earliest phases of the belief in Christ. That Jesus offers himself for the many is a given. However, viewing Jesus as a sacrifice poses a problem, since no sacrifice offers itself. Arguing that Jesus is also the (high) priest, the one who offers the sacrifice aims to solve this. On second thought, however, it still poses a logical difficulty, since no high priest sacrifices his own body. Nonetheless, Christian adherents of the Temple cult could find it illuminating and inspiring.

All of this brings us back to the question of the *dating* of Hebrews. We have seen that there are conflicting considerations as to whether it is written before or after the destruction of the Jerusalem Temple in 70 CE.[144] I would like to point to hints that the letter is written when the Temple cult is no longer in operation.

When readers are assumed already to be cleansed from sin, the author warns them that further offense cannot be atoned for through sacrifice: "For if we willfully persist in sin after having received the knowledge of the truth, there no longer remains a sacrifice for sins; but a fearful prospect of judgment" (10:26–27). This may imply that sacrifices in the Temple can no longer be performed to attain atonement, as they were before (9:13, 23). Another clue is that the heavenly Temple seems to postdate the earthly one: "By this the Holy Spirit indicates that the way into the sanctuary has not yet been disclosed as long as the first Tabernacle is still standing" (9:8). "Tabernacle" in Hebrews probably stands for the Temple. The historical Tabernacle is already out of use under Solomon, but the author certainly does not suggest that the new cult he introduces begins in the early mo- narchic period. His implication is, I suggest, that only after the Temple's destruction can one think of the heavenly Temple. This may also indicate that the author does not intend to polemicize against the Temple cult as a *historical reality*. The heavenly Temple is the heir of the earthly one only when it already has ceased to exist.

We should also make sense of the positive attitude toward sacrifices. The fact that the author relies so heavily on the role of the high priest, sacrifices, and blood for purification as a means of explaining Christ's func- tion and uniqueness shows incredible respect for the Temple cult. I think he cannot expect his readers to accept this argument while the Temple is still active. If he is suggesting that Jesus plays the role of high priest while a Levitical high priest is ministering and sacrifices are still being offered on the altar, he would need to judge the present cult harshly and show that it is invalid, not only theoretically but also practically. This would include pointing out the continuous sins of the Jews or problems in the functioning of the Temple. The idealization of the cult without polemic and focusing only on theological shortcomings that are solved with the coming of Christ coheres with a situation in which there is no reason to argue for the cessa- tion of animal sacrifices, since they have already ceased. The appearance of Christ or Christological beliefs creates a smooth transition of the sacrificial system of the flesh to its spiritual version.

The author uses the sacrificial system to make sense of Christ. In this case he is thinking positively of the cult and believing that it paves the way for Jesus by solving the problem of repetitive sins and sacrifices. If the Temple were still operational at the time of this claim, the author would have a problem. Before using the cult as a model, he would need to go through much harsher criticism and polemic to show that the high priest and sacrifices are ineffective, that they are merely a model and are not *in- tended* to be real to begin with (more like Barnabas and Justin Martyr [see chapter 9]). Hebrews' generally positive assessment of the cult can stand only when it is not practically relevant anymore—when what remains of it is only a memory and a symbol.

For the author, a sense of the Temple, sacrifice, and the image of high priest is illuminating. *Christianity is the direct successor of the sacrificial cult, not its suppressor.* The logic of sacrifice leads to the logic of Christ saving others from sin. If this interpretation is accepted, then Hebrews, being written after 70, does not reject the Temple cult but rather extends it into new realms led by an author devoted to the priestly tradition who nevertheless believes that a second, better phase awaits it.

9 Relating to Judaism, Experiencing the Sacred

Temple and Sacrifices in the New Testament in Perspective

The Historical Jesus is certainly interested in the Temple, but only when he arrives in Jerusalem. He teaches there although not about the Temple per se. His overturning of the tables on the Temple Mount is an act of criticism, not of rejection; nonetheless, it is difficult to infer from the text just *what* is being condemned and why. Undoubtedly Jesus is dissatisfied with the relationship between money and the Temple cult. Many commentators claim that the true target of Jesus's wrath is the Temple cult or those who run it. I disagree with this conclusion. I believe that his problem is with money or, rather, with those corrupt individuals who donate funds to the Temple, thus defiling it with their sins.

There is no textual evidence that Jesus declared that he will bring the imminent demise of the Temple by his own hands, although many Jews in Jerusalem believed that he had. Indeed, this charge seems to be the main reason for his arrest and eventual crucifixion at the hands of the Romans. In depicting his trial, the four evangelists try to dispel the notion that Jesus threatened to destroy the Temple, although Matthew and Luke do mention the coming destruction in the context of grieving its loss. To me, these texts imply that Jesus's disciples do not reject the Temple. With Jesus having been executed as its enemy, however, non-Christian Jews suspected that his followers held a hostile stance toward the Temple.

The Last Supper is a cultic analogy in which the drinking of Jesus's blood and the eating of his flesh become a metaphor for sacrifice. If we consider the analogy an authentic rite proscribed by Jesus, it certainly underscores the impact of sacrificial symbolism on his religious thinking. Presenting himself in terms one would use when describing a sacrifice does not mean that Jesus sought to replace the Temple cult; if anything, by using sacrifice as a metaphor, he demonstrated his high regard for the cult. Interestingly, if the Last Supper was part of a Passover seder in which the Passover lamb was eaten, the Historical Jesus actually consumes sacrificial meat, in addition simply to employing the sacrificial metaphor.

While Paul freely criticizes and limits the relevance of the Law, he does not treat the Temple and its cult in similar fashion. On the contrary, he frequently employs the metaphors of Temple, sacrifice, priesthood, and libation in relation to Christ, the community of believers, and himself as an apostle, thus attesting both to his appreciation for the cult and his belief in the cult's ability to bestow legitimacy on his teachings. Indeed, Paul never says that Jesus's *death* was a sacrifice, nor does he claim that Christ replaces the sacrificial system. On the contrary, absent the religious symbolism that the Jerusalem Temple holds, his metaphors would lack power and appeal. Paul's Temple metaphors are meaningful precisely because the Temple cult denotes God's presence and provides a fundamental means of worship. If we accept Acts' story about Paul in Jerusalem, in which Paul participates in the cult and declares his loyalty to the Temple, this interpretation becomes all the more compelling.

Paul's cultic metaphors provide his readers who turn away from the local Greco-Roman temples an opportunity to experience the sacred in a new way. Through his use of metaphors Paul has made the virtual Temple and sacrifice accessible to his readers. And in doing so, he actually indirectly relates them to the Jewish cultic center and sacred ideas.

Mark depicts numerous conflicts between Jesus and the Temple leadership. He regards both the chief priests and the Zealots who seize control of the Temple during the revolt against Rome as evil and corrupt. Yet despite his harsh criticism of the Temple's leadership, he never rejects the Temple itself. Mark values the cult and its symbolism, as demonstrated by his sayings about the leper's purification by the priest (1:44), the widow's donation to the Temple treasury (12:41–44), and the abomination that causes desolation of the Temple (13:14).

When Mark describes Jesus teaching in the Temple and arguing with his adversaries, his underlying message is the close connection between Jesus and the cult. Such a narrative on the attendance of the Temple and (passive or indirect) participation in the cult has a symbolic meaning. His narrative creates a cultural memory in his readers that helps to shape their religious identity.[1] This applies as well to the stories of Jesus in the Temple found in other gospels as well as to the participation in the Temple cult on the part of Peter, the apostles, and Paul described in the Acts of the Apostles. Jesus selects the Temple as the setting for his teaching in order to emphasize his religious authority. If Mark thought that by teaching in the Temple, Jesus sought to replace it, then the point of the Temple as a means of conferring legitimacy would have been lost. Undoubtedly, he places Jesus in the Temple because he values it as an institution and as a symbol and because he associates its cult with holiness and piety.

In Matthew, Jesus criticizes the Temple through some of his sayings when he emphasizes moral behavior. This leads him to qualify the significance of the Temple cult, declaring that mercy is more important than sacrifice and Jesus (or his ministry) "greater than the Temple." At the same time, several of his sayings underscore the importance and relevance of the Temple to Christian life, such as his declaration that sacrifice first demands reconciliation, that it is pious to swear by the altar and the sanctuary, that the Temple tax should indeed be paid, and, finally, that Judas's blood money cannot be kept in the Temple. The destruction of the Temple, which by the time of Matthew was no longer a dire warning, is certainly made more explicit than in Mark. Yet Jesus's supposed involvement in that destruction is denied by means of the false witnesses, who blame him not for threatening to destroy the Temple but merely for saying that he is "able" to do so. The tearing of the Temple veil describes a positive apocalyptic event that involves the resurrection of the dead, and it is entirely possible that it symbolizes *not* the destruction of the Temple but the end of God's "veiled" presence.

Matthew takes as its aim the enhancement of Temple practices and sensibilities after 70. For him, the Temple holds important symbolic value, which he in turn uses to reinforce Christianity's Jewish origins: By demonstrating the early Christians' commitment to the Temple, he is demonstrating, albeit theoretically, their relation to the Jewish people. His narrative descriptions of Jesus speaking about and at the Temple also serve to heighten his status as an authoritative religious leader. Finally, certain of Jesus's critiques of the Temple shape his image in the eyes of Christian readers, such as when Jesus says that "*something* is greater than the Temple"—which implies, although it is not explicitly stated, that the "something" to which he is referring is in fact himself. Matthew, I believe, does not dare argue explicitly that Jesus is more important than the Temple.

In Luke, Jesus is described as attending the Temple since infancy, and indeed he makes more visits to the Temple here than in Mark and Matthew. Moreover, the Temple charge against Jesus is completely omitted, and in Acts, the apostles (including Paul) visit the Temple, even taking part in the afternoon prayer service. Stephen's speech must not be read as a rejection of the Temple. In speaking out against the tendency to confine God within the Temple's boundaries, Stephen is simply criticizing those who see the Temple as the *only* mode of worshiping God. Acts responds directly to the allegation that Christians threaten the Temple, arguing that they seek involvement in its cult purely on account of its sacredness and that their persecution by the high priest is unjustified. More than any NT author, Luke is a devoted advocate of the Temple.

That Luke has a deep reverence for the Temple as the center of divine worship is clear. But why should Temple piety still be relevant for Luke a generation after the Temple's destruction? For him, attachment to the Temple legitimizes Christianity as a Jewish movement. When Luke–Acts mentions that Jesus, Peter, and Paul attend the Temple, its readers are meant to feel as if they, too, have a stake in Judaism's religious center, which, in any case, is now (ca. 90 CE) relegated to the status of symbol and memory. This legitimation, therefore, operates on numerous levels simultaneously, and the manner by which it occurs is highly complex. We shall see this below in my discussion of the application of ritual studies.

John is undoubtedly replacing the Temple with Jesus in saying that when the hour comes, people will worship in spirit and truth, instead of in Temple Mount. Jesus, too, hints at a substitution for the Temple, but only when implying that the Temple as a cultic institution no longer exists (although John's Jesus never predicts the destruction). In John, the only criticism of the Temple to be found is the "cleansing." Even here, however, Jesus refers to the Temple as "my father's house," and his action is assumed to stem from a zealousness for the Temple. Finally, a certain analogy to the Temple is expressed in the "temple of his body," in which Jesus is described as a temple itself.

When John is placing Jesus in the Temple during the festivals of Passover, Tabernacles, and Hanukkah, he is not rejecting it but instead is expressing his respect for it. His narrative associates Jesus with the sacred. John takes advantage of the Temple setting and its symbolism to characterize Jesus as a holy man who enjoys a special relationship with God; we see this, for example, when Jesus declares his having being sanctified or "dedicated" by God (10:36). To John, the cult is significant and meaningful, if only as a symbol.

The book of Revelation is replete with cultic imagery. At its center lies the heavenly Temple, where the Lamb (designating Christ) is found. We find mentions of the altar, incense, the Menorah, and the sacred Ark. The heavenly Temple itself is described as the locus of God and the Lamb as well as a place of divine judgment. Yet there is nothing in Revelation about the earthly, Jerusalem Temple, save for one provocative sentence about the eschatological New Jerusalem: John, it is said, saw no Temple in the New Jerusalem, since God and the Lamb take its place. The author replaces the Jerusalem Temple with the heavenly one, and with God and the Lamb, in the End of Days.

Still, the worldview of Revelation is decidedly cultic; its Temple imagery is a complex variation of cultic analogy and metaphor. Instead of comparing the worship of Jesus to a Temple visit, an alternative, ideal Temple is visualized. This heavenly Temple was not formulated merely to place Christ's sacrifice in an appropriate cultic setting, however; the Lamb may be adored, but his role in heaven is largely passive. Its cultic status as being slaughtered is surely not the reason for Revelation's creation of a heavenly Temple (indeed, many Jews could perhaps imagine a similar heavenly Temple, albeit without the Lamb, since it does not feature many distinctive Christian characteristics). The author and his readers simply needed a Temple, having been deprived of the earthly one. Moreover, Revelation does not attribute its loss to the Jews at all, and the text's anti-Roman stance implies that the author blames the Romans for destroying the Temple.

Revelation presents an exceedingly positive view of the Jewish cult—that is, on the theoretical level, where building on existing cultic ideas and further developing them is possible. What the author cannot do, by contrast, is relate to the earthly Temple in Jerusalem, since by the time of his writing it is already in ruins. Therefore, he creates a heavenly alternative. But if one were to compare this new, heavenly Temple to the one that once stood in Jerusalem, the former would undoubtedly suit early-Christian beliefs and needs far better than the latter. For John and his readers, there is no coming back from heaven; the next logical step could *only* be a New Jerusalem, with God and the Lamb as its Temple.

This is the only place in which Christ is identified as the Temple (Rev 21:22). Many scholars believe that this equation is customary at that time, and its roots can be seen in the gospel of John. But I can find no clear evidence for this prior to the fourth gospel. In fact, it is the Lamb, *together with God*, that takes the place of the Temple *in the End of Days*. In the heavenly Temple that precedes this phase, however, the Lamb is not equated with the Temple but rather resides within it.

Revelation, then, has nothing to say about the earthly Jerusalem Temple, but its use of Temple imagery nonetheless reveals not only the immense impact of the Temple cult on the author but also his understanding that the void left by the Temple's destruction needed to be filled. This understanding is no doubt related to the text's intense anti-Roman stance.

In Hebrews, Jesus is the high priest of the heavenly Temple, where he provides the ultimate expiatory sacrifice: himself. This role is usually understood as a criticism of the cult in the Jerusalem Temple—which, being unable to offer atonement for the people's sins, requires a replacement—as well as an outright rejection of it. However, I have tried to show that the detailed, yet subtle, manner in which the author builds his argument points to a far more complex approach to the Temple than is generally assumed. The theology of Hebrews is based on the general efficacy of the sacrificial cult and the high priestly office. The author aims to improve upon both, arguing that Christ can grant absolute atonement, that his high priestly office is eternal, and that the heavenly Temple is in truth the original one. Significantly, however, he never criticizes the laws and practices of the sacrificial cult but merely sets out a better alternative. Indeed, Hebrews is written with a great respect for the cult, seeing in it a means of making sense of who Christ is and how he operates as savior.

Since Hebrews seems to be one of the later texts in the NT codex, its attitude vis-à-vis the cult may necessarily reflect an essentially positive sensibility, one articulated by previous generations of believers in Christ. Hebrews is the only NT text that sets out a clear, systematic alternative to the Temple; it is only in Hebrews that Christ takes the place of the high priest and the Temple cult. Yet its driving force is *not* a belief in the Temple's irrelevance or profanity. To the contrary, the Temple and the high priest are necessary to an explanation of Christ's role and purpose.

Assuming that the epistle was written when the Temple was already in ruins, we might say that Hebrews carries on the priestly tradition in a new way—one, we should note, that hews much closer to the original than do many Jewish substitutions, such as prayer or Torah study. (Indeed, one could reasonably argue that even these were not real substitutions, since they already existed before 70 CE.) Thus the author's religious motivation in relating the Temple cult to Christ so closely may have sprung from the very fact of the Temple's destruction.

The Temple in Second- and Third-Century Christianity

In order to gain some perspective on the NT first-century evidence and to see when the early Christian attitude toward the Temple changed and why, we need to see attitudes toward the Temple as they develop in the following centuries. The Temple continues to occupy an important place in early-Christian writings after the first century; the Apostolic Fathers and the authors of the apocryphal texts deal, sometimes quite extensively, with the sacrificial system. Some of them continue approaches found in the NT, while others contain new avenues of criticism and rejection of the Temple. Their treatments of these subjects may be classified into three different but interrelated approaches: utilizing sacrificial or Temple metaphors in the development of new concepts; posing Christian rites and creeds as substitutes for the Temple cult; and condemning the sacrificial cult and the Jerusalem Temple or rejecting them outright.

My discussion will be limited to few examples that show the various uses of Temple imagery and negation of animal sacrifices. I will attempt to introduce the material in each section in chronological order, although the precise dates of composition of some of the texts are unknown.

CULTIC ASSOCIATIONS AND METAPHORS

One of the earliest and most valuable noncanonical Christian texts is the so-called Didache, which contains both a theological manifesto and practical instructions for a life of faith. Most interesting for our purposes is the manner in which the Eucharist is associated with sacrifice in Didache 14:1–3: "On the Lord's Day come together, break bread and hold Eucharist, after confessing your transgressions that your *offering* may be pure; But let none who has a quarrel with his fellow join in your meeting until they be reconciled, that your *sacrifice* be not defiled; For this is that which was spoken by the Lord, 'In every place and time offer me a pure sacrifice, for I am a great king,' saith the Lord, 'and my name is wonderful among the heathen.'"[2]

Here the connection between the Eucharist and sacrifice is not entirely clear.[3] A ritual that is utterly at odds with the Temple cult, the Eucharist—or certain components thereof—is nonetheless designated *as* a sacrifice. It seems as though the preliminary confessional prayer is described

metaphorically as a sacrifice as well.[4] This equation of the Eucharist, including the Eucharistic prayer, with sacrifice somewhat resembles the substitution of sacrifice with prayer in the Qumranic Community Rule, the
Damascus Document, and the Songs of the Sabbath Sacrifices. There is,
however, a notable difference in this case: Unlike the Community Rule and
the Damascus Document, the Didache does not directly discredit sacrifice
by arguing for the superiority of prayer;[5] rather, it simply uses sacrifices as a
conceptual model for the Christian rite.

Assuming that the Didache was composed no earlier than the end of
the first century or very beginning of the second, when the Temple cult no
longer existed, its equation of a community rite with sacrifice should not
necessarily be seen as "anti-sacrificial." Indeed, it is hardly different from
the rabbinical substitution of sacrifice with prayer.[6]

Didache 13:3 also alludes to the priestly system, instructing readers to
give "the firstfruit," including the produce of the winepress, the floor, and
the oxen and sheep, to "the prophets, for they are your high priests." Here
one finds an appropriation of the biblical priestly dues and even an appropriation of the traditional Temple priesthood in the service of establishing a
new type of priesthood for the Christian community. A central component
of Jewish traditional life is followed but at the same time transformed:
By receiving the first fruits the community's religious leaders are acknowledged, implicitly, as taking the place of the Temple priests.

1 Clement, the letter of Clement of Rome to Corinth (usually dated
circa 100 CE), also contains interesting allusions to the Temple cult. Clement declares that Jesus Christ is "the high priest of our offerings" (1 Clem
36.1, following Hebrews). Yet despite this high priestly Christology, the author expresses deep respect and appreciation for the Temple cult. He says
that the priests and the Levites, who serve at God's altar, are the greatest
gifts of God—along with Jesus, the kings of Judah, etc. He also acknowledges their roles and service, including that of the high priest (32; 40.5).
He mentions the command to celebrate sacrifices in their fixed times and
hours, lists the various types of sacrifices, and stresses that they may be
offered only in Jerusalem and inspected only by the high priest and the
ministers (40.1; 41.2). Significantly, all of this is stated in the present tense,
as if Clement were writing in pre-70 Jerusalem.[7]

At first blush it is difficult to understand why these details are relevant
to a Christian leader writing in Rome a generation after the destruction of
the Temple, as if nothing had changed. One possible reason is that Clement

draws an analogy from the priestly offerings and their rules to the church order in relation to offerings and ministrations (41.1). The cult serves as an excellent ready-made model of rules and ordinance granted by God. Indeed, 1 Clement offers an extremely important proof of early-Christian devotion to the sacrificial cult even after 70 CE. Moreover, for Clement, the belief that Christ is the high priest of the Christians' offerings (whatever that might mean) need not contradict the traditional role of the sacrificial system. Clement manages to have it both ways.

Sacrifice imagery is also used by Ignatius of Antioch (writing at the beginning of the second century), who refers to the Eucharist as an "altar."[8] More straightforward identifications of the Eucharist with sacrifice are found in later sources. Justin Martyr (mid-second century) designated the Eucharistic prayers and thanksgivings as sacrifices,[9] while Cyprian of Carthage (also mid-second century) develops further the understanding of the Eucharist as a continuation of that concept which began with sacrifice. For Cyprian, the Eucharist is not the sacrifice of the priest or of the congregation but "the sacrifice(s) of God." He understands "sacrifice" as the consecrated elements that are themselves bound to Jesus's passion, as opposed to the action performed by a pastor in the rite. Hence the sacrificed body and blood of Jesus are sacramentally united with the consecrated bread and wine.[10] It seems that a full equation of the Eucharist rite with sacrifice is attested to only later, in the fourth century.[11]

In Ignatius of Antioch, the entirety of Christian worship is designated the Temple cult. The Christians, he announces, should come together "as to one temple of God, as to one altar, as to one Jesus Christ." For Ignatius, the altar symbolizes unity in the service of God (cf. 1 Cor 10:18). Yet it is not clear whether the text's Temple metaphors pertain to Christ himself, to the assembly, or to the activity of the assembly.[12] Irenaeus of Lyons (late second century) stated that the Christians offer a sacrifice of their own—the "real" one—without defining what exactly this sacrifice is. He also defined the church order as a sacrifice.[13]

Indeed, sacrifice, altar, and Temple become the model of some early Christian authors' conception of piety. Barnabas (early second century) writes, "Let us be spiritual, let us be a temple consecrated to God," while maintaining that "the habitation of our hearts is a shrine holy to the Lord."[14] Such a "spiritualization" of sacrifice can also be found in later texts. Clement of Alexandria (early third century), for example, stressed that the righteous soul is the truly sacred altar, and the incense rising from it a holy prayer.[15] Clement even goes so far as to explain the meaning of sacrifice in a symbolic manner: "The sacrifice of the Law expressed figuratively the piety we practice, and the turtle-dove and the pigeon offered for sins point out that the cleansing of the irrational part of the soul is acceptable to God."[16] Irenaeus of Lyons conceptualized the oblation of the church as pure sacrifices.[17] More specific allusions to Christian worship as sacrifice, such as prayer (following Hos 14:3 and Ps 69:30–21), appear in the early third century. For instance, according to Origen (early third century), one offers unbloody sacrifices by means of his prayers to God.[18]

Interestingly, early-Christian writers considered martyrdom a sacrifice, most likely because Christ's own death was understood as such. Ignatius of Antioch describes the martyr's execution as a libation to God poured out on the altar,[19] and Polycarp of Smyrna (mid-second century) also uses a sacrificial metaphor for describing his own wishful execution "like a noble ram out of a great flock for an offering, a burnt sacrifice made ready and acceptable to God."[20] Less bluntly, Origen in his *Exhortation to Martyrdom* 30 defines martyrdom as a means of achieving forgiveness. Notably, the idea of death as atonement is also found in rabbinic Judaism from the mid-second century.[21]

Christian writers also used architectural Temple imagery as a means of creating a distinctive theology. The gospel of Philip, to give one outstanding example, provides spiritual explanation of the Temple's chambers: The three buildings/chambers in the Jerusalem Temple stand for three concepts in Christianity: baptism, redemption, and the sacrament of the bridal chamber.[22]

Apocryphal legends about Jesus and his relatives also feature a Temple setting, like those of the Lucan Infancy Narrative. In the *Acts of Thomas* 79 (early third century), Jesus the child spends time at the Temple and even participates in the offering of sacrifices. In the Protoevangelium of James (late second or early third century), the author refers repeatedly to the Temple and to Jewish ritual practice (especially that of purity; hence the special chamber that Anna prepares for her infant daughter to protect the young Mary against the taint of impurity). Here Mary and her parents are undeniably observant Jews.[23] The book begins with Joachim, Mary's father, offering sacrifices meant to atone for his own sins as well as for those of Israel (Prot. Jas. 1:1–3). Later, Mary is granted permission to live in the Temple and play at the altar (Prot. Jas. 7:9). Having conceived Jesus, she herself becomes a kind of Temple. She is, we might say, a symbolic sacrifice—not because she replaces the ritual but because, on the contrary, the authors valued its goal and function.[24] For our purposes, it is important to note that ritual purity and Temple piety were used to underscore Mary's holiness and her worthiness as the mother of the Messiah.[25]

REPLACING SACRIFICE

Several early-Christian authors present rites and doctrines as direct substitutions for the sacrificial cult. Barnabas stresses that Jesus offered himself as a sacrifice for our sins (7:3c) and implies that Jesus served as such a sacrifice when referring to the sprinkling of his blood for purification ("The Lord endured to deliver up his flesh to corruption, that we should be sanctified by the remission of sin, that is, by his sprinkled blood," 5:1).

Barnabas 7 creates a link between Jesus's death and the Day of Atonement. The priests' eating of the flesh of the goat (Num 29:11) parallels the Eucharist, which itself equates Jesus's death to a sin offering, like that made on the Day of Atonement. Eating the Eucharist also distinguishes Christians, who do not fast, from Jews. Later in the same chapter the author identifies Jesus with the scapegoat and the goat of the sin offering. He contends that Jesus suffered like the scapegoat and was similarly cursed (on the cross).[26] Jesus is identified not only with the scapegoat of the Day of Atonement but also with the red heifer that purifies the people "from the sins" (8:1–5).[27] Undoubtedly, Barnabas strives to show that everything in the Jewish Scriptures, if read properly, points to Jesus.

Justin Martyr introduces several replacements for the rite of sacrifice. He stresses that God does not seek blood and libations and incense; instead, prayer, thanksgiving, and hymns are more appropriate substitutions.[28] When, according to Justin Martyr, the prophets speak of blood sacrifices or libations presented at the altar at the End of Days (which Justin understands as Christ's Second Advent), they actually refer to authentic spiritual praise (*Dial.* 118.2).

Christ's blood, Justin writes, replaces the purification previously achieved by sacrifices (either by the blood of goats and sheep, the ashes of the heifer, or the offerings of fine flour),[29] since Christ was the eternal priest. He adds that the twelve bells attached to the robe of the high priest symbolize the twelve apostles, who depend on the power of Christ, and that the Christians are the true high priestly race of God.[30] Justin Martyr goes even further, suggesting that the Passover lamb symbolizes Christ, while the two he-goats of the Day of Atonement symbolize his two appearances, since Christ was the offering for all sinners willing to repent.[31]

Irenaeus of Lyons also argues that God wants not sacrifices but faith, obedience, and righteousness. He insists that prayer is equivalent to the offering of incense[32] and that the true sacrifice is observance of church ritual.[33] Clement of Alexandria similarly rejects sacrifice, arguing that true sacrifice is prayer and that the practice of sacrifice should be "spiritualized" following Ps 51:19. According to Clement, just as Jesus sacrificed himself for his believers, the believers must also sacrifice themselves: "We glorify Him who gave Himself in sacrifice for us, we also sacrificing ourselves."[34] While the idea that Christ is a sacrifice offered each day anew prevails in later Christianity,[35] rarely do we find the notion that baptism may replace sacrifices, as in the Pseudo-Clementine *Recognitions*.[36]

The Church Fathers were not the only ones seeking substitutions for sacrifices. Following the destruction of the Temple in 70 CE and the cessation of Jewish sacrifice, the rabbis also developed their own substitutes, such as the concepts of mercy or social justice, prayer, and Torah study.[37] Nonetheless, the need felt by second-century Christians to develop these replacements—and to find justification for them in Scripture—is curious. Guy Stroumsa concludes from this phenomenon that early Christianity is undeniably a sacrifice-centered religion, even if the idea of sacrifice is being reinterpreted. The Christian Anamnesis, he contends, is the reactivation of the sacrifice of the Son of God, performed by the priests. The priests (not the sages) lead the ecclesiastical hierarchy. Sacrifice is thus reoffered perpetually.[38]

ANTI-TEMPLE TEXTS

Plenty of sources from the second to the fourth century reject and resist sacrifice, thus denying the validity of the Jewish sacrificial cult. The author of the Epistle of Barnabas (2:6) for example, utterly rejects the practice of animal sacrifice, arguing that God "has made plain to us through all the Prophets that he needs neither sacrifices nor burnt-offerings nor oblations."[39] Barnabas argues that the relevant biblical commandments related to sacrifices should be read allegorically, since God annulled sacrifices in favor of the new law of Jesus Christ (16:1).

In chapter 16, Barnabas introduces a harsh polemic against the Jerusalem Temple, calling the very notion that God would dwell in a building made by human hands absurd ("the wretched men erred by putting their hope on the building, and not on the God who made them, and is the true house of God," 16.1, recalling Stephen's speech). He even equates the Jewish

Temple with pagan temples (16:2) and argues that the true Temple is not the building, which was rightly destroyed, but the body of the Christian believer.[40]

Most interesting is Barnabas's mockery (16:3–5) of the attempt to rebuild the Temple out of a mistaken belief that God seeks animal sacrifices: "That is happening now. For owing to the war it was destroyed by the enemy; at present even the servants of the enemy will build it up again" (16:4). The author's goal is to show that a transposition has taken place, from a literal Temple that was (in his opinion, rightfully) destroyed to a spiritual Temple that should be understood in Christian terms. The ideas of the remission of sin, of hope in the Name, and of the New Creation in which God dwells (16:8–9) all demonstrate that Barnabas is in fact describing a Christian replacement for the destroyed Temple.[41]

Many scholars realize that Barnabas was reacting to both Jewish *and* Roman plans to rebuild the Jerusalem Temple. His quotation of Isa 49:17 LXX (Barn. 16:5), for example, addresses the rebuilding of the Temple by those who demolished it, that is, the Romans. Peter Richardson and Martin Shukster argue that it relates to the reign of the Roman emperor Nerva (96–98 CE), known for having eased life for the Jews by modifying the *fiscus Iudaicus,* or Jewish tax.[42]

Justin Martyr refuted the Jewish Temple cult on several grounds. First, he declares that God neither needs nor wants sacrifices.[43] Curiously, he offers up an explanation for why sacrifices are commanded in the Torah to begin with: God, he says, commanded them on account of the sins of the Israelites, particularly that of idolatry. Since they made for themselves a golden calf in the wilderness and worshiped other idols, God instructed them to offer sacrifices in His name in order that they not serve idols.[44] This radical argument is also found in later rabbinic sources, attributed to R. Ishmael and R. Levi. It is possible that this view was accepted among some portion of the second-century rabbinic establishment as well, perhaps as a response to the destruction of the Temple.[45]

Second, Justin stresses that God did not need the Temple in Jerusalem as his house or court; on the contrary, the purpose of the Temple is to ensure that the Jews refrain from worshiping idols. Justin goes so far as to argue that the angels defied God when they taught the Israelites to offer sacrifices, incense, and libations.[46] Another reason posited for the rejection of sacrifices in the Temple, this one made by the priests, is that the Jews desecrate God's name.[47] For Justin, the destruction of the Temple is a divine punishment meted out to the Jews.[48] The rejection of the act of sacrifice and of the earthly Temple set the stage for Justin's creed: With the birth of Christ, God nullified the commandments—including sacrifices (*Dial.* 43.1).

Iranaeus of Lyon argues generally that God does not need the material offerings of men, but rather temperance, righteousness, and love of man for his fellow human being.[49] Clement of Alexandria takes a similar approach, maintaining that animal sacrifices are meant to serve merely as an allegory and that God never intended for them to be carried out. Rather, it is Christian prayers that are the best "sacrifices" of all.[50] Clement also boasts that Christianity effectively put an end to animal sacrifice.[51] Tertullian (early third century) mentions that sacrifice has become obsolete now that prayer—the "true" sacrifice—has taken its place. Like Justin, he contends that God never wanted sacrifices in the first place; it was only when the Israelites were prone to idolatry and transgression that God used sacrifices as a ritual means of establishing their connection.[52]

The Pseudo-Clementine collections of the *Homilies* and *Recognitions* (fourth century, based on earlier sources) adopt an extremely hostile approach to the Temple cult,[53] declaring the end of the Temple and sacrifices and insisting that God is not at all pleased by sacrifices.[54] The author/collector of *Recognitions* points to Moses's prophecy in the wilderness to argue that sacrifices were necessary only in order to prevent the Israelites from worshiping idols; that is to say, there was no longer any need of sacrifices when the Law was given to Israel.[55] In fact, Moses told the Israelites that a prophet will arise who will notify them that God desires kindness, not sacrifices (*Recog.* 1.37.1). Moses explained that in the future the Israelites will cease to sacrifice, and baptism will henceforth take its place as a means of securing atonement (*Recog.* 1.39.1–2). Despite his warning, the author adds, the Israelite tyrants abolished the very place that had been predestinated as a house of prayer in preference for a Temple (*Recog.* 1.38.5). The author also claims that the tearing of the Temple veil was a sign of the coming destruction (*Recog.* 1.41.3)

In *Recognitions*, the debate over the Temple and its cult is dramatized through a clash between Peter and James and the Temple's Jewish high priests. While the high priest praises sacrifices and objects to baptism (1.55), Peter argues that the time of sacrifices has already expired; since the Jews do not recognize this truth, the Temple will be destroyed (1.64.1–2; 1.65.1). There follows a public debate in the Temple, attended by James and others who have come to visit.[56] All this may owe its origins to a Jewish-Christian source from around 200 CE.[57]

Strikingly, despite his anti-Temple stance, the author had a deep familiarity with priestly matters, including the laws of purity, anointing oil, etc. (*Recog.* 1.46–48; 1.51.1). In fact, the Pseudo-Clementines were probably law-abiding Jewish-Christians, whose polemic against sacrifices is pursued apart from any broader denigration of Jewish Torah observance.[58]

Epiphanius mentions that in the gospel of the Ebionites Christ said, "I came to do away with sacrifices, and if you cease not sacrificing, the wrath of God will not cease from you."[59] Here too, the rejection of sacrifices does *not* stem from a rejection of the Law.[60] In addition, some so-called Gnostic texts from Nag Hammadi express a critical stance toward sacrifices and relate to Jesus's death as a sacrifice as well. For example, in *The Second Treatise of the Great Seth,* Jesus is described as ripping the Temple veil with his own hands.[61]

CONCLUSIONS: WHY DO LATER CHRISTIANS REJECT THE TEMPLE AND SACRIFICES?

We are now in a position to compare the evidence offered by second- and third-century Christians to the findings presented in the previous chapters of this book. Interestingly, some of the Temple and sacrificial imagery found in the NT texts are also used by later Christian authors: sacrificial imagery of the Eucharist, the Temple as a paradigm of religious piety, the symbolism of the altar, and the ritual observance of laws pertaining to the Temple cult.

In contrast, the rejection of the efficacy of sacrifices—found in the NT, although with substantial reservations, only in Hebrews and hinted at in relation to the End of Days in Revelation—became prevalent only in the second and third centuries. An outright denial of the theoretical validity of sacrifice is nowhere to be found in the NT. Moreover, substitutes for the cult are discussed almost exclusively in the gospel of John and Hebrews. Prayer and the Eucharist as substitutions for sacrifice are not attested in the NT at all, at least not explicitly.

Strikingly, Temple and sacrificial themes continue to occupy the mind of second- and third-century Christians despite the destruction of the Temple and attendant cessation of sacrificial practice among Jews in 70 CE. Although early-Christian polemicists argue against the Jews, the Temple, and sacrifices, they continue to use Temple and cultic imagery when drawing the contours of their religious world.[62] Notably, the very same Apostolic Fathers and writers who reject sacrifices altogether also attempt to find a replacement for the sacrificial cult; many of them use Temple metaphors or analogies for their own conceptions of worship. Sacrifice, the altar, and the Temple, all of which are presented as models of religious piety in Paul's letters, continue to serve the same functions in the writings of Barnabas, Clement of Alexandria, Irenaeus, and Origen.[63]

At first blush it appears as though these authors attempt to resist the idea of sacrifice and its ritual world. On the one hand, they are drawn to them, seeing in them the ultimate expression of devotion to God. Christ, the Eucharist, prayer, and communal togetherness should, they insist, be modeled after sacrificial concepts and practices or even serve as replacements for sacrifices. On the other hand, almost all these authors deny both the necessity and validity of animal sacrifice according to Jewish Law (even though, postdestruction, this was no longer a practical option in any case).

I can think of two general reasons for this attraction–rejection dynamic. First, Gentile Christians writing for non-Jewish readers feel it necessary to address the *general* concept of sacrifice in order to deny their supposed inclination toward pagan cults. Gentile Christians, especially the newly baptized novices, likely miss the (pagan) sacrificial milieu. Their leaders, anxious to chase away the pagan ghosts, set out an alternative: concepts and rites that would themselves be treated as sacrifices, in place of their progenitors.

Second, for those who write in a Jewish setting, such as Barnabas, Justin, and the Pseudo-Clementines, there is a very real sense that the *Jewish* idea of sacrifice—which Jews still very much regard as the ultimate means of serving God—needed to be refuted. To show that Christianity had indeed superseded Judaism, sacrifices had to be discredited and alternative rites preferred. In the general theological struggle between Christianity and Judaism, sacrifices are a veritable battlefield, demonstrated by the fact that even Christian Jews who observe the Law (e.g., Ebionites and Pseudo-Clementines) feel it necessary to reject the Temple cult and to insist that their own concept of sacrifice reigned supreme. The post-70 CE reality of Judaism-sans-Temple grants them an advantage; for them, a religion without sacrifices—by all measures an innovation—is not, as is the case for the Jews, the result of political restraints. Rather, it was a matter of principle and choice.

Nonetheless, I suspect a theology based on the rejection of sacrifice could truly have come into being had the Temple not been razed by Titus.

This leads to a crucial question: Is the rejection of the sacrificial cult not in truth the "natural" and inherent result of the belief in Christ's sacrifice? Two points lead me to answer this in the negative. First, two of the earliest Christian writings not included in the NT, Didache and 1 Clement, do not express a rejection of the Temple and its sacrificial cult. Didache introduces sacrificial analogies as they relate to the Eucharist prayer and the giving of the first fruits to the priest, while 1 Clement expresses admiration for the sacrificial system, albeit with Jesus in the role of high priest. I believe that the reason for their lack of censure toward—indeed, for their embrace of—the Temple cult lies in their not yet having adjusted to Judaism without a Temple.

Second, the multiple analogies to sacrifices found in later sources demonstrate that the positive view of sacrifices found in various NT texts still hold sway in Christians' minds during the second and third centuries. After all, if the Temple and the sacrificial cult are superfluous and inherently idolatrous, why use them as a foundation on which to build the doctrines of Christology, Eucharist, and prayer?[64]

For Barnabas, Justin Martyr, Irenaeus of Lyons, Clement of Alexandria, Tertullian, and others, sacrifices became a kind of boundary separating Christians from both pagans and Jews. Their rejection of the Jewish sacrificial cult is primarily the result of (among other things) social and political factors.[65] As 1 Clement proves, it is far from essential to set the belief in Christ in opposition to devotion to the Jerusalem Temple. Yet the Temple's destruction grants second- and third-century Christians an unprecedented opportunity: They can rid themselves of reliance on the Temple and the sacrificial cult in favor of advancing religious independence. In fact, recent studies by Judith Lieu and Daniel Boyarin conclude that second-century Christian texts portray "the Jews" as the Other, or the counterimage of the Christians, in order to affirm Christians' own identity and legitimize their separate existence.[66]

My intention in making this claim is to shed new light on the NT evidence. Specifically, I argue that one cannot draw conclusions about early Christians' relationship to the Temple on the basis of the critical and polemical perspective of the Apostolic Fathers. They live in a very different political, social, and religious reality from the first-century Christians and have their own, very different, reasons for relating to the Temple as they did.

What we do *not* find in the second- and third-century texts surveyed above (although this is a very partial survey) is also instructive. Whereas many NT scholars find in the gospels and the epistles evidence for the identification of Jesus as the new or eschatological Temple, I cannot find support for their claim in these later texts. Indeed, this idea is not nearly as prevalent as some scholars would assume. For instance, the notion of "the Temple Jesus body" (John 2:21) or Jesus as "greater than the Temple" (Matt 12:6) do seem to appeal to the Apostolic Fathers, but they hardly refer to them. These later authors primarily discuss the concept of sacrifice, as opposed to the Temple, which is contrary to the emphasis in the gospels and Revelation (although Paul uses both).

It is interesting that the characterization of key Christian symbols as sacrificial in both nature and purpose developed gradually: The Eucharist, for example, is only hesitatingly associated with sacrifice; at first, it is only the Eucharistic prayer or confession that is considered sacrificial. Christ, too, is compared to a sacrifice less often than one might expect, and baptism was very rarely regarded as sacrifice, despite its primary value of atonement. Indeed, the appropriation of sacrificial metaphors for Christian rites and beliefs is more complex than Paul's straightforward cultic metaphors would have us believe. Perhaps this is because, as I argued in chapter 2, Paul viewed it mainly a matter of rhetoric, whereas Justin, Clement of Alexandria, and others sought to formulate all-encompassing substitutes for the sacrificial offering. It is easy to say that prayer stood in for sacrifice, since this model is grounded in Psalms and Hosea. But arguing, as many do, that the Eucharist is a type of sacrificial rite is far more difficult. What part of this Christian rite is a natural match for the sacrifice of an animal?

I stress here that the post-NT authors' rejection of the Temple cult was not a natural outgrowth of earlier NT themes or of the interpretation of the gospels. It seems that the Christians of the second and third centuries rarely based their arguments on NT passages. Rather, they more often relied on the prophetic critique of the necessity of sacrifices (esp. Isa 1:11–14; Mal 1:10), a critique that is almost absent in the NT itself.

Ritual Interpretation of the Symbolism of Temple and Sacrifice

The rest of this chapter addresses the meaning and intentions of the NT authors as regards the major themes of the previous chapters. By "meaning" I refer to the perceptions that underlie or guide the authors' claims, and by "intentions" I refer to the more concrete messages directed at their readers.

The main question I seek to address is, *Why* is the Temple so central to the gospels, Hebrews, Revelation, and Paul? This question is relevant to those texts written after 70 CE, when Jews necessarily had to find substitutions for the sacrificial cult and one would naturally expect less interest in the Temple. The question is equally relevant to Paul and Mark, who write before the destruction. Indeed, one would expect that they would have attempted to forge an innovative, independent religiosity. It would be wrong to take for granted the idea that because the gospels describe, time and again, Jesus's acts and teachings in the Temple, the Temple is his focus or the basis of his activity in Jerusalem. We would also miss the point if we failed to consider why Temple imagery is so abundant and potent in Paul's letters and in Revelation, and why Hebrews chooses the high priest as a model for Christ.

By assessing the function of the Temple in NT discourse in light of ritual and other social-scientific models as well as from the perspective of critical theory, I hope to hone the previous chapters into a more concrete thesis. I also hope to analyze what interests and intentions lie beyond these authors' discourse about the Temple, in an effort to understand why they have the Temple play such a major role in their messages.

THE TEMPLE AS A "KEY SYMBOL"

My sociocultural perspective on the multiple uses of the theme of the Temple in the NT follows Sherry Ortner's modeling of "key symbols." The Temple (and the Temple cult) appears in different contexts that together form a "cultural elaboration." In other words, the authors of these texts show a particular interest in the subject. It can therefore be termed, following Ortner, a "key symbol" and analyzed accordingly. The Temple serves as a means not merely of summarizing ideas of sacredness and identity (as it does for ordinary Jews), but also of teasing out complexities and rendering them comprehensible, what Ortner deemed an *"elaborating symbol."*

The Temple-related themes provided a context in which to make sense of the early Christian experience. In addition, they elaborated religious authority. As a key symbol, or central component of early Christian culture, the Temple provides "orientations," that is, cognitive and affective categories, as well as "strategies," or programs of social action in relation to culturally defined goals.[67]

Paul uses the Temple cult as a *root metaphor*. A root metaphor establishes a certain view of the world and suggests an appropriate means of acting within it.[68] Jesus's visits to the Temple may be regarded as such a root metaphor, along with Ortner's "key-scenario," which provides strategies for organizing action experience. Jesus's visits provide a mode of action for successful existence within a culture.[69] For the early Christians, that culture necessarily involved social encounters with non-Christian Jews.

Why does the Temple become such a key? To begin with, the Temple had a broad reach, holding an important cultural meaning for a range of diverse cultural groups. Moreover, the meaning it held for those groups was far more fundamental than were other types of meaning; its content was prior, logically and affectively, to other meanings within the relevant cultural systems.[70] We know for certain that the Temple held pride of place in Jewish society and culture, and it is now clear that the early Christians, as members of this same society and culture, also looked to the Temple as a central pillar of their identity.

TEMPLE AND SACRIFICE AS METAPHORS

A metaphor is a translation of experience from one domain to another, effectively extending the experience. It can even become a plan for ritual behavior or a means of organizing the ritual.[71] Metaphors are translated into actions and become realized by behavior, mainly through the *ritual performance* they describe.[72] A ritual, then, is actually a series of metaphors made manifest through ceremonial rites. This understanding can illuminate the ritual of Eucharist, as established (according to the gospels) by Jesus and practiced as early as the days of Paul. The metaphor of eating Jesus's flesh and drinking his blood is akin to the experience of Jesus as sacrifice. It is an *organizing metaphor,* since "becoming" the body of Christ depends upon a ceremonial act.[73] The sacrificial imagery is intended to create the religious experience and shape the relationship between Jesus and the believer.

Of the cultic metaphors used by Paul and 1 Peter, the most common is that of the community as Temple. In the lexicon of critical theory, this comparison is a type of *conceptual metaphor,* in which the religious experience of the believers relies on the cult. It is a general mental construction that involves many mappings:[74] the Christian community as a Temple or sacrifice (or merely fragrance aroma); Jesus as a sin offering, a Paschal lamb or a *kaporet;* and Paul himself as both a priest or a libation on the altar.

Paul shapes Christian religiosity by using the Temple and its cult as a foundational conceptual metaphor. He organizes extensive portions of experience in light of the Temple and with an aim toward creating more specific metaphors, such as the Christian community as Temple.[75] Usually these mappings have overarching principles.[76] An example is 1 Pet 2:5, which creates a holistic metaphoric system of spiritual Temples, priests, and sacrifices. However, in Paul's letters there are no similar overarching principles to which I can point. On the contrary, Paul uses distinct metaphors, each of which stands entirely on its own.

Nonetheless, Paul's use of so many Temple and cultic metaphors creates an atmosphere of sacred ritual; mundane elements of daily behavior are elevated to the realm of the holy. This is so because metaphors project from the concrete to the abstract.[77] Regardless of whether a given metaphor concerns the community or Jesus, readers are encouraged to feel that they, too, are taking part in a Temple experience. Indeed, the result is an atmosphere not only of sacredness but also of religious action: Readers are told that their very *belief* creates a sense of holiness. Paul thus succeeds in transforming passive ideas into a sense of performance.

The metaphorical meaning of the Temple cult leads us to the concept of ritual. In order to show how Temple discourse helps to shape the early Christians' self-understanding as both a Jewish *and* a New Religious Movement,[78] I will analyze it by means of the ritual-studies model.

APPLYING RITUAL TO TEXT

Every text has a certain effect on its reader. The plot and message touch the reader, alter his or her mind, and sometimes even move him or her to action.[79] Texts may be grasped as cultural entities with real, tangible influence in the world. They serve as guides to action, addressing readers' realities of power and authority.[80] It is even possible to treat certain religious texts as rituals, as they offer their readers an original liturgical celebration, a substitute *locus* of ritual worship and an intimate knowledge of and access to the divine.[81]

I want to define my terms. What, precisely, do I mean by "ritual," and why does the definition matter? In general, ritual is understood as a "rule-governed activity of a symbolic character which draws the attention of its participants to objects of thought and feeling which they hold to be of special significance."[82] Ritual creates mental states, simultaneously expressing and developing a sense of dependence on a moral or spiritual power thought to transcend the realm of the human.[83] It enacts, materializes, or performs a system of symbols. In terms of religion, ritual is a "consecrated behavior": In its ceremonial form, such as the recitation of a myth, ritual performs and objectifies religious beliefs.[84] In this understanding, ritual correlates the individual's internal feelings and imaginative concepts to cultural symbols and accepted social action.[85]

The NT gospels, epistles, and Revelation are not in themselves rituals. Nonetheless, they can be treated as myths, since they each make extensive use of ritual themes: the Temple as idea and symbol; Jesus's visits to the Temple; and sacrifice. Indeed, to better our understanding of NT Temple discourse, we need first to appreciate the connection between myth and ritual.[86] In a sense, we might call the NT passages discussed in this book myths about rituals, since the act of reading the literary treatment of the Temple and its cult operates like a ritual: It transmits the symbolism of the ritual realm and of the consecrated behavior. The reader thinks about the Temple and sacrifices in relation to Jesus or his followers instead of acting in it. Take, for example, the recitation of the order of the high priest's service on the Day of Atonement in the Temple in post-Talmudic ceremonial prayer (the seder 'avoda), which Michael Swartz calls "ritual about myth about ritual." First there was the actual historical rite of the high priest, which was developed into a myth and later recited and reenacted in the minds of the worshipers as a ritual unto itself.[87] In the case of the NT, even if such a rite were only recalled, reread, and discussed (that is, absent the development of a secondary, contemporary ritual ceremony to commemorate it), the ritual concept and symbolism were still transferred to the reader. Like the postrabbinic seder 'avoda, the NT Temple discourse recapitulates a historical event by means of ritual recognition or the verbal recounting of its specific components.

THE EXPERIENCE OF THE SACRED

Literary engagement with the Temple was a way for NT authors to create a religious experience for their readers, one that is analogical to participating in the Temple rites themselves. It is, we might say, their way of playing to their audience or nurturing the cult. Almost any ritual, after all, is a process and an act that heralds change and contains an efficacy all its own.[88]

The general experience relates to two major themes—the holy place itself and the interaction with God that takes place there—that recur throughout the NT. The Temple is holy first and foremost because of its location. For Jews, the Temple Mount is the closest place to God. It is the cosmic *axis mundi*, where heaven and earth meet and the divine presence dwells.[89] The Temple also calls to mind the ritual offerings made to God, of both the public and private type. Even if these sacrifices are rarely mentioned in the NT Temple discourse—they are missing, for instance, in the descriptions of Jesus's visits to the Temple—they are certainly present in the authors' and readers' minds and understood as the very essence of the Temple's existence.

The general purpose of sacrifice, if we recall Henri Hubert and Marcel Mauss, relates to the presence of the divine. The act of offering a sacrifice alters the condition of the person who brings it, transforming both his status and that of his offering from profane to sacred. Sacrifice, then, mediates between the profane and the sacred or the "spirit" or holiness released from the offering to the divine realm.[90] These aspects of religious experience were certainly understood by Christians, even if they did not see themselves as part of the Jewish congregation; they could still relate to the ritual *idea* of sacrifice in a theoretical or imaginary manner.

Ritual performance—even of the literary sort—operates quite effectively on the self. Ritual is a strategy for applying metaphors to individuals' sense of reality, for moving them emotionally, and for provoking a religious experience of empowerment, energy, and euphoria.[91] Clifford Geertz famously argued that religious performances provide not only models *of* belief but also models *for* believing. And indeed, ritual performance induces a set of moods and motivations (i.e., an ethos) and defines a cosmic order or worldview by means of a single set of symbols.[92]

There is no doubt that the meaning and symbolism of the Temple and sacrifice shape the mind of the early Christians. Their idea of the sacred—namely, approaching God's presence—is modeled according to the experience of ritual performance. The early-Christian idea of the holy is, in a sense, evoked by the Temple and its cult: The Temple and sacrifice are models for the experience of the sacred.

For the NT authors, the Temple theme has positive, fundamental religious value. But what was the meaning of this value? What interests does it serve, what goals does it aim to achieve? If ritual is a process that reflects symbolism, what exactly does it symbolize? I shall now turn to an interpretation of the intentions of the ritual experience of Paul and the authors of the gospels, Hebrews, and Revelation, with an eye toward determining what ideas and social functions these texts aimed to promote, and how the Temple discourse advances social processes within the early-Christian communities.

CONNECTING TO THE LOST CENTER OF JUDAISM

One of the characteristics of ritual is its contribution to religious imagination. According to Geertz, "In a ritual, the world as lived and the world as imagined, fused under the agency of a single set of symbolic forms, turn out to be the same world." For Jonathan Z. Smith, ritual adjusts to reality when it reflects on what is and what ought to be and focuses on what is significant in real life.[93] In the gospels, what is imagined and idealized is that Jesus acts and teaches at the Temple with his disciples. In these narratives the early Christians visualize free access to the Temple. Rarely does Jesus speak about the coming destruction, and in most cases the Temple is simply a setting for his other teachings. By creating this ritual background, the texts' authors and readers can imagine that they themselves are still participating in the Temple cult, even though the Temple no longer stands. The Temple setting provides them with an atmosphere of sacredness and closeness to God, just as if Jesus and his followers were still attending it.

This "symbolic attendance" at the Temple provided by the gospels serves a significant social function: compensation for the very real distance from the Temple. The early Christians' exclusion from the Temple is in fact double: First, like the rest of the Jews, the early Christians shared in the loss of the Temple in 70 CE; even if they believed it justified, they too lamented its destruction. Second, according to Acts, they were not welcome in the Temple prior to 70 CE. Peter's and the apostles' teachings there lead to their persecution and (according to my interpretation of later traditions) perhaps also that of James. Many others simply live far away but still look to the Temple and its cult for religious grounding and inspiration. *Imagining proximity to the center of Judaism granted early Christianity legitimation as a Jewish movement, allowing it to share in the core of the Jewish religion (namely, a system of shared beliefs and practices) and cult.*[94]

This analysis answers the question of why the four evangelists described, in great detail, Jesus spending time at the already (or nearly) destroyed Temple. Indeed, far from detaching themselves from the Temple, these authors stress Jesus's relation to it, outlining an intense, complex attachment to the Temple that is a mixture of belief in its centrality to the relationship with God and critique of the Jewish leadership's use of the Temple as a means of gaining social power. In the gospels Jesus reflects this early-Christian position toward the Temple, and the evangelists seek a connection to this sacred heart of Judaism in order both to manifest their Jewishness and to approach God. Even a generation after its destruction, it would seem, the Temple remains for them a marker and a symbol of Jewish identity and closeness to the divine.

Anthropologists claim that ritual is the symbolic enactment of social relations.[95] They believe it regulates the relationship of one human community to another, much like drawing a map of a given society. We may apply this same approach to the Temple narratives in the NT. The descriptions of attending the Temple in the gospels and Acts in effect map out their authors' relations with the main forces in Jewish society. The narratives of visits to the Temple show that the early Christians wish to stay within the bounds of Jewish society, even if powerful Jewish leaders sought to push them outside of it. The conflicts surrounding Jesus and the apostles in and around the Temple symbolized the early Christian struggle to remain within the Jewish realm. In short, the Temple narratives in the gospels and Acts are an act of *belonging* to Judaism.

GAINING RITUAL POWER

One of the social functions of ritual is the production of social power or relationships of power.[96] Ritual exercises power, pointing to the center of authority in society. How does it do so? For starters, ritual plays a cognitive role, rendering intelligible social relationships and serving to organize both people's knowledge of the past and present and their capacity to imagine the future. It helps to define as authoritative certain ways of seeing society and specifies *what* in society is of special significance.[97] Ritual provides institutional legitimation when it unites a particular image of the universe with a strong emotional attachment to that image or symbol.[98]

When the NT authors incorporate the Temple theme into their teachings and draw upon it in their messages, they are utilizing a very effective tool. Instead of neglecting the Temple cult or avoiding the problem of its loss, by granting it pride of place they harness it for the empowerment of their religious discourse.

Early Christianity is based on the new and radical ideas of Jesus as Christ and of the ability of Gentiles to participate in a Jewish religious movement. Christianity being an emergent religion, these ideas made it vulnerable to criticism and attack by mainstream Judaism.[99] Indeed, Paul, Luke, and John all mention that the early Christians were harassed, beaten, and banned from the synagogue. Jews rejected Christianity in theory and its followers in practice. Incorporating the theme of the Temple—albeit in various and alternate forms, such as descriptions of Jesus's and the apostles' attendance; cultic metaphors; and the substitution of a heavenly Temple for the earthly one—therefore balanced the problematic new Christian belief system with more legitimate religious resources. In so doing, Christians not only showed continuity with their Jewish heritage but also shifted the potential ritual power from the Temple cult to the Christian community.

In relating to the Temple and the cult, NT authors argue that they, too, share the belief in the sacredness of the Temple. They too claim to attend the cult before 70, cherish its sacredness, and continue to share some of its characteristics in their daily life. They transfer its ritual power to the Eucharist, think of themselves as analogical to the Temple, and create a heavenly Temple where Christ (the Lamb) resides. Ironically, they seem to own or at least experience the Temple more than any other Jews after 70 CE!

According to Revelation and Hebrews and to lesser degree Paul, Mark, Matthew, Luke, and John, to be a Christian means to have a stake in the Temple, to experience symbolically the Temple cult, and to benefit from the sacred power of proximity to God. The NT Temple discourse is the ultimate compensation for losing the actual Temple, first as Christians (who were barred from it or harassed by Jews into staying away) and then as Jews, when Titus demolished it in 70 CE. The NT Temple imagery also fills the void for Gentile Christians who turned away from pagan cults. Having sworn devotion to God alone, they, like almost every group in antiquity, needed a cultic center they could latch onto. Baptism and the Eucharist simply may not have sufficed to replace the idea of the Temple and sacrifice.

This idea of Temple discourse as empowerment is not intended simply as a means to conform early Christians to mainstream Judaism. As is the case with political rituals, the performance deflects the performer's attention from dissenting elements in society. In so doing, it sometimes underlines the power of specific dominant groups within society and thus discloses social conflicts. Such rituals lead to the "mobilization of bias," or the imposition of values and beliefs by a certain group onto another.[100] In the present case, the ritual power of different types of Temple discourse is attributed to Jesus and the Christians alone. In the Pauline epistles and especially in Hebrews and Revelation, the Temple discourse actually marks the Christians out as different, closer to the sacred than others. Only believers are consecrated in their communities (Paul) or have a Temple in heaven (Revelation) or a heavenly high priest (Hebrews). In this way the early Christians transformed the symbol common to all Jews into a marker of their own.

Despite conventional wisdom, this transformation is effected *without* condemning the Temple (although there is an expressed distaste for the chief priests, mainly in Mark). In the Pauline epistles, Hebrews, and Revelation the alternative Temple discourse is remarkably positive, using new and creative attributes, such as the idea of a holy community, of Christ as a sacrifice, and of a heavenly Temple, to build upon the shared basis of both Judaism and Christianity: the Temple as sacred center.

The gospels' association of Jesus with the Temple offers its readers/believers yet another important element: a sense of *place*, within which to locate Jesus and to situate their own religious imagery. Place, in this context, is not merely a matter of geography. It is, rather, a cultural category, where being is situated and memory is embedded.[101] The NT authors and readers needed a setting for the narratives which contained Jesus in order that his person be clear and vivid in their minds. It is sometimes claimed that in Christianity the people of God become the place of God. Revelation is centered equally on the personality of Jesus, and Paul stresses the dwelling of the Holy Spirit within a community of believers. God is not bounded but encompasses everything.[102] True, the gospels and Acts attest to an opposite process; indeed, in Paul's letters, Revelation, and Hebrews the Temple is transformed from an earthly location into the community or relocated to heaven. Yet the centrality of the Temple as a concept in these texts also attests to the importance attached by their authors to physical location.

IN-GROUP SOCIAL SOLIDARITY AND INTEGRATION

As is true of any ritual act, the power of cultic symbolism brings individuals together as a collective group. Ritual dramatizes collective representations in the course of communal experience.[103] We see this in Paul's presentation of the Eucharist and his use of cultic metaphor (such as the community-as-Temple), which seek to achieve communal integration and solidarity among the Corinthians. The cultic ideas set forth in Revelation can be approached from the same angle: Believers find shelter in the heavenly Temple, a fact that should encourage them during their tribulations.

ADVANCING JESUS'S AUTHORITY

Jesus's activity in the Temple serves another purpose: He demonstrates his authority as a teacher and a leader in the most sacred of places—which, it is later understood, is also the most dangerous place for a Christian leader.

Positing Jesus in close relation to the Jewish ritual center associates him with the very source of power. Anthropological studies have shown that ritual creates hierarchical schemes.[104] To achieve a certain office or rank, one must undergo a rite of incorporation into the new social status. During this rite, one must prove his commitment to the rite itself—namely, to something outside of himself. Thus is the accountability of the office built into the structure of ritual authority.[105]

This may explain why, time and again, the evangelists portray Jesus as behaving quite freely in the Temple (the climax being the "cleansing," or the overturning of the tables), in a style that has led some scholars to suggest that Jesus sees himself as lord of the Temple, effectively taking possession of the place. The authors of the gospels try to give the reader a sense of Jesus's authority by setting him in close proximity to the center of ritual power. In this way, they build his authority as a Jewish leader.

This approach may also apply to the Historical Jesus and the apostles: They all teach in the Temple as a means of acquiring public authority. Proximity to ritual associates them with the power of ritual. But if Jesus's rank as a leader is integrated into the ritual system of the Temple, from the narrative perspective of the evangelists, Jesus identifies with "the system," that is, the Temple cult (albeit with some reservations). This is because ritual, as we now know, is not a neutral production of cultural symbols but is formulated by social and political powers and interests.[106] In coopting the cult's ritual power, the gospels' authors serve their own needs and oppose the dominant power of the Temple institutions that reject Jesus and his teachings.

RITUALS AGAINST THE TEMPLE LEADERSHIP

Rituals sometimes have a negative force, such as when they resist social power. In the so-called Rituals of Rebellion, for instance, we find a dispute about the distribution of power (not about the structure of the system itself). Such rituals give expression to existing social tensions, such as women who seek to assert themselves and princes who behave like kings. These rituals are a type of institutionally sanctioned protest that actually renews and entrenches the authority of "the system." The rite offers an outlet for negative feelings (e.g., in relation to the king) but nonetheless confirms the supremacy of the institution as a whole.[107]

For example, when Jesus experiences rejection by the chief priests and the Pharisees, readers perceive his actions as something akin to ritual resistance. Jesus wants to share in the Temple's ritual power but is not welcomed by the authorities. His teachings there and above all the "cleansing," fulfill the function of a ritual of rebellion, of the quest for authority in the sacred center. Nonetheless, his very attendance at the Temple demonstrates the early-Christian acknowledgment of the ritual system, namely, the Temple cult. This acknowledgment is underscored by the absence of an attack on the high priests' legitimacy (that is, on their traditional role and status, not their moral behavior). Neither Jesus nor his followers seek to wrest control of the Temple away from the Jewish community; on the contrary, they simply want their share of it.

CONCLUSION: RITUAL AND IDENTITY FORMATION

Early Christianity, like any religious system (especially new ones), needs to find expression in symbolic guise. The Temple cult and sacrifices provide a wellspring of powerful symbols that can be harnessed to achieve any number of aims and messages.

First-century early Christianity is a religious and social movement at the beginning of the process of identity formation. Its members have yet to determine who they are: what part of their identity is contiguous with Judaism and what part comprises all-new elements. During this process they undoubtedly look to other non-Christian Jews as a point of reference.[108] Literary engagement with the Temple grants the NT writers and their contemporary readers the opportunity to express their debt to Jewish tradition, while at the same time their distinctiveness from it. Moreover, this engagement enhances their sense of being powerful, genuine, and sacred—that is, close to God. For them, the Temple is a means of experiencing the sacred in both old and new fashion, somewhere on the spectrum between what will later be termed "Judaism" and "Christianity."

10 Concluding Thoughts

Early Christian attitudes toward the Temple originated when Jesus over-turned the tables. By the end of the first century some Christians believed that Christ resides with the Lord in the heavenly Temple or serves there as the high priest for eternity. It is therefore no wonder that until recently many regarded the early-Christian belief system as setting itself *against* the Temple. However, a close analysis reveals that these and many other treatments of the Temple cult are actually not intended to eliminate or su-persede the Jewish concept of the Temple by establishing a radical new re-placement but rather to create a *continuation* of contemporary Jewish ideas relating to the Temple.

Classifying early Christian discourse on the Temple into positive and negative approaches seems to miss the point, since this is not the main thrust of the NT texts. The NT authors do not simply react to the Temple as a "Jewish" (namely, external or remote) cultic institution and symbol. They treat it as a place and a concept that are inherent to their thinking about Jesus and their own identity. The four evangelists situate Jesus in the Temple time and again (although for different reasons) while he teaches the people. Paul coins cultic metaphors to conceptualize the sacred status of Christ, the believers, and himself as an apostle. Hebrews and Revela-tion develop the theme of the Temple through the concept of a heavenly Temple, creating new cultic imagery which draws heavily on the old.

The contents and meaning of all these treatments of the Temple have been summarized and analyzed in the previous chapter. Here I briefly dis-cuss two general issues that build on the previous chapters, namely, the relationship of the early Christians to Judaism and the implications of comprehending the Jerusalem Temple in the first century.

What does the idea of the Temple in early Christianity teach us about its relationship with "Judaism" or with non-Christian Jews? This naturally depends on how one defines early Christian self-identity: Is it a "religion" already separate from "Judaism," a Jewish sect, a (Jewish?) voluntary association, or (as I believe) a new religious movement or Cult within Jewish society and culture (see Regev 2011a; Regev 2016b). Whatever the case, early Christian authors draw heavily on the Temple as a major Jewish institution as well as on the concepts of the Temple and the sacrificial cult. They do so while minimally discrediting the legitimacy of the Jerusalem Temple and the sacrifices, even as they propose alternatives after its destruction. Some refer to the Temple in the conventional Jewish manner as a holy place for worshiping God, a location where all Jews meet with reverence to God and the Torah. Paul and perhaps also John ("the temple of his body") create these metaphors to explain innovative ideas, and Hebrews and Revelation transform them entirely with Christ as a high priest in the heavenly Temple and the Lamb who resides therein.

Whether referring to the Temple in the standard manner or a radical one, these authors are undoubtedly aware that they are sharing this key symbol with non-Christian Jews, and this seems to be one of their hidden messages: that they share the same holy center devoted to the one and only God despite their differences and persecution by fellow Jews. The Temple, real or imagined, is being set against all the nations and cults devoted to other gods in the Greco-Roman world. Thus the intense yet diverse application of Temple-related ideas in early Christian discourse serves a double function: It fosters new avenues of thinking about Christ, his authority, closeness to God, and sacredness, while at the same time these ideas are expressed within a Jewish matrix, relating to the belief in the God of Israel and, to a certain extent, the Torah or the Law (which prescribes the existence of the Temple). Indeed, as the author of Hebrews concedes, the concept of God's Temple cannot be disassociated from the Law.

The Temple in Jerusalem is viewed by Jews and Gentiles alike as a basic institution of the ethnos of the *Ioudaioi*. Josephus and Philo declare that there is "one Temple for one God" (*Against Apion* 2.193; cf. *Ant.* 4.200–201; *Spec. Laws* 1.67), and entry to its sacred precincts is forbidden to Gentiles (*War* 5.194; cf. Acts 21:28). To outsiders this approach toward this specific Temple of the God of Israel must appear to be distinctively Jewish. The early Christian authors themselves probably believe their thinking to be inherent to the Jewish matrix, variations on a theme common to all Jews. For Gentile and Jewish-Christians alike, the Temple discourse is a sort of engagement with and development of the Jewishness of early Christianity. Yet contemporary Jews such as the Sadducean high priests and Pharisaic sages probably did not regard it as a legitimate variation of Jewish principles. To the contrary, transforming this most sensitive key symbol would probably be regarded as blasphemy on a par with Jesus's so-called cleansing of the Temple.

The descriptions of the Temple in NT texts have significant implications for our understanding of the Jerusalem Temple in that period. The many references to the immorality of the high priests and the quarrels related to the Temple are frequently cited, and some even argue that its status as the major place of worship deteriorated when synagogues and rabbis began to compete and flourish. This raises the question of why Jesus and the apostles attended the Temple frequently, or why the early Christian writers associated Jesus with the Temple. If the Temple had become less important, why do Paul, 1 Peter, Hebrews, and Revelation build so heavily upon it as a concept in order to convince their readers that their new ideas about Christ cohere with or continue old cultic conceptions? The Temple and the sacrificial cult are a symbolic field with ample meaning for the early Christians, and with substantive polishing and reshaping it makes sense of their new, radical belief in Jesus. I suggest that the early Christian approaches also indicate many non-Christian Jews who still regard the Temple cult as both the center of their belief and practices and a substantial element of their group/ethnic identity.

The year 70 CE is generally considered to mark the end of the Temple. For the early rabbis and other Jews, the Temple now becomes a memory and the target for substitutions such as prayer, charity, and the study of Torah. Yet while most of the NT authors are writing after its destruction they nevertheless cling to the Temple almost as if it were still standing. At the very least they consider it to be a most vivid symbol. It is the model for prayer, closeness to God, and, above all, for following Jesus! If the Temple has not ceased to be a key symbol of these authors and their readers, it certainly continues to occupy the minds of Jews with a sounder Jewish identity.

Finally, the narratives, imagery, and ideas of the NT authors attest to the richness of the Temple as an institution and as an inspiring symbol.

When Paul and the authors of the gospel of John, Revelation, and Hebrews need to explain who or what Christ is, to formulate new and radical Christologies, and to make them comprehensible to audiences who have at least some knowledge of the Hebrew/Greek Bible, they turn to the Temple and the sacrificial cult. For them, the cult is a vehicle for expressing their spiritual thoughts, experiences, and visions. They neither want the Temple to disappear nor do they want to replace it; rather, they want to recreate the Temple and its cult in a new and symbolic manner.

Notes

Introduction

1. The designation "Christians" is mentioned only three times in the NT (Acts 11:26; 26:28; 1 Pet 4:16). Self-identity of Christianity as distinct from Judaism is first introduced in the second century by Ignatius of Antioch (Magn. 10.3; cf. 8.1; Philad. 6.1). In comparison, while current scholars debate whether the identity of Jews (or Judaeans) and Judaism in antiquity is a matter of religion or ethnicity (Mason 2016:97–220), Jews had a fixed identity in relation to non-Jews.

2. These are discussed in chapter 9.

3. Beale 2004; Wardle 2010; Fassbeck 2001:36–110, 193–214. McKevley 1969 and Daly 1978 deal only with the Temple *or* sacrifices. A short and very partial survey is provided in Turner 1979:106–157.

4. For example, Moule 1950; Cullmann 1958–1959; McKelvey 1969; Gaston 1970:4–5, 240–243; Juel 1977; Fassbeck 2001. For spiritualization, see Klinzing 1971. For example, Wardle 2010:221–226 argues that the transference of Temple terminology to the Christian community occurred very early in the nascent Christian movement. Already the apostles in Jerusalem were not merely analogical to the Temple but "saw themselves as a temple." He suggests that the apostles' "templization of the early Christian" is a reaction against the Temple leadership and its priestly overseers because they were antagonistic to the Christians.

5. Brown 1966:124. Church-Temple: Eph 2:19–21; 1 Pet 2:5; 4:17; Individual-Temple: 1 Cor 3:16; 4:19; Ignatius, Phila 7:2; 2 Clement 9:3; Heaven-Temple: Rev 11:19; Heb 9:11–12; Temple-Jesus Body: John 2:19.

6. E.g., Lieu 1999; Fuglseth 2005; Hogeterp 2006; Horn 2007.

7. Esler 1987:158; Köstenberger 2006:106; Hengel 1981:47,53. In fact, the notion that the Temple and Jesus compete on being the major or perhaps even the sole means of atonement is spelled out by Origen (*Comm. In Joann* 10, 24). Origen argues that Jesus's "cleansing" of the Temple is a symbol of the irrelevance of material sacrifices. According to Daly 1978:3, the concept of Christian sacrifice is built on that of Origen. A further possibility for this approach is modern rejection of animal

sacrifice (on which, see Klawans 2006:6–10). Ullucci 2012:30, 42 criticizes the evolutionary tendency to regard the development of sacrifice in the Greco-Roman world and early Christianity as a progression from crude ritual to "pure religion," as if sacrifices were destined to be replaced.

8. According to Dunn 1993:148–149, the meaning of the Law is limited here to preventing the Gentiles from participating in the grace of God (cf. Gal 3:13–14).

9. Gese 1981:100, 103, to give one example, assumes that in the priestly theology atonement is the basis of the cult. The cult is possible only as an act of atonement, and in the Priestly Code all sacrifices bring atonement. Cf. Janowski 1982. On the daily sacrifice as atoning, see Jub 6:14; 50:11.

10. Klawans 2006:56–73, who also points to the meaning of *imitatio Dei*. See the function of the *tamid* daily sacrifice in Ex 29:42–46.

11. E.g., Ps 27:4–5; 42:3–6; 50:5–9, 13–15, 21–23; 54:8; 96:6; 116:13–19; 118:19–20. See Regev 2004c, where I try to show that sacrifice is a means by which the worshiper approaches God.

12. Crossan 1992:231, following Morton Smith. See also Hengel and Schwemer 2007:316–317.

13. Webb 1991:192–193, 204–205, 211–212 (citations from 204–205, 212). He infers that the Baptist condemns the priestly aristocracy, whose presence or actions defiled the Temple or invalidated its rites, but he does not condemn the actual Temple rites. Joseph 2016:104 follows Webb and also suggests that John influences Jesus's "antipathy towards the Temple." Both are "alternative-temple movements" manifesting suspicion and hostility toward the Temple's current administration. Thomas 1935:esp. 55–56 has already suggested (based on the Church Fathers' evidence on Jewish sects) that ablutions sometimes take the place of sacrifices among certain groups. For assumptions about John the Baptist's priestly authority, see Strelan 2008:128–129.

14. Perrin 2010:38, 42–44. Becker 1998:43–44 even argues that John's baptism and the forgiveness of sins are a form of attack on the Temple cult.

15. Avemarie 1999. He thinks that John was perhaps indifferent to the Temple cult but critical of Essene practices.

16. Taylor 1997:29–31, 108–109. Compare Isa 55:7. In Ps Sol 3:8 and 9:6, atonement is achieved by fasting and affliction or confession. She rejects Thomas's (1935) approach regarding Jewish Baptist movements that regard immersion as a substitution for sacrifices and notes that in contrast to the Baptist groups described by the Church fathers, John's disciples do not practice repeated or daily ablutions.

17. 4Q512 frags. 29–32 vii 8–11; *DJD* 7, 265. See Regev 2016a:esp. 36–37.

18. See, for example, Klawans 2006:114–123. See also the parallelism of the Temple and the Torah in 1 Mac 13:4; 14:29; 2 Mac 2:17; *Against Apion* 2.193–198; m. *Avot* 1:2. For a typology of holiness which relates to the cult, see Regev 2001.

19. *War* 5.14–19. See also 5.397–402. For many other references and an analysis of Josephus's antirebel ideology, see Regev 2011b; Regev 2014a. For Josephus's attitude toward the Temple in *War*, see Tuval 2013:99–110.

20. On the Sadducees and the high priests, see Regev 2005a; 2006.

21. 1QpHab 8:8–13; 12:7–10 (*pesher* on Hab 2:17). Translation follows Horgan 1979.

22. For prayer as a substitute for sacrifices, see also CD 11:20–21. On 1QS 9:3–5, see chapter 2.

23. 4QDᵉ 7 I 15–17 and the parallel in 4QDᵃ 11 1–3. For a broader discussion of moral purity and atonement in Qumran, see Regev 2003; Regev 2007:95–132. Note that Josephus says that the Essenes send only votive offerings to the Temple since they were barred from the Temple and performed their sacrifices "by themselves" (*Ant.* 18:19). According to Philo, they do not offer animal sacrifices at all (*Quod Omis Probus Liber sit* 75).

24. 1QM 2:1–6 (citation from lines 5–6).

25. 4Q174 Florilegium frags. 1 I, 21, 2, lines 3–6.

26. Bauckham 2003; Regev 2007:26 and references.

27. E.g., Schwartz 1997. One of his arguments is the prioritization of the "nation" over the Temple in 2 Mac 5:19. Many texts from Diaspora Judaism do not allude to the Temple at all, although some of them relate to other religious concepts and practices. Tuval 2013:29–89 argues that this attests to their lack of interest in the Temple cult because of the geographic distance and the development of religious substitutes.

28. Cicero, *Pro Flacco* 28:67; *Ant.* 14.227 (donations from Ephesus); Philo, *Leg.* 156–157, 216, 291, 313–316. Josephus mentions eight hundred talents of the Jews' public money, held on the island of Cos (*Ant.* 14.110–118, citing Strabo). See also Regev 2013:73–78. See further Jonathan R. Trotter, "The Jerusalem Temple in the Practice and Thought of Diaspora Jews during the Second Temple Period" (Ph.D. diss., Notre Dame, 2016).

29. Regev 2013:84–89. On Elazar, see *Ps. Aristeas,* 3, 11, 32–33, 38, 46, 121, 123, 126, 128, 170, 320.

30. Regev 2013:89–93.

31. 3 *Sib Or* 3.545–572; (the gifts are brought in 715–731). The Temple is also mentioned in relation to the eschatological scenario in 657–808. On the significance of the Temple in *Sib Or* 3, see Collins 1974a:37–38, 44–47. Collins associates the author with the Temple of Onias IV in Leontopolis (ibid., 52–53).

32. Complaints: *Sib Or* 5.398–413; Collins 1974a:94–95. Rebuilding: *Sib Or* 5.493–511. The destruction is mentioned in 408–413. In contrast, the Fourth Sibylline Oracle rejects the very notion of the Temple. *Sib Or* 4.5–12 is a polemic against idolatry but also declares (8) that God "does not have a house, stone set up as a temple." Lines 24–34 list the virtue of the rejection of all temples and altars and blood sacrifices. Not merely pagan cults are rejected but also a Jewish one (Collins 1974b:367–368), since no positive approach to any Temple is expressed,

and the Jewish one is neglected. Collins 1974b:367–368, 378–380 attributes this text to a post-70 CE Jewish Baptist group and concluded that it developed the rejection of all temples as a reaction to the destruction of the Jerusalem Temple.

33. Fuglseth 2005:193–194.

34. *QE* 2.50; Heir 123. He also mentions pilgrimage to Jerusalem and the Temple tax. See Fuglseth 2005:196–200. Philo has a practical interest in the Temple cult. His personal pilgrimage is mentioned in Prov. 2.64. See Fuglseth 2005:193–195, 218–219 (on the authenticity of this passage, which is quoted from Eusebius, see ibid., 195 n. 22). He also notes that the Jews recognize each other when visiting the Temple, and pilgrimage unites them as a nation (*Spec.* 1.68–70).

35. *Spec.* 1.272–295.

36. *Spec.* 1.293–294; 1.277, respectively.

37. Nikiprowetzky 1967.

38. *Cher.* 99–101; *Somn.* 1.149, 215; Heir 75; Fuglseth 2005:208–212. When God created Adam, he made a sacred Temple for the soul (*Opif.* 137). The gathering of Israel in the wilderness before the erection of the Tabernacle is "the home of the Temple and altar" (*QE* 1:10).

39. Heaven: *Opif.* 55. Cosmos: *Somn.* 1.215.

40. *Spec.* 1.66–67; Fuglseth 2005:208.

41. *Spec.* 1.84–96; *Somn.* 1.214 (breastplate). On the cosmic symbolism of the Temple objects and the high priest's garments, see Goodenough 1935:113–116.

42. Fuglseth 2005:203–206.

43. Goodenough 1935:84.

44. Nikiprowetzky 1967. The analogy of the soul as a temple does not diminish the relevance of the Jerusalem Temple. See Fuglseth 2005:209–210.

45. Gilders 2011. Gilders notes, for example, that in *Spec.* 1.167 animal sacrifices serve as a symbolic means of teaching religious perfection.

46. Henshke 2007. On the Pharisees' approach to the Temple cult and the priesthood, see Regev 2005a.

47. 2 Baruch, written several years after the destruction, expresses grief for the loss of the Temple. 2 Bar 10:18 argues that the priests should throw the Temple's keys to the sky in order that God will guard the Temple since they have failed in doing so. The author proposes two ways of coping with the destruction: recognition that it is a punishment for sins, and a new view of the Temple in which heavenly Jerusalem shifts attention away from the destruction, since heaven is the true dwelling place of God. See Murphy 1987:671, 675, 681–683. On the heavenly Temple, see Lee 2001:146–157, and the discussion in chapter 7. The true Temple was therefore not destroyed and could not be destroyed.

48. B. *Sukkah* 5b; y. *Sukkah* 1, 52b; Nagen 2013:44–53.

49. M. *Menahot* 3:5–6; Nagen 2013:83–93, 98–99.

50. Sifre *Re'eh* 143 (ed. Finkelstein, 196); Henshke 2007:50–56. Charity atones: b. *Bava Batra* 10b (cf. already Dan 4:24; Tobit 12:9).

51. *Avot de-Rabbi Nathan,* version A 4 (ed. Shechter, 21).

52. Siferi *'Ekev* 41 (ed. Finkelstein, 87–88); T. *Berakhot* 3:1; b. *Berakhot* 32b.

53. Rosenfeld 1997.

54. Sifre, *Eeqv* 48 (ed. Finkelstein, 114); Rosenfeld 1997:447–448.

55. *Avot de-Rabbi Nathan* version B, 8 (ed. Shechter, 22). The early Amoraim (ca. 250 CE) state that the study of the Torah is more important than daily sacrifices. See b. *Eruvib* 63b; Rosenfeld 1997:462–463.

56. T. *Bava Qama* 7:6; Rosenfeld 1997:440–441 dates this to R. Yohana b. Zakkai (ca. 80 CE).

57. M. *Rosh ha-Shanah* 4:1; Rosenfeld 1997:442.

58. Neusner 1979:125–127. See, e.g. b. *Menahot* 110a.

Chapter 1. Jesus

1. Sanders 1985:61.

2. Meier 1991:167–195.

3. On the debate about the historicity of the Passion Narrative, its sources, and genre, see Theissen and Merz 1996:444–449; Yarbro Collins 2007:621–639.

4. Dunn 2003:787–788, noting the Son of Man's authority to forgive sins (Mark 2:10; John 20:23). On the same problem concerning John the Baptist, see the introduction. For the view that Jesus identifies himself with the cult, see, e.g., Antwi 1991. However, Congar 1962:112, 117–150 relates to this point while also admitting that Jesus initially has immense respect for the Temple.

5. Ådna 2000:419–430.

6. Theissen and Merz 1996:432–436. See also below on the "cleansing" and the New Temple.

7. Horsley 1987:294–296. See further references in Wardle 2010:223 n. 207 (Wardle 2010:224 believes it postdates Jesus). When scholars refer to the community as a Temple they sometimes confuse it with the eschatological Temple (as noted by Allison 1986:412–413), or the eschatological Temple with the heavenly Temple (such as Draper 1997).

8. Wright 1996:334–437, 362. Similarly, Perrin 2010:esp. 12–14 argues for "embodiment of Yahweh's eschatological Temple." Compare also Borg's theory of Jesus's transformation of holiness and purity (Borg 1984:104–105, 122–123, 133–136, 238), discussed below.

9. Fletcher-Louis 2006; 2007; Pitre 2008:72–78 adds that Jesus actually follows Isa 56:6–8. See also Perrin 2010:146, 167–168.

10. Dunn 2003:796; but, as noted above, he has mixed views on this subject.

11. Paesler 1999:231–232 relies on Matt 5:23–24. Wardle 2010:170–171 enlists Mark. On Jesus's visits and teachings at the Temple, see Mark 11:15, 27; 12:35, 41; 14:49. Luke 2:22, 42 and John 2:14; 6:14; 10:23 incorporate additional visits. Ådna 2011:2673 mentions that Jesus probably accepts at least certain parts of

324 Notes to Pages 20–22

the sacrificial cult as well as the financial support of the Temple. Nevertheless, Ådna still holds to a "replacement theory."

12. E.g., Bornkamm 1960:96–98, although he acknowledges Jesus's departure from rabbinic norms, such as being approachable to children and sinners, not studying the Law like a rabbi, and his statements on rules of purity in Mark 7.

13. Sanders 1985:209, 245–269. For more general concerns, see Moo 1984.

14. Fredriksen 1999:203–207. See also Loader 1996. Meier 2009:342–477 concludes that Mark 7:1–9, 13–23 postdates Jesus; hence there is no evidence that he opposes purity laws.

15. Kazen 2010. Sanders 1985:260. On Mark 7:15 as not an overall rejection of ritual purity system, see Regev 2004a:386–390 and references.

16. Theissen and Merz 1996:361, 366–367. They rely on Papyrus Oxyrinichus X 840 (dated to the second or even fourth century), in which Jesus is accused of not purifying himself before entering the Temple, and on John 13:20, where he declares that washing of the feet suffices, requiring no further cleaning. Thus they conclude that Jesus does not perform the necessary rites of purification, showing a detachment from the Temple (ibid., 432). See also Borg 1994:107–111, who argues that Jesus subverts purity boundaries and introduces an inclusive social vision. Jesus criticizes the purity system, replacing the "politics of purity" with a "politics of compassion."

17. Borg 1994:113 still holds to that view.

18. E.g., Bultmann 1963:36; Theissen 1976; Betz 1997:459; Dunn 2003:636–637 n. 113. Some classify Mark 11:15b as pre-Markan: Paesler 1999:234–242; Ådna 2011:2645.

19. Funk and the Jesus Seminar 1998:122.

20. Buchanan 1991 argues that it is unlikely that the Romans do not interfere immediately. Seely 1993 doubts that the Jews in the Temple do not act against Jesus. Miller 1991 questions the entire methodology of studies on the Historical Jesus to prove its authenticity.

21. Murphy-O'Connor 2000. For further references, see Ådna 2011:2644.

22. E.g., Ådna 2000:191–212. Tan 1997:161 contends that it is inconceivable that authorities would delay their response for three years, as per John's narrative.

23. Bultmann 1963;36; Trocmé 1968; Klinzing 1971:209–210; Sanders 1985:66–67; Marcus 1992:449–451; Ådna 2011:2645–2646. Cf. Tan 1997:181–184. Yarbro Collins 2001:46, 49 notes that Isa 56:7 is omitted in Matthew and Luke and that Jesus does not address the question of the Gentiles' presence at the Temple elsewhere. See also Yarbro Collins 2007:526–527. Seely 1993:270 adds that Jesus is hardly concerned with the Gentiles and does not seem to be interested in public prayer rites.

24. Wright 1996:418–422; Betz 1997:458, 467; Tan 1997:184–185, 188–192; Evans 2001:169; Perrin 2010:83–88; Ådna 2011:2646. Casey 1997, for example, suggests a reconstruction of the Aramaic source of Mark 11:15–18a, maintaining (following Isa 56:7) that Jesus wants to permit the Jews to pray in the outer Gentile court since there is not enough room for them in the inner court on Passover.

Casey connects Jer 7:11 to immoral sins related to the Temple, adding that the Temple tax is not just, since poor people must pay it while rich priests do not. Thus, in citing Jer 7, Jesus opposes the abuse of the poor. Indeed, for those who think that Jesus's power comes from interpretation of Scripture, it is reasonable to assume that he also cites such biblical verses (Casey 1997:320).

25. Sanders 1985:69–70. A symbolic act is "a way of acting on the world and of compensating for the impossibility of such action all at once" (Jameson 1988:151).

26. Wedderburn 2006:18.

27. Dunn 2003:638–639; Evans 1989:238. For similar harsh responses to such words and acts against the Temple, cf. *War* 6.300–309; m. *Sanhedrin* 9:6.

28. Casey 1997:319–320 explains the delay in arguing that Jesus has too much power. Borg 1984:171–173 claims that Jesus does not have enough power or followers to cause immediate interference by the Romans.

29. I do not discuss the view that Jesus tries to occupy the Temple in a militant action and to spark a revolutionary mob action as one of the Zealots. See the rejection of this view by Sanders 1985:68; Fredriksen 2015.

30. On the use of Tyrian shekels, see: t. *Ketubot* 13(12):3 (ed. Zuckermandel, 275); cf. Philo, *Who Heirs the Divine Things* 186. For the half-shekel tribute to the Temple, its origins, history, and ideology, see Regev 2013:73–78.

31. E.g., Evans 1989:248 (following m. *Berakhot* 9:5), commenting that it is not likely to be a later addition since later Gentile readers would not understand this detail.

32. Ådna 1999:446, again following m. *Berakhot* 9:5. Bauckham 1988:78 suggests that this is material sold to the people by the Temple treasury. Ford 1976 concludes that these are money bags (of the money changers or the Temple bank). Others try to relate Jesus's prohibition to the overturning of the tables. Tan 1997:180–181 suggests that this vessel is used for carrying materials for the offerings and that Jesus wishes to halt the selling of these products to the populace. Casey 1997:310–311 relates it to the prohibition on bringing nonsacred vessels into the Temple's holy court (*Against Apion* 2.106) and asserts that it aims at preventing the priests from taking shekels out from the women's court in which they are collected such that the chief priests cannot use them; thus there was no use in collecting them anymore.

33. Betz 1997:461–462; Tan 1997:179; cf. Trocmé 1968:17–19. For further scholarship, see Sanders 1985:62–63.

34. Paesler 1999:243–249. However, it is likely that Zech 14:21 does not refer to "traders" at all (see chapter 6 in relation to the "cleansing").

35. Yarbro Collins 2001:54, 58. In Ezek 44:5–9 foreigners are forbidden to enter the outer court. It is not a civic space but part of the sanctuary. In the Temple Scroll 46:5–12 there is a barrier between the outer court and the city.

36. Nonetheless, some regard Jesus's approach to the Temple as hostile rejection: Neusner 1989:289; Holmén 2001:320–328. See the survey in Joseph 2016:158–159, 165 n. 180.

37. Abrahams 1967:85–89; Klausner 1964:313–315; Sanders 1985:63–65; Fredriksen 1999:208–209; Holmén 2001:316–318.

38. Sanders 1985:76, 89–90.

39. Sanders 1985:70–71, 75. That Jesus's act symbolizes the coming destruction of the Temple and the hope for its rebuilding in light of his discussions of the kingdom of God is already suggested by Bornkamm 1960:158–159; Hiers 1971. Cf. McKelvey 1969:66 on the "cleansing" and the kingdom.

40. Isa 60:13; Tobit 14:5; Jub 1:28; 1 En 91:13; Temple Scroll 29:8–10; Sib Or 3.290–294; 5.414–423. See also the critique below in relation to Mark 14:58.

41. Sanders 1985:77–90 (citations from 87–88). He then proceeds to Jesus's restoration eschatology, ibid., 91–119. Note that Sanders also relies on Jesus's talking about destroying and rebuilding the Temple (Mark 14:58), as discussed below.

42. He is followed, fully or partly, by Hooker 1988:18–19; Meyer 2002:200; Dunn 2003:640, 650; Wardle 2010:173–174; Ådna 2000:25–89, 142–153; 2011:2664–2665, among others.

43. Wright 1996:415–426. He also terms it a "messianic act" (ibid., 651).

44. Fredriksen 1999:210, 232–234. Fredriksen 1990:298 bases this conclusion on Jesus's cursing of the fig tree (Mark 11:12–14) and his prediction of the destruction in Mark 13:1–3. She also refers to the saying attributed to him in Mark 14:58, which is discussed below.

45. Gaston 1970:119, 161–162, 147–154 ("there is no mention of the Messiah at all in the vision of the new Zion in 4 Ezra 10, and Enoch 90:28f. describes the rebuilding of Jerusalem, not the Temple, before the Messiah comes," ibid., 147); Evans 1989:249–250; 1995:319; Seely 1993:264–265. The only parallel Sanders finds is 1 En 90:28–29, which, according to current research, refers not to the Temple at all but to the city of Jerusalem (Tiller 1993:376 and references). For further discussion of Second Temple evidence, see below on Mark 14:58. Joseph 2016:133–167, esp. 138, 156 argues that the "cleansing" is a prediction of the destruction, not a symbolic act of destruction.

46. As Borg 1994:113 notes, only someone who also has restoration eschatology in mind can understand Jesus's act. Evans 1989:esp. 238 argues that Sanders ignores Jesus's hostility toward the (high) priesthood as well as the scriptural data that may motivate Jesus, against which his contemporaries understand his action (but see my own criticism of Evans below). Evans also rightly disagrees with Sanders regarding Mark's embarrassment at Jesus's prediction of the Temple's destruction, since later in 13:2 Mark still mentions the prophecy of destruction.

47. Ådna 1999:464–465, referring to Sanders 1985:70.

48. Evans 1989:239–249.

49. Evans 1989:251–264; 1995. His list includes Hos 4:4–6; 6:6; Isa 1:11; 28:7; Mic 3:9–12; Jer 7:9, 11, 14; Ezek 22:23–31; Lam 4:13; Mal 3:1; Jub 23:21; 1 En 89:73; 1QpHab 8 and 11; 1Q169 pNah 3–4 I 11; Ps Sol 8:11–13 (cf. the Messiah's purg-

ing of Jerusalem in chs. 17–18); T. Mos. 5:3–6:1; *Ant.* 20.181, 206–207; b. *Pesahim* 57a; t. *Menahot* 13:19, 22. This, however, should be balanced by Second Temple sources attesting to the priests' piety (cf. Sanders 1992:91–92, 182–199).

50. Evans 1989:256, 263–264.
51. Evans 1989; 265–267. See Epstein 1964, following b. *Sanhedrin* 41a on the moving of the Sanhedrin from the Temple Mount to the *hanut* forty years before the destruction. Evans raises certain doubts concerning the exact details of Epstein's thesis about the chronology and circumstances of these changes at the Temple Mount. His acknowledgment of doubts about whether Epstein is correct that there is no selling in the Temple Mount before the days of Caiaphas and whether or not Jesus reacted to the change actually puts the validity of his entire thesis in doubt.
52. Horsley 1987:299–300; Hengel 1989a:215 and references; Tan 1997:167–171; Perrin 2010:96–98. Bauckham 1988:176–181, 190–191 links it to Jesus's protest against "commercialism sanctioned by the priestly overseers" and "financial impropriety" or denunciation of "the chief priests' economic malfeasance." In support, he refers to moral criticism of the chief priests on financial grounds such as corruption and greed in both the Qumran scrolls and Josephus (*Life* 193–196)— though he thinks Jesus's view of the Temple is not as negative as in Qumran, as demonstrated by his followers continuing to participate in the cult.
53. Yarbro Collins 2001:52–53; Seely 1993:266, who also adds that the hostility toward the chief priests increases before and during the Jewish War, when social order is breaking down. The sources from the monarchic, postexilic, and Hasmonean periods are chronologically irrelevant.
54. Ådna 2000:335–342; 2011:2655.
55. Sanders 1985:66.
56. Seely 1993:266–267.
57. Compare Weatherly 1994.
58. Theissen 1976.
59. Crossan 1992:355–356, 360, drawing heavily on Jesus's declaration that he will destroy "this house" (Gos. Thomas 71). He connects this saying with the act, arguing that the "cleansing" is an act of symbolic destruction and eventually reaching a conclusion of reconstruction not far from Sanders's thesis (ibid., 359).
60. Betz 1997:469, 472. Knight 1998:182–183 understands it as a protest against the politicization of the Temple by the Herodian dynasty.
61. Horsley 1987:286–300. Borg 1994:114 adds that "the money changers and sellers of birds were part of the temple system that stood at the center of the tributary mode of production, drawing money to the Jerusalem elites." Jesus protests against the Temple becoming "the center of an economically exploitative system dominated by the ruling elites and legitimated by an ideology of purity . . . an indictment of the elites themselves."

62. M. *Bekhorot* 8:7; m. *Sheqalim* 2.4. These coins are extremely common in Judaean archeological sites from the first century CE. For numismatic and archaeological information, see Regev 2013:74 and references; Richardson 1992:512–518.

63. Richardson 1992. He also refers to Jesus's reluctance to pay the tax in Matt 17:24–27, discussed below.

64. Yarbro Collins 2001:60–61. See also Murphy-O'Connor 2000:50.

65. Horbury 1984; Bauckham 1988:74–75. Horbury's main arguments are that the reference to the kings of Israel shows that this is not the post-70 CE Roman *fiscus iudaicus* and that the text makes sense only if applied to a tax levied in the name of God—which is possible only before the destruction. He adds that Jesus's instruction shows concern and respect for the Temple (Horbury 1984:70).

66. Bauckham 1988:76–78, referring to m. *Keritot* 1:7 on the high price of doves for childbirth sacrifice. See also Tan 1997:175–178. Klawans, 2006:237–239 suggests that owing to his renunciation of the accumulating of possessions and wealth, Jesus opposes the notion that the poor are required to pay the Temple tax and to buy offerings since the Temple should not pose a financial burden to the poor. Richardson 1992:518–520 compares this approach to the rejection of the annual Temple tax at Qumran, where it is only a once-in-a-lifetime payment as a "ransom," concluding that Jesus claims that the Temple tax should be paid once in a lifetime as well. On Qumran, see 4Q159 *Ordinances*[a] frags. 1 II + 9, 6–7; Temple Scroll 39:8–11, following Ex 30:11–16.

67. Saldarini 1994:143–147 discusses the question of whether or not the passage goes back to the Historical Jesus, ultimately reaching a negative conclusion.

68. Chilton 1992:esp. 101–102. Cf. m. *Ḥagiga* 2:2–3; t. *Ḥagiga* 2:11; b. *Bezah* 20 a-b. In his reconstruction of the relevant historical background, Chilton again follows Epstein, who accepts rabbinic tradition in b. *Sanhedrin* 41a, inferring that forty years before the destruction (namely, in Jesus's day) Caiaphas (the High Priest) expels the Sanhedrin from the Temple Mount and introduces the traders into it. Selling sacrifices at the Temple is useful for the buyers, since they can then purchase acceptable sacrifices without running the risk of harm befalling the animal on its way to be slaughtered. But the Temple also profits from such trade. Buying the sacrifice causes a breach between the worshiper and the offering in the sacrificial action. Hence Jesus's action is "perfectly explicable within the context of contemporary Pharisaism." Chilton 1992:107–109. Cf. Epstein 1955.

69. Chilton 1992:110–111.

70. Borg 1984:173–175.

71. Borg 1984:175–176, 195 (citation from 175). A similar understanding that Jesus leads a fundamental change of the Temple cult toward the eschatological age is embraced by others. See Davies 1974:350–351 and the survey by Ådna 2011:2658–2663. Cf. also Wright 1992:416–428.

72. Sanders 1985:68–69.

73. Paesler 1999:244. Stegemann 1984 infers that, like the Qumran sectarians (according to his understanding of the scrolls), Jesus believes that God himself

begins to purify everything (Mark 7:1–23), and sacrifices are no longer needed. Those who continue to sacrifice in the Temple do not recognize the eschatological change. The "cleansing" is thus a protest against the continuation of the cult under changed conditions.

74. Crossan 1994:130–131; Ådna 2000:381–386; 2011:2668–2670. Note that this too is heavily dependent on the authenticity of the "den of robbers" citation. On the cult's renewal-replacement, see Ådna 1999:469.

75. Joseph 2016:163–165. This lacks actual textual basis from the gospels and would conflict with Mark's story about Jesus's partaking in the Passover sacrifice (Mark 14:1216). Joseph 2016:167–209, esp. 191 ascribes to the Historical Jesus the rejection of animal sacrifice based on the tradition that Epiphanius (*Panarion* 30.16.4–5) attributes to the Ebionites (see chapter 9). Joseph (2016 esp. ibid., 204) argues that Paul and the gospels eliminate Jesus's opposition to eating meat and sacrifices since this would contradict the doctrine of Jesus as a sacrifice.

76. For an example of Jesus's positive approach toward the sacrificial cult, see Evans 1989:265.

77. The following suggestion first appears in Regev 2004a:397–402.

78. Luke (=Q) 12:16–20, 22–31; Matt 5:3–6//Luke 6:20–31; Matt 6:19–21//Luke 12:33–34; Matt 23:23//Luke 11:42; Mark 10:17–25//Matt 19:16–24//Luke 18:18–25 (on the difficulty of the rich man in entering the Kingdom); Mark 10:21; Luke 14:33; *Gospel of Thomas* 63–65. Cf. Crossan 1992:268–282.

79. Matt 6:24//Luke 16:13. See Hiers 1970:30–36; Betz 1995:454–459; Flusser 1988:169–72 with parallels in rabbinic literature. Its roots can be found in wisdom literature. See Regev 2004a:400 n. 58.

80. Mark 7:15; Luke 11:38–41//Matt 23:25–26; *Gospel of Thomas* 14. Compare Mark 7:18–23 and Luke's parables of mercy (Luke 7:41–43, 10:30–37; 13:6–9; 15:3–7; 15:8–10//Matt 18:10–14; Luke 15:11–32; 18:9–14). Crossan 1992:292, 294 characterizes Jesus's message as the "ethical Kingdom." For moral (im)purity in early Christianity, see Regev 2004a.

81. In the NT, however, moral impurity does not defile the body as in ritual or bodily ("Levitical") impurity and probably does not require ritual purification. Such a view is found only among the Qumran sectarians. See Klawans 2001:85–91.

82. Note that this section begins with a citation of Mal 1:10 as well as a reference to proper sacrificial rites. Since the next sentence in this passage deals with stealing money from the poor and widows, one may presume that this is the act of wickedness that causes defilement. A similar claim that corrupted money pollutes the Temple is mentioned in Jub 23:21. On corrupt wealth in Qumran, see Regev 2007:339–344.

83. See the survey in Theissen and Merz 1996:460–469. My discussion owes much to Winter 1974.

84. Yarbro Collins 2007:621–639. On the debate between those who accept or reject the historicity of the Passion Narrative, see Allison 2010:387–392. Allison defends it.

85. E.g., Fredriksen 1990:301.
86. Sanders 1985:61–76; Dunn 2003:632, 785–786; Crossan 1992:360; 1994:133; Horsley 1987:160–164; Bauckham 1988:86–89.
87. Winter 1974:44–59, 66–67. For the role of the chief priest in general, see Sanders 1985:310–311.
88. E.g., Dunn 2003:784.
89. Sanders 1985:284–287; Dunn 2003:769; Theissen and Merz 1996:465. Indeed, Mark 11:17–18 says that the high priests want his destruction immediately after the "cleansing."
90. Sanders 1985:287. Few scholars view the "cleansing" as minor enough to be overlooked by the Temple authorities. See the survey of Wedderburn 2006:7 n. 30.
91. E.g., Sanders 1985:288, 293. He also adds that anyone who speaks in the name of God and talks about the Kingdom challenges the status quo and that Jesus's message concerning the sinners offends many. On the general Roman perspective on the Jewish Temple, see below.
92. Dunn 2003:628–629.
93. Winter 1974:60–67; Dunn 2003:774. However, Umoh 2004:329–31 argues that *topos* in John 11:48 does not mean the Temple. It is the position/office of the high priests, since the use of the word is general in this case, while elsewhere *topos* is specific.
94. E.g., Fredriksen 1999:234. See the list of references in Regev 2012:218 n. 3. See the *titulus* on the cross "the king of the Jews" (Mark 15:26; John 19:19–21).
95. Theissen and Merz 1996:458.
96. Dunn 2003:652–653.
97. Sanders 1985:204, 238. Allison 2010:234–239 sees the accusation of the desire to destroy and rebuild the Temple as the reason that leads to the messianic charge, which is considered a crime against the state—namely, the Romans.
98. Flusser 2001:139, 141, referring to Zech 6:12 as to where the Messiah will build the Temple; Dunn 2003:633–634, following O. Betz, referring to the Davidic Temple in 2 Sam 7:12–14 and its interpretation in Qumran (4Q174 Florilegium 1.10–13). Perrin 2010:105 suggests that in the "cleansing" Jesus "insinuate[d] his own messianic status" because the Messiah is the one who is expected to rebuild the Temple. See also the thesis that Jesus deems himself the eschatological high priest, as discussed above.
99. Sanders 1985:297–298. Many try to reconstruct the nature of the legal procedure described in Mark 14–15. Clearly, some important details are missing.
100. Crossan 1995:106–108.
101. Mack 1988:263, 288–290.
102. Such as Sanders, Fredriksen, and Allison. However, Borg, Crossan, Mack, Patterson, Hare, and the Jesus Seminar think that Jesus is a noneschatological sage, mainly because of the marginal role of eschatology in Q. See Regev

2006a:14–22. Dunn 2003:697–702 comments that "teacher" is the most common title used for Jesus in the Jesus traditions. Note that Josephus (*Ant.* 18.63) calls him "a wise man" (*sophos aner*). See the refutation of these views in Allison 2010.

103. Wright 1996:543–552 realizes the crux of the problem, concluding that the high priest's Sanhedrin and Pilate are aware of this difference but use the messianic charge only as an excuse to get rid of Jesus. The fact is that they do not arrest his followers.

104. Mark 13:2; Paesler 1999. Sanders 1985:71, 75. Similarly Ådna 2011: 2668–2670. Not a condemnation: Fredriksen 1990:298–299.

105. Dunn 2003:514–515, although with a certain hesitation. More confident are Gärtner 1965:111; Horsley 1987:292–296.

106. Translated by S. Patterson and M. Meyer, *The Gnostic Society Library* website.

107. Brown 1994:448–460; Wardle 2010:183.

108. Authentic words/idea of Jesus: Paesler 1999:11–60; Ådna 2000:127–130, 151–153; and Dunn 2003:632–633. As for the question concerning Jesus's exact words, note that the parallel in John 2:19 (where the Temple is transformed into Jesus's body) is redactional. John combines Jesus's act and sayings. See Paesler 1999:68–69. In contrast, McKelvey 1969:70–71, 79 argues that John's version seems to be the most reliable.

109. Ådna 2011:2654 as well as a group of scholars who relate the saying to the "cleansing." See also Becker 1998:329–331.

110. Sanders 1985:71–72.

111. Cf. Sanders 1985:72; Klinzing 1971:204; Juel 1977:72–73, 123–125. See also below and in chapter 5.

112. Schlosser 1990; Wright 1996:425–442.

113. On the distinction between a sanctuary made with hands (*cheiroptoiēton*) or built without the agency of a hand (*acheiroptoiēto*n) as inauthentic or perhaps Markan, see Juel 144–157; Brown 1994:439–440; Wardle 2010:184. Gaston 1970:161 suspects the influence of Stephen's speech (Acts 7:48). On "within three days" cf. Brown 1994:444; McKelvey 1969:70. Certain doubts are also raised by Bultmann 1963:120–121; Taylor 1959:566. Attributing the words "I will destroy" to Jesus should date before the destruction, since it was not Jesus but Titus who destroys the Temple (Sanders 1985:73–74). Nevertheless, if Mark writes before 70 (see chapter 3) this still may be his own addition.

114. McKelvey 1969:70–71, 79; Sanders 1985:73, 77–87; Dunn 2003:633; Ådna 2000: 25–89; Allison 2010:43; Wardle 2010:184.

115. Wedderburn 2006:16. Cf. Collins 1983:390. Targum Jonathan to Isaiah 53.5 is cited frequently as evidence of the expectation that a Temple will be built by a Messiah (Juel, 1977:185–189; Ådna 2000:81–86). However, Gaston 1970:149 n. 1 already notes that the building of the Temple (unattested in the Hebrew texts of Isaiah) is merely a gloss from TgZechariah 4:9 and 6:13. Shepherd

2014 argues that the *targum* is a harmonization of Isa 53:5 with the renderings of Zech 4 and 6 and Isa 45.26–45.1. The building of the Temple, therefore, does not necessarily reflect the Aramaic translator's own expectations for a messianic temple builder in his own or a later time, but rather his direct interpretation of postexilic Scriptures. Shepherd also points out that TgJon 2 Sam 7:13–14 does not introduce an eschatological interpretation despite the convenient opportunity suggested by Scripture.

116. Wardle 2010:184. Becker 1998:329–331 tries to cope with this difficulty.

117. Positive sayings: Becker 1998:330, 348. See also Borg 1984:180 (adding that Mark 31:2 has only theoretical meaning and that the Temple is not safe). Peter and the apostles: Wedderburn 2006:17–19. He also comments that from the Roman point of view the "cleansing" is a more reasonable reason to put Jesus on trial than blasphemy or speaking against the Temple. Wedderburn suggests that the truth is too embarrassing for the evangelist to admit—that the "cleansing," as a threat on the public order, is the reason for the crucifixion. Mark decides to use the prophecy of the destruction, which seems convincing since it is already fulfilled (ibid., 19). Later accusations against the church: Gaston 1970:65–69.

118. Theissen 1991:125–165 considers it a product of later events, reacting to Caligula's threat on the Temple when the emperor plans to erect his statue there. Becker 1998:331 finds here traces of Markan composition because no explanation is given in this passage for the cause of destruction, probably because such explanation is unnecessary after 70 CE.

119. Juel 1977:120–122; Crossan 1992:357. Cf. Brown 1994:444–448. According to Perrin 2010:103, for Mark, the witnesses are false not because they fabricated the truth but because they twist its meaning.

120. In the gospel of Peter 7:26 (ed. Hennecke and Schneemelcher, 185), the apostles are accused of plotting to burn down the Temple. Similar suspicions are leveled against the *minim* in t. Sanhedrin 13:5 (ed. Zuckermandel, 434).

121. In comparison, Jesus son of Ananias's prediction of destruction leads to his arrest, flogging, and a hearing in front of the Roman governor. He is not executed, but he does not attack the Temple either (*War* 6.300–309). The prediction of destruction by R. Yohanan ben Zakkai (b. *Yoma* 39b), if historical, is not necessarily public and, again, lacks any physical demonstration.

122. For the (heavenly) Temple not made by human hands, see 4 Sib Or 4:11. This text is redacted after 70 CE and is hostile to the Jewish concept of a Temple (Collins 1983:382; Collins 1974; see also the introduction). Acts 7:48 seems to denounce sanctuaries made by human hands (see chapter 5).

123. On his identity, see Winter 1974:44–59; Bond 2004:40–63. Caiaphas serves as a high priest in 18/19–37 CE and probably continues throughout the entire period of Pilate's governorship.

124. His identification as a Sadducee is based on Acts 5:17: "the high priest and all who were with him, that is, the sect of the Sadducees." While the name of the

high priest is not mentioned here Luke's chronology makes it clear that the high priest is Caiaphas. Caiaphas is also mentioned in Acts 4:6.

125. Sadducees: Regev 2005a:esp. 46–48, 318–319. Cf. *Ant.* 13.298; 18.17; 20.199. Pharisees: Winter 1974:174–180.

126. E.g., the burning of the red heifer in a higher degree of purity: m. *Parah* 3.7; t. *Parah* 3.8 (ed. Zuckermandel, 632).

127. Regev 2005a:132–181, 226–241, 383–385; 2006b. One example is the Sadducees' opposition to the pharisaic regulation of the annual half-shekel donation to the Temple, which may undermine the exclusive priestly cultic status (Regev 2005a:132–139).

128. T. *Ḥagigah* 3.35 (ed. Lieberman, 394). In an early nonrabbinic penal code, trespassing in the sancta requires a death penalty, which is probably carried out by stoning, the most common method of execution in prerabbinic halakhah. The early rabbis, however, leave such transgressions to divine punishment (*karet*) and do not require human intervention. Compare Philo, *Leg. ad Gaium* 307; Temple Scroll 35:1–8; 4QD^a 6ii 9–10, with m. *Keritot* 1:1; t. *Sanhedrin* 14:16 (ed. Zuckermandel, 437).

129. *Ant.* 20.189–195. Ishmael follows the Sadducean laws of purity in t. *Parah* 3.6 (ed. Zuckermandel, 632). See Regev 2005a:176–179. Unnamed high priests are involved in demanding that the high priest's garments for the Day of Atonement be kept in the Temple instead of in the custody of the Roman governor, succeeding in their application to Claudius in this matter (*Ant.* 20.6–14).

130. *Annales* 15, 44.

131. The scholarly claim that the Jews are not allowed to execute (following John 18:31) is disproved by Winter 1974;18–23. This is confirmed by the inscription that commands a death sentence for gentiles who enter the holy precincts. See Segal 1989.

132. Hengel 1977:26, 34, 36–38, 40, 46–50.

133. Vestments: *Ant.* 18.90–95; 20.6–14. Sacrifices: Philo, *Leg.* 157, 317; *War* 2.197; *Against Apion* 2.77. Special sacrifices were also offered for the sake of the emperor at specific occasions. See *Leg.* 356.

134. Symbolic center for dominion in Judaea: Goodman 1987:42–43. For the Romanization of the Temple, see Betz 1997:462–465. Roman patronage is also practiced by the manner in which the Roman rulers honor the Temple. See *Ant.* 16.14–15; Philo, *Leg.* 157, 295–297, 310, 319. Imperial cults: Price 1984. See also Regev 2014a.

135. Taylor 2006.

136. Tacitus, *Annales,* 1.57; cf. ibid., 39.

137. Tacitus, *Annales,* 14.31–32.

138. Tacitus, *Histories,* 4.54; Dyson 1975:157–159.

139. *War* 2.409–410. For the Zealots' cultic views and their background in the Jewish and imperial setting, see Regev 2014a.

140. Bowersock 1987; Dyson 1971:258–259, 260–261. Compare also the reestablishment of Galba's statues in response to the revolt in the late 60s CE in northwest Anatolia (Tacitus, *Histories* 3.7).

141. Dio 54: 34: 5–7.

142. Webster 1993:86–89. Note that Claudius prohibits Druidism (Suetonius, *Claud.* 25.5).

143. Tacitus, *Histories*, 4.61.

144. Dio 72.4.

145. MacMullen 1966:128–162.

146. For confrontations between Vespasian and Apollonius, Hadrian and a philosopher, and Caracalla and a Gnostic, see Anderson 1994:151–166.

147. Pesch 1991:364–377; cf. McKnight 2005:323–328, 338.

148. Fitzmyer 2008:427–432, 435–445, noting the parallels and differences in the gospels. Cf. also 1 Cor 10:16–18.

149. Pre-Markan version: Jeremias 1966a:96–105. Jeremias 1966a:185–186, 196–203 suggests that Paul draws on a similar source in Hebrew or Aramaic and that the semantics of Jesus's words in Mark point to their originality.

150. Tan 1997: 202–203 and references.

151. Kodell 1988:22–23, following Bultmann's criticism of the passage as "cultic etiologies."

152. Crossan 1992:360–367, 435–436. Cf. the survey of scholarship in Klawans 2002:4–5.

153. Gese 1981:128–138; Léon-Dufour 1982:54–58, 206–209; Chilton 1994. For the other views, see the detailed survey in Theissen and Merz 1996:407–414.

154. Jeremias 1966a:18–19.

155. Jeremias 1966a:41–62, 86–88. Markus 2013:314–318 stresses that the basic phrase in the Passover seder "this is the (poor) bread" (an invitation to eat the matzah) parallels Jesus's words when distributing the bread, i.e., "this is my body" (Mark 14:22; 1 Cor 11:24). Others who think that the Last Supper is a seder: Klausner 1964:326–329; Dalman 1971:86–93, 101, 106–184; Evans 2001:375.

156. Jeremias 1966a:66–67.

157. McKnight 2005:269–270, 281–282. See also Meier 1991:396.

158. Gese 1981:124–127. He argues that the Last Supper is not a Passover seder because the lamb is not mentioned in the Last Supper and because Paul does not connect it to the Passover.

159. Markus 2013.

160. Klawans 2001. Cf. the survey in Markus 2013:304–307.

161. Theissen and Merz 1996:426–427. They also claim that Jesus's longing to celebrate the Passover (Luke 22:15) does not necessarily mean he actually does so. See also the survey of scholarship in McKnight 2005:264–273.

162. On the problem posed by John, see Jeremias 1966a:16–21. He concludes (ibid., 79–81) that Jesus is crucified on a Sabbath falling on the 15th of Nisan and that John 19:14 is not accurate. Meanwhile, John 19:31 (where Jesus is crucified

on the Sabbath day) fits the synoptic chronology. Jeremias also admits (ibid., 17–18) that Mark 14:12 contradicts itself when it says that the Passover meal takes place on the first day of the feast of Unleavened Bread. This is owing to Mark's style being more accurate in the second part of the sentence with regard to periodization. Dalman 1971:91 suggests that John separates the Last Supper from the Passover by changing the chronology because Jesus's words are not related to the Passover rite.

163. Theissen and Merz 1996:426–427; McKnight 2005:269–270, 281–282; cf. Markus 2013:312–313. Theissen and Merz also mention that Paul refers to "Christ sacrificed as our Passover," (1 Cor 5:5), from which one may conclude that Jesus is put to death at the time of the slaughter of the Passover lambs, as in John—hence the legal proceedings take place before the festival.

164. Klawans 2002; Dunn 2003:772–773. Dunn finds it hard to decide if it is originally a seder. Some argue that this is the result of a Markan redaction that results in linking the Last Supper with a Passover meal: Brown 1998:1.46–57; McKnight 2005:271–273, 304–312.

165. Jub 49:6; Wisdom 18:9; Philo, *Spec.* 2.148. See also Markus 2013:307–311, 323.

166. Markus 2013 suggests that Jesus only uses contemporary prerabbinic characteristics of the Passover meal for his own ceremonial needs.

167. As already noted, some think that Mark redacts the story, inserting the Passover context.

168. Jeremias 1966a:224, noting that this suits the style of double simile or parable (Luke 14:28–32; 15:1–10).

169. Léon-Dufour 1982:54–58, 206–209 identifies the initial phase of the Last Supper with the thanksgiving sacrifice (*todah-shelamim*).

170. Gese 1981:135: "The true proper sacrifice is the body of Jesus himself, his own physical life." Meyer 1988:472 concludes that Jesus fulfills two sacrificial types: the one that seals the covenant and the one that expiates via Jesus's death. Gruenwald 2001:186 suggests that the sacrificial death of Jesus, "the victim," is reenacted ritually by the Christian community. Cf. also Tan 1997:219; Evans 2001:366–368 notes that giving one's life for the sake of the many is attested to in first-century CE Judaism.

171. Jeremias 1966a: 222–226 (citation from 222). See also Wright 1996:557–559.

172. McKnight 2005:281, 326.

173. Added after Jesus's death: Friedrich 1985. Lack expiatory or cultic meaning: Léon-Dufour 1982:169. Meyer 1988 rejects their authenticity since eating Jesus's flesh and drinking his blood make no sense. Jeremias (1966a:209–210) objects to reading Luke 22:16, 18 as such a prediction, since it does not relate to Jesus's direction to share the cup in 22:17. He reads these verses as a declaration of an intent or an oath.

174. Chilton 1994:67–71. Dunn 2003:796 doubts Chilton's thesis because the Last Supper, not the "cleansing," is connected to Jesus's death. Dunn (ibid., 805) reads it as symbolism for death.

175. Chilton 1994:70–71; 1996:124–125. He refers to an attack on the Law as blasphemy in *Ant.* 3.307; *Against Apion* 2.143; 279. Like Chilton, Lang 1992:esp. 469–471 suggests that Jesus's words recall those of the sacrificer who designates a sacrifice as his own, in which the emphasis is on the possessive pronoun. In the Temple cult it is necessary to know to whom the sacrifice belongs. In the Last Supper Jesus promotes more lay involvement than in the Temple cult. After failing to reform the cult in the "cleansing," Jesus forms a new kind of cult in the Eucharist in which he opposes private animal sacrifices. He develops ritual sacred meals using sacrificial language. Bread and wine become the new sacrifice, presented as such by his words. But he does not refer to his own death as Paul seems to presuppose from 1 Cor 11:23–25.

176. Theissen and Merz 1996:433–434. They also see a certain continuation from Jesus to the post-70 CE rabbis: Jesus's detachment from the Temple precedes the rabbis after the destruction, when everyday life and daily meals are hallowed anew. Jesus's conflict with the Temple is therefore a conflict *in* Judaism, not *with* Judaism (ibid., 435). Some argue that the Last Supper is more effective than the Temple cult since its "controverts" or "spiritualizes" the flawed sacrificial worship of ancient Judaism. See Feeley-Harnik 1994:139, 168; Hamerton-Kelly 1994:19–20, 44.

177. McKelvey 1969:184–185. See Chilton 1992:152, who also notes that the body is alluded to as a sacrifice in Heb 10:5 (cf. 10; 13:11). Hebrews, however, lacks an explicit mention of the Last Supper. On the Last Supper in Didache, see chapter 9.

178. Klawans 2002:7.

179. Klawans 2002:9.

180. Klawans 2002:13.

181. Klawans 2002:16–17 with references to previous scholars who point to these aspects, including Jeremias, Léon-Dufour, and Chilton. He notes that some of these sacrificial aspects, such as expiation and Passover, are contradictory (or, I would add, *shelamim*, which relates to thanksgiving).

182. Klawans 2002:14. For purity of meal and prayer, see Regev 2000.

183. Klawans 2002:16.

184. Klawans 2002:11. See also chapter 2.

185. See also Krauss 1989:527 who comments that the Psalm is probably recited at the Temple before the afternoon sacrifice. Cf. Hos 14:3; Ps 119:108.

Chapter 2. Paul's Letters

1. Wenschkewitz 1932:116–132.

2. Wenschkewitz 1932:110–113.

3. Wenschkewitz 1932:130–131.

4. Fraeyman 1947; Newton 1985. See the critical survey in Strack 1994:375–380.

5. Klinzing 1971:214–217, 221.

6. Schüssler Fiorenza 1976:esp. 160–162. She argues that Paul distances himself from the cult in comparison to the Qumran sect.

7. Strack 1994:70, 380, 397.

8. Hogeterp 2006; Lanci 1997; Horn 2007. Gupta 2010:42–46 identifies anti-sacrificial or anti-ritual bias in scholarship on this subject.

9. Böttrich 1999.

10. Vahrenhorst 2008: 225–227, 323–324, 330, 334–338–339.

11. Williams 1999. See also Collins 2008 and the references in Lim 2008:192–193.

12. On these key terms for understanding metaphors, see Lakoff and Johnson 1980.

13. On such projection, see Kövecses 2002:4, 324, 329.

14. Kövecses 2002:6–11.

15. Finlan 2004:47–60 points to several levels of spiritualization: (1) supportive: increasingly symbolic and moralizing interpretation of ritual, attributing new spiritual and abstract meanings to the cult practice (such as adding morality to purification); (2) reforming: internalization of religious values (sacrifice is a broken spirit), in which cultic terms are applied to religious attitude (prayer as incense) and sometimes the correct attitude takes the place of the cult; (3) metaphoric: application of cultic terms to noncultic experience (Maccabean martyr's death as purification and ransom, 4 Mac 6:29; 17:21–22), which sometimes hints at a devaluing of the cult practice; (4) rejection of sacrifice: affirmation of spiritual transformation as the real meaning of piety. Of these, the third is the most relevant to the present discussion.

16. E.g., Fee 1987:147. Liu 2013:122–123 sees here a contrast between the holiness associated with the Temple image and the corruption in a moral sense (on the part of some of the Corinthians), which means defilement. Conzelmann 1975:76 argues for apocalyptic expectation for the eschatological Temple.

17. Hogeterp 2006:327–331. For the holy spirit residing within the community, see 1QS 9:4.

18. Gupta 2010:66–67.

19. Gärtner 1965; Klinzing 1971; Strack 1994:269–272.

20. Fitzmyer 2008:202.

21. Hogeterp 2006:324. Fitzmyer 2008:202 also argues that the metaphorical sense does not imply any antagonism toward the Jerusalem Temple. Compare the idea of the Temple as bringing unity to the Jewish people in Philo's description of pilgrimage, in which the rituals constitute the feeling that all "are of one mind" (Spec. Laws 1.70).

22. Hogeterp 2006:324–325. Paul introduces this claim in a rhetorical question—"do you not know that?"—indicating that he proposes not a new or radical argument but one that is familiar or almost self-evident. See Levison 2006:193. Gärtner 1965:57 n. 2 rejects the view that Paul relates to Mark 14:58—Jesus's alleged rebuilding of the Temple not made with hands "in three days."

23. The idea that Israel is united at the Temple is found in Philo Spec. Laws 1.68–69 in relation to the pilgrimage.
24. McKelvey 1969:105. Cf. Ps 51:12–13; Isa 63:10. The Holy Spirit symbolizes God's *presence* with His people in Isa 32:15; 44:3; Ezek 37:14; 39:29.
25. Individual body: Fee 1987:264. Corporate body: McKelvey 1969:104; Newton 1985:57–58 and the survey in Hogeterp 2006:338–339. On the individual body as expressing the presence of God's Spirit, see Wardle 2010:222–223.
26. Hogeterp 2006:340. He notes that Paul links the Temple to the body, while Philo links it to the soul/mind/wisdom. See Philo, On Creation 137; Spec. Laws 1.269. In Spec. Laws 1.270 Philo does relate holiness to the body through purification (Hogeterp 2006:343–344). See also Wardle 2010:218–219 (building on the parallel in Philo, Virtues 188).
27. Liu 2013:160. Compare the Pauline idea that the believers share Christ's body (1 Cor 6:15; 12:27; Col 1:18, 24; Eph 1:22–23).
28. McKelvey 1969:106–107.
29. Rosner 1998 suggests that Paul here opposes *Temple* prostitution.
30. See the prohibitions against licit and legitimate sexual relations in sacred places, e.g., Ex 19:15; Temple Scroll 45:11–12.
31. Gärtner 1965:54.
32. Liu 2013:201–211, 229–232.
33. Gärtner 1965:50; McKelvey 1969:94–95.
34. Beale 2004:253–254. On the citation and use of these biblical verses, which relate to the Tabernacle/Temple and the dwelling of God's holiness in Israel, see McKelvey 1969:95; Martin 1986:204–205.
35. Fitzmyer 1961. Gärtner 1965:49–56 concludes that there must have been a link between the two groups of texts because of the similar and extraordinary concept of the community as a Temple. Further arguments for post-Pauline interpolation based on *hapax legomena* are challenged by Hogeterp 2006:365–372.
36. Martin 1986:193–195 ("it is difficult to attribute this passage solely to Paul's dictation and originality," ibid., 194); Hogeterp 2006:373.
37. Betz 1973. The Corinthians do not draw boundaries etc.: Levison 2006:209–210. Usually, for Paul, the believers are already purified and sanctified through baptism, viz., 1 Cor 6:11.
38. See also on the Antichrist in the Temple in 2 Thess 2:5; Beale 2004:269–292.
39. Gärtner 1965:64–65; McKelvey 1969:108–110, 117.
40. Because of the parallels in Isa 56:3–8 and 57:13b-15 (which are not alluded to in the text), Beale 2004:262 here regards the Church as the initial phase of the building of the final eschatological Temple. However, these biblical passages do not transform or reduce the Temple into God's Spirit but pertain to the actual Temple or Temple Mount. Rather, in Ephesians the Temple imagery is employed to create an atmosphere of holiness, and its function is to unite Jews and Gentiles. The community as a Temple is restricted to these two senses of holiness and unity. Therefore, I think it is merely a metaphor and not a categoric

new Temple in the full sense of the word. The same applies to 1 Tim 3:15, where the community is God's house and requires appropriate behavior. Cf. Gärtner 1965:68.

41. See, for example, Achtemeier 1995:156, 159 and the references. Elliott 2000:414–418 submits that the meaning of "spiritual house" is "house," not "Temple." He bases this belief on the structure and content of the section in its broader context, relating to "house" imagery in the sense of household. Elliott adds that in the other places in the New Testament where the community is likened to the Temple the term "sanctuary" (*naos*) is used, not "house" (*oikos*). For him, the audience is likened to a household community of priests who bring spiritual sacrifices. Furthermore, they cannot be simultaneously an inanimate Temple and the priests who are offering up sacrifices. Note that in 1 Cor 3:9 the community is God's building and field. Elliott's opinion is rejected by Goppelt 1993:141, who points out that the House of God is also mentioned in 1 Pet 4:17. See also Feldmeier 2008:135–136.

42. Gärtner 1965:73; McKelvey 1969:125–131; Wardle 2010:216–217. Goppelt 1993:14 understands the house as "a dwelling place of God's presence among human beings, the eschatological and new Temple." Gärtner 1965:85–86 assumes that in this new Temple Christ is the high priest who sacrificed himself. Gärtner even assumes that the tradition is based on the idea that Jesus was a high priest who sacrificed himself and in this way put an end to sacrificial service. For the question of whether the priesthood referred to here is a substitute for the priests of the line of the sons of Aaron or a "kingdom of priests and a holy nation" (as referred to in 2:9), see Gäckle 2014:422–429, 444–470. Goppelt 1993:142 maintains that spiritual sacrifices are dedications of the entire person to God, prompted by the Spirit.

43. The Temple imagery is introduced in relation to spiritual attachment to the Lord (he is a living stone, and they are living stones), and the belief in Jesus appears before and after the passage (1 Pet 1:19, 22–23; 2:9). Allison 1986:412 sees in the living stones a hint for living beings in the heavenly Temple.

44. Gärtner 1965; Klinzing 1971, repeated by many others. The relevant passages are 1QS 5:5–6; 8:5–7, 8–10; 9:3–6; 4Q174 Florilegium 1+2+21 6–7.

45. Regev 2017a; Regev forthcoming, which also expand the comparison with the NT texts. The following comparison builds on my previous analysis of the scrolls.

46. The meaning of the Temple of Man (*adam*) is highly debated. See the surveys in Wise 1991. In my view it denotes human adherence to the practices of the Torah. See Regev 2017a:218–221; Regev forthcoming.

47. Gärtner, 1965:22, 25.

48. Martínez and Tigchelaar 2000:89, 91 rightly translate "house."

49. Meaning, through the use of the definite article. Compare Temple Scroll 35:1. For holiness as a ritual degree or level (in relation to the cult, marriage, or descent) and not as a specific place, see 4QMMT B 68, 76, 79.

50. Regev 2017a:225–226; Regev forthcoming. See Flusser 1988:41–44. On the motif of the stone in 1 Peter and in Christian tradition and its Christological significance, see Goppelt 1993:136–140.

51. While Flusser 1988:41–44, argues for Qumranic influence (ibid.). Achtemeier 1995:151–152 rejects direct reliance on the scrolls, and Goppelt 1993:136 emphasizes other differences between 1 Peter and the scrolls.

52. Lanci 1997:10. He supports this by Paul's declaration that he communicates with all people in their own idioms (1 Cor 9:19–23). See also Lim 2010:190–191, 197–201. Similarly, Vahrenhorst 2008:334, 339 argues that Paul's Temple metaphors do not necessitate a Jewish background. Shanor 1988 maintains that Paul's metaphor for building construction (1 Cor 3:12, related to the passage in vss. 16–17) derives from pagan temples.

53. Lanci 1997:90. See also Fee 1987:411–412 (on 1 Cor 9:13).

54. Lanci 1997:95, 104, 107, 111.

55. 1 Cor 8; 10; Gal 5:20; Cf. 1 Thess 4:5. For Paul's belief in one God, the God of Israel, see Dunn 1998:27–50.

56. See Gupta 2010:18–19 (on 1 Cor 6:19).

57. Hogeterp 2006:318–319. It is not clear to what extent Paul's use of *naos* for the sanctuary (in contrast to *hieron*, the entire Temple complex) attests to a distinction between Jewish and pagan temples, See Lanci 1997:91–93; Hogeterp 2006:320–323.

58. Gupta 2010:77–78. On the altar as a Jewish term, see Hogeterp 2006:350–352.

59. Hogeterp 2006:287.

60. Hogeterp 2006:290–291.

61. Gupta 2010:139. For libation in ancient Judaism and the ancient Greek cult, see Reumann 2008:397–398.

62. Wardle 2010:207, 211.

63. McKelvey 1969:123, 180.

64. McKelvey 1969:123–124 notes that Rom 11:26 refers to deliverance from Jerusalem ("Zion"), and he therefore assumes that the *parousia* of Christ will begin in Jerusalem. He is aware, however, of the alternative interpretation that "Zion" is a symbol of the church.

65. Lanci 1997:125, 132–133. He adds that the access of Gentiles to the Corinthian community appears closer to their possible access to Gentile Temples than their limited access to the Jerusalem Temple.

66. Gärtner:138, 140 argued that it was impossible to call both Christ and his community a Temple at one and the same time, and Paul may have decided that the collective aspect had become more prominent. However, as we shall see below, Paul used sacrificial language for both the community and Christ.

67. Fee 2014:454–455 cannot decide whether the imagery relates to Jewish or Greek cultic practice. For Paul's defense of his apostleship, see ibid., 440–442.

68. Paul refers to himself as a *leitourgon*, which is a kind of a public servant and not necessarily a Temple priest, but the term is used in the LXX in relation to the

Temple cult. *Hierourgounta* is a cultic term used in the general sense of performing a cultic service or a sacrifice or consecrating. See Gupta 2010:128–130 based on parallels also from Philo and Josephus. Paul's ministry is already mentioned, without a priestly allusion, in Rom 1:1, 9.

69. Gupta 2010:130–132. Gupta leaves open the question of whether the "offering" is the Gentiles themselves (as believers), the collection to Jerusalem, or Paul's calling for the Romans' obedience. Robinson 1974:231 argues that it pertains to their glorification of God or obedience (cf. Rom 15:9, 18).

70. Hogeterp 2006:288 notes that the "offering of the Gentiles" embraces a Judeocentric perspective.

71. Fitzmyer 1993:712. Dunn 1988:859–860 maintains that the cultic language is transformed (not merely spiritualized) and that the division between cultic and secular has been broken down and abolished. I am not convinced. Newton 1985:60–70 argues that Paul believes himself to be the priest of the new Temple. Lanci 1997:11–12 rejects this view since there is no Christian institutional cult in Paul's letters.

72. Robinson 1974:231 thinks that the metaphor of the Gentiles as an offering conflicts with the one of Jesus as a sacrifice. Daly 1978:247–248 mistakenly regards Jesus as the sacrifice offered by Paul. Here Paul is at Jesus's service, as his agent. Admittedly, there is some confusion about the relationship between Christ and God in this complex metaphor.

73. Robinson 1974:236.

74. These words are not attested to in the NRSV.

75. Fee 2014:519.

76. 1 Cor 10:5–11, 19–21; Fee 1987:470–471.

77. Hogeterp 2006:355–358.

78. Hogeterp 2006:356.

79. Fitzmyer 2008:392.

80. Fee 2014:519.

81. Ullucci 2012:73–74.

82. Renwick 1991:61–94. For the biblical cultic background, cf. Reumann 2008: 712–713.

83. Hogeterp 2006:365. See also Daly 1978:249–250. Furnish 1984:176–177 argues that the cultic meaning is "alien to the context" and that there are no further sacrificial terms in the passage as there are in Phil 4:18 and Eph 5:2. The term is a symbol of the presence of God, as in Sir 45:16. However, Renwick 1991:85 points out that v. 16 relates this to incense, hence to the cult.

84. Renwick 1991:78–79; Gupta 2010:88. Cf. the metaphor that wisdom spreads like fragrance in Sir 24:15.

85. Reumann 2008:712–713. For the sense of partnership and solidarity in the gospel of Christ, see Hogeterp 2006:291; Gupta 2010:149.

86. Gupta 2010:120–123.

87. As suggested, for example, by Käsemann 1980:327, 329. Cf. Fitzmyer 1993:640.

88. Dunn 1988:710.
89. Hogeterp 2006:284–285. This is also implied by the persecution mentioned in Rom 12:14.
90. Libation imagery is also attested to in 2 Tim 4:6 in relation to suffering. For libations in ancient Judaism and the ancient Greek cult, see Reumann 2008:397–398. Gupta 2010:139–140 suggests not only that Paul is referring to a sacrificial service, but also that it is possible that the Philippians are viewed as priests (who perform the service).
91. Gupta 2010:138–139. On the implicit language of sacrifice in Philippians, see Lancaster Patterson 2015:81–115.
92. Communal holiness and atonement: Strack 1994:187–191, 197. Last Supper: Dunn 1998:216–217, following Jeremias 1966a:222–224. So also Hogeterp 2006:335–336.
93. Howard 1969; Finlan 2004:70 maintains that the image of the Paschal lamb "summons up the image of Christ's blood averting the wrath of God just as the apotropaic blood on the doorposts caused the Angel of Death to 'pass over' the Jews." Finlan (ibid., 71) also finds Pauline allusions (1 Cor 11:25; Gal 3:14) to the biblical covenant sacrifice with God and relates it to "the blood of your covenant" in the Eucharist, referring to Gen 15:9–21; Ex 24:6–8; Jer 34:18–20; Zech 9:11. However, Paul never relates to a covenant in this respect.
94. Rom 4:24–25; 8:32; Gal 3:13.
95. Gray 1925:397; Daly 1978:121. Fitzmyer's (2008:242) attempt to find evidence for atonement related to the Passover lamb in Num 28:22 and Ezek 45:22 is off the mark. The sin-offerings he mentions refer not to the Passover lamb but to other sacrificial rites during Passover. Such sin/purification offerings are typical of other festival rites (e.g., Num 28:14, 30; 29:5) or ordained for the consecration of the Temple in Ezek 43:20–22, 25.
96. Philo Spec. Laws 2.147–148; m. *Peshaim* 5:5–7; 7:13–8:3; m. *Zevahim* 5:8.
97. Dunn 1974:133 following Jeremias 1966a:221–222.
98. Fitzmyer 2008:241–242.
99. See also Fredriksen 2010:247.
100. For a literal interpretation of the phrase, see, e.g., Hooker 2008:369. For the view that Paul refers to sin twice, not to sin-offering, see McLean 1992:542–543 and references.
101. Martin 1986:140, 156–157 and references. Martin suggests that the imagery draws on the idea of the Servant of God as a sin-offering in Isa 53:10, perhaps based on earlier tradition. For *hamartian* in the LXX as the rite of the sin-offering (and not the sacrifice itself), see Léopold and Sabourin 1970:252–253. Bell 2002:13–15 resists the view that the second *hamartian* in our passage is not a sin but a sin-offering; in his view Christ becomes a sinner (cf. Gal 3:13). Nonetheless, he points to the concept of sin-offering reflected in 2 Cor 5:14–21.
102. Rom 4:25; 5:8–9; 8:3; Gal 3:13.

103. Note that the bull, male or female goat, and female sheep should be "without [physical] blemish" (*tamim*, Lev 4:3, 23, 28), which could also mean morally innocent. Finlan 2004:99 argues that in 2 Cor 5:14 ("one has died for all; therefore all have died. And he died for all") Jesus is portrayed as a scapegoat, which explains the transformation from sin to no-sin. He modeled it after a ritual of curse transmission where there is an exchange: the victim takes on the community's ills. Cf. Dunn 1998: 181, 217, 219, 22. Unlike Dunn, Finlan rightly insists that the scapegoat is not a sacrifice but a ritual of banishment. He thus concludes that Paul uses the concept of both sacrifice and scapegoat, but this does not mean Paul does not distinguish between the two (ibid., 95). Finlan 2004:101–111 also finds scapegoat imagery in Gal 3:13 ("Christ redeemed us from the curse of the law by becoming a curse for us").
104. E.g., 5:12–13, 20 ("we are ambassadors of Christ"); Hooker 2008:368–369.
105. 2 Cor 6:3–10. See Hooker 2008:372–373.
106. Dunn 1988:422, with bibliography.
107. Finlan 2004:114.
108. Dunn 1988:440–441.
109. Rom 4:25 and 5:8–9 refer to Christ's death for our sins but are even less specific. Rom 3:24–25 seems to make better sense when read along with 8:3. A detailed explanation is introduced later in the Letter to the Hebrews.
110. Best 1998:470. This benefit is detailed throughout the letter: the sins of the Ephesians are forgiven (1:7), they have been raised with Christ and sit with him in the heavens (2:5–6), and they belong to his body (4:7–16).
111. Ex 25:17–22; Heb 9:5; Bell 2002:18–19 and references; Hogeterp 2006:278–279 and references; Finlan 2004:125–126. Campbell 1992:107–112, 130–135 follows Diesmann that the term in the LXX represents the function of the *kaporet*, namely, expiation in general.
112. *War* 5.385; *Ant.* 8.112; 16.182; Hogeterp 2006:278–279. Finlan 2004:136–140 notes that the cognate verbs mean to atone, expiate, propitiate or purify and that the term also exists in Hellenistic usage for votive gifts to the gods (ibid., 125–126).
113. Dunn 1988:17; Finlan 2004:128–129; Vahrenhorst 2008:271–279. However, Stowers 1994:206–213 opposes it since it assumes that Christianity supersedes Judaism, a claim that Paul does not make. Stowers follows Milgrom in arguing that the sprinkling of blood on the *kaporet* grants not atonement but purification. He adds that the original Greek sense of appeasement that the LXX uses has no sacrificial meaning, and also the mention of Christ's blood relates not to the rite of the Day of Atonement but merely to his death.
114. Finlan 2004:143. On the high priestly ritual at the Temple as a rite of purification from sin, see Milgrom 1991:1011–1053.
115. Standing for the Temple and its rituals: Finlan 2004:155, 157. Expiation, medium of atonement, sacrifice, etc.: Dunn 1988:171, also referring to 4 Mac 17:22. In Rom 3:24 Jesus is a *apolutrōseōs*, a redemption, which Dunn (ibid., 169) interprets as a

ransom. Yet one must bear in mind that in Leviticus and ancient Jewish practice what expiates is not the cultic object but the ritual act on Yom Kippur.

116. Newton 1985:76–77. Stökl Ben Ezra 2003:202–204 and Horn 2007:197 survey scholars who hold this position, although they both reject it.

117. Dunn 1998:215–116. For him, anyway, Jesus demonstrates God's righteousness in the present.

118. For these arguments, see Finlan 2004:145–146. He translated v. 25a: "in a bloody death as a mercy seat of faith."

119. Finlan 2004:152–153.

120. Finlan 2004:143–144.

121. Dunn 1988:170; 1998:214–115.

122. Lev 16:2–3 (which stress that the high priest's access to the *kaporet* is the highlight of the entire rite), 13 (the burning incense), 14–16 (the shedding of blood). On the symbolism of the burning of incense on the Day of Atonement, see Regev 2005a:152–159.

123. Rom 3:24–26a is probably a pre-Pauline formula, not so much because of the vocabulary and the syntax as because Paul does not support his claim or explain it, as it is already well known. He also stresses the equal relevance of this claim for both Jews and Gentiles (3:22–23). See Dunn 1988:163–164. For detailed literary arguments, see Meyer 1983 and references.

124. Josephus *War* 5.219 mentions that the holy of holies was an empty chamber.

125. Dunn 1998:216–218; Rom 3:35; 5:9 (cf. Eph 1:7; 2:13; Col 1:20).

126. Rom 4:25; 8:3; 1 Cor 15:3; Gal 1:4.

127. Rom 5:6–8; 8:32; 2 Cor 5:14–15, 21; Gal 2:20; 3:13; 1 Thess 5:9–10. Cf. Eph 5:2, 25.

128. Lev 4:5–7, 16–18, 25, 30, 34–35; 17:11; Dunn 1998:217–218.

129. Dunn 1974:esp. 134, 136–137. While Dunn relies on de Vaux, arguing that in the sin-offering the sacrificed animal atones for the sinner's life, see below for the critical evaluation of Paul's treatment of the sin-offering. In this seminal article Dunn attempts to put forward a symbolism of sacrifice that would appeal to Paul as related or analogical to the death of Christ. Davies 1955:232–237 makes a more far-reaching claim that Paul's use of the idea of Jesus's blood has sacrificial connotations to begin with.

130. Ullucci 2012:74–79 and references.

131. McLean 1992:esp. 546.

132. Finlan 2004:190. There are various suggestions for the origins of the theology of Jesus dying for the sake of others, such as the suffering servant in Isa 53 and the Maccabean Martyrs in 4 Mac. See Joseph 2016:220–231 and references.

133. For example, as *thusia* (probably *shelamin* sacrifices), mentioned in other contexts—but not in relation to Jesus!—in Rom 12:1; Phil 2:17; 4:18; Eph 5:2.

134. Milgrom 1976; 1991:253–264.

135. McLean 1992:432–442 accepts Milgrom's understanding of the *hattat* as purifying the altar and not the person and consequently argues that Paul does not

intend to portray Christ's death as an atoning sacrifice. Since the purificatory function of the *hattat* is echoed in rabbinic sources (e.g., blood and confession atones m. *Shevu'ot* 1:7) and since Paul had a pharisaic background (Phil 3:5), McLean finds it unlikely that he *adapted and transformed* Levitical theology. Yet, despite Paul's background, we shall see that he does not attempt to draw an accurate cultic analogy.

136. Janowski 1982:199–221, 242.

137. Milgrom 1991:253.

138. Bell 2002:8–9. Dunn 1988:171; 1998:218–221 views Jesus as a sin-offering, building on earlier understandings of the sin-offering according to which the sinner is identified with the animal or the animal represents him (cf. Daly 1978:100–106), thus assuming that sin was transferred to the sacrifice.

139. Dunn 1974:133.

140. Dunn 1998:223.

141. Fredriksen 2010:247 concludes that "Paul's use of sacrificial images is confusing and perhaps confused."

142. And in 2 Cor 6:19–7:1—also purity.

143. And in Rom 8:3—also the Law.

144. Johnson 1987:xv; Kövecses 2002:6.

145. For the use of previous knowledge without further details in creating an analogy, see Gentner 1983.

146. Thus Paul's spiritualization of the cult is metaphoric spiritualization. On metaphoric spiritualization in comparison to rejection of sacrifice, see Finlan 2004:47–60.

147. "Any man who [is disciplined . . .] . . . [acc]ept his judgment [wil]lingly, in accordance with what [He sa]id through Moses concerning the soul that sin[s unwittingly, that he shall bring] his sin-offering and [his guilt-offering]." 4QD^e 7 I 15–17 and the parallel in 4QD^a 11 1–3; Regev 2007:122–123. For the text and translation see Baumgarten 1996:76, 163.

148. Cf. Schüssler Fiorenza 1976:164, 168.

149. Opif. 137 (relating to the first Adam): "It was an abode or sacred temple for a reasonable soul which was being made"; Cher. 101: "We call the invisible soul the terrestrial habitation of the invisible God." See Nikiprowetzky 1967. These metaphors are used in a context of a long passage, a systematic analogy with additional metaphors, in which Philo praises the body of first Adam (Opif. 136–138) or the human soul (Cher. 98–107). On Philo's platonic dialectical method (in which there is an ontological dualism between the empirical and ideal worlds) inferring from the specific to the universal or cosmic categories, see Fuglseth 2005:203–205 and references. See also the introduction.

150. See Gilders 2011; Fuglseth 2005:193–195, 209–210, 218–219. On temples of the universe and the soul, see, e.g., Spec. Laws 1.94–97. For pilgrimage, see Prov. 2.64 (on its authenticity, see Fuglseth 2005: 195 n. 22).

151. Dunn 2010:55. Similarly, Frey 2012:460 assumes that for Paul's addressees "the Temple played no major role in the constitution of their new identity, which was decisively defined by the relationship with Christ."

152. Horn 2007:190–192.

153. Finlan 2004:185, 187, 218. Gupta 2010:182 notes that when the believer's body is referred to as a temple (1 Cor 6:19), the implication is that God defines the Temple as "the fortress and the locus of God's life and power."

154. Fredriksen 2010:248.

155. Fredriksen 2014:30–31.

156. Finlan 2004:69 terms this "replacement through fulfillment." He thinks that metaphoric transformation of the cult means that the cult has been transformed into a metaphor (ibid., 218).

157. Horn 2007. However, for Malina and Pilch 2006:75, the gatherings of the Corinthians produce an experience which substitutes for pilgrimage and worship in the Temple.

158. Cf. Hogeterp 2006:280 on this universal means of atonement. Horn 2007:200–202 concludes that in his cultic metaphors Paul removes the barrier in the Temple between Jews and Gentiles.

159. Gupta 2010:206–209 notes the importance of collective Temple metaphors and symbols for social identity, lacking temples like the Greeks, Romans, and Jews.

160. Paul attempts to impart a sense of holiness to the religious life of the members of his communities in several ways. He calls them "holy ones" (Rom 1:7; 1 Cor 1:2; Phil 1:1, etc.) and assigns them holiness and sanctity (1 Thess 5:23; 6:11; 7:14; Rom 11:16). He urges them to act in holiness (1 Thess 3:13; 4:7; Rom 6:19, 22) and poses behavioral demands to set them apart from fornication (1 Thess 4:3). For Paul's language of holiness, see Vahrenhorst 2008.

161. Some interpret Paul's speaking of himself in the past as "being in Judaism" (Gal 1:13–14), as if he no longer considers himself part of the social and religious system known as Judaism. See Porter 2000 and references; Dunn 1999:179. Rudolph 2011:44–45, however, suggests that Paul's words refer to a *specific type* of Judaism, the zeal for the Law, without Christ.

162. Rom 9:3–4; 11:1. See also Gal 2:15; 2 Cor 11:22; Phil 3:5. Dunn 1998:499–532; 1999:181, 187–188. Compare also the declaration "we are the circumcision" (Phil 3:3).

163. Barclay 1996; Campbell 2008:119.

164. Dunn 1988:635.

165. Wagner 2011.

166. Hays 1989.

167. Hays 1989:16. Scripture speaks to Paul's Christians, and they are its addressees since "it is written for our sake" (1 Cor 9:9–10; Rom 4:23–34; cf. Rom 15:4).

168. Hays 1989:2.

169. As Rosner 1994:esp. 186, 189 concludes, Paul's ethics are primarily a development of the religion of Israel.

170. Rom 3:20; see Schreiner 1991, which includes a survey of scholarship.
171. Rom 3:30; Gal 2:16; Räisänen 1985.
172. Gal 3:24; Dunn 1998:141–142.
173. Schreiner 1989.
174. Rosner 2013:121–197.
175. Rosner 2013:204.
176. Sanders 1983:17–64, 100–104, 154–160; Dunn 1985; 1988:lxiii–lxxii, 153–155. Cf. Räisänen 1986:162–177. On the meaning of Paul's works of the Law in light of the parallel term in 4QMMT, see Collins 2017:169–171, and references.
177. Davies 1955:70 points to this passage in concluding that "Paul observed the Law . . . throughout his life." He also notes Acts 13–14; 28:17–25, where Paul is first of all an apostle to the Jews (ibid., 69).
178. Rudolph 2011:73–87 and the references ibid., 85–86 n. 230. See also Bockmuehl 2000:170–172.
179. Rudolph 2011:23–27. This passage, however, raises several other difficulties (Pervo 2009:388–389). Note that in Gal 5:11 Paul seems to react to an accusation that he formerly preached for circumcision.
180. Betz 1979:104, 107 refers to the Jewish way of life, dietary and purity laws.
181. Rudolph 2011:46–47, 51–52. He describes Paul's language as "polemical hyperbole."
182. According to Dunn 1983, in eating with the Gentiles, Peter and Paul merely do not observe the eating of ordinary food in a state of ritual purity (in contrast to eating nonkosher food), which was practiced only by some of the Jews: "The reason why Peter had withdrawn from the table fellowship in the first place was because the purity status of the Gentile believers had been called into question" (ibid., 32).
183. Acts 18:18. For the identification of the vow and haircut as a fulfillment of a Nazarite vow (despite the fact that, in contrast to biblical and rabbinic law, it was cut in the defiled Diaspora), see Chepey 2005:159–165. Koet 1996:139–142 maintains that the Nazarite vow comes in response to the charges against Paul's lawlessness in Acts 18:12–17 and that Luke wants to show his subordination to the Jewish Law.
184. Act 21:21–27 (on which see chapter 5). Other obscure Jewish accusations against Paul and the Law are mentioned in Acts 18:13.
185. Knox 1950:32–43 rejects the general historicity of many of the basic details in Luke's story of Paul. "The Paul of Acts is . . . quite [a] different kind of man and has quite different ideas from the Paul of the letters" (ibid., 32). Knox objects to a harmonization of Paul's letters with Acts, since it is a secondary source: "We may, with proper caution, use Acts to supplement the autobiographical data of the letters, but never to correct them" (ibid., 33); Esler 1987:125–129. Esler (ibid., 110–130) also shows Luke's positive-conservative approach to Jewish Law.
186. Fitzmyer 1998:692 explains Paul's behavior as "making himself all things to all men" (1 Cor 9:22) as follows: "This is not a compromise," since Paul does this "to

keep peace in the Jerusalem church … because he knows that those rites do not undercut his basic allegiance to the risen Christ." However, when Luke's Paul mentions his prayer in the Temple after the revelation of Jesus (22:17) Fitzmyer 1998:707 notes that Luke merely abridges earlier narrative in chapter 9. Pervo 2009:542–543 questions the entire story in Acts 21:17–27, since it does not seem to rely on sound sources and does not deal with the problematics of Paul's teaching but nonetheless does not reject the possibility that Paul purifies himself and pays for the sacrifices, and he is not inclined to see Paul as a hypocrite.

187. Bruce 1976:esp. 295–297.

188. Porter 2001:186–206, esp. 199, 203–205. Porter even maintains that the author of Acts probably has some form of close contact with Paul or his beliefs. Bruce and Porter reject the conclusions of Haenchen 1971:112–116 in relation to the difference between Paul's letters and Acts in relation to theology of Christ and the end of the Law, miracles and gifts, resurrection, as well as Vielhauer 1966 on Paul's speeches in Acts.

189. Lüdemann 1989a:234–236; Bauckham 1995:479; Barrett 1998:1010–1013; Chilton 2004:238–239. Horn 2007:esp. 192 accepts the Acts report on Paul's adherence to Temple practices.

190. Purification and ritual baths before entering the Temple: Regev 2005c (see also in chapter 5). Nazarite: Chepey 2005:169–174. Sponsorship of Nazarites is a manifestation of piety also in the case of Agrippa I in *Ant.* 19.292.

191. Porter 2001:179–182. On the entire problem with survey of scholarship, see Rudolph 2011:53–70.

192. Sanders 1983:100, 185–186; Räisänen, 1986:3–76; Fee 1987:427–428. Cf. the survey in Rudolph 2011:2–12.

193. Nanos 2012. He defines this as "rhetorical adaptability" or "argumentative behavior." Rudolph 2011 interpreted 1 Cor 9:19–23 as related to legal practice, but only in relation to eating ordinary food in a state of ritual purity, similar to Jesus's open commensality (eating with sinners, etc.), because the context (1 Cor 8–10) deals with food and hospitality (e.g., 1 Cor 10:27). When Paul declares that he is no longer "bound to the Torah" he means the pharisaic (strict) halakhah.

Chapter 3. Mark

1. New Temple: Juel 1977:127–215. Anti-Temple, condemned of corruption, Kingdom disassociated: Kelber 1974: 111; 1979:61–62, 65. See also Kloppenborg 2005:427–428.

2. Moloney 2004:87–96. Waetjen 1989:179, 182 regards Jesus's "cleansing" of the Temple an "abolition of the temple institution itself" and names the section discussing it "negation of the temple institution." Waetjen describes the Temple as being responsible for "oppression and dispossession of the Jewish masses" and a "dehumanizing and tyrannical pollution system" without bringing any reference for such biased claims (ibid., 183).

3. Hamerton-Kelly 1994:15–45 (here 16, 19).

4. Evans 1989:269–270. Mack 1988:291–292, 304 stresses that it is Mark who adds Jesus's anti-Temple stance.

5. Broadhead 1992. Gray 2010:86–90 reads the citation of Ps 110 in Mark 12:36 as a sign of Jesus being Lord of the Temple.

6. Juel 1977:122, 128.

7. Juel 1977:123–124.

8. Juel 1977:46.

9. Juel 1977:48, 56.

10. Juel 1977:118, 125.

11. Juel 1977: 129, 130–131, 133–138.

12. Juel 1977:134.

13. Juel 1977:138–139.

14. Myers 1988:375 argues that the New Temple is Jesus's body. The obscurity of the difference between new Temple, eschatological Temple (the heavenly one?), and community as Temple is paradigmatic to NT scholarship.

15. Heil 1997:100.

16. Heil 1997:92–98. Others also suggest deciphering Mark's message through complex literary approaches such as juxtaposing structural elements or intertextuality. See Geddert 1989:145; Gray 2010:200.

17. Juel 1977:121–123.

18. In Life 9 Josephus boasts of assisting the high priests in understanding legal matters. For rabbinic indirect involvement in the cult, see m. *Pe`ah* 2:6; m. *'Orla* 2:12; Regev 2005a:348–377.

19. Marcus 1992:460–461 and references; 2000:35–36 (Mark's "need to inform his readers about Jewish customs suggests that at least some of them are non-Jewish," ibid., 441). Note the common view that Mark is written in Rome, which *may* suggest a Gentile audience: Taylor 1959:26–32; Hengel 1985:1–30, challenged by Marcus 2000:30–37.

20. Yarbro Collins 2007:6; Marcus 2009:944 (who mentions that the Hellenistic sunrise-to-sunrise method of reckoning is also found in Philo and Josephus). Furthermore, note that Mark's Jesus went from Bethany to the city of Jerusalem (cf. 14:3, 13) to eat the Passover sacrifice in accordance with pharisaic Law (Marcus 2009:945).

21. Wong 2009:32–76. Gundry 1993:358–361 argues that Mark 7:3 is accurate and does not portray a Gentile point of view, since hand washing is practiced commonly, not just among Pharisees.

22. Loader 1997:123–125. Yet Loader regards the dismissal of the value of certain laws as related to an anticultic trend, such as the denouncement of the Temple made by hands and the elevation of "the community of faith, the new temple, which fulfills the temple's original purpose of being a house of prayer for all the nations" (ibid., 134–135). Cf. his treatment of the "cleansing" as a rejection of the Temple and introducing the new one (ibid., 96–108). Loader notes that

"to replace the temple by a community is to replace substantial sections of the Torah" (ibid., 104).

23. Crossley 2004:83–98 surveys the debate and argues for general observance of the Law, stressing that Jesus does not abrogate any biblical commandment. So also Wong 2009:32–76, noting that Mark distinguishes his readers from the Jews. But this does not mean he estranges them from Judaism in general. It only shapes the identity of a distinctive Jewish faction. Note that according to Marcus 2000:73–75 there is Pauline influence upon Mark, although he is not of the Pauline school.

24. This is the view of Lane 1974:87–89; Lührmann 1987:54–55; Meyers 1988:152–154.

25. The leper asks Jesus to cleanse him clean, not to cure him, so he can reintegrate into society. But the verb *katharisai* is used for the purpose of physical healing. See Yarbro Collins 2007:178. Cf. Crossley 2004:88.

26. Guelich 1989:77–79; Marcus 2000:210.

27. Räisänen 1982; Gundry 1993:365–367.

28. Dunn 1990:esp. 51; Klawans 2000:147–149. Salyer 1993:161–162 also comments that Mark's Jesus attacks the system of purity Laws from within, thus avoiding setting himself outside of Jewish Law.

29. Yarbro Collins 2007:354–355 with a list of scholars who agree on the Markan insertion. Cf. Taylor 1959:345. Booth 1986:49–50.

30. On the question of whether 19c is a post-Markan gloss, see Booth 1986:49–50 and references.

31. Marcus 2000:457. See also Gundry 1993:356 and the list of references in Rudolph 2002:292.

32. Loader 1997:74–76, 79.

33. Loader 1997:78. Thus Mark 7:19c aims to stress Jesus's authority (ibid., 79).

34. Dunn 1990:45. Yarbro Collins 2007:356 concludes that there is no total abandonment of purity and food laws. The observance of food laws by Jesus's followers in Mark is not obligatory; some of Mark's readers probably observe them, while some do not.

35. Rudolph 2002.

36. Rudolph 2002:308–310 and references; Crossley 2004:204–205.

37. Furstenberg 2008; Kazen 2010:86. On nonpriestly purity in relation to meal prayer and reading the Torah, see Regev 2000.

38. Cf. Crossley 2004:196–197.

39. Heil 1997:77–78.

40. Gray 2010: 30–35 (citation from 34).

41. Kelber 1974:111.

42. Seely 1993:279–280.

43. Evans 2001:179, following Hengel, understands Mark as a warning. Juel 1977:132–133 admits that the den of robbers saying does not fit the context of commerce or dishonest merchants in 11:17 and therefore relates it to another level of the story.

44. Juel 1977:133; cf. Lohmeyer 1962:47.

45. Regev 2005b; Regev 2014. See chapter 5.
46. Juel 1977:131. Yarbro Collins 2007:531 suggests that Mark does not mean that Gentiles will participate in the service of the Temple as Gentiles, but that they will turn to God and adopt Jewish practices.
47. Borg 1984:185–186; Evans 1989:268; Gray 2010:36–37.
48. Hengel 1989a:24–46; Marcus 1992:449–450 and references.
49. Taylor 1959:464; Yarbro Collins 2007:532; Gray 2010:36–38.
50. Gaston 1970:85; Sanders 1985:66–67; Chance 2007:276; Wong 2009:137: Gray 2010:36–37.
51. Marcus 1992:449–451.
52. Yarbro Collins 2007:531. See also Wong 2009:137.
53. Wong 2009:108, 139.
54. Viviano 1989 relates this conflict to the cutting of the high priest's servant's ear (14:47) during Jesus's arrest. He identifies the servants with the deputy high priest—the *segan*—the prefect of the priests, arguing that he is a symbol of the Temple administration. This baseless identification is rejected by Evans 2001:424–425; Yarbro Collins 2007:685. Still, the scene remains odd.
55. Kelber 1979:63 reasonably interprets "these things" as referring to the "cleansing."
56. Heil 1997:81, 85; Gray 2010:46–47, 77–78. Driggers 2007:229, 246 also argues for the exploitive practices of the Jewish leaders in their use of the Temple.
57. Heil 1997:81 argues that these leaders are responsible for "the failure of the temple."
58. Juel 1977:133; Hamerton-Kelly 1994:17–18; Heil 1997:78.
59. Telford 1980; Edwards 1989:207–208; Evans 1989:239–240; Marcus 2009:787–789; Gray 2010:39–43. Some think that Jesus's words "truly I tell you, if you say to this mountain, 'Be taken up and thrown into the sea,' . . . it will be done for you" (11:23) are directed at the end of the Temple Mount and imply its condemnation and doom. See Telford 1980:163; Myers 1988:305; Wright 1996:324–325; Wahlen 2007:253; Gray 2010:48–53. Yet this may also be the Mountain of Olives (11:1; 13:3, discussed below) or any other mountain.
60. Seely 1993:281.
61. Pesch 1991:199–201; Heil 1997:79–80; Wahlen 2007:250–255; Marcus 2009: 788–789.
62. Heil 1997:80; Marcus 2009:796.
63. Gray 2010:53–54.
64. New Temple: Juel 1977:134–136; Gray 2010:53–54. Communal household: Heil 1997:80.
65. Seely 1993:281.
66. Yarbro Collins 2007:531–534 links it to 11:18, where the chief priests and scribes are looking to kill Jesus. Wahlen 2007:258–266 supports this by showing that the "cleansing" has an outer sandwich of passages dealing with Jesus's authority and disputes with the Jewish leaders in 11:1–11; 11:27–12:12. Esler 2005 refuses to link the split of the fig tree episode before and after the "cleansing" to the

theme of the Temple. He suggests that Mark finds the two-stage structure of the episode in an early source—the cursing and discovery of the withered tree within two days. Mark interprets the incident to elicit a message that relates not to judgment but to the centrality of faith and prayer in the life and identity of Jesus's followers. Mark's message in vv. 22–25 is not the coming judgment upon Israel but the power of faith and prayer and the right way to pray. Esler also notes the importance of faith and prayer in Mark (e.g., 9:23, 29).

67. Regev 2014. In Acts 2:42, 47, (communal?) prayers are mentioned, but the apostles continue to pray at the Temple (Acts 3:1). See also chapter 5.

68. Privileged in the Temple: Bauckham 1988:187; Evans 1995; Brooke 1995:286, 294; Heil 1997:81; Yarbro Collins 2007:532; Gray 2010:65–66. Chief priests: Wardle 2010:188–190. Note that in contrast to Isa 5, Jesus's parable does not accuse the vineyard itself, namely, the entire Jewish people, implying that they are not responsible for the rejection of the Son (De Moore 1998:68).

69. De Moore 1998:69–70 and references to previous commentators. He mentions that the Targum interprets the fence in Isa 5:5 as "their temple(s)." See also Gray 2010:62–63.

70. Brooke 1995. He shows that the vineyard in Isa 5:1–7 is interpreted as Jerusalem.

71. Juel 1977:236–237; De Moore 1998:70; Wardle 2010:187; Gray 2010:65. Cf. the survey in Kloppenborg 2006:224–227.

72. Heil 1997:82–83 (designating it as a house of prayer); Moloney 2004:93; Marcus 2009:814–815; Gray 2010:71–72, 75–76 (interpreting the cornerstone as the Temple in light of Zech 4:8, where Zerubbabel lays the foundation of the Temple).

73. Targum Isa: Kloppenborg 2006:95–96, 226. 4Q500: ibid., 101.

74. As suggested by Juel 1977:134. Heil 1997:84 argues that the scribe calls into question "the worth and adequacy" of worship in the Temple and does so in the Temple itself (11:27). Hence total love of God and neighbor surpasses sacrifices as authentic, effective worship.

75. Moo 1984:6–11; Gundry 1993:716–717; Evans 2001:265–266; Yarbro Collins 2007:576. See 1 Sam 15:22; Hos 6:6; Isa 1:11; Jer 6:20; Amos 5:22; Mic 6:6–8; Ps 40:6; 51:16.

76. *Avot de-Rabbi Nathan* version a, ch. 4 (ed. Shechter, 18), version b, ch. 9 (22); Midrash Psalms to Ps 9 (ed. Buber, 80) and Ps 89 (381).

77. Gal 5:14; *Sifra Qedoshim* 4.12 (ed. Weiss, 89b); b. *Shabbat* 31a; *Avot de-Rabbi Nathan* version b, 26 (ed. Shechter, 53).

78. The introduction "truly I tell you" is characteristic of other key teachings of Jesus, producing an expectation of an important, emphatic statement—either prophetic or about discipleship (Yarbro Collins 2007:589–590). In fact, some actually attribute it to the Historical Jesus. See McKelvey 1969:72–73; Evans 2001:509.

79. Cf. *War* 5.200; 6.282; m. *Sheqalim* 6:5.

80. E.g., Yarbro Collins 2007:590.

81. Wright 1982. He also relates the passage to Jesus's objection to similar donations at the expense of one's parents' possessions in the *korban* saying (7:10–13). Yet in the latter passage the problem is that the dedication to God is in conflict with honoring one's parents. Following Wright, Heil 1997:86–87; Driggers 2007:241–243; Gray 2010:78–79 relates the immoral and greedy scribes to the Temple as a den of robbers, though Mark 12:38–40 does not mention the Temple at all but the markets and synagogues.

82. Fitzmyer, 1995:1320–1321; Evans 2001:281–282, 285.

83. Heil 1997:87–89, 93. At the same time, Heil sees the poor widow as an example of total faith in God since she contributes all of her possessions to God, exemplifying the love of God as worth more than sacrifices contributed to the Temple treasury. This assertion is contradictory, since these Temple treasury contributions specifically support the sacrificial cult!

84. Mixed and contradictory attitude: Marcus 2009:861–862. Narrow contextual focus and need to take account of additional sayings: Struthers Malbon 1991.

85. Davies 1974:258; Juel 1977:127–128; Waetjen 1989:196–197; Heil 1997:89; Evans 2001:294–300 (interpreting "wonderful buildings," *oikodonia*, as the Herodian Temple); Kloppenborg 2005:428–430, 449–450. Seely 1993:281 notes that in contrast to the charge in 14:58, Mark does not want to link Jesus to the destruction, since he does not want to show openly a conflict with the Temple for which there is no precedent.

86. Kelber 1974:104–105; Heil 1997:90; Gray 2010:109. Evans 2001:297 rejects the view that leaving the Temple precincts reflects a final break with the Temple. Note that the Mount of Olives is already mentioned in 11:1.

87. Commercial activity and rejecting Jesus: Marcus 2009: 873. Failure of Gentiles' worship: Gray 2010:124. Replacement by Jesus and the Christian community: Geddert 1989:138, 209.

88. Gaston 1970:11–12, 479. He maintains that Mark alters Jesus's original oracle about the Temple based upon an independent tradition (later found in Luke 19:44) which explicitly applies the "no stone on another" tradition concerning Jerusalem (ibid., 64, 242, 424; cf. Dupont 1971). See also Yarbro Collins 2007:761–762. Note that Matt 23:38 and Luke 13:35 find it necessary to add explicit references to the destruction of the Temple which are absent from Mark. Matthew and Luke already know that the Temple is destroyed and are looking for a justification for this disaster.

89. Brandon 1960; Pesch 1991:271; Marcus 1992:460; Gray 2010:98 and references. Incigneri 2003:esp. 118–120 argues that if Mark had written before 70, he would have had to take the risk that the prophecy would turn out to be false.

90. Marxsen 1969:166–189; Lane 1974:17–21; Hengel 1985:1–30 (Mark is written in Rome in 69 CE, and Mark 13 alludes to the situation in the time of Nero); Guelich 1989: xxix–xxxii; Sanders and Davies 1989:16–21; Evans 2001:298. Cf. Yarbro Collins 2007:11–14 and the survey of earlier scholarship in Taylor 1959:31–32.

91. Yarbro Collins 2007:14, 604–605; Hengel 1985:21–23. Marcus 1992:468–460 uses the same argument but nonetheless dates Mark as post-70. See below in the discussion of dating the "abomination of sacrilege." On Simon aspiring to despotic power and high ambitions, see *War* 3.150–151. The people treat his command as if he is a king (*War* 5.510) and he is acclaimed as a savior and protector (*War* 4.575), regarded with reverence and awe (*War* 5.309).

92. Yarbro Collins 2007:601. One of the problems is that Josephus describes the Temple being set on fire by Titus. Titus razes both the city and the Temple afterward (*War* 7.1).

93. Kloppenborg 2005:443–448, esp. 442. However, on page 449 he seems to prefer to see it as Mark's historical narrative based upon earlier tradition. Note that the destruction of a temple entails the belief that the deity has departed. This is already attested to in Ezekiel 8:12; 9:9; and *War* 5.412, and in Josephus there are echoes of the *evocatio* practiced by Titus during the siege (ibid., 441–446).

94. Kloppenborg 2005:444 mentions that the Roman legionaries erect their standards in the court of the Temple and acclaim Titus as *imperator* (*War* 6.316), but he does not discuss whether this should be identified with the "desolating sacrilege" (Mark 13:14). Below we shall see evidence against this possibility.

95. Kloppenborg 2005:450.

96. As does, for example, Evans 2001:318–320.

97. Brandon 1960; Incigneri 2003:128–134. Cf. *War* 6.316. Incigneri prefers the possibility that Titus himself enters the Temple (*War* 6.260) by right of conquest, as Pompey does before him (cf. the desecration in *Ant.* 14.71–73).

98. Hengel 1985:16–17; Yarbro Collins 2007:608–609 (focusing on false messiahs, discussed above); Marcus 1992:454; 2009:890. Kloppenborg 2005:426 notes that the wish that the events leading up to the flight "not occur during the winter" (13:18) does not cohere with Titus's occupation in August 70 CE. Pesch 1991:195–196, 226–227 relates this to the flight to Pella (mentioned by Eusebius). Theissen 1991:125–165 follows previous scholars in finding here echoes of earlier events such as Caligula's attempt to erect his statue at the Temple. He adds that the predictions in 13:7–8 correspond to events in Judaea and its environs in 36–37 CE, such as the war between Antipas and the Nabateans (ibid., 154–155). Yet since Caligula dies before he is able to carry out his decree, it is unlikely that the event makes an impression on Mark almost three decades later (Taylor 1959:511; Evans 2001:318–319).

99. Hengel 1985:21–27. He dates Mark as late as winter 68/69–winter 69/70; that is, before Titus's arrival in Jerusalem, when speculation is raised about a Nero *redivivus* who might desecrate the Temple and inaugurate a period of messianic woes. Hengel notes that the call to flee would be effective before Vespasian's conquest of Judea in 68 since leaving Jerusalem afterward means falling into the hands of the Romans. In this later period people flee from the country to Jerusalem. See also Moloney 2004:92 and the bibliography in 116–117 nn. 34–35.

100. Yarbro Collins 2007:14, 604–605. See also Witherington 2001:345; Wong 2009:187–188.

101. Marcus 1992:454, 446–448. Marcus 2009:890–891 also alludes to the usurpation of the high priesthood by the rebels who elect a high priest by lottery (*War* 4.151–157; 5.5) as a possible desecration of the cult.

102. Markus 1992:454–456. For the Zealots' acts in the Temple, see *War* 2.423; 4.201; 4.241–242; 4.262; 5.402; Hengel 1989a:183–186. For Josephus's descriptions of their sacrilege in the Temple, see Regev 2011.

103. *War* 4.163; cf. ibid., 171, 172, 181. See Regev 2011.

104. Yarbro Collins 2007:609–610. Cf. Evans 2001:318–319.

105. Hengel 1985:25; Evans 2001:292; Yarbro Collins 2007:14, 611. See Taylor 1959:511 and references. Evans 2001:319–320 notes that the abomination of desolation in Daniel envisions the cessation of sacrifice, not the Temple's destruction. He compares it to a prophecy about a man of lawlessness sitting at God's Temple proclaiming himself to be a God (2 Thess 2:3–4), adding that such expectations are raised by Roman rumors of Nero *redivivus* (Suetonius, *Nero* 6.57).

106. Geddert 1989:206–207; Heil 1997:92; Kloppenborg 2005:447–449; Gray 2010: 155.

107. Temple-less age: Kelber 1974:105; Gray 2010:148–149, 155. Community replaces the Temple: Heil 1997:148–149. Gray 2010:144 comments that the Son of Man takes up the role of Isaiah's eschatological Temple in 56:7–8 by gathering all of the nations and the restoration of Israel.

108. Gray 2010:141 admits that in 13:14–23 the Temple is never described as being destroyed, but this is "the very issue that launched this entire discourse . . . the reader is left waiting for the account of the temple's demise—and that account is given in vv. 24–26. Judgment upon the Temple."

109. Yarbro Collins 2007:608–609.

110. Although the deity probably departs (Kloppenborg 2005:447–449), it may be restored, as it has been in the Persian and Hasmonean periods.

111. See also Daly 1978:221–225, 491–508.

112. Heil 1997:94–95.

113. Kalwans 2002:esp. 11–13, followed by Yarbro Collins 2007:655–656.

114. Dunn 2003:772–773; Evans 2001:375. See the discussion in chapter 1.

115. Loader 1997:118, 122. Some argue that Mark redacts the Last Supper as a Passover meal: Brown, 1998:46–57; McKnight 2005:271–273, 304–312.

116. Marcus 2009:947–948. For the term *to pascha* as referring to the sacrifice of the lamb, see Fredriksen 2016:321.

117. Juel 1977:124, 144, 156. The popular argument for this conclusion is that Mark 14:58 echoes the "three days" prediction in 8:31; 9:31; 10:34. See Seely 1993:275, 281; Brown 1998:440, 444; Heil 1997:96, 98; Evans 2001:445; Marcus 2009:1004, 1014.

118. Gray 2010:172–174.

119. For the eschatological Temple built by God's own hands, see 4Q174 Florilegium 1, following Ex 15:17. Cf. Juel 1977:150, 153. Evans 2001:445 notes the Danielic motif of the stone cut from the mountain "by no human hands" which destroys the image of the kingdoms (Dan 7:1) that may be related to "the one like a son of Man" (Dan 7:13).

120. Heil 1997:98. On the three days prediction, see Mark 8:31; 9:31; 10:34.

121. Juel 1977:213.

122. Juel 1977:169–207, referring to 4QFlorilegium and the Targums, where however, the Messiah is *not* the builder of the Temple, as may be implied earlier in Zech 6:12. See also Evans 2001:445–446.

123. Taylor 1959:566 ("a new spiritual system or community"). Juel 1977:145 lists seven scholars who follow this interpretation.

124. Gray 2010:175.

125. Seely 1993:281, following Juel.

126. Lührmann 1980–1981:459–460.

127. In Heb 9:11, 24 it means the heavenly Temple, of which Mark is probably not aware. Even in Hebrews this Temple is not built by Jesus or anyone else but probably exists since creation. Acts 7:48 criticizes the concept of God's dwelling in a Temple made of hands since it resides everywhere without alluding to an alternative Temple. The concept of "made without hands" is attested to in relation to circumcision in Col 2:11.

128. Lohmeyer 1967:347; Hamerton-Kelly 1994:56–57; Evans 2001:509; Marcus 2009:1066; Gray 2010:186. For Seely 1993:282, this seems to be "the final act in the dramatic conflict between Jesus and the Temple." Cf. the survey of scholarship in Yarbro Collins 2007:759–764.

129. Yarbro Collins 2007:760; Gray 2010:188–189. Brown 1998:1110–1113 finds it difficult to identify the specific veil to which the gospels allude. In m. *Yoma* 5:1 there are two veils—at the entrance to the holy and at the entrance to the holy of holies.

130. Chance 2007:285–286.

131. Juel 1977:137, 139, 206; Gray 2010:193–194.

132. Brown 1998:1113–1116, referring to Tacitus, *Hist.* 5.13. R. Johanan Ben Zakkai predicts it owing to a similar sign in j. *Yoma* 6.3, 53c; *Avot de-Rabbi Nathan*, version A, 4 (ed. Shechter, 21, 23); b. *Yoma* 39b. Cf. the astral or cosmic signs in the sky in *War* 6.288–309.

133. *Recognitions* 1.41.3. Cf. the anti-Temple stance, ibid., 39 and 54.1, where the author argues for the cessation of the sacrificial cult. See the edition and comments in Jones 1995:130, 136, 147–149, 156–160. For similar ancient interpretation, see Hippolytus, Pasch. 55.2; John Chrysostom, Hom. Matt 51.32.40. Tertullian, *Adv. Jud.* 13.15 argues that it demonstrates that it is Christ who is the "true Temple."

134. Motyer 1987:155–157; Ulansey 1991:23–25 and bibliography. In addition, in both scenes Jesus is declared (either by the Spirit or by the Roman centurion) to be the Son of God.

135. Gurtner 2007b:300–304. Cf. *War* 5.212–214. See Ulansey 1991.

136. Sabin 2002:108.

137. Yarbro Collins 2007:763–764.

138. B. *Gittin* 90b and parallels. Cf. Mal 2:13–14.

139. As already suggested by Melito of Sardis, *Pasch* 89. On the mourning custom, see Gen 37:34; b. *Bava Metsiah* 59b. Cf. Mark 14:63 in which the high priest rips his garments when hearing Jesus's blasphemy.

140. Milgrom 1976. Compare also the cries of the Temple's court in reaction to the evil deeds of some priests (b. *Pesahim* 57a).

141. On reading Mark as a post-70 reaction to the destruction of the Temple, when belief in Jesus takes the place of the cult and the destruction is explained or even justified, see Seely 1993:276, 277–278, 282; Boring 2006:320–321.

142. Similarly, Yarbro Collins 2007:761–762 questions that there is an anti-Temple theme in Mark 11–15, since predictions of the destruction do not reject the Temple as such. She also reads 14:58 as meaning that the cult is to be renewed, not abolished.

143. Hanson 2000:151–207 and the studies cited ibid., 154 n.9, 159 n. 15, illuminating the narrative role of Jesus's adversaries.

144. Lücking 2002:esp. 162–163.

Chapter 4. Q and Matthew

1. Schultz 1972:99–100; Dettwiler 2009:63–64.

2. Schultz 1972: 166–190, 384; Tuckett 1996:406, 436–438. Wild 1985:113–117 concludes, based on the assumption that Q takes for granted the validity of the Law, that the so-called woe's against the Pharisees in 11:39–42 represent Christian Pharisees who do not dispute the practice of purity observance and tithing, and that Q's criticism arises within a pharisaic context.

3. Translations of Q follow *The International Q Project (The Sayings Gospel Q, 2001)* with slight stylistic changes.

4. Tuckett 1996:407.

5. Kloppenborg 1990a:35–36, 43, 57. For further studies that argue that the Law is acknowledged by Q but is not its initial concern, since Jesus's wisdom teachings are the new means of salvation, see Han 2002:36–37.

6. Kloppenborg 1990a:43. He surmises that the later stage may be a reaction to external social pressure. Cf. Kloppenborg's reconstruction of three literary layers in Q, according to which all of the references to the Law/Torah are found only in the third one (Q³) in Kloppenborg 1987. Compare also his interpretation of Q 11:42c when the scrupulous pharisaic approach to tithing is rebuked (see below).

7. Catchpole 1993:256, 276, 279; Kloppenborg 1990b:154–157 (citation from 157); 2000:199, 212 (on Q³), 256–258 (on the Galilee). He also claims that Q 11:39–41 ridicules the pharisaic distinction between the purity of the cup's inside-outside, using the entire issue as a metaphor. See Kloppenborg 1990a:39–43.

8. In Luke, the temptation in the Temple appears last. In Matthew, it is second. The International Q Project's reconstruction of Q follows Matthew. On the original wording and order of this section in the temptation and the changes made by Luke, see Fleddermann 2005:244–248.

9. Han 2002:133, 142 suggests that Q's Jesus actually implies that God's presence and protection are *not* confined to the Temple.

10. Kloppenborg 1991:99. This interpretation is enhanced in Matthew's version, which relates to the "holy city" (Matt 4:5). One might suggest that the very purpose of the devil's temptation is to force Jesus to perform a miracle and disclose his messianic identity, possibly reflecting special importance for messianic manifestation at the Temple. Yet Davies and Allison 1988:367 deny such messianic overtones, relating merely to Jesus's power as the Son of God, who is totally obedient to God.

11. Han 2002:137, 140. On various views about the message of the temptation story for the Q community, see Kloppenborg 1987:250–256. Kloppenborg, ibid., 253 thinks it promotes dependence upon God.

12. The exact place of the pinnacle, literally the "wing" of the Temple, is uncertain (Eliav 2004). It may refer to a balcony in the Temple wall, perhaps the so-called royal balcony on the south side of the Temple Mount. See Davies and Allison 1988:365–366 and the discussion on James being thrown from the pinnacle in chapter 5.

13. Han 2002:141, referring to Ps 36:8 etc.

14. For the different practices, see Regev 2005a:160–170.

15. Kloppenborg 1990a:42; Han 2002:152, 158.

16. Kloppenborg 1990a:43. Cf. the scholarship discussed in Han 2002:39–40. Recent studies reject this approach. Dettwiler 2009:38–39 argues that given strict rabbinic rules Q 11:42 is not a caricature of pharisaic law but reflects contemporary legal debate. Fleddermann 2005:556 insists that Q 11:42c is not a later addition, since almost all of the woes against the Pharisees in Q have similar additional clauses. The use of "to do" and "to abandon" is characteristic of Q and shows that the clause is original, since Q stresses ethical commandments over ritual ones. In the same vein, it is reasonable to view Q 11:42 as representative of an internal pharisaic debate about tithing and purity without rejecting the Pharisees' basic legal practices or interpretations.

17. Catchpole 1993:264–265; Tuckett 1988:95, 98. Han 2002:149–152 lists scholars who think that Q observes tithes. Kloppenborg 1990a:158 also admits that Q does not reject tithing in its entirety.

18. Han 2002:159–160 following Kloppenborg 1990a:158 (cited). Han refers to the half-shekel tax in Qumran (paid once in a lifetime and not necessarily to the

Temple) and Didache 13:3 (first fruits to the communities' prophets). These examples hardly prove his point, since there is no indication in Q that the tithes are given to anybody other than the priests and Levites.

19. Kloppenborg 1987:145–146; Han 2002:177–180; Luz 2005:154–155. Luz notes that in later rabbinic sources Zechariah is called a prophet and that it is mentioned that he was killed close to the altar.

20. Catchpole 1993:256 does not see any criticism of the Temple here and Tuckett 1996:310–314 holds that this event from the past is not connected to the present adversaries of the Q community. Nonetheless, Han 2002:171–173, 180–183 notes that the author probably implies that the present Temple is still defiled by bloodshed. For the location of the killing of Zechariah in the Temple in later Christian and Jewish tradition, see Eliav 2006:45–55.

21. For identifying "your house" with the Temple, see Han 2002:184; Fleddermann 2005:705. Cf. Jer 12:7; 1 Kings 9:7–8; Tob 1:4. Some scholars perceive negative feelings or even rejection of the Temple here still hold out hope for the future when "the one" returns, namely, the abandonment is temporary. See Catchpole 1993:271, 273–274, 279; Tuckett 1996:314–315. Others reject the Temple under all circumstances: Miller 1988:235, 238–239; Han 2002:184, 187–190, following Schultz, Hoffmann, and Myllykoski. For signs of lament in Matthew's version, see Moffitt 2006.

22. Catchpole, 1993:27. See Q 10:10–12; 11:31–32; 12:42–46; 13:28–29; 17:1–2; 17:33. Kloppenborg 1987:228 sees in Q 13:34–35a a pre-Christian Sophia saying to which the coming of the Son of Man is added.

23. According to Weinert 1982:75–76, when Luke uses *oikos* as Temple he makes clear that this is God's house (Luke 6:4; 11:51; 19:46; Acts 7:47, 49). In addition, Luke usually uses *naos* or *topos* instead. *Oikos* as a domestic house appears in Jer 22 vv. 1, 4, 5, 8. Fitzmyer 1985:1036–37 tends to follow this suggestion. For the blurred relationship between Jerusalem and the Temple in Luke's gospel, cf. Bachmann 1980:13–66.

24. Han 2002:189, 203 (citation); Fleddermann 2005:705.

25. Following Kloppenborg's reconstruction of the literary development of Q, Han 2002:203–207 argues for a more positive approach in 4:9–12 and 11:42c representing a later view. He assumes that the aim here is reducing friction between groups. He also raises the possibility that the later passages are added after the fall of Jerusalem (based on those who think that Q is post-70 CE, which also explains why Q becomes closer to Matthew's approach to the Law). Yet Han (ibid., 207) concludes that Q's group identity has little to do with the Temple: the universalistic vision of the Kingdom has replaced the symbolic centrality of the Temple in Q 4:1–13.

26. Date: see the survey in Davies and Allison 1988:127–138. Galilee: Segal 1991:26–29; Saldarini 1994. Cf. the survey of recent scholarship in Runesson 2008:107 n. 40.

27. Stanton 1992:124–128, 156–157, following Moule, Meier, and Stendhal. For *ecclesia*, see Matt 16:18; 18:17. For the mission to the Gentiles, see Matt 8:5–13; 15:13.

Turning to the Gentiles is usually understood by scholars as crossing the boundary of Jewish consensus. However, Saldarini 1994:78–81 does not see a contradiction between Matthew's Jewish identity and his mission to the Gentiles.

28. Luz 1993:14; Luomanen 1998:164.

29. Overman 1990:142–149; Sim 1998:109–163, esp. 143–148. See especially Saldarini
1994:46–53 and Runesson 2008. Cf. Davies and Allison 1988:23–28, who also
stresses Matthew's Jewish character, such as interest in the Pharisees and Sadducees. The denouncements of the chief priests and Jewish authorities other
than the Pharisees and scribes, however, are less emphatic (Runesson 2008:117).

30. White 1991:241. Cf. Sim 1998:120–123.

31. Runesson 2008:esp. 117, 125. On the synagogue, see ibid., 117–125. I fail to see the
reason for dating the conflict to the pre-70 recent past. Matthew's polemic is
relevant, in my view, only if he still wishes to continue to draw followers from
the Pharisees to his own community.

32. For Luomanen 1998:282 commitment to the law is stressed only for the sake of
legitimation. For Deines 2009:70, 82 the Law is no longer central. More important are love, mercy, and discipleship. The Torah remains God's will and God's
word but does not in and of itself lead to eschatological righteousness or the
Kingdom of God.

33. Generally on the Law: Segal 1991; Stanton 1992:130; Hanger 1993:108. Saldarini
1994:125 notes that the rejection of hand washing (15:20) does not reflect denial
of purity and dietary laws as part of biblical law, since hand washing is a postbiblical practice. Note that Eliezer ben Hanoch was excommunicated because
he doubted the washing of hands (m. *Eduyot* 5:6). For the time limit of the Law,
see Sim 1998:124–126, although others maintain it means "never." Cf. Davies
and Allison 1988:107, 494–495; Luz 1989:265–267. Some argue that Matthew
does not abolish cultic law but does make it inferior to the commandment of
love. See Davies and Allison 1991:104–105; Gurtner 2007b:106.

34. Sim 1998:134–135, 137 and references; Saldarini 1994:125.

35. See the survey of Powell 1995, who suggests that for Matthew the Pharisees
know the Torah only in its technical sense. Yet he denounces their interpretation of it—their teaching and lifestyle—since the interpretation of Scripture
should be made by Jesus and his disciples alone (ibid., 431–435). It is more reasonable, however, that Matthew accepts many precepts of the Pharisees' legal
system (do *whatever* they teach you). I think he denounces their use of legal
practices in order to increase their social and religious status as leaders. See
Regev 2000:199–201.

36. France 2007:889–901, 919–928; cf. the references in Gurtner 2008:129–130 nn. 5–6.

37. Luomanen 1998:228, 283. Hanger 1995:773 regards the Eucharist as an allusion to
sacrifices of atonement in the Temple, while Davies and Allison 1997:473 see
here a sacrifice of a new covenant similar to Ex 24:8. Gerhardsson 1974:31–32
argues that Jesus invites Israel to participate in the spiritual Temple service he
himself carries out and that his followers are to constitute a place of expiation,

a sanctuary of atonement in Israel. Still, Gerhardsson does not think that Matthew invalidates other sacrifices and offerings, and Jesus's own death as ransom does not make the cult superfluous.

38. Saldarini 1994:67; Gurtner 2008:130.

39. Davies and Allison 1988:356 note that in 4:5 (Q) "holy city" is almost certainly redactional, which is Matthean.

40. Runesson 2008:116; cf. Davies and Allison 1997:143. As for why Matthew is the most favorable concerning the Temple, Hanger 1993:lxxiii–lxxv dates the gospel to pre-70, arguing that the positive approach is based upon the period before the destruction. For Hanger, Temple traditions in 5:23–24, 17:24–27, and 23:16–22 are too irrelevant to be added by Matthew after 70, and the verse "pray that your flight may not be in the winter or on a Sabbath" (24:20) makes little sense if the destruction of Jerusalem has already occurred (ibid., lxxiv). In contrast, according to Luz 1993:14 Matthew's memories of the Temple are positive since the Temple no longer exists at the time of the rift between synagogue and community and is irrelevant to this conflict.

41. Davies and Allison 1988:518. The altar here refers to one of the burnt sacrifices (ibid., 248, 517).

42. For the date of the passage, see Davies and Allison 1988:516. Luz 1989:289 points to parallels in ancient Judaism, including the interruption of a guilt sacrifice in a case in which the return of stolen goods has not yet taken place (m. *Bava Qama* 9:1, 12). Similarly, the one who shows mercy offers sacrifices in Prov 15:8; Sir 34:20–21; 35:1–3. The Day of Atonement alone does not expiate offenses against fellow humans (m. *Yoma* 8:9). Welch 2009 argues that the features, ordering, and structure of the Sermon on the Mount all use terms related to the Temple and the cult. However, his list of characteristics—such as righteousness, mercy, peace, anger, sons of God, rejoicing, light, and love—is extremely general and lacks any particular cultic thrust. Others are hardly related to the Temple, including measure for measure (*lex talion*). In most of these cases Welch identifies topics as Temple-related merely because they are mentioned in indirect relation to the Temple elsewhere, e.g., in Psalms.

43. Cultic fidelity: Luz 2001:6; Gurtner 2007b:104–105. Davies and Allison 1991:16 holds that "as a testimony to them" refers to the priests, suggesting proof of Jesus's curing of the leper, his power or authority, and evidence that Jesus observes the Law.

44. Hanger 1993:239.

45. Davies and Allison 1991:105 against the view of a rejection of the Temple, such as in Pseudo-Clementine *Recognitions* 1.37.

46. Gurtner 2008:134; Davies and Allison 1991:105. Cf. Luz 2001:34 who also refers to Targum Hosea.

47. Turner 2008:253–254. Hos 6:6 is used to justify a more radical line of thought, attributed to a contemporary of Matthew, Johanan ben Zakkai, head of the rabbinic school at Yabneh. The latter declares that acts of loving kindness re-

place Temple sacrifices after the destruction of the Temple. See *Avot de-Rabbi Nathan*, version A, 4 (ed. Shechter, 21); Luz 1989:89; Saldarini 1994:130–131.

48. Luz 2001:182.

49. For the reasoning of this analogy, see Davies and Allison 1988:308–312. Note that both Ahimelech the priest and David seem to be unaware of this law and condition the eating of the "sacred bread" by restricting it from women, probably a restriction related to menstrual or semen impurity.

50. Hanger 1993:329. On the Sabbath service in the Temple, see m. *Eruvin* 10:11–15; m. *Pesahim* 6:1–2.

51. Jesus: Davies and Allison 1991:314. His ministry, namely, the phenomenon of his disciples and the reality of the dawning kingdom: Hanger 1993:330, based on the neuter form (*meizdon*) instead of the masculine.

52. Hanger 1993:330. Gerhardsson 1974:28 remarks that the comparison here is between two kinds of worship: the service (*latreia*) which the priests perform in the Temple and the service in which Jesus and his disciples are engaged. Saldarini 1994:130 nonetheless notes that the analogy is strange.

53. Stanton 1992:83, 130; Gurtner 2008:135. Note that Matthew uses other "greater than" statements in relation to the Temple: in 23:17 the Temple is greater than gold, and in 23:19 the altar is greater than the gift given upon it.

54. Saldarini 1994:129 and Luz 2001:182 associate the disciples and their hunger with mercy. Davies and Allison 1991:315 see a greater law here linked both to Jesus himself and to his eschatological purposes.

55. Davies and Allison 1991:603, 627–628. They argue that Matthew ascribes it prior to Easter, unlike Mark 14:58, which notes the phrase "Temple not made by human hands." Matthew omits this latter part of the saying which the witnesses attribute to Jesus (26:61). For community as a Temple, see chapter 2.

56. Barber 2013. Note that the passage in Isa 22:22 refers to "the house of David," and v. 16 probably refers to a domestic house, not the Temple. Despite his discussion of the term "binding and loosing," nowhere are these terms directly related to priests. Barber also attempts to prove that Matthew relates to the priesthood of the disciples, since in Matt 19:28 (and Luke 22:30) the twelve are sitting on the twelve thrones, judging the twelve tribes is a priestly role. However, the only hint of priesthood appears in the next verse, and this too is very vague: the disciples lose land for another kind of inheritance (eternal life) while the priest inherits not the land but work at the Temple (ibid., 951–952).

57. Gurtner 2008:136 rejects the interpretation of Davies and Allison.

58. Civil tax: Cassidy 1979, following several Church fathers; Carter 1999; cf. the references in Garland 1987:200–201. However, we have no evidence for a Roman civil tax at the approximate level of a didrachma (Cassidy's examples are from Egypt). *Fiscus Iudaicus* (cf. *War* 7.218): Saldarini 1994:143–144. He argues that the analogy from the kings of the earth and tolls and tributes fits taxes levied by the imperial government or local rulers. Matthew's group should pay it to show that it is still part of the Jewish community. Yet he admits that "in his narrative,

Matthew keeps up the fiction that the tax is paid to the Temple, but of course by his day, the Temple tax has become a tax levied by Rome." Saldarini reads it along with the Pharisees' question about paying imperial tribute (22:15–22).

59. Flusser 1962; McEleney 1976; Horbury 1984:277 (who cites Wellhausen and argues that the passage goes back to Jesus); Bauckham 1986; Garland 1987:esp. 200, 204; Davies and Allison 1991:740–741; Stanton 1992:141. Some, such as Chilton 1990, argue that the tradition before Matthew originally refers to the Temple tax, but Matthew actually refers to the *fiscus Iudaicus*. On the half-shekel tax, its date, halakhic reasoning, and religious meaning, see Regev 2005a:132–139; Regev 2015:73–78.

60. This is far from being explicated by Matthew and is a matter of dispute. Carter 1999 argues against the logic of the analogy. He interprets "the kings of the earth" not as an analogy to God but in a negative sense following Ps 2; hence Jesus and Peter are not the kings' sons. And who are the strangers? These are Jesus and Peter, who should pay the tax to the Romans. Thus Matthew 17:25–26 is not a parable at all; it does not address a religious relationship but rather contains a straightforward message. This is an intelligent reading, but I find it unconvincing, since a relationship between the kings and their children who are free of taxes does not lead the reader anywhere! It would appear that the children's exemption from payment is presented not in a negative light (as Carter implies) but in a neutral or even positive one. In this sense the kings of the earth do not seem to be hostile earthly figures. Note that in Matthew the Son of God is a key designation (mentioned seventeen times in the gospel, e.g., 16:16, cf. Garland 1987:206), and the children are the first to enter the Kingdom (18:1–5).

61. Pre-70 tradition: Horbury 1984:277; Garland 1987:195; Saldarini 1994:143–144. McEleney 1976:183–184 argues for a Matthean composition because of its vocabulary. Note that, according to the rabbis, the half shekel is not being paid after 70: m. *Sheqalim* 8:8.

62. McEleney 1976:189–190. Stanton 1992:141–142 regards it as a mere legacy concerning past relations. In a similar vein Stanton interprets the avoidance of plight in Jerusalem during the Sabbath (Matt 24:20, ibid., 193–194).

63. Garland 1987:192–193. M. *Sheqalim* 1:3–5 notes that not all of the priests accept it. For the view that the original parable concerns all Jews as children of the king(s), see Flusser 1962.

64. In the Temple Scroll 39:8; 4Q159 *Ordinances*ᵃ the half-shekel payment is established as a once in a lifetime "ransom" (cf. Ex 30:12–13), perhaps because the annulment of payment is not explicated in Scripture. See Flusser 1962:153–155. Note that the half-shekel tribute is founded by the Hasmoneans in conformity with the views of the Pharisees: every Jew can and should be involved in the Temple tax and finance it, but one might see it as a tax even though it is voluntary. The Sadducees probably object to the involvement of the masses in the cult. See Regev 2005a:132–139.

65. Garland 1987:193–194. He notes that the rabbis do not impose the tax upon the priests "for the ways of peace" (m. *Sheqalim* 1:3).

66. Cf. Garland 1987:206–208 and further references.

67. Garland 1987:206–207. Horbury 1984:276 notes that the lesson is that the tax should be paid from lost property rather than the common fund. Fish represent God's grace (or rule) also in Matt 7:10; 14:13–21; 15:36.

68. Matthew pays special attention to similar offenses or scandals. The disciples are scandalized because of Jesus (13:57), they are persecuted and bitten (10:17–18), and Jesus worries about anyone who might put a stumbling block before his followers (18:6).

69. Garland 1987:195, 208 infers that being freed from the tax means that the Temple cult is irrelevant to Matthew. Matthew questions whether Christians are still obligated to the Temple cult after Christ's self-sacrifice, since the disciples are now under the power of the atonement provided by Jesus's death and not the sacrifices of the Temple (referring to Matt 26:28).

70. Flusser 1962:152–153; cf. Horbury 1984:276. Flusser (ibid., 155) adds that the early Christians cannot reject the Temple tax completely since they live in Jerusalem and visit the Temple. This issue is irrelevant to post-70 Matthew.

71. Cf. Gurtner 2007b:110–111, who concludes that "neither the Temple nor its services are portrayed in a negative light" (ibid., 108).

72. Gurtner 2008:139–140 suggests that the relationship between the cleansing and the healing is that by healing the leper he makes it possible for them to enter the Temple. But blind people are excluded from the Temple only in the Qumranic traditions 4QMMT B 49–51, and the lame are not prohibited at all.

73. Gurtner 2008:136. Matthew shortens significantly the fig tree episode, which many commentators on Mark read as anti-Temple (and which in chapter 3 I find unconvincing.) Matthew breaks the Markan sandwich structure of cure-"cleansing"-result and loosens the alleged linkage of this episode to the Temple act. See Telford 1980:79, 81; Gurtner 2008:140–141.

74. Davies and Allison 1997:291 infer that the Pharisees regard as valid only oaths employing the divine name, divine attributes, or the word *korban* (which also means "treasury" of money, see *War* 2.175; Matt 27:6). Thus both the Temple gold and the gift to the altar are binding as part of an oath because they are connected with the term *korban,* while the Temple and the altar, though bold objects, are illegitimate substitutions in an oath formula. Cf. m. *Nedarim* 1:3; m. *Shevuot* 4:13. For the different uses of gold in the Temple, including treasury, utensils and tables, and golden plates of the entire façade, see *War* 5.201–227; 6.387–391; *Ant.* 14.105–109.

75. Stanton 1992:129; Gurtner 2008:143. However, Matthew 23:1–22 is based on an earlier pre-70 source. See Davies and Allison 1988:126–127.

76. Davies and Allison 1997:292–293; Gurtner 2007b:116. Jesus adds the swearing by heaven, which acknowledges God's presence in the Temple (23:22).

77. *Oikos* as Temple: Hanger 1995:680–681, referring to Tob 14:4; Luz 2005:162 because of the other statements on the destruction (24:1–2, 15) and because of the common theme of God's leaving the Temple before the destruction, such as in 2 Bar 8:2 and *War* 6.299 (nevertheless, Luz acknowledges the philological difficulty); Moffitt 2006:306. *oikos* as Jerusalem: Davies and Allison 1997:322.

78. Moffitt 2006:306, 316 sees Jesus leaving the Temple as equivalent to the departure of the divine presence, the Shekhinah, from "the house" because of the shedding of Jesus's blood. For the destruction as a punishment, see also Luz 2005:166.

79. Davies and Allison 1997:334–335. See also Gurtner 2008:146. But Davies and Allison (ibid., 336) also argue that Matthew probably thinks that the old Temple is replaced by a new one, the church (see below on Peter and the *ekklesia* in Matt 16:17–19).

80. Davies and Allison 1997:525–526; Gurtner 2008:148.

81. True witnesses: Hanger 1995:798; Davies and Allison 1997:525. False testimony: Luz 2005:427, following traditional commentators since Origen and owing to the use of the sympathetic term "Temple of God" (see below).

82. According to Hanger 1995:798, Matthew actually alludes to the resurrection of Jesus in three days in 12:40 and 27:63 (and the resurrection on the third day in 16:21; 17:23; 20:19), hence "the accusation thus mixes together two quite separate matters, the destruction of the Temple and the resurrection of Jesus." Yet on page 299 it seems that Hanger is heavily influenced by John 2:19–21. See also Davies and Allison 1997:525. In contrast, Luz 2005:427 plausibly denies any hint of the resurrection, since Jesus only "can" build the Temple but will not.

83. An early version: Bultmann 1963:120. Davies and Allison 1997:525 argue that Matthew wants to reject the idea that Jesus founds the church only after his death, since he already does so before that with Peter (16:17–19), based on the community as a Temple association. For their view that Jesus identifies himself with the Temple, see Davies and Allison 1997:526 n. 38. Their argument that Mark 14:58 refers to Jesus's death and resurrection is flawed, since Mark draws a distinction between the destroyed Temple and "another one" which will be built. It cannot be the same thing but rather something *other* than the one demolished.

84. Luz 2005:427; Gurtner 2008:148. Luz thus concludes that Jesus does not say it.

85. For *naos* as the Temple's inner building, see John 2:20. The payment of thirty shekels and throwing them back into the sanctuary's treasury are both mentioned in Zech 11:12–13 (the LXX renders "treasury" instead of the Masoretic "the potter," which seems to be a scribal error). Davies and Allison 1997:558–559 hold that Matthew is influenced by Zechariah. Note that the context there is a prophecy of destruction.

86. Compare, more generally, Davies and Allison 1997:564–565; Brown 1998:642.

87. Gurtner 2008:150 n. 119.

88. From the Aramaic *korbana*, used in *War* 2.175 and Mark 7:11. See Hanger 1995:813.

89. Cf. Davies and Allison 1997:564 and references. They also maintain that the presence of the blood money there foreshadows the end of the Temple, demonstrated later in the tearing of the Temple's veil.

90. Gurtner 2008:152.

91. Hanger 1995:849; Gurtner 2007b:70–71. This prohibition is depicted graphically by the presence of the woven cherubim on the veil, which resonates with the guardian function they serve in Gen 3:24. As in the case of Mark, it is not entirely clear whether it is the outer or inner veil of the *naos* (the one that separates the *ulam* and the *heikhal* or the one between the *heikhal* and the holy of holies). Outer: Davies and Allison 1997:631, because it must be visible. Inner: Gurtner 2007b:70–71, because it is more sacred.

92. Hanger 1995:632, 849. Cf. Davies and Allison 1997:630–631 and references.

93. Both possibilities are raised by Luz 2005:566, who also notes rabbinic traditions on the destruction in which Titus tore the curtain with his sword: Sifre *ha-'azinu* 328 (ed. Finkelstein, 378–379); b. *Gittin* 56b.

94. Gurtner 2007b:171–173, 185–191.

Chapter 5. Luke–Acts

1. For questions about genre and unity, see Pervo 2009:14–20.

2. Luke as a reliable historian: Cadbury 1958:esp. 299–300; Hengel 1979; Dunn 2009:73–81 and references (noting Luke's knowledge of various small details of Roman Judaea or Greco-Roman politics and culture). Cf. Sterling 1992:16–19, 345–346, 349, 374, 386–389. Sources of Acts: Dupont 1964. Sources on the Temple persecutions (discussed in section II): Lüdemann 1989a:60, 85, 92–93, 234–236, 239, 245–246, 249–251. Cf. studies about how Luke shapes the narrative, e.g., Bond 2004:74–77.

3. On precise geographical knowledge of the Temple (discussed below) and familiarity with the sacrificial rites and security arrangements practiced therein, see Hengel 1983:102–106; Schwartz 2005.

4. Dibelius 2004:14–26; Bonz 2000; Dunn 2009:82–87, 160–164. As far as the internal situation of the Jerusalem church is concerned, Barrett (1998:xxxiii–lxii) concludes that Acts is not entirely accurate, since Luke presents a description more harmonious than reality, which likely includes debates and conflict within the Christian movement.

5. On *hodos*, see Acts 9:2; 19:9, 23; 22:4; 24:14.

6. Conzelmann 1961:145–148, 167; Haenchen 1971:128–129. See further references in Marguerat 2002:131. For Sanders 1987, Luke is anti-Jewish and condemns the Jews for rejecting Jesus.

7. Maddox 1982:36:37 following Haenchen 1963.

8. Wilson 1973:247.

9. Wilson 1983:116.

10. Maddox 1982:43–46.

11. Bovon 2006:378.

12. Gentile audience: e.g., Fitzmyer 1985:57–59. Strelan 2008:102–106 list scholars who think that Luke is a Gentile or God-fearer as well as those who think he is a Jew. Strelan supports the latter position because of the author's deep knowledge of Scripture, and since only a Jew would have authority as a writer.

13. Jervell 1972:141, 142, respectively. See ibid., 41–74. On the promises, see Acts 2:39; 3:25–26; 13:31–32.

14. Tiede 1980; Esler 1987; Tannehill 1990:3, 16; Raven 1995. According to Brawley 1987:151, 159, Luke ties the Gentile mission to Judaism.

15. Marguerat 2002:139–140, 146, respectively.

16. Bovon 2006:493. For the conclusion of both continuity *and* rupture, see Marguerat 2002:129–154. For the conflicting views among scholars, see Tyson 1999.

17. Blomberg 1983 (with bibliographic survey); Wilson 1983:104–108 (citation from 105), respectively. For further examples and discussion, see the survey in Regev 2016c. Note that Wilson 1983:114–115 balances his view with acknowledgment of the importance of the Law for the *Jewish* Christians.

18. Jervell 1972:133–151, esp. 141.

19. Yet Esler also argues that this is not historical since it "runs up against the hard facts," such as the Jewish Christians sharing table-fellowship with Gentiles (Gal 2:11–14; cf. Acts 16:15, 34; 18:7). Luke wants to show that "it was the Jews, especially their leaders, and not the Christians, who had renounced Moses." See Esler 1987:110–130 (citations from 129 and 126, respectively).

20. Loader 1997:273–389, esp. 361, 379, 389.

21. Hengel 1983:107 thinks that this shows an intimate knowledge of Jewish customs.

22. On Paul, see chapter 2. For further examples from Acts and explanation for Luke's stress on Jewish legal practice and piety, see Regev 2016c.

23. Barrett 1998:1011, 2018–2019 thinks that Paul must purify himself because he lives outside of Judaea. He concludes that "Luke was imperfectly informed about the regulations for vows and uncleanness." Fitzmyer 1998:694 understands that the purification Paul undergoes lasts for only "seven days" and also relates it to the impurity of Gentile land. On the period of seven days of purification period as improbable, see Wilson 1983:66; Pervo 2009:546. Note that Luke stresses Paul's purification as piety toward the Temple in Acts 24:18, when Paul mentions that he has been found in the Temple after being purified.

24. For interpreting the archaeological evidence, see Regev 2005c. An extra-purification of already pure persons before they enter the priestly court is mentioned in m. *Yoma* 3:3; t. *Nega'im* 14:3. According to the NRSV, Paul enters the Temple "with them" (21:26), but this is not attested to in the Greek text and is omitted in recent commentaries.

25. On the geographical and theological centrality of Jerusalem for Luke, see Parsons 2007:84–95. Hengel 1983 argues that Luke has fair geographical knowledge of the Temple and Jerusalem.

26. Fay 2006.

27. Bachmann 1980:215–216, 297–302. For the Jerusalem Temple as the place of abode for Israel's sovereign God, see Luke 2:37.

28. Baltzer 1965:esp. 275; Taylor 1999:714; Walton 2004:145–146, 149. Rice 2016 argued for the diminution of the sacerdotal cultic functioning of the Temple, especially in Luke 1–2.

29. McKelvey 1969:84. For Wardle 2010:195, the formation of a communal Christian Temple identity is a reaction to conflict with the chief priests (see also below on the Temple persecutions). For Hamm (2003:216–220), Jesus blesses disciples with his hands as the high priest (Luke 24:50–52) as in Ben Sira 50:20–21, thus perhaps replacing the priestly cult. Cf. Brown 1979:281. Note, however, that the disciples continue to attend the Temple regularly (Luke 24:53).

30. Beale 2004:204–208 sees the coming of the spirit in the Pentecost as a replacement of the Temple by the forgiveness of sin derived from Jesus (Acts 2:38) and speaking in tongues (Acts 2:3) as a theophany which resembles the imagery of the heavenly sanctuary. Beale also reads Acts 15:16–17, in which James cites to Amos 9:11–12, "I will rebuild the tabernacle of David from its ruins," as referring to Jesus's resurrection as an establishment of a new Temple (ibid., 232–238). The verse in Amos, however, refers to a domestic hut, which symbolizes restoration of the Davidic dynasty, not the Temple/Tabernacle (cf. CD 7:16; 4QFlor i 12–13; Fitzmyer 1998:551, 555–556). Note that Koester 1989:66–87 mentions this passage without identifying the tent with the Tabernacle.

31. Chance 1988:35–36, 41–44. Chance (ibid., 44–45) adds that stone imagery in Luke 19:40, 20:17–18, and 21:5–6 alludes to Jesus but not to the Temple.

32. Barrett 1953; Klinzing 1971:201; Grappe 1992:88–115; Bauckham 1995: 442–450; Wardle 2010: 208 n. 151 and references. Note also the (later) allusion in Eph 2.20 to Jesus as the cornerstone of the Temple. Bauckham 1995:423 senses that this perception is problematic in light of Paul's activity in the Temple. He maintains that the Jerusalem community expects that God will remove the Jerusalem Temple, but until that time Christians should continue worshiping in it and should not expect a new Temple *building*.

33. On pillars in Jewish tradition, sometimes in relation to the Temple, see Bauckham 1995:446 n. 104. On the imagery of Rev 3:12, see Aune 1997:241 and the discussion in chapter 7.

34. Elliott 1991:esp. 213, 215–217. For the household scenes, see Acts 1:12–2:45; 4:23–5:11; 6:1–7; 28:30–31. Quite similarly, Le Donne 2013:348, 360 argues that the *ekklesia* is the mediator of the Lord's presence within the Jerusalem Temple. It enacts legitimate Temple worship, and this is demonstrated through legitimate fiscal ethics, such as the offering of Ananias and Sapphira.

35. Brown 1979:241–243. Scholars disagree about the origin of the Infancy Narrative and its relationship to Luke. See Tyson 1999:82–84.

36. Fitzmyer 1981:438; Fay 2006:256.

37. For details, see Fitzmyer 1981:322.

38. Hamm 2003:221. Cf. Head 2004:110.

39. For the Temple prayer, see m. *Tamid* 5:1; Regev 2005b; 2014a. Note that while Zechariah seems to stand alone in the sanctuary, whereas according to m. *Tamid* 5:4–5; 6:1–3 several priests enter the *heikhal* together.

40. Brown 1979:268. In contrast, Taylor (1999:713) argues that the appearance of Gabriel to Zechariah in the *naos* represents the inauguration of the gospel. The significance of the Temple is that "the old covenant . . . having come to an end." In other words, the setting of the Temple is introduced in order to show later that it has been replaced. The question is where Luke intimates such a replacement, if at all.

41. Fitzmyer 1981:425. Brown 1979:447, 449 argues for Luke's confusion and lack of knowledge. Luke does not explicitly say that Jesus's parents redeem him as a firstborn with a sacrifice. In fact, since Mary may be a daughter of a priest (1:36; 1:5), the Law probably does not require this since the Levites take the place of the firstborns (Num 8:16–18). See Brown 1979:449–450. Brown also notes that Luke uses the model of the bringing of Samuel to the sanctuary at Shiloh and that redeeming Jesus as a firstborn would not fit this model.

42. Bovon 2002:99. But he adds that here Luke transfers the holiness from the Temple to Jesus. The observance of Temple practices continues, however, throughout the story.

43. Head 2004:111 notes that here the Temple is again a place of praise, revelation, and proclamation (2:38) as well as hope for renewal and restoration. For Brown 1979:442, the characterization of the widow in the Temple indicates that worship means sacrifices and fasts.

44. Fitzmyer 1981:435–437 argues that the story is independent of the Birth Narrative and probably does not derive from a pre-Lucan source.

45. For the limits of the commandment, see Fitzmyer 1981:440 following m. *Hagiga* 1:1. Josephus and later rabbinic sources mention child pilgrims. Safrai 1965:81–88 therefore concludes that it is customary for the entire family, including women and children, to come to Jerusalem and the Temple for the festival.

46. Head 2004:111, 115 (teaching and learning in the Temple); Brown 1979:448 (foreshadowing debates). Taylor 1999:714, however, believes that the scene represents Jesus's "jurisdiction over the Temple."

47. For the translation and the textual difficulties, see Brown 1979:475–476; Fitzmyer 1981:443–444; Sylva 1987.

48. Brown 1979:490.

49. Brawley 1987:130–131; Rice 2016:58 interprets Jerusalem and its Temple in terms of the abandoned *oikos* of Shiloh (Luke 1–2; 13:35a). He argues for a progressively realized eclipsing or transmuting of the Temple's sacerdotal functions with the arrival (Luke 2:22–40, 41–52), ministry (Luke 5:12–16; 17:11–19; 19:45–48), and finally death (23:45) of the Lord Jesus. He finds thematic and verbal links between Simeon's words and 1 Sam 2:33–35 and so draws a connection between Eli's rejected house and the Jerusalem priesthood of Jesus's day (Rice 2016:77–80). Rice implies that the parallelism between Luke 1–2 and the birth

story of Samuel, and the prophecy on the downfall of the high priestly house of Eli in the sanctuary of Shilo that was destroyed by the Philistines, points to the end of the Jerusalem Temple (83, 86–87). However, since Luke does not refer to Shilo and does not mention any destruction here the implication remains in the mind of the interpreter.

50. The summary style is typical to Luke, who employs it as an editorial statement. See Fitzmyer 1985:1357.

51. This is implied by Conzelmann 1961:75–78, 164–165, 189, who regards the stress on the Temple as a Lukan apologetic claiming that Christianity is heir to Judaism and, as such, fulfills biblical prophecies.

52. Chance 1988:58; Fay 2006:256–257. Josephus and the early rabbis are also not recorded as participating in the sacrificial cult but mainly teaching in the Temple. See the introduction.

53. On Luke's theme of teachers and teaching, see Bachmann 1980:261–289.

54. Inclusion: Fay 2006:257. Bovon 2012:413 thinks that Luke 24:52 shows that the Temple is no longer a place of sacrifice but a place of prayer, as in Acts 3:1. For Bovon, Luke's statement that the apostles are "continually" in the Temple is only "a figure of speech," since the gospel moves from the sacred center to the ends of the earth. Compare Jesus's order to the apostles to stay in Jerusalem and wait for the gift of the holy spirit in Acts 1:4–8, in relation to the eschatological expectations and the so-called delay of Jesus's Second Coming.

55. Some think that the Pentecost also takes place in the Temple, although Luke does not mention any location in Acts 2. See Green 1991:556–557. Green 1994:513 n. 46. Haenchen 1971:168 n. 1 and Bruce 1988:51 n. 9 reject this possibility. Admittedly, the Temple is large enough to hold the assembly of a large crowd of both believers and nonbelievers in Jesus (Acts 2:5, 41). Given Luke's frequent mention of the Temple and the importance of the Temple as a location for the apostles' activity in Acts, it is noteworthy that he does not detail where this event takes place.

56. Brawley 1987:130–131. Angels have an important role in Acts (8:26; 10:3–6).

57. Loyalty to the Temple: Conzelmann 1961:164. Lucan authorship and style: Barrett 1991:350; cf. Pervo 2009:88–89 and references. Pervo calls the summaries "narrative fiction." See also the summary in Acts 4:32–35.

58. Barrett 1991:345, 364–365 addresses it historically and concludes that the apostles are favorable to the Temple. Taylor 1999:717 argues that the apostles do not participate directly in the cult until Paul enters it in Acts 21:23–24, 26–27 but merely synchronize their activity with the sacrificial routine, as in Acts 3:1. Their use of the Temple as a house of prayer and a place of teaching "does not mean they regarded the Temple in the same light as did other Jews" or that they forget Jesus's proclamation of the destruction of the Temple. They simply use the Temple for their preaching in the same manner as Jesus.

59. Corinthian Gate: Schwartz 1991:254; 2005:285. *War* 5.201 and rabbinic sources

(e.g., t. *Kippurim* 2:4, Lieberman ed. 230–231) mention that the Nicanor gate is made of Corinthian bronze, which is said to be as beautiful as gold.

60. Josephus *War* 5.185 mentions that the infrastructure of the eastern portico is built by Solomon.

61. Holmås 2005:413–414 suggests that Acts 10:4, "Your prayers and your alms have ascended as a memorial before God," echoes the pleasing odor of a sacrifice and may serve as a substitute for sacrifice.

62. On Acts 3:1 and 10:3, see Hamm 2003. He suggests as well that Jesus's death at the ninth hour (Luke 23:45; note that Mark 15:33–34 and Matt 27:45–46 refer only to noon) also hints at the time of the afternoon Tamid sacrifice (ibid., 225–226). Schwartz 2005:283–284 argues that Acts 3:1 refers to private prayer.

63. See Ben Sira 50:19; m. Tamid 2:5–3:1. For additional sources as well as historical and cultural analysis, see Regev 2005b; 2014a. Note that Barrett 1991:357 suggests that the prayer in Acts 3:1 is an individual one because the apostles do not offer sacrifices (for more on this, see below). The Temple prayer, however, is practiced when priests bring public sacrifices. In this instance, participants are not required to do anything but pray.

64. In contrast, Holmås 2005:404 argues that Luke is concerned less with the apostles' loyalty to the Temple cult than that it is an allusion to Israel's worship as the actual context for the events that take place.

65. For the question of whether or not Luke refers here to public prayer, see Friedrichsen 2005:105–106. Bailey 1980:145–146 argues that Luke describes "corporate worship, not private devotions," since the two pray in the Temple at the same time and the Temple is a place of a public worship. Cf. Farris 1997:31; Hamm 2003:223. Nevertheless, we cannot know whether they pray immediately after the ceremony of the public prayer. Each expresses his own private words and is by himself—the Pharisee "standing by himself" while the tax collectors "stood apart." Their simultaneous prayers may be simply a result of the narrator contrasting them.

66. Friedrichsen 2005:111–112 concludes that the tax collector probably remains in the outer courtyard, the court of the Gentiles (even though he is probably a Jew).

67. For the question of whether sacrifice is implied here, see Bailey 1980:146–147, 156 (yes); Friedrichsen 2005:115–116 n. 162 (not necessarily).

68. Friedrichsen 2005:114–117.

69. Farris 1997:23–24; Friedrichsen 2005:105. Holmås 2005:415–416 argues that prayer in general reflects in Luke–Acts continuity with Judaism in an attempt to legitimate the young movements.

70. Fitzmyer 1985:1267.

71. Fitzmyer 1985:1261.

72. No functional role: Fitzmyer 1985:1261; no eschatological role: Taylor 1999:715; Holmås 2005:407, 416.

73. Taking possession: Conzelmann 1961:77–79; confrontations with the chief priests: Dawsey 1991:11; not profaned: Bachmann 1980:148, 181–187; restoring it for the eschatological age: Chance 1988:57–58; cf. Weinert 1982:71.

74. In the omission of Jesus's alleged threat to destroy the Temple Taylor 1999:716 sees a separation of the destruction of the Temple from the death of Jesus.

75. Taylor 1999:715; Head 2004:116.

76. Weinert (1982:70) maintains that Luke presents Jesus's saying not so much as an apocalyptic judgment but rather as a prophetic response to the destruction of the Temple. Dawsey 1991 suggests that Luke's story in chs. 19–21 is more plausible than Mark's. The latter suffers from several difficulties. Hence Luke's version seems more original in its essence. This is why Luke is less critical of the Temple than Mark was. While Mark is probably the older of the two gospels, Luke contains the older view.

77. Smith 2017:44–48 argues that the abandonment of your house in Luke 13:34 refers to the Temple based on biblical allusions to "house" as a Temple. However, in Luke 19:41–44 and 21:22–24 (see also 23:28) Jesus predicts the destruction of Jerusalem, not the Temple. Interestingly, Smith 2017:177 is at pains to explain why, if Jesus declares the abandonment of the Temple (13:35), the disciples attend it: they regard it as an appropriate place for prayer and revelatory teaching, but the "eschatological life" they experienced in the Temple "was a life they brought with them through Jesus by the power of the Spirit, not something in the Temple itself."

78. Tiede 1980:65–96, esp. 69–70, 86.

79. Chance 1988:116–117; Tannehill 1990:94. I cannot see why Taylor (2003:63) concludes that Acts should be read in light of Jesus's prophecy about the Temple's destruction and that for the early Christians the Temple comes under judgment. In contrast, Longenecker 2004:98 notes that Luke does not attempt to interpret the destruction of Jerusalem and the Temple as an ironic moment of divine sovereignty. Note that the forthcoming destruction of Jerusalem is understood as a punishment in Luke 13:35 and 19:43–44.

80. Bruce 1988:410. See also Chance 1988:121–122.

81. Turning phase and broken ties: Davies 1974:255–260; the end of blood sacrifice: Bovon 2012:110.

82. Brawley 1987:125–126; Chance 1988:134. The age of divine visitation and defeat of the Gentile are foreseen in the Animal Apocalypse of 1 Enoch 90:17–25. Furthermore, there are possibly indications of hope for the future redemption of Israel. See Luke 2:38; 13:35; 24:21; Acts 28:23–28; Jervell 1972:41–74; Chance 1988:129–138; Tiede 1980:87–96. Cf. Allison 1983.

83. I don't think Luke gives an answer to this grand theological question and would rather leave it open. Brawley (1987:132) thinks that Luke continues to see Jerusalem and the Temple as existing at the navel of the earth and anticipates the restoration of God's favor to the sacred city. He refers to coping with the destruction of the First Temple with new hopes in Ezek 36:8–28 and 43:2–5

(where the glory of the Lord forsaken from the Temple in Ezek 9:3 returns). In contrast, Taylor (1999:719, 721) argues that the post-70 Temple and its destruction are less important to Luke because of his theology of the holy spirit as manifested in the life and expansion of the Church. The divine presence is no longer localized. Thus the restoration of God's presence among the Jewish people is to be sought not through aspiring to rebuild the Temple but in receiving Christianity and the empowerment of the Holy Spirit.

84. Longenecker 2004:98; Head 2004:117 and references. Taylor 1999:717 sees here the lack of divine presence but adds that the Temple already completes its purpose regardless of the death of Jesus.

85. Matera 1985; Green 1991:544; Green 1994:486, 498–499. On the identification of the Temple veil, see chapter 3.

86. Darkness as destruction: Chance 1988:120. Objection: Green 1991:546; last days: Matera 1985:esp. 475; no connection to the veil and the revelation of God: Sylva 1986:esp.245.

87. Sylva 1986. Sylva suggests that the centurion's praise (Luke 23:47) and the crowd's beating their breasts (Luke 23:48; cf. Luke 18:13) also hint at the Temple prayer.

88. Green 1991:551–552; Green 1994:505–506; cf. Matera 1985:482. Green concludes that the barrier between Jews and Gentiles is canceled. The tearing of the veil symbolizes the extension of the good news to those outside of the social boundaries determined by the Temple itself, an obliteration of prior status or ethnic barriers. But note that this applies only to the centurion, not to the crowd, and the centurion already believes in Jesus in Mark.

89. Philips 2009:225–235. From this he concludes that Luke is critical of the priesthood in general and even confronts priestly and prophetic Jewish traditions. Philips does not distinguish chief priests and leaders that persecute Jesus and the Christians from lay priests and the priestly office in general.

90. Chance 1988:36. Rice 2016:97 argues that this does not refer to the Temple cult as an independently valid institution (within Luke's narrative) but merely as one intended to bring about proper recognition of Jesus.

91. Philips (2009:234) suggests that these priests may agree with Stephen's criticism of the Temple, and, regardless, their joining "intensifies Luke's criticism of the priestly tradition." They are converted *from* the priestly tradition. In contrast, Bruce (1988:123) asserts that "the fact that so many priests were joining the community meant that the ties which attached many of the believers to the Temple order would be strengthened. It is not suggested that these priests relinquished their priestly office." Note that Luke also finds it relevant that Barnabas is a Levite (Acts 4:36; cf. also the Levite in the Good Samaritan parable, Luke 10:32).

92. As argued by Strelan 2008. He holds that it is Luke's priestly status that gives him the authority to interpret the traditions, since only a priest can be such an authoritative interpreter of Scripture. The priestly concerns of Luke which Strelan introduces (ibid., 130–145) are too broadly defined.

93. For their roles and history, see Regev 2005a:293–377.

94. Moxnes 1988:68–74. His interest lies in Luke's criticism of the accumulation of wealth and social power. On the chief priests and the Sadducees, see Mason 1995:142–153.

95. Esler 1987:244 n. 43 notes that the law to which Paul refers is "You shall do no injustice in judgment" (Lev 19:15). Barrett 1998:1062 concludes, in contrast to other commentators, that Paul's response is not ironic.

96. The chief priests and other Jewish leaders plan to kill Jesus in Luke 9:22; 19:47; 20:19. They arrest him and hand him to Pilate in Luke 22:2, 4, 50–54, 66; 23:4–20. They arrest the apostles in Acts 4:1–6, 23; 5:17–27; 7:1. Paul involves the high priest in his persecutions of the believers in Jesus in Acts 9:1, 14, 21; 22:5; 26:10–12. The high priest and chief priest persecute or lay charges against Paul in Acts 22:30; 23:2–5, 14; 24:1; 25:2, 15. Cassidy 1983 concludes that the high priests prosecute Jesus because they feel threatened by him. However, as we have already seen, Luke downplays Jesus's deeds and alleged threats against the Temple in the "cleansing," trial, and crucifixion.

97. On the *stratēgos,* see Fitzmyer 1985:1375; Barrett 1998:218–219.

98. Cunningham 1997 concludes that although the Temple plays a role in the rejection of Christ by Jewish leadership, Luke does not attempt to link the rejection of Christianity with the Temple. We do not find in Luke–Acts a direct denunciation and attack on "your high priests and teachers" who caused the cursing of Jesus's name throughout the land, as in Justin Martyr, *Dialogue with Trypho* 117.3.

99. Weatherly 1994. For instance, in Acts 3:17 and 13:27 all of the Jewish leaders are blamed for Jesus's death. In the mockery scene, Luke 23:35 alters *archiereis* (Mark 15:31; Matt 27:41) to *archontes.* The high priests are also omitted in Luke 18:32, altering Mark 10:33–34 (cf. Matt 20:17–18). Luke 19:47 includes the high priests in the plot to kill Jesus but, in comparison to Mark 11:18, broadens the circle of responsibility.

100. Powell 1990. He also shows that Luke is not as harsh as Matthew, who calls them "evil" and condemns them as hopeless. For Luke, the leaders are to be pitied, not hated.

101. Simon 1951:127–128. Simon sees here a tradition that begins before Christ but later develops further in the letter to the Hebrews. For a similar opinion, see, among many others, Klijn 1957; Haenchen 1971:286, 290; Barrett 1998:374 and references; cf. the references cited by Sylva 1986:261–262 nn. 4–5 and Larsson 1993:389–390. Esler 1987:134–135 thinks that the rejection of the Temple is related to Paul's speech on the Areopagus in Athens (Acts 17:24), in which God does not live in dwellings made by man.

102. Dissemination of the divine presence: Taylor 2003:76–77. Christ is the New Temple: Beale 2004:216–228. But as Barrett 1991:351–352, 356–367 notes, this rejection, combined with the acceptance of the Temple in Acts, is exceptional in ancient Judaism.

103. Simon 1951:130–131, suggesting his own interpretation to 2 Sam 7:13 to justify this. See also Haenchen 1971:285. Taylor 2003:77 argues that Stephen approves localized divine presence with no permanent central sanctity. Cf. Koester 1989:98. Koester 1989:84 concludes that while the Tabernacle is in accordance with God's law and prophets, the Temple is not prescribed by these and is not a legitimate sanctuary.

104. Simon 1951:133–135. Cf. Walton 2004:143. For the view that *en cheiropoiētois* refers to the Temple mentioned in the preceding verse and not to the Tabernacle mentioned earlier, see Fitzmeyer, 1998:384; Koester 1989:80. For (heavenly) Temple not made by human hands, see 4Q174Florilegium 1+2+21, 2–4 (citing Ex 16:17) and Sib Or 4:11. The latter is probably a post-70 text written by a baptist group that rejects all earthly Temples (Collins 1974b).

105. Simon 1951; Taylor 2003:76, noting that *pseudos* (in relation to the witnesses against Stephen) has both factual and *ethical* connotations.

106. Simon 1951:132. Wardle 2010:202 argues that his target is the cohort of chief priests, not the Temple—namely, their belief that God could be exclusively contained in a physical building. Few conclude that Stephen opposes the sacrificial cult in principle. See Gaston 1970:156–171 (who also connects Stephen's view to the Samaritans' rejection of the Jerusalem Temple). Koester 1989:85 maintains that the idealization of the Tabernacle does not allow us to assume a rejection of the notion of animal sacrifice, held by some scholars. Taylor 2003:77–78 also opposes the rejection of sacrifices.

107. Esler 1987:154–158, 163 followed by Green 1991:554–555. Esler is influenced by Manson's (1951:25–41) idea that the Letter to the Hebrews is related to Stephen and the Hellenists and presupposes that "Christian faith ultimately sprang from a rejection of the Temple and its cult" (Esler 1987:163). I challenge this position in chapter 8.

108. For Conzelmann 1961:165, the speech actually relates to the post-70 destruction of the Temple. Taylor 2003:80–81 suggests that the original speech refers to Jesus as the agent of destruction, since Jesus proclaims it in Luke 21:6, but speculates that Luke omits this part. He also argues that the speech coheres with the Lukan theme of the dissemination of the divine presence (see also Taylor 1999).

109. Simon 1951:132, 136–137, 146–148. Note that Simon's references to such influences include only post-70 CE texts. Cf. Manson 1951:36, 86, in relation to the Letter to the Hebrews (see chapter 8); Esler 1987:145. Yet Esler correctly notes that the opposition to Stephen arises among other Hellenistic Jews: Cyrenians, Alexandrians, and others from Cilicia and Asia (Acts 6:8).

110. Sterling 1999:212–214 locates the entire speech and the idea that God dwells in Israel outside of Jerusalem and the Temple within the setting of the Jewish Diaspora. There are many suggestions about tracing the traditions behind the speech within Jewish, Samaritan, or early Christian movements (for references, see ibid., 200–201). Sterling concludes that the speech does not reject the Temple but extends Judaism geographically and ethnically (ibid., 216–217).

Also noteworthy is the comment of Barrett 1991:365 that there is no parallel to Stephen's claim in Hellenistic Judaism.

111. Hill 1992:41–67, esp. 80, 101; Larsson 1993:390–395; van de Sandt 2004:58.

112. Hill 1992:67–70, following Dibelius 1956:168. Hill (ibid., 68–70) also points to scholarly bias in the reading of the anti-Temple stance in order to show that Stephen also opposes the Law (though he does praise Moses in his speech) in order to create a bridge to Paul's criticism of the Law. On Luke's view of the false witnesses, see Larsson 1993:382–384.

113. Sylva 1986:264–265; Légasse 1992:62–64; Larsson 1993:390–393; Walton 2004:140–143. Cf. Rhodes 2009:121–122. On this meaning of "the Most high," see Barrett 1998:373.

114. Brawley 1987:122; Rhodes 2009; Hill 1992:71–73 also notes that in Ps 132.5 "until I find a place for the Lord, a dwelling place for the God of Jacob" (partly cited in Acts 7:46b) there is no contrast between these two types of dwelling places.

115. Rhodes 2009:125–128. In Philo, *Vita Moses* 2.28 the Tabernacle is made by hands. For the heavenly sanctuary, see Hebrews 9:11, 24 and chapters 7–8.

116. Sylva 1986:267; Tannehill 1990:93; Larsson 1993:394; Walton 2004:141–142; Marshall 1989:209. Barrett 1998:xcviii–xcix follows this approach and also notes that Stephen's speech does not attack the Law and actually approves of the Mosaic Law.

117. Rhodes 2009:132. Cf. Brawley 1987:121–122. Since Luke is writing when the Temple is already in ruins, Rhodes 2009:135–136 thinks this speech presupposes that the Temple will be destroyed precisely because Stephen's opponents are sinful like their ancestors. God may act again upon his own Temple, just as he has before.

118. Sylva 1986:268–275; Brawley 1987:122. Scholars debate whether the speech is derived from an earlier source (e.g., Taylor 2003:71–76 and references; cf. the survey of Hill 1992:90–101) or is a Lukan composition (e.g., Hill 1992:82–90 and references). One of the concerns is whether it coheres with the narrative of the accusations and trial. An affirmative answer is explained in section II of this chapter.

119. Religious heresy, especially preaching "the gospel of resurrection": Reicke 1984:148–149. Transgression of the Law and eschatological beliefs: Baumbach 1989:185. The chief priests regard the messianism of Jesus and the Church as a threat to their social position: Gaechter 1947. The belief in Jesus: Hultgren 1976. Sanders 1985:281–286 argues for the shortcomings of previous suggestions and concludes that the persecutions are related to the Law and the Temple but also recognizes that this is an incomplete explanation.

120. Most scholars do not accept the view that one of these incidents is a duplication. See Haenchen 1971:254–256. In terms of literary artistry and theological purpose, the second builds upon the first. The second charge is the violation of the Sanhedrin's interdiction, and the result is a beating. See Cunningham 1997:192–194 and references.

121. Haenchen 1971:220–223 surveys the relevant scholarship but leaves the question unresolved. Bond 2004:76–77 suggests the possibility of apocalypticism.

122. Schwartz 1990:119–124 suggests that Agrippa aims to avoid political disturbances.

123. Some maintain that the entire episode is a mixture of two sources, one containing accusations of the Hellenistic Jews and the lynching and the other containing the trial before the Sanhedrin. Cf. Fitzmyer 1998:365, 390–391.

124. Fitzmyer 1998:698; Segal 1989:79–84 with bibliography for inscriptions and Josephus.

125. Acts 21:37–26:32; Rapske 1994.

126. Elliott 1991:223–224. Green 1994 argues for Luke's neutralization of the power of the Temple to regulate socioreligious boundaries of purity and holiness.

127. Wardle 2010:225. He admits that the narrative is *not* rhetorically polemical, explaining this by the fact that these stories are self-referential, interested in internal identity.

128. On the Christians not rebelling against the Temple's dictates, see Dibelius 2004:93. Generally speaking, Luke's detailed presentation of Paul's imprisonment attempts to show that Jewish charges against the Christians are baseless. See Maddox 1982:77–78.

129. To illustrate the rejection of the early Christians, note that Luke uses the self-designation "the Way" (*hodos*, Acts 18:25–26; 22:4; 24:14), while the Christians' opponents use the negative designation *hairesis* (Acts 24:5, 14; 28:22). Compare their banishment from the synagogue (Luke 6:22; Acts 9:20–25; 13:50; 19:9; cf. John 9:22; 12:42; 16:2). The closing of the Temple's doors after Paul is dragged away by the mob (Acts 21:30) can be read in similar fashion.

130. Wardle (2010:196–197, 226) suggests that the persecutions are the chief priests' reaction to the idea of the community as a new Temple. His evidence for this notion is Acts 4:11, where Ps 118:22 is allegedly used as Temple imagery: Jesus is "the stone that was rejected by you, the builders; it has become the cornerstone," building on the relation of the cornerstone to the Temple in 1 Pet 2:4–8 (ibid., 202–206; cf. Beale 2004:216). However, there is scarce and unconvincing evidence for the New Temple in Acts, and its implications are highly hypothetical.

131. *Ant.* 20.200. Translation follows L. H. Feldman in the LCL edition with significant amendments following McLaren 2001:6, 16. For the historical credibility of the passage, despite its reference to "Jesus who was called the Christ," see Meier 1991:56–59.

132. Hengel 2002:552–553; Pratscher 1987:257–259; Martin 1988: lxiv–lxvii.

133. Reicke 1984:152. Bernheim 1997:257 and Martin 1988:lxiii suggest that James is held responsible for Paul's and others' disassociation with the Law but also mention the successful Christian mission as a possible motive.

134. High priests: McLaren 2001:17–19, 25. Common priests: Painter 1999:140–141. Painter infers that James opposes the exploitation of the poorer priests (cf.

Ant. 20.205–207), bearing in mind that the Jerusalem Church is designated as "the poor" (Gal 2:10) and that some priests join it. Cf. also Bernheim 1997:257.

135. Martin 1988:lxvii points to the role of priests among the early Christians in Jerusalem and the socioeconomic defense of the poor and needy set out in the epistle of James.

136. Lüdemann 1989b:62; McLaren 2001:18.

137. McLaren 2001:17–18, 23 states that "Josephus indicates that a variety of means were used by those vying for prominence to assert their influence." He lists kidnapping, robbery, bribery, physical assault, and murder (referring to *Ant.* 20.180–1, 205–207, 208–210, 214). But the murder of Jews by Jews is not mentioned by Josephus; rather, he refers only to the execution of rebels by the Romans.

138. Painter 1999:141; Bernheim 1997:255.

139. Translation follows K. Lake in the LCL edition. For dating Hegesippus to the middle of the second century, see Painter 1999:119–120. For (impossible) identification of the pinnacle (*pterugion*) of the Temple and its significance in early Christian memory, see Eliav 2004.

140. Jones 1995:101–107. The author situates James's teaching in the Temple in spite of the fact that the high priests and the lay priests often beat the Christians for teaching or learning about Jesus (*Recognitions* 1.55.1–2). On the Pseudo-Clementines' negative approach to the Temple, see chapter 9.

141. The mighty cornerstone is identified "in the end of the entrance of the Temple." In *Test. Sol.* 22:7–8.

142. *2 Apoc. Jas.*, Nag Hammadi Coptic Gnostic Library, Codex V 60, 14–62, in Hedrick and Parrott 1996:275.

143. Eusebius, *Historia Ecclesiastica* II, 1.5, referring to Clement of Alexandria, Hypotyposes, 7th book, and repeated ibid., II, 23.3.

144. Lüdemann 1989b:169–177; Painter 1999:116–132, 141, 156–158, 175–177, 179–181, 189; Bauckham 1999; Myllykoski 2007:70–83.

145. Epiphanius, *Panarion* 29.4.2–3 even states that James is permitted to enter the Holy of Holies once a year (like the high priest on the Day of Atonement). Surprisingly, however, Hegesippus does not present this detail as the reason for his execution. Stökl Ben Ezra 2003:247–248 nevertheless thinks that Hegesippus portrays James as a high priest.

146. Eisler argues that James serves as the high priest of the Zealots and that his bold, discourteous entrance into the Holy of Holies leads to his execution at the hands of Ananus. This idiosyncratic interpretation is based on the most unusual detail (and hence probably the most legendary one) described in Hegesippus. On Eisler and his recent followers, cf. Myllykoski 2007:67–68.

147. Bauckham 1999. He also suggests that placing James's martyrdom in the Temple is derived from the Temple imagery attributed to James ("rampart of the people," "the gate of Jesus"). This proposal grants, to my mind, too much credibility to the exact words of James. Note that I have already rejected similar understanding of "the pillars" in Gal 2:9.

148. Evans 1999. Evans (ibid., 249) concludes that Jesus and James might very well advance the same somewhat critical agenda against the Temple establishment.

149. Cf. Bauckham 1999:203–204; Myllykoski 2007:78–79; Gruenwald 1988.

150. For the execution of "any outsider [*zar*] who comes near" (Num 1:51; 3:10, 38; 18:7; cf. Num 4:20), see Philo, *Leg. ad Gaium* 307; Temple Scroll 35:1–8; 4QD^a 6ii 9–10. The early rabbis, however, leave such transgressions up to divine punishment (*karet*) and shy away from human intervention. See m. *Keritot* 1:1; t. *Sanhedrin* 14:16 (ed. Zuckermandel, 437).

151. Mark 14:43, 47, 53–54. Luke 22:52 adds the Temple officers. Matt 26:57 and John 11:49 add Caiaphas's name. For the questions of historical authenticity, see chapter 1.

152. Gospel of Peter 7:26 in Hennecke and Schneemelcher 1963:185; Tosefta *Sanhedrin* 13:5 (ed. Zuckermandel, 434). Admittedly, the identification of these *minim* is problematic.

153. Cf. Fitzmyer 1998:334. The identification with Caiaphas is based on both Luke's chronology and the reference to him in the first prosecution (cf. Acts 4:6). See Bond 2004:7–8, 13, 24; Fitzmyer 1998:299.

154. The high priest who judges Stephen may be Caiaphas, Jonathan son of Ananus, Theophilus son of Ananus, or Simon Cantheras. See Bond 2004:181–182 n. 17 for references. All of these priests are relatives of either Ananus son of Ananus or Caiaphas (of the family of Katros/Cantheras). For Ananias's identification with Ananias son of Nedebaus, see Fitzmyer, 1998:717. Paul's conflict with Ananias implicitly allies the latter with Paul's opponents, and since the Pharisees defend Paul, it appears that Luke considers Ananias a Sadducee. In fact, it is probable that all of the high priests from Herod's time to 68 CE are Sadducees. For the high priestly families and their identification with the Sadducees, see Stern 1976:600–612; Schwartz 1990:185–195.

155. Acts 5:33–40. On the question of the historical reliability of the passage, see Fitzmyer 1998:333–334. Since Gamliel is not mentioned by Josephus, it is possible that Luke follows an early tradition about Gamliel's role in this judicial procedure. As I mentioned above, in *Recognitions* a certain Gamliel is associated with James's followers.

156. However, in Luke's gospel the Pharisees sometimes show respect toward Jesus and sometimes either confront him or are rebuked by him. See Brawley 1987:84–106; Carroll 1988. Note that in Acts some Pharisees become Christians and Paul is identified as a former Pharisee (Acts 15:5; 23:6; 26:5; cf. Phil 3:5). In making this connection, the Christians are associated implicitly with authentic Judaism. Hakola 2009 notes that in the Social Identity Approach the categorization of outside groups may be flexible according to changing social environments: in Acts, the Pharisees legitimate the early Christians' identity.

157. Baumgarten 1983:413–414; Mason 1992:176–177.

158. Pharisees: see the references in McLaren, 2001:7 n. 16, although he nonethe-

less decides against it (ibid., 7–12). Resisting Sadducean law: Martin 1988: xliii; Bauckham 1999:223–224.

159. Luke also stresses the Sadducees' disbelief in resurrection as the reason for their persecution of the Christians; so too he portrays the belief in resurrection as the common ground between the Pharisees and the Christians. See Acts 4:2; 23:6–9; 25:19; Brawley 1987:114–116; Fitzmyer 1998:333, 714–716. That the Sadducees persecute the Christians because of their belief in the resurrection, however, is historically implausible: Although the Pharisees also believe in resurrection, the conflicts between the Pharisees and the Sadducees center on the realm of Jewish law and the Temple cult (Regev 2005a).

160. Regev 2005a:esp. 46–48, 318–319; 2006b.

161. Barrett 1991; Schwartz 2005. The fact that James and eventually Peter also refrain from eating with Gentiles on account of their observance of purity laws (Gal 2:11–14; Dunn 1983) may also imply a similar concern for the sacrificial laws.

162. According to Tyson 1992:184 (following Brandon), "The activity of Peter and the apostles in Acts 1–5 may be read, in part, as their attempt to take control of the Temple," and Paul's entering the Temple is "a final attempt to return the Temple to its proper use."

163. Compare the suggestion that the Last Supper being "in memory" of Jesus (Luke 22:19b) is an iteration of a priestly ritual approach (Carpinelli 1999).

164. E.g., Luke 24:47; Acts 2:28; 5:31; Ravens 1995:139–170. Luke's great concern for the Temple may conform to mainstream Judaism even more if one follows Ravens's thesis that Luke denies Jesus's death as atoning and regards atonement as a direct result of repentance. In this case, the role of the Temple should indeed be related to the Lukan stress on repentance, although Luke weaves them together only in the tax collector's confession at the Temple (Luke 18:13).

165. Conzelmann 1961:209–213. So also Davies 1974:275–278, who sees in the Temple theme only a phase in the transformation from the Jews to the Gentiles.

166. Chance 1988:101–102. On Luke's Judaism, see the introduction to this chapter.

167. Esler 1987:134, 156–158. He notes that the positive approach is foreshadowed by Stephen's speech. However, he actually contradicts himself in presupposing that "Christian faith ultimately sprang from a rejection of the Temple and its cult" (ibid., 163). One can sense here the influence of Manson 1951:25–41 on the antipathy of Hellenistic Jews toward the Temple, which, as I have already noted, has no foundation in Second Temple sources.

Chapter 6. The Gospel of John

1. Brown 1966:lxx, 411; Neyrey 1988:137, 160; Carson 1991:182; Umoh 2004; Attridge 2010. For a bibliographic survey, see Hoskins 2006:10–18. Cullmann 1958–59 relates John to Stephen's speech (Acts 7) and the "Hellenistic" approach to the Temple.

2. Frühwald-König 1998; Lieu 1999; Fuglseth 2005.

3. Kerr 2002:2, 82. See also Thettyil 2007:351–352. Coloe 2001:3 and passim put forward a variant of this thesis: While the Temple "functions in the narrative as a major Christological symbol," the imagery of the Temple "is transferred from Jesus to the Christian community." For a rejection of the idea of the community as Temple in John due to lack of evidence, see Thettyil 2007:433–434. See Beasley-Murray 1999:41.

4. Kinzer 1998.

5. Thettyil 2007:345. Cf. Brown 1966:lxxv, 121.

6. Kerr 2002:34–66, 241; Köstenberger 2006; Draper 1997. However, Frey 2012:488–502 concludes that the destruction has limited impact on early Christian identity and that the Christological use of the Temple is "quite independent of the actual existence or nonexistence of the sanctuary."

7. Heavenly Temple: Kinzer 1998:458. Cf. Draper 1997. Eschatological Temple: Kerr 2002:241, cf. Draper 1997:281; Chanikuzhy 2012:276, 282. Note that Draper does not fully distinguish between the two.

8. Léon-Dufour 1951–52 (relating to the characters and the readers); Martin 2003 (on the Historical Jesus and the Johannine community).

9. Dodd 1968:esp. 133–143; Koester 2003.

10. Compare Moloney 1992.

11. Dodd 1968; Neyrey 1988.

12. E.g., Kotila 1988; Ashton 2007:80. For example, some think that John's Jesus transforms the Sabbath by his miracles and ushers in an eschatological Sabbath through works of salvation and judgment. See Kerr 2002:255–266.

13. Loader 1997:484–485.

14. Loader 1997:528.

15. Pancaro 1975:522–525, 530; cf. ibid., 518–520. He concludes (542) that John 1:17 does *not* mean that Jesus is the new Law. According to Brooke 1988, John 7–10 relates Jesus to Jewish legal practice by mentioning or implying Jesus's relationship with the laws of the Decalogue several times. He concludes that "an interpretation of the Decalogue formed part of the life of the developing Johannine community at some time" (110).

16. Loader 1997:432–491, esp. 485–486. Pointer to Christ: ibid., 488–489. But in the end Loader (ibid., 489) seems to be influenced by Johannine Christology, stating, "Such practices cease to have validity for Christian Jews." The Law "ceased to be the Law of Jesus and the community, except for its Christological function." Note that Loader's interpretation is derived, as he admits, from subordination of John's approach to the Law to John's dualism (flesh/spirit, below/above) and Christology (ibid., 488). Loader (ibid., 489–490) also builds his approach on the "cleansing."

17. Loader 1997:489, 491.

18. Leaders/authorities: Von Wahlde 1982. Elite Jews: Ashton 2007:64–97, following Boyarin 2005. See Beutler 2006:147–151 for bibliographical survey. Beutler thinks that "the Jews" are simply non-Christian Jews.

19. Neyrey 2007:70. In John 1:17; 5:45–47, Jesus is greater than Moses.

20. See especially Martin 2003.

21. Robinson 1962, esp. 109. For those who follow Robinson, including Pancaro himself, see Pancaro 1975:532 n. 112.

22. Thompson 2001:189–193, 209–211. Note also that the Jews are ready to believe in Jesus's authority but continue to argue with him about the meaning of their Abrahamic descent (8:31–32).

23. Brown 1979; Frey 2014:87–95, 149–199.

24. Synoptic version as historical: Lindars 1972:135–136. John's is more accurate: Beasley-Murray 1999:40.

25. Ulrichsen 2003:207; Kerr 2002:79–81. Cf. the survey of Chanikuzhy 2012:251–252.

26. Gnilka 1983:25; Haenchen 1984:183; Mathews 1988:125; Coloe 2001:73; Umoh 2004:323. Note the exaggeration of Coloe 2001:81: "Israel's sacred place is empty . . . there is an anticipation of a new mode of worship." Dodd 1968:301 argues that the "cleansing" signifies the destruction of the Temple and the replacement of the sacrificial cult through the resurrection of Christ. Chanikuzhy 2012:252–53 suggests that John adds the animals to the description found in the synoptic gospels in order to symbolize opposition to the slaughter of animals.

27. Chanikuzhy 2012:260–61 builds on the supposed prophecy of the ceasing of trade at the Temple: "And there shall no longer be *traders* [*kna'ani*] in the house of the Lord of hosts on that day" (Zech 14:21, NRSV). He regards it as attesting to Jesus's view of an eschatological Temple without trade. This verse is hardly implied in John 2. See also Paesler 1999:247–248.

28. Chanikuzhy 2012:262–266.

29. Ironic remark: Beasley-Murray 1999:40. Foreseeing the destruction: Köstenberger 2006:100.

30. Brown 1966:115, 123. Cf. Kerr 2002:87–90; On John's two levels of meaning, see Léon-Dufour 1951–1952. Thus the double meaning applies to both the Temple and Jesus. See Chanikuzhy 2012:309–310. Thompson 2001:212 argues that only the death of Jesus (and not the destruction of the Temple) is implied here. While the rebuilding in three days is usually taken as referring to Jesus's resurrection after three days, this can be inferred only from the chronology in 19:31 and 20:1 (as in Mark 15:42 and 16:1). It is doubtful that the reader can understand this when first reading John 2. Three days may also mean a short period of time (cf. Luke 13:32–33). See Hoskins 2006:115.

31. Jesus's resurrection: Haenchen 1984:185; Kinzer 1998:448; Hartman 1989; Mathews 1988:121; Coloe 2001:84; Hoskins 2006:114–116. Thus the expectations for rebuilding the Temple are fulfilled in a new manner (e.g., Umoh 2004:324; Chanikuzhy 2012:315). Physical Temple: Chanikuzhy 2012:311. According to Coloe 2000:50–54, Jesus's title "the Nazarene" (19:18) is messianic (Heb. *netzer*, Isa 4:2; 11:1, etc.), hence Jesus is framed as the one who is expected to build a new Temple. Frühwald-König 1998:221, however, rejects the dichotomy be-

tween Jesus and the Temple and suggests that Jesus's presence gives the Temple its sacredness.

32. Beasley-Murray 1999:40. On "the Temple of his body" as referring to Jesus as the new Temple, see Barrett 1955:167; McKelvey 1969:78–79; Hartman 1989:70–71, 76–78; Moloney 1990; Schnelle 1996:366–371; Frey 2012:484.

33. Chanikuzhy 2012:317–322 (referring to John 10:17–18; 1 Cor 15:4); McPolin 1979:29; Hartman 1989; Kerr 2002:93. For Dodd 1968:302–303, Jesus's body as the new Temple symbolizes the Church, as in 1 Cor 3:16; 2 Cor 6:16, following Origen, *Comm. In Joann* x. 35. But Hoskins 2006:114 n. 28 rightly notes that the Church is not destroyed and raised after three days.

34. Draper 1997:281 argues that Jesus builds this Temple at the end of time as a seed of David, following 2 Sam 7.

35. Kerr 2002:81 claims that John echoes the eschatological prophecy concerning no traders in the Temple in Zech 14:21. Schneiders 2006:esp. 346–347 links the identification of Jesus with the Temple to Ezek 37:26–28, whereby the resurrection of Israel is related to the rebuilding of the sanctuary. He points to linkage between Jesus's body and the Temple elsewhere in John, interpreting Jesus's call to drink water from him (John 7:37–39, see also 19:34–37) as symbolizing the Temple, based on Ezek. 47:1–12, where water flows from the Temple. But even if one agrees that John has these complex intertextual hints in mind, how would his readers grasp them?

36. Lee 2002:27. See also Thettyil 2007:387–398.

37. Neyrey 2007:70; cf. Neyrey 1988:131–137. It is also argued that the narrative context of the first sign at Cana implies Jesus's innovation of traditional Judaism, e.g., new wine takes the place of old wine, symbolizing the new age. Brown 1966:104. Cf. Chanikuzhy 2012:234–236.

38. Beasley-Murray 1999:39–40. Cf. Koester 2003:86–88.

39. The term "zeal" reflects piety toward God, the Torah, and the Temple. See Hengel 1989a:146–228. Brown 1966:124 and Moloney 1990:443 ignore the problem when they read the zeal motif as implying that the Temple action would lead to Jesus's execution. Chanikuzhy 2012:276–282 (cf. also Hartman 1989:76) maintains that this zeal may be directed only toward the eschatological Temple, namely, Jesus himself.

40. Beasley-Murray 1999:39–40 sees zeal as an indication of a positive attitude about the Temple ("Jesus has come to open up the way to the true worship of God") but relates it to the eschatological Temple. It is fair to say that zeal for God's house can be understood in a totally different manner. It is the zeal of those who sentence Jesus that "consumes" him. Yet the context here is Jesus's act, not the trial and crucifixion. Hence John probably alludes to the "cleansing" as an act of zeal.

41. Lindars 1972:137.

42. As I mentioned earlier, some argue that the objection to commerce alludes to

384 Notes to Pages 203–207

Zech 14:21, which describes the Temple in the End of Days, concluding that John hints at the eschatological Temple. There is, however, a philological flaw in this interpretation. The NRSV reads, "And there shall no longer be traders in the house of the Lord of hosts on that day." But the Hebrew reads *kena'ani* (Canaanite). The LXX reads *Chananaios*. Zechariah may refer not to a commercial occupation but to an ethnic distinction, objecting to the presence of non-Judeans in the house of God. See Meyers and Meyers 1993:505–507, who connect the term to several other such ethnic titles of Gentiles in the chapter, e.g., Egyptians. Furthermore, John mentions the Temple as a trading place (*oikon emporiou*), not alluding directly to merchants. John does not cite Zechariah directly. There is no indication whatsoever that he alludes to the eschatological Temple.

43. A critical modern reader may find here a clue that the Jewish leaders are responsible for the destruction. Such an accusation—common in Josephus's *Jewish War*, in which the rebels and the opponents blame each other (Regev 2014a)—cannot be found in the NT, despite its relevance to the situation of the early Christians in post-70 CE. For Thomas's version, where Jesus declares that he will destroy the Temple, see chapter 1.

44. Fuglseth 2005:173, 176, 184 concludes that while Jesus's body is *a* temple, it is not stated that it is *the* Temple, substituting for the earthly one. This means that there is not a complete break with the Temple, not even a reinterpretation of the Temple.

45. The believers are "one body in Christ" (Rom 12:5). See also 1 Cor 12:12–27.

46. Note that John also relates to (figurative) physical union with Christ in 14:20–23; 15:1–11.

47. Koester 2003:8.

48. *Ant.* 11.310; 12:7–10; 13:74–79.

49. Bultmann, Haenchen, and others argue that the "we" who worship for what "we know" actually refers to the Christians or even the Johannine community, since these scholars cannot accept that John favors conventional Judaism (see below about "salvation is from the Jews"). Yet the verse clearly poses opposition between Samaritans and Jews. See Brown 1966:172; Thettyil 2007:87–88.

50. John leaves open the question as to what exactly the Samaritans do not know. See Thettyil 2007:79–86.

51. Thettyil 2007:86–87.

52. John 7:28b; 8:54–55; 15:21. See Thettyil 2007:87. Some argue that it is a later interpolation. Bultmann 1971:189–190 n. 6 relies on John 1:11; 8:41, where the Jews are not the chosen and saved people, as well as the fact that Jesus disassociates himself from the Jews in 8:17; 10:34; 13:33. Haenchen 1984:222 insists that salvation for John comes only from God and Christ. Others, however, think this is not an appropriate gloss (Lindars 1972:188–189; Carson 1991:223). The actual point of the debate is indeed John's approach to Judaism. Kerr 2002:184–187 argues that the saying

coheres with the Jewish character of John's Jesus (Jesus is identified as a Jew in 4:9). Throughout the gospel he disassociates himself not from the Jews, but from the Law—or at least the Jewish interpretation of the Law. The Jews that Jesus opposes (e.g., 8:44) are only a certain portion of the Jews. In other cases, John views the Jews positively (e.g., 11:19, 31). Kerr also argues that this provocative phrase is integral to the thought and structure of the narrative, since vv. 21 and 23 relate to salvation at the eschatological hour. See also Brown 1966:172; Van Belle 2001.

53. Thettyil 2007:90–93, 102–105.

54. Betz 1981. Cf. also Dodd 1968:223, 314; Lindras 1972:189–190. For discussion, see Thettyil 2007:126–127, 129, 134. Betz 1981:62–64 points to worship in spirit and truth in the Qumran *yahad*, e.g., "to establish the spirit of holiness in truth eternal in order to atone" (1QS 9:3–4). This passage introduces an alternative to the Temple cult through prayer and moral behavior. See Regev 2003:267–275.

55. E.g., Ex. 34:6; Isa. 38:18; Ps. 25:10; 31:6; 86:15. The Torah is truth in Ps 119:142, 151.

56. Dodd 1968:177, 226.

57. Um 2006:173. Cf. Köstenberger 2006:102. One of the meanings of the spirit is an eschatological power which creates new life (Jub 1:23; Jos. Asen. 8:9; 1 Bar 23:5).

58. Kerr 2002:194–195; Thettyil 2007:137–150, 156–158. See Cullmann 1958–1959:169–170. For Hoskins 2006:143–145, worship in spirit and truth makes the Jerusalem Temple unnecessary, surpassing it. This is "based upon fuller experience of God's abundant provision ('spirit') and fuller revelation ('truth')." Um 2006:140–159 sees hints at the belief in Jesus—namely, Temple Christology—in John 4:6–15: Jesus as running water relates to cultic and messianic senses of water in Isa 58:11; Ezek 43:1–5; 47:1–9; Joel 4:18. See Grelot 1963.

59. Kerr 2002:188, 195.

60. Lee 1994:64–94.

61. Attridge 2010:265 notices that the coming of the hour in 4:23 implies the destruction.

62. Neyrey 2009:70. Cf. Neyrey 1988:160. Thettyil 2007:108, 164 regards it as superior to the Jerusalem Temple. Dodd 1968:170 stresses that God is spirit, comparing this to an inferior "shadowy ritual which either counterfeits or at best merely symbolizes the approach to God."

63. Um 2006:166, 173, 187, basing this assertion on John 1:14; 2:13–22; 4:10; 7:37–39. See Bultmann 1971:189–192; Brown 1966:180.

64. In contrast to Köstenberger 2006: 102.

65. Post-70 CE: Köstenberger 2006:93. See also Fuglseth 2005:184–185. Answer to the fall of the Temple: Kerr 2002:199.

66. Regev 2013:70–71 and references.

67. Brown 1979:38–39 relates the opposition to the Temple cult ("in spirit and truth") to Samaritan strains (and their Jewish associates) in the second phase of the Johannine community. Yet Samaritans would probably be offended by this plain preference for Jewish worship in Jerusalem.

68. Brown 1966:32–34; Coloe 2001:15; Köstenberger 2006: 98; Thettyil 2007: 370–372.

69. Manifests God's presence: Thettyil 2007:372. True temple: Coloe 2000:57. Surpasses the Temple: Köstenberger 2006:99. See also Schnelle 1996:369. Meagher 1969 suggests that it alludes to the community as a Temple. Note, however, that Pancaro 1975:542 argues that in 1:17 Jesus is *not* the new Law.

70. Koester 1989:102–108. Some argue that Jesus is also the Temple in John 1:51: "You will see heaven opened and the angels of God ascending and descending upon the Son of Man." For Brown 1966:90–91, Jesus is the ladder, the "localization of the *shekhina.*" Jesus takes the place of Bethel (the cultic center of the Israelite monarchy, where Jacob builds an altar) as the house of God to "become the locus of divine glory." See also Um 2006:153–154; Thettyil 2007:378–382; Attridge 2010:263; Frey 2012:482. While in John 1:51 the Son of Man connects heaven and earth in a manner that may be associated with the Temple, this does not point to a direct relationship to the Temple, nor does John mention Bethel at all. The reference to Jacob's letter is a more general way to ascribe sacredness and mysticism to Jesus. See Kerr 2002:166.

71. Shekhina: Beasley-Murray 1999:14. A noncultic use: Haenchen 1984:119. LXX: e.g., Lot dwelt/put his tent (*eskēnōsen*) in Gen 13:12.

72. Ezek 43:9 (the future Temple is mentioned in the previous verses) and Zech 2:14, although Hoskins 2006:118 uses these verses to prove the cultic meaning of the verb.

73. Brown 1966:33; Coloe 2000:49–50 takes a further step and identifies this new Temple with the Christian community in which the Father, Jesus, and the Spirit all dwell together.

74. John 2:16; McCaffrey 1988:30, followed by Coloe 2001:160–162, who identifies the house with the community of believers as a living Temple. Note that in John God dwells where Jesus is going (16:28; 17:11–13). *Oikos* as Temple: Zech 14:21; McCaffrey 1988:49–50, 54–55, 60–64. "Many rooms" with chambers: McCaffrey 1988:67, 75. See Neh 13:7; Ezek 40:17; 1 Chr 28:11–12. But, as he admits, in none of the passages *monai*, or rooms, are used.

75. McCaffrey 1988:98–107, 130. See John 11:48; Acts 6:13–14; Coloe 2001:164–166, who interprets the *topos*/house as the eschatological Temple.

76. McCaffrey 1988:132 suggests that since the phrase "my father's house" is attributed to David in 2 Sam 7:14, it suits Jesus as the Son of David. However, the passage does not designate David's house as a Temple. Furthermore, in Johannine Christology Jesus is never designated as the Son of David. In the single place in which the Messiah Son of David is mentioned (John 7:42) he is not identical with Jesus, who lacks a Davidic pedigree (Bultmann 1971:305–306). John's readers cannot link "my house" with the biblical King David and understand that Jesus actually alludes to the heavenly Temple.

77. McCaffrey 1988:177 follows the two levels of meaning of Léon-Dufour 1951–1952.

78. Dwelling as a spiritual experience: Gundry 1967. Household: Sverre 1962. Compare the mansions in heaven 1 En 45:3; 2 En 61:2 cf. 1 En 39:4–8; 41:2.

79. Beasley-Murray 1999:249, following Fischer 1975:58–74. This latter house in heaven (2 Cor 5:1) is not a heavenly Temple. See McKelvey 1969:141, 146–147. For the question of whether it relates to the resurrection of the body, see Furnish 1984:265.

80. Haenchen 1984:182. Cf. Frühwald-König 1998:231. Kerr 2002:266–267 adds that instead of spending the Passover in Jerusalem he undergoes his own consecration in the house of Bethany (11:55; 12:3) and that there seems to be an underlying critique of the festivals running through chapters 5–11.

81. Brown 2003:302–305. Cf. Léon-Dufour 1951–1952:171–173.

82. Coloe 2001:3. Her thesis claims that what is said of Jesus will be applied to the Christian community in the future (4:23; 7:38–39; 14:2). Hence the Temple gives the community a clear sense of identity.

83. Kerr 2002:211–226. On Jesus as the Passover lamb, see below in the conclusions section of this chapter.

84. Hoskins 2006:176–180. See John Chrysostom *Hom. Jo.* 46.

85. Grelot 1963:44–45. Cf. m. *Sukkah* 4:9–10.

86. Kerr 2002:245–246, followed by Thettyil 2007:413–416. For this ceremony, see m. *Sukkah* 5:3–4.

87. Grelot 1963:44–45 notes the use of these verses when commenting on the meaning of the water libation in t. *Sukkah* 3:3–18. See also Kerr 2002:237–241. Note that Zech 14:16–19 refers to the festival of Tabernacles. According to Grelot 1963, John 7:38 alludes to Num 21:20 and Zech 14:8.

88. Hoskins 2006:161–166. He proposes that John 7:37–39 is also based on the eschatological meaning of the abundance of water from the rock in the new age in Isa 48:21.

89. Hoskins 2006:167–170. Cf. also Thettyil 2007:413–416. On fire and light in the Tabernacle, Mount Zion, and the Temple, see Ex 40:38; Isa 4:5; Ezek 43:3. According to Coloe 2001:135–136, since the pillars of cloud and fire in the wilderness settle upon the Tabernacle (Num 9:15, 17) and later fill the Temple (1 Kings 8:4–11), "Jesus offers a light surpassing the wilderness cloud." However, the link between the light and cloud of God's presence is unclear. Coloe 2001:142, 203 also sees Jesus's fivefold repetition of the phrase "I am" in John 8 while standing at the Temple at the feast of Tabernacle as a kind of theophany, a new manifestation of God's presence there.

90. Jesus leaves the Temple and is sanctified: Davies 1974:291–296 (based on the theological weight of Jesus's "I am" claims at the Temple during Tabernacles); followed by Coloe 2001:143. Jesus returns: Kerr 2002:249.

91. As Barrett 1955:320 concludes, "As Moses sanctified the Tabernacle and its contents . . . so God sanctified Jesus for his mission." See also Kerr 2002:255; Hoskins 2006:173, 175; Thettyil 2007:413–421. For *hēgiasen* as consecration of the Tabernacle, see Num 7:1, 10–11. Hoskins also notes here that Jesus resembles the Temple because prayer in Jesus's name (e.g., John 16:23–26) is similar to the Temple as a house of prayer (1 Kings 8), hence prayer in Jesus's name is

meant to fulfill and replace prayer in or toward the Temple. For a survey of various ways scholars related Hanukkah to John's portrayal of Jesus, see Dennert 2013. According to Dennert, John's focus on Jesus's "works" suits the festival of Hanukkah because of a tendency to associate Hanukkah with miracles.

92. Coloe 2001:154–155.

93. John 2:14; 5:14; 7:14, 28; 8:2, 20, 59; 8:23; 18:20. See below in the conclusions section of this chapter.

94. Frühwald-König 1998:224–233 regards Jesus's attendance in the Temple during the festivals merely as a platform for Christological presentation of Jesus using the Temple as a legitimate background. I think, however, that there is a relationship of sacredness between Jesus and the Temple.

95. Cf. Schnelle 1996:370.

96. During the celebration no sacrifices are offered, and some of it takes place in the Women's Court, some distance from the altar. There is no sign that priests participate in it except for the libation of the water on the altar, which is rejected by the Boethusians. Cf. t. *Sukkah* 3:16; cf. m. *Sukkah* 4:9; Regev 2005a:159–160. On the popular and "ordinary" character of the celebration, in which the masses participate, see t. *Sukkah* 4:5. The Temple is characterized as the life of the world in b. *Bava Batra* 4a.

97. Lindras 1972:299–301.

98. Regev 2008; 2013:36–57. In 1 Mac 1:59, its name is "the days of the dedication of the altar. Cf. also 2 Mac 2:9.

99. Ordinary sacrifices are called sacred things by the Rabbis (e.g., m. *Zenahim* 5:1, 6–7). In the Community Rule, lay Israelite members are called "a holy house for Israel" and priests are called the "holy of holies for Aaron" (1QS 8:5–6).

100. Brown 1966:411, for example, argues that Jesus is consecrated in a manner similar to a priest ("set aside for important work or high office"). See also Barrett 1978:385.

101. See above for the references. Luke, by comparison, mentions his presence there only five times. Some even explain this attention to the Temple, following Polycrates, by saying that John's Beloved Disciple was a priest. See Hengel 1989b:109–110, 118, 124–126.

102. Lieu 1999:53–54.

103. Frühwald-König 1998:220–221.

104. The problems with the Jewish authorities in John take place in the synagogue rather than in the Temple (cf. the exclusion from the synagogue in 9:22; 12:42; 16:2). See Frühwald-König 1998:223–224.

105. Fuglseth 2005:117–284, esp. 243–249, 284. On Philo's Temple analogies and Qumranic criticism and temporal rejection, see the introduction and chapter 3.

106. Carey 1981 provides a bibliographic survey and defends its centrality for Johannine theology.

107. Dodd 1968:233. Cf. Barrett 1955:68. The only traces of removal of sin, or rather the sinfulness of those who reject Jesus, is discussed in John 8:21, 24, 34. In

1 John 1:7, however, Jesus's blood purifies from sin as in the sin/purification offering at the Temple (cf. Milgrom 1991:253–292), and Jesus is presented as atonement for the world's sins (2:2, cf. 3:5).

108. Carey 1981; Carson 1991:148–151; Nielsen 2006:225–228. Carson identifies it with "the apocalyptic lamb" (e.g., 1 Enoch 90:9–12), but this lamb is related to judgment and destruction rather than expiatory sacrifice. Nielsen argues for corporal integration of Isa 53 and the Paschal lamb.

109. Nielsen 2006:252–253; Coloe 2001:191–196. Cf. Brown 1970:882–883, 930.

110. Grigsby 1982 and references. Cf. Carey 1981 and references.

111. Its nonexpiatory character is recognized by Carey 1981:101–102. Forced attempts to see a certain type of expiation in Ex 12 (Coloe 2001:194–196; Nielsen 2006:234–235) are irrelevant to the Second Temple reality of a commemoration ritual with no sense of blame. Hillel the elder prescribes the Paschal lamb a status similar to that of a public sacrifice of the Sabbath's burnt offering. See t. *Pesha* 4:13 (ed. Leiberman, 165). On the Paschal lamb in comparison to the other sacrifices, see Tabory 1996:34–59.

112. Barrett 1955:147.

113. Consecrated: Brown 1970:766–767; Coloe 2001:203–206; Bond 2004:140. Save the people and sacrifice himself: Heil 1995. Heil does not decide whether he is trying to show that Jesus is the good shepherd, a king, or a unique Jewish high priest. Heil also argues for Jesus's superiority over the Jewish high priest during the trial (18:20–22), but this, I submit, does not make him the high priest. On Jesus's priestly image based on overly general features—legal authority and communal meals—see Cirafesi 2011–12. Jesus's farewell prayer in John 17 is regarded by some as of high priestly character, mainly because of the language of sanctification or consecration in truth in vv. 17, 19. For the history of research, see Attridge 2013. Attridge concludes that the author is only "gesturing" toward a "priestly" reading of Jesus (ibid., 12).

114. Caiaphas actually supports the early Christian belief that the death of Jesus promises salvation to the believers (Brown 1966:442–443). On the prophetic power of the high priest, see ibid., 444. Some interpret Jesus's undivided tunic (19:23), which allegedly resembles that of the high priest, as a symbol of his being a kind of high priest himself. Yet this is too general a feature to be related to the high priest. The tunic may symbolize perfection and holiness in general. De la Potterie 1979 rejects the high priestly imagery and suggests that the tunic represents the unity of the People of God.

115. Glorification: 2:11; 7:39; 12:16, 23; 13:31; 17:1, 5. Exaltation: 3:14; 8:28; 12:32.

116. Contra Hoskins 2006:147, 156, who tries to connect Jesus's glory (*doxa*) with the Temple's glory. *Doxa*, the honor of God, is not related to the Temple in Deut 5:24; Josh 7:19; Ps 19:1.

117. Schneiders 1977:esp. 223. According to Ricoeur 1976:45–69, a symbol creates a new semantic reality. Regarding symbolism in John, see Koester 2003.

Chapter 7. The Book of Revelation

1. Collins 1979:9.
2. Aune 1997:l, cxxi; Yarbro Collins 1984:46–50. Note, for example, the use of Hebrew *harmagedon* (Rev 16:16), following the Hebrew text of Zech 12:11. See,
   however, the general reservations of Koester 2014:69. On similarities to Qumran, see Elgvin 2009; Ulfgard 2009 (and see also below on the Songs of the
   Sabbath Sacrifices and the New Jerusalem Scroll). Elgvin 2009:277 concludes
   that the author is not influenced directly by the scrolls but by the "common
   Israelite background" of priestly strands represented at Qumran. On 2 Baruch
   and 4 Ezra, see below.
3. Irenaeus in Eusebius *Hist. eccl.* 3.18.3; 5.30, where he refers to Domitian's persecution of the Christians. Aune 1997:lxiv–lxx notes that there is no reason to
   think that Domitian persecuted the Christians in particular nor to date Revelation specifically to his reign. Koester 2014:74–78 adds that Irenaeus cannot be
   trusted because he assumes that John is the apostle, which may be the reason
   for his dating of Revelation.
4. Yarbro Collins 1984:54–83: dated to the end of the reign of Domitian; Aune
   1997:lxvii–lxi: the final edition is completed toward the end of the reign of
   Domitian or even at the beginning of Trajan, though the first edition is based
   on traditions from the 60s; Koester 2014:65, 71, 79–80: in the period 80–100
   CE. Rev 17:9–11 refers to seven kings, nourishing many speculations on their
   identity—hence the chronology of Revelation. Aune 1997:lxi–lxiii, for example,
   sees here a reference to emperors after Nero (who dies in 68). Yarbro Collins
   1984:58–64 explores different possibilities and concludes that there is no reason
   to date Revelation later than Domitian. Cf. the critique of such attempts by
   Koester 2014:73–79.
5. Thompson 1990; Stevenson 2001. For language and symbols recognizable also to
   Greek and Romans, see, for example, Stevenson 2001:264, 297–298.
6. Yarbro Collins 1986:312.
7. See Aune 1998a:440–445 for survey of scholarship. Aune argues that it includes
   both Jews and Gentiles. So also Yarbro Collins 1998:405.
8. Stevenson 2001:252–257.
9. Stevenson 2001:225–228 with bibliographic survey of other suggestions. Cf. Yarbro Collins 1986:310–311; Bauckham 1993:124.
10. Yarbro Collins 1986:314. On the social situation of crisis and conflict with other
    Jews on the belief in Jesus, see Yarbro Collins 1984:85–87.
11. The Temple is opened here and in 15:5. Cf. opening the Temple's doors in 1 Kings
    3:15; 1 Chr 9:27; 2 Chr 29:3; Spatafora 1997:171. Elgvin 2009:269 notes that this
    may be either a manifestation of sanctity (he refers to the closed gate in the
    Temple court in m. *Tamid* 3:7) or a sign of destruction.
12. In Roman and Jewish sources a voice from the Temple might announce divine
    wrath. See Koester 2014:646. For Spatafora 1997:190–191, harvest is a metaphor
    for judgment. Koester 2014:628–662, however, sees it as potentially both posi-

tive or destructive. The grain harvest 14:15 recalls that the time of judgment has come in 14:7. Harvest has a negative meaning in many biblical sources, e.g., Joel 3:12; Isa 17:5; Matt 3:12. But Koester (ibid., 629) interprets the grain harvest as the ingathering of the faithful at the final coming of Christ.

13. "To pour out" (*ekchein*) has a cultic meaning, like pouring libations (Phil 2:17). See Aune 1998a:883. On angels in Revelation, see Aune 1998a:840–842.

14. Stevenson 2001:220–221. Stevenson (ibid., 235) states that the heavenly Temple mediates between the divine and the human. However, the humans present there are the ones exalted to heaven, while those on earth are judged for destruction. This is not a mediation of the sacred in the manner found in earthly Temples.

15. Koester 2014:628.

16. Aune 1998a:437. See also below.

17. For an example of viewing the heavenly Temple as representing the Endtime, see Beasely-Murray 1978:148. See Spatafora 1997:156–158, 297, 300; Beale 2004:317 for a coping with such confusion.

18. On these heavenly Temples, see Himmelfarb 1993.

19. Spatafora 1997:158, 253–257, 297–300.

20. For *mishkan* (dwellings) and *skēnēs* in ancient Jewish writings also designating the Jerusalem Temple, see Aune 1998a:876–878; Koester 2009:644. Koester notes the tradition that Moses sees the heavenly sanctuary (Wis 9:8; 2 Bar 4:5; Heb 8:1–6), implying that the heavenly Tabernacle in Revelation is the one that serves as a model for the Mosaic earthly one.

21. For this interpretation of smoke as theophany in light of biblical passages, see Aune 1998a:879–881. Cf. Ex 40:34–35. For inaccessibility to the sacred, see Ex 19:12–13; Lev 16:2; 2 Chron 7:1–2.

22. For a study of the throne and its Jewish origins, see Gallusz 2014.

23. Bauckham 1993:31.

24. Koester 2014:368.

25. Stevenson 2001:233–334, who also points to cultic elements in the throne scenes. For the Temple as the place of the throne, see Bauckham 1993:33.

26. Aune 1998a:404. Compare the souls' place under the throne in *Avot de-Rabbi Nathan*, version A, 26 (ed. Shechter, 82); b. Shabb 152b. Stevenson 2001:287–289 notes the meaning of asylum as protection and justice in Greco-Roman traditions, but this is already found in Ex 21:14 and 1 Kings 2:28–29. He sees here a sign that God executes justice and judgment from the altar (ibid., 301).

27. Aune 1998a:888 translates "someone from the altar," arguing that here the altar is not personified. He suggests that the voice belongs to one of the martyrs under the altar in 6:10 whose request for vengeance has not been answered yet. Koester 2009:648 maintains that the voice does not come from the altar itself. Rather, the author used metonymy, calling something by the name of something else in close relation to it, and the voice actually comes from the martyrs under the altar (6:9–11), just as a voice from the throne is a voice of someone on

or near the throne (16:17; 19:5). Koester 2009:465–466 prefers the possibility that the altar represents an angel in 9:13–14. The motif of a voice (*bat qol*) coming from the Temple (especially the holy of holies) manifests in rabbinic literature as a divine message. See, e.g., on the revelation to John (Hyrcanus), the high priest in b. *Sotah* 33a and par. Cf. Isa 66:6.

28. Allison 1986:410–411, referring to 4Q403 frag. 1, Col I, 38–46.

29. Aune 1998a:606 identifies it with the offerings altar, citing the use of the definite article in 11:1. Daly 1978:301 objects to this conclusion (referring to several others who have held it). He argues that there is no pouring of blood at the foot of the altar, and John merely means that the souls are preserved in proximity to God. Daly identifies it with the incense golden altar, but his reference to martyrdom as a sacrificial offering (Phil 2:17; 2 Tim 4:6, cf. Rom 12:1) does not support this identification, since these do not relate to incense.

30. According to Aune 1998a:536, the altar of the burnt offerings is mentioned on 6:9; 11:1 (see above); 14:18; 16:7. The incense altar is referred to in 8:3, 5; 9:13. For Spatafora 1997:169, most of the references are to the incense altar, but 6:9— which relates to the souls of the martyrs—is probably the sacrifice altar. Koester 2014:398 sees only a single altar, though it has multiple functions.

31. McKelvey 1969:166 n. 3 maintains that there is only one type of altar, as in other Jewish apocalyptic texts in which only the altar of the burnt offering appears. But, curiously, he adds that in Revelation this altar of blood sacrifices is spiritualized as the altar of incense. For Spatafora 1997:169, John spiritualizes the notion of sacrifice in referring to offering of incense and the sacrifices of the martyrs, whereas in 11:1 the altar is not real but rather symbolizes the Christian notion of sacrifice.

32. Koester 2014:398. He notes the similarity to the rite in which the blood of sacrificial victims is poured out at the base of the altar (Lev 4:7). This shows that God has received their death as a sacrifice (on humans' death as atonement, see 4 Macc 6:29; 17:22).

33. Aune 1997:356–359 notes the possible Jewish cultic background for the bowls of incense but adds that they may also echo Greek religion. Cf. Koester 2014:378. Note that in 15:7–16:21 the offering bowls bring judgment to earth.

34. Aune 1998a:515–518. Aune refers to a similar episode in Ezek 10:2 where an angel is commanded to fill his hands with burning coals from between the *cherubim* and scatter them over the city as a sign of judgment. Cf. the interpretation in b. Yoma 77a. He concludes that John applies this to the punishment of the pagans.

35. Ex 30:7–10; Lev 16:12–13; Num 17:11–15; m. *Tamid* 5:4–5.

36. Aune 1997:358, in relation to Rev 5:7. Koester 2014:379 confuses incense with the odor and fragrance of the sacrifice in Eph 5:2 and Phil 4:18 (they are all related to smoke: see chapter 2) and regards it as a metaphor for the acts of love.

37. Daly 1978:301–302. He refers to Philo's interpretation of the golden altar and incense as superior over the stone altar of bloody sacrifice (Spec. 1.273–277).

38. On the syntactical relationship between incense and prayers in 8:3–4, see Aune 1998a:512. Aune (ibid., 513) notes that in the latter case the incense is not a metaphor for prayer; rather, there is smoke from its burning, closely associated with prayer. He refers to prayer as incense in other contemporary sources, including Par. Jer. 9:1–4. Spatafora 1997:194 unwarrantedly states that the altar is a symbol of prayer.

39. For prayer (of the righteous) taking the place of sacrifice (of the wicked) in Qumran, see CD 11:20–21; 1QS 9:3–5 (regarding which see also chapter 2). This concept is probably the basis of the Songs of the Sabbath Sacrifices. On Didache, see chapter 9. For the manner in which prayer was modeled after the Temple cult in Second Temple Judaism, see Regev 2014b.

40. Aune 1997:88. The lampstand symbolizes the worship in the Temple in 4 Ezra 10:22. Its symbolism in Revelation may be rooted in the basic positive sense of light in the NT: Matt 5:14–16; John 8:12; Rev 4:5, etc.

41. Stevenson 2001:239. On the lampstand as the church, see Aune 1997:93–94; Koester 2014:245.

42. It is not clear whether the ark is destroyed (4 Ezra 10:22) or hidden to be restored in the future (2 Mac 2:4–8). Cf. the Samaritans' search for the holy vessels buried on Mount Gerizim (*Ant.* 18.85–86).

43. Compare Aune 1998a:677; Koester 2014:541. On the heavenly model of the Tabernacle, see Wis 9:8; *Ant.* 3.181; Philo QE 2.68; b. *Hag* 12b; Gen Rab 55.7.

44. Spatafora 1997:181–184.

45. McKelvey 1969:164.

46. For example, Schüssler Fiorenza 1972:142 views priesthood here as synonymous with holiness.

47. Schüssler Fiorenza 1972:336–338; Aune 1998b:1093.

48. Rev 5:7–8; 7:11, 15; 8:3–5; 15:5; 22:3–4 (in the New Jerusalem). See Stevenson 2001:239–240; Elgvin 2009:261–263. Elgvin 2009:263 comments that in 7:3 and 9:4 God's servants on earth are sealed with the name of the Lamb on their foreheads (cf. 14:1; Ezek 9:4). This seal symbolizes priestly ministry since the high priest wears the inscription "sanctified to the Lord" (Ex 28:36–37). McKelvey 1969:164 suggests that the white robes (15:5) are similar to the high priest's garments on the Day of Atonement. On white and clean clothes in 3:4–5, 18; 6:9–11; 22:14, see Elgvin 2009:265–266. These, however, are not distinctive priestly characteristics. As for the martyrs who wash their robes and make them white in the blood of the Lamb (7:14–15), Aune 1998a:475 notes that they are able to stand before God's throne only because of their purity, which is based upon the atoning death of Christ.

49. See Schüssler Fiorenza 1972:77–78.

50. For such an understanding, see Ulfgard 2009:258. Cf. Schüssler Fiorenza 1972:418–420.

51. 4Q400ShirShab 1 I, 3, 9, 12; 2 6–7, where they praise God and give Him glory, quite like Revelation. See Ulfgard 2009:260, 262.

52. Aune 1998b:1093. In 22:5 John stresses that they will rule for ever and ever after the millennium.

53. On the significance of the Christians' rule (kingship) in 1:6 and 5:10, see Schüssler Fiorenza 1972:227–236. On kingship in the Hellenistic world, see the survey in Regev 2013:131–133. For the high priesthood as associated with kingly authority, see ibid., 104–107, 171–173.

54. The Lamb is mentioned in Revelation twenty-eight times. See Bauckham 1993:66.

55. Aune 1997:353. Slaughter of the Lamb is also stressed in 5:12 and 13:8.

56. Daly 1978:298–300. According to Koester 2014:376–377, the slaughtered lamb, or the lamb who seems to have been slaughtered, symbolizes the sacrifice of deliverance (Passover) or the sacrifice of atonement. Yet there is no hint of Passover in relation to the Lamb. Daly 1978:301 notes the possible reflection of the suffering servant (Isa 53:7, cf. Jer 11:19).

57. Koester 2014:388.

58. Elgvin 2009:268.

59. As Bauckham 1993:64, summarizes, "Christ's sacrificial death belongs to the way God rules the world."

60. At times the Lamb is worshiped together with God (5:11; 7:9). In fact, the Lamb is not only worshiped but also paired with God. Yet it is subordinated to God in 22:3–4. On the Christology of Revelation and the worship of Christ, see Bauckham 1993:58–65.

61. According to McKelvey 1969:162, "The author selected what was the supreme moment in the life of every Jew and interpreted it spiritually in the light of Christ's Paschal victory and subsequent reign."

62. Aune 1997:241–242. In Philo, Q.E. 1.21, "Good men are the pillars of the whole community." In 1 Tim 3:15, the household of God, namely, the church, is the pillar of truth. Cf. Prov 9:1. On the pillars of the Christian community in Jerusalem in Gal 2:9, see chapter 5.

63. E.g., Aune 1997:241.

64. Aune 1997:242–243. Cf. the inscribing of God's name on Aaron's rosette (*tzitz*) in Ex 28:36–38; 39:30–31. Cf. b. *Sotah* 5a.

65. Koester 2009:265, 270–272.

66. For the various suggestions on the meaning of the tree of life and paradise, see Koester 2009:265–266; Stevenson 2001:245–249. For the present interpretation, see Koester 2009:271; Stevenson 2001:248. Cf. the description of paradise in the new creation in Rev 22:1–5. Stevenson 2001:250 adds that this promise fulfills the statement in 3:8 that Christ provides an open door of access to the kingdom.

67. Daly 1978:304 suggests that John alludes to the idea of the community as Temple but not consciously. See also Elgvin 2009:269. For others, the Temple is the one in the Endtime, in a metaphorical sense, which is united with the divine presence. See Spatafora 1997:146. Cf. ibid., 127–145. I find this idea obscure and unfounded.

68. Aune 1997:241. He refers to the pillars of the eschatological house in 1 En 90:29, but these are related to Enoch's New Jerusalem, not to the Temple.

69. Allison 1986:esp. 411. See 4Q403 frag. 1, Col I, 38–46.

70. Cf. Stevenson 2001:270.

71. Yarbro Collins 1984:66.

72. Aune 1998a:603. Cf. 1 Kings 22:11; Isa 8:1–4; 20:1–6; Jer 13:3–11; 27:1–28:16; Ezek 24:3; Acts 21:11. For the present interpretation, see Stevenson 2001:260, 262; Beale 2004:314–315.

73. Aune 1998a:594.

74. Charles 1920:1.270–273 (surveying previous scholarship); Beasley-Murray 1978:176–177; Briggs 1999:24–25 and n. 78. See the survey in Aune 1998a:594–596. Flusser 1988:390–452 reconstructs a Jewish source from the period before the First Revolt against Rome which is allegedly used by the author.

75. Yarbro Collins 1984:67–69 notes that John can hardly call the earthly historical city of Jerusalem "the holy city" (11:2), since he refers to it as Sodom and Egypt, where the Lord is crucified (11:8). She sees the passage as using a pre-70 tradition which serves as a response to the destruction after the rebels had believed that the Temple would not fall to the Romans (*War* 6.283–286). Nevertheless, it is not clear what kind of eschatological expectations are introduced here, since John adds that the city will be taken by the enemies.

76. Yarbro Collins 1984:67; Bauckham 1993:127; Aune 1998a:597–598; Spatafora 1997:169–170 (for whom the altar symbolizes the Christian notion of sacrifice). Koester 2014:284 suggests that the altar shows that God is preserving a community where true worship can take place. His identification of the Temple with the community is based upon the designation of the church as a lampstand, his interpretation of the pillar (3:12) as related to the Temple-community, and the idea that the believers are akin to priests (although we have seen that this is a designation of holiness and that the believers usually are not ministering as priests). See Beale 2004:314–320, although he also identifies the true Temple with Christ. For Beale, Revelation "depicts the Temple of the age to come as having broken into the present age" (ibid., 317). Beale builds his notion of the Temple as a community on the Qumranic identification of the saints with the heavenly community.

77. Koester 2014:485–486; Stevenson 2001:257–265. Compare the vulnerability of the witnesses in 11:8–10. Koester rightly notes that being trampled does not necessarily mean destruction but rather political domination. Beasley-Murray 1978:182 suggests that the outer court alludes to the court of Gentiles in the Temple and represents the unbelievers.

78. Giblin 1984:438–440. So Bachmann 1994, also because no other Temple is mentioned in Revelation.

79. Spatafora 1997:167; Briggs 1999:24–25 and n. 78.

80. Koester 2014:484–485.

81. Translation follows Koester 2014:793.

82. The twelve gates symbolize the twelve tribes of Israel, as in Ezek 48:33–34 and 5Q15 *NJar* 1:10. See Aune 1998b:1165; Lee 2001:276, 281.

83. On the list of stones or gems, see Koester 2014:817–818. He favors the idea that the people of the New Jerusalem resemble the high priest.

84. Bauckham 1993:129. Compare 21:27 with 17:4–5.

85. Rev 21:1–2; Lee 2001:270.

86. McKelvey 1969:170.

87. McKelvey 1969:177; Stevenson 2001:267–268. There is disagreement as to whether the New Jerusalem actually symbolizes the saints. McKelvey 167–176 holds that it does, and Schüssler Fiorenza 1972:348–350 claims it does not. Aune 1998b:1122 notes that saints dwell here.

88. As argued by Lee 2001:277; Stevenson 2001:272. Compare the conversion of Gentiles in 11:13; 14:14–16; 15:4. Cf. Bauckham 1993:138–139.

89. Lee 2001:271, 301–302.

90. Note that the heavenly Jerusalem represents the new covenant of freedom in Gal 4:26. Cf. the disappearance of heaven and earth in Mark 13:31 and Matt 5:18. Compare the expectations for the New Creation, e.g., Jub 1:29; 4:26; 4 Ezra 7:75; Sib. Or. 5.212; Matt 19:28; 2 Pet 3:13, and perhaps also 1 En 91:16.

91. This also explains the origins of the idea of the brightness of the New Jerusalem in Rev 21:23; 22:5a. Cf. the brightness of the Heavenly Temple in 1 En 14:20–2; Lee 2001:293–294.

92. 2 Bar 32:6; 44:12; 49:3; 57:2; 73–74; 4 Ezra 7:26, 30–31; 10:54; 13:36; Lee 2001:129–139, 146–157. See also Aune 1998b:1116–1118, also noting Greek parallels from the second century BCE.

93. Aune 1998b:1122–1123; Koester 2014:797. For God's presence in the holy city, see also Isa 1:26; Jer 3:17; Ezek 48:35; Zech 8:3.

94. Isa 2:2; Zech 14:16–21; Tob 1:4; 14:5; 1 En 91:13 (the Apocalypse of Weeks); Jub 1:17, 28; 2 Bar 32:2–4; 11Q18 10 I, 2; Sib. Or. 5.422.

95. Lee 2001:282.

96. McKelvey 1969:176. On the holy of holies, see 1 Kings 6:2; m. *Middot* 4.6. Cf. Lee 2001:283–284. McKelvey refers to the pillar in 3:12 as proof of the existence of this new Temple, but, as explained above, the passage probably relates to the heavenly one.

97. Bauckham 1993:132–139.

98. 2 Sam 6; 24; Ps 132:5–14. For the Temple Scroll, Jerusalem is "the city of the Temple" (e.g., 45:7–17).

99. Beale 2004:317; Aune 1998b:1166–1167.

100. Koester 2014:821. He also notes that for Paul the Temple is a metaphor not for Christ but for the Church. Hence we should not confuse Revelation's approach toward the Lamb in relation to the true Temple with other early Christian variations of the Temple theme.

101. Hoffman 2001:155, 166. He notes that at the time of the prophecy the Ark is no longer available. The last mention of it is in the reign of Josiah (2 Chr 35:3),

when the prophet has lost hope for its return. Jeremiah thus rejects tangible religious symbols (such as swearing upon the Ark) owing to preference for belief in the covenant with God. On the Cheruvim as God's throne, see 1 Sam 4:4; 2 Sam 6:2; Isa 37:16; Ps 99:1; cf. Num 7:89.

102. Tiller 1993:41–50 (following Dimant). Cf. the Tabernacle as tower in 1 En 89:32–33 and the impure tower in the restoration period in 1 En 89:73. Flusser 1988:454–565 tries to explain how John reaches the conclusion that there will be no Temple in the city in the messianic age. Based on a much later rabbinic midrash regarding the Messiah as the "lamp" instead of the Temple, Flusser reconstructs an earlier Jewish exegesis (on which John allegedly depends) which identifies the Messiah with "the lamp" based on Isa 60:19 and Ps 132:17.

103. Stone 1990:324 n. 43 and references. This absence is surprising given the lament on the loss of sacrifices and the Temple (4 Ezra 3:24; 10:21; cf. 10:45–46). See also the rebuilding of the city but not the Temple in 4 Ezra 3:24. Lee 2001:131–132 argues that the author identifies the Temple with Jerusalem. Najman 2014:108–125 argues that 4 Ezra 3:6; 10:27, 44; 13:36 (cf. 2 Bar 4:1–4) discusses not only paradise and the New City of Zion but also the building by God of the eschatological Temple. Nevertheless, she admits that this is expressed "elliptically" and that the author does not "portray" the divine restoration of the Temple (ibid., 121, 124).

104. No distinction: Murphy 1987:671; a relative lack of interest in the eschaton, ibid., 682–683.

105. Young 1972:311–312. Cf. Aune 1998b:1168.

106. Koester 2014:831–832; Lee 2001:279, 229. In a sense, the city, the New Jerusalem, becomes a theophany, a direct encounter with God. But it does not become a Temple by itself (contra McKelvey 1969:176) since God and the Lamb are its Temple. See Spatafora 1997:239–240. Compare the later postrabbinic view that in the world to come God will forgive sins without need of sacrifices (following Isa 43:25): Tanhuma *shmini* 6 (ed. Buber, 24).

107. As does, for example, Lee 2001:283, 302–303.

108. Stevenson 2001:268–270. For the parallels, see also Lee 2001:302. Stevenson (ibid., 270–271) points to similarities to Ezek 40–48 which link the New Jerusalem to the Temple: measuring (21:15–17; Ezek 40:3–42:20); river (22:1–2; Ezek 47:1–12); a voice that promises to live with the people (21:3; Ezek 43:6–7); and God's throne (21:3, 5; 22:1, 3; Ezek 43:7). All of these show how Revelation transforms Ezekiel's imagery and that the New Jerusalem fulfills Ezek 37:26–27, which describes God's dwelling place. Stevenson maintains that the New Jerusalem fulfills earlier references to the Temple in 3:12 and 7:15, as those who serve God in the city actually serve in his Temple. This seems improbable since the author explicitly denies the existence of a Temple in the New Jerusalem.

109. See McKelvey 1969:177; Yarbro Collins 1984:67.

110. For the rebels' Temple ideology, see Regev 2014a.

111. Murphy 1987:676 similarly concludes that the heavenly city serves the purpose of directing the attention of readers away from the catastrophe of 70 CE toward heaven. The absence of the Temple causes the author to focus on the heavenly world and to deemphasize the rebuilding of the Temple. On shifting attention to the other world, see ibid., 681. For 4 Ezra's approach to the Temple, see Najman 2014. For early rabbinic preference of the Torah over the Temple, see the introduction.

112. The main clue is the holding of palm branches and renouncing of God's salvation (as in the *hallel* prayer at the Temple, m. *Sukkah* 4:5) in 7:10. On 7:9–17 as hinting at the feast of Booths, see McKelvey 1969:163, 169 (who also finds similar imagery in the New Jerusalem); Draper 1985. See, however, the criticism of Aune 1998a:448–450.

113. 1 En 14: 8–25; T. Levi 3:5–8; 18:6; Apoc. Abr. 29:17–18; Himmelfarb 1993. Cf. the Temple's divine template in Wis 9:8; 2 Bar 4:3.

114. The Heikhalot literature continues priestly tradition and the Temple-centered worldview. It also discusses high priests and refers to the altar. See Elior 1995:348–351.

115. For introduction and critical edition, see Charlesworth and Newsom 1999. The idea of heavenly worship of God is mentioned elsewhere in the Dead Sea Scrolls, see Regev 2007:369–371.

116. The Songs distinguish between the *'ulam* and *devir* (the outer and inner sanctum) in 4Q405 frags. 14–15, col 1, 10–13. The *devir* is mentioned frequently in the Songs (e.g., 4Q403 1 b 32–38). See also references to the Temple veil, e.g., 4Q405 frags. 15+16 3, 5.

117. The throne is mentioned in Songs in 4Q405 frags. 20–22, col. 2, 2–4. 9; frag. 23, col. 1, 3.

118. 11Q17 frags. 21–22 col. 9, 4–5 (in the 13th song, perhaps at the culmination of the liturgy). It is impossible to say whether it refers to blood sacrifices, since the context is missing owing to the fragmentary nature of the preservation of the entire scroll.

119. Himmelfarb 1993:33–36. T. Levi 3:6 mentions bloodless sacrifices and offerings. Plain sacrifices are mentioned in Apoc. Abr. 29:17–18. In the Songs the angels atone for the sins of those who repent (4Q400 1, 16).

120. E.g., Yarbro Collins 1984:89–110, 121–124, 314–316. On Roman religious institutions, see Scherrer 1984. On Revelation's polemic against Roman imperial cult, see the list of references in Scherrer 1984:599 n. 1.

121. Cf. Yarbro Collins 1986:314, 394–396.

122. Although there is no evidence for organized persecution by Domitian, Asian Christians are harassed, ridiculed, and oppressed in the early 90s. Rev 2–3 refers to their suffering. John also fears upcoming executions (16:6; 17:6). See Slater 1998; cf. Yarbro Collins 1984:85, 98.

123. Yarbro Collins 1986:315–316.

124. Bauckham 1993:8–9, 35, 38.

125. Yarbro Collins 1984:152–154, 165–166.
126. Compare the common view that in Heikhalot literature the heavenly Temple is a reaction or compensation for the destruction of the Temple. See Elior, 1995:345–347.
127. Yarbro Collins 1984:99–100. Cf. above Aune's conclusion regarding the author's Judaean origins. Yarbro Collins also argues that the author makes sense of the destruction by blaming Jerusalem for the rejection of Jesus. She also concludes that New Jerusalem language compensates for the loss of the city and the Temple (ibid., 99). However, the compensation of the heavenly Temple is far more immediate.
128. On the heavenly Temple as a symbol of early Christian communal identity, see Stevenson 2001:235–236, 279.

Chapter 8. Hebrews

1. Manson 1951:vi. Cf. Gäbel 2006:472–483; McKelvey 2013:205; the references in Ribbens 2016:136 n. 240. See, for example, Salevao 2002: esp. 208–210, who also claims (and attempts to explain) Hebrews' separation from Judaism (e.g., ibid., 171, 197).
2. Manson 1951:32, 34, 169. He also argues that Hebrews puts "an end to the Law and the Cultus of Israel."
3. Church 2017:esp. 404–421, building on Heb 9:11, in which Jesus passed *through* (*dia*) the heavenly Temple, and *hupodeigma kai skia* (8:5) as symbolic fore-shadowing.
4. Koester 2001:46–47. He also notes references to the "descendants of Abraham" (2:16) and allusions to the Law in 13:9–10. However, Koester also lists possible indications for a mixed audience of Jews and Gentiles, such as warnings about falling away from the living God (3:12). On the Old Testament citations, compare the intertextual (and traditional) priestly discourse pointed out by deSilva 2006. Dunnill 1992:24–25 notes that the author does not raise the problem of circumcision. For Jewish-Christian readers, see also Manson 1951:156–158 and passim. Some think that the readers are Christians who intend to return to Judaism, e.g., Bruce 1965: xxiii–xxx.
5. Lane 1991:lxi–lxii. He refers to the danger of apostasy and mentions that some are interested in listening to preaching and Scripture (2:1; 2:7–4:13; 12:25). On the thesis that the danger is that readers will return to Judaism, see the final section of this chapter.
6. Lane 1991:lxii. On the very obscure internal and external clues for dating, see Koester 2001:50–54.
7. Lane 1991:lxii–lxiii; Attridge 1989:6.
8. Attridge 1989:9; Salevao 2002:107–108 (who also adds the Epistle of Barnabas).
9. Attridge 1989:8.
10. Koester 2001:52–53; Lindars 1991:4. Lane 1991:218 adds that the Tabernacle also relates to the old covenant in contrast to the new one.

11. Attridge 1989:8.
12. Schenck 2007:196–197.
13. Isaacs 1992:43–44, 67; cf. Koester 2001:53.
14. Schenck 2007:196. Cf. Brown and Meier 1983:150–151. Another possible chronological indication is that the sacrificial cult is being referred to in the present
tense as if it still operates in the Temple. This, however, is only a literary style. It
does not necessarily allude to contemporary practices prior to 70. Other writers
also use the present tense in writing about the Temple cult when it is no longer
extant. Attridge 1989:8; Koester 2001:53. Cf. *Ant.* 4.224–257; *Against Apion* 2.77,
193–198; 1 Clem 41.2. See Lane 1991:lxiii, 218.
15. Lane 1991:lxiv–lxvi; Salevao 2002:104–108. Cf. Attridge 1989:8.
16. Koester 2001:53–54 notes scholars who date Hebrews before 70 mainly because
the destruction is not mentioned and those dating it to the 80–90s because
they assume that it is a reaction to the loss of the Temple. For pre-70 dating, see
also Lindars 1991:19, 87; Walker 1994; Church 2017:14–16, with a bibliographic
survey.
17. Attridge 1989:217–218. Christ is called simply a priest in 7:3, 11, 15; 8:14, but this
seems to be a shortened form for high priest, as in Ps 110:4.
18. Regev 2013:104. Note that Philo sees the priesthood as perfect and moral
while Josephus argues that the priests are of highest character. See Koester
2001:358–359.
19. Cf. Stuart 1968.
20. 4Q543 *Visions of Amram^a ar* frag. 3, 1; 4Q541 *Aaron A* 9 i (otherwise known
as *4QTestament of Levi^a(?)* or *4QApocryphe de Lévi^b?* ar); Fletcher-Louis
2002:187–192. See also the later T. Levi 2–5.
21. 1QSb 4:24–26. Translation follows Fletcher-Louis 2002:150. See the scholarship
and discussion in Fletcher-Louis 2002:151–158.
22. Fletcher-Louis 2002:152–153; Regev 2007:361–362.
23. The *nezer*, mentioned in 1QSb 4:28, bears God's most holy name, the *tetragram-
maton*. Cf. Ex. 29:6; 39:30; Lev 8:9; Fletcher-Louis 2002:155.
24. See *Ant.* 11.317–319. On the debate about the political role of the high priests in
these periods, see Regev 2013:105–107.
25. CD 12:23–13:1; 14:19; 19:10–11; 19:35–20:1; 1QS 9:11. Messianic meal: 1QSa 2:11–22.
Compare the priority of the priest in the meals of the *yahad* (1QS 6:4–5). The
War Rule refers to both the prince (*nasi*) of the congregation and the leading
priest (1QM 5:1; 15:4; 16:13; 19:12). See also Mason 2008:83–109. The phenomenon of two messianic figures is attested to in the pre-Qumranic 4Q213 *Levi^a
ar* 1 II + 2, 15–19.
26. Yadin 1958. Danielou 1958:111–113 relates it to Essenes. See the survey in Isaacs
1992:38–41.
27. For detailed and cautious assessment, see Braun 1966:1.241–278; 2.181–184. He
concludes that the similarities relate to scriptural citations and exegetical methods but nonetheless reflect different ideas. Isaac 1992:40–41 lists differences be-

tween Hebrews and Qumran, concluding against a direct link with Hebrews, preferring a common Jewish heritage. See also Attridge 2004.

28. Attridge 1989:99, 103 notes that in 11QMelk (discussed below) and perhaps also T. Levi 18, the priestly messiah is an angel. Since angels serve in the heavenly cult, he suggests that priestly angels are the basis of the understanding of Christ as a high priest. On the debate concerning Hebrews portraying Jesus as an angel, see Mason 2008:133–137.

29. Manson 1951:54, 108–109. See the survey in Lane 1991: cxl–cxli, cl. In chapter 1 I mentioned the thesis that the Historical Jesus already sees himself as the new high priest.

30. Attridge 1989:102. See Ignatius Phld. 9:1; Mart. Pal 14.3; Polycarp Phil. 12.2.

31. Koester 2001:109.

32. Koester 2001:296, 298.

33. Haber 2005:106, 112.

34. Ribbens2016 . According to deSilva 2006 Hebrews introduces Jesus as a reenactment of the Levitical priests' ministry in a quite conservative manner.

35. Koester 2001:373.

36. Horbury 1983:50–51, 64–65. He also notes the close relationship between the red heifer rite and the Day of Atonement (as attested to in rabbinic sources).

37. Lane 1991:194 sees here a major argument for the ineffectiveness of the Levitical high priests: How can a person who needs to atone for his own sins also do the same for others?

38. Koester 2001:373.

39. Attridge 1989:200. Another advantage of Jesus is that "we do not have a high priest who is unable to sympathize with our weaknesses, but we have one who in every respect has been tested as we are, yet without sin" (4:15). This, however, does not really conflict with the Levitical high priest, since the latter also "is able to deal gently with the ignorant and wayward, since he himself is subject to weakness" and first offers sacrifices for himself (5:2–3).

40. The passage implies that Christ "remains" in his office and thus belongs to the divine realm of spirit and power because of his heavenly perfection. See Attridge 1989:209–210. On Christ's perfection, see Ribbens 2016:169–177. As we will see shortly, the basis for the new priesthood is the biblical verse "you are a priest *for ever*" (Ps 110:4), which may imply that this high priest will live forever.

41. Lane 1991:cxli; Koester 2001:346. Lindars 1991:76 notes the similarity between Melchizedek and the Son of God (cf. Ps 2:7 cited in Heb 5:5). Cf. Attridge 1989:145–147. On Jesus as the Son of God, see Heb 7:3, 28; 10:29 (cf. Mark 1:11; 9:7).

42. Koester 2001:287.

43. *War* 6.438. See also Philo's admiration of him as the "king of peace" and "having, as its inheritance the true God, and entertaining lofty and sublime and magnificent ideas about him" (*Leg. Alleg.* 3.79–82).

44. Koester 2001:345–347. Cf. Callaway 2013:153.

45. Attridge 1989:187; Lane 1991:169, 171. Dunnill 1992:165–166 notes that the author integrates priestly and kingly functions.
46. 11Q13*Melchizedek* II 5–25; Mason 2008:184–186. Interestingly, Melchi Zedek, identified as the Prince of Light, and the angel Michael are mentioned in 4Q544*Visions of Amram* 3 IV 2–3. See Mason 2008:167–168.
47. Attridge 1989:191–192. On Melchizedek's character, see Philo, *Leg. Alleg.* 3.79–82. In 11Q13*Melchizedek* II 6–8, he "will make them return . . . to free them from [the debt of] all their iniquities . . . in which atonement shall be made for all the sons of [light and] for the men [of] the lot of Mel[chi]zedek."
48. According to Mason 2008:200, the portrait of Melchizedek in 11Q13*Melchizedek* bears more similarities to Hebrews' presentation of Jesus than to the latter's discussion of Melchizedek.
49. Attridge 2004:332–333.
50. Confirms the new eternal priesthood: Attridge 1989:207. More binding than the Law: Lane 1991:194–195.
51. Lane 1991:184; Koester 2001:109.
52. Cf. Attridge 1989:142–144.
53. Lane 1991:119 suggests that Jesus's offering (*prosenegkas*) of prayers parallels the high priest's gifts and sacrifices. On similar terminology of offering in Hebrews, cf. ibid., 186, 192.
54. Koester 2001:282.
55. Brooks 1970:206; Daly 1978:267–269. Cf. Koester 2001:359.
56. Koester 2001:109–110 discusses these two aspects and refers to the debate about whether or not Christ's priesthood begins on earth in his earthly life, without pointing out the contradiction that this entails. See also Moffitt 2011.
57. Koester 2001:293–294 notes that his sinlessness does not derive from being a high priest. See Stewart 1967–1968, who observes that ancient Jewish sources seldom portray the high priest as sinless. Attridge 1989:212, on the other hand, relates his being holy, blameless, undefiled, and separated from sinners to the priestly features listed in Lev 21:11, 17.
58. Attridge 1989:210; Koester 2001:365.
59. Manson 1951:115 relates them all to his high priesthood, although the priestly title is defined only in relation to some of them.
60. Koester 2001:360–361.
61. Lane 1991:194. On the Day of Atonement pattern, see Moffitt 2011:217–220, 256–285.
62. The latter act is an inaccurate simplification of Scripture, since Moses sprinkles the blood only on the altar and the priestly garments (Lev 8:15, 19, 24, 30; 9:9, 12).
63. Cf. Attridge 1989:257; Koester 2001:415. Heb 9:13 does not conform to the Jewish rite since there is no sprinkling of blood of goats and bulls on defiled persons. There is no reason to associate the sprinkling of the red heifer ashes, which are used for cleansing in cases of corpse impurity, with sin-offering (*contra* At-

tridge 1989:248). Daly 1978:272–273 argues that the author is not concerned with presenting the Old Testament accurately but freely uses the cultic institutions to serve his own argumentative purposes.

64. Lane 1991:542. Cf. Moffitt 2011:277. Koester 1962 argues that the author intends to show that the sacrifice of Jesus, which makes people clean, is performed outside of the camp. That is, his act of cleansing is performed in a profane place, *abolishing* all cultic performances. Lane 1991:445 criticizes this approach, since the text has no cultic sense of a profane space but merely of a hostile environment. Note that the author pushes this metaphor further when he portrays the Christians' life as taking place also "outside the camp," where they are abused, looking for "the city that is to come" (13:13–14).

65. Ribbens 2016:149–163, esp. 160, 162: "That Christ's sacrifice is greater does not diminish the assumption that the old covenant sacrifices achieved forgiveness of sins. . . . Christ's sacrifice must follow the pattern of the levitical sacrifice for it to be accepted as an atoning sacrifice." Cf. Manson 1951:144–145. Eberhart 2005:60 maintained that Heb 10:14 denies the validity of the sacrificial cult. However, 9:13 uses the effectiveness of the cult as the foundation of the metaphor engaging Christ's sacrifice.

66. Koester 2001:414, referring to Heb 10:1.

67. Dunnill 1992:237.

68. Koester 2001:121. He notes that atonement also means "averting God's wrath" (Num 17:11–16; 25:11). On the priestly sensitivity to impurity and desecration, see Regev 2001. On the cult and the fear of God's wrath in Qumran, see the introduction.

69. Lindars 1991:10, 14, 59.

70. Koester 2001:298–299.

71. Attridge 1989:250–151.

72. Lane 1991:193.

73. Koester 2001:110.

74. Attridge 1989:245. Heb 13:10 mentions that "we have an altar from which those who officiate in the Tabernacle have no right to eat," but it is unclear to what contemporary practice the author refers. Suggestions include the Eucharist and the heavenly Temple. See Stott 1962–1963:66; Lane 1991:537–538.

75. Brooks 1970:209–210. On Christ's blood and its effect following the priestly Law, see Moffitt 2011:257–271. Ribbens 2016:154–159 points out that the blood (of the sacrificed animal) achieves forgiveness for sins (cf. 5:1, 3; 7:27; 9:7) in the new covenant, despite the denial of sacrifice and blood to accomplish forgiveness in 10:4, 11.

76. Lane 1991:472; Attridge 1989:250. However, in 12:24 Jesus's blood is *sprinkled* to signify the new covenant. See Attridge 1989:376. On sprinkling for the inauguration of a new covenant or consecration of the priest, see Heb 9:18–21, discussed above.

77. Lane 1991:238, 240. Some regard the shedding of Jesus's blood as real: Attridge 1989:248; Cockerill 2012:394; cf. Ribbens 2016:118.

78. Koester 2001:415–416. For many, Jesus atones/purifies "by means of" (*dia*) his blood, without actually performing the priestly rite: Brooks 1970:209–210; Gäbel 2006:284–285, 288; Moffitt 2011:224, 273.

79. On Jesus's death, see Rom 5:6–8; 6:6; Phil 2:7; Dunn 1974. Hebrews does refer to Jesus's death elsewhere (2:14; 9:15). On Jesus's blood, see Rom 3:25; 5:9; Eph 1:7; 2:13; Col 1:20.

80. Claims for Christ's death removing sin and purifying are found in Acts 15:9; Tit 2:14; 1 John 1:7, 9. However, in Hebrews the dominant image is more complex and builds on priestly imagery: the pouring of blood on the altar removes sin ritually (cf. Ex 30:10). See Attridge 1989:250. Cf. Koester 2001:412–413.

81. On the purification of the heavenly Tabernacle, see Jamieson 2016. On the sin as its target, see Moret 2016. Some interpret the purification of the heavenly Tabernacle (9:23) as a metaphor for cleansing one's conscience (e.g., Attridge 1989:262) perhaps because 9:22 relates purification to forgiveness. Many think it actually purifies the Temple in heaven (Dunnill 1992:232–234; Lane 2000:247; Koester 2001:421, 427), which may be supported by parallels from Second Temple literature. Ribbens 2016:120–124 concludes that Christ actually inaugurates the heavenly sanctuary (as Moses inaugurates the old covenant in 9:18): in one offering Christ consecrates the heavenly sanctuary, inaugurates the new covenant, and atones for sins.

82. Eberhart 2005:56–57; Dunnill 1992:140. Cf. Brooks 1970:208; Lindars 1991:84.

83. Attridge 1989:183, 185 concludes that this relates to his sacrificial death and that the veil encloses the presence of God.

84. Calaway 2013:113. Cf. Lane 1991:224.

85. Compare the spiritual aspect of the *asham* sacrifice (guilt offering, Lev 5), in Milgrom 1976.

86. Eberhart 2005:60.

87. Here, the author implies that the sacrifices are brought annually, probably referring to those of the Day of Atonement. This is repeated in 9:25–26. However, in 10:11 the problem is with the ordinary priest's daily sacrifice for sin ("and every priest stands day after day at his service, offering again and again the same sacrifices that can never take away sins"). However, the daily sacrifices (*tamid*) are not sin-offerings but whole-burnt sacrifice (Ex 29:41–42).

88. Koester 2001:399; Ribbens 2016:178.

89. On the platonic aspect of this argument, see Attridge 1989:270. See, however, Lane 2000:259.

90. In assuming that the high priest is required to offer *day-by-day* sacrifice—first for his own sins and then for the people's—the author (erroneously?) conflates daily and Day of Atonement sacrifices (Attridge 1989:213; Koester 2001:367–368). Lane suggests that he echoes the tradition that Aaron or the high priest offer daily sacrifices both for himself and the people (Sir 45:14; Philo, *Spec.*

Laws 3.131 also refer to daily blessings for the sake of the people). In any event, this serves the author well, implying that the high priest needs to atone for his own guilt day by day.

91. Lane 1991:194–195; Koester 2001:428.

92. Lane 1991:206.

93. Ribbens 2016:163–184.

94. Lindars 1991:78.

95. Calaway 2013:138. The question remains whether Jesus's self-sacrifice in 7:27 is metaphorical. Compare other sacrificial metaphors pertaining to the crucifixion in 1 John 1:7 and Rev 7:14 and the different sacrificial metaphors in Rom 12:1; Eph 5:2, etc. See Eberhart 2005:56–57.

96. Gäbel 2006:425–466.

97. Brooks 1970:212. Cf. Eberhart 2005:59.

98. Calaway 2013:160. Scholer 1991 reads the call to draw near (see 10:19, 22) as priestly imagery describing approaching the altar. However, the believers are not designated as priests. In fact, their position is precarious; it would be improper to suggest that they enjoy some sacerdotal privilege or right of divine favor. They are totally dependent on God's grace. Also, they are not supposed to sacrifice anything. All mediation is exercised by Christ (Dunnill 1992:234, 259).

99. Heb 13:10 declares that "we have an altar," but the meaning is obscure. Scholars disagree whether there is any reference to the Eucharist in Hebrews. For skepticism, see Swetnam 1966; Williamson 1975; Lindars 1991:10, 77, 96; Attridge 1989:392–396. Koester 2001:127–129 argues that the lack of mention of the Eucharist is coincidental and does not imply its rejection. Heb 5:7 stresses Jesus's prayer before his death and later refers to the believers' (communal?) prayer as a sacrifice: "Let us continually offer a sacrifice of praise to God"; that is, the fruit of lips that confess his name (13:15). However, here (and in Rev 5:8; 8:3–4), prayer does not replace sacrifice (Koester 2001:378), although throughout the epistle sacrifice is "spiritualized." It is interesting that despite his alternative to the sacrificial cult, the author still needs to portray the institute of prayer as modeled upon sacrifice. See the discussion in chapter 7. This is but one sacrificial metaphor among many in Hebrews. On prayer as sacrifice here in light of other biblical texts, see Daly 1978:283; Attridge 1989:400.

100. A heavenly Temple not made by human hands is mentioned in the Sibylline Oracles 4.11, which are redacted after 70 CE (Collins 1983:382; Sib. Or. 4.116 refers to the Temple's destruction by Rome). Attridge 1989:223 points out similarities to Philo's dichotomy between earthly and heavenly temples, preferring the transcendent Temple as the true and perhaps also moral one.

101. Lane 1991:207–208 associates the heavenly Temple with an eschatological one, probably because it is supposed to last forever. However, I would stress that for the believers the heavenly one is already present.

102. Beale 2004:296–297.

103. Attridge 1989:220.
104. The problem is introduced by MacRae 1978; cf. Hurst 1990:24–27, 42–66. For heaven as a Temple, see Philo, *Spec.* 1.66 (see the equation of the holy of holies to heaven in *Ant.* 3.123, 181); McKelvey 1969:151. For a Temple in heaven, see Calaway 2013:105, 113; cf. Moffitt 2016:69–81. Compare the heavenly city in Heb 11:16; 12:22, which probably does not mean that the entire heaven is a city.
105. Koester 2001:383. See Wis 9:8; Philo, *Vit. Mos.* 2.74 (on which, see Attridge 1989:219). Lane 1991:207 notes that in Hebrews there is no strict Platonic dualism between the material and the spiritual, since the distinction between the Tabernacle and the heavenly Temple is dependent on a historical situation. Actually, in Second Temple Judaism the heavenly cult served to legitimize its earthly counterpart. See Ribbens 2016:52–81, 81, 137.
106. Lane 1991:206. McKelvey 1969:149 takes the comparison too far in concluding that "by representing the heavenly sanctuary as the true sanctuary and its earthly counterpart as its shadow the writer very effectively demonstrates the transcendence and superiority of Christianity over Judaism." One should also bear in mind that the author does use the conceptions of Judaism or Christianity.
107. On *hupodeigma* as pattern, blueprint, or preliminary sketch to be followed (8:5; 9:23), see Hurst 1990:13–17. A similar distinction of shadow and reality applies to the Law in 10:1.
108. Attridge 1989:260–261; Calaway 2013:107.
109. Koester 2001:427, noting that "the law has only a shadow of the good things to come" (10:1). Others see here an inauguration of Jesus's high priesthood (Spicq) or the purification of the heavenly sanctuary (Gäbel). See the survey in Calaway 2013:157–158.
110. On the Day of Atonement imagery, see Attridge 1989:248; Moffitt 2011:217–220, 256–285. On the red heifer typology (10:22), see Gäbel 2006:375–392.
111. Church 2017:esp. 273, 404–411 argues that it is a metaphor for the eschatological Temple, the dwelling of God with His people. However, Moffitt 2011:275–276, 298 and Ribbens 2016:129 rightly conclude that the Temple is real, not metaphoric. It is the "true Tabernacle" (8:2), analogical to the sacrificial cult. See also Stegemann and Stegemann 2005:15–18. Moffitt 2016:275–276 maintains that Jesus's high priestly office in heaven, his sacrifice, and blood are not metaphors but part of an analogy to the sacrificial cult.
112. Attridge 1989:245–247, 263–264. Brooks 1970:210–211 rightly notes that in Hebrews *skēnē* cannot represent Jesus's body (cf. John 2:21), since Jesus passes through it (9:11). In fact, Hebrews diverges from the cultic symbolism in Mark 15:29 or John 2:21, which use *naos* when it uses *skēnē* or *hagia*. Furthermore, in Hebrews the cult is replaced not by the church but by Jesus, in addition to being relocated to heaven. See Isaacs 1992:109, 146–147, 150.
113. Gäbel 2006:252–253.

114. Moffitt 2011:42, 216–220, 228–230, 276, followed by Ribben 2016:108, 135. Just as the Day of Atonement sacrifice involved a process that included slaughter and blood application, so also Hebrews describes Christ's sacrifice as a process that includes his death as a victim on earth, entrance into the heavenly sanctuary via his ascension, and presentation of the offering in the heavenly Holy of Holies. Thus while Christ's sacrifice begins on earth, he does not act as priest until he is in the heavenly realm, where his priestly act of sacrifice includes the presentation of himself as an offering.

115. On the identification and character of the curtain, see Calaway 2013:114 n. 49.

116. Attridge 1989:217 (and scholars cited in n. 22), 285, 287; Lane 1991:218–219, 223. Cf. Moffitt 2011:222, 282–283; Ribbens 2016:116–117, 165. Koester 2001:409 and Schenck 2016:249–250 do not accept this distinction. Note that the author is mistaken in placing the golden altar of incense in the inner sanctum.

117. Schenck 2016:254.

118. Attridge 1989:262.

119. For broader discussion, see Regev 2017b.

120. Koester 2001:354–355. See also Attridge 1989:203–205 and a quite similar idea in Rom 5:20.

121. Koester 2001:360.

122. Manson 1951:114.

123. Daly 1978:266–267.

124. Manson 1951:114–115. He also notes the differences between the two (ibid., 193, 195–196) concerning ideas of atonement and relationship with God.

125. Heb 13:9 speaks obscurely against "regulations about food." Lindars 1991:10–11 interprets them as ritual meals; Walker 1994 reads them as festival meals; Koester 2001:560–561 as food practices and perhaps the blessing over them; and Attridge 1989:395 entertains the suggestion that the passage repudiates the Eucharist.

126. Joslin 2008:158–164. Koester 2001:115, 359 points out that Hebrews' attitude toward the Law is much more complex than simple rejection.

127. Transformation: Joslin 2008:133–134, 166–167, following BDAG. See similar use of the word in Ps. Arist. 160; Philo *De Gigantibus,* 66; Josephus *Against Apion* 1.286.

128. Heb 7:16–19; 9:10–11; 10:1. See Lane 1991:181–182; Lane 2000:482. On the cultic context of the Law's shadow (10:1), see Ribbens 2016:186–188.

129. Attridge 1989:131 and Lane 1991:101–102 agree that this terminology refers to Sabbath observance.

130. Dunnill 1992. On Mount Zion, see ibid., 144–146.

131. Lindars 1991:46–47.

132. Lindars 1991:59, 63.

133. Manson 1951:vi, 24 (citations), 32, 34, 169. For references to additional scholars holding the same view, see Koester 2001:57 n. 123.

134. Koester 2001:57. On the Tabernacle in Stephen's speech, see Koester 1989:82–85.

135. For a survey of theories on the situation of the readers and what the letter responds to, see Lindars 1991:4–8.
136. Isaacs 1992:25 n. 2 reviews scholars who argue that the author addresses Christians who desire to return to Judaism. Cf. also Moule 1950:37; Motyer 2004:189.
137. Lindars 1991:90. On Philo, see Nikiprowetzky 1967.
138. Motyer 2004.
139. Koester, 2001:382, 428; Gäbel 2006:484–488. Brown sees here a threat of reversion to the Jewish sacrificial system by Christians in Rome after 70, reviving the cult based on the Tabernacle (Brown and Meier 1983:151–158). Moule 1950:35, 37–39 suggests that Hebrews aims to explain why only Christianity has no sacrificial system. In quite a different vein, Koester 2001:78–79 suggests that Hebrews is competing with Greco-Roman cults, since it gives the readers "a focus for their worship that allows their community to maintain an identity distinct from groups associated with other sanctuaries." However, the author's examples and explanations are restricted to the Torah and contemporary Jewish practice.
140. See my earlier conclusions in Regev 2004b:32–33.
141. Pauline Christology may have been confusing, requiring clarification and interpretation, as Dunn 1998:231 notes: "The significance of Christ's death could be adequately expressed only in imagery and metaphor. . . . Paul uses a rich and varied range of metaphors in his attempt to spell out the significance of Christ's death . . . no one metaphor is adequate to unfold the full significance of Christ's death . . . they do not always fit well together (Col. 2.11–15!)."
142. Scholars find it difficult to reconcile Hebrews with Paul's doctrine. Cf. Ribbens 2016:107–108, 135; Jamieson 2017. For example, Koester 2001:109–110, 382 n. 264 argues that Jesus's atoning sacrifice was exclusively on earth, whereas Attridge 1989:251, 271 thinks Christ's heavenly ministry is, in a sense, equivalent to and simultaneous with his earthly death on the cross.
143. Schenck 2016:243–245.
144. Church 2017:15–16 argues that the author's claim that if sacrifices could have made the people perfect they would no longer have been offered (10:1–2) shows that the author presumes that they are still being practiced. However, the sting of the passage is theoretical—*one single* sacrifice should suffice to attain perfection, just like Christ's—and the context, the "shadow" of the Law, is also theoretical, not historical.

Chapter 9. Relating to Judaism

1. Compare Kirk and Thatcher 2005; Baker 2011. On how historical narrative builds group identity, see Liu and László 2007.
2. Translations of the Didache follow K. Lake, *The Apostolic Fathers*, LCL edition.

3. Daly 1978:312–313. Ullucci 2012:96–97 simply states that the Lord's Day is a sacrifice. He also notes the departure from other understandings of Christian sacrifice that I will discuss below: First, there is no comparison of Jesus, and certainly not of his death, to a sacrifice. The sacrifice is made by the community. Moreover, sins must be dealt with before the rite; hence the sacrifice itself does not release one from sin.

4. On prayer (praise and thanksgiving) as sacrifice, see Daly 1978:503; Niederwimmer 1998:196–97 with bibliographic survey. Niederwimmer prefers a very general definition of sacrifice but also considers the possibilities of the Eucharist itself (as in later Christian sources) and Eucharistic prayers. See also Claussen 2005:155–158. On the Eucharistic prayer, see Did 9:1–7; 10:5–6.

5. On the Qumranic view that the sectarians' prayer is preferable to the (unrighteous) sacrifices offered in the Temple, see Regev 2005b; Regev 2014b.

6. On the problem of dating the Didache, see, e.g., Betz 1996:244–245. On rabbinic views of prayer as taking the place of sacrifice after 70, see the introduction.

7. On the dependence of 1 Clement on Hebrews as well as on Jewish traditions, see Lampe 2003:75–77 with bibliographic survey.

8. Ignatius, Philadelphians 4; Ferguson 1980:1169.

9. Justin, *Dial.* 43.3; 117.1. The cereal offering of the skin-diseased person (Lev 14:10) is a symbol of the Eucharist bread in *Dial.* 41.1. See Ferguson 1980:1173–1174.

10. Cyprian, Epistle 62.1, 9, 12 (ANF 5:361); Epistle 75.6 (ANF 5:398); Mayes 2010:313–315. Note also the altar and the sacrifices of the bishop in Epistle 15.1; 16.3. Ullucci 2012:114–117 comments that Cyprian uses this argument for the sake of staking out a position in relation to the correct practice of the Eucharist, not as a set doctrine of Christian sacrifice.

11. E.g., Eusebius, *Demonstratio Evangelica*, 5:3.

12. Ignatius, *Magnesians* 7.2. See Ferguson 1980:1168, who also notes that the emphasis here is on the meeting under the ministers' leadership. On the use of Temple imagery in describing the communal order in the second century, see Eliav 2006:155.

13. Irenaeus, *Against Heresies* 4:17–18; Ullucci 2012:104–107.

14. Barnabas 4:11 and 6:15, respectively. Translations of the Epistle of Barnabas follow K. Lake in the LCL edition. Its date is discussed below.

15. Clement of Alexandria Strom 7.6.

16. Clement of Alexandria Strom 7.6. See also Strom 5.11 on the spiritual meaning of sacrifice. Translations of Clement of Alexandria follow Roberts and Donaldson, *The Ante-Nicene Fathers*, vol. 2.

17. Irenaeus of Lyon, *Against Heresies* 4.18.1.

18. Origen, C. Cels. 8.21. For similar arguments by Clement of Alexandria, see Ferguson 1980:1181–1182. See also below on prayer as a substitute for sacrifice.

19. Ignatius, Romans 2.2. On martyrdom as a sacrifice, see ibid., 4.2.

20. Martyrdom of Polycarp of Smyrna, 14:1 trans. Lightfoot in the LCL edition. See Ullucci 2012:100–101.

21. T. *Yom Kippurim* 4:6–10 (ed. Lieberman, 251); m. *Sanhedrin* 6:2; Mekhilta of Rabbi Ishmael, *Bahodesh* 6 (ed. Horovitz-Rabin); b *Peshaim* 50a, 53b; Boyarin 1999:93–126.

22. Gospel of Philip 69.14–26 (Robinson 1996:151). On the Gnostic concept of the bridal chamber as conjugal unions on high, see Irenaeus, *Against Heresies* 1.21.3. Note that the next paragraph in the gospel of Philip relates to the tearing of the veil of the most inner chamber.

23. Vuong 2014. See also Vuong 2012.

24. Vuong 2012:121–122. Note, however, that while the text approves of the efficacy of the Temple, it also depicts conflicts with the Temple priests.

25. Vuong 2012:219–221.

26. Stökl Ben Ezra 2003:152–154 on Barn. 7:1–5 and 7:6–11.

27. On Christ as the red heifer, see Daly 1978:432 (however, the law of the red heifer rite in Num 19 does not mention sin but merely bodily ritual purity). Despite the harsh polemic, the author is very much aware of Jewish and even rabbinic law and appropriates the halakhic details to his Christological doctrine. Alon 1957:297 points to knowledge of rabbinic halakhah in the involvement of undefiled children in the making of the ashes (m. *Parah* 3:2–3). He also compares the ritual symbolism of the epistle with rabbinic halakhah, including the idea that the ashes enable atonement, and finds echoes of rabbinic tradition in people's treatment of the scapegoat (ibid., 299–305).

28. 1 *Apology* 13; see also 1 *Apology* 10; *Dial.* 117.2; Daly 1978:331–333; Ferguson 1980:1172–1173. In *Dial.* 117.2, Justin maintains that prayers and thanksgivings (by the appropriate people) are the only perfect sacrifices. He also refers to the same concept as held by Diaspora Jews.

29. *Dial.* 13.1; Daly 1978:325, 328–330 concludes that Christ's sacrifice fulfills the Old Testament sacrificial rites.

30. Twelve bells: *Dial.* 42.1; 116.1; 118:2; Ferguson 1980:1173; true high priestly race: *Dial.* 116.3, quoting Mal 1:11.

31. *Dial.* 40.1–4; Daly 1978:328–329.

32. Irenaeus, *Against Heresies* 4.17.

33. Irenaeus, *Against Heresies* 4:18.

34. Clement of Alexandria, *Stromata* 7.6–8; *Paedagogus* 3.12 (quoting Isa. 1:11–14); *Strom* 7.3, respectively. For one's body and self as a living sacrifice, see Ferguson 1980:1179–1180.

35. E.g., John Chrysostom, *Hom. In Heb.* 17:3 (on Heb 9:24–26).

36. *Recog.* 1.48.6; 1.54.1. On the Pseudo-Clementines, see below.

37. Stroumsa 2009:66–69. See the introduction.

38. Stroumsa 2009:72–73. He referred to John Chrysostom, *Hom. In Heb.* 17:3. The patristic liturgical language developed a sacrificial vocabulary that continues in the vein of the ancient tradition. See Ferguson 1990:816–818.

39. Barn. 2:4, later quoting Isa 1:11–13. See Ullucci 2012:97–98.

40. Barn. 16:6–10. He also declares, "God dwells in us" (16:8–9), and "a spiritual temple being built for the Lord" (16:10).
41. Richardson and Shukster 1983:34.
42. Richardson and Shukster 1983 with a summary of previous dating of the epistle. On dating it to Nerva's reign, see ibid., 41–44.
43. 1 *Apology* 10:1; 13:1; *Dial.* 10:3; 22.
44. *Dial* 19.6; 22.1, 11; Cf. also *Dial.* 43.1; 67.8; 92.4.
45. R. Levi: Leviticus Rabbah 22.8; R. Ishmael: Tanhuma, *akhrei mot* 17 (ed. Buber, 69–70). Note, however, that these rabbinic sources are much later than Justin.
46. Temple: *Dial.* 22.11; Angels: 2 *Apology* 5, 3–4. He also brings Old Testament quotations against sacrifice in *Dial.* 22.3 (Amos 5:21–25); 28.5 (Mal. 1:110–12).
47. *Dial.* 41.2; 117.2 (following Mal. 1:10–12).
48. *Dial.* 16.2; 40.2. Eliav 2006:158–160 concludes that Barnabas and Justin discuss the desolation of the Temple Mount and regard it as a punishment for the rejection of Christ. See Barn. 11; Justin, *Dial.* 25.1–26.1.
49. Irenaeus of Lyon, *Adv. haer.* 4.18.1; Ferguson 1980:1177.
50. Strom 7.6; see also *Strom* 7.3; Ferguson 1980:1881–1882; Ullucci 2012:108–110.
51. Clement, *Protrepticus* (also known as Exhortation to the Greeks) 3.42.
52. On prayer instead of sacrifice: Tertullian *De Oratione* 28; Ferguson 1980:1184. On sacrifices as commanded only as a means of preventing idolatry: *Adversus Marcionem* 2.18.
53. On the Pseudo-Clementines and their place within so-called Jewish-Christianity, associating themselves with Peter and James (*Recog.* 1.43.2; 44.1), and as against Paul, see Yoshiko Reed 2003.
54. *Recog.* 1.27 and 1.64; *Homilies* 111.45, respectively. Citations of *Recognitions* follow the edition of Jones 1995.
55. *Recog.* 1.35; 1.36.1; 37.4.
56. *Recog.* 1.66.2 ff. On the death of James, see chapter 5. It is interesting that the author located James's teaching in the Temple in spite of the fact that the high priests and the lay priests had often beaten the Christians for teaching or learning about Jesus (*Recog.* 1.55.1–2).
57. Jones 1995:163. Bourgel 2015 suggests that *Recog.* 1.27–71 was written as a response to the Jews' failure to rebuild the Temple during the Bar-Kockba revolt (132–135 CE).
58. Yoshiko Reed 2003:197–198, 204–213, esp. 209.
59. Epiphanius, *Panarion* (or *Against Heresies*) 30.16.4–5. Translation follows Hennecke 1991:158. Hennecke dates this gospel to the first half of the second century (ibid., 156). *Panarion* 30.16.7 contains orders against the Temple and sacrifices, and the fire on the altar is attributed to the "Ascents of James."
60. According to Epiphanius, *Refutation of All* 30:1–2, Ebion, the founder of the Ebionites, emerged from the Nazarenes and adhered to Judaism's Law of the Sabbath, circumcision, and all other Jewish observances. The Nazarenes also observe that Law (ibid., 5.4; 7.5; 8.1).

61. See the survey of the so-called Gnostic texts in Roukema 2014. For *The Second Treatise of the Great Seth,* see Nag Hammadi Codex VII 2. 58.26–29; Robinson 1996:366; Roukema 2014:159.

62. Cf. Eliav 2006:153.

63. On the symbol of the Temple as a model for second-century ecclesiology, see Fassbeck 2001.

64. According to Ullucci 2012:135, "Christians did not create a rational rejection of sacrifice that they then lived out. Historical circumstances ended animal sacrifice for Christians first. It was left to later Christian cultural producers to make sense of this situation and rationalize and defend the fact that Christians did not sacrifice."

65. To illustrate this boundary, suffice it to mention that Ignatius of Antioch urged his audience to abandon ancient customs and to celebrate the Lord's Day rather than the Sabbath (*Magn.* 9.1). He also says that the disciples of Jesus should be called Christians (literally, those who live in accordance with *Christianismos*); whoever is called by another name is not "of God" (*Magn.* 10.1). Ignatius may be objecting to the fact that some disciples were claiming the name "Jew" for themselves.

66. Lieu 1996. Boyarin 2004:37–73, esp. 43–44 argues that Christian texts from the second and third centuries, such as Justin's *Dialogue with Trypho,* are trying to differentiate between Christianity and Judaism. Rabbinic texts from the same period are engaged in a parallel endeavor. This quest for Christianity's distinctiveness is probably a response to the existence of traits common to Christians and Jews, particularly Jewish rabbis, as well as the fact that the boundaries between Judaism and Christianity in the second and third centuries were blurred. See Boyarin 1999.

67. Ortner 1973.

68. On root metaphor, see Ortner 1973:1340–1341.

69. Ortner 1973:1341–1342.

70. On the key aspect of key symbols, see Ortner 1973:1343.

71. Fernandez 1986:3–27.

72. Fernandez 1986:21–23, 41–50. Cf. Turner 1974.

73. Fernandez 1986:43.

74. On mental constructions, their mappings and overarching principles, see Fauconnier and Turner 2008:53.

75. On foundational conceptual metaphors and specific metaphors, see Kövecses 2006:144.

76. On these overarching principles, see Fauconnier and Turner 2008:53.

77. Kövecses 2002:6. Cf. the discussion in chapter 3.

78. On early Christianity as a New Religious Movement or Cult, see Regev 2016b.

79. For Roland Barthes, for example, the meaning of the text is accessible only as an activity or a production. Texts should be understood in terms of what they

do and what readers do with them. The text, in other words, is *experienced*. See Roland Barthes, "From Work to Text." In Harari 1979:75.

80. Said 1983:33–35, 45–48. In addition, Ricoeur and Jameson maintain that social action can be interpreted similarly to a text. See Bell 1992:44–45.

81. Balsamo 2004:esp. 16, discussing mainly James Joyce. See also the sacramental and sacrificial reenactments of the Eucharist in Joyce (ibid., 112–123).

82. Lukes 1975:291.

83. Bell 1997:28, following Radcliffe-Brown.

84. Geertz 1973:112–114; Bell 1992:27.

85. Munn 1973:esp. 579, 583, following Durkheim.

86. Ritual and myth are interconnected in the study of religion. See Bell 1997:3–10 on the myth and ritual school of thought. Eliade pointed to the mythical aspects of ritual, namely, the ritual reenactment or recounting of a cosmogenic event or story (ibid., 10–11 and references). See, for example, the Eucharist in 1 Cor 10:16; Luke 22:19b.

87. For myth about ritual, see Doniger O'Flaherty 1988:esp. 97, 101, on which Swartz 1997 builds. Doniger O'Flaherty 1988:103 maintains that myths, which exist in the realm of imagination, provide tools to expose the illusory nature of rituals. According to Swartz 1997:152–153, the Day of Atonement prayer addresses the problem of the absence of sacrifice in a system to which it was once central, through rituals of recitation. That is, by recounting a lost ritual verbally, a community develops a way of memorializing that ritual through an act that is *itself* a ritual. This is an actualization of sacred space in time.

88. See Handelman 2004:2, 3–4, 23 on ritual in its own right.

89. Clifford 1972:131–189.

90. Hubert and Mauss 1964:13, 51–52, 97–98, 102–103.

91. Fernandez 1986:esp. 43. On the social function of ritual and performance, see Bell 1997:73–76.

92. Geertz 1973:114, 118–119.

93. Geertz 1973:112; Smith 1980.

94. Note that even in the Damascus Document, in which the Temple is treated as polluted (CD 6:11–16), tributes are sent to the Temple by pure messengers (CD 10:18–21).

95. E.g., Gluckman 1962:2, 15, 26, 33, 37, 50.

96. Bell 1992:196–223.

97. Lukes 1975:esp. 301 (albeit concerning political ritual).

98. Kertzer 1988:40–46, following Turner.

99. Regev 2016b.

100. Lukes 1975:300–301, 305.

101. Sheldrake 2001:4–8, 16.

102. Sheldrake 2001:33–89, esp. 37–38, 66–67.

103. Durkheim 1965, esp. 427–428; Lukes 1973:463, 471–472. On the contribution of ritual to social organization and solidarity, see Kertzer 1988:15–34, 57–76.

104. Bell 1992:104, 177–181.
105. Fortes 1962:56–57, 74. In ritual, authority is both dramatized and glamorized. See Kertzer 1988:104.
106. Asad 1983, criticizing Geertz's "Religion as Cultural System" (Geertz 1973: 87–125).
107. Gluckman 1963:112, 128. Cf. transformative rituals of social change and political revolution in Bell 1992:169.
108. For a survey of the scholarship on general approaches to early Christian identity, see Holmberg 2008. Lieu 2004 explores the next phase of the shaping of a more distinct identity in the second century.

Bibliography

Abrahams, I. 1967 [1917]. *Studies in Pharisaism and the Gospels.* New York: Ktav.

Achtemeier, P. J. 1995. *1 Peter.* Hermeneia. Minneapolis: Fortress.

Ådna, J. 1999. "Jesus' Symbolic Act in the Temple (Mark 11:15–17): The Replacement of the Sacrificial Cult by His Atoning Death." In B. Ego, A. Lange, and P. Pilhofe, eds., *Gemeinde ohne Tempel—Community Without Temple.* WUNT 118. Tübingen: Mohr-Siebeck, 461–475.

———. 2000. *Jesu Stellung zum Tempel: Die Tempelaktion und das Tempelwort als Ausdruck seiner messianischen Sendung.* WUNT II 119. Tübingen: Mohr.

———. 2011. "Jesus and the Temple." In T. Holmén and S. E. Porter, eds., *Handbook for the Study of the Historical Jesus.* Leiden: Brill, 3:2635–2675.

Allison, D. C. 1983. "Matt. 23:39 = Luke 13:35b as a Conditional Prophecy." *NTS* 18: 75–84.

———. 1986. "4Q 403 Fargm. I Col I, 38–46 and the Revelation to John." *RevQ* 12: 409–414.

———. 2010. *Constructing Jesus: Memory, Imagination, and History.* Grand Rapids: Baker.

Alon, G. 1957. "The Halakhah in the Epistle of Barnabas." In *Studies in Jewish History in the Times of the Second Temple, the Mishna, and the Talmud.* Tel Aviv: Hakibutz Hameuchad, 1:295–312 (Hebrew).

Anderson, G. 1994. *Sage, Saint and Sophist: Holy Men and Their Associates in the Early Roman Empire.* London: Routledge.

Antwi, D. J. 1991. "Did Jesus Consider His Death to Be an Atoning Sacrifice?" *Interpretation* 45: 17–28.

Asad T. 1983. "Anthropological Conceptions of Religion: Reflections on Geertz." *Man* 18, no. 2: 237–259.

Ashton, J. 2007. *Understanding the Fourth Gospel.* 2d ed. Oxford: Oxford University Press.

Attridge, H. W. 1989. *The Epistle to the Hebrews.* Hermeneia. Philadelphia: Fortress.

———. 2004. "The Epistle to the Hebrews and the Scrolls." In A. J. Avery-Peck et al., eds., *When Judaism and Christianity Began: Essays in Memory of Anthony J. Saldarini.* Leiden: Brill, 2:315–342.

————. 2010. "Temple, Tabernacle, Time, and Space in John and Hebrews." *Early Christianity* 1: 261–274.

————. 2013. "How Priestly Is the 'High Priestly Prayer' in John 17?" *CBQ* 75: 1–14.

Aune, D. E. 1997. *Revelation 1–5*. WBC 52. Dallas: Word.

————. 1998a. *Revelation 6–16*. WBC 52B. Nashville: Thomas Nelson.

————. 1998b. *Revelation 17–22*. WBC 52C. Nashville: Thomas Nelson.

Avemarie, F. 1999. "Ist die Johannestaufe ein Ausdruck von Tempelkritik? Skizze eines methodischen Problems." In B. Ego, A. Lange, and P. Pilhofer, eds., *Gemeinde ohne Tempel—Community Without Temple*. WUNT 118. Tübingen, Mohr Siebeck, 395–410.

Bachmann, M. 1980. *Jerusalem und der Tempel: Die geographisch-theologischen Elemente in der lukanischen Sicht des judischen Kultzentrums*. Stuttgart: Kohlhammer.

————. 1994. "Himmlisch. der 'Tempel Gottes' von Apk 11,1." *NTS* 40: 474–480.

Bailey, K. E. 1980. *Through Peasant Eyes*. Grand Rapids: Eerdmans.

Baker, C. A. 2011. *Identity, Memory, and Narrative in Early Christianity: Peter, Paul, and Recategorization in the Book of Acts*. Eugene, OR: Pickwick.

Balsamo, G. 2004. *Rituals of Literature: Joyce, Dante, Aquinas, and the Tradition of Christian Epic*. Lewisburg: Bucknell University Press.

Baltzer, K. 1965. "The Meaning of the Temple in the Lukan Writings." *HTR*, 58: 263–277.

Barber, M. P. 2013. "Jesus as the Davidic Temple Builder and Peter's Priestly Role in Matthew 16:16–19." *JBL* 132, no. 4: 935–953.

Barclay, J. M. G. 1996. "Do We Undermine the Law? A Study of Romans 14:1–16:6." In J. D. G. Dunn, ed., *Paul and the Mosaic Law*. WUNT 89. Tübingen: Mohr, 287–308.

Barrett, C. K. 1953. "Paul and the 'Pillar Apostles,'" in J. N. Sevenster and W. C. van Unnik, eds., *Studia Paulina in honorem Johannis De Zwann Septuagenarii*. Haarlem: Bohn, 1–19.

————. 1955. *The Gospel According to St. John* London: SPCK.

————. 1978. *The Gospel According to St. John*. 2d ed. London: SPCK.

————. 1991. "Attitudes to the Temple in the Acts of the Apostles." In W. Horbury, ed., *Templum Amicitiae: Essays on the Second Temple Presented to Ernst Bammel*. JSNTSup 48. Sheffield: JSOT Press, 345–367.

————. 1998. *A Critical and Exegetical Commentary on the Acts of the Apostles*. 2 vols. ICC. London: T & T Clark International.

Bauckham, R. 1986. "The Coin in the Fish's Mouth." In D. Wenham and C. Blomberg, eds., *Gospel Perspectives VI: Miracles in the Gospels*. Sheffield: JSOT Press, 219–252.

————. 1988. "Jesus' Demonstration in the Temple." In B. Lindars, ed., *Law and Religion: Essays on the Place of Law in Israel and Early Christianity*. Cambridge: James Clarke, 72–89.

————. 1993. *The Theology of the Book of Revelation*. Cambridge: Cambridge University Press.

————. 1995. "James and the Jerusalem Church." In B. W. Winter, ed., *The Book of Acts in Its Palestinian Setting*. Vol. 4 of *The Book of Acts in Its First Century Setting*. Carlisle, UK: Paternoster, 415–480.

————. 1999. "For What Offence Was James Put to Death?" In B. Chilton and C. A. Evans, eds., *James the Just and Christian Origins*. Leiden: Brill, 199–232.

————. 2003. "The Early Jerusalem Church, Qumran and the Essenes." In J. R. Davila, ed., *The Dead Sea Scrolls as Background to Postbiblical Judaism and Early Christianity*. Leiden: Brill, 63–89.

Baumbach, G. 1989. "The Sadducees in Josephus." In L. H. Feldman and G. Hata, eds., *Josephus, the Bible and History*. Leiden: Brill, 173–195.

Baumgarten, A. I. 1983. "The Name of the Pharisees." *JBL* 102, no. 3:411–428.

Baumgarten, J. M. 1996. *Qumran Cave 4.XIII: The Damascus Document (4Q266–273)*. DJD 18. Oxford: Clarendon Press.

Beale, G. K. 2004. *The Temple and the Church's Mission: A Biblical Theology of the Dwelling Place of God*. Nottingham: Apollos.

Beasley-Murray, G. R. 1978. *The Book of Revelation*. Grand Rapids: Eerdmans.

————. 1999. *John*. WBC 36. 2d ed. Nashville: Thomas Nelson.

Becker, J. 1998. *Jesus of Nazareth*. Berlin: de Gruyter.

Bell, C. 1992. *Ritual Theory, Ritual Practice*. Oxford: Oxford University Press.

————. 1997. *Ritual: Perspectives and Dimensions*. Oxford: Oxford University Press.

Bell, R. H. 2002. "Sacrifice and Christology in Paul." *JTS* 53.1: 1–27.

Bernheim, P.-A. 1997. *James, the Brother of Jesus*. London: SCM Press.

Best, E. 1998. *Ephesians*. ICC. Edinburgh: T & T Clark.

Betz, H. D. 1973. "2 Cor 6:14–7:1: An Anti-Pauline Fragment?" *JBL* 92: 88–108.

————. 1979. *Galatians*. Hermeneia. Philadelphia: Fortress.

————. 1997. "Jesus and the Purity of the Temple (Mark 11:15–18): A Comparative Religion Approach." *JBL* 116: 455–472.

Betz, J. 1996. "The Eucharist in the Didache." In J. A. Draper, ed., *The Didache in Modern Research*. Leiden: Brill, 244–275.

Betz, O. 1981. "'To Worship God in Spirit and in Truth': Reflections on John 4, 20–26." In A. Finkel and R. Frizzel, eds., *Standing Before God: Studies on Prayer in Scripture and in Tradition with Essays in Honor of John M. Oesterreicher*. New York: Ktav, 53–72.

Beutler, J. 2006. *Judaism and the Jews in the Gospel of John*. Roma: Pontificio Istituto Biblico.

Blatzer, K. 1965. "The Meaning of the Temple in the Lukan Writings." *HTR* 58: 263–277.

Blomberg, C. L. 1983. "The Law in Luke–Acts." *JNST* 22: 53–80.

Bockmuehl, M. 2000. *Jewish Law in Gentile Churches*. Edinburgh: T & T Clark.

Bond, H. K. 2004. *Caiaphas: Friend of Rome and Judge of Jesus?* Louisville: Westminster/John Knox.

Bonz, M. P. 2000. *The Past as Legacy: Luke–Acts and Ancient Epic*. Philadelphia: Fortress.

Booth, R. P. 1986. *Jesus and the Laws of Purity: Tradition, History and Legal History in Mark 7.* Sheffield: JSOT Press.

Borg, M. J. 1984. *Conflict, Holiness and Politics in the Teaching of Jesus.* New York: Edwin Mellen.

———. 1987. *Jesus: A New Vision.* New York: Harper & Row.

———. 1994. *Jesus in Contemporary Scholarship.* Valley Forge, PA: Trinity Press International.

Boring, M. E. 2006. *Mark: A Commentary.* NTL. Louisville: Westminster/John Knox.

Bornkamm, G. 1960. *Jesus of Nazareth.* New York: Harper & Row.

Böttrich V. 1999. "'Ihr seid der Tempel Gottes.' Tempelmetaphorik und Gemeinde bei Paulus." In B. Ego, A. Lange, and P. Pilhofer, eds., *Gemeinde ohne Temple— Community Without Temple.* Tübingen: Mohr, 411–425.

Bourgel, J. 2015. "Reconnaissances 1.27–71, ou la réponse d'un groupe judéo-chrétien de Judée au désastre du soulèvement de Bar-Kokhba." *NTS* 61, no. 1: 30–49.

Bovon, F. 2002. *Luke 1: A Commentary on the Gospel of Luke 1:1–9:50.* Hermeneia. Minneapolis: Fortress.

———. 2006. *Luke the Theologian: Fifty-Five Years of Research (1950–2005).* 2d rev. ed. Waco: Baylor University Press.

———. 2012. *Luke 3: A Commentary on the Gospel of Luke 19:28–24:23.* Hermeneia. Minneapolis: Fortress.

Bowersock, G. W. 1987. "The Mechanics of Subversion in the Roman Provinces." In A. Giovanini and D. van Berchem, eds., *Opposition et Résistances a l'empire d'Auguste a Trajan.* Geneva: Foundation Hardt, 291–317.

Boyarin, D. 1999. *Dying for God: Martyrdom and the Making of Christianity and Judaism.* Stanford: Stanford University Press.

———. 2004. *Border Lines: The Partition of Judaeo-Christianity.* Philadelphia: University of Pennsylvania Press.

———. 2005. "What Kind of a Jew Is an Evangelist?" In G. Aichele and R. Walsh, eds., *Non-Canonical Readings of Canonical Gospels.* London: T & T Clark, 109–153.

Brandon, S. G. F. 1960. "The Date of the Markan Gospel." *NTS* 7: 126–141.

Braun, H. 1966. *Qumran und das Neue Testament.* 2 vols. Tübingen: Mohr.

Brawley, R. L. 1987. *Luke–Acts and the Jews: Conflict, Apology and Conciliation.* SBLMS 33. Atlanta: Scholars Press.

Briggs, R. A. 1999. *Jewish Temple Imagery in the Book of Revelation.* New York: Peter Lang.

Broadhead, E. K. 1992. "Christology as Polemic and Apologetic: The Priestly Portrait of Jesus in the Gospel of Mark." *JSNT* 47: 21–34.

Brooke, G. J. 1988. "Christ and the Law in John 7–10." In B. Lindars, ed., *Law and Religion: Essays on the Place of the Law in Israel and Early Christianity.* Cambridge: James Clarke, 102–112.

———. 1995. "4Q500 1 and the Use of Scripture in the Parable of the Vineyard." *DSD* 2: 268–294.

Brooks, W. E. 1970. "The Perpetuity of Christ's Sacrifice in the Epistle to the Hebrews." *JBL* 89: 205–214.

Brown, R. E. 1966. *The Gospel According to John i–xii.* AB 29. New York: Doubleday.

———. 1970. *The Gospel According to John (xiv–xxi).* AB 29A. New York: Doubleday.

———. 1979a. *The Birth of the Messiah: A Commentary on the Infancy Narratives in Matthew and Luke.* New York: Doubleday.

———. 1979b. *The Community of the Beloved Disciple: The Life, Loves and Hates of an Individual Church in New Testament Times.* New York: Paulist Press.

———. 1998. *The Death of the Messiah.* 2 vols. New York: Doubleday.

———. 2003. *An Introduction to the Gospel of John.* New York: Doubleday.

———, and J. P. Meier. 1983. *Antioch and Rome.* London: Geoffrey Chapman.

Bruce, F. F. 1965. *The Epistle to the Hebrews.* New London Commentary. London: Harper Collins.

———. 1976. "Is the Paul of Acts the Real Paul?" *BJRL* 58: 282–302.

———. 1988. *The Book of the Acts.* Rev. ed. NICNT; Grand Rapids: Eerdmans.

Buchanan, G. W. 1991. "Symbolic Money-Changers in the Temple." *NTS* 37: 280–290.

Bultmann, R. K. 1963. *The History of the Synoptic Tradition.* Oxford: Blackwell.

———. 1971. *The Gospel of John: A Commentary.* Philadelphia: Westminster.

Cadbury, H. J. 1958. *The Making of Luke–Acts.* Repr. London: SPCK.

Calaway, J. C. 2013. *The Sabbath and the Sanctuary: Access to God in the Letter to the Hebrews and Its Priestly Context.* WUNT 2.349. Tübingen: Mohr.

Campbell, W. S. 2008. *Paul and the Creation of Christian Identity.* London: T & T Clark.

Carey, G. L. 1981. "The Lamb of God and Atonement Theories." *TynBul* 32: 97–122.

Carpinelli, F. G. 1999. "'Do This as My Memorial' (Luke 22:19): Lucan Soteriology of Atonement." *CBQ* 61: 74–91.

Carroll, J. T. 1988. "Luke's Portrayal of the Pharisees." *CBQ* 50: 604–621.

Carson, D. A. 1991. *The Gospel According to John.* The Pillar New Testament Commentary. Grand Rapids: Eerdmans.

Carter, W. 1999. "Paying the Tax to Rome as Subversive Praxis: Matthew 17.24–27." *JSNT* 76: 3–31.

Casey, P. M. 1997. "Culture and Historicity: The Cleansing of the Temple." *CBQ* 59: 306–332.

Cassidy, R. J. 1979. "Matthew 17.24–27—A Word on Civil Taxes." *CBQ* 41: 571–580.

———. 1983. "Luke's Audience, the Chief Priests, and the Motive for Jesus Death." In R. J. Cassidy and P. J. Scharper (eds.), *Political Issues in Luke–Acts.* Maryknoll, NY: Orbis Books, 146–167.

Catchpole, D. 1993. *The Quest for Q.* Edinburgh: T & T Clark.

Chance, J. B. 1988. *Jerusalem, the Temple, and the New Age in Luke–Acts.* Macon, GA: Mercer University Press.

———. 2007. "The Cursing of the Temple and the Tearing of the Veil in the Gospel of Mark." *Biblical Interpretation* 15: 268–291.

Chanikuzhy, J. 2012. *Jesus, the Eschatological Temple: An Exegetical Study of John 2,13–22 in the Light of the Pre-70 C.E. Eschatological Temple Hopes and the Synoptic Temple Action.* Leuven: Peeters.

Charles, R. H. 1920. *A Critical and Exegetical Commentary on the Revelation of St. John.* 2 vols. ICC. Edinburgh: T & T Clark.

Charlesworth, J. H., and C. Newsom (eds.). 1999. *Angelic Liturgy: Songs of a Sabbath Sacrifice. The Dead Sea Scrolls: Hebrew, Aramaic, and Greek Texts with English Translations.* Princeton Theological Seminary Dead Sea Scrolls Project 4B. Tübingen: Mohr.

Chepey, S. 2005. *Nazarites in Late Second Temple Period.* AJEC 60. Leiden: Brill.

Chilton, B. 1990. "A Coin of Three Realms (Matthew 17:24–27)." In D. J. A. Clines, S. E. Fowl, and S. E. Porter, eds., *The Bible in Three Dimensions.* Sheffield: Sheffield Academic Press, 269–282.

———. 1992. *The Temple of Jesus: His Sacrificial Program Within a Cultural History of Sacrifice.* University Park: Pennsylvania State University Press.

———. 1994. *A Feast of Meanings: Eucharistic Theologies from Jesus Through Johannine Circles.* SNT 72. Leiden: Brill.

———. 1996. *Pure Kingdom: Jesus' Vision of God.* Grand Rapids: Eerdmans.

———. 2004. *Rabbi Paul: An Intellectual Biography.* New York: Doubleday.

Church, P. 2017. *Hebrews and the Temple: Attitudes to the Temple in Second Temple Judaism and in Hebrews.* SNT 171. Leiden: Brill.

Cirafesi, W. V. 2011–12. "The Priestly Portrait of Jesus in the Gospel of John in the Light of 1QS, 1QSa and 1QSb." *Journal of Greco-Roman Christianity and Judaism* 8: 83–105.

Claussen, C. 2005. "The Eucharist in the Gospel of John and the Didache." In A. Gregory and C. Tuckett, eds., *Trajectories Through the New Testament and the Apostolic Fathers.* Oxford: Oxford University Press, 135–163.

Clifford, R. J. 1972. *The Cosmic Mountain in Canaan and in the Old Testament.* Cambridge: Harvard University Press.

Cockerill. G. L. 2012. *The Epistle to the Hebrews.* NICNT. Grand Rapids: Eerdmans.

Collins, J. J. 1974a. "The Sibylline Oracles of Egyptian Judaism." *SBLDS* 13. Montana: SBL.

———. 1974b. "The Place of the Fourth Sibyl in the Development of the Jewish Sibyllina." *JJS* 25, no. 3: 365–380.

———. 1979. "Introduction: Towards the Morphology of a Genre." *Semeia* 14: 1–20.

———. 1983. "Sibylline Oracles." In J. H. Charlesworth, ed., *The Old Testament Pseudepigrapha.* New York: Doubleday, 1:317–472.

———. 2017. *The Invention of Judaism: Torah and Jewish Identity from Deuteronomy to Paul.* Oakland: University of California Press.

Collins, R. F. 2008. *The Power of the Image in Paul.* Collegeville, MN: Liturgical Press.

Coloe, M. L. 2000. "Raising the Johannine Temple (Jn 19:19–29)." *Australian Biblical Review* 48: 47–58.

———. 2001. *God Dwells with Us: Temple Symbolism in the Fourth Gospel.* Collegeville, MN: Liturgical Press.

Congar, Y. M.-J. 1962. *The Mystery of the Temple* Trans. R. F. Trevett. London: Burns & Oates.

Conzelmann, H. 1961. *The Theology of St. Luke.* New York: Harper & Row.

———. 1975. *1 Corinthians.* Philadelphia: Fortress.

Coppens, J. 1973. "The Spiritual Temple in the Pauline Letters and Its Background." *Studia Evangelica* 6: 53–60.

Cortez, F. H. 2006. "From the Holy to the Most Holy Place: The Period of Hebrews 9:6–10 and the Day of Atonement as a Metaphor of Transition." *JBL* 125.3: 527–547.

Crossan, J. D. 1992. *The Historical Jesus: The Life of a Mediterranean Jewish Peasant.* New York: HarperCollins.

———. 1995. *Who Killed Jesus? Exposing the Roots of Anti-Semitism in the Gospel Story of the Death of Jesus.* New York: HarperCollins.

Crossley, J. G. 2004. *The Date of Mark's Gospel: Insight from the Law in Earliest Christianity.* London: T & T Clark.

Cullmann, O. 1958–1959. "L'Opposition contre le temple de Jerusalem, motif commun de la theologie johannique et du monde ambiant." *NTS* 5: 157–173.

Cunningham, S. 1997. *"Through Many Tribulations": The Theology of Persecution in Luke–Acts.* Sheffield: Sheffield Academic Press.

Dalman, G. 1971 [1929]. *Jesus–Jeshua: Studies in the Gospels.* New York: Ktav.

Daly, R. J. 1978. *Christian Sacrifice: The Judaeo-Christian Background before Origen.* Washington: Catholic University of America Press.

Danielou, J. 1958. *The Dead Sea Scrolls and Primitive Christianity.* Baltimore: Helicon.

Daube, D. 1956. *The New Testament and Rabbinic Judaism.* London: Athlone.

Davies, P. R. 1996. *Sects and Scrolls: Essays on Qumran and Related Topics.* Atlanta: Scholars Press.

Davies, W. D. 1955. *Paul and Rabbinic Judaism.* London: SPCK.

———. 1974. *The Gospel and the Land: Early Christianity and Jewish Territorial Doctrine.* Berkeley: University of California Press.

———, and D. C. Allison. 1988. *The Gospel According to Saint Matthew, I.* ICC. Edinburgh: T & T Clark.

———. 1991. *The Gospel According to Saint Matthew, II.* ICC. Edinburgh: T & T Clark.

———. 1997. *The Gospel According to Saint Matthew, III.* ICC. Edinburgh: T & T Clark.

Dawsey, J. M. 1991. "The Origin of Luke's Positive Perception of the Temple." *Perspectives in Religious Studies* 18, no. 2: 5–22.

Deines, R. 2009. "Not the Law but the Messiah: Law and Righteousness in the Gospel of Matthew—An Ongoing Debate." In D. M. Gurtner and J. Nolland, eds., *Built upon the Rock: Studies in the Gospel of Matthew.* Grand Rapids: Eerdmans, 53–84.

De la Potterie, I. 1979. "La tunique sans couture, symbole du Christ grand prêtre?" *Bib* 60: 255–269.

De Moor, J. C. 1998. "The Targumic Background of Mark 12:1–12: The Parable of the Wicked Tenants." *JSJ* 29: 63–80.

Dennert, B. C. 2103. "Hanukkah and the Testimony of Jesus' Works (John 10:22–39)." *JBL* 132, no. 2: 431–451.

deSilva, D. A. 2006. "The Invention and Argumentative Function of Priestly Discourse in the Epistle to the Hebrews." *Bulletin for Biblical Research* 16.2: 295–323.

Dettwiler, A. 2009. "The Source Q and the Torah." In M. Tait and P. Pakes, eds., *Torah in the New Testament.* London: T & T Clark, 32–64.

Dibelius, M. 1956. *Studies in the Acts of the Apostles.* London: SCM.

———. 2004. "The First Christian Historian." *The Book of Acts: Form, Style and Theology.* Repr. Minneapolis: Fortress.

Dimant, D. 1986. "4QFlorilegium and the Idea of the Community as Temple." In M. Hadas-Lebel, A. Caquot, and J. Riaud, eds., *Hellenica et Judaica: Hommage à Valentin Nikiprowetzky.* Paris: Peeters, 165–189.

Dodd, C. H. 1952. *Rediscovering the Parables of the Kingdom.* London: Nisbet.

———. 1968. *The Interpretation of the Fourth Gospel.* Cambridge: Cambridge University Press.

Doniger O'Flaherty, W. 1988. *Other People's Myths: The Cave of Echoes.* New York: Collier Macmillan.

Draper, J. A. 1983. "The Heavenly Feast of Tabernacle: Revelation 7:1–17." *JSNT* 19: 133–147.

———. 1997. "Temple, Tabernacle, and Mystical Experience in John." *Neotestamentica* 31–32: 263–288.

Driggers, I. B. 2007. "The Politics of Divine Presence: Temple as Locus of Conflict in the Gospel of Mark." *Biblical Interpretation* 15: 227–247.

Dunn, J. D. G. 1974. "Paul's Understanding of the Death of Jesus." In Robert Banks, ed., *Reconciliation and Hope: New Testament Essays on Atonement and Eschatology Presented to L. L. Morris on His 60th Birthday.* Carlisle, UK: Paternoster, 125–141.

———. 1983. "The Incident at Antioch (Gal. 2:11–18)." *JSNT* 5/18: 3–57.

———. 1985. "Works of the Law and the Curse of the Law (Galatians 3,10–14)." *NTS* 31: 523–554.

———. 1988. *Romans.* 2 vols. WBC 38A-B. Waco: Word.

———. 1990. "Jesus and Ritual Purity: A Study of the Tradition-History of Mark 7.15." In *Jesus, Paul and the Law: Studies in Mark and Galatians.* Louisville: Westminster/John Knox, 37–60.

———. 1993. *The Epistle to the Galatians.* Black's New Testament Commentaries. London: T & T Clark.

———. 1998. *The Theology of Paul the Apostle.* Grand Rapids: Eerdmans.

———. 1999. "Who Did Paul Think He Was? A Study of Jewish-Christian Identity." *NTS* 45: 174–193.

———. 2003. *Jesus Remembered.* Grand Rapids: Eerdmans.

———. 2009. "Beginning from Jerusalem." In *Christianity in the Making,* vol. 2. Grand Rapids: Eerdmans.

———. 2010. *Did the First Christians Worship Jesus?* London: Westminster/John Knox.

Dunnill, J. 1992. *Covenant and Sacrifice in the Letter to the Hebrews.* Cambridge: Cambridge University Press.

Dupont, J. 1964. *The Sources of Acts: The Present Position.* London: Darton, Longman & Todd; New York: Herder and Herder.

———. 1971. "Il n'en sera pas laissée pierre sur pierre (Mc 13,2; Luc 19,44)." *Bib* 52, 301–320.

Durkheim, E. 1965 [1915]. *The Elementary Forms of Religious Life.* Trans. J. W. Swain. New York: Free Press.

Dyson, S. L. 1971. "Native Revolts in the Roman Empire." *Historia* 20: 239–274.

———. 1975. "Native Revolt Patterns in the Roman Empire." *ANRW* II.3:138–175.

Eagleton, T. 1983. *Literary Theory: An Introduction.* Minneapolis: University of Minnesota Press.

Eberhart, C. A. 2005. "Characteristics of Sacrificial Metaphors in Hebrews." In G. Gelardini, ed., *Hebrews: Contemporary Methods—New Insights.* Atlanta: SBL, 37–64.

Edwards, J. R. 1989. "Markan Sandwiches: The Significance of Interpretations in Markan Narratives." *NT* 31: 193–216.

Elgvin, T. 2009. "Priests on Earth and in Heaven: Jewish Light on the Book of Revelation." In F. García Martínez, ed., *Echoes from the Caves: Qumran and the New Testament.* Leiden: Brill, 257–278.

Eliav, Y. Z. 2004. "The Tomb of James, Brother of Jesus, as *Locus Memoriae.*" *HTR* 97, no. 1: 33–59.

———. 2006. *God's Mountain: The Temple Mount in Time, Place, and Memory.* Baltimore: Johns Hopkins University Press.

Elior, R. 1995. "From Earthly Temple to Heavenly Shrines: Prayer and Sacred Liturgy in the *Hekhalot* Literature and Its Relation to Temple Traditions." *Tarbiz* 64, no. 3: 341–380 (Hebrew).

Elliott, J. H. 1991. "Temple versus Household in Luke–Acts: A Contrast in Social Institutions." In J. H. Neyrey, ed., *The Social World of Luke–Acts: Models for Interpretation.* Peabody, MA: Hendrickson, 211–240.

———. 2000. *1 Peter.* AB 37B. New York: Doubleday.

Epstein, V. 1964. "The Historicity of the Gospel Account of the Cleansing of the Temple." *ZNW* 55: 42–58.

Esler, P. F. 1987. *Community and Gospel in Luke–Acts.* Cambridge: Cambridge University Press.

———. 2005. "The Incident of the Withered Fig Tree in Mark 11: A New Source and Redactional Explanation." *JSNT* 28, no. 1: 41–67.

Evans, C. A. 1989. "Jesus' Action in the Temple: Cleansing or Portent Destruction." *CBQ* 51, no. 2: 237–270.

———. 1992. "Opposition to the Temple: Jesus and the Dead Sea Scrolls." In J. H. Charlesworth, ed., *Jesus and the Dead Sea Scrolls*. New York: Doubleday, 235–253.

———. 1995a. "Jesus' Action in the Temple and Evidence of Corruption in the First-Century Temple." In *Jesus and His Contemporaries: Comparative Studies*. Leiden: Brill, 219–344.

———. 1995b. "God's Vineyard and Its Caretakers." In *Jesus and His Contemporaries: Comparative Studies*. Leiden: Brill, 381–406.

———. 1999. "Jesus and James: Martyrs of the Temple." In *James the Just and Christian Origins*, B. Chilton and C. A. Evans, eds., SNT 98. Leiden: Brill, 233–249.

———. 2001. *Mark 8:28–16:20*. WBC 34B. Waco: Word.

Farris, M. 1997. "A Tale of Two Taxations (Luke 18:10–14b): The Parable of the Pharisee and the Toll Collector." In V. G. Shillington, ed., *Jesus and His Parables: Interpreting the Parables of Jesus Today*. Edinburgh: T & T Clark, 23–33.

Fassbeck, G. 2001. *Der Tempel der Christen: traditionsgeschichtliche Untersuchungen zur Aufnahme des Tempelkonzepts im frühen Christentum*. Tübingen: Francke.

Fauconnier, G., and M. Turner. 2008. "Rethinking Metaphor." In R. W. Gibbs, ed., *The Cambridge Handbook of Metaphor and Thought*. Cambridge: Cambridge University Press, 53–66.

Fay, R. C. 2006. "The Narrative Function of the Temple in Luke–Acts." *Trinity Journal* 27, no. 2: 255–270.

Fee, G. D. 1987. *The First Epistle to the Corinthians*. NICOT. Grand Rapids: Eerdmans.

———. 2014. *The First Epistle to the Corinthians*. NICOT. Rev. ed. Grand Rapids: Eerdmans.

Feeley-Harnik, G. 1994. *The Lord's Table: The Meaning of Food in Early Judaism and Christianity*. Washington" Smithsonian Institution Press.

Feldmeier, R. 2008. *The First Letter of Peter: A Commentary on the Greek Text*. Waco: Baylor University Press.

Ferguson, E. 1980. "Spiritual Sacrifice in Early Christianity and Its Environment." *ANRW* 23.2: 1151–1189.

———. 1990. "Sacrifice." In E. Ferguson et al., eds., *Encyclopedia of Early Christianity*. New York: Garland.

Fernandez, J. W. 1986. *Persuasions and Performances: The Play of Tropes in Culture*. Bloomington: Indiana University Press.

Finkel, A., and R. Frizzel (eds.). 1981. *Standing Before God: Studies on Prayer in Scripture and in Tradition with Essays in Honor of John M. Oesterreicher*. New York: Ktav, 53–72.

Finlan, S. 2004. *The Background and Content of Paul's Cultic Atonement Metaphors.* Atlanta: Society of Biblical Literature.

Fischer, G. 1975. *Die himmlischen Wohungen. Untersuchungen zu Joh 14,2f.* Frankfurt/ Main: Lang, 58–74.

Fitzmyer, J. A. 1961. "Qumran and the Interpolated Paragraph in 2 Cor 6:14–7:1." *CBQ* 23: 271–280.

———.1981. *The Gospel According to Luke I–IX.* AB 28. New York: Doubleday.

———.1985. *The Gospel According to Luke X–XXIV.* AB 28A. New York: Doubleday.

———. 1993. *Romans.* AB 33. New York: Doubleday.

———.1998. *The Acts of the Apostles.* AB 31. New York: Doubleday.

———.2008. *1 Corinthians.* AB 32. New York: Doubleday.

Fleddermann, H. T. 2005. *Q: A Reconstruction and Commentary.* Leuven: Peeters.

Fletcher-Louis, C. H. T. 2002. *All the Glory of Adam: Liturgical Anthropology in the Dead Sea Scrolls.* STDJ 42. Leiden: Brill.

———. 2006. "Jesus as the High Priestly Messiah: Part 1." *Journal for the Study of the Historical Jesus* 4, no. 2: 155–175.

———.2007. "Jesus as the High Priestly Messiah: Part 2." *Journal for the Study of the Historical Jesus* 5, no. 1: 57–79.

Flusser, D. 1962. "Matthew XVII 24–27 and the Dead Sea Sect." *Tarbiz* 31.2: 150–156 (Hebrew).

———. 1988. *Judaism and the Origins of Christianity.* Jerusalem: Magnes.

———. 2001. *Jesus.* Jerusalem: Magnes.

Ford, M. J. 1976. "Money Bags in the Temple (Mk. 11, 16)." *Bib* 57: 249–253.

Fortes, M. 1962. "Ritual and Office in Tribal Society." In M. Gluckman, ed., *Essays on Ritual and Social Relations.* Manchester: Manchester University Press, 53–88.

Fraeyman, M. 1947. "La spiritualization de l'idée du temple dans les éprites pauliniennes." *ETL* 23: 378–412.

France, R. T. 2007. *The Gospel of Matthew.* NICNT; Grand Rapids: Eerdmans.

Fredriksen, P. 1990. "Jesus and the Temple, Mark and the War," *SBL 1990 Seminar Papers,* 293–310.

———. 1999. *Jesus of Nazareth: King of the Jews.* New York: Vintage Books.

———. 2010. "Judaizing the Nations: The Ritual Demands of Paul's Gospel." *NTS* 56: 232–252.

———. 2014. "How Later Contexts Affect Pauline Content, or: Retrospect Is the Mother of Anachronism." In P. J. Tomson and J. Schwartz, eds., *Jews and Christians in the First and Second Centuries: How to Write Their History.* CRINT 13. Leiden: Brill, 17–51.

———. 2015. "Arms and the Man: A Response to Dale Martin's 'Jesus in Jerusalem: Armed and Not Dangerous.'" *JSNT* 37, no. 3: 312–325.

Frey, J. 2012. "Temple and Identity in Early Christianity and in the Johannine Community: Reflections on the 'Parting of the Ways.'" In D. R. Schwartz and Z. Weiss, eds., *Was 70 CE a Watershed in Jewish History? On Jews and Judaism*

Before and After the Destruction of the Second Temple. Ancient Judaism and Early Christianity v.78. Leiden: Brill, 447–507.

———. 2014. *The Gospel According to John: From the Jews and for the World*. Beer Sheva: Ben Gurion University of the Negev (Hebrew).

Friedrich, G. 1985. *Die Verkuendigung des Todes Jesu im Neuen Testament*. 2d ed. Dusseldorf: Neuenkirchener.

Friedrichsen, T. A. 2005. "The Temple, a Pharisee, a Tax Collector, and the Kingdom of God: Rereading a Jesus Parable (Luke 18:10–14A)." *JBL* 124, no.1: 89–119.

Frühwald-König, J. 1998. *Tempel und Kult. Ein Beitrag zur Christologische des Johannesevangeliums*. BU 37. Regensburg: Verlag Friedrich Pustet.

Fuglseth, K. S. 2005. *Johannine Sectarianism in Perspective: A Sociological, Historical, and Comparative Analysis of Temple and Social Relationships in the Gospel of John, Philo, and Qumran*. Sup. NT 119. Leiden: Brill.

Funk, R. W., and the Jesus Seminar. 1998. *The Acts of Jesus: What Did Jesus Really Do? The Search for the Authentic Deeds of Jesus*. New York: HarperCollins.

Furnish, V. P. 1984. *II Corinthians*. AB 32. New York: Doubleday.

Furstenberg, Y. 2008. "Defilement Penetrating the Body: A New Understanding of Contamination in Mark 7.15." *NTS* 54: 176–200.

Gäbel, G. 2006. *Die Kulttheologie des Hebräerbreifes: Eine exegetisch-religionsgeschlichtliche Studie*. WUNT 2.212. Tübingen: Mohr.

Gäckle, V. 2104. *Allgemeines Priestertum: Zur Metaphorisierung des Priestertitels im Frühjudentum und Neuen Testament*. Tübingen: Mohr Siebeck.

Gaechter, P. 1947. "The Hatred of the House of Annas." *Theological Studies* 8: 3–34.

Gallusz, L. 2014. *The Throne Motif in the Book of Revelation: Profiles from History of Interpretation*. Bloomsbury: T & T Clark.

García Martínez, F., and J. C. Tigchelaar. 2000. *The Dead Sea Scroll Study Edition*, 2 vols. Grand Rapids: Eerdmans.

Garland, D. E. 1987. "Matthew's Understanding of the Temple Tax (Matt 17:24–27)." *SBL Seminar Papers* 26, 190–209.

Gärtner, B. 1965. *The Temple and the Community in Qumran and the New Testament*. Cambridge: Cambridge University Press.

Gaston, L. 1970. *No Stone on Another: Studies in the Significance of the Fall of Jerusalem in the Synoptic Gospels*. Leiden: Brill.

Geddert, T. J. 1989. *Watchwords: Mark 13 in Markan Eschatology*. Sheffield: JSOT Press.

Geertz, C. 1973. *The Interpretation of Cultures*. New York: Basic Books.

Gentner, D. 1983. "Structure-Mapping: A Theoretical Framework for Analogy." *Cognitive Science* 7: 155–170.

Gerhardsson, B. 1974. "Sacrificial Service and Atonement in the Gospel of Matthew." In R. Banks, ed., *Reconciliation and Hope: New Testament Essays on Atonement and Eschatology Presented to L. L. Morris on His 60th Birthday*. Exeter, UK: Paternoster, 25–35.

Gese, H. 1981. *Essays on Biblical Theology*. Minneapolis: Augsburg.

Giblin, C. H. 1984. "Revelation 11.1–13: Its Form, Function, and Contextual Integration." *NTS* 30: 433–459.

Gilders, W. K. 2011. "Jewish Sacrifice: Its Nature and Function (According to Philo)." In J. W. Knust and Z. Várhelyi, eds., *Ancient Mediterranean Sacrifice*. Oxford: Oxford University Press, 94–122.

Gluckman, M. 1962. "Les rites de passage." In M. Gluckman, ed., *Essays on Ritual and Social Relations*. Manchester: Manchester University Press, 1–52.

———. 1963. "Rituals of Rebellion in South East Africa." In *Order and Rebellion in Tribal Africa*. London: Cohen & West, 110–136.

Gnilka, J. 1983. *Johannesevangelium*. Die Neue Echter Bibel. Würzburg: Echter Verlag.

Goodenough, E. R. 1935. *By Light, Light: The Mystic Gospel of Hellenistic Judaism*. New Haven: Yale University Press.

Goodman, M. D. 1987. *The Ruling Class in Judaea*. Cambridge: Cambridge University Press.

Goppelt, L. 1993. *A Commentary on I Peter*. Grand Rapids: Eerdmans.

Grappe, C. 1992. *D'un Temple à l'autre: Pierre et l'Eglise primitive de Jérusalem*. Études d'histoire et de philosophie religieuses 71. Paris: Presses Universitaires de France.

Gray, G. B. 1925. *Sacrifice in the Old Testament*. Oxford: Clarendon.

Gray, T. C. 2008. *The Temple in the Gospel of Mark: A Study in Its Narrative Role*. WUNT II/242. Tübingen: Mohr.

———. 2010. *The Temple in the Gospel of Mark: A Study in Its Narrative Role*. Grand Rapids: Baker Academic.

Green, J. B. 1991. "The Death of Jesus and the Rending of the Temple Veil: A Window into Luke's Understanding of Jesus and the Temple." *SBLSP* 30: 543–557.

———. 1994. "The Demise of the Temple as 'Cultural Center' in Luke–Acts: An Exploration of the Rending of the Temple Veil (Luke 23.44–49)." *RB* 101, no. 4: 495–515.

Grelot, P. 1963. "Jean Vii, 38: eau du rocher ou source du Temple." *RB* 70: 43–51.

Grigsby, B. 1982. "The Cross as an Expiatory Sacrifice in the Fourth Gospel." *JSNT* 15: 51–80.

Gruenwald, I. 1988. "Halakhic Material in Codex Gnosticus V, 4: The Second Apocalypse of James?" In *From Apocalypticism to Gnosticism*. Frankfurt: Peter Lang, 279–294.

———. 2001. "Paul and Ritual Theory: The Case of the 'Lords' Supper' in 1 Corinthians 10 and 11." In A. Y. Collins and M. M. Mitchell, eds., *Antiquity and Humanity: Essays on Ancient Religion and Philosophy*. Tübingen: Mohr Siebeck, 157–187.

Guelich, R. 1989. *Mark 1–8:26*. WBC 34A. Dallas: Word.

Gundry, R. H. 1967. "In My Father's House Are Many Monai." *ZNW* 58: 68–72.

———. 1993. *Mark: A Commentary of His Apology for the Cross,* 2 vols. Grand Rapids: Eerdmans.

Gupta, N. K. 2010. *Worship That Makes Sense to Paul: A New Approach to the Theology and Ethics of Paul's Cultic Metaphors.* Berlin: de Gruyter.

Gurtner, D. M. 2007a. "The Rending of the Veil and Markan Christology: 'Unveiling' the ΥΙΟΣ ΘΕΟΥ (Mark 15:38–39)." *Biblical Interpretation* 15: 307–322.

———. 2007b. *The Torn Veil: Matthew's Exposition of the Death of Jesus.* Cambridge: Cambridge University Press.

———. 2008. "Matthew's Theology of the Temple and the 'Parting of the Ways': Christian Origins and the First Gospel." In D. M. Gurtner and J. Nolland, eds., *Built Upon the Rock: Studies in the Gospel of Matthew.* Grand Rapids: Eerdmans, 128–153.

Haber, S. 2005. "From Priestly Torah to Christ Cultus: The Re-Vision of Covenant and Cult in Hebrews." *JSNT* 28, no. 2: 105–124.

Haenchen, E. 1963. "Judentum und Christentum der Apostelgeschicte." *ZNW* 54: 155–187.

———. 1971. *The Acts of the Apostles.* Oxford: Blackwell.

———. 1984. *John 1.* Hermeneia; Philadelphia: Fortress.

Hahn, S. W. 2008. "Temple, Sign and Sacrament: Towards a New Perspective on the Gospel of John." In *Temple and Contemplation: God's Presence in the Cosmos, Church, and Human Heart, Letter and Spirit* 4: 107–143.

Hakola, R. 2009. "Friendly Pharisees and Social Identity in Acts." In T. E. Phillips, ed., *Contemporary Studies in Acts.* Macon, GA: Mercer University Press, 181–200.

Hamerton-Kelly, R. G. 1994. *The Gospel and the Sacred: Poetics of Violence in Mark.* Minneapolis: Fortress.

Hamm, D. 2003. "The Tamid Service in Luke–Acts: The Cultic Background Behind Luke's Theology of Worship (Luke 1:5–25; 18:9–14; 24:50–53; Acts 3:1; 10:3, 30)." *CBQ* 65: 215–231.

Han, K. S. 2002. *Jerusalem and the Early Jesus Movement: The Q Community's Attitude Toward the Temple.* Sheffield: Sheffield Academic Press.

Handelman, D. 2004. "Introduction: Why Ritual in Its Own Right?" in D. Handelman and G. Lindquist, eds., *Ritual in Its Own Right: Exploring the Dynamics of Transformation.* New York: Berghahn Books, 1–32.

Hanger, D. A. 1993. *Matthew 1–13.* WBC 33A. Dallas: Word.

———. 1995. *Matthew 14–28.* WBC 33B. Dallas: Word.

Hanson, J. S. 2000. *The Endangered Promises: Conflict in Mark.* Atlanta: SBL.

Harari, J. (ed.). 1979. *Textual Strategies: Perspectives in Post-Structuralist Criticism.* Ithaca: Cornell University Press.

Hartman, L. 1966. *Prophecy Interpreted: The Formation of Some Jewish Apocalyptic Texts and of the Eschatological Discourse Mark 13 Par.* ConBNT 1; Lund: Gleerup.

———. 1989. "'He Spoke of the Temple of His Body' (Jn 2:13–22)." *Svensk ex- egetisk årsbok* 54: 70–79.

Hays, R. B. 1989. *Echoes of Scripture in the Letters of Paul.* New Haven and London: Yale University Press.

Head, P. 2004. "The Temple in Luke's Gospel." In T. D. Alexander and S. Gathercole, eds., *Heaven on Earth: The Temple in Biblical Theology.* Carlisle, UK: Paternoster, 101–119.

Hedrick, C. W., and D. M. Parrott. 1996. "The Second Apocalypse of James (V, 4)." In J. M. Robinson, ed., *The Nag Hammadi Library in English.* Rev. ed. Leiden: Brill, 270–276.

Heil, J. P. 1995. "Jesus as a Unique High Priest in the Gospel of John." *CBQ* 57: 729–745.

———. 1997. "The Narrative Strategy and Pragmatics of the Temple Theme in Mark." *CBQ* 59: 76–100.

Hengel, M. 1977. *Crucifixion.* Philadelphia: Fortress.

———. 1979. *Acts and the History of Earliest Christianity.* Philadelphia: Fortress.

———. 1981. *The Atonement: The Origins of the Doctrine in the New Testament.* Minneapolis: Fortress.

———. 1983. "Luke the Historian and the Geography of Palestine in the Acts of the Apostles." *Between Jesus and Paul: Studies in the Earliest History of Christianity.* London: SCM, 97–128.

———. 1985. *Studies in the Gospel of Mark.* Minneapolis: Fortress.

———. 1989a. *The Zealots.* Trans. D. Smith. Edinburgh: T & T Clark.

———. 1989b. *The Johannine Question.* London: SCM Press.

———. 2002. "Jakobus der Herrenbruder—der erste Papst?" *Paulus und Jakobus: Kleine Schriften III.* WUNT 141. Tübingen: Mohr Siebeck, 549–582.

Hengel, M., and A. M. Schwemer. 2007. *Jesus und das Judentum.* Tübingen: Mohr.

Hennecke, E. 1991. *New Testament Apocrypha,* in W. Schneemelcher (ed. and trans.), Volume 1: *Gospels and Related Writings.* Trans. R. M. Wilson. Philadelphia: Westminster.

———, and W. Schneemelcher (eds.). 1963. *New Testament Apocrypha.* 2 vols. Philadelphia: Westminster.

Henshke, D. 2007. *Festival Joy in Tannaitic Discourse.* Jerusalem: Magnes (Hebrew).

Hiers, R. H. 1970. "Friends by Unrighteous Mammon." *JAAR* 38: 30–36.

———. 1971. "Purification of the Temple: Preparation for the Kingdom of God." *JBL* 90, 82–90.

Hill, C. C. 1992. *Hellenists and Hebrews: Reappraising Division Within the Earliest Church.* Minneapolis: Fortress.

Himmelfarb, M. 1993. *Ascent to Heaven in Jewish and Christian Apocalypses.* Oxford: Oxford University Press.

Hoffman, Y. 2001. *Jeremiah: Introduction and Commentary.* Vol. 1, chapters 1–25. Tel Aviv: Am Oved and Magnes (Hebrew).

Hogeterp, A. L. A. 2006. *Paul and God's Temple: A Historical Interpretation of Cultic Imagery in the Corinthian Correspondence.* Biblical Tools and Studies 2. Leuven: Peeters.

Holmås, G. R. 2005. "'My House Shall Be a House of Prayer:' Reading the Temple as a Place of Prayer in Acts within the Context of Luke's Apologetical Objective." *JSNT* 27, no. 4: 393–416.

Holmberg, B. 2008. "Understanding the First Hundred Years of Christian Identity." In B. Holmberg, ed., *Exploring Early Christian Identity*. Tübingen: Mohr, 1–32.

Holmén, T. 2001. *Jesus and the Jewish Covenant Thinking*. Leiden: Brill.

Hooker, M. D. 1988. "Traditions About the Temple in the Sayings of Jesus." *BJRL* 70: 7–19.

———. 2008. "On Becoming the Righteousness of God: Another Look at 2 Cor 5:21." *NT* 50, no. 4: 358–375.

Horbury, W. 1983. "The Aaronic Priesthood in the Epistle to the Hebrews." *JSNT* 19: 43–71.

———. 1984. "The Temple Tax." In E. Bammel and C. F. D. Moule, eds., *Jesus and the Politics of His Day*. Cambridge: Cambridge University Press, 265–286.

Horgan, M. P. 1979. *Pesharim: Qumran Interpretations of Biblical Books*. CBQMS 8. Washington: Catholic Biblical Association of America.

Horn, F. W. 2007. "Paulus und der Herodianische Tempel." *NTS* 53: 184–203.

Horsley, R. 1987. *Jesus and the Spiral of Violence: Popular Jewish Resistance in Roman Palestine*. San Francisco: Harper & Row.

Hoskins, P. M. 2006. *Jesus as the Fulfillment of the Temple in the Gospel of John*. Milton Keynes, UK: Paternoster.

———. 2007. *Jesus as the Fulfillment of the Temple in the Gospel of John*. Paternoster Biblical Monographs. Eugene, OR: Wipf and Stock.

Howard, J. K. 1969. "Christ Our Passover." *EvQ* 41: 97–108.

Hubert, H., and M. Mauss. 1964 [1898]. *Sacrifice: Its Nature and Function*. London: Cohen & West.

Hultgren, A. J. 1976. "Paul's Pre-Christian Persecutions of the Church: Their Purpose, Locale, and Nature." *JBL* 95: 97–111.

Hurst, L. D. 1990. *The Epistle to the Hebrews: Its Background of Thought*. Cambridge: Cambridge University Press.

Hurtado, L. W. 2003. *Lord Jesus Christ: Devotion to Jesus in Earliest Christianity*. Grand Rapids: Eerdmans.

Incigneri, B. J. 2003. *The Gospel to the Romans: The Setting and Rhetoric of Mark's Gospel*. Leiden: Brill.

Isaacs, M. E. 1992. *Sacred Space: An Approach to the Theology of the Epistle of Hebrews*. Sheffield: JSOT Press.

Jameson, T. 1988. "The Symbolic Inference; or Kenneth Burke and Ideological Analysis." In *The Ideologies of Theory: Essays 1971–1986*. Minneapolis: University of Minnesota Press, 137–152.

Jamieson, R. B. 2016. "Hebrews 9.23: Cult Inauguration, Yom Kippur and the Cleansing of the Heavenly Tabernacle." *NTS* 62: 569–587.

———. 2017. "When and Where Did Jesus Offer Himself? A Taxonomy of Recent Scholarship on Hebrews." *Currents in Biblical Research* 15.3: 338–368.

Janowski, B. 1982. *Sühne als Heilsgeschehen: Studien zur Sühnetheologie der Priester-schrift und zur Wurzel KPR im Alten Orient und im Alten Testament.* WMANT 55; Neukirchen-Vluyn: Neukirchener Verlag.

Jensen, P. 1992. *Graded Holiness: A Key to the Priestly Conception of the World.* JSOT-Sup 106, Sheffield: Sheffield Academic Press.

Jeremias, J. 1966a. *The Eucharist Words of Jesus.* Trans. N. Perrin. London: SCM.

———. 1966b. *Rediscovering the Parables of Jesus.* New York: Charles Scribner's Sons.

Jervell, J. 1972 [2002]. *Luke and the People of God: A New Look at Luke–Acts.* Philadelphia: Augsburg Fortress.

Johnson, M. 1987. *The Body in the Mind: The Bodily Basis of Reason and Imagination.* Chicago: University of Chicago Press.

Johnson, R. 2001. *Going Outside the Camp: The Sociological Function of the Levitical Critique in the Epistle to the Hebrews.* London: Sheffield Academic Press.

Jones, F. S. 1995. *An Ancient Jewish Christian Source, Pseudo-Clementine Recognitions 1.27–71.* Atlanta: Society for Biblical Literature.

Joseph, S. J. 2016. *Jesus and the Temple: The Crucifixion in Its Jewish Context.* Cambridge: Cambridge University Press.

Joslin, B. 2008. *Christ, the Law, and the Theology of the Mosaic Law in Hebrews 7:1–10:18.* Eugene, OR: Paternoster.

Juel, D. 1977. *Messiah and Temple: The Trial of Jesus in the Gospel of Mark.* Atlanta: Scholars Press.

Käsemann, E. 1980. *Commentary on Romans.* Trans. G. W. Bromile. Grand Rapids: Eerdmans.

Kazen, T. 2010. *Jesus and Purity Halakhah: Was Jesus Indifferent to Impurity?* Winona Lake, IN: Eisenbrauns.

Kelber, W. H. 1974. The Kingdom in Mark: A New Place and a New Time. Philadelphia: Fortress.

———. 1979. *Mark's Story of Jesus.* Philadelphia: Fortress.

Kerr, A. R. 2002. *The Temple of Jesus' Body: The Temple Theme in the Gospel of John.* London: Sheffield Academic Press.

Kertzer, D. I. 1988. *Ritual, Politics, and Power.* New Haven and London: Yale University Press.

Kilpatrick, G. D. 1946. *The Origins of the Gospel According to St. Matthew,* Oxford: Clarendon Press.

Kinzer, M. S. 1998. "Temple Christology in the Gospel of John." *SBL Seminar Papers,* 37, no. 1: 447–464.

Kirk, A., and T. Thatcher (eds.). 2005. *Memory Tradition and Text: Uses of the Past in Early Christianity.* Leiden: Brill.

Klausner, J. 1964 [1925]. *Jesus of Nazareth: His Life, Time and Teaching.* Boston: Beacon Press.

Klawans, J. 2000. *Impurity and Sin in Ancient Judaism.* Oxford: Oxford University Press.

———. 2001. "Was Jesus' Last Supper a Seder?" *Bible Review* 17.5, 24–33, 47.

———. 2002. "Interpreting the Last Supper: Sacrifice, Anti-Spiritualization and Anti-Sacrifice." *NTS* 48:1–17.

———. 2006. *Purity, Sacrifice and the Temple: Symbolism and Supersessionism in the Study of Ancient Judaism.* Oxford: Oxford University Press.

Klijn, A. F. J. 1957. "Stephen's Speech—Acts 7:2–53." *NTS* 4: 25–31.

Klinzing, G. 1971. *Die Umdeutung des Kultus in der Qumrangemeinde und im NT.* Göttingen: Vandenhoeck & Ruprecht.

Kloppenborg, J. S. 1987. *The Formation of Q: Trajectories in Ancient Wisdom Collections.* Minneapolis: Fortress.

———. 1990a. "Nomos and Ethos in Q." In J. E. Goehring et al., eds., *Gospel Origins and Christian Beginnings in Honor of James M. Robinson.* Sonoma, CA: Polebride, 35–48.

———. 1990b. "City and Wasteland: Narrative World and the Beginning of the Saying Gospel (Q)." In D. Smith, ed., *How Gospels Begin, Semeia* 52. Atlanta: Scholars Press, 145–160.

———. 1991. "Literary Convention, Self-Evidence and Social History of the Q People." *Semeia* 55. Atlanta: Scholars Press, 77–102.

———. 2000. *Excavating Q: The History and Setting of the Saying Gospel.* Minneapolis: Fortress.

———. 2005. "Evocatio Deorum and the Date of Mark." *JBL* 124: 419–450.

———. 2006. *The Tenants in the Vineyard: Ideology, Economics, and Agrarian Conflict in Jewish Palestine.* WUNT 195. Tübingen: Mohr, 71–105.

Knight, J. 1998. *Luke's Gospel.* London: Routledge.

Knox, J. 1950. *Chapters in a Life of Paul.* New York: Abingdon/Cokesbury. Reprint, Macon, Ga: Mercer, 1987.

Kodell, J. 1988. *The Eucharist in the New Testament.* Wilmington, DE: Glazier.

Koester, C. R. 1989. *The Dwelling of God: The Tabernacle in the Old Testament, Intertestamental Jewish Literature, and the New Testament.* CBQMS 22. Washington: Catholic Biblical Association of America.

———. 2001. *Hebrews.* AB 36. New York: Doubleday.

———. 2003. *Symbolism in the Fourth Gospel: Meaning, Mystery, Community.* Minneapolis: Fortress.

———. 2014. *Revelation.* AB 38A. New Haven and London: Yale University Press.

Koester, H. 1962. "'Outside the Camp': Hebrews 13, 9–14." *HTR* 55: 299–315.

Koet, J. 1996. "Why Did Paul Shave His Hair (Acts 18:18)? Nazirite and Temple in the Book of Acts." In M. Poorthuis and C. Safrai, eds., *The Centrality of Jerusalem: Historical Perspectives.* Kampen, Netherlands: Kok Pharos, 128–142.

Köstenberger, A. J. 2006. "The Destruction of the Second Temple and the Composition of the Fourth Gospel." In J. Lierman, ed., *Challenging Perspectives on the Gospel of John.* WUNT 2/219. Tübingen: Mohr, 69–107.

Kotila, M. 1988. *Umstrittene Zeuge. Studien zur Stellung des Gesetzes in der johanneischen Teologiegeschichte.* Helsinki: Suomalainen Tiedeakatemia.

Kövecses, Z. 2002. *Metaphor: A Practical Introduction.* New York: Oxford University Press.

———. 2006. *Language, Mind and Culture. A Practical Introduction.* New York: Oxford University Press.

Krauss, H.-J. 1989. *Psalms 61–150: A Commentary.* Minneapolis: Fortress.

Lakoff, G., and M. Johnson. 1980. *Metaphors We Live By.* Chicago: University of Chicago Press.

Lampe, P. 2003. *Christians at Rome in the First Two Centuries: From Paul to Valentinus.* London: Continuum.

Lancaster Patterson, J. 2015. *Keeping the Feast: Metaphors of Sacrifice in 1 Corinthians and Philippians.* Atlanta: SBL.

Lanci, J. R. 1997. *A New Temple for Corinth: Rhetorical and Archaeological Approaches to Pauline Imagery.* New York: Peter Lang.

Lane, W. L. 1974. *The Gospel According to Mark: The English Text with Introduction, Exposition, and Notes.* NICNT; Grand Rapids: Eerdmans.

———. 1991. *Hebrews 1–8.* WBC 47A. Mexico City: Thomas Nelson.

———. 2000. *Hebrews 9–13.* WBC 47B. Mexico City: Thomas Nelson.

Lang, B. 1992. "The Roots of the Eucharist in Jesus' Praxis." *SBL Seminar Papers,* 467–472.

Larsson, E. 1993. "Temple-Criticism and the Jewish Heritage: Some Reflections on Acts 6–7." *NTS* 39: 379–395.

Leaney, A. R. C. 1966. *The Rule of Qumran and Its Meaning.* Philadelphia: Westminster.

Le Donne, A. 2013. "The Improper Temple Offering of Ananias and Sapphira." *NTS* 59: 346–364.

Lee, D. A. 1994. *The Symbolic Narratives of the Fourth Gospel: The Interplay of Form and Meaning.* Sheffield: JSOT Press.

———. 2002. *Flesh and Glory: Symbolism, Gender and Theology in the Gospel of John.* New York: Herder and Herder.

Lee, P. 2001. *The New Jerusalem in the Book of Revelation: A Study of Revelation 21–22 in the Light of Its Background in Jewish Tradition.* WUNT 2/129. Tübingen: Mohr-Siebeck.

Légasse, S. 1992. *Stephanos: histoire et discours d'Etienne dans les Actes des Apôtres.* Paris: Cerf.

Léon-Dufour, X. 1951–1952. "Le signe du temple selon saint Jean." *Recherches de Science Religieuse* 39: 155–175.

———. 1982. *Le partage du pain eucharistique selon le Nouveau Testament.* Paris: Editions du Seuil.

Léopold, S., and L. Sabourin. 1970. *Sin, Redemption and Sacrifice: A Biblical and Patristic Study.* Roma: Pontificio Istituto Biblico.

Levison, J. R. 2006. "The Spirit and the Temple in Paul's Letters to the Corinthians." In S. E. Porter, ed., *Paul and His Theology.* Leiden: Brill, 189–215.

Licthenberger, H. 1999. "Zion and the Destruction of the Temple in 4 Ezra 9–10." In B. Ego et al., eds., *Gemeinde ohne Tempel—Community Without Temple.* WUNT 118, Tübingen: Mohr, 239–249.

Lieu, J. M. 1996. *Image and Reality: The Jews in the World of the Christians in the Second Century.* Edinburgh: T & T Clark.

———. 1999. "Temple and Synagogue in John." *NTS* 45: 51–69.

———. 2004. *Christian Identity in the Jewish and Graeco-Roman World.* New York: Oxford University Press.

Lim, K. Y. 2010. "Paul's Use of Temple Imagery in the Corinthian Correspondence: The Creation of Christian Identity." In K. Ehrensperger and J. B. Tucker, eds., *Reading Paul in Context: Explorations in Identity Formation, Essays in Honour of William S. Campbell.* London: Bloomsbury T & T Clark, 189–205.

Lindars, B. 1972. *The Gospel of John.* NCBC 25. London: Oliphants.

———. 1991. *The Theology of the Letter to the Hebrews.* Cambridge: Cambridge University Press.

Liu, J. H., and J. László. 2007. "Narrative Theory of History and Identity: Social Identity, Social Representations, Society and the Individual." In G. Moloney and I. Walker, eds., *Social Representations and Identity: Content, Process and Power.* New York: Palgrave Macmillan, 85–108.

Liu, Y. 2013. *Temple Purity in 1–2 Corinthians.* WUNT 2.343. Tübingen: Mohr.

Loader, W. R. G. 1992. *The Christology of the Fourth Gospel.* 2d ed. Frankfurt: Peter Lang.

———. 1996. "Challenged at the Boundaries: A Conservative Jesus in Mark's Tradition." *JSNT* 63: 45–61.

———. 1997. *Jesus' Attitude Towards the Law: A Study of the Gospels.* Tübingen: Mohr-Siebeck.

Lohmeyer, E. 1956. *Das Evangelium des Matthäus. Nachgelassene Ausarbeitungen und Entwürfe.* KEK I,1. Göttingen, Vandenhoeck & Ruprecht.

———. 1962. *Lord of the Temple: A Study of the Relation Between Cult and Gospel.* Richmond: John Knox Press.

———. 1967. *Das Evangelium des Markus übersetzt und erklärt.* 17th ed. Göttingen: Vandenhoeck & Ruprecht.

Longenecker, B. W. 2004. "Rome's Victory and God's Honour: The Spirit and the Temple in Lukan Theodicy." In G. N. Stanton, B. W. Longenecker, and S. C. Barton, eds., *The Holy Spirit and Christian Origins: Festschrift for James D. G. Dunn.* Grand Rapids: Eerdmans, 90–102.

Lücking, S. 2002. "Die *Zerstörung* des Tempels 70 n. Chr. als Krisenerfahrung der frühen Christen." In J. Hahn, ed., *Zerstörungen des Jerusalemer Tempels: Geschehen—Wahrnehmung—Bewältigung.* WUNT 147. Tübingen: Mohr, 140–165.

Lüdemann, G. 1989a. *Early Christianity According to the Traditions in Acts: A Commentary.* Trans. J. Bowden. Minneapolis: Fortress.

———. 1989b. *Opposition to Paul in Jewish Christianity.* Philadelphia: Fortress.

Lührmann, D. 1981. "Markus 14.55–64. Christologie und Zerstörung des Tempels im Markusevngelium." *NTS* 27: 457–474.

———. 1987. *Das Markusevangelium.* HNT 2. Tübingen: Mohr.

Lukes, S. 1973. *Emile Durkheim, His Life and Work: A Historical and Critical Study.* Stanford: Stanford University Press.

———. 1975. "Political Power and Social Integration." *Sociology: Journal of the British Sociological Association* 9, no. 2: 289–308.

Luomanen, P. 1998. *Entering the Kingdom of Heaven: A Study of the Structure of Matthew's View of Salvation.* WUNT 2.101. Tübingen: Mohr.

Luz, U. 1989. *Matthew 1–7.* Hermeneia. Minneapolis: Fortress.

———. 1993. *The Theology of the Gospel of Matthew.* Cambridge: Cambridge University Press.

———. 2001. *Matthew 8–20.* Hermeneia. Minneapolis: Fortress.

———. 2005. *Matthew 21–28.* Hermeneia. Minneapolis: Fortress.

Mack, B. 1988. *A Myth of Innocence: Mark and Christian Origins.* Philadelphia: Fortress.

Mackie, S. D. 2007. *Eschatology and Exhortation in the Epistle to the Hebrews.* WUNT II/223. Tübingen: Mohr.

MacMullen, R. 1966. *Enemies of the Roman Order.* Cambridge: Harvard University Press.

MacRae, G. W. 1978. "Heavenly Temple and Eschatology in the Letter to the Hebrews" *Semeia* 12: 179–200.

Maddox, R. 1982. *The Purpose of Luke–Acts.* Edinburgh: T & T Clark.

Malina, B. J., and J. J. Pilch. 2006. *Social Science Commentary on the Letters of Paul.* Minneapolis: Augsburg.

Manson, W. 1951. *The Epistle to the Hebrews.* London: Hodder and Stoughton.

Marcus, J. 1992. "The Jewish War and the *Sitz im Leben* of Mark." *JBL* 111: 441–462.

———. 2000. *Mark 1–8.* AB27. New York: Doubleday.

———. 2009. *Mark 8–16.* AB27A. New Haven and London: Yale University Press.

———. 2013. "Passover and Last Supper Revisited." *NTS* 59: 303–323.

Marguerat, D. 2002. "Jews and Christians in Conflict." *The First Christian Historian: Writing the Acts of the Apostles.* SNTSMS 121. Cambridge: Cambridge University Press, 129–154.

Marshall, I. H. 1989. "Church and Temple in the New Testament." *Tyndale Bulletin* 40:203–222.

Martin, R. P. 1986. *2 Corinthians.* WBC 40. Waco: Word.

———. 1988. *James.* WBC 48. Waco: Word.

Martyn, J. L. 2003 [1968]. *History and Theology in the Fourth Gospel.* 3rd ed. Louisville: Westminster/John Knox.

Marxsen, W. 1969. *Mark the Evangelist: Studies in the Redaction History of the Gospel.* Nashville: Abingdon.

Mason, E. F. 2008. *"You Are a Priest Forever": Second Temple Jewish Messianism and the Priestly Christology of the Epistle to the Hebrews.* STDJ 74. Leiden: Brill.

Mason, S. 1992. *Josephus and the New Testament.* Peabody, MA: Hendrickson.

———. 1995. "Chief Priests, Sadducees, Pharisees and Sanhedrin in Acts." In R. Bauckham, ed., *The Book of Acts in Its First Century Setting, VI: The Book of Acts in Its Palestinian Setting.* Grand Rapids: Eerdmans, 119–177.

———. 2016. *Orientation to the History of Roman Judaea.* Eugene, OR: Cascade.

Matera, F. J. 1985. "The Death of Jesus According to Luke: A Question of Sources." *CBQ* 47: 469–485.

Mathews, K. A. 1988. "John, Jesus and the Essenes: Trouble in the Temple." *Criswell Theological Review* 3.1: 101–126.

Mayes, R. J. H. 2010. "The Lord's Supper in the Theology of Cyprian of Carthage." *Concordia Theological Quarterly* 74: 307–324.

McCaffrey, J. 1988. *The House With Many Rooms: The Temple Theme of Jn. 14,2–3.* Analecta Biblica 114. Rome: Pontificio Istituto Biblico.

McEleney, N. J. 1976. "MT 17:24–27—Who Paid the Temple Tax? A Lesson in Avoidance of Scandal." *CBQ* 38.2: 178–192.

McKelvey, R. J. 1969. *The New Temple: The Church in the New Testament.* Oxford: Oxford University Press.

———. 2013. *Pioneer and Priest: Jesus Christ in the Epistle to the Hebrews.* Eugene, OR: Pickwick.

McKnight, S. 1999. "Jesus and James on Israel and Purity." In B. Chilton and C. A. Evans, eds., *James the Just and Christian Origins.* SNT 98. Leiden: Brill, 83–129.

———. 2005. *Jesus and His Death: Historiography, the Historical Jesus, and Atonement Theory.* Waco: Baylor University Press.

McLaren, J. S. 2001. "Ananus, James, and the Earliest Christianity: Josephus's Account of the Death of James." *JTS* 52: 1–25.

McLean, B. H. 1992. "The Absence of Atoning Sacrifice in Paul's Soteriology." *NTS* 38: 531–535.

McPolin, J. 1979. *John.* New Testament Message 6. Dublin: Veritas.

Meagher, J. C. 1969. "John 1:14 and the New Temple." *JBL* 88, no. 1: 57–68.

Meeks, W. A. 1983. *First Urban Christians: The Social World of the Apostle Paul.* New Haven and London: Yale University Press.

Meier, J. P. 1991. *A Marginal Jew: Rethinking the Historical Jesus.* Vol. 1: *The Roots of the Problem and the Person.* New York: Doubleday.

Meyer, B. F. 1983. "The Pre-Pauline Formula in Rom. 3:25–26a." *NTS* 29: 198–208.

———. 1988. "The Expiation Motif and the Eucharistic Words: A Key to the History of Jesus?" *Gregorianum* 69: 461–487.

———. 2002. *The Aims of Jesus.* London: SCM.

Meyers, C., and E. M. Meyers. 1993. *Zechariah 9–14.* AB 25C. New York: Doubleday.

Milgrom, J. 1976. "Israel's Sanctuary: The Priestly 'Picture of Dorian Gray.'" *RB* 83: 390–399.

———. 1991. *Leviticus 1–16*. AB 3. New York: Doubleday.

Miller, R. J. 1988. "The Rejection of the Prophets in Q." *JBL* 107: 225–240.

———. 1991. "The (A)historicity of Jesus. Temple Demonstration: A Test Case in Methodology." *SBL 1991 Seminar Papers*, 235–252.

Moffitt, D. M. 2006. "Righteous Bloodshed, Matthew's Passion Narrative, and the Temple's Destruction: Lamentations as a Matthean Intertext." *JBL* 125: 299–320.

———. 2011. *Atonement and the Logic of Resurrection in the Epistle to the Hebrews*. SNT 141. Leiden: Brill.

———. 2016. "Serving in the Tabernacle in Heaven: Sacred Space, Jesus's High-Priestly Sacrifice, and Hebrews' Analogical Theology." In G. Gelardini and H. W. Attridge, eds., *Hebrews in Contexts*. AJEC 91. Leiden; Brill, 259–279.

Moloney, F. J. 1990. "Reading John 2:13–22: The Purification of the Temple." *RB* 97: 432–452.

———. 1992. "Who Is 'the Reader' in/of the Fourth Gospel?" *Australian Biblical Review* 40: 20–33.

———. 2004. *Mark: Storyteller, Interpreter, Evangelist*. Peabody, MA: Hendrickson.

Moo, D. 1984. "Jesus and the Authority of the Mosaic Law." *JSNT* 20: 3–49.

Moret, J.-R. 2016. "Le rôle du concept de purification dans l'Épître aux Hébreux: une réaction à quelques propositions de David M. Moffitt." *NTS* 62: 289–307.

Motyer, S. 1987. "The Rending of the Veil: A Markan Pentecost." *NTS* 33: 155–157.

———. 2004. "The Temple in Hebrews: Is It There?" In T. D. Alexander and S. Gathercole, eds., *Heaven on Earth. The Temple in Biblical Theology*. Carlisle, UK: Paternoster, 177–189.

Moule, C. F. D. 1950. "Sanctuary and Sacrifice in the Church of the New Testament." *JTS* 1: 29–41.

Moxnes, H. 1988. *The Economy of the Kingdom: Social Conflict and Economic Relations in Luke's Gospel*. Minneapolis: Fortress.

Munn, N. D. 1973. "Symbolism in a Ritual Context." In J. J. Honigmann, ed., *Handbook of Social and Cultural Anthropology*. Chicago: Rand McNally, 579–612.

Murphy, F. J. 1987. "The Temple in the Syriac Apocalypse of Baruch." *JBL* 106: 670–683.

Murphy-O'Connor, J. M. 2000. "Jesus and the Money Changers." *RB* 107: 42–55.

Myers, C. 1988. *Binding the Strong Man: A Political Reading of Mark's Story of Jesus*. Maryknoll, NY: Orbis.

Myllykoski, M. 2007. "James the Just in History and Tradition: Perspectives on Past and Present Scholarship (Part II)." *Currents in Biblical Research* 6, no. 1: 11–98.

Nagen, Y. 2013. *Water, Creation and Immanence: The Philosophy of the Festival of Sukkot*. Jerusalem: Magid [Hebrew].

Najman, H. 2014. *Losing the Temple and Recovering the Future: An Analysis of 4 Ezra*. New York: Cambridge University Press.

Nanos, M. D. 2012. "Paul's Relationship to Torah in Light of His Strategy 'to Become Everything to Everyone' (1 Corinthians 9:19–22)." In R. Bieringer and

D. Pollefeyt, eds., *Paul and Judaism: Crosscurrents in Pauline Exegesis and the Study of Jewish-Christian Relations*. London: Continuum, 106–140.

Neusner, J. 1979. "Map Without Territory: The Mishnah's System of Sacrifice." *History of Religions* 19: 103–127.

———. 1989. "Money Changers in the Temple: The Mishna's Explanation." *NTS* 35: 287–290.

Newton, M. 1985. *The Concept of Purity at Qumran in the Letters of Paul*. Cambridge: Cambridge University Press.

Neyrey, J. H. 1988. *An Ideology of Revolt: John's Christology in Social-Science Perspective*. Minneapolis: Fortress.

———. 2007. *The Gospel of John*. NCBC. Cambridge: Cambridge University Press.

———. 2009. *The Gospel of John in Cultural and Rhetorical Perspective*. Grand Rapids: Eerdmans.

Niederwimmer, K. 1998. *The Didache*. Hermeneia. Minneapolis: Fortress.

Nielsen, J. T. 2006. "The Lamb of God: The Cognitive Structure of a Johannine Metaphor." In J. Frey, J. G. Van der Watt, and R. Zimmermann, eds., *Imagery in the Gospel of John*. WUNT 200. Tübingen: Mohr, 217–256.

Nikiprowetzky, V. 1967. "La Spiritualisation des Sacrifices et le Culte Sacrificiel au Temple de Jérusalem Chez Philon d'Alexandrie." *Semitica* 17: 97–116.

Ortner, S. B. 1973. "On Key Symbols." *American Anthropologist* 75: 1228–1346.

Overmann, J. A. 1990. *Matthew's Gospel and Formative Judaism: The Social World of the Matthean Community*. Minneapolis: Fortress.

Paesler, K. 1999. *Das Tempelwort Jesu. Die Traditionen von Tempelzerstörung und Tempelerneuerung im Neuen Testament*. FRLANT 184. Göttingen: Vandenhoeck & Ruprecht.

Painter, J. 1999. *Just James: The Brother of Jesus in History and Tradition*. Minneapolis: Fortress.

Pancaro, S. 1975. *The Law in the Fourth Gospel*. Leiden: Brill.

Parsons, M. C. 2007. *Luke: Storyteller, Interpreter, Evangelist*. Peabody, MA: Hendrickson.

Paulien, J. 1995. "The Role of the Hebrew Cultus, Sanctuary, and Temple in the Plot and Structure of the Book of Revelation." *Andrews University Seminary Studies* 33.2: 245–264.

Perrin, N. 2010. *Jesus the Temple*. London: SPCK.

Pervo, R. I. 2009. *Acts*. Hermeneia. Minneapolis: Fortress.

Pesch, R. J. 1977. *Das Markusevangelium*, I. Einleitung und Kommentar zu Kap. 1,1–8:26; HTKNT 2/1. 2d ed. Freiburg/Basel/Vienna: Herder.

———. 1991. *Das Markusevangelium, II. Kommentar zu Kap. 8,27–16,20*. HTKNT, Bd. 2,2. Freiburg: Herder.

Philips, T. A. 2009. "Prophets, Priests and Godfearing Readers." In T. E. Phillips, ed., *Contemporary Studies in Acts*. Macon, GA: Mercer University Press, 222–239.

Pitre, B. 2008. "Jesus, the New Temple, and the New Priesthood." *Letter & Spirit* 4: 47–83.

Price, S. R. F. 1984. *Rituals of Power: The Roman Imperial Cult in Asia Minor.* Cambridge: Cambridge University Press.

Porter, S. E. 2000. "Was Paul a Good Jew? Fundamental Issues in a Current Debate." In B. W. Pearson and S. E. Porter, eds., *Christian–Jewish Relations Through the Centuries.* Sheffield: Sheffield Academic Press, 148–174.

———. 2001. *Paul in Acts.* Peabody, MA: Hendrickson.

Powell, M. A. 1990. "The Religious Leaders in Luke: A Literary-Critical Study." *JBL* 109, no. 1: 93–110.

———. 1995. "Do and Keep What Moses Says (Matthew 23:2–7)." *JBL* 114, no. 3: 419–435.

Pratscher, W. 1987. *Der Herrenbruder Jakobus und die Jakobustradition.* FRLANT, 139. Göttingen: Vandenhoeck & Ruprecht.

Räisänen, H. 1982. "Jesus and the Food Laws: Reflection on Mark 7:15." *NTS* 16: 79–100.

———. 1985. "Galatians 2.16 and Paul's Break with Judaism." *NTS* 31.4: 543–553.

———. 1986. *Paul and the Law.* Philadelphia: Fortress.

Rapske, B. 1994. *The Book of Acts in Its First-Century Setting.* Vol. 3: *The Book of Acts and Paul in Roman Custody.* Carlisle, UK: Paternoster; Grand Rapids: Eerdmans.

Ravens, D. 1995. *Luke and the Restoration of Israel.* Sheffield: Sheffield Academic Press.

Regev, E. 2000. "Pure Individualism: The Idea of Non-Priestly Purity in Ancient Judaism." *Journal for the Study of Judaism in the Persian, Hellenistic and Roman Period* 31: 176–202.

———. 2001. "Priestly Dynamic Holiness and Deuteronomistic Static Holiness." *Vetus Testamentum* 51: 243–261.

———. 2003. "Abominated Temple and a Holy Community: The Formation of the Concepts of Purity and Impurity in Qumran." *Dead Sea Discoveries* 10.2: 243–278.

———. 2004a. "Moral Impurity and the Temple in Early Christianity in Light of Qumranic Ideology and Ancient Greek Practice." *HTR* 79.4: 383–411.

———. 2004b. "A Kingdom of Priests or a Holy (Gentile) People: The Temple in Early Christian Life and Thought." *Cathedra* 113: 5–34 (Hebrew).

———. 2004c. "Sacrifices of Righteousness: Visiting the Temple and Bringing Sacrifices as Religious Experience in Psalms." *Tarbiz* 73, no. 3: 365–386 (Hebrew).

———. 2005a. *The Sadducees and Their Halakhah: Religion and Society in the Second Temple Period.* Yad Izhak ben Zvi (Hebrew).

———. 2005b. "Temple Prayer as the Origin of the Fixed Prayer (On the Evolution of Prayer During the Period of the Second Temple)." *Zion* 70.1: 5–30 (Hebrew).

———. 2005c. "The Ritual Baths Near the Temple Mount and the Extra-Purification Before Entering the Temple Courts." *Israel Exploration Journal* 55, no. 2: 194–204.

———. 2006a. "Temple or Messiah? On the Trial of Jesus, the Temple and the Roman Policy." *Cathedra* 119: 13–36 (Hebrew).

————. 2006b. "The Sadducees, the Pharisees and the Sacred: Meaning and Ideology in the Halakhic Controversies Between the Sadducees and the Pharisees." *Review of Rabbinic Judaism* 9: 126–140.

————. 2007. *Sectarianism in Qumran: A Cross-Cultural Perspective.* Religion and Society Series 45. Berlin: Walter de Gruyter.

————. 2008. "Hanukkah and the Temple of the Maccabees: Ritual and Ideology from Judas Maccabeus to Simon." *Jewish Studies Quarterly* 15, no. 2: 87–114.

————. 2009. "Temple and Righteousness in Qumran and Early Christianity: Tracing the Social Differences Between the Two Movements." In D. R. Schwartz and R. A. Clements, eds., *Text, Thought, and Practice in Qumran and Early Christianity.* Leiden: Brill, 64–87.

————. 2010a. "Temple Concerns and High-Priestly Persecutions from Peter to James: Between Narrative and History." *New Testament Studies* 56: 64–89.

————. 2010b. "The Temple in Mark: A Case Study About the Early-Christian Attitude Toward the Temple." In D. Jaffé, ed., *Studies in Rabbinic Judaism and Early Christianity: Text and Context.* Leiden: Brill, 139–159.

————. 2011a. "Were the Early Christians Sectarians?" *Journal of Biblical Literature* 130.4: 771–793.

————. 2011b. "Josephus, the Temple, and the Jewish War." In J. Pastor, P. Stern, and M. Mor, eds., *Flavius Josephus: Interpretation and History.* Supplements to the Journal for the Study of Judaism 146. Leiden: Brill, 279–293.

————. 2012. "The Trial of Jesus and the Temple: Sadducean and Roman Perspectives." In B. Chilton, A. Donne, and J. Neusner, eds., *Soundings in the Religion of Jesus.* Minneapolis: Fortress, 97–107, 218–224.

————. 2013. *The Hasmoneans: Ideology, Archaeology, Identity.* Journal of Ancient Judaism Supplements 10. Göttingen: Vandenhoeck & Ruprecht.

————. 2014a. "The Temple Cult, Romanization, and the Rebels: The Roman Setting for the Rebels' Religious Ideology." *Journal of Ancient Judaism* 5: 40–60.

————. 2014b. "Prayer Within and Without the Temple from Ancient Judaism to Early Christianity." *Henoch: Historical and Textual Studies in Ancient and Medieval Judaism and Christianity* 36: 118–138.

————. 2016a. "Washing, Repentance and Atonement in Early Christian Baptism and Qumranic Purification Liturgies." *Journal for the Jesus Movement in Its Jewish Setting* 3: 33–60.

————. 2016b. "Early Christianity in Light of New Religious Movements." *Numen* 63: 483–510.

————. 2016c. "Jewish Legal Practice and Piety in the Acts of the Apostles: Apologetics or Identity Marker?" In A. Hautman et al., eds., *Religious Stories in Transformation: Conflict, Revision and Reception.* Jewish and Christian Perspectives. Leiden: Brill, 126–143.

————. 2017a. "Almost a Temple: The Community-Temple Identification in Qumran and the New Testament, Their Differences and Relationships." *Megilot* 13: 197–229 (Hebrew).

———. 2017b. "What Has Been Changed in the Law of Hebrews." *Biblica* 98.4: 582–599.

———. Forthcoming. "Community as Temple: Revisiting Cultic Metaphors in Qumran and the New Testament." *Bulletin for Biblical Research.*

Reicke, B. 1984. "Judaeo-Christianity and Jewish Establishment, A.D. 33–66." In E. Bammel and C. F. D. Moulde, eds., *Jesus and the Politics of His Day.* Cambridge: Cambridge University Press, 145–152.

Renwick, D. A. 1991. *Paul, the Temple, and the Presence of God.* BJS 224. Atlanta: Scholars Press.

Reumann, J. 2008. *Philippians.* AB 33B. New Haven and London: Yale University Press.

Rhodes, J. N. 2009. "Tabernacle and Temple: Rethinking the Rhetorical Function of Acts 7:44–50." In T. E. Phillips, ed., *Contemporary Studies in Acts.* Macon, GA: Mercer University Press, 119–137.

Ribbens, B. J. 2016. *Levitical Sacrifice and Heavenly Cult in Hebrews.* Berlin: de Gruyter.

Rice, P. H. 2016. *Behold, Your House Is Left to You: The Theological and Narrative Place of the Jerusalem Temple in Luke's Gospel.* Eugene, OR: Pickwick.

Richardson, P. 1992. "Why Turn the Tables? Jesus' Protest in the Temple Precincts." *SBL Seminar Papers*, SBLSP 31. Atlanta: Scholars Press, 507–523.

———, and M. B. Shukster. 1983. "Barnabas, Nerva, and the Yavnean Rabbis." *JTS* 34: 31–55.

Ricoeur, P. 1976. *Interpretation Theory: Discourse and the Surplus of Meaning.* Fort Worth: Texas Christian University Press.

Robinson, D. W. B. 1974. "The Priesthood of Paul in the Gospel of Hope." In R. Banks, ed., *Reconciliation and Hope: New Testament Essays on Atonement and Eschatology Presented to L. L. Morris on His 60th Birthday.* Grand Rapids: Eerdmans, 231–245.

Robinson, J. A. T. 1962. "The Destination and Purpose of John's Gospel." *Twelve New Testament Studies*, SBT 34. London: SCM, 107–125 [= *NTS* 6 (1960): 117–131].

Robinson, J. M., ed. 1996. *The Nag Hammadi Library in English.* 4th rev. ed. Leiden: Brill.

Rosenfeld, B. Z. 1997. "Sage and Temple in Rabbinic Thought After the Destruction of the Second Temple." *Journal for the Study of Judaism in the Persian, Hellenistic and Roman Period* 28: 437–463.

Rosner, B. S. 1994. *Paul Scripture and Ethics: A Study of 1 Corinthians 5–7.* Leiden: Brill.

———. 1998. "Temple Prostitution in 1 Corinthians 6:12–20." *Novum Testamentum* 40: 336–351.

———. 2013. *Paul and the Law: Keeping the Commandments.* Downers Grove, IL: InterVarsity.

Roukema, R. 2014. "Sacrifice in 'Gnostic' Testimonies of the Second and Third Centuries CE." In A. Houtman et al., eds., *The Actuality of Sacrifice: Past and Present*. Leiden: Brill, 153–169.

Rudolph, D. J. 2002. "Jesus and the Food Laws: A Reassessment of Mark 7:19b." *Evangelical Quarterly* 74, no. 4: 291–311.

———. 2011. *A Jew to the Jews: Jewish Contours of Pauline Flexibility in 1 Corinthians 9:19–23*. WUNT 2.304. Tübingen: Mohr.

Runesson, A. 2008. "Rethinking Early Jewish–Christian Relations: Matthean Community History as Pharisaic Intragroup Conflict." *JBL* 127, no. 1: 95–132.

Sabin, M. N. 2002. *Reopening the World: Reading Mark as Theology in the Context of Early Judaism*. New York: Oxford University Press.

Safrai, S. 1965. *Pilgrimage at the Time of the Second Temple*. Tel Aviv: An Hassefer (Hebrew).

Said, E. W. 1983. *The World, the Text, and the Critic*. Cambridge: Harvard University Press.

Saldarini, A. J. 1994. *Matthew's Christian-Jewish Community*. Chicago: University of Chicago Press.

Salevao, I. 2002. *Legitimation in the Letter to the Hebrews: The Construction and Maintenance of a Symbolic Universe*. Sheffield: Sheffield Academic Press.

Salyer, G. 1993. "Rhetoric, Purity and Play: Aspects of Mark 7:1–23." *Semeia* 64: 139–170.

Sanders, E. P. 1977. *Paul and Palestinian Judaism: A Comparison of Patterns of Religion*. Philadelphia: Fortress.

———. 1983. *Paul, the Law and the Jewish People*. Philadelphia: Fortress.

———. 1985. *Jesus and Judaism*. London: SCM Press.

———. 1992. *Judaism: Practice and Belief 63 b.c.e.–66 c.e.* London: SCM.

———, and M. Davies 1989. *Studying the Synoptic Gospels*. London: SCM; Philadelphia: Trinity Press International.

Sanders, J. T. 1987. *The Jews in Luke–Acts*. Philadelphia: Fortress.

Sandt, H. van de. 2004. "The Presence and Transcendence of God: An Investigation of Acts 7, 44–50 in the Light of the LXX." *ETL* 80: 30–59.

Schenck, K. L. 2007. *Cosmology and Eschatology in Hebrews: The Setting of the Sacrifice*. Cambridge: Cambridge University Press.

———. 2016. "An Archaeology of Hebrews' Tabernacle Imagery." In G. Gelardini and H. W. Attridge, eds., *Hebrews in Contexts*. AJEC 91. Leiden; Brill, 238–258.

Scherrer, S. J. 1984. "Signs and Wonders in the Imperial Cult: A New Look at a Roman Religious Institution in the Light of Rev 13:13–15." *JBL* 103: 599–610.

Schlosser, J. 1990. "La parole de Jésus sur la fin du Temple." *NTS* 36: 398–414.

Schnackenburg, R. 1987. *The Gospel According to St. John*. Vol. 2. New York: Crossroad.

Schneiders, S. M. 1977. "Symbolism and the Sacramental Principle in the Fourth Gospel." In P.-R. Tragan, ed., *Segni e Sacramenti nel Vangelo di Giovanni*. Rome: Editrice Anselmiana, 221–235.

———. 2006. "The Raising of the New Temple: John 20:19–23 and Johannine Ecclesiology." *NTS* 52, no. 3: 337–355.

Schnelle, U. 1996. "Die Tempelreinigung und die Christologie des Johannesevangeliums." *NTS* 42: 359–373.

Schoedel, W. R. 1985. *Ignatius of Antioch: A Commentary on the Letters of Ignatius of Antioch.* Philadelphia: Fortress Press.

Scholer, J. 1991. *Proleptic Priests: Priesthood in the Epistle to the Hebrews.* JSNTSup 49. Sheffield: JSOT Press.

Schreiner, T. R. 1989. "The Abolition and Fulfillment of the Law in Paul." *JSNT* 35: 47–74.

———. 1991. "Works of the Law in Paul." *NT* 33, no. 3: 217–244.

Schultz, S. 1972. *Q: Die Spruchquelle der Evangelisten.* Zurich: Theologischer Verlag.

Schüssler Fiorenza, E. 1972. *Priester für Gott: Studien zum Herrschafts und Priestermotiv in der Apokalypse.* Munster: Aschendorff.

———. 1976. "Cultic Language in Qumran and in the NT." *CBQ* 38: 159–177.

Schwartz, D. R. 1979. "The Three Temples of 4Q Florilegium." *Revue de Qumran* 10.1: 83–91.

———. 1990. *Agrippa I: The Last King of Judaea.* Tübingen: Mohr-Siebeck.

———. 1997. "The Jews of Egypt Between the Temple of Onias, the Temple of Jerusalem, and Heaven." *Zion* 57: 5–22 (Hebrew).

Schwartz, J. 1991. "Once More on the Nicanor Gate." *Hebrew Union College Annual* 62: 245–284.

———. 2005. "Temple and Temple Mount in the Book of Acts: Early Christian Activity, Topography and Halachah." In J. Pastor and M. Mor, eds., *The Beginnings of Christianity.* Jerusalem: Yad ben Zvi, 279–295.

Seely, D. 1993. "Jesus' Temple Act." *CBQ* 55: 263–283.

Segal, A. F. 1991. "Matthew's Jewish Voice." In D. Balch, ed., *Social History of the Matthean Community: Cross-Disciplinary Approaches.* Minneapolis: Fortress, 3–37.

Segal, P. 1989. "The Penalty of the Warning Inscription from the Temple of Jerusalem." *IEJ* 39: 79–84.

Shanor, J. 1988. "Paul as Master Builder: Construction Terms in First Corinthians." *NTS* 34: 461–471.

Sheldrake, P. 2001. *Spaces for the Sacred: Place, Memory, and Identity.* London: SCM Press.

Shepherd, D. 2014. "When He Comes, Will He Build It? Temple, Messiah and Targum Jonathan." *Aramaic Studies* 12, no. 1: 89–107.

Sim, D. C. 1998. *The Gospel of Matthew and Christian Judaism: The History and Social Setting of the Matthean Community.* Edinburgh: T & T Clark.

Simon, M. 1951. "St. Stephen and the Jerusalem Temple." *Journal of Ecclesiastical History* 2: 127–142.

Slater, T. B. 1998. "On the Social Setting of the Revelation to John." *NTS* 44: 232–256.

Smith, J. Z. 1980. "The Bare Facts of Ritual." *History of Religions* 20: 112–127.

Smith, S. 2017. *The Fate of the Jerusalem Temple in Luke–Acts: An Intertextual Approach to Jesus' Laments Over Jerusalem and Stephen's Speech*. London: Bloomsbury T & T Clark.

Spatafora, A. 1997. *From the "Temple of God" to God as the Temple: A Biblical Theological Study of the Temple in the Book of Revelation*. Roma: Editrice Pontificia Università Gregoriana.

Stanton, G. N. 1992. *A Gospel for a New People: Studies in Matthew*. Louisville: Westminster/John Knox.

Stegemann, E. W., and W. Stegemann. 2005. "Does the Cultic Language in Hebrews Represent Sacrificial Metaphors? Reflections on Some Basic Problems." In G. Gelardini, ed., *Hebrews: Contemporary Methods—New Insights*. Atlanta: SBL, 13–23.

Stegemann, H. 1984. "Some Aspects of Eschatology in Texts from the Qumran Community and in the Teaching of Jesus." In J. Amitai, ed., *Biblical Archaeology Today*. Jerusalem: Israel Exploration Society, 408–426.

Sterling, G. 1992. *Historiography and Self-Definition: Josephus, Luke–Acts, and Apologetic Historiography*. NovTSup 64. Leiden: Brill.

———. 1999. "'Opening the Scriptures': The Legitimation of the Jewish Diaspora and Early Christian Mission." In D. P. Moessner, ed., *Jesus and the Heritage of Israel: Luke's Narrative Claim upon Israel's Legacy*. Harrisburg: Trinity Press International, 199–217.

Stern, M. 1976. "Aspects of Jewish Society: The Priesthood and Other Classes." In S. Safrai et al., eds., *The Jewish People in the First Century*, II, *CRINT* I. Assen/Amsterdam: Van Gorcum, 561–630.

Stevenson, G. 2001. *Power and Place: Temple and Identity in the Book of Revelation*. BZNW 107. Berlin: de Gruyter.

Stewart, R. A. 1967–1968. "The Sinless High-Priest." *NTS* 14: 126–135.

Stökl Ben Ezra, D. 2003. *The Impact of Yom Kippur on Early Christianity*. WUNT 163. Tübingen: Mohr.

Stone, M. E. 1990. *Fourth Ezra*. Hermeneia. Minneapolis: Fortress.

Stott, W. 1962–1963. "The Conception of 'Offering' in the Epistle to the Hebrews." *NTS* 9: 62–67.

Stowers, S. 1994. *A Rereading of Romans: Justice, Jews and Gentiles*. New Haven and London: Yale University Press.

Strack, W. 1994. *Kultische Terminologie in ekklesiologischen Kontexten in den Briefen des Paulus*. Weinheim: Beltz Athenäum.

Strelan, R. 2008. *Luke the Priest: The Authority of the Author of the Third Gospel*. Aldershot: Ashgate.

Stroumsa, G. G. 2009. *The End of Sacrifice: Religious Transformations in Late Antiquity*. Chicago: University of Chicago Press.

Struthers Malbon, E. 1991. "The Poor Widow in Mark and Her Poor Rich Readers." *CBQ* 53: 589–604.

Sverre, A. 1962. "'Reign' and 'House' in the Kingdom of God in the Gospels." *NTS* 8: 215–240.

Swartz, M. D. 1997. "Ritual about Myth about Ritual: Towards an Understanding of the 'Avodah' in the Rabbinic Period." *Journal of Jewish Thought & Philosophy* 6: 135–155.

Swetnam, J. 1966. "On the Imagery and Significance of Heb. 9.9–10." *CBQ* 28: 155–173.

Sylva, D. D. 1986. "The Temple Curtain and Jesus' Death in the Gospel of Luke." *JBL* 105: 239–250.

———. 1987. "The Cryptic Clause *en tois tou patros mou dei einai me* in Luke 2:49b." *ZAW* 78: 132–140.

Tabory, Y. 1996. *The Passover Ritual Throughout the Generations.* Tel Aviv: Hakibbutz Hameuchad (Hebrew).

Tan, K. H. 1997. *The Zion Traditions and the Aims of Jesus.* Cambridge: Cambridge University Press.

Tannehill, R. C. 1990. *The Narrative Unity of Luke–Acts: A Literary Interpretation.* Vol. 2: *The Acts of the Apostles.* Minneapolis: Fortress.

Taylor, J. E. 1997. *The Immerser: John the Baptist Within Second Temple Judaism.* Grand Rapids: Eerdmans.

———. 2006. "Pontius Pilate and the Imperial Cult in Roman Judaea." *NTS* 52: 555–582.

Taylor, N. H. 1999. "Luke–Acts and the Temple." In J. Verheyden, ed., *The Unity of Luke–Acts.* BHTL 142. Leuven: University of Leuven and Peeters, 709–721.

———. 2003. "Stephen, the Temple, and Early Christian Eschatology." *RB* 110: 62–85.

Taylor, V. 1959. *The Gospel According to St. Mark.* London: Macmillan.

Telford, W. R. 1980. *The Barren Temple and the Withered Fig Tree: A Redactional-Critical Analysis of the Cursing of the Fig-Tree Pericope in Mark's Gospel and Its Relation to the Cleansing of the Temple Tradition.* JSNTSup 1. Sheffield: JSOT Press.

Theissen, G. 1976. "Die Tempelweissagung Jesu. Prophetie im Spannungsfeld von Stadt und Land." *Theologische Zeitschrift* 32: 144–158.

———. 1991. *The Gospels in Context: Social and Political History in the Synoptic Tradition.* Minneapolis: Fortress.

———, and A. Merz. 1996. *The Historical Jesus: A Comprehensive Guide.* Minneapolis: Fortress.

Thettyil, B. 2007. *In Spirit and Truth: An Exegetical Study of John 4:19–26 and a Theological Investigation of the Replacement Theme in the Fourth Gospel.* Leuven: Peeters.

Thomas, J. 1935. *Le mouvement baptiste en Palestine et Syrie (150 av J.C–300 ap. J.C.).* Gembloux: Duculot.

Thompson, J. W. 1979. "Hebrews 9 and Hellenistic Concepts of Sacrifice." *JBL* 98, no. 4: 567–578.

Thompson, L. L. 1990. *The Book of Revelation: Apocalypse and Empire.* Oxford: Oxford University Press.

Thompson, M. M. 2001. *The God of the Gospel of John.* Grand Rapids: Eerdmans.

Tiede, D. L. 1980. *Prophecy and History in Luke–Acts.* Philadelphia: Fortress.

Tiller, P. A. 1993. *A Commentary on the Animal Apocalypse of I Enoch.* Atlanta: Scholars Press.

Trocmé, É. 1968. "L'expulsion des marchands du Temple." *NTS* 15: 1–22.

Trotter, Jonathan R. "The Jerusalem Temple in the Practice and Thought of Diaspora Jews During the Second Temple Period." Ph.D. diss., Notre Dame, 2016.

Tuckett, C. M. 1988. "Q, the Law and Judaism." In B. Lindars, ed., *Law and Religion.* Cambridge: Cambridge University Press, 90–101.

———. 1996. *Q and the History of Early Christianity: Studies on Q.* Peabody, MA: Hendrickson.

Turner, D. L. 2008. *Matthew.* Baker exegetical commentary of the New Testament. Michigan: Baker Academic.

Turner, H. W. 1979. *From Temple to Meeting House: The Phenomenology and Theology of Places of Worship.* The Hague: Mouton.

Turner, V. 1974. *Dramas, Fields and Metaphors: Symbolic Action in Human Society.* Ithaca: Cornell University Press.

Tuval, M. 2013. *From Jerusalem Priest to Roman Jew: On Josephus and the Paradigms of Ancient Judaism.* WUNT 2.357. Tübingen: Mohr.

Tyson, J. B. 1992. *Images of Judaism in Luke Acts.* Columbia: University of South Carolina Press.

———. 1999. *Luke, Judaism and the Scholars: Critical Approaches to Luke–Acts.* Columbia: University of South Carolina Press.

Ulansey, D. 1991. "The Heavenly Veil Torn: Mark's Cosmic 'Inclusio.'" *JBL* 110: 23–25.

Ulfgard, H. 2009. "The Songs of the Sabbath Sacrifice and the Heavenly Scene of the Book of Revelation." In A. Klostergaard Petersen et al., eds., *Northern Lights on the Dead Sea Scrolls: Proceedings of the Nordic Qumran Network 2003–2006.* Leiden: Brill, 251–266.

Ullucci, D. C. 2012. *The Christian Rejection of Animal Sacrifice.* Oxford: Oxford University Press.

Ulrichsen J. H. 2003. "Jesus—der neue Tempel? Ein Kritischer Blick auf die Auslegung vin Joh 2,13–22." In D. E. Aune, T. Seland, and J. H. Ulrichsen, eds., *Neotestamentica et Philonica: Studies in Honor of Peder Borgen. Supplements to Novum Testamentum 106.* Leiden: Brill, 202–214.

Um, S. 2006. *The Theme of Temple Christology in John's Gospel.* London: T & T Clark.

Umoh, C. 2004. "The Temple in the Fourth Gospel." In M. Labahn, K. Scholtissek, and A. Strotmann, eds., *Israel und siene Heilstraditionen in Johannesevangelium. Festgabe für Johannes Beutler SJ zum 70. Geburtstag.* Paderborn: Ferdinand Schöningh, 314–333.

Vahrenhorst, M. 2008. *Kultische Sprache in den Paulusbriefen.* WUNT 230. Tübingen: Mohr.

Van Belle, G. 2001. "'Salvation Is from the Jews': The Parenthesis in Jn 4,22." In R. Bieringer, D. Pollefeyt, and F. Vanneuville, eds., *Anti-Judaism and the Fourth Gospel: Papers from the Leuven Colloquium, January 2000 (Jewish and Christian Heritage Series, 1).* Assen: Van Gorcum, 368–398.

Verheyden, J., et al., eds. 2014. *Studies in the Gospel of John and Its Christology: Festschrift Gilbert Van Belle.* Leuven: Peeters.

Vielhauer P. 1966. "On the 'Paulism' of Acts." In L. E. Keck and J. L. Martyn, eds., *Studies in Luke–Acts.* Philadelphia: Fortress, 33–50.

Viviano, B. T. 1989. "The High Priest's Servant's Ear: Mark 14:47." *RB* 96: 71–80.

Vuong, L. 2012. "Purity, Piety, and the Purposes of the Protevangelium of James." In L. M. McDonald and J. H. Charlesworth, eds., *Non-Canonical Religious Texts in Early Judaism and Early Christianity.* London: T & T Clark, 205–221.

———. 2014. "The Temple Persists: Collective Memories of the Jewish Temple in Christian Narrative Imagination." In J. D. Rosenblum, L. Vuong, and N. DesRosiers, eds., *Religious Competition in the Third Century CE: Jews, Christians, and the Greco-Roman World.* Göttingen: Vandenhoeck & Ruprecht, 114–125.

Waetjen, H. C. 1989. *A Reordering of Power: A Socio-Political Reading of Mark's Gospel.* Minneapolis: Fortress.

Wagner, J. R. 2011. "Paul and Scripture." In S. Westerholm, ed., *The Blackwell Companion to Paul.* Oxford: Blackwell, 154–171.

Wahlde, U. C. von. 1982. "The Johannine 'Jews': A Critical Survey." *NTS* 28, no. 1: 33–60.

Wahlen, C. 2007. "The Temple in Mark and Contested Authority." *Biblical Interpretation* 15: 248–267.

Walker, P. W. L. 1994. "Jerusalem in Hebrews 13:9–14 and the Dating of the Epistle." *TynBul* 45: 39–71.

Walton, S. 2004. "A Tale of Two Perspectives? The Place of the Temple in Acts." In T. D. Alexander and S. Gathercole, eds., *Heaven on Earth: The Temple in Biblical Theology.* Carlisle, UK: Paternoster, 135–149.

Wardle, T. 2010. *The Jewish Temple and Early Christian Identity.* WUNT II/291. Tübingen: Mohr.

Wead, D. W. 1970. *The Literary Design of the Fourth Gospel.* Basel: Komm.

Weatherly, J. A. 1994. *Jewish Responsibility for the Death of Jesus in Luke–Acts.* Sheffield: Sheffield Academic Press.

Webb, R. L. 1991. *John the Baptizer and Prophet: A Socio-Historical Study.* JSNTSup 62. Sheffield: JSOT Press.

Webster, G. 1993. *Boudica: The Roman Conquest of Britain.* London: Batsford.

Wedderburn, A. J. M. 2006. "Jesus Action in the Temple: A Key or a Puzzle." *ZNW* 96: 1–22.

Weinert, F. D. 1982. "Luke, the Temple and Jesus' Saying About Jerusalem's Abandoned House (Luke 13:34–35)." *CBQ* 44: 68–76.

Welch, J. W. 2009. *The Sermon on the Mount in the Light of the Temple*. Farnham and Burlington: Ashgate.

Wenschkewitz, H. 1932. *Die Spiritualisierung der Kultusbegriffe: Tempel, Priester und Opfer im Neuen Testament*. Angelos-Beiheft 4. Leipzig: Eduard Pfeiffer, 70–230.

White, L. M. 1991. "Crisis Management and Boundary Maintenance: The Social Location of the Matthean Community." In D. Balch, ed., *Social History of the Matthean Community: Cross-Disciplinary Approaches*. Minneapolis: Fortress, 211–247.

Wienert, F. D. 1982. "Luke, the Temple and Jesus' Saying About Jerusalem's Abandoned House (Luke 13:34–35)." *CBQ* 44, no. 1: 68–76.

Wild, R. A. 1985. "The Encounter Between Pharisaic and Christian Judaism: Some Early Gospel Evidence" *NT* 27: 105–124.

Williams, D. J. 1999. *Paul's Metaphors: Their Context and Character*. Peabody, MA: Hendrickson.

Williamson, R. 1975. "The Eucharist in the Epistle to the Hebrews." *NTS* 21: 300–312.

Wilson, S. G. 1973. *Gentiles and Gentile Mission in Luke–Acts*. Cambridge: Cambridge University Press.

———. 1983. *Luke and the Law*. Cambridge: Cambridge University Press.

Winter, P. 1974. *On the Trial of Jesus*, rev. ed. Berlin: de Gruyter.

Wise, M. O. 1991. "4QFlorilegium and the Temple of Adam." *Revue de Qumran* 15: 103–132.

Witherington, B. 2001. *The Gospel of Mark: A Socio-Rhetorical Commentary*. Grand Rapids: Eerdmans.

Wong, S. H. 2009. *The Temple Incident in Mark 11,15–19: The Disclosure of Jesus and the Marcan Faction*. Frankfurt am Main: Peter Lang.

Wright, A. G. 1982. "The Widow's Mites: Praise or Lament?" *CBQ* 44:256–265.

Wright, N. T. 1996. *Jesus and the Victory of God*. Minneapolis: Fortress.

Yadin, Y. 1958. "The Dead Sea Scrolls and the Epistle to the Hebrews." *Scripta Hierosolymitana* 4: 36–55.

Yarbro Collins, A. 1984. *Crisis and Catharsis: The Power of the Apocalypse*. Philadelphia: Westminster.

———. 1985. "Insiders and Outsiders in the Book of Revelation and Its Social Context." In J. Neusner and E. S. Frerichs, eds., *"To See Ourselves as Others See Us": Christians, Jews, "Others" in Late Antiquity*. Chico, CA: Scholars Press, 187–218.

———. 1986. "Vilification and Self-Definition in the Book of Revelation." *HTR* 79: 308–320.

———. 1998. "The Book of Revelation." In J. J. Collins, ed., *The Origins of Apocalypticism in Judaism and Christianity*, in B. McGinn, J. J. Collins, and S. J. Stein, eds., *The Encyclopedia of Apocalypticism*. New York: Continuum, 1:384–414.

———. 1999. "Jesus and the Jerusalem Temple." In *International Rennert Guest Lectures Series* 5. Ramat Gan: Bar-Ilan University and the Hebrew University of Jerusalem.

————. 2001. "Jesus' Action in Herod's Temple." In A. Yarbro Collins and M. M. Mitchell, eds., *Antiquity and Humanity: Essays on Ancient Religion and Philosophy.* Tübingen: Mohr Siebeck, 45–61.

————. 2007. *Mark.* Hermeneia. Minneapolis: Fortress.

Yoshiko Reed, A. 2003. "'Jewish Christianity' After the 'Parting of the Ways': Approaches to Historiography and Self-Definition in the Pseudo-Clementine Literature." In A. H. Becker and A. Yoshiko Reed, eds., *The Ways That Never Parted: Jews and Christians in Late Antiquity and the Early Middle Ages.* TSAJ 95. Tübingen: Mohr Siebeck, 189–232.

Young, E. J. 1972. *The Book of Isaiah, I, 1–18.* NICOT. Grand Rapids: Eerdmans.

General Index

Agrippa II, 8, 42, 182, 192
Ananias, son of Nedebaus, 174, 182, 191, 379n154
Animal Apocalypses (1 Enoch 85–90), 242 244, 372
Annaus, son of Annaus, 118
Ark of the Covenant, 78, 80, 83, 228, 264
Aroma, 7, 71–72, 73, 84, 85, 86, 304
Attridge, Harold, 256

Baptism, 155, 269, 294, 298, 310, 338n37; John's, 6, 108, 320n14; replacing sacrifices, 7, 296, 302
Bauckham, Richard, 28, 29, 187
The Beautiful Gate, 164, 179
blasphemy, 36, 49, 181, 188, 214, 316, 332n117, 336n175, 357n139
Borg, Marcus, 30

Caiaphas, Joseph, 26, 35, 36, 42, 179, 190–191, 196, 220, 327n51, 329n68, 332n123, 333n125, 379n151, 379nn153–154, 389n114
Chilton, Bruce, 29, 46, 49
Christology, Temple, 210, 219, 221, 385n58
Clement of Alexandria, 187, 188, 293–294, 296, 298, 300, 301, 302
coin, 133, 148, 200; copper, 113; figures on, 28, 51, 248; Tyrian, 23, 28, 328n62
Commemoration of sacrifices, 48, 220; of Temple, 15, 216, 389n111

Community-as-Temple, 60, 62, 66, 78, 100, 226, 245, 311
condemning the Temple, 26, 37, 96, 97, 108, 109, 176, 183, 192, 291, 311
corruption: of priests, 25–27, 31, 107, 199, 327n52; Temple, 96, 105
Crossan, John Dominique, 6, 27, 31, 35, 46

Daily sacrifice (*Tamid*), 159, 172, 194, 255, 323n55, 404n87, 404n90
Dead Sea Scrolls, 9, 398n115
Desecration of the Temple, 10, 42, 102, 117, 119–120, 149, 180, 192
Diaspora Judaism, 12–14, 321n27
Dunn, James, 35, 36, 72, 74, 79, 80, 83, 92, 104

Elliott, John, 158, 339n41
Emergent religion, 309
End of Days, 227, 241, 244, 246, 295, 299; and Temple, 39, 41, 240, 243, 244, 289–290, 384n42
Esler, Philip, 4, 155, 176–177, 195
ethics, ethical, 33, 53, 68, 91, 94, 133, 139, 150–151; behavior, 90, 132, 136; dimensions of the Law, 130
Evans, Craig, 25–26, 27, 96, 119, 188
Ezekiel, 23, 397n108

festival(s), 14, 46–48, 93, 203, 212–217, 288; Dedication, 214–215; Hanukkah, 12, 216–217, 388n91; Passover,

451

Index of Ancient Sources